ADWEEK/ART DIRECTORS'
INDEX

ADWEEK /ART DIRECTORS'
INDEX
USA · VOLUME

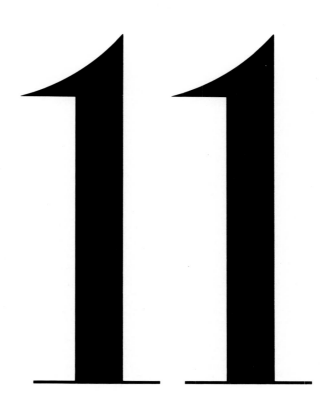

Published Under License in the U.S.A. by ASM Communications, Inc.

Published Internationally by Rotovision, SA

Published under license in the USA by:
ASM Communications, Inc.
820 Second Avenue
New York
New York 10017
Tel. 212-661 8080

Published internationally by:
RotoVision SA
Case Postale 434–10, rue de l'Arquebuse
CH-1211 Geneva 11–Switzerland
Tel. 022-212121–Telex 421479 rovi ch

Cover and divider page design:
Elana Gutman

ISBN 2-88046-049-2

© 1985 RotoVision, SA

Special thanks to:

Barbara Baskin, Sandie Capelli, Carolyn
Doyle, Robin Fried, Sheri Gasché, Merry
Greene, Janice Loeb, Bobbi Mencher,
Trish Parks, Sharon Sherman,
Joan Webster.

Andresen Typographics, Wenche Huang,
Lighthouse Graphics, Repro Color,
Toppan Printing Co., and Judy Walker.

Printed in Japan

From all of us to each of you . . .

Our heartfelt thanks to all the artists who made this volume and to you in the creative community for your enthusiasm and support.

We continue our search for the best of America's creative talent and hope this INDEX will make your job simpler and more enjoyable.

Your comments and suggestions are always welcome; we look forward to serving you for many years to come.

Elana Gutman, Director for
The Staff at ADWEEK/Art Directors' Index
and RotoVision SA

ADWEEK/East
820 Second Avenue, New York, New York 10017 (212) 661-8080

ADWEEK/Southeast
75 Third Street, N.W., Atlanta, Georgia 30365 (404) 881-6442

ADWEEK/Midwest
435 North Michigan Avenue, Chicago, Illinois 60611 (312) 467-6500

ADWEEK/Southwest
2909 Cole Avenue, Dallas, Texas 75204 (214) 747-2385

ADWEEK/West
514 Shatto Place, Los Angeles, California 90020 (213) 384-7100

Table of Contents

• Illustration, Design, Art Direction & Related Services

• Photography & Stock Photography

• Illustrators' & Photographers' Representatives

• Printing, Production & Related Services

• Actors, Models & Talent

• Additional Support Services

Alphabetical Index to Advertisers

Illustrators

Ajin **10**
Tel. 212-760-0919

Allen, Terry **11**
Tel. 718-624-1210

Anthony Illustration, Mitchell **12**
Tel. 415-322-1376

Anton, Jerry **13-15**
Tel. 212-689-5886

Artists Associates **16-21**
Tel. 212-755-1365/6

Artists International **22-25**
Tel. 212-334-9310

Art Staff, Inc. **26-31**
Tel. 313-963-8240

Battes, Greg **32**
Design & Illustration
Tel. 214-620-7685

Bendell, Norman **114**
Tel. 212-807-6627

Bennett, Dianne **33**
Graphic Illustration and Design
Tel. 213-558-3697

Bingham, Sid **34**
Tel. 818-957-0163

Björkman, Steve **35**
Tel. 714-261-1411

Blanchette, Dan **36**
Tel. 312-332-1339

Bleck, Cathie **37**
Tel. 214-942-4639

Bolle, Frank **40-41**
Tel. 212-247-1130

Bralds, Braldt **38**
Tel. 212-243-7063

Braught, Mark **39**
Tel. 812-234-6135

Bruck, J.S. **40-65**
Artists Management
Tel. 212-247-1130

Caras, Peter **42, 43**
Tel. 212-247-1130

Catalano, Sal **66**
Tel. 201-447-5318

Cellini, Eva **44, 45**
Tel. 212-247-1130

Cellini, Joseph **46, 47**
Tel. 212-247-1130

Chan, Ron **67**
Tel. 415-441-4544

Chang, Warren **68**
Tel. 415-964-1701

Chinchar, Al **48, 49**
Tel. 212-247-1130

Cigliano, William V. **69**
Tel. 212-980-8061

Clark, Tim **70**
Illustration/Graphics
Tel. 213-202-1044

Cobane, Russell **78**
Tel. 313-625-6132

Cobb & Associates, Lisa
32, 37, 122, 139, 165, 174, 178
Tel. 214-939-0032

Coleman Presents, Inc.,
Woody **71-77**
Tel. 216-621-1771

Connally, Connie **79**
Tel. 214-340-7818

Consani, Chris **133**
Tel. 213-934-3395   213-936-2757

Craft, Kinuko Y. **80**
Tel. 212-486-9644

Craig, John **81**
Tel. 608-872-2371

Curry, Tom **82**
Tel. 512-443-8427

Dacey, Bob **50, 51**
Tel. 212-247-1130

Daniels & Daniels **83**
Artistic Licence
Tel. 805-498-1923

Dedell, Jacqueline **84, 85**
Artist Representative
Tel. 212-741-2539

Diffenderfer, Ed **86**
Tel. 415-254-8235

Dudash, Michael **52, 53**
Tel. 212-247-1130

Dudzinski, Andrzej **87**
Tel. 212-628-6959

Eberbach, Andrea **88**
Tel. 317-253-0421

Ella **90, 91**
Tel. 617-266-3858

English, Mark **17**
Tel. 212-755-1365/6

Ericksen, Marc W. **89**
Tel. 415-362-1214

Erlacher, Bill **16-21**
Artists Associates
Tel. 212-755-1365/6

Evans, Robert **92**
Tel. 415-397-5322

Fernandes, Stanislaw **94, 95**
Tel. 212-533-2648

Fisher, Dave **74**
Tel. 913-831-0835

Flesher, Vivienne **93**
Tel. 212-505-6731

Franké, Phil **120**
Tel. 212-679-1358

Frazee, Marla **136**
Tel. 213-934-3395   213-936-2757

Fromentin, Christine **54, 55**
Tel. 212-247-1130

Furukawa, Mel **121**
Tel. 212-679-1358

Gillot, Carol **96**
Tel. 212-243-6448

Giusti, Robert **97**
Tel. 212-752-0179

Goldammer, Ken **98**
Tel. 312-836-0143

Goldman Agency, David **114**
Tel. 212-807-6627

Graham, William **154**
Tel. 312-467-0330

Greathead Studio **99**
Tel. 404-952-5067

Green, Norman **13**
Tel. 212-689-5886

Grove, David **100**
Tel. 415-433-2100

Guarnaccia, Steven **101**
Tel. 212-420-0108

Guetary, Hélène **121**
Tel. 212-679-1358

Harris, Diane Teske **102**
Tel. 212-719-9879

Heck, Cathy **118**
Tel. 212-679-1358

Heindel, Robert **18**
Tel. 212-755-1365/6

Hess, Mark **103**
Tel. 914-232-5870

Hess, Richard **104**
Tel. 203-354-2921

Hodges/Illustration, Ken **105**
Tel. 213-431-4343

Hull, Scott **106**
Artist Representative
Tel. 513-433-8383

Hunt, Robert **107**
Tel. 415-824-1824

Jarvis, David **108**
Tel. 904-255-1296

Johnson, B.E./Concept One **109**
Tel. 716-461-4240

Joyner, Eric **110**
Tel. 415-626-9890

Kenyon, Chris **111**
Tel. 415-923-1363

Kilroy, John **112**
Tel. 617-925-0582

Kimble, David **113**
Tel. 213-849-1576

Kimura, Hiro **134**
Tel. 213-934-3395   213-936-2757

Kingston, Jim **114**
Tel. 212-807-6627

Kirchoff/Wohlberg, Inc. **115**
Tel. 212-644-2020

Klein, Renee **116**
Tel. 718-624-1210   212-841-4464

Kordic, Vladimir **117**
Tel. 216-951-4026

Krepel, Dick **19**
Tel. 212-755-1365/6

Photographers

Segrest Photography Inc., Jerry
302
Tel. 214-426-6360

Sellers Photography, Dan   303
Tel. 214-631-4705

Seltzer Studios, Inc., Abe   304
Tel. 212-807-0660

Siegel, David M.   305
Tel. 602-257-9509

Simko, Robert   306
Tel. 212-912-1192

Soorenko, Barry A./   307
Photogroup Inc.
Tel. 301-652-1303

Stafford, Vern/Commercial   311
Photographic Services, Inc.
Tel. 615-246-9578

Stettner, Bill   308-310
Tel. 212-460-8180

Stevens, Bob   312, 313
Tel. 213-271-8123

Stoecklein, David R.   314, 315
Tel. 208-726-5191

Stolk Photography, Robert   316
Tel. 415-621-4649

Toto, Joe   317-319
Tel. 212-620-0755

Turner, Pete   320, 321
Tel. 212-765-1733

Unangst, Andrew   322
Tel. 212-889-4888

Vullo, Phillip   323
Tel. 404-874-0822

Wahlstrom Photography, Inc.,
Richard   324, 325
Tel. 415-550-1400

Watson, Alan   326
Tel. 619-239-5555

Wien, Jeffrey   327
Tel. 212-243-7028

Wilkes, Stephen   328-331
Tel. 212-475-4010

Wojcik, James   332
Tel. 212-807-0593

Designers

Artfile   183
Tel. 919-781-5087

Cronan, Michael Patrick
184, 185
Tel. 415-543-6745

Girvin Design, Inc., Tim   186
Tel. 206-623-7808

Pushpin Lubalin Peckolick
188, 189
Tel. 212-674-8080

Ross Design Associates, Inc.
190, 191
Tel. 212-206-0044

Schwab Design, Michael   187
Tel. 415-546-7559

Sekiguchi, Yoshi   194
Tel. 312-433-4140

Unlimited Swan Inc.   192, 193
Tel. 203-637-4840

Stock Photography

Photo Researchers   335
Tel. 212-758-3420

West Stock, Inc.   336-339
Tel. 206-621-1611

Creative Services

G.S. Litho
Tel. 201-933-8585

Kinetics
Tel. 312-644-2767

Moebius
Tel. 213-458-4194

Photo 85
Tel. 203-852-0500

Photo District News
Tel. 212-677-8418

Professional Color Service
Tel. 818-787-7333

Serindipity
Tel. 404-237-4040

Geographic Regions

East
Connecticut, Delaware, Maine,
Maryland, Massachusetts, New
Hampshire, New Jersey, New York,
Pennsylvania, Rhode Island,
Vermont, Washington, D.C.,
West Virginia

Southeast
Alabama, Florida, Georgia,
Mississippi, North Carolina, South
Carolina, Tennessee, Virginia

Midwest
Illinois, Indiana, Iowa, Kansas,
Kentucky, Michigan, Minnesota,
Missouri, Nebraska, North Dakota,
Ohio, South-Dakota, Wisconsin

Southwest
Arkansas, Colorado, Louisiana,
New Mexico, Oklahoma, Texas

West
Alaska, Arizona, California, Hawaii,
Idaho, Montana, Nevada, Oregon,
Utah, Washington, Wyoming

ILLUSTRATION

Index
to
Illustrators

AJIN

Represented by:
Raymond Stringer
251 West 30th Street
Suite 5 E
New York, NY 10001
Tel. 212-760 0919

27th recipient of Japan's coveted Bunshun Manga Award. Residing in New York City since April, 1983. Sculptures by Ajin appear monthly in Esquire's "The New America."

American clients include: The New York Times, Fortune, Time, Harpers, 50 Plus, Geo, Personal Computing, Games, Corporate Design, Pepsi-Cola International, National Lampoon, Children's Television Workshop, C.B.S. Entertainment.

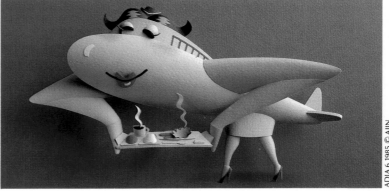

ADIA 6 1985 © AJIN

10

Terry Allen

291 Carroll Street
Brooklyn, New York 11231
Tel. 718-624 1210

Mitchell Anthony

San Francisco Studio:
Tel. 415-322 1376

For prompt and courteous service, contact my rep Mark Halcomb, in San Francisco at 415/982-8833.

I work fast with an ability to conceptualize and build on your layout through my use of scale and saturated color.

I enjoy working with a diversified clientele in both consumer and trade markets. Recently I've had the pleasure of working with PG&E, Atari, Corvus Systems, Intel Corporation, Valid Logic Systems, Daystar Learning Corporation, Pizza Hut, San Francisco Magazine, Emmy Magazine, Micro Communications Magazine, Koala Corporation and Abekas Corporation.

Transparency portfolio available upon request.

A.D.s: Gary Silverstein & John Griesel

creating circuits
at the speed of thought

Client: Daystar Learning Corporation
A.D.: Max Heim

Client: Valid Logic Systems
A.D.s: Gary Silverstein & John Griesel

ADIA 6 1985 © Mitchell Anthony

Jerry Anton/Norman Green

Represented by:
Jerry Anton
107 East 38th Street
New York, NY 10016
Tel. 212-689 5886

Clients include:
American Express, California Canners & Growers Assoc., Ciba-Geigy, Henson Associates, Botanic Garden Seed Co., N.Y. Zoological Society, Rockefeller Foundation, Pajama Corporation of America, Columbia Pictures, Ash Le Donne, Fisher, N.W. Ayer, Benton & Bowles, Young & Rubicam, Scali, McCabe & Sloves, Marsteller, Wells, Rich & Greene, D-F-S, McCann-Erickson, J.W. Thompson, Ogilvy & Mather, Good Housekeeping, Ladies Home Journal, Redbook, Travel & Leisure, Simon & Schuster, Random House, Workman Publishing, Celestial Seasonings, Sunrise Publications.

ADIA 6 1985 © Norman Green

13

Jerry Anton/Bob Ziering

Agent:
Jerry Anton
107 East 38th Street
New York, NY 10016
Tel. 212-689 5886

Corporate clients include:
IBM, Exxon, Mobil Oil Corp.,
Channel 13, Film Society of
Lincoln Center, Paul Taylor Dance
Company, City of Boston, NY
Zoological Society, McCarter
Theater, Parke-Davis, Ciba-Geigy,
NY University, American Express
Co., AT&T, National Endowment
for the Humanities, Control Data
Corporation, First National Bank
of Boston

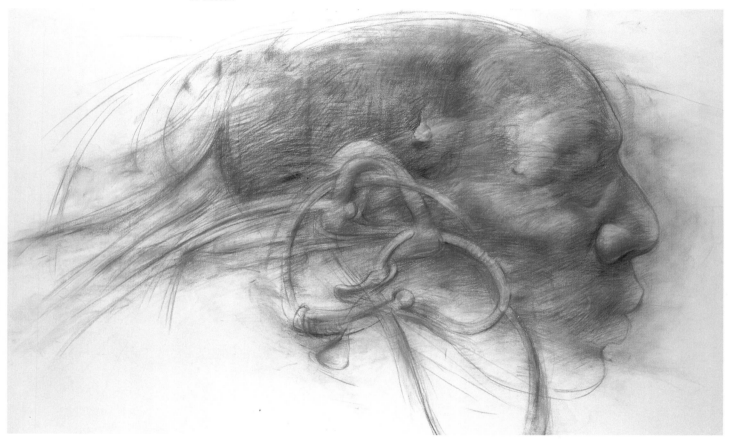

14

Jerry Anton/Bob Ziering

Agent:
Jerry Anton
107 East 38th Street
New York, NY 10016
Tel. 212-689 5886

Clients include:
Ash/LeDonne/Fisher, N.W. Ayer, Burson-Marsteller, Benton & Bowles, Doyle, Dane & Bernbach, McCaffrey & McCall, Tracy-Locke, Lord, Geller, Federico.& Einstein, Young & Rubicam, McCann- Erickson, Howard Merrell & Partners, United Artists, ABC, NBC, CBS, American Heritage, Time, Inc., Random House, Print, Runner Magazine, Humphrey, Browning, MacDougall.

ADIA 6 1985 © Bob Ziering

15

BILL ERLACHER ARTISTS ASSOCIATES

211 EAST 51 STREET, NEW YORK, NEW YORK 10022 (212) 755-1365/6 ASSOCIATE: NICOLE EDELL

ARTISTS REPRESENTED

NORMAN ADAMS

DON BRAUTIGAM

MICHAEL DEAS

MARK ENGLISH

ALEX GNIDZIEJKO

ROBERT HEINDEL

STEVE KARCHIN

DICK KREPEL

SKIP LIEPKE

RICK McCOLLUM

FRED OTNES

DANIEL SCHWARTZ

Artists Associates/Mark English

Agent:
Bill Erlacher
211 East 51st Street
New York, NY 10022
Tel. 212-755 1365/6

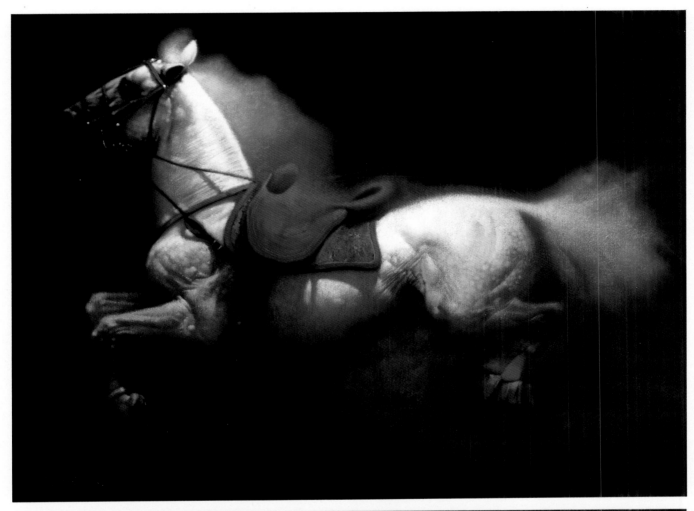

ADIA 6 1985 © Mark English

Artists Associates/Bob Heindel

Agent:
Bill Erlacher
211 East 51st Street
New York, NY 10022
Tel. 212-755 1365/6

ADJA 6 1985 © Robert Heindel

211 East 51st Street
New York, NY 10022

18

Artists Associates/Dick Krepel

Agent:
Bill Erlacher
211 East 51st Street
New York, NY 10022
Tel. 212-755 1365/6

Artists Associates/Skip Liepke

Agent:
Bill Erlacher
211 East 51st Street
New York, NY 10022
Tel. 212-755 1365/6

Artists Associates/Skip Liepke

Artists Associates/Fred Otnes

Agent:
Bill Erlacher
211 East 51st Street
New York, NY 10022
Tel. 212-755 1365/6

ADIA 6 1985 © Fred Otnes

Artists International

225 Lafayette Street #1102
Soho, N.Y.C. 10012
Tel. 212-334 9310

Agent:
Michael G. Brodie

Norman MacDonald

Tony Chen

Jody Lee

Gino D'Achille

Artists International

225 Lafayette Street #1102
Soho, N.Y.C. 10012
Tel. 212-334 9310

Agent:
Michael G. Brodie

David Chestnutt

David Chestnutt

Richard Walz

Gino D'Achille

Artists International

225 Lafayette Street #1102
Soho, N.Y.C. 10012
Tel. 212-334 9310

Agent:
Michael G. Brodie

Bill Cleaver

Bill Cleaver
Jerry Harston

Norman MacDonald
Laura Westlake

Artists International

225 Lafayette Street #1102
Soho, N.Y.C. 10012
Tel. 212-334 9310

Agent:
Michael G. Brodie

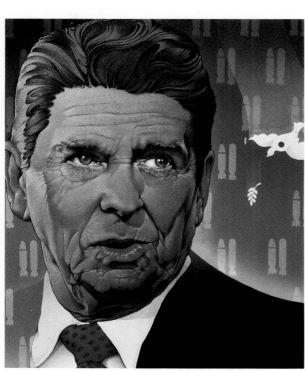

Jeffrey Oh

John Nez

Jody Lee

Art Staff, Inc.

1200 City National Bank Building
Detroit, Michigan 48226
Tel. 313-963 8240

The world's finest automotive and
product illustrators add new
dimensions to their portfolio.

Agents:
Ben Jaroslaw
Dick Meissner

Merry Christmas to all

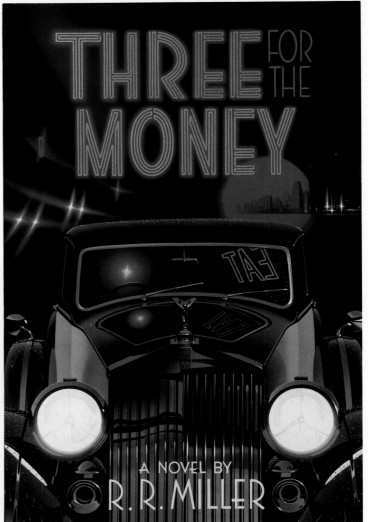

Art Staff, Inc.

1200 City National Bank Building
Detroit, Michigan 48226
Tel. 313-963 8240

Agents:
Ben Jaroslaw
Dick Meissner

Representation: Specialization:

John Arvan	Ben Jaroslaw	Lou Perkowski
Joy Brosious	Baron Lesperance	Debbie Peterson
Ralph Brunke	Linda Meek	Jeff Ridky
Larry Cory	Dick Meissner	Al Schrank
Sheryl DeMorris	Heidi Meissner	Jim Slater
Kevin Fales	Delynn Meyer	Linda Stetter
Susan Fiorello	Dick Miller	Ken Taylor
Pat Fisher	Kathy Miller	Lisa Valentine
Janet Gaffka	Jerry Monteleon	Bill Westman
Jim Gutheil	Sandy Nelson	Alan Wilson
Vicki Hayes	Lora Parlove	Lilly Zamanian

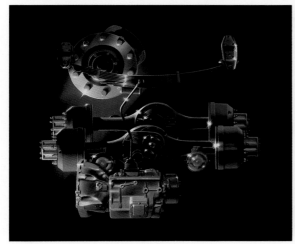

Art Staff, Inc.

1200 City National Bank Building
Detroit, Michigan 48226
Tel. 313-963 8240

Fabulous technical illustrations for
the world's prestigious clients.

Agents:
Ben Jaroslaw
Dick Meissner

Art Staff, Inc.

1200 City National Bank Building
Detroit, Michigan 48226
Tel. 313-963 8240

Agents:
Ben Jaroslaw
Dick Meissner

Award winning performances in
all media.

Art Staff, Inc.

1200 City National Bank Building
Detroit, Michigan 48226
Tel. 313-963 8240

Fantastic interpretations of new products.

Agents:
Ben Jaroslaw
Dick Meissner

Art Staff, Inc.

1200 City National Bank Building
Detroit, Michigan 48226
Tel. 313-963 8240

Agents:
Ben Jaroslaw
Dick Meissner

Problem solving solutions to every
assignment.

Greg Battes Design & Illustration

2954 Satsuma Drive
Dallas, Texas 75229
Tel. 214-620 7685

Represented by:
Lisa Cobb & Associates
2200 N. Lamar
Suite 202
Dallas, TX 75202
Tel. 214-939 0032

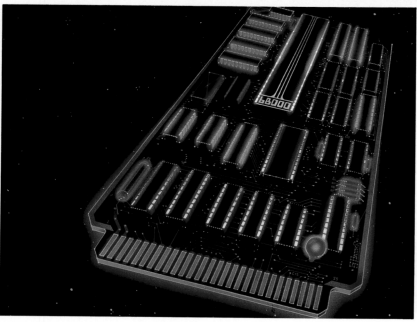

Dianne Bennett   Graphic Illustration and Design

8800 Venice Blvd.
Los Angeles, California 90034
Tel. 213-558 3697

Clients include:
Collins Foods International,
Carnation Company, Host
International, Kentucky Fried
Chicken, Teleflora, Admarketing
Advertising, Keye Donna Pearlstein
Advertising, Kauffman and
Associates Advertising, Brentwood
Publishing, Eastman Publishing,
Intro Magazine, Flowers &
Magazine.

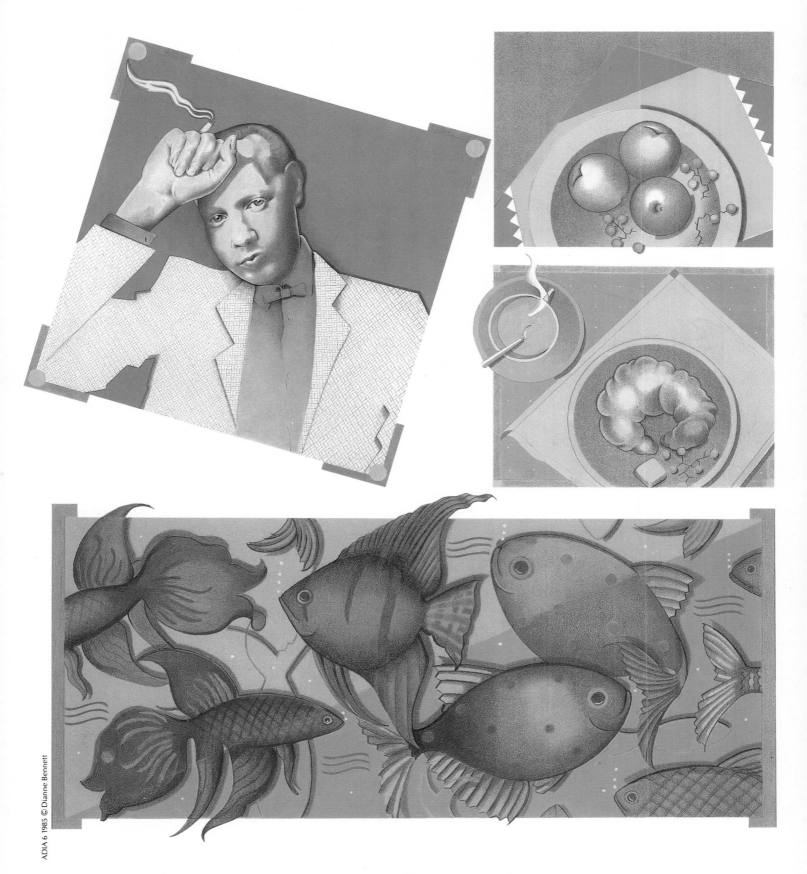

ADIA 6 1985 © Dianne Bennett

33

Sid Bingham/Richard Kriegler

Sid Bingham
2550 Kemper
La Crescenta, California
Tel. 818-957 0163

Richard Kriegler
2814 3rd Street
Santa Monica, California
Tel. 213-396 9087

Agent:
Nancy George
Tel. 213-935 4696

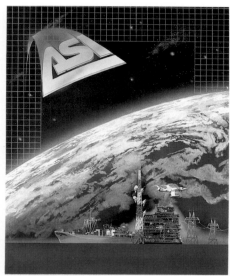

Sid Bingham

Richard Kriegler

Steve Björkman

1711 Langley
Irvine, California 92714
Tel. 714-261 1411

Represented in Los Angeles by:
Laurie Pribble
Tel. 818-574 0288

Represented in San Francisco by:
Mark Halcomb
Tel. 415-982 8833

Dan Blanchette

185 North Wabash Avenue
Chicago, Illinois 60601
Tel. 312-332 1339

Agent: Joni Tuke
368 West Huron
Chicago, Illinois 60610
Tel. 312-787 6826

Clients include:
Kraft, Kroger, Pillsbury, Miles
Laboratories, Abbott Labs,
Michelob, York Steak House,
McDonald's, Taco Bell, Grandma's
Cookies, Upsher-Smith
Pharmaceuticals, Allstate
Insurance, and the American Dairy
Association.

Who constructs the building blocks of taste?

In processed meats, snack foods, canned and frozen foods and dry groceries, no-one has more experience than Griffith Laboratories in helping food processors develop and deliver their own unique flavor profiles; making sure that their individual product tastes remain consistent, time after time.

Griffith technicians have a special familiarity with the essential components of taste and flavor. It enables them to consistently create products basic to the food processing industry. In recent years, we've made important advances in such areas as cures, tenderizers, liquid smokes, encapsulated spices, hydrolyzed vegetable proteins, soy protein concentrates and more. This pioneering, problem-solving approach is put to work for each Griffith customer.

Working with "building blocks" like these makes the job of a food processing technician easier.

When you want to be sure that that the basics are right before you set to work, talk to Griffith. We're the Taste Technologists.

Write or call:
Griffith Laboratories U.S.A.
12200 S. Central Ave.
Alsip, Illinois 60658
312-371-0900.

GRIFFITH LABORATORIES U.S.A.
The Taste Technologists.

Cathie Bleck

1019 North Clinton
Dallas, Texas 75208
Tel. 214-942 4639

Agent in Dallas:
Lisa Cobb & Assoc.
Tel. 214-939 0032

Agent in Chicago:
Vince Kamin & Assoc.
Tel. 312-787 8834

Clients include:
American Airlines, Advertising Age, Boston, Boston Globe, Boys Life, Chicago Tribune, Coca Cola, Cunningham & Walsh, Dallas Times Herald, "D," Focus, Houston, Houghton Mifflin, Richards Group, Scott Foresman, Southland, Texas Monthly, Tracy Locke, BBDO

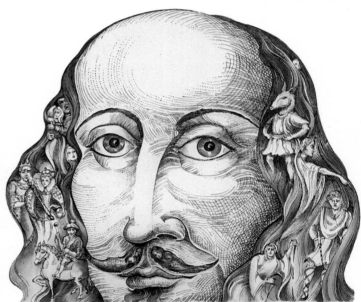

Braldt Bralds

Tel. 212-243 7063

Represented by:
Milton Newborn Associates
135 East 54th Street
New York, NY 10022
Tel. 212-421 0050

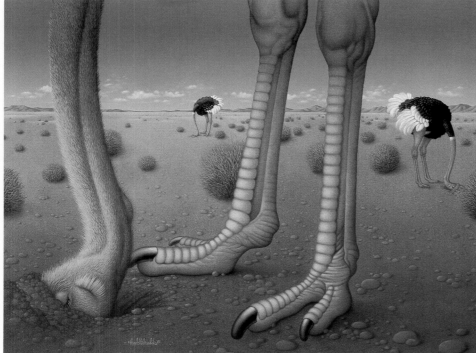

Mark Braught

Room 18, Commerce Building
629 Cherry Street
Terre Haute, Indiana 47807 USA
Tel. 812-234 6135

Agent:
Scott Hull
Tel. 513-433 8383

Clients include:
Metropolitan Life Insurance,
Quinn & Johnson/BBDO, General
Housewares Corporation, Florida
Trend Magazine, Marten House
Hotel, American Dairy
Association, Anheiser-Busch,
Scott Foresman Publishing,
NW Ayer/Chicago, and others.

If you have any questions or would
like additional samples please
don't hesitate to call. Until
then . . . thank you.

Wenn Sie irgendwelche Fragen
haben sollten, oder wenn Sie
zusätzliche Proben haben
möchten, bitte rufen Sie an!
Bis dahin . . . danke schön.

Si vous avez des questions ou
si vous voulez les échantillons
supplémentaires n'hésitez pas
à nous donner un coup de fil.
A bientôt . . . merci.

J.S. Bruck/Frank Bolle

Artists Management
157 West 57th Street
New York, NY 10019
Tel. 212-247 1130

J. S. Bruck/Frank Bolle

Artists Management
157 West 57th Street
New York, NY 10019
Tel. 212-247 1130

J. S. Bruck/Peter Caras

Artists Management
157 West 57th Street
New York, NY 10019
Tel. 212-247 1130

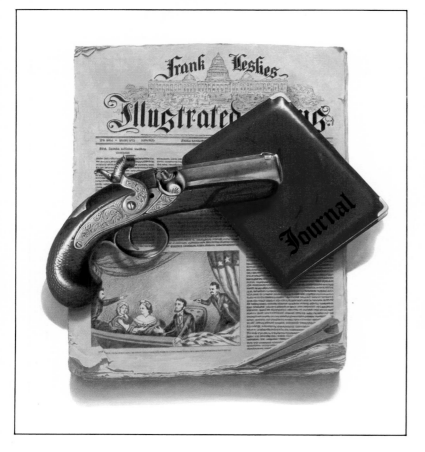

J.S. Bruck/Peter Caras

Artists Management
157 West 57th Street
New York, NY 10019
Tel. 212-247 1130

J. S. Bruck/Eva Cellini

Artists Management
157 West 57th Street
New York, NY 10019
Tel. 212-247 1130

J.S. Bruck/Eva Cellini

Artists Management
157 West 57th Street
New York, NY 10019
Tel. 212-247 1130

ADIA 6 1985 © Eva Cellini

J. S. Bruck/Joseph Cellini

Artists Management
157 West 57th Street
New York, NY 10019
Tel. 212-247 1130

J. S. Bruck/Joseph Cellini

Artists Management
157 West 57th Street
New York, NY 10019
Tel. 212-247 1130

J.S. Bruck/Al Chinchar

Artists Management
157 West 57th Street
New York, NY 10019
Tel. 212-247 1130

J.S. Bruck/Al Chinchar

Artists Management
157 West 57th Street
New York, NY 10019
Tel. 212-247 1130

J. S. Bruck/Bob Dacey

Artists Management
157 West 57th Street
New York, NY 10019
Tel. 212-247 1130

J. S. Bruck/Bob Dacey

Artists Management
157 West 57th Street
New York, NY 10019
Tel. 212-247 1130

ADIA 6 1985 © Bob Dacey

J. S. Bruck/Michael Dudash

Artists Management
157 West 57th Street
New York, NY 10019
Tel. 212-247 1130

THE FINANCIAL SOURCE: Innovation upon innovation! Now INTERPLEX™ gives you the ability to track your dollar resources and evaluate your investment activities. Automatically.

To anyone close to the financial management arena, INTERPLEX is proof that Manufacturers Hanover is committed. To lead. Because INTERPLEX has established a new standard in this fast-moving, vital field.

Now you can control both your corporate finances and your corporate investments through the INTERPLEX family of services.

INTERPLEX is a microcomputer-based management system that

gathers, formats, stores, retrieves, and manipulates corporate financial information. Automatically. Giving you precious extra time to plan and make decisions.

The Treasury Management Source™ automatically collects data from your banks and has it waiting for your arrival early in the morning. It enables you to project the end of day cash position, analyze target balances.

forecast cash flows, transfer funds. And more. Much more.

The Investment Management Source™ swiftly and automatically tracks your corporate portfolios. It enables you to access your Transactions Pending Report, your Maturity Report, your Broker Report—to name just a few. What's more, it performs portfolio analysis, screens your security database, even accrues interest—among its

many functions.

Together or separately, these members of the INTERPLEX family give you a whole new ability. The ability to act rather than react.

Learn how you can enter the new age of INTERPLEX and gain total control. Automatically. Contact George Chelius, Vice President, MH Financial Management Systems, Inc., a subsidiary of Manufacturers Hanover Trust Company, at 1-800-MHT-PLEX.

MH Financial Management Systems, Inc.

H MANUFACTURERS HANOVER
The Financial Source™ Worldwide.

J. S. Bruck/Michael Dudash

Artists Management
157 West 57th Street
New York, NY 10019
Tel. 212-247 1130

"Half of me is the Earl
of Greystoke.
The other half
is wild."

ADIA 6 1985 © Michael Dudash

GREYSTOKE
THE LEGEND OF
TARZAN
LORD OF THE APES

J.S. Bruck/Christine Fromentin

Artists Management
157 West 57th Street
New York, NY 10019
Tel. 212-247 1130

ADIA 6 1985 © Christine Fromentin

54

J.S. Bruck/Christine Fromentin

Artists Management
157 West 57th Street
New York, NY 10019
Tel. 212-247 1130

ADIA 6 1985 © Christine Fromentin

J.S. Bruck/Jimmy Mathewuse

Artists Management
157 West 57th Street
New York, NY 10019
Tel. 212-247 1130

56

J.S. Bruck/Jimmy Mathewuse

Artists Management
157 West 57th Street
New York, NY 10019
Tel. 212-247 1130

57

J. S. Bruck/Lew McCance

Artists Management
157 West 57th Street
New York, NY 10019
Tel. 212-247 1130

58

J.S. Bruck/Lew McCance

Artists Management
157 West 57th Street
New York, NY 10019
Tel. 212-247 1130

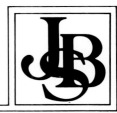

J.S. Bruck/Richard Newton

Artists Management
157 West 57th Street
New York, NY 10019
Tel. 212-247 1130

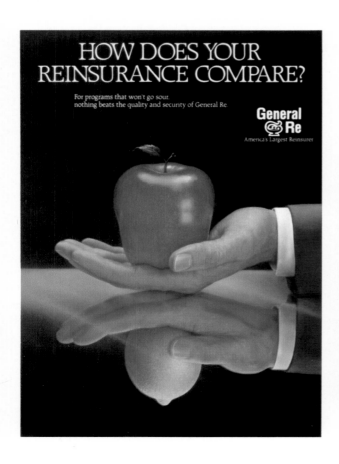

ADIA 6 1985 © Richard Newton

J.S. Bruck/Richard Newton

Artists Management
157 West 57th Street
New York, NY 10019
Tel. 212-247 1130

J.S. Bruck/Jo Anne Scribner

Artists Management
157 West 57th Street
New York, NY 10019
Tel. 212-247 1130

J.S. Bruck/Jo Anne Scribner

Artists Management
157 West 57th Street
New York, NY 10019
Tel. 212-247 1130

J. S. Bruck/Sally Vitsky

Artists Management
157 West 57th Street
New York, NY 10019
Tel. 212-247 1130

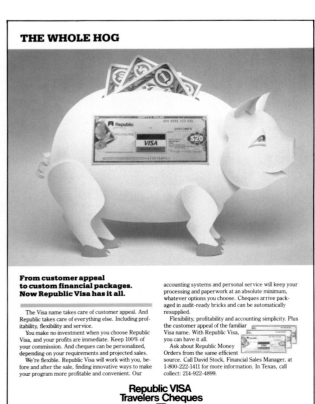

64

J. S. Bruck/Sally Vitsky

Artists Management
157 West 57th Street
New York, NY 10019
Tel. 212-247 1130

Sal Catalano

114 Boyce Place
Ridgewood, New Jersey 07450
Tel. 201-447 5318

Clients include:
National Audubon Society, Ciba-Geigy, American Motors, CBS, NBC, Coca Cola, General Foods, New York Zoological Society, Canada Dry, ABC, Time-Life, Pepsi Cola, Citibank, Travenol, U.S. Government, Upjohn, Lederle, Pfizer, Burger King, IBM, United Artists, Panasonic, Borden, McGraw-Hill, RCA, TWA, McNeil, Squibb, Bayer, Wyeth, Seagram, N.J. Bell, Sterling, American Cyanimid, Roche, American Distillers, Paramount Studios, Merck International, Doyle Dane Bernbach, J. Walter Thompson, Grey, Ogilvy-Mather, Marsteller, Benton & Bowles, Ted Bates, Foote Cone & Belding, McCaffrey-McCall, Kallir, Philips, Ross, McCann Erickson, Dancer-Fitzgerald-Sample, T.V. Guide, Redbook, Reader's Digest, Esquire, Avon Books, N.Y. Times.

Ron Chan

1717 Union Street
San Francisco, California 94123
Tel. 415-441 4544

Clients include:
Vicom Associates
Computerland
Sierra Magazine
West Magazine
Bank of America
California Living
Goodby, Berlin & Silverstein
San Francisco Symphony

Atari
Flowers& Magazine
Focus Magazine
Wells Fargo
J. Walter Thompson
Foote, Cone & Belding/Honig

Warren Chang

1243 Vicente Drive, #72
Sunnyvale, California 94086
Tel. 415-964 1701

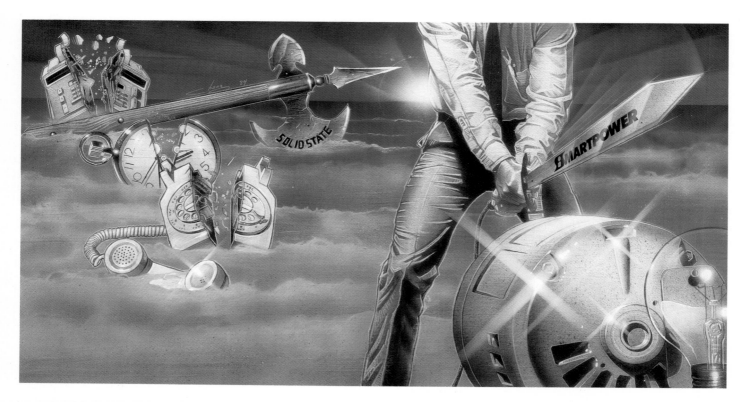

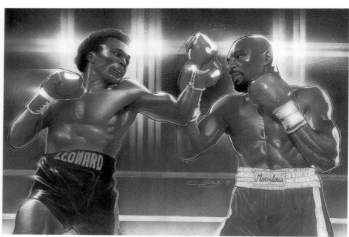

William V. Cigliano

Agent:
Eileen Moss
333 East 49th Street
New York, NY 10017
Tel. 212-980 8061

In Chicago call:
Tel. 312-878 1659

Clients include:
Abbott Laboratories, AG Becker, Arista Records, Ballantine Books, Burry, Canteen Corporation, Chicago Magazine, Gerber, Guideposts, Kraft Foods, Lanier, MacMillan Publishing, Mazola, Miller Breweries, Modern Healthcare, Morton Salt, International Harvester, N.Y. Art Director's Club, Proctor & Gamble, Rockwell International, Savings Institutions, Sealed Air Corporation, Seven-Up, Standard Oil, Stanley Hardware, Strohs Breweries, Success Magazine, United Airlines, US Gypsum, Viking Penguin Books.

Tim Clark Illustration/Graphics

8800 Venice Boulevard
Los Angeles, California 90034
Tel. 213-202 1044

Working until eleven since
sixty-seven.

Clients include:
Warner Brothers, MCA, Columbia, Capital Records, Motown Records, Needham, Harper and Steers Advertising, Grey Advertising, Cunningham and Walsh Advertising, Ogilvy and Mather Advertising, Marsteller Advertising, Parker Advertising, California Magazine, California Business Magazine, Texas Monthly Magazine, California Federal, McDonalds Restaurants, Mattel Toys, Carnation.

Woody Coleman Presents/John Letostak

7801 Fernhill Avenue
Parma, Ohio 44129

Agent:
Woody Coleman Presents, Inc.
1295 Old River Road
Cleveland, Ohio 44113
Tel. 216-621 1771

John's carefully crafted oil paintings are pure Americana, a style that easily lends itself to a nostalgic approach in the marketing of many goods and services. Although John has ten years experience in editorial illustration and dozens of national awards, he has only recently

applied his talents to advertising and is considered an emerging national talent. The images below represent works done for the Saturday Evening Post (cover contest), Cuna Supply, Turface, and Georgia Food & Nut Processors.

Woody Coleman
PRESENTS, INC.   (216) 621-1771

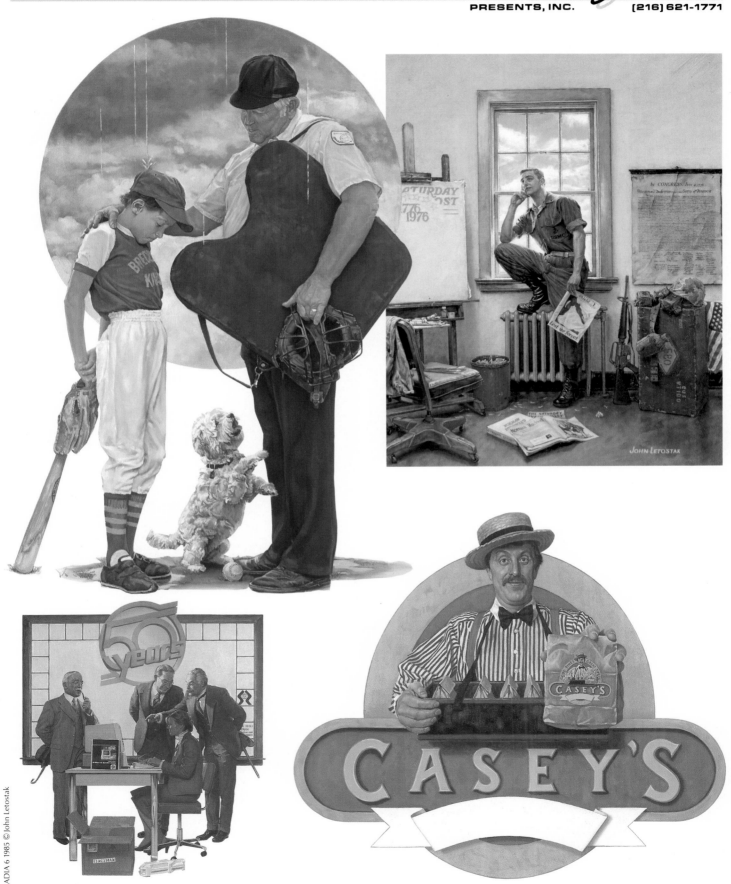

Woody Coleman Presents/Ezra N. Tucker

4634 Woodman Avenue
Sherman Oaks, California 91432

Agent:
Woody Coleman Presents, Inc.
1295 Old River Road
Cleveland, Ohio 44113
Tel. 216-621 1771

Clients include:
Anheuser-Busch, Inc., Levi-Straus,
Sunrise Publications, 20th Century
Fox, Universal Studios, Warner
Brothers, Adolph Coors Co., Ace
Books, Playboy Magazine, CBS
Records, Bridge Communications,
Bank of America, MCA Records,
Agememnon Productions,
Bostik Co., Miller Breweries,
NBC-TV, etc.

PRESENTS, INC.   (216) 621-1771

Woody Coleman Presents/Bob Novak

5356 Huron Road
Lyndhurst, Ohio 44124

Agent:
Woody Coleman Presents, Inc.
1295 Old River Road
Cleveland, Ohio 44113
Tel. 216-621 1771

Bob's style combines extraordinary perspectives and precise craftsmanship giving a new and unusually creative twist to any marketing strategy.

Advertising, institutional and editorial illustration done with attention to detail and deadlines have earned him local and national awards and a partial client list that includes Ardell, Inc., BF Goodrich,

Budweiser, Chessie Systems, Firestone, Foster & Kleiser, General Electric, GTE, Goodyear, HBJ Publications, Inc., NBC, Nutri-Systems, Ohio Bell, Penton IPC, Pepsi Cola and Stouffers.

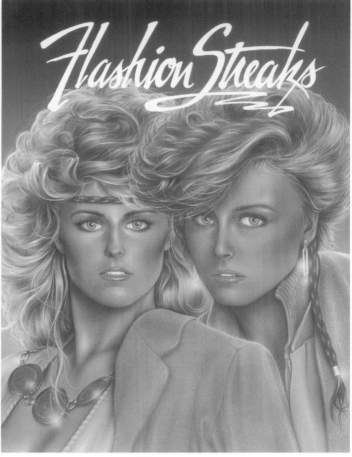

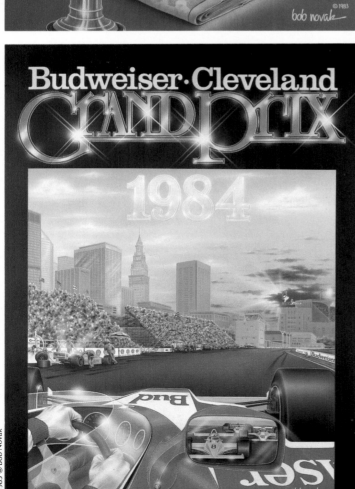

ADIA 6 1985 © Bob Novak

73

Woody Coleman Presents/Dave Fisher

3451 Houston Road
Waynesville, Ohio 45068

Agent:
Woody Coleman Presents, Inc.
1295 Old River Road
Cleveland, Ohio 44113
Tel. 216-621 1771

Partial client lists:
ITT, NCR, Bluecross-Blue Shield,
Coca-Cola, Cooper Industries
World Book, Inc., Cincinnati
Opera, Royal Air, Procter &
Gamble, Owens-Illinois, David
C. Cook Publishing, EG & G
Ortec, Opryland USA, Howard
Paper Mills, Antioch Publishing
Co., Firestone, Union Carbide,
General Electric.

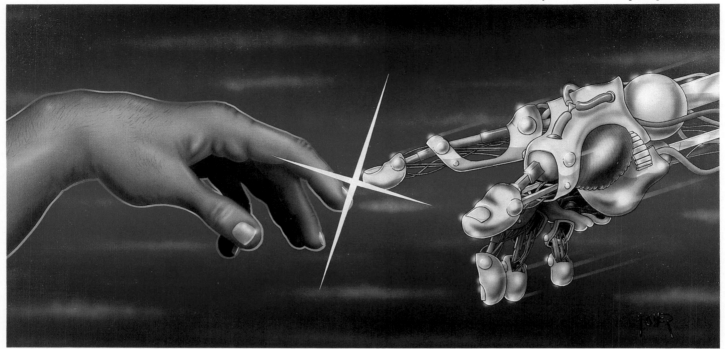

ADIA 6 1985 © Dave Fisher

74

Woody Coleman Presents/Ernest Norcia

7309 West 67th Street
Overland Park, Kansas 66202

Agent:
Woody Coleman Presents, Inc.
1295 Old River Road
Cleveland, Ohio 44113
Tel. 216-621 1771

Armed with Fresh Ideas
and a Gleam in my Eye
I Create Immortal Imagery
you can't Pass By.

Yes, from beyond the horizon
comes the artist whose quest is
to erase those demons of design
who darken the pages of our
graphic souls.

Rescuing clients from the
dungeons of dullness, he seeks
not the technical facts, but the
illustrious truth.

PRESENTS, INC. (216) 621-1771

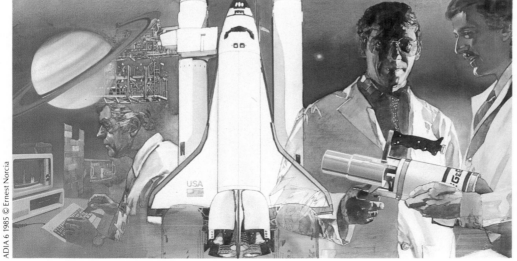

ADIA 6 1985 © Ernest Norcia

AL MARGOLIS

5094 Lansdowne Rd.
Solon, OH 44139

Woody Coleman Presents, Inc.
1295 Old River Road
Cleveland, OH 44113

Al Margolis's drawings render the world from a slightly off-center vantage point. His round-eyed people are irresistibly loveable, regardless of what problems they are mired in or how unbelieveable their situations may be. Al has been producing his gang of characters for twelve years, and has had them perform their antics in black and white and color for scores of clients including IBM-PC, Harvest Publishing, American Greetings, Penton Publishing, Scholastic Magazine and Argus Communications.

PRESENTS, INC.   [216] 621-1771

STUART C. WALTON

26151 Lake Shore Blvd.
Euclid, OH 44132

Woody Coleman Presents, Inc.
1295 Old River Road
Cleveland, OH 44113

In the years Stuart C. Walton has been a free-lance illustrator, he has done work for Picker Corp., Ameritrust, Childers, The Zoological Society and many of the areas largest ad agencies. He has become known for his distinctive line technique used particularly in editorial and institutional material.
He is specifically interested in wildlife, environmental, and technological subjects. One of his recent endeavors was to design a calendar on endangered species for Reuter/Stokes Co. The dolphin below is an example.

PRESENTS, INC.   [216] 621-1771

ERNIE NORCIA

3451 Houston Road
Waynesville, OH 45068

Woody Coleman Presents, Inc.
1295 Old River Road
Cleveland, OH 44113

Ernie's artistic talents lie in fine arts, full color illustrations (see preceeding page) and black & white line. The examples below show a clean "corporate" flair. They are used by P.R. firms and agencies for newsletters, annual reports and facility brochures. His portrait likenesses are perfect; as are his figure group situations. Prolific and fast, he works in line, charcoal, line & wash and a variety of other mediums to satisfy the most particular of art directors. Truly a "professional."

Woody Coleman

PRESENTS, INC.   [216] 621-1771

ADIA 6 1985 © Norcia/Shephard

TOM SHEPHARD

28914 Buchanan Drive
Bay Village, OH 44140

Woody Coleman Presents, Inc.
1295 Old River Road
Cleveland, OH 44113

A product of the depression, Tom Shephard knew hard times. For seven years his family lived in a Christmas tree his father found abandoned on a corner lot. Determined to make his mark in the world of art he used only available media, this samples of his earlier work can be found carved in desk tops, scrawled on men's room walls and etched in public booths. Today you can find him giggling, scribbling and napping in his studio overlooking an uncut lawn.

Woody Coleman

PRESENTS, INC.   [216] 621-1771

ADIA 6 1985 © Norcia/Shephard

Russell Cobane

8291 Allen Road
Clarkston, Michigan 48016
Tel. 313-625 6132

Agent:
Carol Chislovsky Inc.
420 Madison Avenue
New York, NY 10017
Tel. 212-980 3510

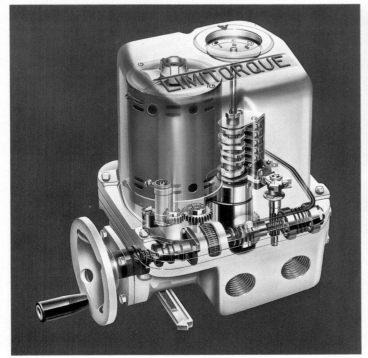

Connie Connally

7818 Ridgemar
Dallas, Texas 75231
Tel. 214-340 7818

Agent:
Sandra Freeman
3333 Elm
Dallas, Texas 75226
Tel. 214-742 4302—Dallas
Tel. 212-254 0866—New York

Kinuko Y. Craft

Represented by:
Fran Seigel
515 Madison Avenue
New York, NY 10022
Tel. 212-486 9644

Time, Inc.

Infodata Systems, Inc.

John Craig

Rural Route 2, Box 81
Soldiers Grove, Wisconsin 54655
Tel. 608-872 2371

Agent:
Carolyn Potts & Associates
3 East Ontario #25
Chicago, Illinois 60611
Tel. 312-935 1707

Partial client list:
A+ Magazine, Ad Age Magazine, American Airlines, American Way, Album Graphics, Anheuser-Busch (Budweiser, Bud Light & Natural Light), Chicago, Cracker Jack, CENTEL, Cuisine, Games, Horizon, Minnesota Public Radio, Northwest Orient, Peat Marwick, Philadelphia, PC World, Playboy, Public Agenda Foundation, Ruby Street Cards, Runner, Scott Foresman, & Co., Sesame Street, Success, Sieber & McIntyre, 7-Up, 13-30 Corporation, TWA Ambassador, Williams Pinball, Henry Weinhard Beer (Ogilvy & Mather/SFO), General Electric, U.S. Gypsum.

Further examples of work can be seen in: Society of Illustrators Vols. 23, 25 & 26, American Illustration Vols. 1 & 3, American Showcase Vols. 7 & 8, CA Art Annual '80, Chicago Talent Sourcebook 1983, Creativity 80 & 82.

ADIA 6 1985 © John Craig

81

Tom Curry

309 East Live Oak
Austin, Texas 78704
Tel. 512-443-8427

Represented in New York by:
Eileen Moss
333 East 49th Street
New York, NY 10017
Tel. 212-980 8061

Client list includes:
Adweek, American Airlines, American Bank, Anheuser Busch, Apple Computer, Boys' Life, California Dreamers, Chicago Magazine, Continental Airlines, Del Taco, Discipleship Journal, Dr. Pepper, Emergency Medicine Magazine, Exxon, Financial World, Holiday Inn, Holt Caterpillar, IBM, Murine, Newsweek, Northwest Mall, Paul Broadhead & Associates, Random House, Republic Bank, Selsun Blue, Southwest Airlines, Schlotzsky's, Steak and Ale Restaurants, Texas Instruments, Texas Monthly, The Cleveland Plain Dealer, The Dallas Times Herald

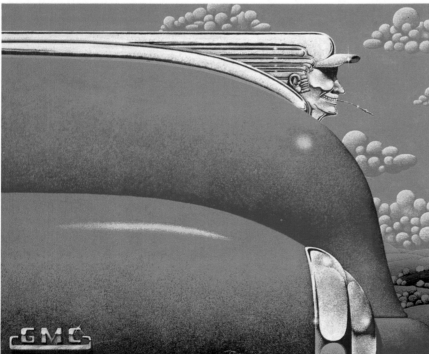

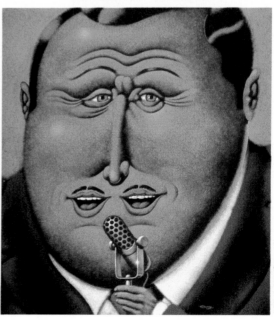

Daniels & Daniels   Artistic Licence

14 South Madrid
Newbury Park, California 91320
Tel. 805-498 1923

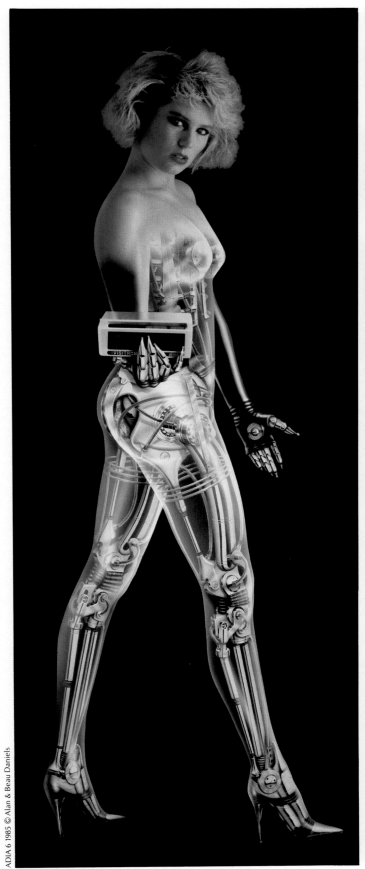

Jacqueline Dedell Artist Representative

58 West 15th Street
New York, NY 10011
Tel. 212-741 2539

Illustration:
Ivan Chermayeff
Teresa Fasolino
Ivan Powell
Barry Root
Richard Williams

Design:
Chermayeff and Geismar
Associates
Call for separate brochure.

Photography:
Henry Wolf

Please call for our full color brochure showing a selection of each artist's work. Upon request, portfolios will be sent overnight to any city in the U.S.A., Canada, London or Paris. Delivery to other European cities and Japan take slightly longer.

Richard Williams   Barry Root   Henry Wolf   Jacqueline Dedell   Ivan Powell   Teresa Fasolino   Ivan Chermayeff

Jacqueline Dedell Artist Representative

Veuillez téléphoner pour demander notre brochure en couleurs figurant une sélection du travail de chaque artiste. On peut envoyer les portefeuilles pour arriver le lendemain à n'importe quelle ville aux Etats-unis, ainsi qu'au Canada, à Londres ou à Paris. Livraison à d'autres villes européennes et au Japon pourraient prendre plus longtemps.

各アーティストの作品を掲載したブローシュア を御希望の方は御一報ください。連絡を受け 次第、アメリカ国内、カナダの各都市及びロン ドン、パリには一晩でポートフォリオをお送りし ます。他のヨーロッパの都市及び日本へは、 少し時間がかかります。

Bitte rufen Sie an, um unsere Farbbroschüre zu bekommen, worin ein Probestück von dem Werk jedes Künstlers wieder-gegeben ist. Auf Wunsch werden Kollektionen übernacht an irgendeine Stadt in den U.S.A., Kanada, London oder Paris versendet. Zustellungen an andere europäische Städte, sowie Japan dauern etwas länger.

58 West 15th Street
New York, NY 10011
Tel. 212-741 2539

Barry Root

Ivan Powell

Teresa Fasolino

Richard Williams

ADIA 6 1985 © Jacqueline Dedell

Ivan Chermayeff

Ed Diffenderfer

32 Cabernet Court
Lafayette, California 94549
Tel. 415-254 8235

Illustrations have appeared in Time, Fortune, Newsweek, Reader's Digest, Argosy, Chevron World.

Portrait assignments include Prince Philip, Sir Edmund Hillary, Ted Williams, Henry J. Kaiser, Gen. Jimmy Doolittle.

Clients include:
Chevron Corporation, Bank of America, Sears Roebuck, Pendleton, General Electric, United Technologies, Westinghouse, U.S. Leasing, Lone Star Industries, Atari, Barclay's Bank, Department of Interior, U.S. Air Force, Bechtel Power Corp., Crocker Bank International.

Andrzej Dudzinski

52 East 81st Street
New York, NY 10028
Tel. 212-628 6959

Clients include:
The Atlantic, Ted Bates, The Boston
Globe, Geo, Grey Advertising, GQ,
Money, Newsweek, The New York
Times, Rolling Stone, Scholastic
Publications, San Jose Mercury
News, Texas Monthly, J.W.
Thompson, TWA Ambassador,
Vanity Fair, Ziff Davies Publications.

ADIA 6 1985 © Andrzej Dudzinski

87

Andrea Eberbach

5301 North Delaware
Indianapolis, Indiana 46220
Tel. 317-253 0421

Advertising, Editorial, Publishing
Art.

Conception artistique pour les
maisons d'édition.

Werbung, Redaktion,
Kunstveröffentlichung.

A partial client list includes:
Addison-Wesley Publishing,
American Dental Association,
Better Homes and Gardens,
Borden's, Citizen's Gas, Indiana
Bell Telephone, Laidlaw
Publishing, Lincoln National Life,
Mayflower, McDougal-Littell

Publishing, McGraw-Hill
Publishing, Merchant's Bank,
National Geographic, Parent's
Magazine, The Saturday Evening
Post, Scott-Foresman, Sunrise
Publications, Walden Books, and
others.

ADIA 6 1985 © Andrea Eberbach

Marc W. Ericksen

1045 Sansome Street
Studio 306
San Francisco, California 94111
Tel. 415-362 1214

Los Angeles clients please call:
Chuck DuBow
Tel. 213-938 5177

Fantasy and Technology

Partial client list:
Amdahl
Activision
Atari
Anthem, Inc.
Broderbund, Inc.
Bank of America
Crown Zellerbach
Destek, Inc.

East West Network
Hewlett Packard
Hesware
Hexcel
Jacuzzi
Kelsey Hayes
Masport America
Prolog Computers

San Francisco Magazine
Searle, Inc.
Siemiens, Inc.
Trans International Airlines
Tronix Software
United Airlines
Viacom
Zehntel, Inc.

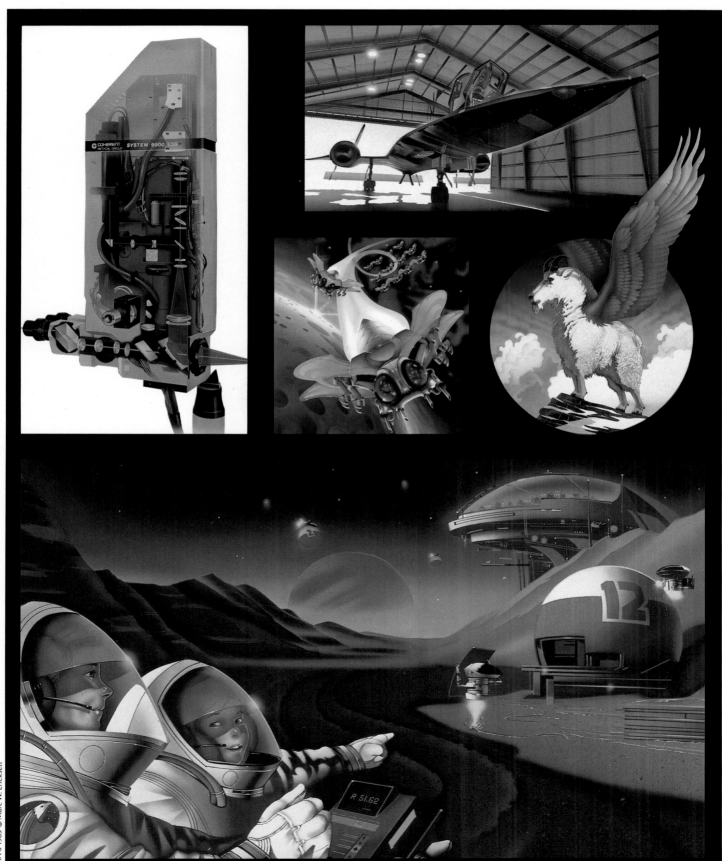

ADIA 6 1985 © Marc W. Ericksen

Ella

Photographers' & Artists'
Representative
229 Berkeley Street
Boston, Massachusetts 02116
Tel. 617-266 3858

ANNA DAVIDIAN

ROGER LEYONMARK

ROB CLINE

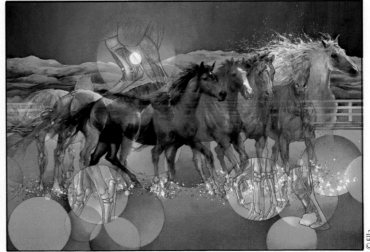

BENTE ADLER

ADIA 6 1985 © Ella

Ella

Photographers' & Artists'
Representative
229 Berkeley Street
Boston, Massachusetts 02116
Tel. 617-266 3858

ANATOLY DVERIN

JACK CROMPTON

SUSAN DODGE

RON TOELKE

Robert Evans

1045 Sansome Street, Studio 306
San Francisco, California 94111
Tel. 415-397 5322

Clients include:
J. Walter Thompson, Soskin-Thompson, McCann-Erickson, Foote Cone & Belding, David W. Evans, Doyle Dane & Bernbach, Allen & Dorward, Dailey & Associates, Pat Mountain Design, Blue Cross, Learning Magazine,

Specialized Bicycling Components, A+ Magazine, AT&T, Apple, Epson, Onyx Systems, Hewlett-Packard, Paperback Software, By-Video, Margaux Controls

ADIA 6 1985 © Robert Evans

92

Vivienne Flesher

23 East 10th Street
New York City, NY 10003
Tel. 212-505 6731

Clients include:
Time Magazine, New York
Magazine, Fortune Magazine,
Elizabeth Arden, Bloomingdales,
Macys, Henri Bendel, CBS
Records, Random House, featured
in Graphis 229, several paintings
are to be used in the movie
"Almost You," has worked
extensively in Europe and Japan.

Eames Chaise: Herman Miller Catalogue

Vogue Magazine: Fashion

New York Times: Poster and Magazine Advertisement

Rolling Stone Magazine: Cover

H Magazine: Fitness

Stanislaw Fernandes

35 East 12th Street
New York, NY 10003
Tel. 212-533 2648

Art and Design for advertising, editorial and corporate assignments.

Please call for full color brochure.

Clients include:
AIWA, Almay Cosmetics, American Express, American International Pictures, AT&T, Avco Embassy Pictures, Avon Cosmetics, Ballantine Books, Business Week, Canadian Club, Chase Bank, Chemical Bank, Columbia Pictures, Cyba Geigy, Deknatel, Ellesse, Exxon, Foster Grant, Hammermill Paper,

Jim Henson Associates, Hoescht, IBM, International Paper, Eli Lilly, Miller Beer, Money Magazine, Newsweek, New York Lottery, Norelco, Ownes Corning, Philips, Procter & Gamble, RCA, St. Regis Paper, Schweppes, Seagrams, Sony, Teleprompter, Toshiba, Twentieth Century Fox, U.S. Steel, Western Electric, Wranglers.

ADIA 6 1985 © Stanislaw Fernandes

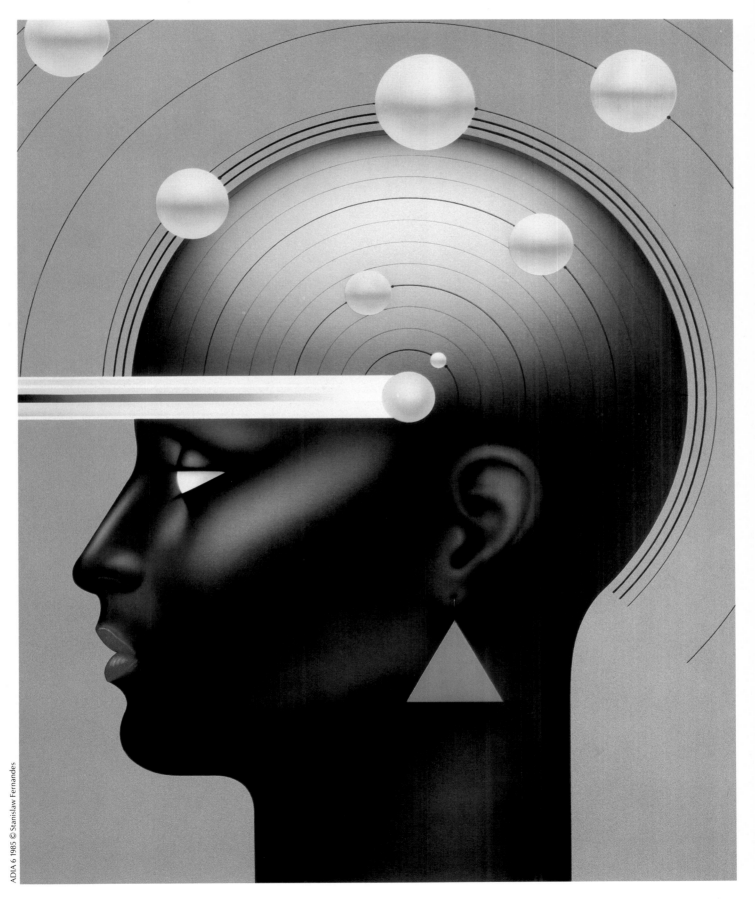

Carol Gillot

162 West 13th Street, Apartment 66
New York, NY 10011
Tel. 212-243 6448

Airbrush pharmaceutical and
technical illustration and design.

Clients include:
AT&T, CBS, Colgate, Creamer,
Discover, Fortune, Grey, Gross
Townsend Frank, Kallir Phillips
Ross, Microsystems, P.C., Readers
Digest, Rolf W. Rosenthal, Time.

Member:
Graphic Artists Guild.

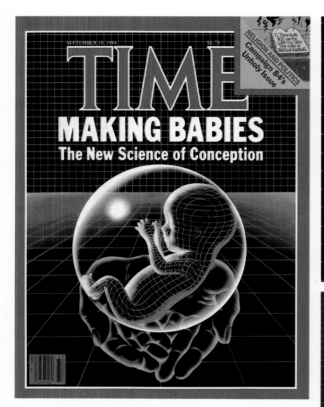

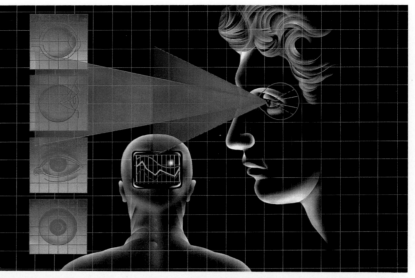

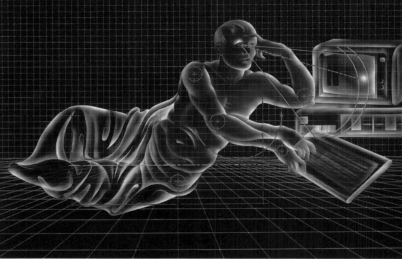

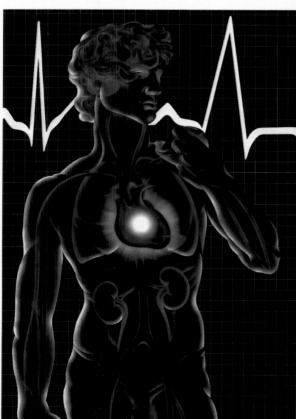

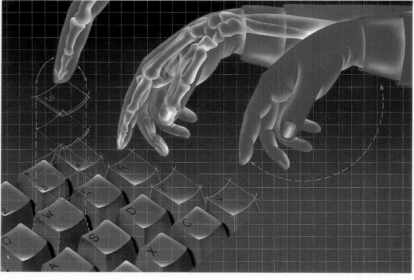

Robert Giusti

Tel. 212-752 0179

Represented by:
Milton Newborn Associates
135 East 54th Street
New York, NY 10022
Tel. 212-421 0050

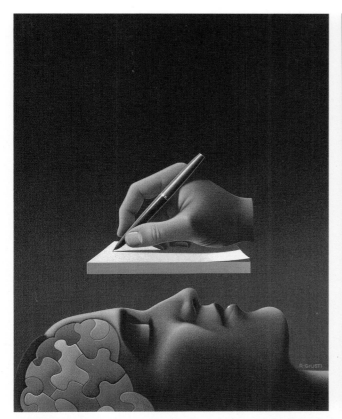

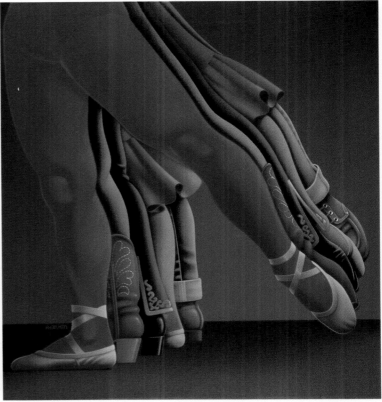

Ken Goldammer

405 North Wabash Avenue
Chicago, Illinois 60611
Tel. 312-836 0143

Midwest Agent:
Joni Tuke
368 West Huron
Chicago, Illinois 60601
Tel. 312-787 6826

A partial client list includes:
Anheuser Busch, Avco Embassy
Pictures, United Airlines,
American Motors, Rockwell
International, Proctor and Gamble,
International Harvester, Schwinn,
American Veterinary Medical
Association, U.S. News And World
Report, U.S. Robotics

Member Graphic Artists Guild

Greathead Studio

2975 Christopher's Court
Marietta, Georgia 30062
Tel. 404-952 5067

Contact:
Ian Greathead

Clients include:
Alamo, Allegheny, Amoco, Burger King, Busch Gardens, Delta Airlines, C&S, Coca Cola, Contel, Firestone, Georgia Pacific, Harris, Hayes, Hunter Douglas, IBM, International Harvester, Intertec,

J. Walter Thompson, John Harland, MSA, NAPA, Nokia, Ogilvy & Mather, Peachtree Software, Quadram, Seth Thomas, Siemans-Allis, Smith & Nephew, Snapper, Wrangler.

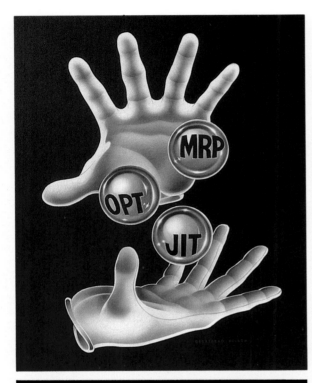

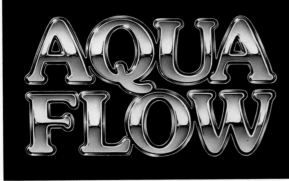

David Grove

382 Union Street
San Francisco, California 94133
Tel. 415-433 2100

Steven Guarnaccia

89 Bleecker Street 6B
New York, NY 10012
Tel. 212-420 0108

Insert for 1984 Herman Miller Annual Report

Animated Multigroup TV spot for Altman & Manley, Cambridge

1984 MCI Annual Report

Diane Teske Harris

Represented by:
Marion Moskowitz Represents Inc.
342 Madison
New York, NY 10017
Tel. 212-719 9879

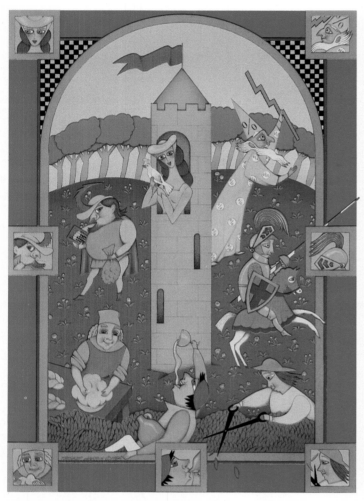

Mark Hess

Tel. 914-232 5870

Represented by:
Milton Newborn Associates
135 East 54th Street
New York, NY 10022
Tel. 212-421 0050

Richard Hess

Tel. 203-354 2921

Represented by:
Milton Newborn Associates
135 East 54th Street
New York, NY 10022
Tel. 212-421 0050

ADIA 6 1985 © Richard Hess

Ken Hodges/Illustration

12401 Bellwood Road
Los Alamitos, CA 90720
Tel. 213-431 4343

Agent:
Jeanette Hodges
Ken Hodges, Inc.
12401 Bellwood Road
Los Alamitos, California 90720
Tel. 213-431 4343

Ken Hodges, specialist in full color illustration and design. Extensive experience in the defense, aerospace, and electronics industries as well as with commercial and industrial corporations.

Works from blueprints, photography, or prototypes.

Cleared for secret material.

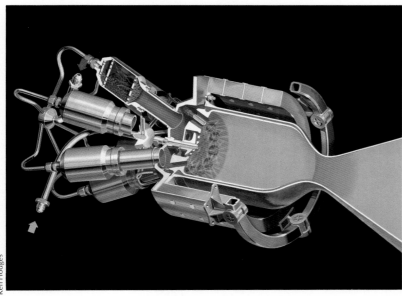

Scott Hull Artist Representative

20 Lynn Rae Circle
Dayton, Ohio 45459
Tel. 513-433 8383

Representing some of America's
leading artists. For portfolios on
the artists, call or write.

Price Waterhouse

Don Vanderbeek

John Maggard

Howard Paper

Illustrators & Designers Workshop

David Groff

Budweiser

Tracy Britt

David Lesh

Huffy Corporation

Robert Hunt

4376 21st Street
San Francisco, California 94114
Tel. 415-824 1824

New York Representative:
Barbara Gordon Assoc.
Tel. 212-686 3514

San Francisco Representative:
Jan Collier
Tel. 415-552 4252

Additional illustrations may be
seen in American Showcase,
Volumes 6 and 7, and Art Directors
Index, Volumes 9 and 10.

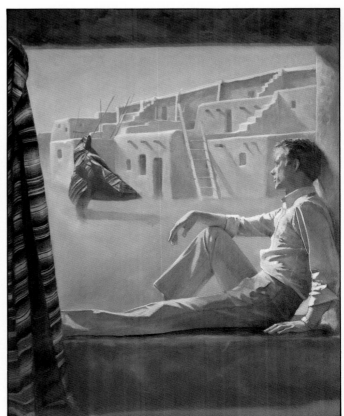

David Jarvis

275 Indigo Drive, Daytona Beach
Florida 32014   Tel. 904-255 1296

Representatives:
JOE MENDOLA   212-986 5680
420 Lexington Avenue, Suite 2911
New York City, NY 10170

CHUCK DUBOW   213-938 5177
7461 Beverly Boulevard, Suite 405
Los Angeles, California 90036

Clients:
20th Century Fox, Paramount, Disney Studios, MCA, Universal, MGM/UA, Lorimar, NBC Premiere, Diener Hauser Bates, Bill Gold, ABC TV, ABC Records, RCA Records, Warner Electra Atlantic, Motown, Redbook, Architectural Digest, Cosmopolitan, Psychology Today, Fortune, Motor Trend, Newsweek, Reader's Digest.

Goodyear, Chrysler de Mexico, Toyota, Nissan, Nippon Denso, Hughes Aircraft, Mattel, ARCO, Continental Airlines, Clairol, Holland America Cruise Lines, Nautilus Sports/Medical, Coors, Nabisco, Gallo, Aim Toothpaste, MacDonalds, Benchmark Bourbon, Bantam, Ballantine, Pinnacle, Berkeley/Jove, Dell, Harlequin, Ace, Scholastic Books.

BBD&O, Y&R, JWT, NW Ayer, Grey, Foote Cone Belding, Leo Burnett, Doyle Dane Bernbach, Chiat Day, Needham Harper & Steers, Benton & Bowles, Cunningham Root Craig, D'Arcy MacManus & Masius, Bozell & Jacobs, Dancer Fitzgerald Sample, McCaffrey & McCall, Kenyon & Eckardt, Eisaman Johns & Laws, McCann Erickson, MSIA.

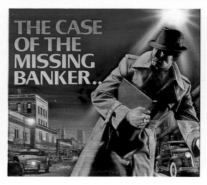

B.E. Johnson / Concept One

366 Oxford Street
Rochester, New York 14607
Tel. 716-461 4240

Los Angeles:
Robert Jones
10889 Wilshire Boulevard
Los Angeles, California 90024
Tel. 213-208 5093

Technical and Astronomical Art.
Special Effects Design

It is a fine thread that contains
the volatile balance between
accuracy, clarity and creativity.
The art of a fine illustrator is his
ability to strain these connections
without breaking the thread.

それは正確さ、明白さ及び創造性の間にある
変り易いバランスを有する細い糸の様なもので
ある。優れたイラストレーターの技巧としては、
彼がその糸を切らずにこれらのつながりをぴん
と張る事が出来る能力があるという事である。

Technology
and the Art to understand it,

Nature
and the Art to appreciate it,

The Unknown
and the Art to experience it.

DESIGNERS ILLUSTRATORS CONSTRUCTORS

Eric Joyner

#21 Lapidge Street #4
San Francisco, California 94110
Tel. 415-626 9890

Clients include:
Activision, Electronic Arts,
Harcourt Brace Jovanovich, Inc.,
Pacific Telephone, Creative
BioMolecules, The Mind's Eye,
Dionex, Wescor, Edusoft, Miller
Freeman Publishers, Devoluy
Lynch, Explorama, McDaniels
& Assoc.

Chris Kenyon

14 Wilmot
San Francisco, CA 94115
Tel. 415-923 1363

281 Castle Hill Ranch Road
Walnut Creek, California 94595
Tel. 415-934 5844

John Kilroy

28 Fairmount Way
Nantasket, Massachusetts 02045
Tel.: 617-925 0582

Clients include:
BASF, ComputerWorld Magazine/
CW Communications, Dynamic
Graphics Inc., W.R. Grace & Co.,
Graphic-Sha Publishing Co. Ltd.,
Gunn Assoc., HHCC, Howard
Johnsons, Myasthenia Gravis
Foundation, Parker Bros., Polaroid
Corp., Osborne Computers,
Saltwater Sportsman Magazine,
Spaulding Corp., Yankee

Magazine. Direct and with affiliate
agencies. Slide portfolio available.

Unter seinen Kunden befinden
sich:
BASF, ComputerWorld Magazine/
CW Communications, Dynamic
Graphics Inc., W.R. Grace & Co.,
Graphic-Sha Publishing Co. Ltd.,
Gunn Assoc., HHCC, Howard

Johnsons, Myasthenia Gravis
Foundation, Parker Bros., Polaroid
Corp., Osborne Computers,
Saltwater Sportsman Magazine,
Spaulding Corp., Yankee Magazine.
Direkt und mit Filialagenturen.
Diakollektion erhältlich.

ADIA 6 1985 © John Kilroy

David Kimble

711 South Flower
Burbank, California 91502
Tel. 213-849 1576

Agent:
John Steinberg, Inc.
10434 Corfu Lane
Los Angeles, California 90077
Tel. 213-279 1775

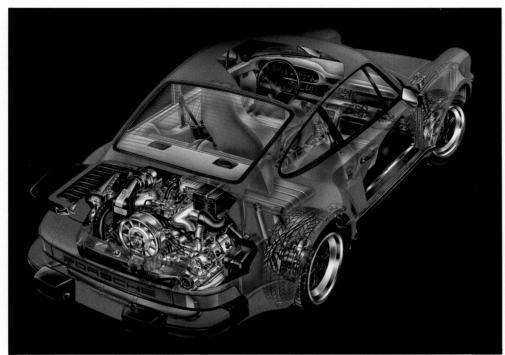

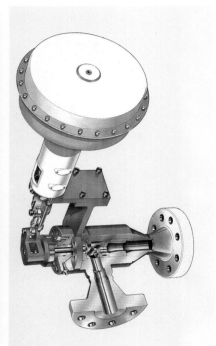

Jim Kingston
Norman Bendell

Agent:
David Goldman Agency
18 East 17th Street
New York, NY 10003
Tel. 212-807 6627

Kingston

Kingston

Bendell

Bendell

Kirchoff/Wohlberg, Inc.

866 United Nations Plaza
New York, NY 10017
Tel. 212-644 2020

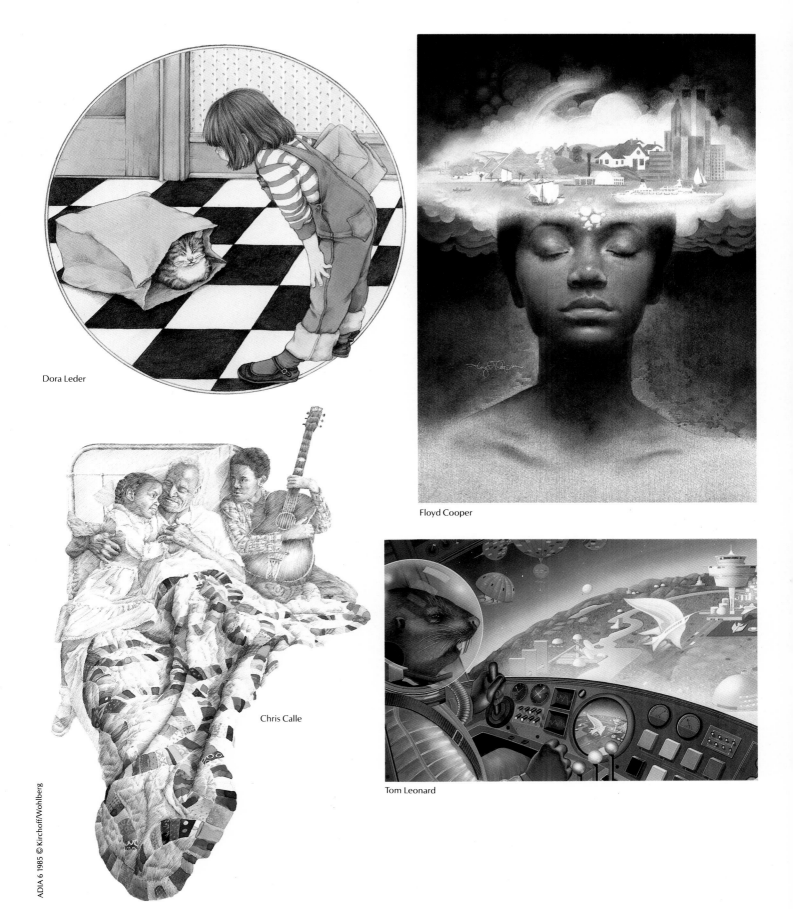

Dora Leder

Floyd Cooper

Chris Calle

Tom Leonard

115

Renee Klein

291 Carroll Street
Brooklyn, New York 11231
Tel. 212-841 4464
      718-624 1210

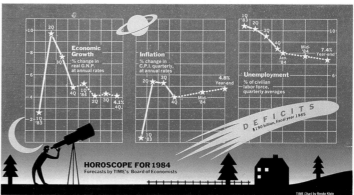

HOROSCOPE FOR 1984
Forecasts by TIME's Board of Economists

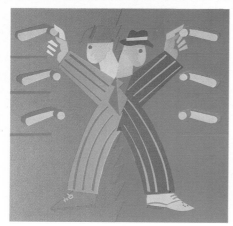

NETTING THE BIG ONES
Top five mergers

Buyer/Seller	Price in billions (date announced)	Combined annual sales at merger in billions
1 Socal/Gulf Oil	$13.2 (March 5, '84)	$57.3
2 Texaco/Getty Oil	10.1 (Jan. 6, '84)	53.1
3 Du Pont/Conoco	8.0 (July 6, '81)	31.7
4 U.S. Steel/Marathon Oil	6.6 (Nov. 19, '81)	23.7
5 Santa Fe Industries/Southern Pacific	5.1 (Sept. 27, '83)	6.0

Source: W. T. Grimm & Co.   TIME Chart by Renée Klein

Vladimir Kordic

35351 Grovewood Drive
Eastlake, Ohio 44094
Tel. 216-951 4026

Agents:
Woody Coleman
Tel. 216-621 1771

Joel Harlib
Tel. 312-329 1370

Lander/Osborne • Cathy Heck

Represented by:
LANDER/OSBORNE
A Division of Jane Lander
Associates
333 East 30th Street
New York, NY 10016
Tel. 212-679 1358

Clients include:
Young & Rubicam, Scali McCabe &
Sloves, Bozell & Jacobs, BBD&O,
Backer & Spielvogel, Benton
& Bowles, AT&T, Hertz, Jello,
Mrs. Paul's, Commodore
Computers, Scholastic Magazine,
Woman's Day, Pocket Books,
Banbury Books, Texas
International

ADIA 6 1985 © Cathy Heck

Lander/Osborne • Frank Riley

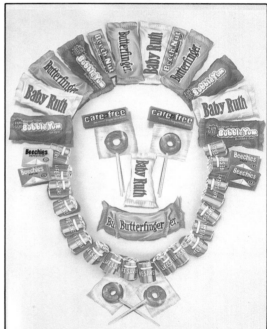

ADIA 6 1985 © Frank Riley

119

Lander/Osborne • Phil Franké

Represented by:
LANDER/OSBORNE
A Division of Jane Lander
Associates
333 East 30th Street
New York, NY 10016
Tel. 212-679 1358

Clients include:
AT&T, ABC, CBS, NBC, Young & Rubicam, Ted Bates, Bill Gold Advertising, Paramount Pictures, Warner Brothers, 20th Century Fox, Burger King, Coleco, Associated Press, Sportschannel, Goodyear, Foote Cone & Belding, Ogilvy & Mather, Geer Dubois, McCann-Erickson, Doyle Dane Bernbach, BBD&O, Kallir Phillips Ross, Golf Digest, Science Digest, Field & Stream, Bradbury Press, Popular Mechanics.

ADIA 6 1985 © Phil Franké

120

Lander/Osborne • Guetary/Lambert/Furukawa

Represented by:
LANDER/OSBORNE
A Division of Jane Lander
Associates
333 East 30th Street
New York, NY 10016
Tel. 212-679 1358

Guetary clients include:
NBC, Gillette, Benton & Bowles,
Ted Bates, Ash le Donne,
McCaffrey & McCall, N.W. Ayer,
A.C.&R., Medicus Intercon,
Cosmopolitan, Bergdorf
Goodman, Young Miss, Tennis
Magazine.

Lambert clients include:
Sports Illustrated, New York

Times, Newsweek, Columbia
Records, Life, Bell Telephone,
DHL, Medical Economics,
Ted Bates Advertising.

Furukawa clients include:
Maxell, AT&T, INA, New York
Times, J. Walter Thompson, Foote
Cone & Belding, A.C.&R., Geer
Dubois, Ogilvy Mather/2, Rolf
Werner Rosenthal, GQ

Helene Guetary

Saul Lambert

Mel Furukawa

Narda Lebo

4851 Cedar Springs
Dallas, Texas 75219
Tel. 214-528 0375

Agent in Dallas:
Lisa Cobb and Associates
2200 N. Lamar
Suite 202
Dallas, TX 75202
Tel. 214-939 0032

Agent in New York:
Michele Manasse
Tel. 212-873 3797

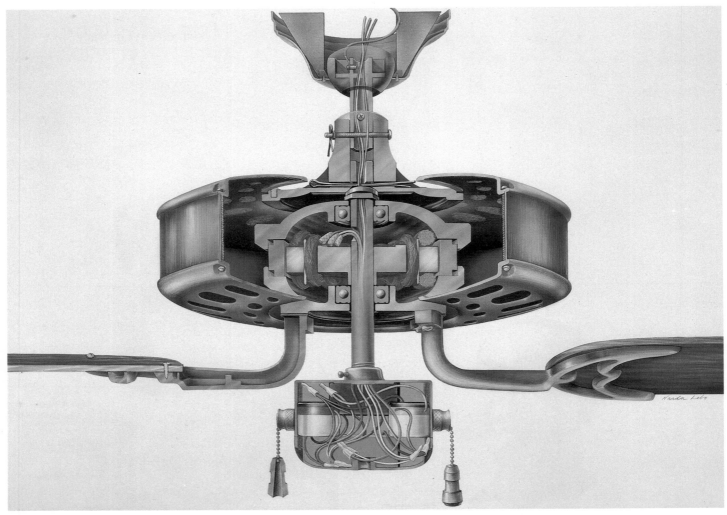

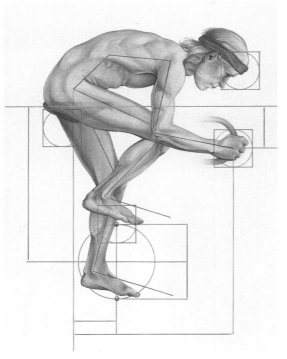

Arnie Levin

Represented by:
Marion Moskowitz Represents Inc.
342 Madison Avenue
New York, NY 10017
Tel. 212-719 9879

Panter Cigars/BBDO Amsterdam

Exxon Office Systems/Marsteller

The New Yorker Magazine, Inc., 1978 ©

The New Yorker Magazine Inc., 1984 ©

David Lesh

6021 Rosslyn Avenue
Indianapolis, Indiana 46220
Tel. 317-253 3141

Agents:

New York:
Joanne Palulian
Tel. 203-866 3734

San Francisco:
Diane Sullivan
Tel. 415-563 8884

Midwest:
Scott Hull
Tel. 513-433 8383

I've had the pleasure of working with Newsweek, Sports Illustrated, Jonson, Pedersen, Hinrichs & Shakery, Doyle Dane Bernbach, Ketchum Advertising, Memorex, Pacific Bell, NCR, Science 84, Book of the Month Club, Anthony Russell Inc., TV Guide, Apple, and others in cities like New York, San Francisco, Montreal, Boston, and Los Angeles. If you have any questions or would like additional samples, please don't hesitate to call. Until then . . . thank you.

Broom & Broom/San Francisco

David Lesh

6021 Rosslyn Avenue
Indianapolis, Indiana 46220
Tel. 317-253 3141

Agents:

New York:
Joanne Palulian
Tel. 203-866 3734

San Francisco:
Diane Sullivan
Tel. 415-563 8884

Midwest:
Scott Hull
Tel. 513-433 8383

I've had the pleasure of working with Newsweek, Sports Illustrated, Jonson, Pedersen, Hinrichs & Shakery, Doyle Dane Bernbach, Ketchum Advertising, Memorex, Pacific Bell, NCR, Science 84, Book of the Month Club, Anthony Russell Inc., TV Guide, Apple, and others in cities like New York, San Francisco, Montreal, Boston, and Los Angeles. If you have any questions or would like additional samples, please don't hesitate to call. Until then...thank you.

Jeffrey Dawson Associates/Boston

Edward H. Lim

348 Locust Street #2
San Francisco, California 94118
Tel. 415-921 1374

126

John Littleboy

7 Ninth Avenue
San Francisco, California 94118
Tel. 415-387 9718

Francis Livingston

1537 Franklin Street, Suite 105
San Francisco, California 94109
Tel. 415-776 1531

Agent:
Freda Scott
1440 Bush Street
San Francisco, California 94109
Tel. 415-775 6564

John Lytle

P.O. Box 5155
Sonora, California 95370
Tel. 209-928 4849

ABC Sports' unprecedented coverage of the
Games of the XXIII Olympiad begins in Los Angeles.
abc 9:00PM 7

ADIA 6 1985 © John Lytle

Some people think Bank of America only works with industrial giants.

Richard Martin

485 Hilda Street
East Meadow, New York 11554
Tel. 516-221 3630

Member:
Graphic Artists Guild.

◆

Representing Illustrators
GENE ALLISON
CHRIS CONSANI
JIM ENDICOTT
MARLA FRAZEE
ALETA JENKS
HIRO KIMURA
GARY PIERAZZI
ROBERT PRYOR
PAUL ROGERS
GREG ROWE
GARY RUDDELL
DICK SAKAHARA

Photographer
DENNIS GRAY

◆

RITA MARIE & FRIENDS

A R T I S T S'   R E P R E S E N T A T I V E S

6376 West 5th Street ◆ Los Angeles, California 90048

West Coast
RITA MARIE
Office: (213) 934-3395
Messages: (213) 936-2757

Chicago-Midwest
RODNEY RAY
Office: (312) 222-0337
Messages: (312) 472-6550

TELECOPIER IN OFFICE

◆

Rita Marie & Friends/Dick Sakahara

28826 Cedarbluff Drive
Rancho Palos Verdes,
California 90274
Tel. 213-541 8187

West Coast Representative:
Rita Marie
6376 West 5th Street
Los Angeles, California 90048
Tel. 213-936 2757

Chicago/Mid-West
Representative:
Rodney Ray
405 North Wabash Avenue, # 3106
Chicago, Illinois 60611
Tel 312-222 0337

Tokyo Representative:
Tim Okamoto
Ko-Po-Ai # 202
2-24-17 Takaido
Higashi, Suginami-ku
Tokyo 168 Japan

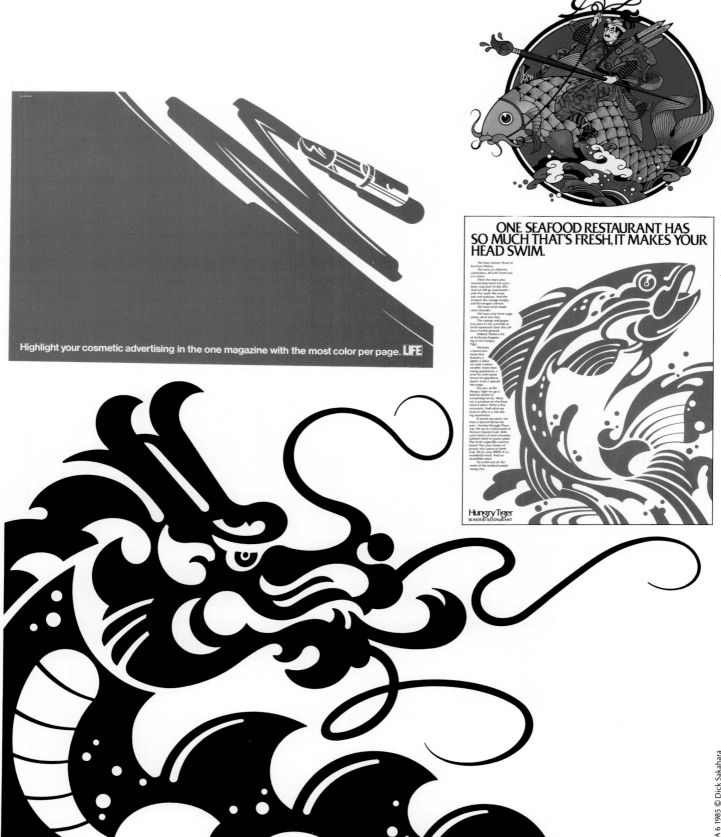

Highlight your cosmetic advertising in the one magazine with the most color per page. **LIFE**

ONE SEAFOOD RESTAURANT HAS SO MUCH THAT'S FRESH, IT MAKES YOUR HEAD SWIM.

Hungry Tiger
SEAFOOD RESTAURANT

Rita Marie & Friends/Chris Consani

Rita Marie
Office: Tel. 213-934 3395
Messages: Tel. 213-936 2757

Rodney Ray
Office: Tel. 312-222 0337
Messages: Tel. 312-472 6550

Rita Marie & Friends/Hiro Kimura

Rita Marie
Office: Tel. 213-934 3395
Messages: Tel. 213-936 2757

Rodney Ray
Office: Tel. 312-222 0337
Messages: Tel. 312-472 6550

Rita Marie & Friends/Paul Rogers

Rita Marie
Office: Tel. 213-934 3395
Messages: Tel. 213- 936 2757

Rodney Ray
Office: Tel. 312-222 0337
Messages: Tel. 312-472 6550

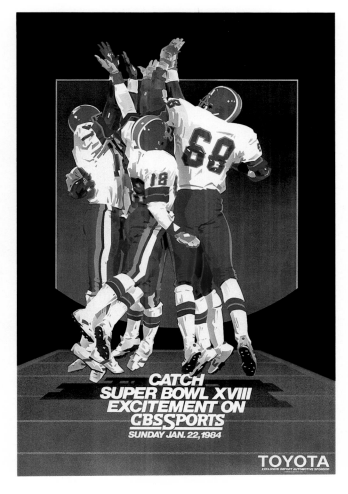

Rita Marie & Friends/Marla Frazee

Rita Marie
Office: Tel. 213-934 3395
Messages: Tel. 213-936 2757

Rodney Ray
Office: Tel. 312-222 0337
Messages: Tel. 312-472 6550

ADIA 6 1985 © Marla Frazee

136

Gary Ruddell

Represented in LA by
Rita Marie Tel. 213-934 3395
Messages: Tel. 213-936 2757

Represented in Chicago by
Rodney Ray Tel. 312-222 0337
Messages: Tel. 312-472 6550

Represented in NYC by
Barnie Kane Tel. 212-206 0322

Clients include:
Avon Books, Budweiser Beer, Boise Cascade, Blue Diamond Almonds, Bantom Books, Coors Beer, Carnation, Fantasy Records, Bank of America, United Artists, 20th Century Fox, Universal Studios, Playboy Magazine, National Lampoon, Ballantine Books, Kawasaki Motorcycles, Levi-Strauss, Papermoon Graphics, Putnam & Sons, Rolling Stone, Selway Tool Company, New York Title Insurance, Swiss Miss, Wayne Dog Food, Busch Beer, Penthouse Magazine, Advanced Micro Devices, Steven Spielberg, Kraft Foods, Pinnacle Books, Chic Magazine, Fawcett Books, Processor Technology, Harrison Computers, Texas Instruments, Mattel Toys, Western Graphics, Liberty Records, Speedo Swimwear, Standard Oil, Hills Bros. Corp., NBC Sports, Michelob Beer

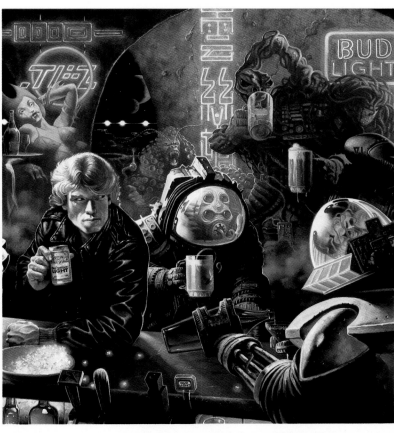

ADIA 6 1985 © Gary Ruddell

Bill Mayer

240 Forkner Drive
Decatur, Georgia 30030
Tel. 404-378 0686

Dan Sell, Chicago
Tel. 312-565 2701

Agents:

Phil Williams, Atlanta
Tel. 404-873 2287

Tricia Webber, New York
Tel. 212-460 5690

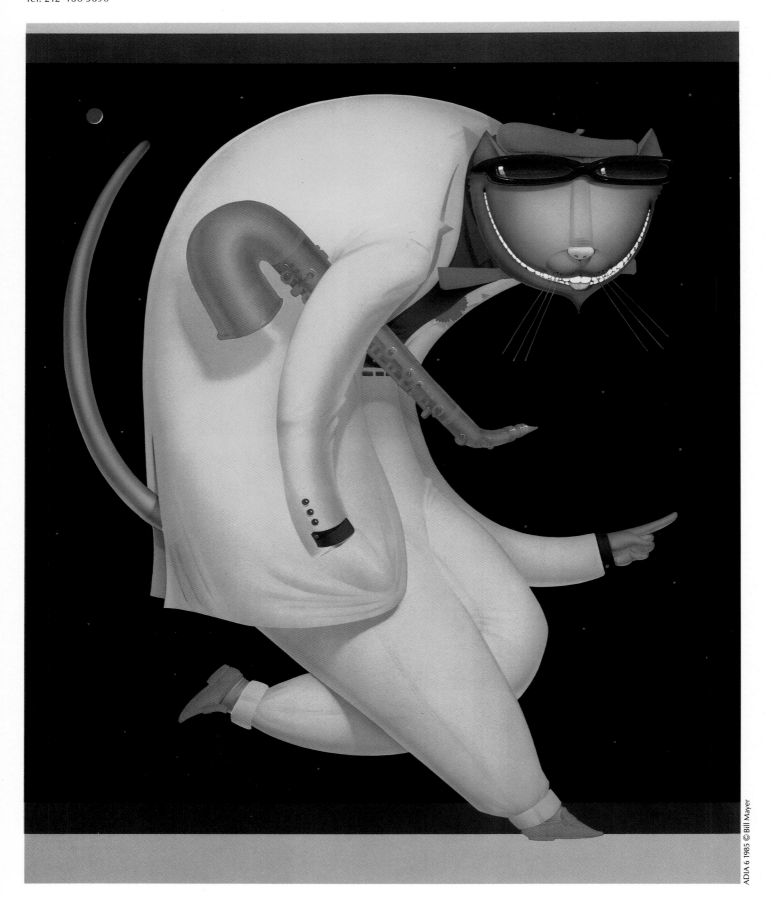

ADIA 6 1985 © Bill Mayer

Michael McGar

3330 Irwindell Boulevard
Dallas, Texas 75211
Tel. 214-339 0672

Agent:
Lisa Cobb and Associates
2200 N. Lamar
Suite 202
Dallas, TX 75202
Tel. 214-939 0032

Southwest Texas State University,
Art Center College of Design.
Included in American Illustration
II.

Clients include:
Republic Bank Corporation,
Trammel Crow, University Savings,
Frito-Lay, Muse Air, Texas Monthly,
D-Magazine, Boston Magazine,
Houston City Magazine, Dallas
Times Herald, Texas Business
Magazine.

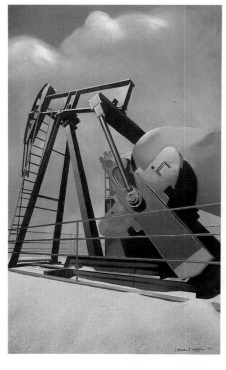

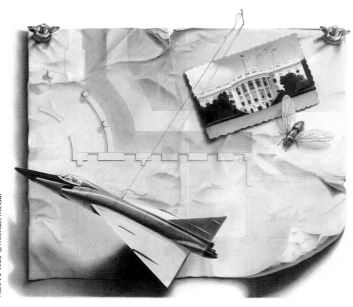

McNamara Associates, Inc.

McNamara Associates, Inc.

We've got a reputation to live up to.

Quality. Experience. Talent. Service. Innovation. For more than thirty-five years, McNamara Associates Inc. has proven itself to be one of the foremost graphic art sources in the industry. A fine reputation doesn't come easy.

It has taken dedicated and talented people who have made that extra effort to achieve excellence. To view a complete presentation of our design and illustration capabilities for corporate identification, full media advertising, annual reports, literature or sales promotion programs, please ask our representative, or call us direct.

When we begin, your problems end.

McNamara Associates, Inc.

James L. Maniere
President and General Manager
1250 Stephenson Highway
Troy, Michigan 48083
Tel. 313-583 9200

211 East 51st Street
New York, NY 10022
Tel. 212-759 5910/11

980 Yonge Street
Toronto, Ontario
Canada M4W 2J9
Tel. 416-924 3371

100 East Ohio Street
Chicago, Illinois 60611
Tel. 312-642 5328

142

McNamara Associates, Inc.

Design:
Willie Levitt
Gary Shortt
Dave Steffen
Martin Stewart
Bill Tite
Rob Graves Wesolosky

Illustrators:
Max Altekruse
Bob Boston
Gary Ciccarelli
Garry Colby
Perry Cooper
Garth Glazier
Rick Jacobi
Konrad Kahl
Hank Kolodziej
Chuck Passarelli

Mechanical Illustration:
Paul Adams
Ted Kubit
Rainer Laubach
Tony Randazzo
Gary Richardson
Bryan Stolzenburg
Walt Trussel
Don Wieland

Photo Retouching:
Dan Clancy
Les Hardy
Ted Kubit
Dick Scullin
Mike Tiderington
Bill Windsor

Paul Meisel

90 Hudson Street, 5E
New York, NY 10013
Tel. 212-226 5463

Richard Milholland

8271 West Norton Avenue
West Hollywood, California
90046
Tel. 213-462 6565
Tel. 201-793 4329

Clients include:

Advertising:
BBD&O, N.W. Ayer, Chiat/Day,
J. Walter Thompson, Dancer
Fitzgerald Sample, Benton
& Bowles, keye donna pearlstein,
Grey, DJMC, Abert Newhoff &
Burr, Della Femina Travisano,
Needham Harper & Steers, Hall &
Levine, Rod Dyer, New York West.

Publications:
Los Angeles Times, Herald
Examiner, California Magazine,
Playgirl, California Business, Oui,
Screen Actors Magazine,
Songwriters Magazine, Chic,
Selections Magazine,
New York Times.

Record Companies:
Elektra/Asylum, Warner Bros.,
CBS, A&M, Casablanca.

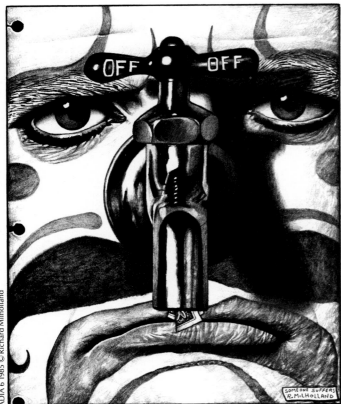

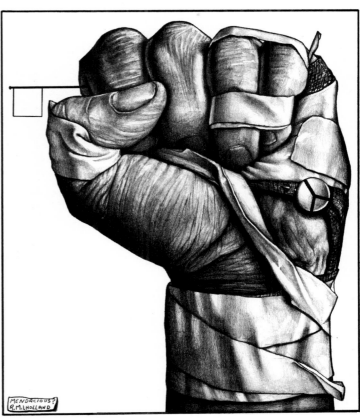

Geoffrey Moss

Represented by:
Marion Moskowitz Represents Inc.
342 Madison Avenue
New York, NY 10017
Tel. 212-719 9879

Union Carbide Annual Report 1983

Clabir Corporation Annual Report 1983

Emergency Medicine

Barbara Nessim

240 East 15th Street
New York, NY 10003
Tel. 212-677 8888

Barbara Nessim is a principal in Nessim & Associates. Her illustration and design have won awards in major shows since 1961.

An impressive list of clients include AT&T; BBDO; Doyle, Dane, Bernbach; Benton & Bowles; Mobil; Young & Rubicam; Exxon; Daniel & Charles; McCann-Erickson; American Express; Ogilvey & Mather; Revlon and many others. Her work has steadily appeared in major magazines over the past 20 years including New York Magazine, Esquire, Fortune & Time. Over 30 in-depth articles have been written about her work worldwide and she is currently putting together a book of her work with the major part devoted to her computer art. Publication date is currently scheduled for Fall 1985.

For more samples see full color pages in the Black Book 1980, '81 and '83.

All types of computer generated images available for print and video.

Ann Neumann

444 Broome Street
New York, NY 10013
Tel. 212-431 7141

Pamela Noftsinger

7 Cornelia Street
New York, NY 10014
Tel. 212-807 8861

ABC
NBC
RCA Records
Showtime Cable Network
Warner Communications
Business Week Magazine
Forbes Magazine
Fortune Magazine
New York Magazine
Avon Books

American Express
Avis
Candie's
Dannon Yogurt
Kool Aid
Levi's
Revlon
Stroh's Beer
Toys 'R Us
20th Century Fox

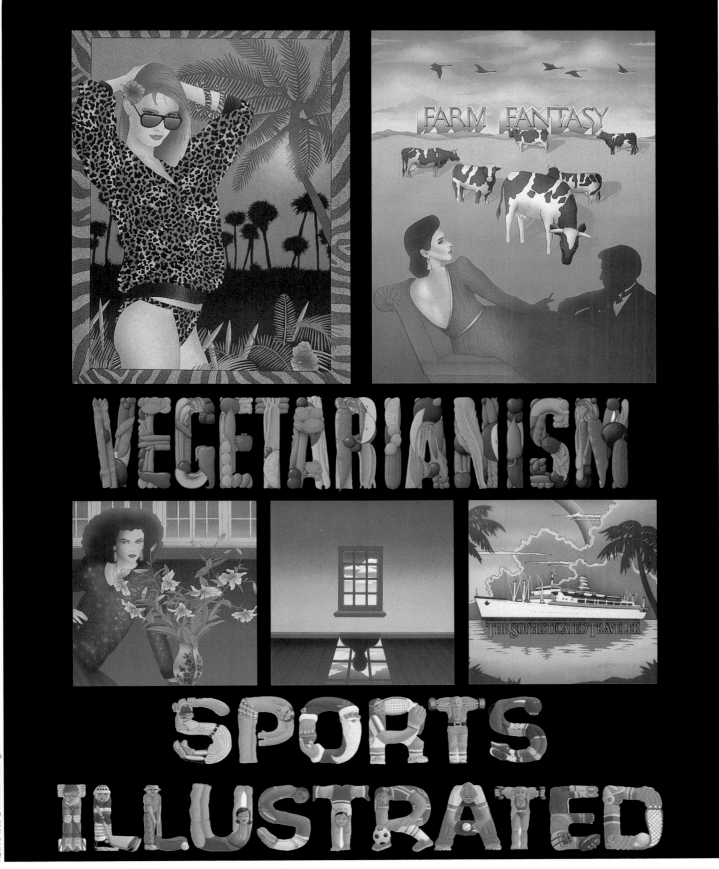

Robert A. Olson

15215 Buchanan Court
Eden Prairie, Minnesota 55344
Tel. 612-934 5767

Clients include:
AT&T, Control Data, Lindenmeyer
Paper Co., Northwest Orient,
Putnam Publishing, Ralston Purina,
Gelco, Reader's Digest, Republic
Airlines, Postgraduate Medicine,
Remmele Engineering, Windemere
Collection, Sports Medicine
Magazine, Westlaw, 3M, Drug
Therapy Magazine, etc.

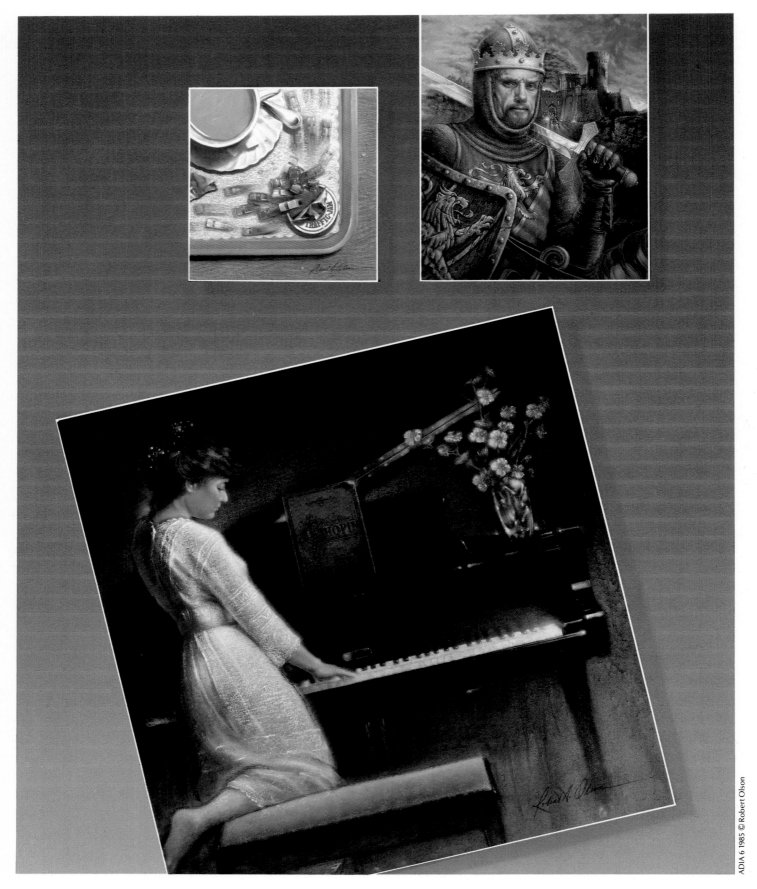

ADIA 6 1985 © Robert Olson

Dickran Palulian

Agent:
Joanne Palulian
18 McKinley Street
Rowayton, Connecticut 06853
Tel. 203-866 3734

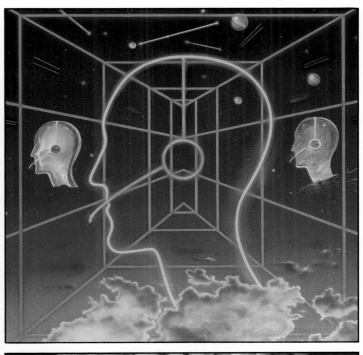

Jean François Podevin

223 South Kenmore
Los Angeles, California 90004
Tel. 213-739 5083

Agent:
Vicki Prentice-Ostan
Ostan-Prentice-Ostan
13802 Northwest Passage,
Suite 203
Marina Del Rey, California 90292
Tel. 213-823 4440

New York Agent:
Frank and Jeff Lavaty & Assoc.
50 East 50th Street
New York, NY 10022
Tel. 212-355 0910

►·OSTAN·PRENTICE·OSTAN·

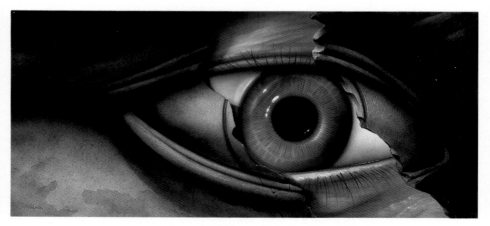

ADIA 6 1985 © Jean François Podevin

Bill Prochnow

1717 Union Street
San Francisco, California 94123
Tel. 415-673 0825

Drawings, Calligraphy, Woodcuts
& Paintings

Clients have included:
Adventure Travel, California
Academy of Sciences, California
Living, Communication Arts,
Dancer Fitzgerald Sample, Fairchild,
Foote Cone Belding/Honig, Frisco,
Mother Jones, National Semi-
Conductor, Oceans, Pacific Bell,
Pacific Discovery, San Francisco
Examiner-Chronicle, San Jose
Mercury News, Sierra Club, Sports
Illustrated, West

PLATE 9

DRAWN FROM PHOTOS by BILL PROCHNOW

Artists Who Draw from Life.
BISON·REMINGTONICS

"I used to hide in the hold of the boat when my father was sleeping. Then, when the boat began to rock, I'd know we were outside the Gate, and out I'd come. My parents tried everything: part-time school, beatings, everything, but I'd just run away. Finally at seventh grade they gave up. I won."

153

William Graham

116 W. Illinois
Chicago, IL 60610
Tel. 312-467 0330

Technical and Medical Illustration
from layouts, from blueprints,
or from life.

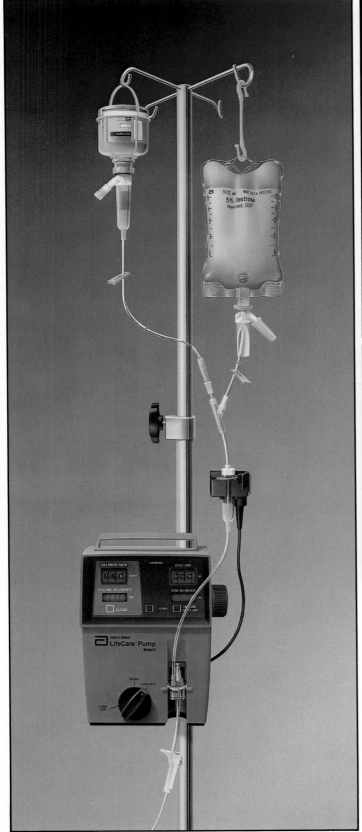

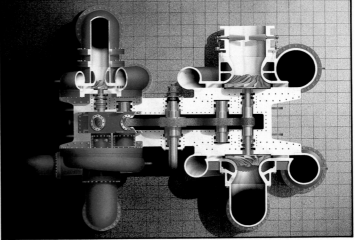

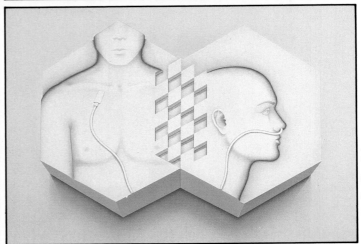

Carolyn Potts & Associates/Leslie Wolf

Agent:
Carolyn Potts & Associates
3 East Ontario, Suite 25
Chicago, Illinois 60611
Tel. 312-935 1707

Partial client list:
Advertising Age, American Dental
Association, Centel, McDonald's,
Hardee's, Northern Illinois Gas,
Oscar Mayer, Illinois Bell
Telephone, Kellogg's, Kraft, Hyatt
Hotels, United Airlines, Dorsey
Labs, Thomson Vacation, Scott,
Foresman and Co., Holt-Miflin
Publishers, Yankee Magazine

More work can be seen in:
Volume 7, American Showcase
Illustration pg. 187
Chicago Talent Sourcebook
1982, 1983, 1984

ADIA 6 1985 © Leslie Wolf

155

Chuck Pyle

146 Tenth Avenue
San Francisco, California 94118
Tel. 415-751 8087

President, San Francisco Society
of Illustrators. Member, Graphic
Artists' Guild.

Clients include:
Atari, Gemco/Lucky Stores, Hearst
Newspapers, J. Walter Thompson,
Lone Star Gas, Ogilvy Mather,
Safeway Stores, and the U.S. Air
Force.

156

Radenstudio

210 West 67th Terrace
Kansas City, Missouri 64113
Tel. 816-421 5079
(No answer, call 816-421 5076)

Paper sculpture as a form of illustration by Michael.

Papierskulptur als Abbildungsform, von Michael.

Michael fait des sculptures en papier comme type d'illustration.

Scott Reynolds

308 West 30th Street #9/B
New York, NY 10001
Tel. 212-239 0009

Agent:
Jim Lilie—West Coast
Representative
1801 Franklin Street
Apartment 404
San Francisco, California 94109
Tel. 415-441 4384

Clients:
Time Magazine, American
Express, AT&T, Random House,
Texas Monthly, McGraw Hill, The
New York Times, Guy Laroche
Parfum, The Boston Globe,
Business Week, The Franklin
Library, etc.

ADIA 6 1985 © Scott Reynolds

158

Marc Rosenthal

230 Clinton Street
Brooklyn, New York 11201
Tel. 718-855 3071

Clients include:
Fortune, Connoisseur, Discover,
Savvy, The New York Times, The
Boston Globe, Adweek, PC World,
AT&T, the USA National Pavilion
at Expo '85, Japan

HAVE YOU SEEN ROSENTHAL LATELY?

Roger Roth

Michele Manasse
1960 Broadway Suite 2 East
New York, NY 10023
Tel. 212-873 3797

From Left to right and top to bottom:
1. The New York Times Magazine:
"The Androgenous Man"
2. Henry Kissinger
3. Nikolai Gogol: "The Nose"
4. The New York Times Magazine
"The Ideological Election"

Sue Rother

1537 Franklin Street, Suite #103
San Francisco, California 94109
Tel. 415-441 8893

Clients include:
Chevron Chemical, Crocker
National Bank, Pacific Telephone,
Amfac Inc., Blue Shield, Blue
Cross, Oakland A's, Syntex,
Activision, Atari Inc., Koala
Technologies Corp., Apple
Magazine, Fafco Inc.,
Computerland, Inc. Falcon Cable
T.V., Inc., Dell Publishing, Inc.,
J. Walter Thompson

161

Kazuhiko Sano

105 Stadium Avenue
Mill Valley, California 94941
Tel. 415-381 6377

Clients:
Activision, Atari, Bank of America,
Bantam Books, Crocker Bank, Del
Monte, Dell Publishing, G.E., Levi
Strauss, Lucasfilm, Rockwell, 20th
Century Fox, Visa, Warner Bros.

162

Jim Sharpe

5 Side Hill Road
Westport, Connecticut 06880
Tel. 203-226 9984

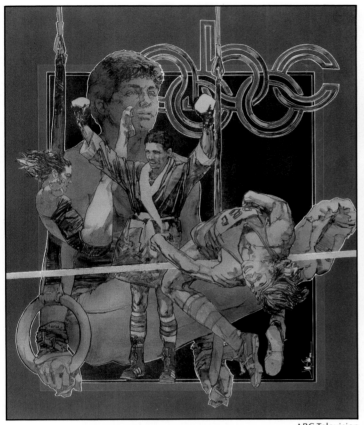

ABC Television

TV Guide

TV Guide

NFL Properties

Gini Shurtleff

c/o S.I. International
43 East 19th Street
New York, NY 10003

Agent:
Herb Spiers/Director/
S.I. International
43 East 19th Street
New York, NY 10003
Tel. 212-254 4996

Specializing in surreal, fantasy, mystical, science fiction and children's illustrations.

ADIA 6 1985 © Gini Shurtleff

James Noel Smith

1011 North Clinton
Dallas, Texas 75208
Tel. 214-946 4255

Agent:
Lisa Cobb and Associates
2200 N. Lamar
Suite 202
Dallas, TX 75202
Tel. 214-939 0032

Randy South

48 2nd Street, 5th Floor
San Francisco, California 94105
Tel. 415-543 1170

Agent:
Betsy Hillman
San Francisco
Tel. 415-563 2243

Michel Happe
Los Angeles
Tel. 213-684 3037

Partial list of clients:
J. Walter Thompson Co., Grey
Adv., Ketchum Adv., Chiat Day
Adv., Dancer Fitzgerald Sample,
Inc., Doyle Dane Bernbach/West,
Foote Cone & Belding/Honig Inc.,
Ogilvy & Mather, Inc., Needham
Harper & Steers Adv., McCann
Erickson, Inc., D'Arcy Mac Manus
& Masius, BBDO West, Dyer/Kahn
Inc.

Ed Soyka

231 Lafayette Avenue
Peekskill, New York 10566
Tel. 914-737 2230

I am able to come up with original concepts to meet your need or work from your design.

I prefer to work directly with the art director for maximum flexibility and creativity.

I have received well over 100 awards for artistic achievement.

Clients include:
AT&T, Time, Esquire, Forbes, Ciba-Geigy, TV Guide, W R Grace, Fortune, Sudler & Hennessey, Wm. Douglas McAdams, Columbia Records, Pocket Books, Science Digest, Psychology Today, Frankfurt Communications, Grey Advertising, and Atlantic Records

ADIA 6 1985 © Joe Spencer

Joe Spencer/Design & Illustration

11201 Valley Spring Lane
Studio City, California 91602
Tel. 818-760 0216

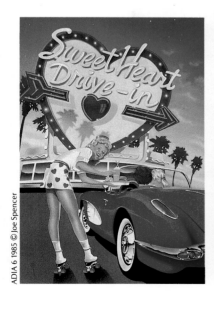

ADIA 6 1985 © Joe Spencer

Mark Stearney

405 North Wabash
Chicago, Illinois 60611
Tel. 312-644 6669

Clients include:
American Dental Association,
Ameritech, Anheiser-Busch,
Beatrice Foods, Dow-Corning,
Chicago Sun-Times, Kemper
Insurance, Illinois Bell, Quaker
Oats, Rockwell International,
TRW, Union Carbide, Scott-
Foresman Publishing, WLS-TV,
Raintree Publishing

Robert Gantt Steele

14 Wilmot Street
San Francisco, California 94115
Tel. 415-885 2611

Agent:
Jan Collier
Tel. 415-552 4252

Jonathan Stewart

113 South Twenthieth Street
Philadelphia, Pennsylvania 19103
Tel. 215-561 0805

Jözef Sumichrast

Represented in New York by:
Madeline Renard
Tel. 212-490 2450

Represented in Chicago by:
Jim Berntsen
Tel. 312-822 0560

Studio:
Tel. 312-945 6353

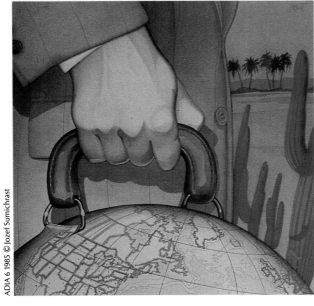

173

James E. Tennison

713 Highland Drive
Arlington, Texas 76010
Tel. 817-861 1550

Southwest Agent:
Lisa Cobb
2200 N. Lamar
Suite 202
Dallas, TX
Tel. 214-939 0032

New York Agent:
Joan Sigman
Tel. 212-421 0050
Tel. 212-832 7980

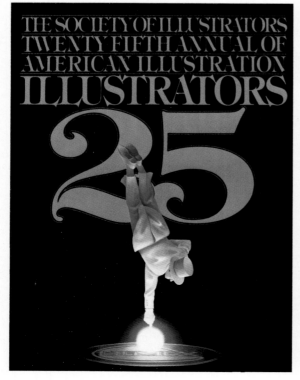

Paul Vaccarello

1749 North Wells Street
Chicago, Illinois 60614
Tel. 312-664 2233

Clients include:
Abbott Laboratories, Campbell-Mithun, Chicago Tribune, Chicago White Sox, CNA Insurance, Consumers Digest, R.S. Feldman & Co., Foote, Cone & Belding, Frankel & Co., Gorman Publishing Co., Hartmarx, Household Finance Corp., Inryco, Inc., Inside Sports, Inc., Leo Burnett Co., Mandabach & Simms, McDonald's, Miller Brewery Co., Mobium, Montgomery Ward Enterprises, Needham Harper & Steers, Inc., N.W. Ayer, Inc., Ogilvy & Mather, Playboy Enterprises, Procter & Gamble, Scott Foresman & Co., United Airlines, Westinghouse Electric Corp.

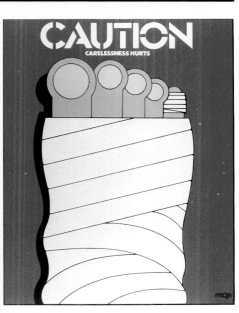

Kurt Vargö

111 East 12th Street
New York, NY 10003
Tel. 212-982 6098

Knapp Communications

Ziff Davis

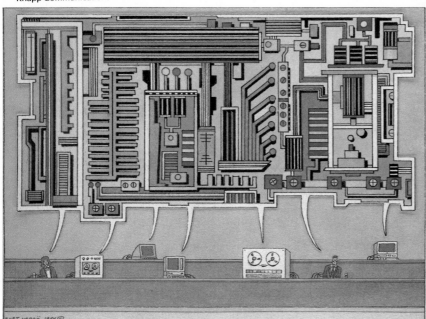

Psychology Today

Art Direction

John S.P. Walker

47 Jane Street
New York, NY 10014
Tel. 212-242 3435

Michele Warner

1011 North Clinton
Dallas, Texas 75208
Tel. 214-946 4255

Agent:
Lisa Cobb and Associates
2200 North Lamar
Suite 202
Dallas, Texas 75202
Tel. 214-939 0032

ADIA 6 1985 © Michele Warner

Susan Wells, Artists' Representative

5134 Timber Trail, NE
Atlanta, Georgia 30342
Tel. 404-255 1430

Illustrators:
Richard Loehle
Tel. 404-325 9580
Beth White
Tel. 615-297 6853
Monte Varah
Tel. 404-487 5973

Richard Loehle

Beth White

ADIA 6 1985 © Susan Wells

Monte Varah

David Wilcox

Tel. 201-832 7368

Represented by:
Milton Newborn Associates
135 East 54th Street
New York, NY 10022
Tel. 212-421 0050

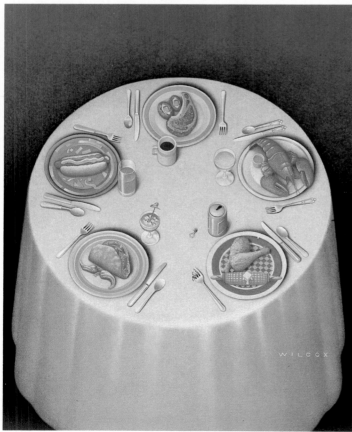

DESIGN

ARTFILE

P.O. Box 1024
Cary, North Carolina 27511
Tel. 919-781 5087

ARTFILE represents the most talented and sought after graphic designers, photographers, and illustrators in North Carolina. ARTFILE specializes in brokering free-lance art talent to agencies and corporations in the Research Triangle area. A unique opportunity to obtain the highly professional talent your project needs, locally.

ARTFILE vertritt die begabtesten und begehrtesten Graphiker, Fotografen und Abbilder in Nord-Karolinien, ARTFILE spezialisiert sich darauf, freischaffende Künstler an Agenturen und Handelsgesellschaften in der Gegend Research Triangle zu makeln. Eine einmalige Gelegenheit, die sehr professionellen Künstler zu bekommen, die Sie brauchen, in Ihrer eigenen Gegend.

アートファイルは、北カロライナの才能あふれるグラフィック・デザイナー、写真家、イラストレーターを代表しています。アートファイルは、フリーランスのデザイナーをリサーチ、トライアングル・エリアの広告代理店や企業に仲介することを専門としています。貴プロジェクトが必要とする、高度に専門的知識をもつデザイナーを手近に得られるユニークなところです。

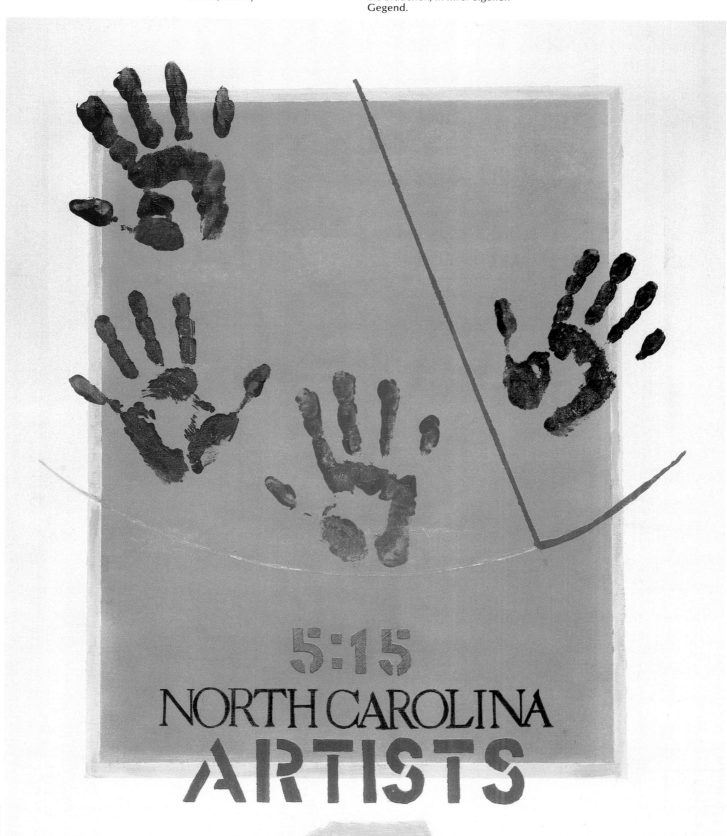

ADIA 6 1985 © Artfile

183

Michael Patrick Cronan

Michael Patrick Cronan/
Design Inc.
1 Zoe Street
San Francisco, California 94107
Tel. 415-543 6745

For those who believe
good design is good business.

Für diejenigen, die glauben, dass
guter Entwurf ein gutes Geschäft
ist.

Pour ceux qui croient que la bonne
conception est une bonne affaire.

Michael Patrick Cronan

Michael Patrick Cronan/
Design Inc.
1 Zoe Street
San Francisco, California 94107
Tel. 415-543 6745

Tim Girvin Design, Inc.

911 Western Avenue, Suite 408
Seattle, Washington 98104
Tel. 206-623 7808/7918
Telecopier 206-623-7816

Tim Girvin Design, Inc., has worked on projects throughout the United States, Canada, Europe and the Far East with architects, interior designers, art directors, graphic and industrial designers as well as client direct.

In addition to specialized lettering treatments, typographic and alphabet design, this office has developed packaging, signage, all types of print collateral as well as campaign, film and corporate identity.

Our clients include American Express, Apple Computers, AT&T, Bloomingdale's, Leo Burnett, Diamond Shamrock, Walt Disney Productions, Hewlett Packard, Hilton, Microsoft, Herman Miller, Nordstrom, Ogilvy Mather, Pennzoil, Sheraton, Texas Instruments, United Vintners, and Westin Hotels.

For additional information and samples, please communicate with our office on your company letterhead.

Michael Schwab Design

118 King Street
San Francisco, California 94107
Tel. 415-546 7559

Partial client list:
Levi Strauss and Co., Atlantic
Richfield, Anheuser Busch, Merrill
Lynch, American Express, New
York Times Magazine, Wilkes
Bashford, A & M Records.

Pushpin, Lubalin, Peckolick, Inc.

67 Irving Place
New York, NY 10003
Tel. 212-674 8080

Contact:
Phyliss Rich Flood,
Senior Vice President

Under the direction of Seymour Chwast and Alan Peckolick this graphic communications company is a leader in the field specializing in corporate identity, logos, annual reports, brochures, posters, publication design, product development, film graphics and animation, packaging, illustration, architectural/environmental design including trade shows, exhibits and pavilions. Pushpin Lubalin Peckolick corporate clients include: IBM, Sony, Mobil, Forbes, Digital, Associated Merchandising Corporation, Time Inc., Avnet Electronics, Cablevision, and Borg Warner. The company also works with advertising agencies and publishing companies both here and abroad.

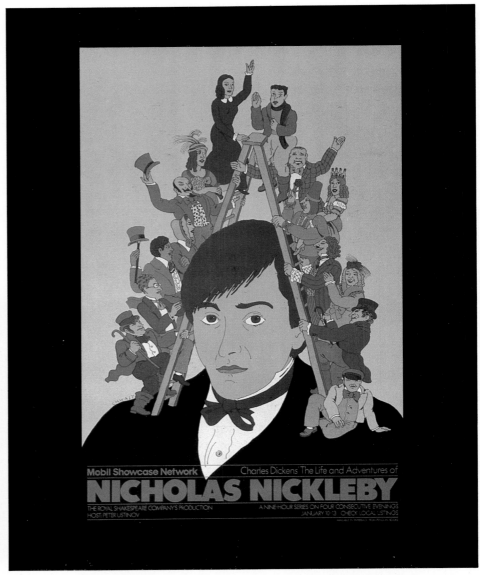

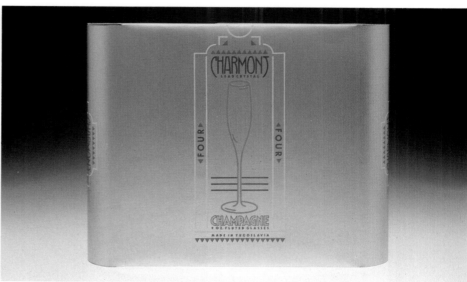

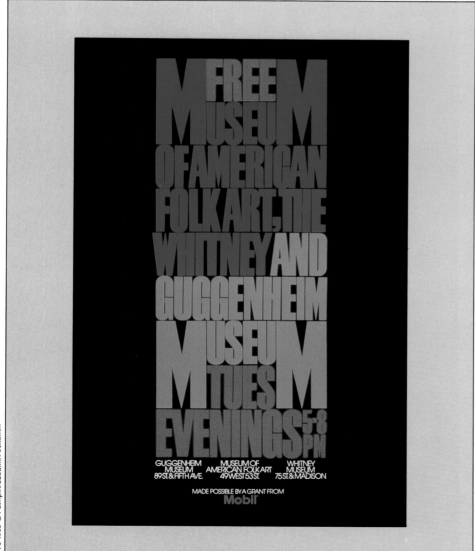

Ross Design Associates, Inc.

27 West 20th Street
New York, NY 10011
Tel. 212-206 0044

Peter Ross and Mecca Culbert
Designers/Partners

D.K. Holland
Designer/Account Executive

Bud Lavery
Designer

Publishing: Esquire's book on men's fashion and grooming—design concept through pross supervision; Peanut, design of a new computer magazine including all advertising materials

Advertising: American International Group's ongoing trade advertising campaign

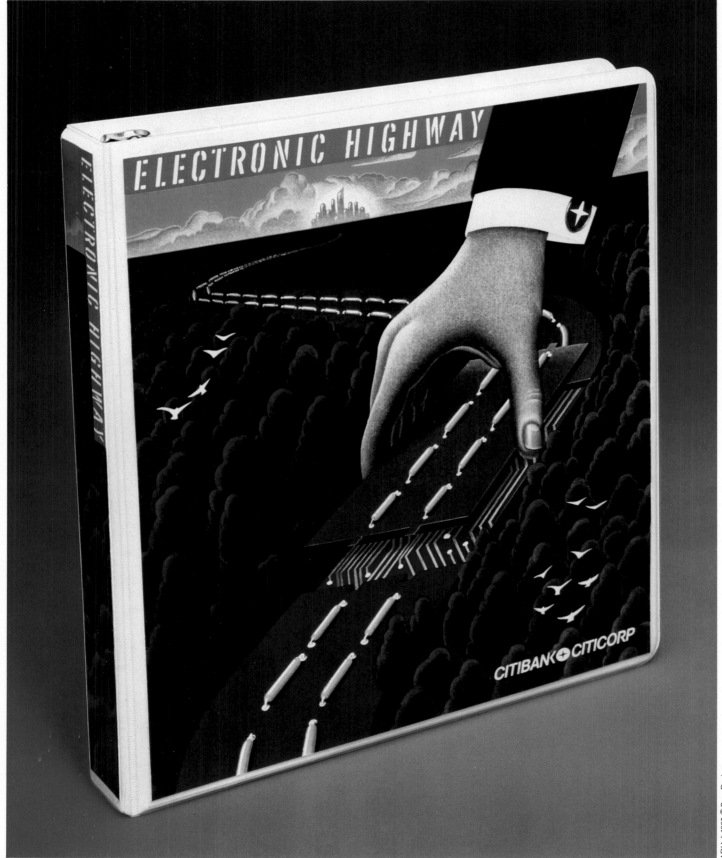

ADIA 6 1985 © Ross Design

Corporate Communications: Citicorp Credit Services promotion package—design through tight comprehensives for focus group to creation of final printed pieces; Noble Lowndes International's new corporate identity program

Product Development: Tree Communications' corporate identity and creation of a line of wrapping papers plus point-of-purchase displays and promotional materials; Waverly Schumacher's Old Sturbridge Village wallpaper and fabric sample books—design concept through actual production of three separate books

Additional Client List: American Telephone and Telegraph (AT&T), Brooklyn Academy of Music, Ink Tank, IBM, MTV, Madison Square Press, The Museum of Modern Art, Pintchik Paints, Pushpin Lubalin Peckolick, Rolling Stone Magazine, Time Magazine, Tudor Investment

Additional Capabilities: Art Direction, Illustration, Copywriting, Photography

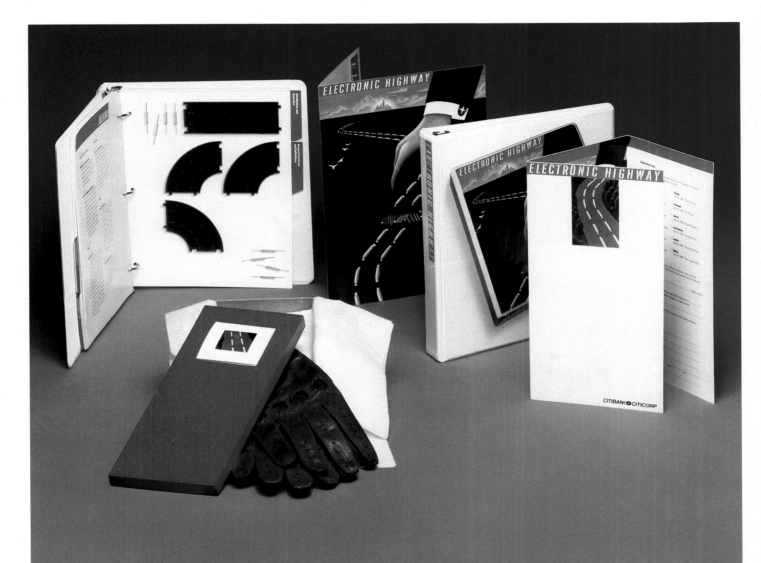

The Perfect Client

ADIA 6 1985 © Ross Design

WHAT DO YOU DO WHEN your company has a major communications hurdle to overcome?

Well if you're anything like Citibank, you sit back and do nothing.

Nothing but think, that is, until you've thought it through and thoroughly defined the problem.

At Ross Design we appreciate clients who take this thinking, analytical approach to corporate communications.

Because we believe that a clear statement of the problem brings you halfway to a solution from the very beginning.

The following case pro-

vides a perfect illustration.

CITIBANK PLANNED TO intensify its marketing of corporate cash management services to financial officers of major companies.

Having decided to present it through a series of roadshows entitled "Electronic Highway," they needed a full-scale graphic package that would do it all—generate interest, educate Citibank personnel as well as potential clients, present complex information in inviting form.

What kind of graphic

approach was required?

By means of a few well-considered questions and answers we got to the heart of the problem—how to lead an audience best characterized as risk-averse into an area best characterized as untried—

And created the comprehensives pictured here.

Futuristic in style yet humanistic in feeling, the look we designed would portray Citibank as a daring innovator and pioneer in the field of electronic banking while at the same time inspiring

confidence and trust.

Every design element was added to reinforce this dual purpose.

We designed a total package, seven pieces in all. And even added a special post-seminar gift—a pair of driving gloves to thank the customer for travelling the "Electronic Highway" with us.

So if you like the kind of problem-solving approach we took in Citibank's case, why not give us a call yourself?

TOGETHER WE'LL CREATE the kind of perfect graphic solution that can only come about through perfect communication between client and designer.

Unlimited Swan Inc.

272 Riverside Avenue
Riverside, CT 06878
Tel. 203-637 4840

Unlimited Swan is Jim Swan. For
twenty years a source for unusual
and distinctive advertising and
graphic design.

Past projects include:
Brochures, catalogs, corporate
identity, advertising, packaging,
environment, film, commercials,
constructions, posters, cards
and more. To all, creativity
professionally applied.

Thanks to: Linda Mevorach / L
ou Di Joseph / Jerry Murff / Tim
Newman / Dennis Powers / Ra
y Lofaro / Barney Melsky / San
dra Swan / Lenny Friedman /
Denny Tillman / Don Batters
hall / Phil Peppis / Henry Holt
zman / Joseph Feury / Lee Gr
ant / Saul Landa / Neil Tardio /
Jeff Lovinger / Randi Kirshb
aum / Jeffery Metzner / Brian
Mitchell / Murray Bruce / Bo
b Cox / John Lucci / Art Kan
e / Peter Gerquest / Ed Bian
chi / Andy Gutelle / Barbie J
ackson / Carol Phillips / Dick
Jayson / Ken Blancato / Jer
ry Cotts / Camile Lane / Bob
Curtis / Jean Claude Kauf
man / Dan Roth / Brett She
vack / Robert Bricken / Pa
cy Markman / Earl Rath /
Jack Wiswal / Roger Faw
cett / Toni Ficalora / Rob
Mounsey / Ken Yagoda /

Unlimited Swan est Jim Swan. Depuis vingt ans, une source de créations publicitaires et graphiques originaux et distinctifs. Parmi nos réalisations passées: Brochures, catalogues, identités corporatives, publicités, emballages, environnement, films, publicités télévisées, constructions, posters, cartes et autres... Tous ces projects ont été réalisés avec créativité et professionalisme.

Unlimited Swan (Unbegrenzter Swan) heißt Jim Swan. Seit zwanzig Jahren eine Quelle sowohl von außergewöhnlichen und unverwechselbaren Reklamen als auch von Abbildungskunst. Frühere Projekte schließen Broschüren, Kataloge, Geschäftsidentität, Werbung, Verpackung, Umweltschutz, Filme, Reklamen, Konstruktionen, Posters, Karten und so weiter ein. Kreativität wird in allen Sachen geübt.

アンリミテッド スワンとはジム スワンのことです。20年間に亘って、ユニークな特徴のある広告とグラフィックデザインのソースとなってきました。過去のプロジェクト：ブローシュア、カタログ、CI、広告、パッケージング、環境デザイン、映画、コマーシャル、建設、ポスター、カードその他。全てにプロフェッショナルな創造性が発揮されています。

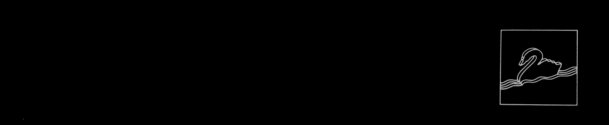

Steve Frankfurt / Nicholas Gaetano / Roger Lewis / R.Y.C. / George Cohen / Helen Berling / Susan Hamilton / Dr. Thomas Henley / Pat McDonald / Jake Holmes / Larry Read / Tom Ragland / Jeff Dell / Phylis Witreol / Robert Dalrymple / Al Ames / Myron Slosberg / Mel Abfire / Lee Kowalski / Ken Roman / Ted Chin / Susan Turnbull / Dick Gildersleeve / Phil Kaczor / Nancy Gilkyson / Allen Rozek / Randy Ross / Phillip Collins / Jean Mallet / Bob Steigleman / John Roughan / Alfio Maugeri / Bob Lelle / Ras Apenes / Chuck Pfeifer / Mike Smith / Lou Puopolo / Sandy Rand / Ron Lockhart / Earl Cavanagh / Bob Geller / Jim Turnbull / Jerry Ansel / Skip Swan / Joe Kardwell / Kan Nakai / Dave Ottey / Jimmy Carrol / et al.

Yoshi Sekiguchi

Design 1
437 Marshman Street
Highland Park, Illinois 60035
Tel. 312-433 4140

In today's market with ever-increasing competition, the need to represent your organization, product or service with an imaginative, innovative identity is imperative. A good symbol should make it possible to communicate instantly and capture the viewer's attention with visual magnetism.

情報氾濫時代の今日、企業や製品、サービス等を表わすシンボル・マークは、より独創的な個性を持つ必要性が増した。良いマークは、業種、性質、将来への姿勢等を表現し、他の競争相手より優れているというイメージを、即時に大衆の心に深く焼き付ける事が可能である。関口余士のデザイン・1（ワン）は、日米両国で多数のシンボル・マークとその適用プログラムを創造し、多くのデザイン関係の賞を与えられている。

Symbols To Communicate

U.S. Ski Writers Association

Nebraska Air National Guard
(Known as Cornhusker Guard)

U.S. Peace Academy

Arakawa Chemical (Japan)

Maple Bluff Racquet Club

RESTAURANT
Royal Host

Royal Host (Japan)
(Chain Restaurants)

American Federal Savings

Medical Gas Piping Systems

Nebraska Division of
U.S. Air Force

Chicago Futaba-kai
Japanese School
("Futaba" — Two young leaves
out of a seed)

McDonald's Kids' Classic
(Golf Tournament)

Chicago Tofu
("Tofu" — Soybean curd)

Mazda Hall of Fame
Championship
(Golf Tournament)

Health, Inc. (Japan)

Illinois Professional
Writers Association

Lone Star Trading Co.
(Import/export firm in Texas)

PHOTOGRAPHY

Index
to
Photographers

Kent Barker

2039 Farrington
Dallas, TX 75207
Tel. 214-760 7470

Agent:
Sally Nicolaou
Tel. 214-526 1406

Fashion/beauty and styled portraiture for advertising and editorial.

Partial client list includes: Frost Bros., Sanger Harris, J.C. Penney, Herrell Inc., The Horchow Collection, St. Bernard Sports, Piz Buin Suntan Oil, The Dallas Ballet, The Richards Group, D Magazine, Texas Monthly Magazine, Australian Vogue

ADIP 11 1985 © Kent Barker

198

Richard Berenholtz

600 West 111th Street,
New York, NY 10025
Tel. 212-222 1302

Original and Stock Photography.
Specializing in New York City.

Hank Benson Photography

653 Bryant Street
San Francisco, California 94107
Tel. 415-543 8153

Represented in San Francisco by:
Ellen Phillips
Tel. 415-928 6336/543 8153

Hank Benson Photography

653 Bryant Street
San Francisco, California 94107
Tel. 415-543 8153

Represented in San Francisco by:
Ellen Phillips
Tel. 415-928 6336/543 8153

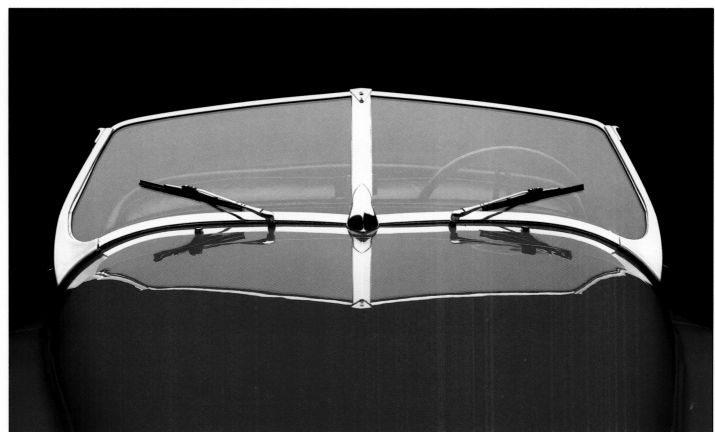

ADIP 11 1985 © Hank Benson

Alan Bergman

8241 West 4th Street
Los Angeles, California 90048
Tel. 213-852 1408

I bring out the best in people. All kinds of people in all kinds of places. For all types of ads, annual reports, and publications. So give me a call. Because there's no better people photographer.

A partial list of my clients includes: ABC Television; ARCO; BBDO; Bell Telephone; Cole & Weber; Foote, Cone & Belding; General Telephone; IBM; Mammoth Mountain Ski Area; MCA Records; Ogilvy & Mather; State of Alaska; Time/Life, Inc.; Wells, Rich, Greene; Young & Rubicam/Dentsu.

ADIP 11 1985 © Alan Bergman

Black Box Studios, Inc.

824 Exposition, Suite 215
Dallas, Texas 75226
Tel. 214-826 3348

Representative:
Judy Dennis
1118 Brunner
Dallas, Texas 75224
Tel. 214-948 1700

BLACK BOX STUDIOS, INC.

Barbara Bordnick

39 East 19th Street
New York, NY 10003
Tel. 212-533 1180

Print and film. Fashion/beauty
advertising, editorial and
illustration. Corporate and
celebrity portraiture. ASMP,
APA member.

Bill Boyd Photography

614 Santa Barbara Street
Santa Barbara, California 93101
Tel. 805-962 9193

Agent:
Lorna Boyd
614 Santa Barbara Street
Santa Barbara, California 93101
Tel. 805-962 9193

Still life, architecture, food,
illustration, corporate and stock.
For these clients and more: Owens
Corning Fiberglas, Libbey Glass,
Champion Spark Plugs, American
Motors General, General Tire,
LucasFilms, Catch It Swimwear,
Made In Paradise, Dripcut
Corporation, Sears, Shell Oil,
Guardian Glass, Pritikin Center.

Charles William Bush

7623 Beverly Boulevard
Los Angeles, California 90036
Tel. 213-937 8246

Representatives:

Los Angeles:
Ellen Knable, Linda Carlson,
Eve Diamond
Tel. 213-855 8855

Chicago:
Bill Rabin & Associates
Tel. 312-944 6655

New York:
Madelaine Renard
Tel. 212-490 2450

San Francisco:
Nadine Hyatt & Associates
Tel. 415-543 8944

Industrial revolution.

ADIP 11 1985 © Charles William Bush

206

Charles William Bush

7623 Beverly Boulevard
Los Angeles, California 90036
Tel. 213-937 8246

Representatives:

Los Angeles:
Ellen Knable, Linda Carlson,
Eve Diamond
Tel. 213-855 8855

Chicago:
Bill Rabin & Associates
Tel. 312-944 6655

New York:
Madelaine Renard
Tel. 212-490 2450

San Francisco:
Nadine Hyatt & Associates
Tel. 415-543 8944

YOU MADE VISA A CLASSIC.

C&I Photography, Inc.

C&I Photography, Inc.
3523 Ryder Street
Santa Clara, California 95051
Tel. 408-733 5855

EasyLink Mail Box Address
62807100
Telex 910333 9995

"Execution with Imagination"

Advertising
Corporate and Industrial
Editorial
Photomicrography
Studio and Location

Five full-time staff photographers.

Fully equipped in-house
laboratory.

Portfolio by mail on request.

ADIP 11 1985 © C & I Photography

208

Stan Cacitti

589 Howard Street
San Francisco, California 94105
Tel. 415-974 5668

In the studio or on location, assignments specializing in still life, illustration, editorial, corporate, architectural and annual reports.

Clients have included:
Joseph E. Seagram & Sons, Paul Masson, Halpern Sounds, Reluxtrol, Pacific Telephone, Carma Developers, Fairmont Hotel, Vicom Assoc., Grosvenor Hotel, San Francisco Magazine, Yakima Products, Whole Earth Restaurants, Vis Art Films, Williams Sonoma, Skidmore Owings & Merrill, Unigraphics, Shaklee Corp., The Blake Agency, Taurus Computers, Gifford Computers, Young & Rubicam/Dentsu, Autotex, SAGA Corp., San Francisco Vacation Council, San Mateo County Convention & Visitors Bureau, Western Insurance Co., Charles Bonn & Assoc., Multi-Asian Properties, Ted Thompson Period, Quinn's Cooler, Guild Wineries, United Vintners, Inglenook Wine, Souverain Wine, Petri Wine, Jacaré Wine, Cribari Wine, Cresta Blanca Wine, Colony Wine, Taylor California Wine, VISA U.S.A. Inc., Hilton Hotels, San Francisco Symphony, California Wine Assoc.

Christopher Casler ASMP

Casler Communications
1600 Viewmont Drive
Los Angeles, California 90069
Tel. 213-854 7733

Agent:
Paul Wheeler
Wheeler Pictures
50 West 29th Street
New York, NY 10001
Tel. 212-696 9832

Clients include:
I.B.M.
Chevron U.S.A.
Merrill Lynch Realty
Northrop Corporation
Wells Fargo Bank
Home Box Office
McDonald's

Commercial & Editorial, Fine Art
& Architectural Photography.

Sowohl Werbungs—und
redaktionelle Fotografie als auch
Kunst—und Baukunstfotografie.

Texte biographique: Commercial
et editorial, beaux arts et
photographie architecturale.

コマーシャル・編集写真、美術・建築写真

James Caulfield APA

114 West Kinzie Street
Chicago, Illinois 60610
Tel. 312-828 0004

Represented by:
Rick Wainman
Tel. 312-337 3960

CAULFIELD

Paul Chauncey Photography

388 North Hydraulic
Wichita, Kansas 67214
Tel. 316-262 6733

Represented by:
Michele Chauncey

ADIP 11 1985 © Paul Chauncey

Paul Chauncey Photography

388 North Hydraulic
Wichita, Kansas 67214
Tel. 316-262 6733

Represented by:
Michele Chauncey

213

Walter Chrynwski

154 West 18th Street
New York NY 10011
Tel. 212-675 1906

214

Ric Cohn

156 Fifth Avenue
New York, NY 10010
Tel. 212-924 6749

Agent:
Elise Caputo
Tel. 212-949 2440

For more of Ric's work, see our ads in: Art Directors' Index Vol. 9 and Vol. 10, The Creative Black Book 1982, 1983, 1984, and 1985, and the 1985 Northeast Revue. Or call Elise Caputo to see the complete portfolio.

ADIP 11 1985 © Ric Cohn

RIC COHN

Bruno

35 West 36th Street
New York, NY 10018
Tel. 212-563 2730

Represented by:
Holly Kaplan
35 West 36th Street
New York, NY 10018
Tel. 212-563 2730

In association with Cosimo's
Studio Inc. All photos below are
studio creations.

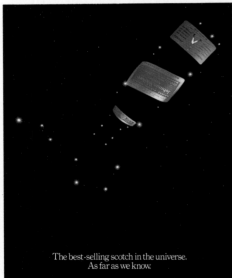

The best-selling scotch in the universe.
As far as we know.

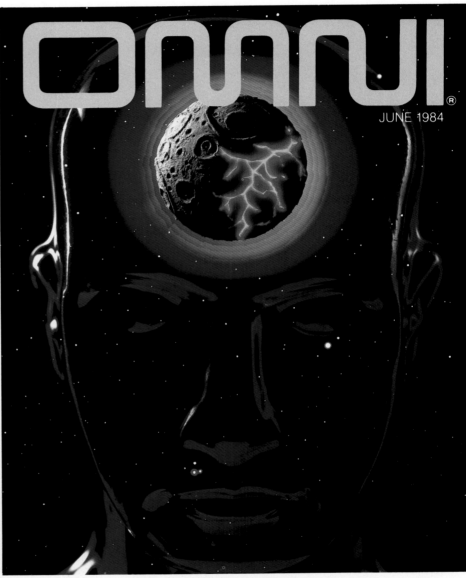

JUNE 1984

A FEW MICHELIN DEALERS STILL HAVE TO WAIT MORE THAN 48 HOURS FOR DELIVERY.

Granted, there are many Michelin dealers who receive same-day delivery. And many more who get their Michelins before 48 hours have passed.

But, frankly, there are still a few who must wait over 48 hours. That's the price they pay for working in the peace and solitude of the countryside.

But, no matter where you're located in the United States (or where any of your branches are located)

the Michelin tires you want.

Our plan in '84 is to stock the tires and sizes you want most and ship to you the day you order.

That's just one of the remarkable advantages of Michelin's extensive sales and distribution system.

You not only get product first — you get Michelin service fast. And it doesn't make any difference how large or small you are.

quality among consumers, and you've got a combination that's very hard to beat when it comes to selling radials.

This year, the Michelin line becomes even more complete. Joining the full line of passenger car and performance tires is what may be the finest all-season radial ever made: the Michelin XA4.

But sometimes making the best isn't enough.

why Michelin is supporting the XA4 with one of the largest advertising campaigns in company history.

For more information on how Michelin's service organization, sales force and advertising can make selling Michelins even easier, contact your Michelin Distribution Center or your Michelin Representative.

They've got the answers. No matter where

ADIP 11 1985 © Bruno

216

Cosimo

35 West 36th Street
New York, NY 10018
Tel 212-563 2730

Represented by:
Holly Kaplan
35 West 36th Street
New York, NY 10018
Tel. 212-563 2730

T.V. Reel on request. All photos
below are studio creations.

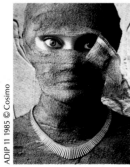

**UNTIL MICHELIN'S XA4, WHEN YOU BOUGHT ALL-SEASON TIRES
YOU MADE TWO COMPROMISES.**

ONE HERE.

ONE HERE.

A DISASTER IS ABOUT TO HAPPEN.

Frank Cowan Studio Inc.

5 East 16th Street
New York, NY 10003
Tel. 212-675 5960

FRANK COWAN

Partial client list:
A&P
AT&T
Aim Toothpaste
Air Force
American Express
Army
Avon
Bayer Aspirin
Beefeaters Gin
Bell Telephone
Betty Crocker
Boeing
Budweiser
Campari
Carrier
Cheerios
Chemical Bank
Citibank
Coca Cola
Colgate
Coors Beer
Dean Witter Reynolds
Dentu Creme
Desitin
Dial Soap
Dow Chemicals
DuPont
Esquire
Exxon
Falstaff Beer
Fisher Price
Fleischmanns
Ford
Gainesburgers
General Mills
General Motors
General Electric
Gillette
Gleem
Gravy Train
Hart Shaffner & Marx
Hathaway Shirts
Heinz
Holiday Inn
International Paper
ITT
Ivory
Johnson & Johnson
Kelloggs
Kentucky Fried Chicken
Kimbies Diapers
Kodak
Kraft
Lego Toys
Levis
Life Magazine
Lipton Tea
Luvs Diapers
MacDonalds
McGraw Hill
Mead Paper
Motorola
National Airlines
Navy
Nedicks
Nestles
Owens-Corning
Pampers
PanAm
Pepsi Cola
Pitney Bowes
Pizza Hut
Playtex
Polaroid
Procter & Gamble
Prudential
Q-tips
RCA
Sanka
Scope
Sealy
Sheraton Hotels
Shout
Sperry Univac
Sylvania
Talon Zippers
Thom Mc An
Time Magazine
Trident Gum
TWA
United Airlines
Volkswagen
Weight Watchers
Wrangler

ADIP 11 1985 © Frank Cowan

Tony Curatola

18 East 17th Street
New York, NY 10003
Tel. 212-243 5478

David Deahl Photography, Inc. 312-644-3187   Represented by Rosemary Ferreri

Len DeLessio

7 East 17th Street
New York, NY 10003
Tel. 212-206 8725

Still-Life Photography for Print, TV, and Fotomatic. Sample reel available.

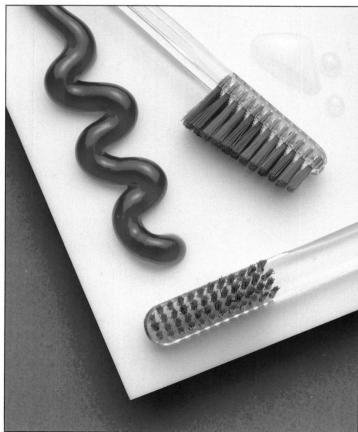

Douglas Dubler Photography

162 East 92nd Street
New York, NY 10128
Tel. 212-410 6300

Agent:
S. Dianne Dubler
Tel. 212-410 5300

Beauty and fashion photography.

Partial client list:
Revlon, Max Factor, Charles of the
Ritz, Avon, Redken, Chapstick,
Levi Strauss, Catalina, Jantzen,
Audio Vox, Rolex, BMW,
Hasselblad, Nikon, Vogue,
Harper's Bazaar, Cosmopolitan,
McCall's, Popular Photography

(All Photos: Hair and Make-up: David Frank Ray, Styling: Holly Henley) Background: Charles Broderson

ADIP 11 1985 © Douglas Dubler

223

Dennis Dubiel

1313 West Randolph Street
Chicago, Illinois 60607
Tel. 312-666 0136

A Dennis Dubiel continuous-tone poster is available for the asking. Please make request on company letterhead. Poster not shown below.

Un poster ton-continue Dennis Dubiel est à votre disposition, vous n'avez qu'à le demander. Veuillez bien nous écrire sur papier de lettres de votre société. Le poster n'est pas à voir en-dessous.

デニス デュビイエルのポスターを御希望の方は会社の用箋にてお申し込みください。提供できるポスターは掲載のものとは違います。
アート・ディレクター：ワルド パチェコ
ホーム・エコノミスト：マージョリー リヒテンバーグ

Dennis Dubiel

1313 West Randolph Street
Chicago, Illinois 60607
Tel. 312-666 0136

A Dennis Dubiel continuous-tone poster is available for the asking. Please make request on company letterhead. Poster not shown below.

Un poster ton-continue Dennis Dubiel est à votre disposition, vous n'avez qu'à le demander. Veuillez bien nous écrire sur papier de lettres de votre société. Le poster n'est pas à voir en-dessous.

Art Director—Waldo Pacheco
Home Economist—Marjory Lichtenberg

Directeur artistique—
Waldo Pacheco
Economiste domestique—
Marjory Lichtenberg

デニス デュビイエルのポスターを御希望の方は会社の用箋にてお申し込みください。提供できるポスターは掲載のものとは違います。
アート・ディレクター：ワルド パチェコ
ホーム・エコノミスト：マージョリー リヒテンバーグ

ADIP 11 1985 © Dennis Dubiel

Elle

Ellen Schuster
3719 Gilbert Avenue
Dallas, Texas 75219
Tel. 214-526 6712

American Airlines

Neiman-Marcus

Fisher Controls

Elle

Ellen Schuster
3719 Gilbert Avenue
Dallas, Texas 75219
Tel. 214-526 6712

Recovery Records

Stock

Maxim's—Landscape: David Muench

ADIP 11 1985 © Elle

John Paul Endress

254 West 31 Street   6,100 sq. feet fully equipped

Suzanne Estel Studios

2325 Third Street
San Francisco, California 94107
Tel. 415-864 3661

Specializing in advertising
illustration, fashion photography
and television photomatics.

Clients include:
Armor-Dial, Atari, BankAmerica
Corporation, Beef Industry
Council, Blue Cross, Boysen
Paints, Bullock's, Fairmont Hotels,
Gumps, Fila Sportswear, Hunt-
Wessen Foods, I. Magnin, Jantzen,
Jordache, Joseph Magnin, Koret of

California, Lancome Cosmetics,
Levi Strauss, Logo of Paris, Macy's,
National Raisin Board, Pendleton
Woolen Mills, Philippine Airlines,
Regis Corporation, Fromm &
Sichel, Shaklee Corporation,
California Milk Advisory Board,
Simpson Paper Co., Speedo
International, United Vintners,
Victoria's Secret, Visa U.S.A. Inc.,
St. Regis Wine.

230

Stefan Findel, Inc.

1133 Spring Street, NW
Atlanta, Georgia 30309
Tel. 404-872 8103

Charlie Freeman Photography

3333 Elm Street
Dallas, Texas 75226
Tel. 214-742 1446;
NY 212-254 0866

Represented by:
Sandra Freeman
3333 Elm Street, Suite 100
Dallas, Texas 75226
Tel. 214-742 4302

ADIP 11 1985 © Charlie Freeman

Michael Furman

115 Arch Street
Philadelphia, Pennsylvania 19106
Tel. 215-925 4233

Agent:
Victoria Satterthwaite
Tel. 215-925 4233

234

Beth Galton

130 West 25th Street
New York, NY 10001
Tel. 212-242 2266

Agent:
Ms. Rosemary Samuels
Tel. 212-477 3567

ADIA 6 1985 © Beth Galton

WESTVACO; McCAFFREY McCALL

Larry Gatz

8610 Sunny Ridge Drive
Houston, Texas 77095
Tel. 713-550 8455

A West Coast style on the
Gulf Coast.

Clients include:
Bozell & Jacobs, McCann-Erickson,
MDR, Inc., Ogilvy & Mather, Rives,
Smith, Baldwin & Carlberg/Young
& Rubicam; Beechcraft, Conoco,
Exxon, Houston Astros, Gulf Oil,

Lane Telecommunications, Martin-
Decker, Nissan, NL Industries,
Soltex, Shell Chemical, Teledyne
Marine, Texas Instruments, Toyota,
and Wilson Foods.

Animatic/McCANN-ERICKSON

ADIP 11 1985 © Larry Gatz

Mark E. Gibson is California Color

P.O. Box 14542
San Francisco, California 94114
Tel. 415-431 5411

Vivid chromes for advertising,
corporate, and editorial clients.
Assignment and stock.

ADIP 11 1985 © Mark E. Gibson

237

Elliot Gilbert

311 North Curson Avenue
Los Angeles, California 90036
Tel. 213-939 1846

"Kit" Travel Trailers

Teleflora

Teleflora

Teleflora

Lois Greenfield

35 West 31 Street
New York, NY 10001
Tel. 212-947 0898, 212-595 2759

Agent:
Christine Simoneau
Tel. 212-696 2085

LOIS GREENFIELD

LEGWEAR

YOU'RE A STAR IN CAPEZIO

Christopher Gould Photography

224 West Huron
Chicago, Illinois 60610
Tel. 312-944 5545

Represented by:
David Montagano
Tel. 312-944 1125

ADIP 11 1985 © Christopher Gould

Christopher Gould Photography

224 West Huron
Chicago, Illinois 60610
Tel. 312-944 5545

Represented by:
David Montagano
Tel. 312-944 1125

241

ADIP 11 1985 © Christopher Gould

Bart Harris

Bart Harris Photography Inc.
Print & Film
70 West Hubbard
Chicago, Illnois 60610

Agent:
O'Brien—Steiber
Tel. 312-580 0880

Bart is equally confortable
shooting in studio and on location.
APA and AICP.

Sandi Hedrich

Hedrich Blessing
11 West Illinois Street
Chicago, Illinois 60610
Tel. 312-321 1151

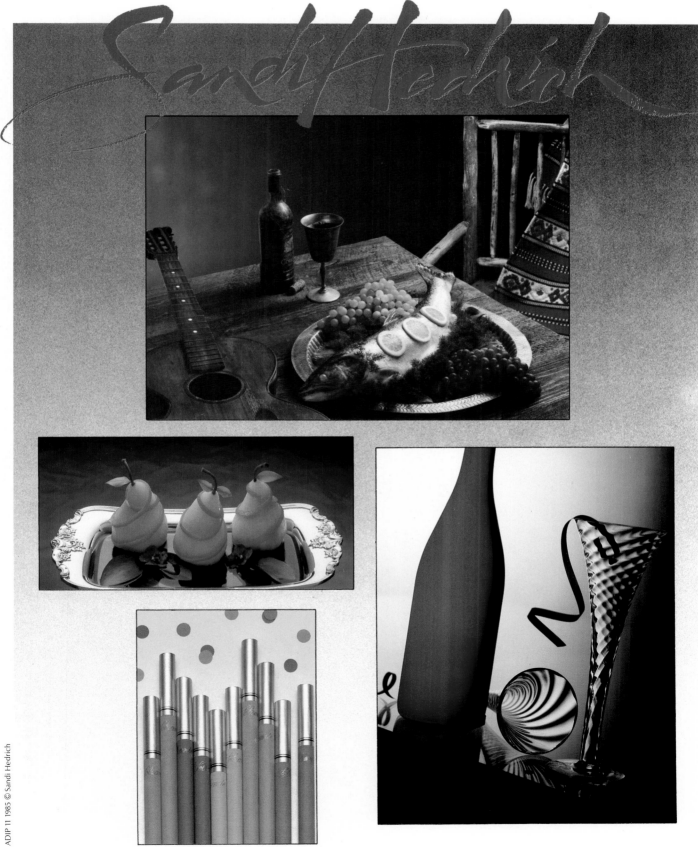

PAT HILL

37 West 26th Street • New York City 10010
(212) 679-0884 • (212) 532-3479

With Special Thanks:
Kriss Ziemer, Model • Judi Muscio, Stylist
Gareth Green, Hair & Makeup
John Muth, Production Coordinator
R.J. Luzzi Ltd., Design

© 1985 PAT HILL

Ryszard Horowitz

103 Fifth Avenue
New York, NY 10003
Tel. 212-243 6440

New York Agent:
Sol Shamilzadeh
1155 Broadway
New York, NY 10001
Tel. 212-532 1977

Paris agent:
Evelyn Menascé
PPP, 16, rue Guillaume Tell
75017 Paris
Tel. 227 24 82

London agent:
Effie Hillier
17 Blomfield Road
London W9
Tel. 286 01 89

Tokyo agent: PPS, Tokyo
CPO Box 2051
Tel. 03- 264 3821
     06- 531 5577

With illustration by Andrzej Dudzinski

Imbrogno

411 North LaSalle Street
Chicago, Illinois 60610
Tel. 312-644 7333

Agent (East Coast):
Jim Taylor
Tel. 718-875 7350

Clients include:
Chas A Stevens, Chicago
Magazine, Dow Corning, Ft.
Howard Paper, Gast, Gianni
Furniture, Hubbell Steel, Illinois
State Lottery, Micro Data Base
Systems, NBC, Nichicon, OSI,
Playboy Magazine, Reliable
Electric, Reliance Comm/Tec,
Square-D

Imbrogno

411 North LaSalle Street
Chicago, Illinois 60610
Tel. 312-644 7333

Agent (East Coast):
Jim Taylor
Tel. 718-875 7350

Clients include:
Chas A Stevens, Chicago
Magazine, Dow Corning, Ft.
Howard Paper, Gast, Gianni
Furniture, Hubbell Steel, Illinois
State Lottery, Micro Data Base
Systems, NBC, Nichicon, OSI,
Playboy Magazine, Reliable
Electric, Reliance Comm/Tec,
Square-D

ADIP 11 1985 © Imbrogno

Mark Johnson Photographer

P.O. Box 57561
Dallas, TX 75207
Tel. 214-939 0213

Representatives:

In New Orleans:
Nancy LaNasa
Tel. 504-944 9068

In Los Angeles:
Amy Allen
Tel. 714-675 5751

Ron Johnson

2460 Eliot Street
Denver, Colorado 80211
Tel. 303-458 0288

Photography of architecture, interior design, related products, furnishings, and accessories.

Photographie d'architecture, décoration intérieure et produits de décoration, meubles et accessoires.

建築、インテリア、関連商品、家具、アクセサリーの写真

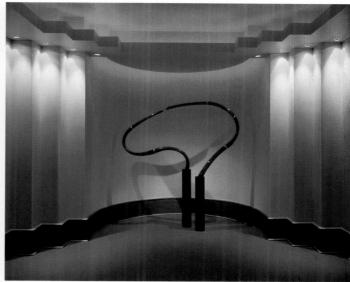

ADIP 11 1985 © Ron Johnson

Geof Kern

1337 Crampton
Dallas, Texas 75207
Tel. 214-630 0856

Agent:
Lisa Cobb & Associates
2200 N. Lamar
Suite 202
Dallas, TX 75202
Tel. 214-939 0032

Awards include a Silver and
Honorable Mention at the 63rd
New York Art Directors Club
Exhibition in the brochure
category.

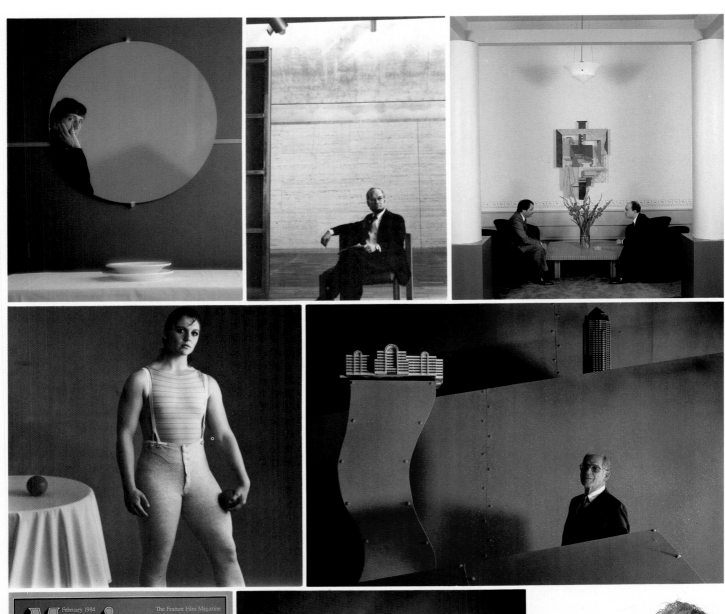

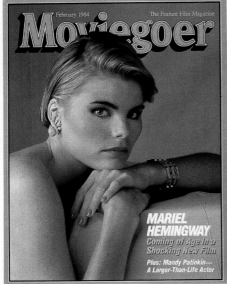

ADIP 11 1985 © Geof Kern

Geof Kern

1337 Crampton
Dallas, Texas 75207
Tel. 214-630 0856

Agent:
Lisa Cobb & Associates
2200 N. Lamar
Suite 202
Dallas, TX 75202
Tel. 214-939 0032

Awards include a Silver and
Honorable Mention at the 63rd
New York Art Directors Club
Exhibition in the brochure
category.

ADIP 11 1985 © Geof Kern

Kathryn Kleinman

542 Natoma Street
San Francisco, California 94103
Tel. 415-864 2406

KATHRYN KLEINMAN

Rick Koehler Studios

1622 Moulton Parkway Suite A
Tustin, California 92680
Tel. 714-730 5982

Agent:
Deborah Gordon

Clients include:
Toshiba America Inc., Pertec
Computer Corporation, R.B.
Furniture, U.S. Divers, Angels
Home Centers, Microdata
Corporation, Zee Medical/
McKesson, Buick, Esmark/Hunt-
Wesson, Plus/Millcreek, Hilton,
Richlife Foods, Adolph Coors.

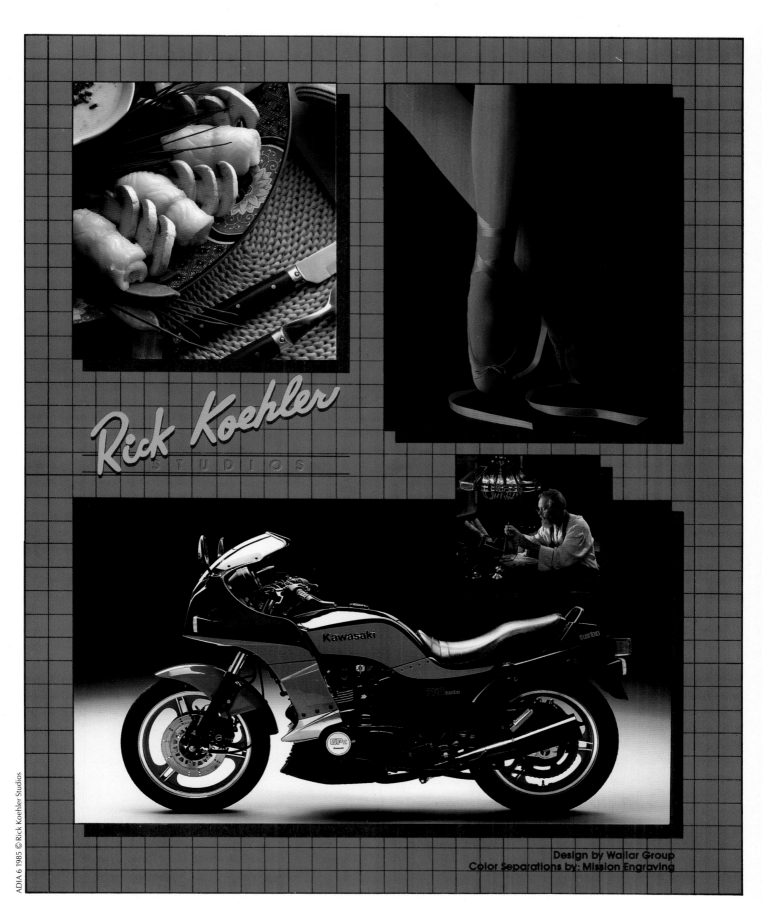

Design by Wallar Group
Color Separations by: Mission Engraving

PARISH

PARISH KOHANIM
1130 WEST PEACHTREE ST. N.W.
ATLANTA, GA 30309
ATLANTA (404) 892-0099
NEW YORK (212) 662-6611

254

Dan Kozan

32 West 22nd Street
New York, NY 10011
Tel. 212-691 2288, 212-688 0245

Agent:
Michael Ginsburg & Associates
339 East 58th Street
New York, NY 10022
Tel. 212-628 2379

Clients:
American Bell, American Express,
Brown & Williamson, Burger King,
Charles of the Ritz, Cover Girl,
Cuisine Magazine, Elizabeth
Arden, Estee Lauder, General
Electric, General Foods, Halston
Fragrances, Heublein, IBM,
Minolta, Orlane, Panasonic,
Pepsico, Proctor & Gamble, Ralph
Lauren, Revlon, Seagrams.

Mark Kozlowski Photography

39 West 28th Street
New York, NY 10001
Tel. 212-684 7487

Photographs © 1984
Mark Kozlowski
Portfolio and photomatic reel
available.

IS REPRESENTED BY
JANE MAUTNER
(212) 777-9024

Mark Kozlowski Photography

39 West 28th Street
New York, NY 10001
Tel. 212-684 7487

Well orchestrated, quality photography of large and small productions, with care in every detail.

Photographs ©1984 Mark Kozlowski

Crisco Oil Photomatic

Kaz Kurisu

819-1/2 North Fairfax Avenue
Los Angeles, California 90046
Tel. 213-655 7287

Agent:
Japan—
Office Makiyama
Tel. 03-423 4797

Bobbi Lane

7213 Santa Monica Boulevard
Los Angeles, California 90046
Tel. 213-874 0557

Advertising, annual reports,
corporate, audio-visual.
In the studio or on location.

Complete studio totalling
2400 square-feet.

Stock available.

American Bell, Summa Corp.,
Pentax, Mattel Electonics, Mattel
Toys, Westwood One, Honda,
Beverly Hills Workout, Milton-
Meyer Corp. Infinity. Kenwood,
Everest & Jennings, Marantz,
Fostex, Alpine/Luxman, Kodak,
Universal Studios Tour, Esso-Uniflo,
Cosmerica, Tokina, American
Telecommunications.

First Interstate Bank, Sheraton,
Uniden, Richlife, Lawry's, Teledyne
Inet, Chapperal, California
Magazine, ITT Cannon, Tajone
Ranch, Cinema Group, Nakamichi,
Janeil.

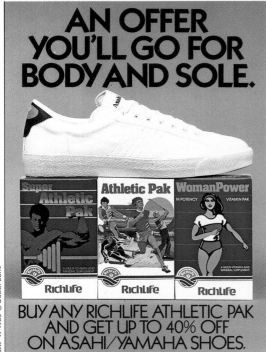

ADIP 11 1985 © Bobbi Lane

259

David Langley

536 West 50th Street
New York, NY 10019
Tel. 212-581 3930

TV reel available

Glenn Gill   Ogilvy & Mather

Bill Nollman   Wells Rich & Greene

Mike Withers   Travelers Ins.   Ally & Gargano

Martin Connolly   Tenderleaf Tea   DFS

Lisa Fisher   Columbia Pictures   Greenberg Assoc.

David Langley

536 West 50th Street
New York, NY 10019
Tel. 212-581 3930

TV reel available

The $40 Billion Baby That the World Hasn't Adopted Yet

FIRST BOSTON

Paul Basile   Della Femina Travisano

BODYGARD FROM SIMONIZ.
THE LEGENDARY SHINE WITHOUT
THE LEGENDARY SWEAT.

Mike Withers   Ally & Gargano

TOYOTA GRAND PRIX OF LONG BEACH

Paul Nelson   DFS-LA

OUR ENGINEERS WOULDN'T CHOOSE
BETWEEN PERFORMANCE OR MILEAGE.
SO YOU GET BOTH.

Marie Castellano   Della Femina Travisano

THE COMMUNICATIONS BREAKTHROUGH THAT
BUSINESSMEN HAVE BEEN WAITING FOR SINCE 1905.

NYNEX
Mobile Communications

Ron Hartley   Wunderman Ricotta & Kline

Gilles Larrain

95 Grand Street
New York, NY 10013
Tel. 212-925 8494

Mikhail Baryshnikov

Elaine Kudo

Miles Davis

Jane Seymour

Gilles Larrain

95 Grand Street
New York, NY 10013
Tel. 212-925 8494

Johan Renvall

LEGNAME

Rudi Legname

389 Clementina
San Francisco, California 94103
Tel. 415-777 9569

Los Angeles: 213-855 8855
Chicago: 312-944 6655
London: 499-1258

Dick Luria Photography, Inc.

5 East 16th Street
New York, NY 10003
Tel. 212-929 7575

266

Dick Luria Photography, Inc.

5 East 16th Street
New York, NY 10003
Tel. 212-929 7575

Brian Leng

1021-1/2 North La Brea
Los Angeles, California 90038
Tel. 213-850 0995

Agent:
Jill Youmans
1021-1/2 North La Brea
Los Angeles, California 90038
Tel. 213-850 0995

Specializing in photographing
people and people with products
in the studio and on location.

6,000 sq. ft. studio with full
kitchen and cove accomodates
large products and sets.

"Stock also available."

Advertising, editorial and
corporate clients include:
Casio, Columbia Pictures Home
Video, Softsel, Levi Strauss, Nike,
Maxell, IBM, MicroSoft, Hyatt
Hotels, KLH Systems, Pioneer
Stereo, U.S. Manufacturing, PSI
Telecommunications, Penn Reels,

Brunton-Lakota, Pachmayr,
Universal Piano, Young & Rubicam,
D'Arcy-McManus & Masius,
Doremus/West, Oglivy & Mather,
Los Angeles Magazine,
Inc. Magazine.

BRIAN LENG

ADIP 11 1985 © Brian Leng

John Manno Photography

20 West 22nd Street
New York, NY 10010
Tel. 212-243 7353

Agents:
Marge Casey & Lou Arroyo
245 East 63rd Street
New York, NY 10021
Tel. 212-486 9575

MANNO

Jay Maisel

190 Bowery
New York, NY 10012
Tel. 212-431 5013

Clients include:
AGFA, Alitalia, American Airlines, American Express, AT&T, Avis, Avon, Bausch and Lomb, Benson and Hedges, BMW, Bristol Myers, Buick, Carborundum, CBS, Champion, Chase Manhattan Bank, Chemical Bank, Chesebrough Ponds, Ciba-Geigy, Citicorp, Coca-Cola, Datsun, Dayco, Debeers, Dupont, Eastern Airlines, Eastman Kodak, Exxon, Ford, Fuji, Gannett, Goodyear, Gulf, Hallmark, Health-tex, Heinz, Hertz, Hilton, Hyatt, IBM, ITT, Kimberly Clark, KLM, Knoll, Manufacturers Hanover Trust, Metropolitan Life, MGM, Miller Beer, NBC, Nikon, Otis, Pan Am, Pepsico, Puegeot, Phillip Morris, Polaroid, RCA, Renault, Revlon, R.J. Reynolds, Schlumberger, Seagrams, Sony, Swissair, Texaco, 3M, Union Carbide, United Airlines, United Technologies, Vantage, Visa, Volvo, Western Union, Westinghouse, Westvaco, Xerox.

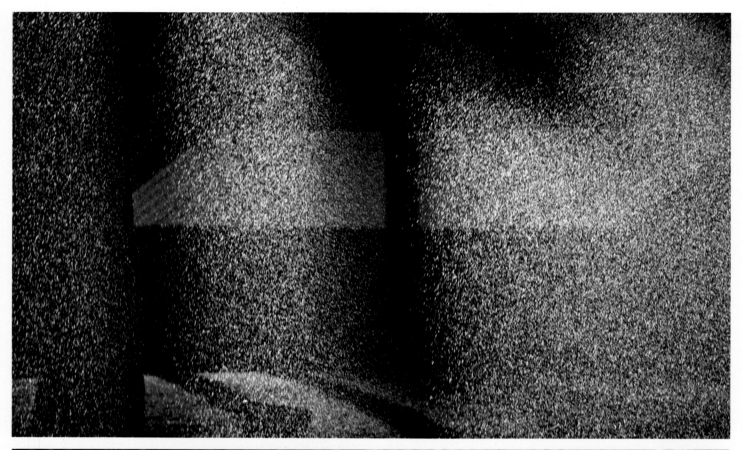

Jay Maisel

190 Bowery
New York, NY 10012
Tel. 212-431 5013

For stock or assignment photography with a different point of view, call Jay Maisel and ask for Oyv, Tom or Emily.

Für Standard- oder Auftragsfotografie mit einer anderen Perspektive, rufen Sie Jay Maisel, und fragen Sie nach Oyv, Tom oder Emily.

Pour des photographies de stock ou pour un objectif specifique, téléphoner à Jay Maisel et demander Oyv, Tom ou Emily.

あらゆる観点からのストック写真、課題写真をお求めの方はJay Maiselに電話しOyvかTomかEmilyにお尋ねください。

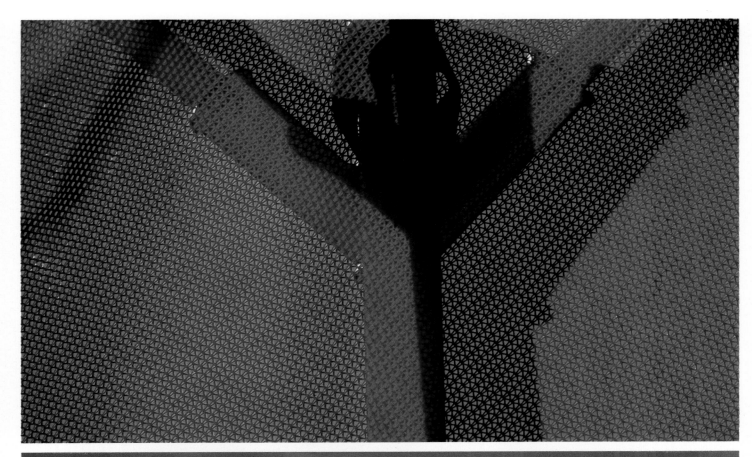

ADIP 11 1985 © Jay Maisel

Dennis Manarchy

229 West Illinois Street
Chicago, Illinois 60610
Tel. 312-828 9272

Agent:
Mary Atols

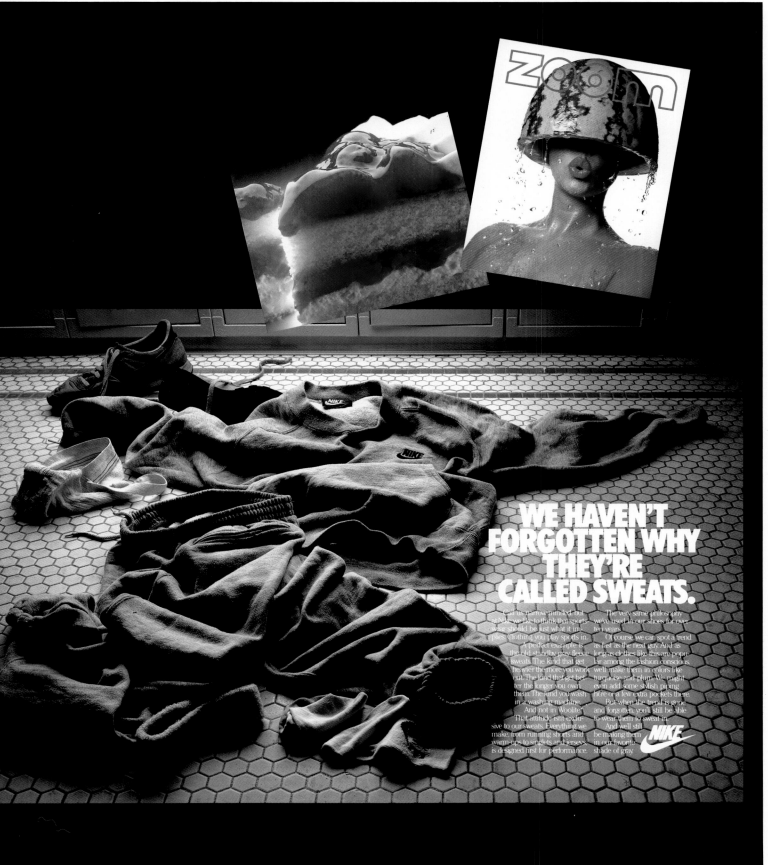

WE HAVEN'T FORGOTTEN WHY THEY'RE CALLED SWEATS.

Call us narrow-minded, but at Nike we like to think that sportswear should be just what it implies. Clothing you play sports in.

A perfect example is the old standby gray fleece sweats. The kind that get heavier the more you work out. The kind that get better the longer you own them. The kind you wash in a washing machine. And not in Woolite.

That attitude isn't exclusive to our sweats. Everything we make, from running shorts and warm-ups to singlets and jerseys, is designed first for performance.

The very same philosophy we've used in our shoes for over ten years.

Of course, we can spot a trend as fast as the next guy. And as long as clothes like this are popular among the fashion conscious, we'll make them in colors like turquoise and plum. We might even add some stylish piping here or a few extra pockets there.

But when the trend is gone and forgotten, you'll still be able to wear them to sweat in.

And we'll still be making them in our favorite shade of gray.

NIKE

Jim Marchese

200 West 20th Street
New York, NY 10011
Tel. 212-242 1087

Represented by Mary Lamont

Color and b/w photography for advertising, corporate, editorial, and travel. AIGA, Andy, Art Directors Club and CA awards. Member ASMP.

Clients have included: American Express, Analog & Digital Systems, Arthur Young & Co., Avenue, Ballantine Books, Barron's, Capitol/EMI, Chemical Bank, Colorado Heritage Center, Crown Publishers, DelMonte Canada, Discover, Exxon, Federal Express, Grow Group, Hanover Square Securities, Hitachi, Liberace, Life of Virginia, Merrill Lynch, New York Magazine, OTB, Pan Am, Peabody Intl., Print, Reader's Digest Intl., Saks Fifth Avenue, G. Schirmer, South Bronx Development Corp., Bruce Springsteen, T. Rowe Price, TIAA, Texaco, TWA, Western Union, Wall Street Journal (Creative Directors campaign).

See also American Showcase 6, 7, and 8, and Corporate Showcase 3.
© 1985 Jim Marchese

Bill Backer for The Wall Street Journal

Percy Knauth, writer

Rosser Reeves for Ted Bates

Merrill Lynch

TIAA Insurance

Arthur Young & Co.

Gerald R. Ford/Peabody Intl.

ADIP 11 1985 © Jim Marchese

Frank Maresca

F R A N K
MARESCA

236 W. 26TH STREET • NEW YORK, NEW YORK • 212-620-0955

Member APA

Represented by:
Lauri Lorenzo
212-620-0961

promotional posters
on request

David Martinez

2325 Third Street #433
San Francisco, California 94107
Tel. 415 558-8088

Specializes in photographing people
in editorial situations for advertising.
Equipped to shoot on location or
in the studio.

Ed Masterson

11211 Sorrento Valley Road, Suite S
San Diego, California 92121
Tel. 619-457 3251

Partial client list:
United Airlines, Ted Bates Adv.,
Jantzen, ESPN, Time Magazine,
EDN Magazine, Frito-Lay, Sony, J.
Walter Thompson, Tatham-Laird &
Kudner, Spiro & Associates, 3-M,
SZF Adv., WSB T.V., Spiro, U.S.
Navy, Rogers & Cowans, Jeans
West, Aitkin-Kynett, Radisson
Hotels, Dunfey Hotels, Burell
Adv., Braymes & Assoc.,

Colony Resorts, McDonald &
Seigenthalter, Parade Mag.,
Coleco, Shorts Aircraft, D Kobs &
Brady Adv., Winterkorn & Lillis
Adv., Ralston-Purina, Richter &
Carr Adv., Govatos & Dunn Adv.,
Oak Tree Stores, Palm Springs
Racquet Club, National Enquirer,
Sears Roebuck

ADIP 11 1985 © Ed Masterson

Phil Matt

Box 10406
Rochester, NY 14610
Tel. 716-461 5977

The three most important things to
know about Phil are location,
location, and location.

Some of the clients who know
include:
Barron's, Bausch & Lomb, Business
Week, Changing Times, Chase
Manhattan Bank, Chubb Group,
Eastman Kodak Company,
Eastman School of Music, Essence,
Forbes, Goulds Pumps, GM/Delco,
Graduate School of Management/
University of Rochester,

Hutchins/Young & Rubicam,
I.B.M., Inc., Lincoln First Bank,
Nalge Company, Newsweek, The
New York Times, Rochester
Philharmonic Orchestra,
Rochester Telephone, Rumrill-
Hoyt, Sybron Corporation, Sykes
Datatronics, Time, United Press
International, USA Today, Venture,
Xerox Corporation.

Extensive color and B/W stock—
fully computerized cross-
reference. See our ad in American
Showcase Volume 8, p. 204.

Member:
ASMP, NPPA.

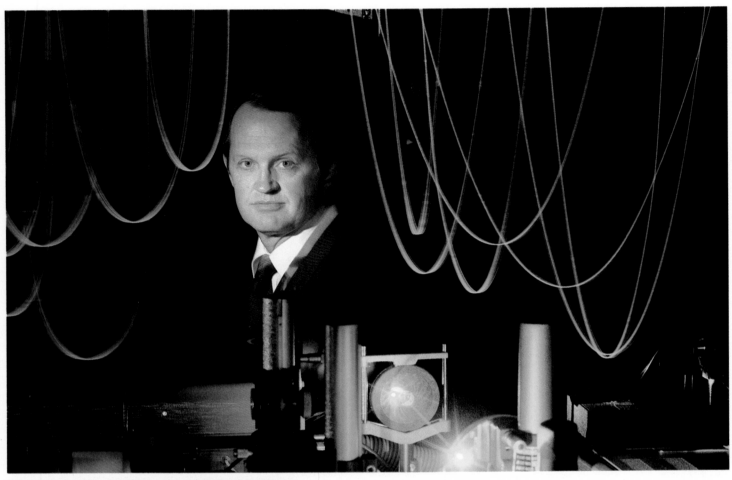

ADIP 11 1985 © Phil Matt

Robert Maxham

319 East Huisache
San Antonio, Texas 78212
Tel. 512-735 3537

279

James McLoughlin

148 West 24th Street
New York, NY 10011
Tel. 212-206 8207

Agent:
John Kenney Associates
342 Madison Avenue
New York, NY 10017
Tel. 212-697 8370

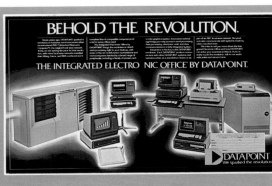

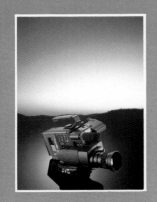

280

Merle Norman

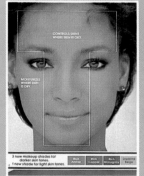

Avon

McLoughlin

Represented by John Kenney Associates • 342 Madison Ave., NYC 10017 • (212) 697-8370

Reid Miles

brings romance back to tabletop!

When more is at stake than just clicking the shutter!

Telephone this studio for your local representative at (213) 462-6106 . . . or send your layouts direct
to our telecopier machine at. . . (213) 462-8816

The Reid Miles Studio, Inc., 1136 North Las Palmas, Hollywood, California 90038

ADIP 11 1985 © Reid Miles

Chris Moore

20 West 22nd Street
New York, NY 10010
Tel. 212-242 0553

Agent:
H. Martyn Williams
Tel. 212-242 0553

ADIP 11 1985 © Chris Moore

Gary R. Moore

1125 East Orange Avenue
Monrovia, California 91016
Tel. 818-359 9414

Still Photography
Film and Video

Member:
IATSE Local 659
International Film Producers
Association
Academy of Television Arts
and Sciences
International Association of
Business Communicators

As a Motion Picture Cameraman
and Commercial Photographer,
I intermix, as a matter of course,
the best of both arts.

I have complete studio facilities
and an exceptional mobile location
package for on-site photography,
cinematography, and video.

Clients include:
Walt Disney Productions,
Disneyland, The Disney Channel,
ABC, Tomy Toys, American Honda,
Eastman Kodak, GEON, Weber-
Redline, General Can Co.,
Universal Studios, many others

ADIP 11 1985 © Gary Moore

285

Nancy Moran

143 Greene Street
New York, NY 10012
Tel. 212-505 9620

Represented in Los Angeles by:
Françoise Kirkland
Tel. 213-855 1349

Clients include:
Citibank, Lucasfilm, Ltd., Life, GEO, Rolling Stone, Newsweek, Robert A. Becker, Inc., Lally McFarland & Pantello, Inc., Cosgrove Assoc., Workman Publishing, People, Paramount Pictures Corp., MGM/UA, Fortune, Money, Warner Communications, Inc., Henson Assoc., Inc., FAO Schwarz, Vanity Fair, GQ, New York Magazine, Time, Sports Illustrated, The New York Times Magazine, Walt Disney.

OUTSIDE: Diana Nyad in New York Harbor for Quest Magazine.

MORAN

INSIDE: Donald Sutherland for MGM/UA. Teddy Bear for Workman Publishing. Man with Bad Cold for Lally, McFarland & Pantello, Inc.

Steve Newby Photography

4501 Swiss Avenue
Dallas, Texas 75204
Tel. 214-821 0231

People. Places. Product. 110%
thought and effort goes into every
shot and project, whether it be
corporate, industrial, advertising,
or product illustration. And it
shows.

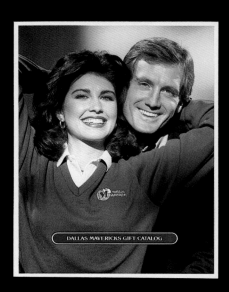

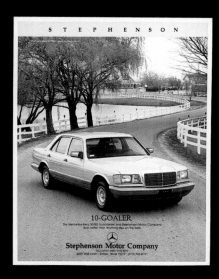

Jim Olvera

2700 Commerce Street
Dallas, Texas 75226
Tel. 214-939 0550

Here are a few of my still lifes. No tricks or gimmicks—just pictures, pure and simple

I make photographs of people the same way. If you'd like to see some, take a look at page 370 in ADI 10. Or better yet, call me and I'll send you a portfolio.

Then you can see what I've done for my clients, who include American Airlines, Cadillac Fairview, The Dallas Museum of Art, Diamond Shamrock, Diners Club, Dr. Pepper, Faberge, TGI Friday's, Northern Telecom, Woody Pirtle, The Richards Group, Southern Methodist University, Steak and Ale, and Ziff-Davis Publishing.

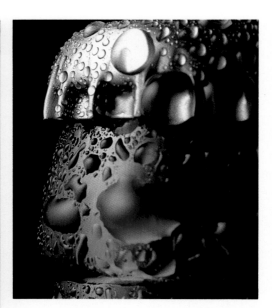

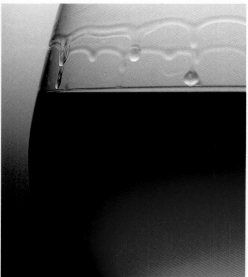

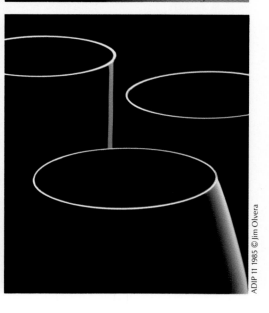

ADIP 11 1985 © Jim Olvera

Gary Perweiler

873 Broadway
New York, NY 10003

Agents:
Stephen Madris
Tel. 212-744 6668

Diane Henning
Tel. 212-246 8484

Print portfolio and film reel
available on request.

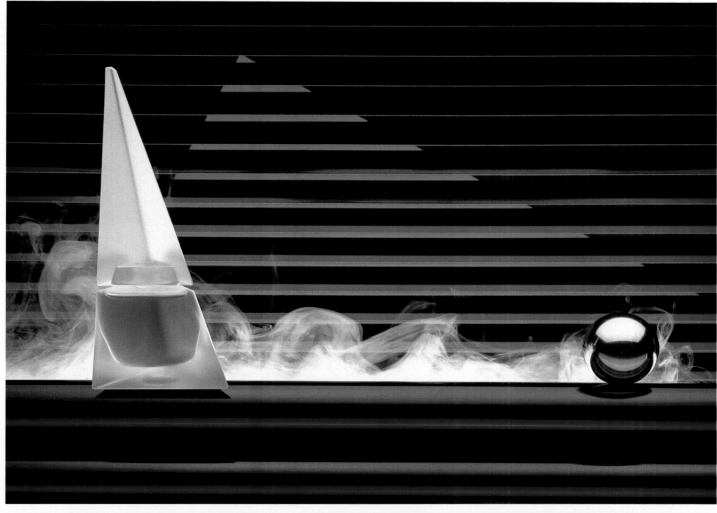

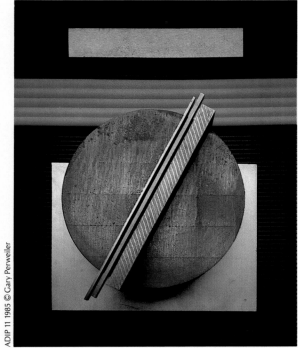

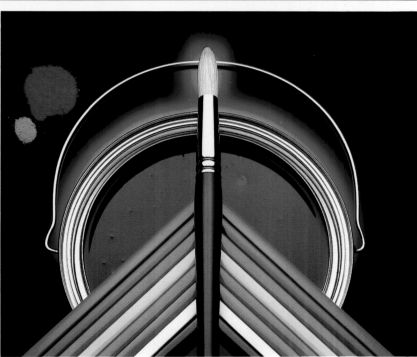

Photographic Communications

2004 Martin Avenue
Santa Clara, California 95050
Tel. 408-727 2233

Corporate Rep:
Richard Cassidy

Studio Rep:
Laurie Haugaard

Photographic Communications, located in Silicon Valley, is dedicated to the high tech industry. We work with the finest art directors and corporate communications people when creating the concepts, themes and motifs that are setting the pace for the high tech market.

Our 10,800 square-feet studio allows for multiple shoots and large-scale projects. Our staff regularly handles the fabrication of large studio sets, complex location and table top sets. Propping, styling and casting are integral in our set engineering and design functions. Our own in-house lab handles E6 chromes to meet last minute deadlines and strict quality control.

We have developed a range of styles from classic clean shots to exotic, complex and progressive special effects. Our special effects work is designed for single chrome delivery without retouching, by utilizing multiple cameras and/or optical printing/cel animation techniques.

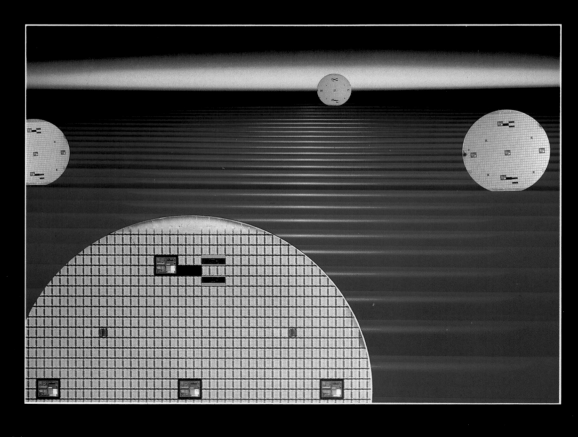

Ron Pomerantz

325 West Huron Street
Chicago, Illinois 60610 U.S.A.
Tel. 312-787 6407

Agent:
Susan Dannenberg
Tel. 312-787 6407

IMAGINATION.

Our clients include:
AT&T, Bang & Olfsun, Baby Ruth, Beecham Labs, Blistex, Boise Cascade, Bon Ami, Leo Burnett, Canadian Mist, Chicago Tribune, Chicago Mercantile Exch., CNA, Coleco/CBS, Conti-Commodities, Fort Howard, French's, Grey-North, Helene Curtis, IBM, Illinois Bell, Kimberly-Clark, Knight-Ridder, Littlefuse, Lucky Strike, Mandabach & Simms, Marsteller, Midas, Midland Hotel, Needham/Harper, Old Forester, Polygram, Quaker Oats, Rust-Oleum, G.D. Searle, Teletype Corp., Tyson Foods, Usher's, Westwood Pharmaceutical, 1984 World's Fair.

ADIP 11 1985 © Ron Pomerantz

Jim Polaski

215 West Superior 6th.
Chicago, Illinois 60610
Tel. 312-751 2526

Agent:
Tom Erickson
Tel. 312-751 2534

We shoot food.

Our posters are available by request on your company letterhead. We also shoot Tabletop & product.

Wir machen auch Aufnahmen von Tischoberfläche und Erzeugnis.

Unsere Poster sind nach Wunsch auf Ihrem Geschäftspapier erhältlich. Wir machen auch Aufnahmen von Essen.

Nous photographions également les produits sur table.

Nos posters avec entête de votre compagnie sont disponibles sur commande spéciale. Nous photographions également la nourriture.

ADIP 11 1985 © Jim Polaski

Jim Polaski

215 West Superior 6th.
Chicago, Illinois 60610
Tel. 312-751 2526

Agent:
Tom Erickson
Tel. 312-751 2534

We shoot Tabletop & product.

Our posters are available by request on your company letterhead. We also shoot food.

Wir machen auch Aufnahmen von Tischoberfläche und Erzeugnis.

Unsere Poster sind nach Wunsch auf Ihrem Geschäftspapier erhältlich. Wir machen auch Aufnahmen von Essen.

Nous photographions également les produits sur table.

Nos posters avec entête de votre compagnie sont disponibles sur commande spéciale. Nous photographions également la nourriture.

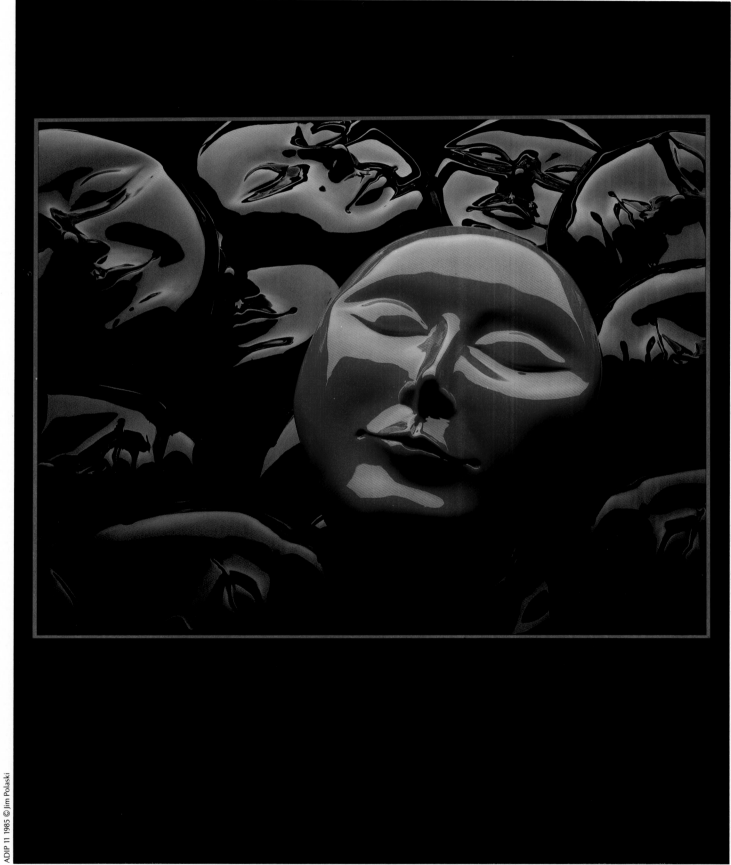

Donovan Reese

4801 Lemmon Avenue
Dallas, Texas 75219
Tel. 214-526 5851

Worldwide Location Photography
for Advertising, Annual Report,
Architectural, Corporate and
Travel Clients. Full format studio
also available.

Stock Available upon request.

Lawrence Robins/Gil Cope

50 West 17th Street
New York, NY 10011
Tel. 212-206 0436

Representative:
Jenny Macfie

Representative in Chicago:
Ken Feldman
Tel. 312-337 0447

Full service print production co.

Société de production de toutes
sortes d'éreuves.

Vollständige Graphikhandlung.

プリントのことなら何でも行います。

Tom Ryan Photography

1821 Levee
Dallas, Texas 75207
Tel. 214-651 7085

Agent:
Lisa Cobb & Associates
2200 N. Lamar
Suite 202
Dallas, TX 75202

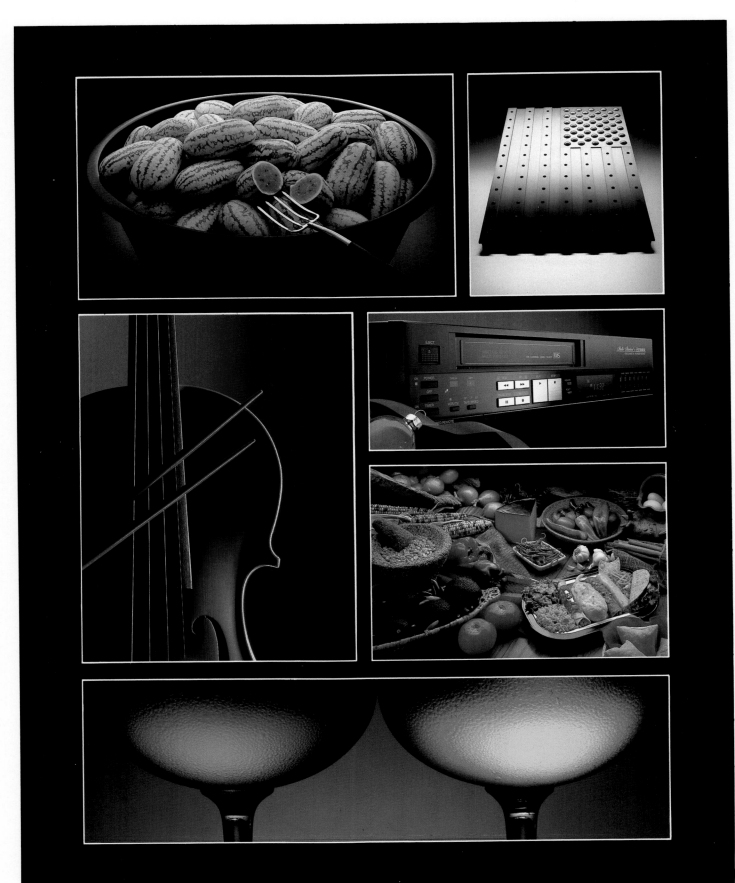

Sato Photography, Inc.

152 West 26th Street
New York, NY 10001
212-741 0688

Client List:
Nina Ricci, African Art Magazine,
Arts D'Afrique Noir Magazine,
Country-Style Ceramics
International

297

SAVAS
PHOTOGRAPHY

James Savas Suite 1105
37 West 20th Street
New York, New York 10011

212/620-0067

P H O T O G R A P H Y

James Savas
Suite 1105
37 West 20th Street
New York, New York 10011

212/620-0067

ADIP 11 1985 © Jim Savas

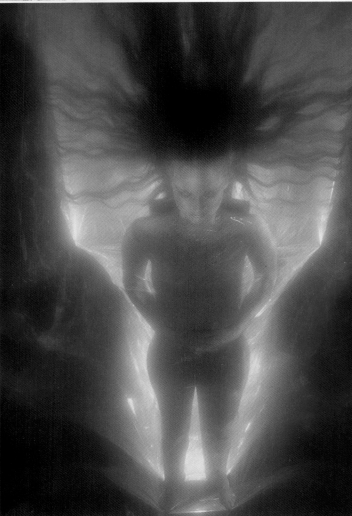

Jerry Segrest Photography, Inc.

1707 South Ervay
Dallas, Texas 75215
Tel. 214-426 6360

Agent:
Melanie Spiegel
Photocom, Inc.
Dallas, Texas
Tel. 214-428 8781

Problem-solving photo
illustration. People, places,
products. Location or extensive
studio facilities in converted
1930's movie theatre in downtown
Dallas. Portfolio upon request.

American Airlines, Frito-Lay,
Glenmore/Kentucky Tavern,
Libby's/Crosse & Blackwell,
Marion Laboratories, Pepsi Cola
Co., Rockwell International,
Texas Instruments, Xerox.

SEGREST

Dan Sellers Photography

2258 Vantage Street
Dallas, Texas 75207
Tel. 214-631 4705

Some clients I have worked with
include:
American Express, Alabama Metal
Products Co., CBS Records, EBSCO
Industries, Inc., Frito-Lay, Holiday
Inn, IBM, Jason Younger Sportswear,
Marriott, Miller Brewing, Gillette,
Pizza Hut, Texas Art Gallery,
United Technologies.

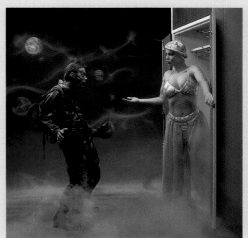

Abe Seltzer Studios, Inc.

524 West 23rd Street
New York, NY 10011
Tel. 212-807 0660

Agent:
Doug Brown
New York
Tel. 212-980 4971

Television reel upon request.

Bobine d'échantillons télévision
sur demande.

Fernsehspule auf Wunsch.

テレビ用フィルムも承ります。

Set photographed in studio for Y&R, Inc., New York

David M. Siegel: Arizona

224 North 5th Avenue
Phoenix, Arizona 85003
Tel. 602-257 9509

David is long experienced in Arizona shooting. This state makes working easy because we have every possible type of location: low desert to snow-topped mountains. Permits are rarely required, good shooting weather & beautiful sunsets are year round. Our studio is well established and facilitates studio work as well as location. We have 8000 sq. ft. of shooting space, full kitchen, B&W lab, offices, conference room, and downtown location close to all rental and travel services. We've taken years of in-studio expertise and brought them on location. Please review our previous work in ADI # 9 and # 10.

Partial client list: Arizona Bank, Arizona Biltmore, Armour Foods, Bozell & Jacobs, Cramer/Krasselt, Doubletree Hotels, First Interstate Bank, Motorola, Oglivey & Mather, Phillips-Ramsey, U-Haul, Valley National Bank, Wells Rich & Greene, Western Savings, Chiat-Day, J. Walter Thompson, Ray Vote Graphics, Aaron, Sautu, + G.

ADIP 11 1985 © David M. Siegel

305

Robert Simko

375 South End Avenue 30L
New York, NY 10280
Tel. 212-912 1192

Barry A. Soorenko/Photogroup Inc.

5161 River Road, Building 2-B
Washington, DC 20816
Tel. 301-652 1303

Bill Stettner

118 East 25th Street
New York, NY 10010
Tel. 212-460 8180

Agent:
Mary Anne James
Tel. 212-370 3769

Stettner

Bill Stettner

118 East 25th Street
New York, NY 10010
Tel. 212-460 8180

Agent:
Mary Anne James
Tel. 212-370 3769

Clients include:
Citibank, Fabergé, Fiat, Cutty Sark, Gordon's Gin, Bacardi Rum, Bankers Trust, Polydor Records, Timex, Miller Beer, Pioneer Stereo, Winston Cigarettes, Gilbey's Gin, Teachers Scotch, Kentucky Fried Chicken, Jameson Irish Whiskey, Coca-Cola, Panasonic, Columbia Records, Saab, Polaroid, General Foods,

Travelers Life Insurance, Atlantic Records, AT&T, Xerox, Pan Am, Shulton, Sony, Revlon, Texaco, Camel Cigarettes, Arista Records, Jack In The Box, Barney's, U.S. Army, Chase Manhattan Bank, Smirnoff, Metropolitan Life Insurance, GTE, American Airlines, Philip Morris, Campari, IBM,

Procter & Gamble, M&M/Mars, General Electric, R.J. Reynolds, Bristol-Myers, Chesebrough-Ponds, Heublein, Nabisco, American Tobacco, British Airways, Bulova, NY Telephone, Brown & Williamson, Caeser's Hotels, Duncan Hines, U.S. Post Office, Jim Beam

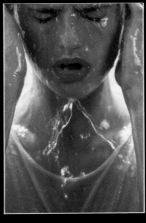

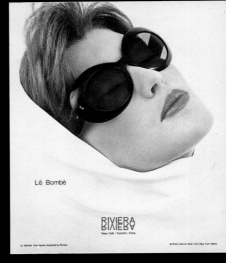

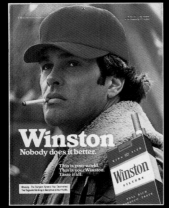

STETTNER

Vern Stafford

Commercial Photographic Services
P.O. Box 1971
222 Commerce Street
Kingsport, Tennessee 37662
Tel. 615-246 9578
TWX 810-574 5180

I specialize in location advertising, fashion, and beauty—"people and products." As an art director, you must rely on my ability to interpret, visualize, create, and execute. On every shot, someone's job is on the line. If you don't please your client, you lose the account. If I don't please you, I lose the account. I don't lose accounts; do you?

Be sure every time, call or send a TWX. I'm available for location work worldwide.

ADIP 11 1985 © Vern Stafford

Bob Stevens

9048 Santa Monica Boulevard
Los Angeles, California 90069
Tel. 213-271 8123

Agent in Chicago:
Vicki Peterson
Tel. 312-467 0780

Agent in Texas:
Tila Newhaus
Tel. 713-529 7913

TV reel on request.

Robert Stevens Productions
9048 Santa Monica Boulevard
Los Angeles, California 90069
Tel. 213-271 0145

Bob Stevens goes both ways.

Still photographer. Film director. For Bob, the two go hand in hand.
Whether he's shooting layouts or storyboards, Bob brings something to each job.
His own creative style. That's how he made his reputation. And how he keeps it up.
So for a great job, call Bob Stevens.
Either way, he definitely goes out of his way.

STEVENS

ADIP 11 1985 © Bob Stevens

Bob Stevens

9048 Santa Monica Boulevard
Los Angeles, California 90069
Tel. 213-271 8123

Agent in Chicago:
Vicki Peterson
Tel. 312-467 0780

Agent in Texas:
Tila Newhaus
Tel. 713-529 7913

TV reel on request.

Robert Stevens Productions
9048 Santa Monica Boulevard
Los Angeles, California 90069
Tel. 213-271 0145

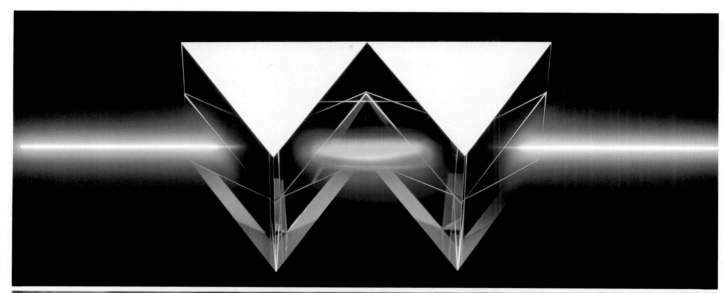

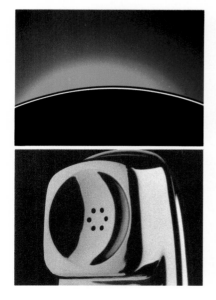
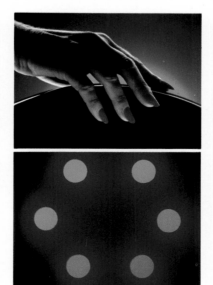

ADIP 11 1985 © Bob Stevens

313

David R. Stoecklein

Ketchum, Idaho
Tel. 208-726 5191

Represented by:
PhotoUnique
New York/Los Angeles

West Stock
Seattle

Clients:
Fila, North Face, Serac, Olin,
Nordica, Dynastar, Smith Goggles,
Look Bindings, Reflex Poles,
San Marco

With Destination Photography
Used by:
United, Eastern, TWA and
American Airlines

"I shoot people and product in any
type of outdoor setting. I carefully
coordinate an atmosphere that
will create a unique marketing
opportunity for my client. I use
locations around the world that
most photographers have never
been exposed to."

David R. Stoecklein

Ketchum, Idaho
Tel. 208-726 5191

Represented by:
PhotoUnique
New York/Los Angeles

West Stock
Seattle

Clients:
Fila, North Face, Serac, Olin,
Nordica, Dynastar, Smith Goggles,
Look Bindings, Reflex Poles,
San Marco

With Destination Photography
Used by:
United, Eastern, TWA and
American Airlines

"I shoot people and product in any
type of outdoor setting. I carefully
coordinate an atmosphere that
will create a unique marketing
opportunity for my client. I use
locations around the world that
most photographers have never
been exposed to."

Stolk Studios

1970 Harrison Street
San Francisco, California 94103
Tel. 415-621 4649

Agent:
David Wiley
1535 Green Street, Suite 207
San Francisco, California 94123
Tel. 415-441 1623

WHAT'S A TOTO?

"A truly heavy photographer."

ED WOLPER
ART DIRECTOR
SCALI, McCABE, SLOVES, INC.

Joe Toto

148 West 24th Street
New York, NY 10011
Tel. 212-620 0755

Represented in New York City by:
Elise Caputo
Tel. 212-949 2440

ADIP 11 1985 © Joe Toto

Joe Toto

148 West 24th Street
New York, NY 10011
Tel. 212-620 0755

Represented in New York City by:
Elise Caputo
Tel. 212-949 2440

CLIENT: SEAGRAMS
TITLE: LOUIS PASTEUR
ART DIRECTOR: CRAIG SPAULDING
AGENCY: WARWICK

CLIENT: WALT DISNEY PRODUCTIONS
TITLE: SANTA'S HELPERS
ART DIRECTOR: MIKE RANDAZZO
AGENCY: MINGO-JONES

CLIENT: CONTROL DATA
TITLE: PAYROLL PANIC
ART DIRECTOR: JULES SCHAEFFER
AGENCY: HICKS & GREIST

CLIENT: HERTZ
TITLE: GOALIE
ART DIRECTOR: STEPHEN MONTGOMERY
AGENCY: SCALI, MCCABE, SLOVES

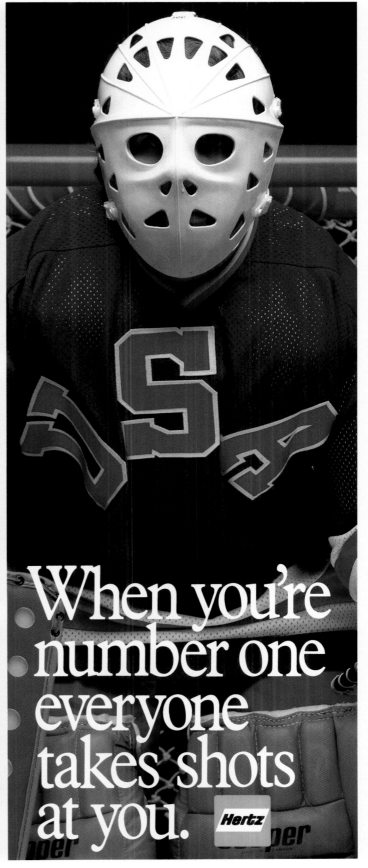

ADIP 11 1985 © Joe Toto

319

Peter Turner

154 West 57th Street
New York, NY 10019
Tel. 212-765 1733

London Representative
Annette Ponsford
Tel. 44-1-789 5976

Stock
The Image Bank
Tel. 212-953 0303

Peter Turner

154 West 57th Street
New York, NY 10019
Tel. 212-765 1733

London Representative
Annette Ponsford
Tel. 44-1-789 5976

Stock
The Image Bank
Tel. 212-953 0303

Andrew Unangst

381 Park Avenue South
New York, NY 10016
Tel. 212-889 4888

Agent:
Doug Brown
400 Madison Avenue
New York, NY 10022
Tel. 212-980 4971

Phillip Vullo APA

565 Dutch Valley Road
Atlanta, Georgia 30324
Tel. 404-874 0822

Agent:
Jennifer Vullo
Tel. 404-874 0822

Clients include:
AMF, Bell South, Blue Cross, Burton Campbell, Columbia Pictures, Compton Advertising, Contel, Coca-Cola, Diversified Products, Farmbest, Genesco, Georgia Pacific, Goldkist, Great Western, Grolsch, Hewlett Packard, Holiday Inn, IBM, Jerico, Krystal, McCann Erickson, Simmons USA, Sonat Inc., J. P. Stevens, Textron, J. Walter Thompson, Union Carbide, WTBS, Whirlpool, Wilkinson Sword, Young & Rubican, Ziff Davis

ADIP 11 1985 © Phillip Vullo

Richard Wahlstrom Photography Inc.

650 Alabama Street
San Francisco, California 94110
Tel. 415-550 1400

Agents:
Elka Kovac
743 Wisconsin Street
San Francisco, California 94107
Tel. 415-550-7755

Melanie Speigel
155 Pittsburg Street
Dallas, Texas 75207
Tel. 214-428 8781

Ken Feldman
30 Huron Street
Chicago, Illinois 60611
Tel. 312-337 0447

Larry Lynch
3317 Montrose, # 1130
Houston, Texas 77006
Tel. 713-520 9938

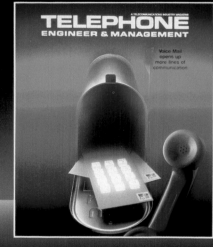

Alan Watson

San Diego, California
Tel. 619-239 5555

Agent:
Mary Kay Burns
Box 135
Barboursville, Virginia 22923
Tel. 703-832 2037

Studio and location photography of people, products and food for advertising and industry from the comfortable climate of San Diego, the hassle free gateway to the west.

Photographie en atelier et en extérieur de personnes, produits et aliments pour la publicité et le commerce. Nous travaillons dans le climat confortable de San Diego, la porte sans ennuis vers l'Ouest des Etats-unis.

広告用、一般企業向けの人物、商品、食品の スタジオ写真、ロケーション撮影は、西への 環境の良い、自由な玄関口のサンディエゴの 快適な気候から得られます。

Jeffrey Wien

160 Fifth Avenue
New York, NY 10010
Tel. 212-243 7028

Clients include:
Charles of the Ritz, Opium, YSL,
Bain de Soleil, Jean Naté, Calvin
Klein Cosmetics, Polo, Chaps,
Gloria Vanderbilt, Ralph Lauren,
Tuxedo, Almay Inc., Revlon Inc.,
Estée Lauder Inc., Aqua Velva,
Tanqueray Gin, Johnnie Walker
Scotch, Blue Nun, Self Magazine,
Andrew Geller, Cacharel, Anne
Klein, ABC Inc., Showtime Inc.

JEFFREY WIEN

ADIP 11 1985 © Jeffrey Wein

Stephen Wilkes

48 East 13th Street
New York, NY 10003
Tel. 212-475 4010

Color...Advertising—corporate, industrial, editorial and fine art. Stock photography available upon request...

Couleur...Publicité—entreprise, industrie, rédaction et beaux-arts. Photothèque disponible sur demande.

Farbe...Werbung—Gesellschaft, Redaktion und schöne Künste. Bildarchiv erhältlich auf Anfrage.

Partial client list includes: Associated Dry Goods, AT&T, ADP, Boston Five Bank, Church & Dwight, Citicorp, Colt Industries, Computer Vision, Digital Equipment, E.F. Hutton, Chase Manhattan Bank, Fischer Brothers Investment Builders, General Electric, Great Lakes Carbon, Hoechst and Roussel, Impell Corporation, Marine Midland, Olympia & York, PepsiCo,

Raytheon Co., Sandoz Pharmaceutical, Sterling Roman, St. Regis, Phillip Morris Co., Diners Club, Money Magazine, Donaldson Lufkin & Jenrette, Kodak, Manufacturers Hanover. Digital Equip., Fisher Bros. Investment Builders, Nike, Peat, Marwick Mitchell & Co.

Money Magazine

Aix en Province, France

ADIP 11 1985 © Stephen Wilkes

Stephen Wilkes

48 East 13th Street
New York, NY 10003
Tel. 212-475 4010

Color...Advertising—corporate, industrial, editorial and fine art. Stock photography available upon request...

Couleur...Publicité—entreprise, industrie, rédaction et beaux-arts. Photothèque disponible sur demande.

Farbe...Werbung—Gesellschaft, Redaktion und schöne Künste. Bildarchiv erhältlich auf Anfrage.

Partial client list includes: Associated Dry Goods, AT&T, ADP, Boston Five Bank, Church & Dwight, Citicorp, Colt Industries, Computer Vision, Digital Equipment, E.F. Hutton, Chase Manhattan Bank, Fischer Brothers Investment Builders, General Electric, Great Lakes Carbon, Hoechst and Roussel, Impell Corporation, Marine Midland, Olympia & York, PepsiCo,

Raytheon Co., Sandoz Pharmaceutical, Sterling Roman, St. Regis, Phillip Morris Co., Diners Club, Money Magazine, Donaldson Lufkin & Jenrette, Kodak, Manufacturers Hanover. Digital Equip., Fisher Bros. Investment Builders, Nike, Peat, Marwick Mitchell & Co.

PepsiCo

PepsiCo

Stephen Wilkes

48 East 13th Street
New York, NY 10003
Tel. 212-475 4010

Color...Advertising—corporate, industrial, editorial and fine art. Stock photography available upon request...

Couleur...Publicité—entreprise, industrie, rédaction et beaux-arts. Photothèque disponible sur demande.

Farbe...Werbung—Gesellschaft, Redaktion und schöne Künste. Bildarchiv erhältlich auf Anfrage.

Partial client list includes: Associated Dry Goods, AT&T, ADP, Boston Five Bank, Church & Dwight, Citicorp, Colt Industries, Computer Vision, Digital Equipment, E.F. Hutton, Chase Manhattan Bank, Fischer Brothers Investment Builders, General Electric, Great Lakes Carbon, Hoechst and Roussel, Impell Corporation, Marine Midland, Olympia & York, PepsiCo,

Raytheon Co., Sandoz Pharmaceutical, Sterling Roman, St. Regis, Phillip Morris Co., Diners Club, Money Magazine, Donaldson Lufkin & Jenrette, Kodak, Manufacturers Hanover. Digital Equip., Fisher Bros. Investment Builders, Nike, Peat, Marwick Mitchell & Co.

ADIP 11 1985 © Stephen Wilkes

Citicorp

330

Stephen Wilkes

48 East 13th Street
New York, NY 10003
Tel. 212-475 4010

Color...Advertising—corporate,
industrial, editorial and fine art.
Stock photography available upon
request...

Couleur...Publicité—entreprise,
industrie, rédaction et beaux-arts.
Photothèque disponible sur
demande.

Farbe...Werbung—Gesellschaft,
Redaktion und schöne Künste.
Bildarchiv erhältlich auf Anfrage.

Partial client list includes:
Associated Dry Goods, AT&T,
ADP, Boston Five Bank, Church &
Dwight, Citicorp, Colt Industries,
Computer Vision, Digital
Equipment, E.F. Hutton, Chase
Manhattan Bank, Fischer Brothers
Investment Builders, General
Electric, Great Lakes Carbon,
Hoechst and Roussel, Impell
Corporation, Marine Midland,
Olympia & York, PepsiCo,

Raytheon Co., Sandoz
Pharmaceutical, Sterling Roman,
St. Regis, Phillip Morris Co.,
Diners Club, Money Magazine,
Donaldson Lufkin & Jenrette,
Kodak, Manufacturers Hanover.
Digital Equip., Fisher Bros.
Investment Builders, Nike, Peat,
Marwick Mitchell & Co.

ADIP 11 1985 © Stephen Wilkes

St. Regis Paper Company

James Wojcik

95 Vandam Street
New York City, NY 10013
Tel. 212-807 0593

Agent:
Jim Berns
Tel. 212-929 6421

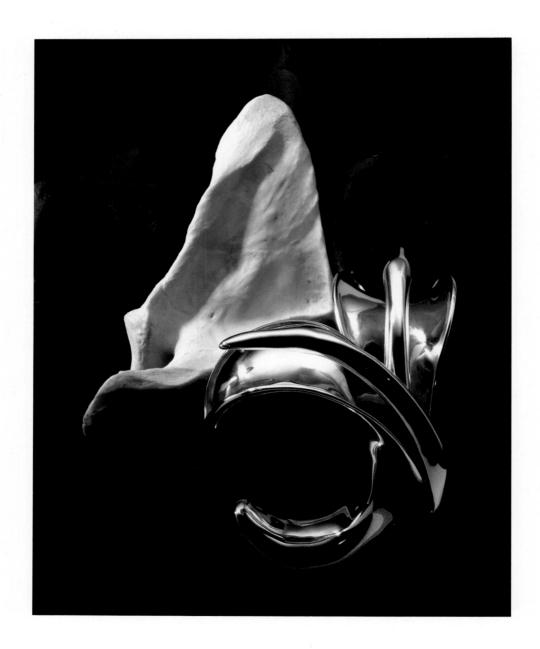

STOCK PHOTOGRAPHY

There is
one perfect
image
for your job.

PHOTO RESEARCHERS, INC.
60 East 56 Street New York, NY 10022 Telephone: 212.758.3420 Cable: FOTOSEARCH New York Telex: 428532 Photony

Almost anything you'll need in color or black & white—people, sports, travel, abstracts, medical,
high technology, and The National Audubon Society Collection of wildlife and plants.

West Stock, Inc.

157 Yesler, Suite 600
Seattle, Washington 98104
Tel. 206-621 1611

"Existing photography of
practically everything."

Tim Heneghan

David Stoecklein

Keith Gunnar

Don Graham

David Stoecklein

Don Graham

David Stoecklein

ADIP 11 1985 © West Stock, Inc.

336

West Stock, Inc.

157 Yesler, Suite 600
Seattle, Washington 98104
Tel. 206-621 1611

"Existing photography of
practically everything."

WEST STOCK

Doug Wilson

John Luke

Doug Wilson

Bill Staley

John Luke

Jeff Miller

Charles Pearson

ADIP 11 1985 © West Stock, Inc.

West Stock, Inc.

157 Yesler, Suite 600
Seattle, Washington 98104
Tel. 206-621 1611

"Existing photography of
practically everything."

WEST STOCK

David Falconer

Jason Rubinsteen

Don Normark

Jay Lurie

Jeffry Myers

Walter Hodges

Ben Marra

West Stock, Inc.

157 Yesler, Suite 600
Seattle, Washington 98104
Tel. 206-621 1611

"Existing photography of
practically everything."

WEST STOCK

Paul Kotz

Steve Meltzer

Bill Staley

Jeff Gnass

Matt Brown

Rick Morley

Mike Nakamura

339

CREATIVE SERVICES

CREATIVE SERVICES
CONTENTS

ILLUSTRATION

DESIGN, ART DIRECTION, CREATIVE SERVICES

PHOTOGRAPHY
       Photographers
       Stock Photo Houses

REPS: ILLUSTRATORS AND PHOTOGRAPHERS

PRINTING, PRODUCTION
       Prints, Chromes, Retouchers
       Printers and Engravers
       Typographers
       Paper Suppliers

TALENT, MISCELLANEOUS SERVICES
       Actors, Models, Talent
       Props, Services, Locations, Supplies
       Copywriters

ILLUSTRATION

Abel, Ray/ 180 Vasser Place, Scarsdale, NY .... (914) 725-1899
Abraham, Daniel Ethan/ 425 Fifth Avenue, Brooklyn, NY .... (212) 499-4006
Abrams, Kathie/ 41 Union Square West Rm. 1001, New York, NY .. (212) 741-1333
Accornero, Franco/ 420 Lexington Ave., New York, NY .... (212) 697-8525
Accurso, Anthony/ 5309-7th Avenue 1st Floor, Brooklyn, NY........ (212) 435-1323
Acuna, Ed/ 353 W 53 St Ste 1W, New York, NY......................... (212) 682-2462
Adam, Gaylord Inc/ 236 E. 36th Street, New York, NY .... (212) 684-4625
Adams & Braverman Inc/ 1420 Walnut St, Philadelphia, PA......... (215) 735-3562
Adams, Jeanette/ 261 Broadway, New York, NY .... (212) 732-3878
Adams, Jeffrey/ 15 W. 72nd St., New York, NY .... (212) 799-2231
Addams, Charles/ New York, NY .... (203) 227-7806
Adler, Bente/ 103 Broad St., Boston, MA................................ (617) 266-3858
Adler Graphics/ 28 Kansas Street, Hackensack, NJ .... (201) 343-3358
Admore Inc/ 56 Summer St, Shrewsbury, MA .... (617) 845-6321
Advertising Bull-Pen Graphics/ Box 446, Greens Farms, CT.......... (203) 255-3301
A F A-Art For Advertising/ 420 Lexington Ave, New York, NY .... (212) 953-7951
Affiliated Artist/Designers/ 222 E 46th St, New York, NY .... (212) 661-1520
Aiese, Bob/ 12 Charles, Lynbrook, NY .... (516) 887-1367
Airstream/ 60 E 42nd Street, New York, NY .... (212) 682-1490
Aitken, Amy/ 227 Waverly Place, New York, NY .... (212) 691-8753
AJIN/ 251 W. 30th St. 5e, New York, NY .... (212) 760-0919
   See our ad on page 10
AKM Associates/ 41 E 42nd, New York, NY .... (212) 687-7636
Albahae, Andrea/Illustrator/ Brooklyn, NY .... (718) 934-7004
Albano, Chuck/ 192 N Second St, Bethpage, NY .... (516) 938-0821
Alcorn, Robert/ 114 E 32nd St Suite 902, New York, NY .... (212) 685-2770
Alcorn, Stephen/ 135 E 54th, New York, NY .... (212) 421-0050
Alderman New York/ 360 Park Ave S, New York, NY .... (212) 683-2266
Alexander, Paul R/ 37 Pine Mt Rd, West Redding, CT .... (203) 544-9293
Allaux, Jean Francois/ 21 W. 86th Street, New York, NY .... (212) 873-8404
Alleman, Annie/ 38 E. 21st St., New York, NY .... (212) 477-4185
Allen, Gary/ Box 302 HC1, Samsonville, NY .... (914) 657-6473
Allen, Julian/ 31 Walker Street, New York, NY .... (212) 925-6550
Allen, Julian/ 6 Jane St, New York, NY .... (212) 989-7074
ALLEN, TERRY/ 291 Carroll St., Brooklyn, NY .... (718) 624-1210
   See our ad on page 11
Alley, Rob/ 201 East 28th Street, New York, NY .... (212) 532-0928
Allner, Walter/ 110 Riverside Dr, New York, NY .... (212) 288-8010
Almquist, Don/ 166 Grovers Avenue, Bridgeport, CT .... (203) 336-5649
Almquist, Don/ 353 West 53rd Street, New York, NY .... (212) 730-0144
Alpert, Alan/ 405 E. 54th Street, New York, NY .... (212) 421-8160
Alpert, Olive/ 9511 Shore Rd., New York, NY .... (212) 833-3092
Ameijide, Ray/ 251 E. 51st Street, New York, NY .... (212) 832-3214
Ames, Lee/ 6500 Jericho Tpke, Commack, NY .... (516) 499-2222
Amicosante, Vincent/ 264 Under Cliff Avenue, Edgewater, NJ........ (201) 943-3340
Amity, Elana/ 339 E. 77th Street, New York, NY .... (212) 879-4690
Amsel, Richard/ 353 E. 83rd Street, New York, NY .... (212) 744-5599
Anderson, Richard/ 157 West 57th Street Suite 304,
   New York, NY... (212) 247-1130
Anderson, Robert/ 44 W. 69th Street, New York, NY .... (212) 787-7380
Angelini, George/ 185 East 85th Street, New York, NY .... (212) 369-1925
Angus, Martha/ New York, NY .... (212) 355-1316
Ansado, John/ 400 East 55th Street, New York, NY .... (212) 929-0487
Anspach-Grossman Portugal/ 711 3rd Avenue, New York, NY ...... (212) 692-9000
Anthony Inc., Robert/ 10 23rd Street, New York, NY .... (212) 673-3011
ANTHONY, MITCHELL ILLUSTRATION/ 516 E. Maude Ave.,
   Sunnyvale, CA .... (408) 738-3729
   See our ad on page 12
Antonios, Tony/ 60 E 42nd Street, New York, NY .... (212) 682-1490
Antoni, Volker E.H./ 889 Pacific Street, Brooklyn, NY .... (212) 636-4670
ANTON, JERRY/ 107 E. 38th St., New York, NY .... (212) 689-5886
   See our ad on pages 13-15
Appel, Albert/ 119 West 23rd Street, New York, NY .... (212) 989-6585
Appleby, Ellen/ 310 E. 46th Street, New York, NY .... (212) 953-1008
Arcelle, Joan/ 430 W. 24th Street, New York, NY .... (212) 924-1865
Archambault, David/ 450 West 31 St, New York, NY .... (212) 683-5451
Arisman, Marshall/ 314 W 100th, New York, NY .... (212) 662-2289
Aristovulos, Nick/ 16 E 30th, New York, NY............................ (212) 725-2454
Art Department Inc/ 2 W 46th St, New York, NY....................... (212) 391-1826
Artery, The/ 12 W Biddle St, Baltimore, MD .... (301) 752-2979
Art Farm Inc/ 420 Lexington Ave, New York, NY .... (212) 688-4555
Articy Advertising/ 2566 Washington Street, Boston, MA .... (617) 442-7600
Artistic Innovations/ 99 Madison Avenue, New York, NY .... (212) 686-4646
Artist International/ 225 Lafayette Street, New York, NY .... (212) 334-9310
ARTISTS ASSOCIATES/ 211 E. 51st St., New York, NY............... (212) 755-1365
   See our ad on pages 16-21

ARTISTS INTERNATIONAL/ 225 Lafayette St. #1102,
   Soho New York, NY.. (212) 334-9310
   See our ad on pages 22-25
Arton Assoc/ 216 East 45 Street, New York, NY .... (212) 661-0850
Art Plus Studio Inc./ 30 W. 32nd Street, New York, NY .... (212) 564-8258
Art Source, The/ 201 King St, Chapaqua, NY .... (914) 238-4221
Art Staff Inc/ 275 Madison Ave, New York, NY .... (212) 685-0900
ART STAFF, INC./ 1200 City National Bank Bldg.,
   Detroit, MI... (313) 963-8240
   See our ad on pages 26-31
Art Studio, The/ 140 Sylvan Ave, Englewood Clfs, NJ................. (201) 461-0520
A-S-H Associates/ 250 5th Ave, New York, NY .... (212) 889-2100
Ashmead, Hal/ 353 West 53rd Street, New York, NY .... (212) 730-0144
Ashmead, Hal/ Woodbury, CT .... (203) 263-3466
Assel, Steven/ New York, NY... (212) 789-1725
Bacchus, Hamid/ 1370 Carroll St, Brooklyn, NY .... (212) 493-6942
Backhaus, R.B. Art & Design/ 280 West End Avenue,
   New York, NY... (212) 877-4792
Bacon Design Studio, Paul/ 881 7th Avenue, New York, NY .... (212) 247-4760
Badenhop, Mary/ 807 Madison Avenue, New York, NY .... (212) 861-4133
Bagu, Delores/ 155 E 38 Street, New York, NY .... (212) 697-6170
Bahm, Joan Landis/ 6 Jane Street, New York, NY .... (212) 989-7074
Baker, Bernard & Lowery Design/ 1365 E 51st St,
   Brooklyn, NY... (212) 763-1340
Balin, Racquel/ 334 W 87th Street PH-B, New York, NY.............. (212) 496-8358
Ballenger, Tom/ 333 E 30 St, New York, NY............................ (212) 679-1358
Ballentine, Joyce/ 353 W 53rd Street Suite 1W, New York, NY..... (212) 682-2462
Bang, Molly Garrett/ Box 299, Woods Hole, MA .... (617) 548-7135
Barberis, Juan/ New York, NY .... (212) 737-5062
Barber, Ray/ 295 Washington Ave, Brooklyn, NY .... (212) 857-2941
Baren, Joan/ 105 East 16th Street, New York, NY .... (212) 477-6071
Barkley, James/ 25 Brook Manor, Pleasantville, NY .... (914) 769-5207
Barkley, Jim/ 342 Madison Ave., New York, NY .... (212) 697-8525
Barlowe, Wayne D./ 459 W. 24th Street, New York, NY.............. (212) 924-7026
Barrera, Alberto/ 463 West St. Apt. 1017d, New York, NY .... (212) 724-3638
Barrett, Ron/ 2112 Broadway, New York, NY .... (212) 874-1370
Barr, Ken/ 342 Madison Avenue, New York, NY .... (212) 697-8525
Barry, James E/ 69 W. 68th Street, New York, NY .... (212) 873-6787
Barry, Rick/ 159 W. 23rd Street, New York, NY .... (212) 691-0038
Barry, Ron/ 165 E. 32nd St., New York, NY .... (212) 686-3514
Barton, Bernard/ 16 Dover Road, Westport, CT .... (203) 227-2071
Barton, David/ 495 Broom Street, New York, NY .... (212) 966-1757
Barton, Gillet Co/ 17 Commerce St, Baltimore, MD .... (301) 685-3626
Bascove/ 319 E. 52nd Street, New York, NY .... (212) 888-0038
Basnite, Ray/ 120 W 44th Penthouse 1701, New York, NY.......... (212) 997-0048
Bass, Bob/ 43 E. 19th St., New York, NY .... (212) 254-4996
BATTES, GREG/ 2954 Satsuma Dr., Dallas, TX .... (214) 620-7685
   See our ad on page 32
Bauer, Carla/ 156 Fifth Ave, New York, NY .... (212) 807-8305
Bauman, Jill/ PO Box 152, Jamaica, NY .... (718) 631-3160
Bazzel, Debrah/ 114 E 32nd St Suite 902, New York, NY............ (212) 685-2770
Beatty, Mary/ 4 Patton Place, Huntington, NY........................ (516) 427-7713
Becker, Ron/ 265 E 78th, New York, NY .... (212) 535-8052
Bego, Dolores/ 155 E. 38th Street, New York, NY .... (212) 697-6170
Bellows, Amelia/ 3014 Dent Place NW #16E, Washington, DC ...... (202) 337-0412
Belser, Burkey/ 1337 Corcoran Street N.W., Washington, DC ...... (202) 462-1482
Ben-Ami, Doron/ 206 Lincoln Place, Brooklyn, NY .... (212) 638-6675
Benas, Jeanne A/ 14 Sparrowbush Rd, Latham, NY .... (518) 783-9556
BENDELL, NORMAN/ 18 E. 17th St., New York, NY.................. (212) 807-6627
   See our ad on page 114
Bengo, Dolores/ 155 E 38th Street, New York, NY .... (212) 697-6170
Benjamin, Bernard/ 1763 2nd Ave 37K, New York City, NY .... (212) 722-7773
BENNETT, DIANNE/ 8800 Venice Blvd., Los Angeles, CA .... (213) 558-3697
   See our ad on page 33
Berger, Charles J/ 53 Maplewood Dr, Plainview, NY .... (516) 931-5085
Bergman, Barbara/ 41 E 41st St, New York, NY .... (212) 687-6754
Bermudez, Frank/ 1466 Broadway, New York, NY .... (212) 398-1070
Bernhard, Annika/ 230 E. 80th Street, New York, NY .... (212) 744-5039
Bernhardt & Fudyma/ 133 E. 36th Street, New York, NY .... (212) 889-9337
Bernstein & Andriulli, Inc./ 60 East 42, New York, NY .... (212) 682-1490
Berran, Robert/ New York, NY .... (212) 986-5680
Berson, Julie/ 18 Fairport Rd, Westport, CT .... (203) 255-0681
Big Apple Sign Corp/ 240 W 35th St, New York, NY .... (212) 575-0706
Billout, Guy/ 222 W. 15th St., New York, NY .... (212) 255-2023
BINGHAM, SID/ 2550 Kemper, La Cresenta, CA...................... (818) 957-0163
   See our ad on page 34

Biondo, Charles Design Assoc/ 227 E 44th St, New York, NY........ (212) 867-0760
Birkey, Randall/ 420 Madison Ave, New York, NY...................... (212) 980-3510
Birmingham, Lloyd/ Peekskill Hollow Road, Putnam Valley, NY ..... (914) 528-3207
BJORKMAN, STEVE/ 1711 Langley, Irvine, CA .... (714) 261-1411
See our ad on page 35
Black, Ben/ 1 Salem, Malden, MA.. (617) 322-2830
Blackwell, Garie/ 60 E. 42nd St. #505, New York, NY .... (212) 682-1490
Blakeney, Barbara/ 61 Horatio Street Apt. 2A, New York, NY........ (212) 243-0109
BLANCHETTE, DAN/ 185 N. Wabash Ave., Chicago, IL .... (312) 332-1339
See our ad on page 36
BLECK, CATHIE/ 1019 N. Clinton, Dallas, TX .... (214) 942-4639
See our ad on page 37
Block, Kenneth Paul/ 140 Riverside Dr, New York, NY .... (212) 873-3291
Blossom, David/ 152 Goodhill Road, Weston, CT .... (203) 227-4065
Blum, Z./Edward T. Riley, Inc./ 215 E. 31 St., New York, NY ...... (212) 684-3448
Boker Group/ 232 Madison Ave, New York, NY .... (212) 686-1132
BOLLE, FRANK/ 157 W. 57th St., New York, NY .... (212) 247-1130
See our ad on pages 40, 41
Bomzer Associates/ 66 Canal St, Boston, MA............................ (617) 227-5151
Bonforte, Lisa/ 201 East 28th Street, New York, NY .... (212) 532-0928
Bonhomme, Bernard/ 111 Wooster St. Phc, New York, NY .... (212) 925-0491
Bono, Peter Illustration/ 59 Van Houten Avenue, Passaic, NJ........ (201) 778-5489
Boone, Charles/ 39 W 16th, New York, NY .... (212) 371-4838
Booth, George/ New York, NY .... (203) 227-7806
Bossert, Jill/ 154 E. 64th Street, New York, NY .... (212) 752-7657
Boston-Pacific Design Group/ 251 Elm St, Buffalo, NY .... (716) 856-1150
Bouffard, John J/ 250 Fifth Ave, New York, NY .... (212) 689-4333
Boyd, Harvey/ 24 Fifth Ave, New York, NY .... (212) 475-5235
Boyd, Kris Illustrates/ 318 E 89 St, New York, NY .... (212) 876-4361
Bozzo, Frank/ 400 E. 85th Street, New York, NY .... (212) 535-9182
Bracken, Carolyn/ 201 East 28th Street, New York, NY .... (212) 532-0928
Brainin, Max/ 135 5th Ave, New York, NY .... (212) 254-9608
BRALDS, BRALDT/ 135 E. 54th St., New York, NY .... (212) 243-7063
See our ad on page 38
Bramhall, W./E. T. Riley, Inc./ 215 E. 31 St., New York, NY .... (212) 684-3448
Brandegee Assoc/ 1722 Murray Ave, Pittsburgh, PA .... (412) 422-8310
Brangwynne Ad Art/ 46 Summer Street, Boston, MA .... (617) 542-2086
BRAUGHT, MARK/ 629 Cherry St. Rm. 18,
Terre Haute, IN .... (812) 234-6135
See our ad on page 39
Brautigam, Don/ New York, NY .... (212) 755-1365
Brayman, Kari/ 333 W 55th St, New York, NY .... (212) 582-6137
Breeden, Paul M./ Sullivan Harbor Farm, Sullivan, ME .... (301) 371-6817
Breiner, Joanne/ 11 Webster Street, Medford, MA.................... (617) 395-0865
Brickman, Robin Dee/ 381 Morris Avenue, Providence, RI .... (401) 273-7372
Brickner, Alice/ 4720 Grosvenor Ave, Bronx, NY .... (212) 549-5909
Bridy, Dan/ 353 West 53rd Street, New York, NY .... (212) 730-0144
Bridy, Dan Visuals/ 119 1st Avenue, Pittsburgh, PA .... (412) 288-9362
Brillhart, Ralph/ 310 Madison Ave. #1225, New York, NY .... (212) 867-8092
Broderson, Charles/ 873 Broadway, New York, NY .... (212) 925-9392
Brodie, Michael/ 225 Lafayette St., New York, NY .... (212) 334-9310
Brofsky, Miriam/ 186 Riverside Drive, New York, NY .... (212) 595-8094
Brooks, Harold/ 20 W. 87th Street, New York, NY .... (212) 595-5980
Brooks, Lou/ 415 W. 55th Street, New York, NY .... (212) 245-3632
Brooks, Walter/ Appletree Lane RR2, Norwalk, CT .... (203) 847-3366
Brotman, Zoe/ 38 Macdougal St., New York, NY .... (212) 777-5747
Broussard, Edwin Scott/ 43 E. Grand Avenue, Montvale, NJ .... (201) 391-1877
Brown, Bob/ 267 Fifth Ave., New York, NY .... (212) 686-5576
Brown, Dan/ New York, NY .... (212) 986-5680
Browne, Pema Ltd/ 185 E. 85th Street, New York, NY .... (212) 369-1925
Brown, Huntley/ New York, NY .... (212) 737-5062
Brown Ink Associates/ 267 Fifth Avenue Room 803,
New York, NY.. (212) 686-5576
Brown, Judith Gwyn/ 522 E. 85th Street, New York, NY .... (212) 288-1599
Brown, Margaret/ New York, NY .... (212) 355-1316
Brown, Michael David/ 108 E 35th St, New York, NY .... (212) 751-4656
Brown, Richard/ 3979 York Rd, Furlong, PA.......................... (215) 794-8186
Brown, Robert/ 1665 Kaufers Lane, Fort Lee, NJ .... (212) 686-5576
Brown, Robert/ 353 West 53rd Street, New York, NY .... (212) 730-0144
Brown, Robert S./ 221 Erlanger Blvd., North Babyton, NY .... (516) 586-6874
Bruce, Emmett/ 285 Park Place, Brooklyn, NY .... (212) 636-5263
BRUCK, J. S./ 157 W. 57th St., New York, NY .... (212) 247-1130
See our ad on pages 40-65
Brundage, D/ New York, NY.. (212) 689-3902
Brusca, Jack/ 43 E. 19th St., New York, NY .... (212) 254-4996

Bryan, Diana/ 200 E. 16th St., New York, NY...................... (212) 475-7927
Bryan, William Park/ New York, NY .... (212) 288-8010
Buchanan, Yvonne/ 411 14th St., Brooklyn, NY .... (212) 965-3021
Buckett Assocs. Inc., Bill/ 137 Gibbs Street, Rochester, NY .... (716) 546-6580
Buckley, William/ 187 Bowery, New York, NY .... (212) 674-4275
Buctel, George/ 160 West End Avenue, New York, NY .... (212) 362-3381
Bugg, Bob/ New York, NY .... (212) 986-5680
Bujold, Marcia/ 73 Sherman Avenue, Staten Island, NY .... (212) 273-3098
Burger, Robert/ 111 Wooster St., New York, NY .... (212) 925-0491
Burgoyne, John/ 200 E 78th St #8C, New York, NY................ (212) 570-9069
Burleson, Joe/ 185 East 85th Street, New York, NY .... (212) 369-1925
Burns, Ray/ 27 Warncke Road, Wilton, CT .... (203) 762-5286
Burrows & Associates, Bill/ 103 E. Read Street,
Baltimore, MD .... (301) 752-4615
Buschini, Maryanne Illustrator/ 602 N 16th St Apt 0,
Philadelphia, PA.. (215) 235-7838
Buschman, Llynne E./ 186 Franklin Street, New York, NY .... (212) 925-4701
Bush, Lon/ 108 E 35th St, New York, NY .... (212) 889-3337
Butcher, Jim/ 1357 E MacPhal Road, Belair, MD .... (301) 879-6380
Byrd, Bob/ 353 W. 53rd Street #1W, New York, NY .... (212) 682-2462
Cabarga, Leslie/ 258 W Tulpehocken St, Philadelphia, PA............ (215) 438-9954
Cagle, Daryl/ 320 Stamford Av, Stamford, CT .... (203) 359-3780
Cain, David/ 200 W. 20th Street, New York, NY .... (212) 691-5783
Campbell, James/ 485 Elm Street, Monroe, CT .... (203) 261-0247
Campbell, Jim/ New York, NY.. (212) 986-5680
Campbell, Mary/ 258 Clinton Ave, Brooklyn, NY .... (212) 857-6734
Cannella, Vito/ 224 Ave B, New York, NY .... (212) 477-0401
Cantarella, Virginia Hoyt/ 107 Sterling Place, Brooklyn, NY........ (212) 622-2061
CARAS, PETER/ 157 W. 57th St., New York, NY .... (212) 247-1130
See our ad on pages 42, 43
Carbone, Kye/ 101 Charles Street, New York, NY .... (212) 242-5630
Cardi, Nick/ New York, NY.. (212) 683-8525
Caricatures By Sherry Lane/ 155 Bank Street Studio 404,
New York, NY.. (212) 675-6224
Carloni Associates/ 205 E 42nd St, New York, NY .... (212) 661-3070
Carlson, David/ 201 East 28th Street, New York, NY .... (212) 532-0928
Carr, Barbara/ 245 E. 40th Street, New York, NY .... (212) 370-1663
Carson, Jim/ 18 Orchard St., Cambridge, MA...................... (617) 661-3321
Carter, Bunny/ 200 E 78th St #8C, New York, NY .... (212) 570-9069
Cartoonmix/ Box 108, Village Station, NY .... (212) 929-4825
Casado, Ralph/ 333 East 23 Street, New York, NY .... (212) 689-0435
Cassler, Carl/ 420 Lexington Ave., New York, NY .... (212) 986-5680
Castelnovo, Ann/ 219 Front Street, Weymouth, MA .... (617) 337-8480
CATALANO, SAL/ 114 Boyce Pl., Ridgewood, NJ .... (201) 447-5318
See our ad on page 66
Caulos Co Goldie Kleiner/ 295 Central Park West,
New York, NY.. (212) 799-8050
Cavanagh, Dorothe/ 752 West End Avenue Suite 23J,
New York, NY.. (212) 662-1490
Cavanagh, Jim/ 300 Ocean Parkway Apt 1-N, Brooklyn, NY .... (212) 871-1881
Cayea, John/ 39 Lafayette Street, Cornwall-On-Hud, NY .... (914) 534-2942
CELLINI, EVA/ 157 W. 57th St., New York, NY .... (212) 247-1130
See our ad on pages 44, 45
CELLINI, JOSEPH/ 157 W. 57th St., New York, NY .... (212) 247-1130
See our ad on pages 46, 47
Censoni, Robert/ 400 E. 59th Street #7G, New York, NY .... (212) 758-0052
Certa, Liz/ 1468 White Plains Rd, New York, NY .... (212) 863-1420
Cesc/Edward T. Riley, Inc./ 215 E. 31 St., New York, NY .... (212) 684-3448
Chabrian, Debbi/ 185 Goodhill Road, Weston, CT.................. (203) 226-7674
Chandler, Jean/ 385 Oakwood Drive, Wyckoff, NJ .... (201) 891-2381
Chang, Kuan/ 30 E Tenth St, New York, NY .... (212) 777-6102
CHANG, WARREN/ 1243 Vicente Dr. #72, Sunnyvale, CA .... (415) 964-1701
See our ad on page 68
CHAN, RON/ 1717 Union St., San Francisco, CA.................... (415) 441-4544
See our ad on page 67
Charmatz, Bill/ 25 West 68th Street, New York, NY .... (212) 595-3907
Chasan & Yaris Inc/ 274 Madison Ave, New York, NY .... (212) 683-6900
Chatalbash, Ron/ 522 Huckleberry Lane, Franklin Lakes, NJ .... (201) 891-7381
Chenault Assocs/ 605 Third Ave, New York, NY...................... (212) 557-0600
Cheng, Judith/ 185 Goodhill Road, Weston, CT .... (203) 226-7674
Chen, Tony/ 225 Lafayette, New York, NY .... (212) 334-9310
Chermayeff & Geismar Assocs/ 15 E 26 St, New York, NY .... (212) 532-4499
Chermayeff, Ivan/ 58 W 15th St, New York, NY .... (212) 741-2539
Cherry, Jim/ 336 E 30th St, New York, NY .... (212) 686-0861
Cheryl Cooper/ New York, NY .... (212) 929-7217

Tools of the trade.

ILLUSTRATION/East

Chessare, Michele/ 10 Crestmont Rd Apt 1C, Montclair, NJ.......... (201) 746-4918
Chestnutt, David/ 225 Lafayette St., New York, NY.................... (212) 334-9310
CHINCHAR, AL/ 157 W. 57th St., New York, NY................. (212) 247-1130
    See our ad on pages 48, 49
Chislovsky, Carol/ 420 Madison Ave, New York, NY .... (212) 980-3510
Chorao, Kay/ 290 Riverside Drive, New York, NY.................... (212) 749-8256
Christe, John/ 95 W 95th St, New York, NY .... (212) 222-2538
Christopher, Tom/ New York, NY.................................... (212) 986-3282
Chronister, Robert/ Highland, NY................................... (914) 691-2531
Church, Marilyn/ 160 W. 97th Street, New York, NY................. (212) 865-4447
Chwast, Jacqueline/ 490 W. End Avenue, New York, NY .... (212) 873-5033
Chwast, Seymour/ 67 Irving Place, New York, NY.................... (212) 674-8080
Ciardiello, Joe/ 203 Center St., Staten Island, NY................... (212) 351-2289
Cicarelli, Gary/ 353 W. 53rd Street #1-W, New York, NY .... (212) 682-2462
Ciccariello, Peter Gerard/ 7 Morrell, East Hampton, NY............ (516) 324-7922
Ciesiel, Christine G./ 101 MacDougal Street, New York, NY........ (212) 982-9461
CIGLIANO, WILLIAM/ 832 W. Gunnison, Chicago, IL .... (312) 878-1659
    See our ad on page 69
Clarke, Bob/ 159 W 53rd St, New York, NY .... (212) 581-4045
Clarke Caricatures/ 67 Burr St, Easton, CT .... (203) 259-1932
Clarke, Norman Graphics/ 39-12 58 St Woodside, New York, NY ... (212) 335-2381
Clarke, Robert J./ 46 Washburn Park, Rochester, NY .... (716) 442-8686
Clarke, Terence/ 31 Dunton Ave, E Patchogue, NY .... (516) 475-5299
CLARK, TIM/ 8800 Venice Blvd., Los Angeles, CA................. (213) 202-1044
    See our ad on page 70
Clayton, Robert/ New York, NY.................................... (212) 737-5062
Cleveland, J Design/ 31 Hillcrest Drive, Wayne, NJ .... (201) 628-0416
Cline, Rob/ 229 Berkeley #52, Boston, MA.......................... (617) 266-3858
Cobane, Russell/ C/O C. Chilovsky 420 Madison, New York, NY.... (212) 980-3510
COBANE, RUSSELL/ 8291 Allen Rd., Clarkston, MI .... (313) 625-6132
    See our ad on page 78
COBB, LISA & ASSOCIATES/ 2200 N. Lamar #202,
    Dallas, TX .... (214) 939-0032
    See our ad on pages 32, 37, 122, 139, 165, 174, 178
Cocca, Mary Ann/ 5 Edison Street, Saugus, MA...................... (617) 233-3512
Cochet, Paulette/ Cresskill, NJ .... (201) 568-1436
Coester, Michael/ New York, NY .... (212) 986-5680
Cole, Lynn A./ 403 3rd Street, Brooklyn, NY .... (212) 499-6839
COLEMAN, WOODY PRESENTS, INC./ 1295 Old River Rd.,
    Cleveland, OH.. (216) 621-1771
    See our ad on pages 71-77
Collier, John/ 501 5th Ave #1407, New York, NY.................... (212) 490-2450
Collier, Roberta L./ 100 3rd Avenue, New York, NY .... (212) 260-7299
Collins, Jeanne A/ 2710 Keystone Drive, Harrisburg, PA .... (717) 657-9555
Colona, Bernie/ 185 Goodhill Road, Weston, CT .... (203) 226-7674
Comp Art Plus/ 12 W 27th St, New York, NY .... (212) 689-8670
Concept One/Gizmo/ 366 Oxford St., Rochester, NY .... (716) 461-4240
Condon, J&M Inc/ 126 Fifth Ave, New York, NY .... (212) 242-7811
CONNALLY, CONNIE/ 7818 Ridgemar, Dallas, TX .... (214) 340-7818
    See our ad on page 79
Conner, Marsha/ 16 Douglas Place, Verona, NJ .... (201) 239-1408
CONSANI, CHRIS/ P.O. Box 7000-763,
    Redondo Beach, CA.. (213) 930-0811
    See our ad on page 133
Console, Carmen/ 8 Gettysburg Dr, Voorheese, NJ .... (609) 424-8735
Continuity Assoc/ 62 W 45th Street, New York, NY .... (212) 869-4170
Conway-Designs/ 104 Broad St, Boston, MA.......................... (617) 451-1031
Cook, David/ 310 Madison Ave. #1225, New York, NY .... (212) 867-8092
Cooley, D. Gary/ 23 West Thirty Fifth St., New York, NY .... (212) 695-2426
Cooper, Cheryl/ 515 Madison Ave., New York, NY.................. (212) 486-9644
Cooper, Richard/ 105-40 62nd Road, Rego Park, NY................. (212) 699-0365
Cooper, Robert/ 420 Madison Avenue, New York, NY.............. (212) 980-3510
Corben, Richard/ 43 E. 19th St., New York, NY.................... (212) 254-4996
Corey, Lee Studios/ 299 Madison Avenue, New York, NY........... (212) 682-5048
Cornell, Jeff/ 58 Noyes Rd, Fairfield, CT .... (203) 259-7715
Cornell, Laura/ 120 W 81st, New York, NY .... (212) 580-1321
Corvi, Donna A./ 1591 Second Ave, New York, NY .... (212) 628-4868
Corwin, Judith Hoffman/ 333 E. 30th Street, New York, NY .... (212) 889-1059
Costabel, Eva/ 33-43 Crescent Street, Astoria, NY.................. (212) 278-1315
Couratin, Patrick/ 333 E 30th St, New York, NY .... (212) 679-1358
Courtney, Richard/ 43 E. 19th St., New York, NY .... (212) 254-4996
CRAFT, KINUKO Y./ 515 Madison Ave., New York, NY............. (212) 486-9644
    See our ad on page 80
CRAIG, JOHN/ R.R. 2 Box 81, Soldiers Grove, WI .... (608) 872-2371
    See our ad on page 81

Crair, Mel/ 1439 East 84th Street, Brooklyn, NY .... (212) 444-6940
Cramer, D. L./ 10 Beechwood Dr., Wayne, NJ .... (201) 628-8793
Crandell, Louise/ 177 Hudson St, New York, NY..................... (212) 966-4863
Craven Design Studios Inc/ 461 Park Ave S, New York, NY .... (212) 696-4680
Crawford, Margery/ 237 E. 31st Street, New York, NY.............. (212) 686-6883
Crawford, Robert/ 340 E 93rd Street #9l, New York, NY .... (212) 722-4964
Creative Annex Inc/ 39 W 29th St, New York, NY .... (212) 730-0740
Creative Freelancers Inc.// 62 West 45th Street,
    New York, NY... (212) 398-9540
Crews, Donald/ 653 Carroll Street, Brooklyn, NY .... (212) 636-5773
Crofut, Bob/ 225 Peaceable St, Ridgefield, CT .... (203) 431-4304
Cronin, E T/ New York, NY .... (212) 243-1481
Cross, Peter/ 645 West End Ave. #9e, New York, NY .... (212) 362-3338
Cruz, Raymond/ 162 W. 13th Street #55, New York, NY .... (212) 243-1199
Csatari, Joe/ New York, NY .... (212) 986-5680
Csatari, Joseph/ South River, NJ .... (201) 257-4660
Cummins, Jim/ 185 Goodhill Rd, Weston, CT........................ (203) 226-7674
Cunningham, Robert M/ 177 Waverly Place Apt 4F,
    New York, NY... (212) 675-1731
CURRY, TOM/ 309 E. Live Oak, Austin, TX .... (512) 443-8427
    See our ad on page 82
Curtis Design Inc/ 29 E 32nd St, New York, NY .... (212) 685-0670
Cusack, Margaret/ 124 Hoyt Street, Brooklyn, NY .... (212) 237-0145
Dabocvich, Lydia/ 29 Sargent-Beechwood, Brookline, MA .... (617) 232-7628
DACEY, BOB/ 157 W. 57th St., New York, NY .... (212) 247-1130
    See our ad on pages 50, 51
D'Achille, Gino/ New York, NY .... (212) 929-5840
Daily, Don/ 1007 Lombard Street, Philadelphia, PA.................. (215) 922-1124
Dale, Robert/ 1573 York Ave., New York, NY .... (212) 737-1771
Dallasta, Ray/ 353 West 53rd Street, New York, NY .... (212) 730-0144
Dallison, Ken/ 108 W 35th St, New York, NY .... (212) 889-3337
Daly, Gerry/ 69-40 Yellowstone Blvd Apt 116,
    Forest Hills, NY.. (212) 897-5395
Daly, Sean/ 85 South Street, New York, NY .... (212) 668-0031
Daly, Tom/ 47 E. Edsel Avenue, Palisades Park, NJ .... (201) 943-1837
Damaskos, Steve/ 78 Metropolitan Avenue, Roslendale, MA .... (617) 323-0143
D'Amico, George Advertisng Inc/ 565 Fifth Avenue,
    New York, NY... (212) 682-8676
Danby, Ken/ New York, NY... (212) 737-5062
Daniel, Alan/ 185 Goodhill Rd., Weston, CT........................ (203) 226-7674
Daniels, Alan/ 120 E. 32 St., New York, NY .... (212) 689-3233
DANIELS & DANIELS/ 14 S. Madrid, Newbury Park, CA............ (805) 498-1923
    See our ad on page 83
Dani, Cartoon Personalities/ Box 275, Lincoln, RI .... (401) 724-5365
Darden, Howard/ 56 Roosevelt Avenue, Butler, NJ .... (201) 838-3706
Darrow, Whitney Jr/ 331 Newtown Turnpike, Wilton, CT .... (203) 762-9062
Dauber, Liz/ New York, NY... (212) 737-5062
Davidian, Anna/ 229 Berkeley #52, Boston, MA..................... (617) 266-3858
Davidson, Everett/ 60 E. 42nd Street, New York, NY .... (212) 682-1490
Davidson, Karen A./ 64 Wilson Street, North Billerica, MA .... (617) 667-7869
Davis, Allen/ 141-10 25th Road, Flushing, NY...................... (212) 428-1471
Davis, Brian/ C/O Blumenthal 810 7th Ave, New York, NY .... (212) 541-9615
Davis, Jack/ 108 E. 35th Street, New York, NY .... (212) 889-3337
Davis, Jack/ New York, NY .... (212) 751-4656
Davis, Marshall/ Topping Ln, S Norwalk, CT .... (203) 866-7900
Davis, Michael/ 333 E. 49th St., New York, NY .... (212) 980-8061
Davis, Paul/ 14 East 4th, New York, NY .... (212) 420-8789
Dawson, John/ 310 Madison Ave. #1225, New York, NY .... (212) 867-8092
De Araujo, Betty/ 201 East 28th Street, New York, NY .... (212) 532-0928
De Berardinis, Olivia/ PO Box 541 Midtown Station,
    New York, NY... (212) 580-9846
Decamps, Craig/ 341 W. 38th Street, New York, NY .... (212) 564-2691
DEDELL, JACQUELINE/ 58 W. 15th St., New York, NY .... (212) 741-2539
    See our ad on pages 84, 85
Deeter, Catherine/ 60 E. 42nd St. #505, New York, NY .... (212) 682-1490
Defiore, Gabe/ 353 West 53 St Suite 1W, New York, NY........... (212) 682-2462
Degen, Paul/ 135 Eastern Parkway, Brooklyn, NY .... (212) 636-8299
Deigan, Jim/ 625 Stanwix Street #2501, Pittsburgh, PA............. (412) 391-1698
Deigan, Jim/ 353 West 53rd Street, New York, NY................. (212) 730-0144
Dekeifte, Kees/ 185 Goodhill Road, Weston, CT.................... (203) 226-7674
Delattre, Georgette/ 100 Central Park South, New York, NY .... (212) 247-6850
Della Piana, Elissa/ 201 Elm Street, Medford, MA.................. (617) 395-2197
Delli Carpini, Kaylor Inc/ 118 E 28th St, New York, NY .... (212) 684-3463
De Michiell, Robert/ 43 E. 19th St., New York, NY .... (212) 254-4996
Demiskey, Sheri/ 463 West Street, New York, NY .... (212) 989-6743

GET SMART.

Making it in this business involves a great deal more than just pressing a shutter release. There are terms like self promotion, copyright protection, fee negotiation, and options in incorporation that stand between you and success. Unfortunately, most photographers become pros because they're good at taking pictures, not because they're good at running a business.

Last year, PHOTO '84 attracted more than 6,000 photographers from all over the country. And for good reason. It provided an opportunity to see and hear more than 60 industry professionals speak on a wide variety of important topics, from creating a winning portfolio to techniques in food photography. In addition, a 30,000 square foot exhibition was packed with 200 exhibitors displaying every conceivable product and service of interest to the working pro. Collectively, it was quite an experience.

On November 22-24, PHOTO '85 will return to the New York Coliseum with the largest collection of exhibits and seminars this industry has ever seen. Two years of feedback has fine tuned this event. The focus, however, will remain the same: to help make all of us a little smarter.

So, get smart. Order your PHOTO '85 program brochure detailing the seminar program, special events and exhibition by calling Lydia today at (203) 852-0500, or writing Conference Management Corporation, 17 Washington Street, Norwalk, CT 06854.

November 22-24, 1985
The New York Coliseum, New York City

Sponsored by *Photo District News*. Managed by Conference Management Corporation.

Derosa, Dee/ 3409 Pleasant Valley Road, Syracuse, NY .... (315) 673-2308
Deschamps, Rob/ 108 E 35th St, New York, NY .... (212) 889-3337
De Seve, Peter/ 321 East 12th Street, New York, NY .... (212) 533-2717
Design Consortium/ 413 Walnut St, Harrisburg, PA.................... (717) 234-6414
Detrich, Susan/ 253 Baltic Street, Brooklyn, NY .... (212) 237-9174
Devlin, Bill/ 108 East 35th St, New York, NY .... (212) 751-4656
Devlin, Harry/ 433 Hillside Avenue, Mountainside, NJ .... (201) 233-1280
Dewey, Kenneth Francis/ New York, NY .... (212) 755-4945
Di Blasi, Sharon/ 201 East 28th Street, New York, NY .... (212) 532-0928
DiCianni, Ron/ 342 Madison Ave., New York, NY .... (212) 697-8525
DiComo, Charles & Assocs./ 12 W. 27th Street, New York, NY ..... (212) 689-8670
Dietz, Jim/ 165 E. 32nd St., New York, NY .... (212) 686-3514
Difate, Vincen/ 12 Ritter Drive, Wappingers Fall, NY .... (914) 297-6842
DIFFENDERFER, ED/ 32 Cabernet Ct., Lafayette, CA................ (415) 254-8235
    See our ad on page 86
Difranza-Williamson/ 1414 6th Ave, New York, NY .... (212) 832-2343
Dilakian, Hovik/ 111 Wooster St. #Phc, New York, NY .... (212) 925-0491
Dillon, Diane & Leo/ 221 Kane Street, Brooklyn, NY .... (212) 624-0023
Dilorenzo, John R/ 525 Bronxville Rd, Bronxville, NY .... (914) 961-9286
Dinnerstein, Harvey/ 933 President Street, Brooklyn, NY .... (212) 783-6879
Dior, Jerry/ 9 Old Hickory Lane, Edison, NJ .... (201) 561-6536
Dittrich, Dennis/ 42 W. 72nd St. #12b, New York, NY .... (212) 595-9773
Dodds, Glenn/ 392 Central Parkway W., New York, NY .... (212) 679-3630
Domingo, Ray/ 108 E. 35th Street, New York, NY .... (212) 889-3337
Donnelly, Liza/ 121 W. 79th Street Apt. 3C, New York, NY .... (212) 873-1270
Doret, Michael/ 61 Lexington Ave., New York, NY .... (212) 889-0490
D'Ortenzio, Alfred/ 353 W. 53rd Street, New York, NY .... (212) 682-2462
Downey, William/ 21 Vista Place, Red Bank, NJ .... (201) 842-5965
Drate, Spencer/ 160 5th Ave Rm 613, New York, NY .... (212) 620-4672
Drawings Etc/ 330 E 49th, New York, NY .... (212) 752-4967
Drovetto, Richard/ 355 E. 72nd Street, New York, NY .... (212) 861-0927
Drucker, Mort/ 42 Juneau Blvd., Woodbury, NY .... (516) 367-4920
Dryden, Patty/ 575 West End Ave, New York, NY .... (212) 724-4900
Duarte, Mary Young/ 350 1st Avenue, New York, NY .... (212) 674-4513
DUDASH, MICHAEL/ 157 W. 57th St., New York, NY................ (212) 247-1130
    See our ad on pages 52, 53
DUDZINSKI, ANDRZEJ/ 52 E. 81st St., New York, NY.............. (212) 628-6959
    See our ad on page 87
Duke, Christine/ Maple Avenue, Millbrook, NY .... (914) 677-9510
Dupont, Lane/ 353 West 53rd Street, New York, NY .... (212) 730-0144
Dyno, George/Ind. Graphics/ P.O. Box 491, Farmington, CT .... (203) 582-6631
Eagle, Mike/ 7 Captains Lane, Old Saybrook, CT...................... (203) 388-5654
Eastman, Bryant/ New York, NY .... (212) 697-8525
East Village Enterprises/ 231 W 29th St Room 807,
    New York, NY .... (212) 563-5722
Ebel, Alex/ 30 Newport Road, Yonkers, NY .... (914) 961-4058
EBERBACH, ANDREA/ 5301 N. Delaware,
    Indianapolis, IN .... (317) 253-0421
    See our ad on page 88
Ebert, Leonard/ Rd 2, Douglassville, PA .... (215) 689-9872
Echevarria, Abe/ Box 98 Anderson Rd, Sherman, CT .... (203) 355-1254
Edelman Studios Inc/ 8 E 12th St, New York, NY .... (212) 255-7250
Edwards, Sandie/ 317 W. 87th Street #4D, New York, NY .... (212) 664-5656
Eggers Films/ 8 East 48th Street, New York, NY .... (212) 751-9044
Eggert, John/ New York, NY .... (212) 986-5680
Egielski, Richard/ 463 West Street, New York, NY .... (212) 255-9328
Einsel, Naiad/ Westport, CT .... (203) 226-0709
Einsel, Walter/ 26 S. Morningside Drive, Westport, CT .... (203) 226-0709
Elios, Irene/ 171 Mystic Street, Arlington, MA .... (617) 643-8403
ELLA/ 229 Berkeley St., Boston, MA................................. (617) 266-3858
    See our ad on pages 90, 91
Elliot, John Highmount Studios/ 304 High Mount Terr,
    Upper Nyack, NY .... (914) 353-2483
Ellis, Dean/ 30 E 20th St, New York, NY .... (212) 254-7590
Ely, Creston/ 74 Glen Road, Sandy Hook, CT .... (203) 426-8115
Ely, Richard/ 207 W. 86th Street, New York, NY .... (212) 874-4816
Emberley, Barbara/ 6 Water Street, Ipswich, MA .... (617) 356-2805
Emmett, Bruce/ 285 Park Place, Brooklyn, NY .... (212) 636-5263
Endewelt, Jack/ 50 Riverside Drive, New York, NY .... (212) 877-0575
Endicott, James/ 15 E 76th St, New York, NY .... (212) 288-8010
ENGLISH, MARK/ 211 E. 51st St., New York, NY .... (212) 755-1365
    See our ad on page 17
Enik, Ted/ 82 Jane Street #4A, New York, NY .... (212) 620-5972
Ennis, John/ 310 Madison Ave. #1225, New York, NY .... (212) 867-8092
Enos, Randall/ 11 Court of Oaks, Westport, CT .... (203) 227-4785

Epstein, Dave Inc./ Dowes Lane, Irvington, NY .... (914) 591-7470
Epstein, Len/ 720 Montgomery Avenue, Narberth, PA .... (215) 664-4700
Erdner Studios/ 210 E McMurray Rd, Mcmurray, PA .... (412) 561-6769
ERICKSEN, MARC W./ 1045 Sansome St. #306,
    San Francisco, CA.. (415) 362-1214
    See our ad on page 89
ERLACHER, BILL/ 211 E. 51st St., New York, NY .... (212) 755-1365
    See our ad on pages 16-21
Erwin, Jane/ 1 Walker Court, Cambridge, MA.......................... (617) 547-3273
Eucalyptus Tree Studio/ 22220 N. Charles Street,
    Baltimore, MD .... (301) 243-0211
Eucalyptus Tree Studio/ 353 West 53rd Street, New York, NY....... (212) 730-0144
Eutemey, Loring/ 51 Fifth Avenue, New York, NY .... (212) 741-0140
Evans, Dilys/ 40 Park Avenue, New York, NY .... (212) 683-2039
EVANS, ROBERT/ 1045 Sansome St. #306,
    San Francisco, CA.. (415) 397-5322
    See our ad on page 92
Evcimen, Al/ 305 Lexington Ave., New York, NY .... (212) 889-2995
Falcon, Dennis R./ 185 Bronx River Road, Yonkers, NY .... (914) 237-7079
Falcone & Associates/ 13 Watchung Avenue PO 637,
    Chatham, NJ .... (201) 635-2900
Falkins, Richard Adv Design/ 15 W 44th St, New York, NY .... (212) 840-3040
Fallin, Kenneth/ 155 Riverside Dr Apt 1B, New York, NY............. (212) 362-7646
Familton, Herb/ 59 W 10th St, New York, NY .... (212) 254-2943
Farina, Michael/ New York, NY .... (212) 355-1316
Farnsworth, Bill/ 267 Fifth Ave., New York, NY .... (212) 686-5576
Farris, Joseph/ Long Meadow Lane, Bethel, CT........................ (203) 743-3660
Fasolino, Teresa/ 233 E. 21st Street, New York, NY .... (212) 741-2539
Febland, David/ 670 West End Avenue, New York, NY .... (212) 580-9299
Feinenan, Jeff/ 333 East 49th Street, New York, NY .... (212) 734-4533
FERNANDES, STANISLAW/ 35 E. 12th St., New York, NY.......... (212) 533-2648
    See our ad on pages 94, 95
Ferrara, Lidia/ 301 E. 78th Street #14D, New York, NY .... (212) 861-3891
Ferris, Carlisle Keith/ 50 Moraine Road, Morris Plains, NJ .... (201) 539-3363
Fery, Guy/ New York, NY .... (213) 383-0498
Fieramosca, Kathy Krantz/ 222 E 21st St, New York, NY .... (212) 777-9446
Fijal, Theodore A/ 51 Rzasa Dr, Chicopee, MA........................ (413) 592-4230
Finewood, Bill/ 201 East 28th Street, New York, NY .... (212) 532-0928
Fiore, Peter/ Graybar Bld. 420 Lexington Av., New York, NY........ (212) 986-5680
Fischer, Rick/ New York, NY .... (212) 684-4255
FISHER, DAVE/ 1295 Old River Rd., Cleveland, OH .... (216) 621-1771
    See our ad on page 74
Fisher, Mark/ 233 Rindge Avenue, Cambridge, MA .... (617) 876-9721
Fitzgerald, Frank/ 212 East 89 Street, New York, NY .... (212) 722-6793
Flagg, Elliott/ 63 Avenue A, New York, NY .... (212) 475-5915
Flaherty, Darren/ W Cornwall, CT .... (203) 672-6163
Fleischer, Barbara/ 333 E. 53rd Street, New York, NY .... (212) 355-1954
Fleischer, Justin/ 85 Barrow St, New York, NY .... (212) 242-5299
Fleminger, Irwin/ 565 First St, Brooklyn, NY .... (212) 499-0541
Fleming, Marge/ 15 St Pauls Pl, Garden City, NY .... (516) 746-0818
FLESHER, VIVIENNE/ 23 E. 10th St. #1204,
    New York, NY .... (212) 505-6731
    See our ad on page 93
Flex Inc/ 342 Madison Ave, New York, NY .... (212) 682-3042
Flynn, Thomas/ 44 Marion Street, Brookline, MA .... (617) 734-2177
Forbes, Bart/ New York, NY .... (212) 490-2450
Ford/Scott Transgraphics Corp/ 100 Crown St, New Haven, CT..... (203) 777-2426
Foster, B. Lynne/ 540 Fort Washington Ave. #3d,
    New York, NY .... (212) 781-1055
Fowler, Eric Nicholas/ 268 East 7 Street, New York, NY .... (212) 982-8793
Fox, Barbara/ 301 W. 53rd Street, New York, NY .... (212) 245-7564
Francis, Judy/ 110 W 96th, New York, NY .... (212) 866-7204
FRANKE, PHIL/ 333 E. 30th St., New York, NY...................... (212) 679-1358
    See our ad on page 120
Fraser, Betty/ 240 Central Park South, New York, NY .... (212) 247-1937
FRAZEE, MARLA/ , ...(213) 934-3395
    See our ad on page 136
Freas, John/ 353 W 53rd St Apt 1W, New York, NY .... (212) 682-2462
Freelancers' Registry/ 1506 19th St Nw, Washington, DC .... (202) 232-8572
Freeman, Irving/ 145 4th Avenue Apt. 9K, New York, NY .... (212) 674-6705
Friedman, Gary/ 463 West St, New York, NY .... (212) 691-0859
Friedman, Marvin/ Hopewell, NJ .... (609) 466-2730
Friedman, Wendy Rebecca/ 23 E. 10th Street, New York, NY .... (212) 598-0393
Frinta, Dagmar/ 87 Hope St, Providence, RI .... (401) 273-6125
FROMENTIN, CHRISTINE/ 157 W. 57th St., New York, NY........ (212) 247-1130
    See our ad on pages 54, 55

Frost, Lesa/ 201 E 36th St, New York, NY .... (212) 689-1379
Frost, Ralph/ 170 Polk Avenue Apt 6, Syracuse, NY .... (315) 445-0064
Fuchs, Bernard/ 3 Tanglewood Lane, Westport, CT .... (203) 227-4295
Fulgoni, Louis/ 233 W. 21st Street #4D, New York, NY .... (212) 243-2959
Furchgott-Scott, Carol/ 242 Barren Hill Rd, Spring Mill, PA......... (215) 828-3446
FURUKAWA, MEL/ 333 E. 30th St., New York, NY .... (212) 679-1358
    See our ad on page 121
Gaadt, David/ 310 Madison Ave. #1225, New York, NY .... (212) 867-8092
Gaadt, George/ 353 West 53rd Street, New York, NY .... (212) 730-0144
Gabriele, Tony/ 420 Lexington Ave, New York, NY .... (212) 986-5680
Gadino, Victor, Jr./ 1601 3rd Avenue #20K, New York, NY .... (212) 534-7206
Gaetano, Nicholas/ 821 Broadway 6th Floor, New York, NY .... (212) 674-5749
Galarza Inc., James/ 580 Sylvan Avenue, Englewood Cliff, NJ... .... (201) 568-5008
Gala, Tom/ New York, NY.. (212) 986-5680
Gale, Cynthia/ 229 E. 88th St., New York, NY .... (212) 860-5429
Galub, Meg/ 405 W. 57th St., New York, NY .... (212) 489-8544
Gambale, David/ 268 E. 7th St., New York, NY .... (212) 982-8793
Gampert, John/ 8300 Talbot Street, Kew Gardens, NY .... (212) 441-2321
Gardner, Jean/ 1929 Chestnut St, Philadelphia, PA .... (215) 564-2021
Garrido, Hector/ New York, NY .... (212) 986-5680
Gartel, Laurence Computer Gra./ 152-18 Jamacia Estates,
    New York, NY .... (212) 580-2800
Gaydos, John A/ 709 Orchard Rd, Kinnelon, NJ .... (201) 838-3869
Gehm, Charles/ 342 Madison Ave., New York, NY .... (212) 697-8525
Gem Studio/ 420 Lexington Ave., New York, NY .... (212) 687-3460
Genkins, Arnold/ 301 E. 48th Street, New York, NY .... (212) 758-4907
Gentile, John & Anthony/ 850 Seventh Avenue, New York, NY....... (212) 757-1966
Gerber, Mark and Stephanie/ 159 Madison Avenue,
    New York, NY .... (212) 684-7137
Gerson, Elizabeth/ 30 Nassau Street, Princeton, NJ .... (609) 924-8715
Gersten, Gerry/ 1380 Riverside Drive, New York, NY .... (212) 928-7957
Geyer, Jackie/ 353 West 53rd Street, New York, NY .... (212) 730-0144
Giamas, Tony/ 38 Sherman Avenue, Closter, NJ .... (201) 767-8209
Giese, William A/ 100 Kaufman Drive, Peterborough, NH .... (603) 924-3569
Giglio, Richard/ 299 W. 12th Street, New York, NY .... (212) 675-7642
Gignilliat, Elaine/ 150 E. 56th Street, New York, NY .... (212) 935-1943
GILLOT, CAROL/ 162 W. 13th St. #66, New York, NY .... (212) 243-6448
    See our ad on page 96
Gilpin, John/ 209 Wengin Way, West Chester, PA .... (215) 692-3445
Gioia, Louis/ 105 W. 13th Street, New York, NY .... (212) 741-4170
Giordano, Richard/ 105 Red Coach Drive, Stratford, CT .... (203) 377-4904
Giovanni Design Associates/ 137 E 36th St, New York, NY .... (212) 725-8536
Giovanopoulos, Paul/ 119 Prince Street, New York, NY .... (212) 677-5919
Gist, Linda E./ 224 Madison Avenue, Fort Washington, PA .... (215) 643-3757
GIUSTI, ROBERT/ 135 E. 54th St., New York, NY .... (212) 421-0050
    See our ad on page 97
Givotovsky, Marina/ 41 E Seventh St, New York, NY .... (212) 260-2242
Gladych-Broderick, Marianne/ 25 Prince Street, New York, NY ..... (212) 925-9712
Glanzman, Louis S./ 154 Handsome Avenue, Sayville, NY............ (516) 589-2613
Glasbergen, Randy Jay/ P.O. Box 687, Earlville, NY .... (315) 691-2424
Glaser, Milton Inc/ 207 E. 32nd Street, New York, NY .... (212) 889-3161
Glazer Associates/ 2 Tudor Pl, New York, NY .... (212) 687-0937
Glazer, Theodor Lloyd/ 28 Westview Road, Spring Valley, NY .... (914) 354-1524
Gleason, Paul/ 310 Madison Ave. #1225, New York, NY .... (212) 867-8092
Glessner, Marc/ 24 Evergreen Road, Somerset, NJ .... (201) 249-5038
Glickman, Risa D./ 99 St James Place, Brooklyn, NY .... (212) 332-0354
Gnatek Associates, Michael/ 6642 Barnaby St NW,
    Washington, DC .... (202) 363-6803
Gnidziejko, Alex/ 37 Alexander Avenue, Madison, NJ .... (201) 377-2664
Gold, Albert/ 6814 McCallum Street, Philadelphia, PA............... (215) 848-5568
GOLDAMMER, KEN/ 405 N. Wabash Ave. Ste 3611,
    Chicago, IL.. (312) 836-0143
    See our ad on page 98
Goldberg, Bill/ 2043 Moravian St, Philadelphia, PA .... (215) 567-1499
Goldberg, Richard A./ 368 Congress St, Boston, MA .... (617) 876-7360
GOLDMAN, DAVID AGENCY/ 18 E. 17th St., New York, NY ...... (212) 807-6627
    See our ad on page 114
Goldman, Marvin/ Rt 3 Gipsy Trail Road, Carmel, NY .... (914) 225-8611
Gold, Marcy/ 200 E 28th St, New York, NY .... (212) 685-4974
Goldsmith, Bill/ 300 E. 59th Street, New York, NY .... (212) 838-6420
Goldstrom, Robert/ 336 E 54th St Apt 14, New York, NY .... (212) 832-7980
Gonzalez, Dan/ 286 Clinton Avenue Apt. 4A, Brooklyn, NY .... (212) 636-3524
Goodelman, Suzanne/ 300 E. 69th Street, New York, NY .... (212) 472-8612
Goodman, J.E./ 214 W. 21st Street #4D, New York, NY .... (212) 691-3546
Gordon & Assoc/ 165 E 32nd St, New York, NY .... (212) 686-3514

Gorman, W Chris Assoc/ 12 E 41st St, New York, NY .... (212) 696-9377
Gothard, David/E.T.Riley,Inc./ 215 E. 31 St., New York, NY .... (212) 684-3448
Gottfried, Max/ 82-60 116 St #CC3, Kew Gardens, NY .... (718) 441-9868
Gottlieb, Dale/ 487 4th St, Brooklyn, NY............................. (212) 499-2776
Graboff, Abner/ New York, NY .... (212) 737-5062
Graddon, Julian/ 114 E 32nd St Suite 902, New York, NY .... (212) 685-2770
Graddon, Julian/ 545 Washington Ave, Brentwood, NY .... (516) 231-6655
Graham, Mark/ 40 Harrison Street #32C, New York, NY .... (212) 349-3480
Graham Studios, Mariah/ 670 West End Avenue, New York, NY..... (212) 580-8061
GRAHAM, WILLIAM/ 116 W. Illinois, Chicago, IL .... (312) 467-0330
    See our ad on page 154
Graphica Inc/ 375 Sylvan Ave, Englewood Clfs, NJ .... (201) 567-8026
Graphic Expression Inc, The/ 150 East 58 Street,
    New York, NY.. (212) 759-7788
Graphic People, The/ 62 W 39th St, New York, NY .... (212) 944-0330
Graphics Plus Assoc/ 214 Blvd of Allies, Pittsburgh, PA .... (412) 566-1010
Graphic Workshop/ 466 Old Hook Rd, Emerson, NJ .... (201) 967-8500
Grashow,James/E.T.Riley,Inc./ 215 E. 31 St., New York, NY .... (212) 684-3448
Gray, Barbara E./ 169 East 69 St., New York, NY .... (212) 744-2945
Gray, George/ 385 West End Avenue, New York, NY .... (212) 873-3607
Gray, John/ 420 Madison Ave, New York, NY .... (212) 980-3510
Gray, John E./ 264 Van Duzer Street, Staten Island, NY .... (212) 447-6466
Gray, Susan/ 42 West 12th Street, New York City, NY .... (212) 787-5400
GREATHEAD STUDIO/ 2975 Christopher's Ct.,
    Marietta, GA... (404) 952-5067
    See our ad on page 99
Greenapple Sales Prom Inc/ 47 E 19th St, New York, NY............. (212) 254-9575
Green, Dan/ Route 1 PO Box 203, High Falls, NY .... (914) 687-9370
GREEN, NORMAN/ 11 Seventy Acres Rd.,
    West Redding, CT .... (203) 438-9909
    See our ad on page 13
Gregori, Lee/ 400 East 56 St., New York, NY......................... (212) 758-1662
Grien, Anita/ 155 E. 38th Street, New York, NY .... (212) 697-6170
Griesbach/Martucci/ 35 Sterling Pl., New York, NY.................. (212) 622-1831
Grifalconi, Ann/ 124 Waverly Place, New York, NY.................. (212) 777-9042
Griffel, Barbara/ New York, NY... (212) 446-0285
Griffin, Jim/ 310 Madison Ave. #1225, New York, NY .... (212) 867-8092
Griffin, Virginia Sing/ 317 Washington Avenue #1A,
    Brooklyn, NY.. (212) 857-8993
Grimm, Jean/ 201 E. 21st Street #8R, New York, NY .... (212) 533-8309
Grossberg, Manuel/ 1200 Broadway, New York, NY................. (212) 532-3335
Grossman, Robert/ 19 Crosby Street, New York, NY .... (212) 925-1965
Grote, Rich/ 114 E. 32nd St. #902, New York, NY .... (212) 685-2770
Groth, John/ New York, NY .... (212) 737-5062
Group East Studio/ 114 Lexington Ave, New York, NY .... (212) 725-9545
Group West Inc./Ren Wicks/ 5455 Wilshire Blvd. 1212,
    Los Angeles, CA... (213) 937-4472
Grove, Al/ Box 510 Hemlock Dr, Hopewell, NY .... (914) 226-8916
GROVE, DAVID/ 382 Union St., San Francisco, CA .... (415) 433-2100
    See our ad on page 100
Grushkin, Philip/ 86 E. Linden Avenue, Englewood, NJ .... (201) 568-6686
GUARNACCIA, STEVEN/ 89 Bleecker St. #6b,
    New York, NY.. (212) 420-0108
    See our ad on page 101
GUETARY, HELENE/ 333 E. 30th St., New York, NY .... (212) 679-1358
    See our ad on page 121
Gufstafson, Dale/ New York, NY .... (212) 986-5680
Guice, Brad/ 333 East 49th Street, New York, NY .... (212) 734-4533
Gulacy, Paul/ 6201 Blvd. East Apt. #4AS, West New York, NJ ...... (201) 854-1537
Gumen, Murad/ 33-25 90th St. Ste. 6k, Jackson Heights, NY........ (718) 478-7267
Gunn Assoc/ 275 Newbury, Boston, MA .... (617) 267-0618
Gunn, Robert/ 201 East 28th Street, New York, NY .... (212) 532-0928
Gurganus, Nancy/ 8112 Carroll Ln, Silver Spring, MD .... (301) 585-3726
Gustafson, Dale/ 56 Fourbrooks Rd., Stamford, CT .... (203) 322-5667
Gustavson, Mat/ 425 W 23 St Rm 17A, New York, NY .... (212) 243-2750
Guzzi, George/ 11 Randlett Park, West Newton, MA .... (617) 244-2932
Haas, Arie/ 35 West 38 Street, New York, NY .... (212) 382-1677
Haber, Vera/ 333 East 49th Street, New York, NY .... (212) 734-4533
Hadfield Art Services, J.J./ PO Box 336, Ashton, RI .... (401) 333-6322
Hafner, Marylin/ 185 Holoworthy Street, Cambridge, MA .... (617) 354-0696
Hallgren, Gary/ 6 West 37th St #5, New York, NY .... (212) 947-1054
Hall, Joan/ 155 Bank Street #H954, New York, NY .... (212) 243-6059
Hamagami, John/ 353 West 53rd Street, New York, NY .... (212) 730-0144
Hamberger, John/ RD #4 Box 415, Monroe, NY .... (914) 986-6616
Hamilton, Ken C/ 845 West End Ave #11-D, New York, NY .... (212) 749-1647

ILLUSTRATION/East

Hamilton, Marcus/ 342 Madison Ave Room 261, New York, NY..... (212) 986-3282
Hamilton, William/ Box 8, West Port, CT.................................. (203) 227-7806
Hampton, Blake/ 64 Steephill Road, Weston, CT...................... (203) 227-1681
Hamrick, Chuck/ Graybar Bld. 420 Lexington Av.,
  New York, NY... (212) 986-5680
Handlesman, Bud/ PO Box 8, Westport, CT............................. (203) 227-7806
Handville, Bob/ 99 Woodland Dr, Pleasantville, NY .... (914) 769-3582
Hann, Jacquie/ 40 Harrison Street, New York, NY .... (212) 233-5851
Hardy, Neil/ 2 Woods Grove Road, Westport, CT .... (203) 226-4446
Harkins, George/ New York, NY .... (212) 980-3510
Harmon, Lily/ New York, NY .... (212) 737-5062
Harmuth, Will/ 201 E 28th St, New York, NY .... (212) 532-0928
Harrington, Glenn/ 165 E. 32nd St., New York, NY .... (212) 686-3514
HARRIS, DIANE TESKE/ 342 Madison Ave., New York, NY .... (212) 719-9879
  See our ad on page 102
Harrison, Sean/ 1349 Lexington Avenue, New York, NY .... (212) 369-3831
Harrison, William/ New York, NY .... (212) 689-3233
Harris, Sidney/ 8 Polo Road, Great Neck, NY .... (516) 466-6143 .
Harsh, Fred/ 185 Goodhill Rd, Weston, CT............................. (203) 226-7674
Harston, Jerry/ New York, NY .... (212) 929-5840
Hart, Veronika/ 60 E 42nd Street, New York, NY .... (212) 682-1490
Harvey, Richard/ 420 Lexington Ave, New York, NY .... (212) 867-9535
Havey, Paula/ 301 W. 53rd St., New York, NY .... (212) 245-6118
Haynes, Michael/ 420 Madison Av, New York, NY .... (212) 980-3510
Hearn, Diane Dawson/ 22 Spring St, Pawling, NY .... (914) 855-1152
Heath, R. Mark/ 4338 Roland Springs Dr., Baltimore, MD .... (301) 366-4633
Heatley, William Paul/ 11 Tilghman Dr, Wayne, NJ .... (201) 694-1290
HECK, CATHY/ 333 E. 30th St., New York, NY .... (212) 679-1358
  See our ad on page 118
HEINDEL, ROBERT/ 211 E. 51st St., New York, NY .... (212) 755-1365
  See our ad on page 18
Heiner, Joe/ 194 Third Avenue, New York, NY .... (212) 475-0440
Hejja, Attila/ 300 Edward Street, Roselyn Heights, NY .... (516) 621-8054
Henderson, Alan/ 420 Madison Ave Suite 401, New York, NY ...... (212) 980-3510
Henderson, Meryl/ 555 Main Street #308, Roosevelt Islan, NY ..... (212) 688-8329
Hendrix, Bryan/ 79 Willoughby Ave, Brooklyn, NY .... (212) 857-9442
Henselmann, Casper/ 21 Bond Street, New York, NY .... (212) 533-0430
Herder, Edwin/ 310 Madison Ave. #1225, New York, NY............ (212) 867-8092
Hering, Al C/O Shelley Kopel/ 342 Madison Ave, New York, NY .... (212) 986-3282
Herman, Tim/ 420 Madison Ave, New York, NY........................ (212) 980-3510
Hernandez, Richard/ 144 Chambers Street, New York, NY........... (212) 732-3474
Herrick, George/ 384 Farmington Avenue, Hartford, CT .... (203) 527-1940
Herring, Michael/ 244 W. 103rd St., New York, NY .... (212) 663-2848
Hersh, Helen/ 34 Plaza St, Brooklyn, NY .... (212) 638-2343
HESS, MARK/ 135 E. 54th St., New York, NY .... (212) 421-0050
  See our ad on page 103
Hess, Milo/ 69-39 Yellowstone Blvd., Forest Hills, NY.............. (718) 268-3394
HESS, RICHARD/ 135 E. 54th St., New York, NY................... (212) 421-0050
  See our ad on page 104
Hill, Amy Incadescent Ink Inc/ 111 Wooster Street,
  New York, NY... (212) 925-0491
Hillman, Ben/ 137 East 25th Street, New York, NY .... (212) 679-2670
Hinlicky, Gregg/ PO Box 1521, Toms River, NJ .... (201) 269-4867
Hiroko/ 67-12 Yellowstone Blvd, New York, NY .... (212) 896-2712
Hirschfield, Al/ 122 E. 95th Street, New York, NY .... (212) 534-6172
Hitech Weapon System Art Group/ 212 W Rt 38, Moorestown, NJ . (609) 234-1200
HODGES, KEN/ILLUSTRATION/ 12401 Bellwood Rd.,
  Los Alamitos, CA.. (213) 431-4343
  See our ad on page 105
Hoffmann, Ginny/ 108 East 35th St, New York, NY .... (212) 889-3337
Hogarth, Paul/ 215 E 31 St, New York, NY .... (212) 684-3448
Hogarth, William/ 207 Carpenter Avenue, Sea Cliff, NY .... (516) 676-2374
Holland, Brad/ 96 Greene Street, New York, NY .... (212) 226-3675
Hooks, Mitchell/ 321 E. 83rd Street, New York, NY .... (212) 737-1853
Hopkins, Chris/ 353 West 53rd Street, New York, NY .... (212) 730-0144
Horowitz, Amy/ New York, NY .... (212) 925-0491
Hortens, Walter/ 154 E. 64th Street, New York, NY .... (212) 838-0014
Hosner, William/ 420 Madison Ave, New York, NY .... (212) 980-3510
Hostovich, Michael/ 470 W. 23rd St., New York, NY .... (212) 242-6367
Ho, Tien/ 201 East 28th Street, New York, NY .... (212) 532-0928
Houghtelling, Ayres/ 60 Sutton Place S., New York, NY .... (212) 752-8696
Howard, H John/ 336 East 54th St, New York, NY.................... (212) 832-7980
Howitt, Karen/ 1136 Fifth Ave, New York, NY .... (212) 534-1423
Howland, Deborah/ 58 Steephill Road, Weston, CT .... (203) 227-3647
Hsin, Fuh-Lin/ 185 Goodhill Road, Weston, CT........................ (203) 226-7674

Huehnergarth, John/ 196 Snowden Lane, Princeton, NJ .... (609) 921-3211
Huelsman, Amy/ 24 S. Calumet Avenue, Hastings On Hud, NY ...... (914) 478-0596
Huerta, Catherine/ 60 E. 42nd St. #505, New York, NY .... (212) 682-1490
Huerta, Gerard/ 1059 3rd Avenue, New York, NY .... (212) 753-2895
Huffaker, Sandy/ 375 Snowden, Princeton, NJ .... (609) 924-2883
Huffman, Tom/ 130 W. 47th Street, New York, NY .... (212) 819-0211
Hull, Cathy/ 236 East 36 Street, New York, NY .... (212) 683-8559
HULL, SCOTT/ 20 Lynn Rae Cir., Dayton, OH .... (513) 433-8383
  See our ad on page 106
Hulme, Norman D/ One ADP Boulevard, Roseland, NJ .... (201) 994-5566
Hulsey, John/ Route 9D Lawes Lane, Garrison, NY................... (914) 424-3544
Hunter,Graham Adv Cartoon Svcs/ 42 Clonavor Road,
  West Orange, NJ .... (201) 731-6322
Hunter, Stanley/ Maple Ave, Millbrook, NY .... (914) 677-9510
Hunt, Jim/ 420 Madison Ave, New York, NY .... (212) 980-3510
HUNT, ROBERT/ 4376 21st St., San Francisco, CA................. (415) 824-1824
  See our ad on page 107
Hurwitz, Joyce/ 7314 Burdette Court, Bethesda, MD .... (301) 365-0340
Huyssen, Roger/ 1059 Third Ave., New York, NY .... (212) 888-9193
Hyatt, John/ 31 Mercer St, New York, NY .... (212) 431-4980
Hyers/Smith Inc/ 750 Summer St, Stamford, CT .... (203) 327-1017
Hyman, Trina Schart/ Brick Hill Road, Lyme, NH .... (603) 795-2180
Ian, M/ New York, NY... (212) 724-2800
Identitia Incorp./ 10 Harris Street, Newburyport, MA .... (617) 462-3146
Illustrations Done/ 4209 20th St NE, Washington, DC .... (202) 529-0429
Image Factory Inc/ 645 West End Ave, New York City, NY .... (212) 877-1739
Imgrund, Paul/ 75 Stockton Lake Blvd., Manasquan, NJ .... (201) 449-6647
Incandescent, Inc./ 111 Wooster Street Penthouse C,
  New York, NY... (212) 925-0491
Intersight Design, Inc./ 419 Park Ave S., New York, NY .... (212) 696-0700
Iosa, Ann/ 185 Goodhill Road, Weston, CT............................. (203) 226-7674
Iris, Joyce/ 11 Riverside Drive, New York, NY .... (212) 877-6161
Ivens, Rosalind/ 1312 Walnut Street, Philadelphia, PA .... (215) 732-8366
Jaben, Seth/ 47 E. 3rd St. #3, New York, NY .... (212) 260-7859
Jaksevic, Nenad/ 165 E. 32nd St., New York, NY .... (212) 686-3514
Jamieson, Doug/ 42-20 69th St, Woodside, NY .... (212) 565-6034
Janovitz, Kiki-Marilyn/ New York, NY .... (212) 689-3902
JARVIS, DAVID/ 725 Indigo Drive, Daytona Beach, FL.............. (904) 255-1296
  See our ad on page 108
Jasper, Jackie/ 165 E. 32nd St., New York, NY .... (212) 686-3514
Jazwiecki, Leonard P./ 34-26 85 Street, Jackson Heights, NY .... (212) 639-7317
Jean, Carol/ 371 Sagamore Ave, Mineola, NY .... (212) 742-3322
Jeffers, Kathy/ 106 E 19th St, New York, NY .... (212) 475-1756
Jenkins-Klem/ 17 Stuyvesant Apt 19, New York, NY .... (212) 533-2689
Jenkins, Steve/ 65 Fourth Ave, New York, NY .... (212) 982-8266
Jetter, Frances/ 390 West End Avenue, New York, NY .... (212) 580-3720
J & M Condon/ 126 Fifth Ave, New York, NY .... (212) 242-7811
Joffe, Vera/ 4 Park Avenue Suite 16 N, New York, NY .... (212) 686-0448
JOHNSON, B. E./ 366 Oxford St., Rochester, NY .... (716) 461-4240
  See our ad on page 109
Johnson, Doug/ 45 E 19th, New York, NY .... (212) 260-1880
Johnson, Evelyn Assoc/ 201 E 28th Str, New York, NY.............. (212) 532-0928
Johnson, Kristin/ 902 Broadway Room 1609, New York, NY........ (212) 477-4033
Johnson, Pam/ 49 Richmondville Avenue, Westport, CT .... (203) 226-3233
Johnston, Shaun & Susan/ 890 West End Avenue Apt 11E,
  New York, NY... (212) 663-4686
Jones Anastasi & Mitchell Adv/ 502 W Sixth St, Erie, PA .... (814) 453-6635
Jones, Bob/ 420 Lexington Ave. #2911, New York, NY .... (212) 986-5680
Jones, George H/ 52 Old Highway, Wilton, CT......................... (203) 762-7242
Jones, Roger/ 15 Waldo Avenue, Somerville, MA .... (617) 628-1487
Jones, Ron/ 185 East 85th Street, New York, NY .... (212) 369-1925
Jordan, Laurie/ 185 Goodhill Road, Weston, CT .... (203) 226-7674
Jorg, Elizabeth/ 121 Brompton Rd, Garden City, NY .... (516) 248-7036
Joseph, Paula/ 147 W 13th St, New York, NY .... (212) 242-6137
Joudrey, Ken/ 15 W. 72nd St., New York, NY .... (212) 799-2231
JOYNER, ERIC/ 21 Lapidge St. #4, San Francisco, CA .... (415) 626-9890
  See our ad on page 110
Joy Street Studio Inc/ 64 Long Wharf, Boston, MA................... (617) 742-8077
Just, Hal/ 155 E 38th St, New York, NY .... (212) 697-6170
Kahn, Donald/ New York, NY .... (212) 682-2555
Kalish, Lional/ 108 E 35th St, New York, NY .... (212) 889-3337
Kanarek, Michael/ 114 E. 32nd St., New York, NY .... (212) 685-2770
Kaneda, Shirley/ 34 W. 56th Street, New York, NY .... (212) 246-6335
Kane, Harry/ 310 E. 49th Street, New York, NY .... (212) 486-0180
Kane, Kid/ 60 E. 42nd Street, New York, NY .... (212) 682-1490

Kanelous, George/ 9 E. 32nd St., New York, NY .... (212) 688-1080
Kane, Michael/ 15 W. 72nd St., New York, NY........................ (212) 799-2231
Kane, Morgan/ 500 E. 77th Street, New York, NY .... (212) 288-0243
Kaplan, Alan/ 2143 73rd Street, Brooklyn, NY .... (212) 259-0178
Kaplan, Joanne/ 500 E 77th St, New York, NY .... (212) 734-3533
Kaplan, Mark/ 2738 Ocean Ave, Brooklyn, NY........................ (718) 743-0657
Kappes, Werner/ 33 E 22nd St, New York, NY .... (212) 673-2484
Karapelou, John W./ 280 Sedore Avenue, Fairview, NJ .... (201) 943-0432
Kardwell Assoc/ 21 E 40th St, New York, NY .... (212) 532-8866
Karlin, Eugene/ 39-73 48th Street, Sunnyside, NY.................. (212) 457-5086
Karlin, James/Technical Illustr/ Box 213, Fairport, NY .... (716) 223-5678
Karl, Jerry/ 1045 Eglon Court, North Merrick, NY .... (516) 485-7462
Kass Graphics Inc., Warren/ 505 8th Avenue, New York, NY ..... (212) 868-3133
Katinas, Charles C./ 61 E. 11th Street, New York, NY .... (212) 228-6352
Katz, Les/ 451 Westminster Rd, Brooklyn, NY .... (212) 284-4779
Kaufman, Robert/ Hoboken, NJ .... (201) 653-5203
Kaye Graphics Inc./ 151 Lexington Ave., New York, NY .... (212) 889-8240
Keller, Carol/ 58 Burside Ave, Somerville, MA........................ (617) 547-2930
Kelly, Susannah Rep Les Mince/ 111 Wooster St, New York, NY.... (212) 925-0491
Kendrick, Dennis/ 99 Bank Street Apt. 3G, New York, NY .... (212) 924-3085
Kenny, Pat/ 2914 Barker Street, Silver Spring, MD .... (301) 496-2192
KENYON, CHRIS/ 14 Wilmot, San Francisco, CA .... (415) 923-1363
    See our ad on page 111
Kerbs, Larry Studios Inc/ 419 Park Ave S, New York, NY .... (212) 686-9420
Kershner Studios/ 70 Ward Park, Grand Island, NY .... (716) 773-1468
Ketchum, Ron Assoc Inc/ 8 Prince St, Rochester, NY .... (716) 271-2380
Kibbee, Gordon/ 6 Jane Street, New York, NY .... (212) 989-7074
KILROY, JOHN/ 28 Fairmount Way, Nantasket, MA .... (617) 925-0582
    See our ad on page 112
KIMBLE, DAVID/ 711 S. Flower, Burbank, CA .... (213) 849-1576
    See our ad on page 113
KIMURA, HIRO/ 862 W. 24th St. #2e, New York, NY .... (212) 929-3266
    See our ad on page 134
Kingsley, Melinda/ 120 E. 79th Street, New York, NY .... (212) 879-2042
KINGSTON, JIM/ 18 E. 17th St., New York, NY .... (212) 807-6627
    See our ad on page 114
King, William/ Box 1867, East Hampton, NY .... (516) 324-7653
Kinstrey, Jim/ 35 Bryant Place, Lodi, NJ .... (201) 772-1781
KIRCHOFF/WOHLBERG, INC./ 866 United Nations Plz.,
New York, NY .... (212) 644-2020
    See our ad on page 115
Kirk, Daniel/ 85 South St. #6n, New York, NY .... (212) 825-0190
Klaboe & Siwek Assocs/ 2315 Broadway, New York, NY .... (212) 362-6666
Klavins, Uldis/ 30 Topcrest Lane, Ridgefield, CT .... (203) 438-3904
Klein, David F./ 281 A Henry Street, Brooklyn, NY.................. (212) 875-1656
KLEIN, RENEE/ 291 Carroll St., Brooklyn, NY .... (718) 624-1210
    See our ad on page 116
Klenca, George/ New York, NY .... (212) 737-5062
Klimt, Bill & Maurine (Rep)/ 15 W 72nd Street, New York, NY ... (212) 799-2231
Kliros, Thea/ 313 E. 18th Street, New York, NY .... (212) 254-2574
Kluglein, Karen/ 88 Lexington Ave, New York, NY.................. (212) 684-2974
Knettell, Sharon/ 108 E 35th St, New York, NY .... (212) 889-3337
Knight, Hilary/ 300 E. 51st Street, New York, NY .... (212) 755-4047
Koda-Callan, Elizabeth/ 792 Columbus Avenue, New York, NY ... (212) 663-6720
Koester, Michael/ Graybar Bld. 420 Lexington Av.,
New York, NY.. (212) 986-5680
Kohfield, Dick/ 71 Aiken St #R-10, Norwalk, CT .... (203) 846-0015
Kondo, Yokio/ 201 East 28th Street, New York, NY .... (212) 532-0928
Bliss Brothers/ 342 Madison Ave. #261, New York, NY .... (212) 986-3282
KORDIC, VLADIMIR/ 35351 Grovewood Dr., Eastlake, OH .... (216) 951-4026
    See our ad on page 117
Koren, Edward/ 215 E 31 St, New York, NY .... (212) 684-3448
Korotkin, J Biegeleisen/ 12 Glenwood Road, Montclair, NJ .... (201) 783-1463
Koslow, Howard/ 26 Highwood Road, East Norwich, NY.......... (516) 922-7427
Kossin, Sanford/ 143 Cow Neck Road, Port Washington, NY ...... (516) 883-3038
Kotschnig, Enid/ 220 W. 98th Street #10F, New York, NY .... (212) 866-5099
Kovalcik, Terry/ 88 Union Ave., Clifton, NJ .... (201) 478-1191
Krakovitz, Harlan/ New York, NY.. (212) 689-3902
Krantz-Fieramosca, Kathy/ New York, NY .... (212) 689-3902
KREPEL, DICK/ 211 E. 51st St., New York, NY .... (212) 755-1365
    See our ad on page 19
Kretschmann, Karin/ 323 W 75th St, New York, NY .... (212) 724-5001
Kretzschmar, Hubert Studio/ 211 West Broadway, New York, NY ... (212) 431-8517
KRIEGLER, RICHARD/ 2814 3rd St., Santa Monica, CA .... (213) 396-9087
    See our ad on page 34

Kroll, Eric/ 118 E 28th St Ste 1005, New York, NY.................. (212) 684-2465
Krug, Kenneth/ 60 2nd Avenue #22, New York, NY .... (212) 677-1572
Kubinyi, Laszlo/ New York, NY .... (212) 755-4945
Kunstler, Mort/ Cove Neck Road, Oyster Bay, NY .... (516) 922-6760
Kursar, Raymond/ 1 Lincoln Plaza, New York, NY.................. (212) 873-5605
Kursh, Stephen/ 684 Ave of the Americas, New York, NY.......... (212) 947-0122
Kyle, Ron/ 186 Lincoln St, Boston, MA .... (617) 426-5942
Lacano, Frank/ 336 Sherwood Rd, Union, NJ .... (201) 688-9251
Lackow, Andy/ 114 E 32nd St Suite 902, New York, NY .... (212) 685-2770
Ladas, George/ 157 Prince St, New York, NY........................ (212) 673-2208
Laffoley, Paul/ 36 Bromfield Street, Rm 200, Boston, MA .... (617) 482-9044
Lakeman, Steven/ 115 W. 85th Street, New York, NY .... (212) 877-8888
LAMBERT, SAUL/ 333 E. 30th St., New York, NY .... (212) 679-1358
    See our ad on page 121
Lam Design Assocs Inc/ 661 N Broadway, White Plains, NY ...... (914) 948-4777
Lamut, Sonya/ 165 E. 32nd St., New York, NY .... (212) 686-3514
LANDER/OSBORNE/ 333 E. 30th St., New York, NY .... (212) 679-1358
    See our ad on pages 118-121
Landis, Joan/ 6 Jane St, New York, NY .... (212) 989-7074
Lang, Cecily/ 19 Jones Street, New York, NY .... (212) 924-1942
Langdon, John/ 106 S. Marion Ave., Wenonah, NJ .... (609) 468-7868
Lang, Gary/ 342 Madison Avenue, New York, NY .... (212) 697-8525
Lanza, Barbara/ Box 118, Pine Island, NY .... (914) 258-4601
La Padula, Thomas/ 1296 Midland Ave, Yonkers, NY .... (914) 237-0675
Lapaqula, Tom/ 201 East 28th Street, New York, NY .... (212) 532-0928
Lapinski, Joe/ 420 Madison Ave, New York, NY .... (212) 980-3510
Lapsley, Robert/ New York, NY .... (212) 689-3902
Laquatra, Jack/ 1221 Glencoe Avenue, Pittsburgh, PA .... (412) 279-6210
La Raja, Diane/ 250 W 27th St, New York, NY .... (212) 243-3240
Lasher, Mary Ann/ 60 E. 42nd St., New York, NY .... (212) 682-1490
Laslo, Larry/ 179 E. 71st Street, New York, NY .... (212) 737-2340
Laslo, Rudy/ New York, NY .... (212) 683-8525
Lavaty Artists Representatives/ 50 E 50th St, New York, NY ...... (212) 355-0910
Lawrence, Edward Studio/ 856 Western Ave, Pittsburgh, PA ...... (412) 322-1444
Lawrence, Matthew Co/ 62 West 45 Street, New York, NY .... (212) 869-1150
Lawrence, Vint/ 3221 Macomb Street N.W., Washington, DC ...... (202) 244-2516
Lawton, April/ 31 Hampshire Drive, Farmingdale, NY.............. (516) 454-0868
Lawton, Nancy/ 8 Shelterview Dr., New York, NY .... (212) 720-0157
Lazarevich, Mila/ 225 E. 63rd Street Apt. 9F, New York, NY ...... (212) 371-9173
Leake, Donald/ 124 W. 80th Street, New York, NY .... (212) 877-8405
Leamon, Tom/ 18 Main Street, Amherst, MA .... (413) 256-8423
Lebbad, James A./ 220 Fifth Ave, New York, NY .... (212) 679-2234
LEBO, NARDA/ 4851 Cedar Springs, Dallas, TX .... (214) 528-0375
    See our ad on page 122
Lebron, Michael/ 36 Cooper Sq. Rm. 7f, New York, NY .... (212) 477-0748
Lee, Robert J/ Rd 1 PO Box 24, Carmel, NY .... (914) 225-4934
Leff, Jerry Associates/ 342 Madison Avenue, New York, NY .... (212) 697-8525
Lehew, Ron/ Philadelphia, PA .... (215) 928-0918
Leigh, Thomas/ Rd 1 Box 84, Sheffield, MA .... (413) 229-3353
Lemericse, Bruce/ 410 W. 24th Street #6K, New York, NY .... (212) 989-0749
Lent, Blair/ 10 Dana Street Apt. 208N, Cambridge, MA .... (617) 547-4572
LESH, DAVID/ 6021 Rosslyn Ave., Indianapolis, IN .... (317) 253-3141
    See our ad on pages 124, 125
Lesser, Ron/ 342 Madison Ave., New York, NY .... (212) 697-8525
Le-Tan, Pierre/E.T.Riley,Inc./ 215 E. 31 St., New York, NY .... (212) 684-3448
LETOSTAK, JOHN/ 1295 Old River Rd., Cleveland, OH .... (216) 621-1771
    See our ad on page 71
Lettick, Birney/ 121 E 35th, New York, NY .... (212) 532-0535
Levering, Robert/ 330 E. 79th Street, New York, NY .... (212) 535-4618
LEVIN, ARNIE/ 342 Madison Ave., New York, NY .... (212) 719-9879
    See our ad on page 123
Levine, Andy/ 1558 2nd Ave Apt 2R, New York City, NY .... (212) 288-2481
Levine, Bette/ 60 East 42nd Street, New York, NY .... (212) 682-1490
Levine, Ned/ 1462 First Ave, New York, NY .... (212) 861-8374
Levine, Ron/ 1 West 85th Street, New York, NY .... (212) 787-7415
Levin, Lynne/ 70 East 96th Apt 5C, New York, NY .... (212) 722-2706
Levin, Sue/ 9111 Burdette Rd, Bethesda, MD .... (301) 983-1029
Levirne, Joel/ 151 W. 46th Street, New York, NY .... (212) 869-8370
Levy, Robert S/ 333 East 49th Street, New York, NY .... (212) 734-4533
Lewin, Ted/ 152 Willoughby Ave, Brooklyn, NY .... (212) 622-3882
Lewis, John D/ 61 E Hillside Ave, Plymouth, PA .... (717) 779-9055
Lewis, Tim/ 194 Third Ave., New York, NY .... (212) 475-0440
Leyonmark, Roger/ 139 Sumner Street, Newton, MA .... (617) 965-0930
Liberatore, Gaetano/ 43 E. 19th St., New York, NY .... (212) 254-4996
Lidbeck, Karin/ 185 Goodhill Road, Weston, CT.................... (203) 226-7674

Lieberman, Ron/ 109 W. 28th Street, New York, NY .... (212) 947-0653
LIEPKE, SKIP/ 211 E. 51st St., New York, NY .... (212) 755-1365
See our ad on page 20
Lilly, Charles/ 56 W. 82nd Street #15, New York, NY .... (212) 873-3608
Lilly Graphics/ 54 Munroe Road, Lexington, MA .... (617) 861-8151
LIM, EDWARD H./ 348 Locust St. #2,
    San Francisco, CA .... (415) 921-1374
    See our ad on page 126
Lindlof, Ed/ 353 W. 53rd St., New York, NY .... (212) 682-2462
Lindman, Sven/ 500 E. 87th Street, New York, NY .... (212) 794-9085
Lion House/ PO Box 217, Lahaska, PA................................... (212) 682-1490
Lipton, Martha/ 392 Central Park West, New York, NY .... (212) 666-9226
Little Apple Art/ 409 6th Ave., Brooklyn, NY .... (212) 499-7045
LITTLEBOY, JOHN/ 7 Ninth Ave., San Francisco, CA .... (415) 387-9718
    See our ad on page 127
LIVINGSTON, FRANCIS/ 1537 Franklin St. #105,
    San Francisco, CA .... (415) 776-1531
    See our ad on page 128
Lloyd, Peter/ 120 E. 32 St., New York, NY .... (212) 689-3233
Loccisano, Karen/ 185 Goodhill Road, Weston, CT .... (203) 226-7674
Lodigensky, Ted/ 120 E. 32 St., New York, NY .... (212) 689-3233
Logos Logos Logos/ 355 Lexington Avenue, New York, NY .... (212) 682-0830
Longtemps, Kenneth/ 362 Clinton St., Brooklyn, NY .... (212) 852-2178
Lopez, Antonio/ 31 Union Square W., New York, NY .... (212) 924-2060
Lorenz, Al/ 185 Goodhill Road, Weston, CT .... (203) 226-7674
Lorenz, Albert Studio/ 49 Pine Ave, Floral Park, NY .... (516) 354-5530
Lorenz, Lee/ PO Box 8, Westport, CT................................... (203) 227-7806
Loscalzo, Glee/ 185 East 85th Street, New York, NY .... (212) 369-1925
Lubey, Dick/ 726 Harvard Street, Rochester, NY .... (716) 442-6075
Luebbers, Robert M. Inc./ 2010 Chancellor Street,
    Philadelphia, PA.. (215) 567-2360
Lukac, Maria/ 10 Martling Street, East Norwich, NY .... (516) 922-1274
Lurio, Eric A./ 250 W 15th Street, New York, NY .... (212) 929-3071
Lutz, Bill/ 22 W 38th, New York, NY .... (212) 398-1990
Luzak, Dennis/ PO Box 342, Redding Ridge, CT....................... (203) 938-3158
Lyall, Dennis/ 353 W 53rd St Apt 1W, New York, NY .... (212) 682-2462
Lyman, Kenvin/ New York, NY .... (212) 683-8525
Lynch, Don/ 532 N. Broadway, Upper Nyack, NY .... (914) 358-3939
LYTLE, JOHN/ P.O. Box 5155, Sonora, CA .... (209) 928-4849
    See our ad on page 129
MacArthur, David/ 147B E Bradford Ave, Cedar Grove, NJ .... (201) 857-1046
MacDonald, Jay/ 161 S Woodland St, Englewood, NJ.................. (201) 568-0053
Mack, John/ 11 Columbia Place, Brooklyn Hts, NY .... (212) 568-8591
Mack, Stan/ New York, NY .... (212) 755-4945
Maddalone, John/ 1123 Broadway #310, New York, NY .... (212) 807-6087
Maestro, Giulio/ 702 Summer Hill Road, Madison, CT................. (203) 421-3788
Maffia, Daniel/ 44 N. Dean Street, Englewood, NJ .... (201) 871-0435
Magagna, Anna Marie/ 2 Tudor City Place, New York, NY .... (212) 840-1234
Magdich, Dennis/ 342 Madison Ave., New York, NY .... (212) 697-8525
Magee, Alan/ Pleasant Point Road, Cushing, ME....................... (207) 354-8838
Magna Graphics Corp/ 37 Elm St, Westfield, NJ .... (201) 233-0801
Maguire Advertising Assocs/ 584 Delaware Ave, Buffalo, NY .... (716) 882-1041
Mahoney, Katherine/ 60 Hurd Rd., Belmont, MA .... (617) 661-8385
Mahoney, Ron/ 353 West 53rd Street, New York, NY .... (212) 730-0144
Mahon, Rich/ 120 E. 32 St., New York, NY .... (212) 689-3233
Main Idea, The/ 345 Morgantown Rd, Reading, PA .... (215) 376-4871
Malsberg, Edward/ 11 White Birch Drive, Ossining, NY .... (914) 941-3613
Mambach, Alex/ 102-35 64th Road, Forest Hills, NY .... (212) 275-4269
Mandel, Saul/ 163 Maytime Dr, Jericho, NY .... (516) 681-3530
Mangiat, Jeff/ Graybar Bld. 420 Lexington Av., New York, NY .... (212) 986-5680
Manhattan Model Makers/ New York, NY .... (212) 620-0398
Mannone, Lorraine L/ 652 W 163rd St, New York, NY .... (212) 781-8274
Manos, Jim Illustrator/ Maple Shade, NJ .... (609) 235-2174
Mantel, Richard/ 194 Third Ave., New York, NY .... (212) 475-0440
Manya, Julia/ 353 West 53rd Street, New York, NY .... (212) 730-0144
Marckrey Design Group Inc/ 10 E 23rd St, New York, NY .... (212) 475-2822
Mardon, Allan/ 108 E 35th St, New York, NY .... (212) 889-3337
Margaret & Frank & Friends Inc/ 124 Hoyt Street,
    Brooklyn, NY.. (212) 237-0145
MARGOLIS, AL/ 1295 Old River Rd., Cleveland, OH .... (216) 621-1771
    See our ad on page 76
Marguerita/ 430 E 63rd St, New York, NY .... (212) 832-3279
Marich, Felix/ 420 Madison Avenue, New York, NY .... (212) 980-3510
MARIE, RITA & FRIENDS/ 6376 W. 5th St.,
    Los Angeles, CA. .... (213) 934-3395
    See our ad on pages 131-137

Mariuzza, Peter/ 146 Hardscrabble Road, Briarcliff Mano, NY .... (914) 769-3310
Mark-Burton Inc/ 300 Summer St, Boston, MA .... (617) 426-3971
Markel, Freda/ 1060 Park Avenue, New York, NY .... (212) 534-7521
Mark, Mona/ 712 Broadway, New York, NY .... (212) 473-7255
Marshall, Bradley/ 105 W 72nd St, New York, NY .... (212) 865-9459
Martin, David Stone/ New York, NY .... (212) 737-5062
Martinez, Sergio/ 43 E. 19th St., New York, NY .... (212) 254-4996
Martin, Jerome/ 322 Second Ave, New York, NY .... (212) 475-1473
Martin, John/ New York, NY .... (212) 490-2450
Martinot, Claude/ 55 Bethune St., New York, NY .... (212) 242-1407
MARTIN, RICHARD/ 485 Hilda St., East Meadow, NY .... (516) 221-3630
    See our ad on page 130
Mascio, Tony/ New York, NY .... (212) 355-1316
Mascio, Tony/ 4 Teton Ct., Voorhees, NJ .... (215) 567-1585
Masi, George/ 111 Wooster St. #PHC, New York, NY .... (212) 925-0491
Maslen, Barbara/ 226 E. 29th Street, New York, NY .... (212) 686-6559
Mason, Fred/ 20 Wynnwood Road, Greenwich, CT..................... (203) 661-7947
MATHEWUSE, JIMMY/ 157 W. 57th St., New York, NY .... (212) 247-1130
    See our ad on pages 56, 57
Mathieu, Joseph/ 215 E 31 St, New York, NY .... (212) 684-3448
Mattelson, Marvin/ 88 Lexington Ave., New York, NY .... (212) 684-2974
Mattingly, David B./ 466 Washington St. #2e, New York, NY .... (212) 219-0689
Matt, Margaret/ 201 E 28th Street, New York, NY .... (212) 532-0928
Max, Peter/ 118 Riverside Dr, New York, NY .... (212) 873-9800
Maxwell, Bill/ 235 W 22 St., New York, NY .... (212) 675-3112
Maxwell, Brookie/ 53 Irving Place, New York, NY .... (212) 475-6909
MAYER, BILL/ 240 Forkner Dr., Decatur, GA .... (404) 378-0686
    See our ad on page 138
Mayer, Mercer/ Beach Hill Rd, Bridgewater, CT....................... (203) 354-5852
McAfee, Mara/ 345 E. 86th Street, New York, NY .... (212) 348-9284
MCCANCE, LEW/ 157 W. 57th St., New York, NY. .... (212) 247-1130
    See our ad on pages 58, 59
McClelland, John/ 612 Laurel Rd, New Canaan, CT .... (203) 966-3083
McConnell and Borow/ 10 E. 23rd Street, New York, NY .... (212) 254-1486
McCormack, Geoffrey/ New York, NY .... (212) 986-5680
McCormack, Geoffrey/ Graybar Bld. 420 Lexington Av.,
    New York, NY.. (212) 986-5680
McCoy, Terrence L/ 105 Market Street, Pittsburgh, PA............... (412) 261-0460
McCrady, Lady/ 17 Park Avenue, New York, NY .... (212) 532-6317
McDaniel, Jerry/ 155 E 38th Street, New York, NY .... (212) 697-6170
McDonough, Vincent/ 6669 Fresh Pond Road, Ridgewood, NY....... (212) 799-1727
MCGAR, MICHAEL/ 3330 Irwin Dell Blvd., Dallas, TX .... (214) 339-0672
    See our ad on page 139
McGinnis, Bob/ 13 Arcadia, Old Greenwich, CT .... (203) 637-5055
McGinty, Nick/ 353 West 53rd Street, New York, NY .... (212) 730-0144
McIntosh, Jon/ 268 Woodward Street, Waban, MA .... (617) 964-6292
McKie, Roy/ 215 E 31 St, New York, NY .... (212) 684-3448
McLean, Wilson/ 902 Broadway, New York, NY .... (212) 473-5554
McLean, Wilson/ 50 East 50th Street, New York, NY .... (212) 752-8490
McLoughlin, Wayne/ 194 Third Avenue, New York, NY .... (212) 475-0440
McLoughlin, Wayne/ 194 Third Ave., New York, NY .... (212) 475-0440
MCNAMARA ASSOCIATES, INC./ 1250 Stephenson Hwy.,
    Troy, MI .... (313) 583-9200
    See our ad on pages 140-143
McVicker, Charles/ 4 Willow St, Princeton, NJ .... (609) 924-2660
Medbery, Sherrell/ 301 W. 108th Street, New York, NY .... (212) 222-5853
Mehlman, Elwyn/ 108 East 35th Street, New York, NY .... (212) 751-4656
Meisel, Ann/ 420 Lexington Ave. #2911, New York, NY .... (212) 986-5680
MEISEL, PAUL/ 90 Hudson St. 5E, New York, NY .... (212) 226-5463
    See our ad on page 144
Melendez, Robert/ New York, NY .... (212) 355-1316
Mello, John/ 161 W. 54th Street, New York, NY .... (212) 265-2658
Meltzoff, Stanley/ 128 Grange Avenue, Fair Haven, NJ .... (201) 747-4415
Mendola Ltd/ 420 Lexington Ave., New York, NY .... (212) 986-5680
Mercie, Tina/ 111 Wooster St. #PHC, New York, NY .... (212) 925-0491
Meritet, Michael/ 273 W. 73rd Street Apt. 1B, New York, NY .... (212) 580-2773
Merrill, Abigail/ 153 E. 57th Street, New York, NY .... (212) 753-7565
Metcalf, Roger/ 9 E. 32nd St., New York, NY .... (212) 688-1080
Meyerowitz, Michael/ 210 E. 38th Street, New York, NY .... (212) 682-0989
Meyerowitz, Rick/ 68 Jane Street, New York, NY .... (212) 989-2446
Meyers, Lou/ 108 E 35 Street, New York, NY .... (212) 889-3337
Michaels, Bob/ 304 East 49 St., New York, NY .... (212) 752-1185
Michal, Marie/ 108 E. 35th Street, New York, NY .... (212) 889-3337
Michaud, Roland/ 73 O'Toole, Westwood, NJ .... (201) 664-3128
Michels, Dale/ 1122 Avery St, Parkersburg, WV .... (304) 422-1147

Midda, Sara/E. T. Riley, Inc./ 215 E. 31 St., New York, NY.......... (212) 684-3448
Mihaesco, Eugene/ 25 Tudor City Place Apt 1423,
New York, NY.. (212) 692-9271
Mikolaycak, Charles/ 64 E 91st Str, New York, NY.................. (212) 427-9628
Mikos, Mike/ Graybar Bld. 420 Lexington Av., New York, NY....... (212) 986-5680
Milbourn, Patrick D./ 327 W. 22nd Street, New York, NY .... (212) 989-4594
MILHOLLAND, RICHARD/ 8271 W. Norton Ave.,
West Hollywood, CA .... (213) 462-6565
See our ad on page 145
Millman, David/ 884 West End Ave. Apt. 51, New York, NY .... (212) 866-1747
Milnazik, Kim/ 210 Locust Street #3F, Philadelphia, PA............. (215) 922-5440
Milne, Jonathan/ Graybar Bld. 420 Lexington Av.,
New York, NY.. (212) 986-5680
Minor, Wendell/ 277 W. 4th Street, New York, NY .... (212) 691-6925
Minor, Wendell/ 277 W. 4th St., New York, NY .... (212) 691-6925
Mintzer, Judy/ 526 E. 83rd Street, New York, NY .... (212) 737-3166
Mistretta, Andrea/ 5 Bohnert Place, Waldwick, NJ .... (201) 652-5325
Mitsuhashi, Yoko/ 43 E. 29th Street, New York, NY .... (212) 683-7312
Miyake, Yoshi/ 185 Goodhill Road, Weston, CT .... (203) 226-7674
Miyamoto, Lance R/ 53 Smithfield Road, Waldwick, NJ .... (201) 447-6682
Miyamoto, Linda/ PO Box 2310, Brooklyn, NY .... (718) 596-4787
Mizumura, Kazue/ 316 Ocean Drive E., Stamford, CT .... (203) 348-8347
MOEBINS/ 225 Santa Monica Blvd., Santa Monica, CA .... (213) 458-4195
Moldoff, Kirk/ 18 McKinley Street, Piermont, CT .... (914) 365-0336
Moll, Charles/ 124 Waverly Place, New York, NY .... (212) 673-4823
Molno, Carl/ 60-11 Broadway, Woodside, NY .... (212) 687-7636
Montiel, David/ 115 W. 16th St. #211, New York, NY .... (212) 989-7426
Mooney, Gerry/ New York, NY .... (212) 781-3209
Moonlight Studio: S Wagner/ 3816 Albemarle Street NW,
Washington, DC .... (202) 244-2801
Moore, Daryl/ 185 Goodhill Road, Weston, CT .... (203) 226-7674
Moraes, Greg/ 310 Madison Ave. #1225, New York, NY .... (212) 867-8092
Morgan, Henry/ PO Box 8, Westport, CT .... (203) 227-7806
Morgan, Jacqui/ 315 E. 58th Street, New York, NY .... (212) 421-0766
Morgan, Vicki/ 194 Third Avenue, New York, NY .... (212) 475-0440
Morgen, Barry/ 425 West End Ave., New York, NY .... (212) 595-6835
Moriarty, Jerome/ 51 W. 28th Street, New York, NY .... (212) 689-4974
Morley, Carol/ 143 Bennett Ave, New York, NY .... (212) 927-6805
Morrill, Rowena/ 344 W. 72nd Street #6H, New York, NY .... (212) 362-7742
Morris, Frank/ 15 W. 72nd St., New York, NY .... (212) 799-2231
Morrison, Bill/ 68 Glandore Road, Westwood, MA................... (617) 329-5288
Morton, Lucy/ 42 St Austins Pl, Staten Island, NY .... (212) 447-6344
Mosberg, Stewart Design/ 11 West Seventy Third Street,
New York, NY.. (212) 873-6130
Moseley, Marshall & Richie/ 409 6th Ave, Brooklyn, NY .... (212) 499-7045
Moskof & Assoc Inc, Martin/ 154 West 57th Street,
New York, NY.. (212) 765-4810
Moskonitz, Steve/ 909 Beacon Street, Boston, MA .... (617) 266-2680
MOSKOWITZ, M. REPRESENTS, INC./ 342 Madison Ave.,
New York, NY .... (212) 719-9879
See our ad on pages 102, 123, 146
Moss, Donald/ 232 Peaceable Street, Ridgefield, CT .... (203) 438-5633
MOSS, GEOFFREY/ 342 Madison Ave., New York, NY .... (212) 719-9879
See our ad on page 146
Moyler, Alan/ Umpawaug Rd, West Redding, CT .... (203) 938-2168
Munger, Nancy/ 185 Goodhill Road, Weston, CT.................... (203) 226-7674
Murawski, Alex/ 108 E 35th St, New York, NY .... (212) 751-4656
Murray, John/ PO Box M, Bairstown, NJ .... (201) 362-6835
Murray, Steve/ 334 E. 77th Street, New York, NY .... (212) 861-4736
Myers, David/ 228 Bleecker Street, New York, NY .... (212) 989-5260
Myers, Lou/ New York, NY .... (212) 751-4656
Myers, Sylvia F./ 2301 Lombard, Philadelphia, PA .... (215) 925-1747
Najaka, Marlies/ 241 Central Park West, New York, NY .... (212) 580-0058
Nakai Sacco & Crowell/ 466 Lexington Ave., New York, NY .... (212) 210-6905
Naprstek, Joel F./ 76 Park Place, Morris Plains, NJ................. (201) 285-0692
Nason Design Assoc Inc/ 329 Newbury Street, Boston, MA .... (617) 266-7286
Neff, Leland/ 506 Amsterdam Avenue #61, New York, NY .... (212) 724-1884
Neibart, Wally/ 1715 Walnut St., Philadelphia, PA .... (215) 564-5167
Nejman-Levikova, Marina/ 155 E 38 St, New York, NY .... (212) 697-6170
Nemirov, Meredith/ 110 Kent St, Brooklyn, NY .... (212) 389-5972
Neski, Peter/ 315 E 68th St, New York, NY .... (212) 737-2521
NESSIM, BARBARA/ 240 E. 15th St., New York, NY .... (212) 677-8888
See our ad on page 147
Neubecker, Robert/ 395 Broadway Ave, New York, NY .... (212) 674-6806
Neumann, Ann/ 444 Broome Street, New York, NY .... (212) 431-7141

NEUMANN, ANN/ 444 Broome St., New York, NY .... (212) 431-7141
See our ad on page 148
NEWBORN, MILTON ASSOCIATES/ 135 E. 54th St.,
New York, NY .... (212) 421-0050
See our ad on pages 38, 97, 103, 104, 180
Newman Design Associates Inc/ 133 Mulberry St, New York, NY ... (212) 226-9801
New Studio Inc/ 210 E 52nd St, New York, NY...................... (212) 752-8686
NEWTON, RICHARD/ 157 W. 57th St., New York, NY .... (212) 247-1130
See our ad on pages 60, 61
Neyman-Levikova, Marina/ 155 E 38 Street, New York, NY .... (212) 697-6170
Ng, Michael Studios/ 84-20 60th Ave, Elmhurst, NY .... (212) 651-1913
Nicastre, Michael/ 342 Madison Ave., New York, NY .... (212) 697-8525
Nicotra, Roseann/ 342 Madison Ave., New York, NY .... (212) 697-8525
Nighthawk Studio/ 420 Madison Ave, New York, NY .... (212) 980-3510
Niles, David A./ 36 Coburn Hill Road, Concord, MA .... (617) 369-4584
Nilson, Judith/ 3 Washington Square Village, New York, NY .... (212) 533-2465
Nix, Jonathon J./ 175 Fifth Ave. #1112, New York, NY .... (212) 447-8027
NOFTSINGER, PAMELA/ 7 Cornelia St., New York, NY .... (212) 807-8861
See our ad on page 149
Nolan, Diane A/ 68 Crest Road, Middletown, NJ .... (201) 671-0820
Noma, Juki/ 142-02 84 Drive Apt LA, Briarwood, NY .... (212) 657-3728
Noonan, Julia/ 873 President St., Brooklyn, NY .... (212) 622-9268
NORCIA, ERNEST/ 1295 Old River Rd., Cleveland, OH .... (216) 621-1771
See our ad on pages 75, 77
Norman, Marty/ 5 Radcliff Blvd., Glen Head, NY .... (516) 671-4482
Norris, Edgar/ 160 East 38th St Apt 34H, New York, NY .... (212) 687-1686
North, Chas W Studios/ 40 W 20th St, New York, NY .... (212) 686-5740
Norton Graphics/ 69 Charles St #3, Boston, MA .... (617) 523-4934
Nostradamus Advertising/ 250 West 57 St #1128A,
New York, NY.. (212) 581-1362
Notarile, Chris/ Graybar Bld. 420 Lexington Av.,
New York, NY.. (212) 986-5680
NOVAK, BOB/ 1295 Old River Rd., Cleveland, OH................. (216) 621-1771
See our ad on page 73
Oberman Arline & Marvin/ 119 Morris Street, Yonkers, NY .... (914) 963-6906
O'Brien, John/ 201 East 28th Street, New York, NY .... (212) 532-0928
Odom, Mel/ 252 W. 76th Street, New York, NY .... (212) 724-9320
Oelbaum, Fran/ 196 W. 10th St., New York, NY .... (212) 691-3422
Olanoff, Greg/ 310 Madison Ave. #1225, New York, NY .... (212) 867-8092
Olbinski, Rafal/ 470 W. 23rd St., New York, NY .... (212) 242-6367
Oliver, Sandi/ PO Box 1203, Weston, CT .... (203) 226-4469
Olson, Maribeth/ 75 Huntington Ave, Scarsdale, NY .... (914) 472-2381
OLSON, ROBERT A./ 15215 Buchanan Ct.,
Eden Prairie, MN .... (612) 934-5767
See our ad on page 150
Omnigraphics Inc/ 19 Mt Auburn St, Cambridge, MA .... (617) 354-7444
Opticalusions/ 9 E. 32nd St., New York, NY .... (212) 688-1080
Orloff, Denis E/ 310 E Ninth St, New York, NY .... (212) 982-8341
Ormai, Stella/ 26 E Manning Street, Providence, RI................. (401) 272-0407
Osser, Stephanie Fleischer/ 150 Winding River Rd,
Needham, MA .... (617) 237-1116
O'Sullivan, Tom/ New York, NY .... (212) 737-5062
Osyczka, Bohdan D./ Summit Avenue, Peekskill, NY .... (914) 737-5119
OTNES, FRED/ 211 E. 51st St., New York, NY .... (212) 755-1365
See our ad on page 21
Overacre, Gary/ New York, NY .... (212) 751-4656
Ovies, Joe/ 420 Madison Ave, New York, NY .... (212) 980-3510
Palladini, David/ 60 E 42nd St, New York, NY .... (212) 682-1490
PALULIAN, DICKRAN/ 18 McKinley St., Rowayton, CT .... (203) 866-3734
See our ad on page 151
Pando, Leo/ 138 Montague St, Brooklyn, NY .... (212) 852-0617
Panero, Roxanne/ 301 W. 17th Street, New York, NY .... (212) 242-0735
Parios Studio/ 18 E 48th St, New York, NY .... (212) 421-1680
Parisi, Annette/ 87-60 97th Street, Woodhaven, NY .... (212) 846-4650
Parker, Ed/ 45 Newbury St, Boston, MA .... (617) 437-7726
Parker, Nancy W./ 51 E. 74th Street, New York, NY .... (212) 734-0858
Parker, Robert Andrew/ 215 E 31 St, New York, NY .... (212) 684-3448
Parle Portraits/ 100 Lasalle St., New York, NY .... (212) 663-7361
Parry, Ivor A./ 4 Lorraine Dr., Eastchester, NY.................... (212) 889-0619
Parshall, C. A. Inc./ 200 Henry Street, Stamford, CT .... (212) 685-6370
Parsons, John/ 342 Madison Ave., New York, NY .... (212) 697-8525
Parubchenko, Zina/ 28 York Street, Lambertville, NJ .... (609) 397-0947
Paslavsky, Ivan/ 510-7 Main Street N., New York, NY .... (212) 759-3985
Passalacqua, David/ 325 Versa Place, Sayville, NY .... (516) 589-1663
Pastor, Perico/ 334 The Bowery, New York, NY .... (212) 228-5692

Paul, Tony/ 467 W 57 St, New York, NY .... (212) 307-6188
Peak, Bob/ 50 East 50th Street, New York, NY .... (212) 752-8490
Peele, Lynwood/ 344 W 88th St, New York, NY .... (212) 799-3305
Pelavin, Daniel/ 45 Carmine St., New York, NY .... (212) 929-2706
Pels, Winslow Pinney/ 226 E. 53 #3c, New York, NY .... (212) 355-7670
Pema Browne/ 185 E 85 St, New York, NY .... (212) 369-1925
Penelope/ 342 Madison Ave., New York, NY .... (212) 697-8525
Pepper, Bob/ 157 Clinton Street, Brooklyn, NY .... (212) 875-3236
Pepper, Brenda/ 157 Clinton Street, Brooklyn, NY .... (212) 875-3236
Perina, Jim/ 33 Regent St., N. Plainfield, NJ .... (201) 757-3010
Perrott, Jennifer/ New York, NY .... (212) 929-5840
Perry, Constance A./ 178 Florence Street, Melrose, MA .... (617) 665-9641
Perry, E Stephen/ 150 Mountain Ave, Pompton Plains, NJ .. (201) 839-0873
Peterson, Cheryl/ 215 E 31 St, New York, NY .... (212) 684-3448
Peterson, Joyce/ 60 Hickory Lane, Old Lyme, CT .... (203) 434-8156
Peterson, Judy/ 96 Greene Street, New York, NY .... (212) 226-3675
Petragnani, Vincent/ 420 Madison Avenue, New York, NY .... (212) 980-3510
Pettingill, Ondre/ 245 Bennett Avenue, New York, NY .... (212) 942-1993
PFC Advertising Svce Co/ 130 West 42 St, New York, NY .... (212) 391-8030
Phllis Bek-Gran/ New York, NY .... (212) 689-3902
Pimsler, Al/ 101 Central Park W, New York, NY .... (212) 787-4967
Pinkney, Jerry/ 41 Furnace Dock Road, Croton-On-Hudson, NY ...... (914) 271-5238
Pisano, Al/ 21 Skyline Drive, Upper Saddle Ri, NJ .... (201) 327-6716
Pitt Studios/ 105 Market St, Pittsburgh, PA..................... (412) 261-0460
Plato Taleporos/ 400 Second Ave., New York, NY .... (212) 689-3138
Plotkin, Barnett/ 126 Wooleys Lane, Great Neck, NY .... (516) 487-7457
Plourde, David/ 185 East 85th Street, New York, NY .... (212) 369-1925
Plumb Design Group Inc/ 57 East 11th St 7th Flr,
   New York, NY... (217) 673-3490
Plumer, Paul Associates/ 16 Warren Street, Hallowell, ME .. (207) 622-1812
Plumridge Artworks Inc./ 10215 Fernwood Road, Bethesda, MD .... (301) 530-9624
Pluzynski & Assoc Inc/ 512 7th Ave 44th Floor, New York, NY..... (212) 221-5998
PODEVIN, JEAN FRANCOIS/ 223 S. Kenmore,
   Los Angeles, CA... (213) 739-5083
   See our ad on page 152
Podwil, Jerry/ 108 W. 14th Street, New York, NY .... (212) 255-9464
Poersch, Enno/ 80 Hoyt Street, Brooklyn, NY .... (212) 403-9833
Pohl, Dennis/ 159 W. 4th Street, New York, NY .... (212) 255-8540
Pollack, Scott/ 11 Trinity Pl., Hewlett, NY .... (516) 295-4026
Porter, Ray/ 330 E 33rd St, New York, NY .... (212) 685-2375
POTTS, CAROLYN & ASSOCIATES/ 3 E. Ontario #25,
   Chicago, IL.. (312) 935-1707
   See our ad on page 155
Powell, Ivan/ 58 W. 15th Street, New York, NY .... (212) 741-2539
Powers, Lisa/ 18 E. 65th Street, New York, NY .... (212) 249-9307
Powers, Richard/ 34 Bloomer Road, Ridgefield, CT........... (203) 438-2511
Price, George/ Tenafly, NJ .... (201) 568-2880
Priestley, S. J., Illustration/ 241 West Emerson Street,
   Melrose, MA.. (617) 665-5892
Prime Design/ 37 Elm St, Westfield, NJ .... (201) 233-6689
PROCHNOW, BILL/ 1717 Union St., San Francisco, CA .... (415) 673-0825
   See our ad on page 153
Provensen, Alice and Martin/ Box 171 Meadowbrook Lane,
   R D Staatsburg, NY .... (914) 266-3245
Pruyn, Glen/ 800 Cottman #105a, Philadelphia, PA .... (215) 722-1323
Publishers Graphics Inc/ 49 Richmondville Avenue,
   Westport, CT... (203) 226-3233
Pucci, Albert John/ New York, NY .... (212) 737-5062
Punchatz, Don Ivan/ 6 Jane St, New York, NY .... (212) 989-7074
Punz/ New York, NY.. (212) 355-1316
Purdom, Bill/ 780 Madison Avenue Apt. 7A, New York, NY .... (212) 988-4566
Pushpin Lubalin Peckolick/ 67 Irving Place, New York, NY .... (212) 674-8080
Putkowski, Gregory/ 169 Glascoe Avenue, Staten Island, NY .... (212) 981-0555
Putt, Glenna/ 101 W 81st Street, New York, NY .... (212) 677-0427
Pyk, Jan/ 340 East 93rd Street, New York, NY .... (212) 876-9749
PYLE, CHUCK/ 146 Tenth Ave., San Francisco, CA .... (415) 751-8087
   See our ad on page 156
Quon, Mike Design Office/ 53 Spring St., New York, NY ..... (212) 226-6024
RADEN STUDIO/ 210 W. 67th Ter., Kansas City, MO .... (816) 421-5079
   See our ad on page 157
Radigan, Bob/ 353 West 53rd Street, New York, NY .... (212) 730-0144
Radiomayonnaise Productions/ 112a Appleton St, Boston, MA ...... (617) 536-5440
Rafkin-Rubin, Inc/ 1466 Broadway, New York, NY .... (212) 869-2540
Raglin, Tim/ 138 W. 74th Street, New York, NY .... (213) 873-0538
Randall, Deborah K./ 128 Elmwood Avenue, Norberth, PA........... (215) 667-5923

Rane, Walter/ 310 Madison Ave. #1225, New York, NY .... (212) 867-8092
Rapecis Associates Inc/ 17 E 45th St, New York, NY .... (212) 697-1760
Rapp, Gerald & Cullen Inc/ 108 East 35th Street #4,
   New York, NY... (212) 889-3337
Raymond, Larry/ PO Box 304, Scaneateles, NY .... (315) 685-8620
Redell, Jacqueline/ 58 W. 15th Street, New York, NY .... (212) 741-2539
Reinert, Kirk/ 310 Madison Ave. #1225, New York, NY ..... (212) 867-8092
Reingold, Alan/ 155 E 38th St, New York, NY .... (212) 697-6170
Reinharz, Hedy/ 222 E. 75th Street, New York, NY .... (212) 988-8009
Remington, Barbara/ 9 E 17th St, New York, NY .... (212) 675-8418
Renard, Madeline/ 501 5th Ave #1407, New York, NY ..... (212) 490-2450
Renfro, Ed/ 353 West 53rd Street, New York, NY .... (212) 582-0023
Reott, Paul/ 51-10 Van Horn St., Queens, NY .... (212) 426-1928
Resicoff, Joel/ 121 Second Ave, New York, NY .... (212) 254-0746
Reynard, June/ 75 Perry St, New York, NY .... (212) 989-5186
REYNOLDS, SCOTT/ 308 W. 30th St. #9b, New York, NY .... (212) 239-0009
   See our ad on page 158
Richards, Linda/ 128 E. 91st St., New York, NY .... (212) 348-3781
Rich Art Graphics/ 1305 Vine St, Philadelphia, PA........... (215) 922-1539
Richer, Paul/ 113 W 74th St, Belle Harbor, NY .... (212) 799-5622
Rickerd, David/ 18 University Ave., Chatham, NJ .... (201) 635-9513
Rigo, Martin/ 43 E. 19th St., New York, NY..................... (212) 254-4996
RILEY, FRANK/ 333 E. 30th St., New York, NY .... (212) 679-1358
   See our ad on page 119
Ritter, Edward/ 10 Tulane Road, Glen Cove, NY .... (516) 671-4493
Rivkin, Miriam C./ 96 5th Avenue Apt. 2F, New York, NY .... (212) 989-9352
Rixford, Ellen/ 308 W. 97th Street #71, New York, NY ..... (212) 865-5686
Rizzo, George A/ 323 East 53 Street, New York, NY .... (212) 688-5441
Rizzotto, Rick/ 149 Leavitt Street, Hingman, MA .... (617) 749-2453
Robbins, Carrie/ 11 W 30th Street 15th Floor,
   New York City, NY .... (212) 564-8625
Roberts, Cheryl/ 200 E 78th St, New York, NY .... (212) 570-9069
Roberts Media/ 3 E. Elm St. Suite 3E, Greenwich, CT ..... (203) 869-5265
Roberts,Stefan K. Assoc., Inc./ 155 East 47th Street,
   New York, NY... (212) 688-9798
Rodericks, Michael/ 15 W. 72nd St., New York, NY .... (212) 799-2231
Rodico Prato/ 154 West 57th Street, New York, NY .... (212) 245-5854
Rodin, Christine/ 38 Morton St., New York, NY .... (212) 242-3260
Rodriguez, Bob/ 501 5th Ave #1407, New York, NY .... (212) 490-2450
Rodriguez, Jon/ 172 W. 79th Street, New York, NY .... (212) 787-6518
Rogers, Howard/ Walnut Lane, Weston, CT .... (203) 227-2273
ROGERS, PAUL/ 6376 W. 6th St., Los Angeles, CA .... (213) 934-3395
   See our ad on page 135
Rolnick, Karen/ 366 W 23rd, New York, NY .... (212) 989-4336
Romas/ Graybar Bld. 420 Lexington Av., New York, NY ..... (212) 986-5680
Rongaus, Wayne C./ 395 New Castle Avenue, Sharon, PA .... (412) 946-8321
Rosenbaum, Jonathan/ 185 East 85th Street, New York, NY ...... (212) 369-1925
Rosenberg, Jane/ 1720 2nd Avenue #3C, New York, NY ..... (212) 722-0326
Rosenblatt, Ralph Barre/ 333 East 84 Street, New York, NY .... (212) 535-3978
Rosenbloom Richard/ New York, NY................................ (212) 986-3282
Rosen, Lauren/ 309 W 104th Street Apt 4C, New York, NY .... (212) 222-3810
Rosenthal, Audrey/ 110 New England Avenue, Stamford, CT ...... (203) 322-0882
Rosenthal, Doug/ 24 Fifth Ave., New York, NY................ (212) 475-9422
ROSENTHAL, MARC/ 230 Cointon St., Brooklyn, NY .... (718) 855-3071
   See our ad on page 159
Rosenthal, Sidney J., Ph.D./ Arrco Medical Art 909 Beacon,
   Boston, MA.. (617) 266-2680
Rosner, Meryl/ 342 Madison Ave Room 261, New York, NY ..... (212) 986-3282
Ross, Barry/ 211 W 102nd St, New York, NY .... (212) 663-7386
Ross Design Assoc./ 27 W. 20th St., New York, NY .... (212) 206-0044
Rosse, Allainora/ Court Street, Haverhill, NH.................. (603) 989-5522
Ross, Geremy/ 26 Vautrinot Avenue, Hull, MA .... (617) 925-0176
Rossin Creative Group Inc/ 1 E 42nd St, New York, NY ..... (212) 599-0173
Ross, Jamie L./ 238 E. 58 St., New York, NY .... (212) 838-0738
Ross, Larry/ 53 Sairview Ave, Madison, NJ .... (201) 377-6859
Ross, Richard/ 71 Redbrook Road, Great Neck, NY .... (516) 466-3339
Roth, Adele Studio/ 24 W 55th St, New York, NY .... (212) 247-6297
ROTHER, SUE/ 1537 Franklin St. #103,
   San Francisco, CA.. (415) 441-8893
   See our ad on page 161
ROTH, ROGER/ 1960 Broadway #2E, New York, NY .... (212) 873-3797
   See our ad on page 160
Ruan, Roy/ 175-20 Wexford Terrace, Jamaica Estates, NY .... (212) 297-7911
RUDDELL, GARY/ 6376 W. 6th St., Los Angeles, CA............ (213) 934-3395
   See our ad on page 137

Ruddell, Gary/Rep: Barney Kane/ 120 E. 32nd St.,
New York, NY.. (212) 206-0322
Ruenitz, George/ 21 Carlin St., Norwalk, CT .... (203) 846-9249
Ruff, Donna/ 42 E. 23rd St., New York, NY .... (212) 505-6913
Ruffins, Reynold/ 38 E. 21st Street, New York, NY .... (212) 674-8150
Ruland, Mike/ 353 West 53 St Suite 1W, New York, NY .... (212) 682-2462
Rush, John/ 185 East 85th Street, New York, NY .... (212) 369-1925
Russell, Anthony Inc/ 170 Fifth Ave, New York, NY .... (212) 255-0650
Rutherford, Jenny/ 185 Goodhill Road, Weston, CT .... (203) 226-7674
Ryan, Terry/ 9 E. 32nd, New York, NY .... (212) 688-1080
Sabin, Bob/ 310 Madison Ave. #1225, New York, NY .... (212) 867-8092
Sabin, Mark/ 115 Central Park W, New York, NY .... (212) 362-6965
Sacks, Shelly/ 406 Crosby Avenue, West Deal, NJ .... (201) 531-4431
SAKAHARA, DICK/ 28826 Cedarbluff Dr.,
Palos Verdes, CA .... (213) 541-8187
See our ad on page 132
Saldutti, Denise/ 463 West Street Apt 354 H, New York, NY .... (212) 255-9328
Salerno, Steve/ 120 W 81st Street, New York, NY .... (212) 580-1321
Salmon - Greene, Meryl/ 401 East 74 Street, New York, NY .... (212) 734-4964
Sametz, Roger/ 40 W. Newton Street, Boston, MA .... (617) 266-8577
Sanderson, Ruth/ 185 Goodhill Rd., Weston, CT .... (203) 226-7674
SANO, KAZUHIKO/ 105 Stadium Ave., Mill Valley, CA .... (415) 381-6377
See our ad on page 162
Santore, Charles/ 138 S. 20th Street, Philadelphia, PA .... (215) 563-0430
Santoro, Christopher/ 80 Seaman Ave, New York, NY .... (212) 532-0928
Sargent, Claudia Karabaic/ 15-38 126th Street,
College Point, NY .... (718) 461-8280
Saris, Anthony/ 103 E. 86th Street, New York, NY .... (212) 831-6353
Sarsony, Robert/ 60 Gristmill Road, Randolph, NJ .... (201) 328-8988
Sassafras Studios/ 307 Fourth St, Annapolis, MD .... (301) 263-3364
Sauber, Rob/ Graybar Bld. 420 Lexington Av., New York, NY .... (212) 986-5680
Saunders, Gail/ 1 Longfellow Place, Boston, MA .... (617) 723-6277
Saunders, Hoyt/ 205 E 42nd Street, New York, NY .... (212) 599-0280
Savitt, Sam/ Dingle Ridge, North Salem, NY .... (914) 669-5428
Scarmato, Tony Inc/ 16 W 46th St, New York, NY .... (212) 869-8787
Schaare, Harry/ 310 Madison Ave. #1225, New York, NY .... (212) 867-8092
Schatzky, Sidney/ 23 E 20th St, New York, NY .... (212) 777-5966
Scherman, John/ 310 E 12th St, New York, NY .... (212) 473-7237
Schiffrin, Rebecca/ 22 W. 95th Street, New York, NY .... (212) 866-0602
Schlegel, Donald/ 208 E. 84th Street, New York, NY .... (212) 879-4829
Schleinkofer, David/ Graybar Bld. 420 Lexington Av.,
New York, NY.. (212) 986-5680
Schmidt, Bill/ 310 Madison Ave. #1225, New York, NY .... (212) 867-8092
Schmidt, Chuck/ 420 Madison Ave, New York, NY .... (212) 980-3510
Schneider, Frederick & Grafis/ 260 Montague Road,
Leverett, MA .... (413) 549-0704
Schongut, Emanuel/ 194 Third Ave., New York, NY .... (212) 475-0440
Schorr, Kathy Staico/ New York, NY .... (212) 684-3598
Schorr, Todd/ 353 W 53 St Apt 1W, New York, NY .... (212) 682-2462
Schottland, Miriam/ 470 W. 23rd St., New York, NY .... (212) 242-6367
Schuman, Harold/ 359 Boylston St, Boston, MA .... (617) 266-0911
Schwab, Michael/ 501 5th Ave #1407, New York, NY .... (212) 490-2450
Schwartz, Daniel/ 48 E. 13th Street, New York, NY .... (212) 533-0237
Schwartz, Frank/ New York, NY .... (212) 689-3902
Schwarz, Jill/ 80 N Moore St, New York, NY .... (212) 227-2444
Schwenk, George/ Rd 2, Garrison, NY .... (914) 265-2855
Scott, Louis Assoc Inc/ 22 E 21st St, New York, NY .... (212) 674-0215
SCRIBNER, JO ANNE/ 157 W. 57th St., New York, NY .... (212) 247-1130
See our ad on pages 62, 63
Scrofani, Joe C/O America Art/ 353 W 53rd Street Suite 1W,
New York, NY.. (212) 682-2462
Seaver, Jeff/ 130 W. 24th Street, New York, NY .... (212) 255-8299
Selby, Bill/ 342 Madison Ave., New York, NY .... (212) 697-8525
Sell, Michael/ 253 W 72nd Street, New York, NY .... (212) 580-1321
Sempe, Jean J./E.T.Riley,Inc./ 215 E. 31 St., New York, NY .... (212) 684-3448
Service Art Studio Inc/ 49 W 45th St, New York, NY .... (212) 398-1212
Severance, Gail/ New York, NY .... (212) 689-3902
Shalansky, Len/ 59 Darling St, Warwick, RI............................. (401) 738-3215
Shanner & Pappas/ 528 Clinton Ave, Bridgeport, CT .... (203) 576-1516
Shap, Sandra/ 420 Madison Avenue, New York, NY .... (212) 980-3510
Shareff, Ira/ 81 Irving Pl, New York, NY .... (212) 475-3963
Sharnn, Matthew/ 267 Fifth Ave., New York, NY .... (212) 686-5576
SHARPE, JIM/ 5 Side Hill Rd., Westport, CT .... (203) 226-9984
See our ad on page 163
Shaw & Koulermos Inc/ 110 E 59th St, New York, NY .... (212) 688-5290

Shea, Mary Anne/ 224 W. 29th Street, New York, NY .... (212) 239-1076
Sheba, Ross/ New York, NY .... (212) 799-8783
Sheila Camera/ 229 East 79th Street, New York, NY .... (212) 532-0928
Shekerjian, Haig & Regina/ New York, NY.............................. (212) 737-5062
Shelley, Lee Graphics/ 37 Hale Ave, Cypress Hills, NY .... (212) 277-9376
SHEPHARD, TOM/ 1295 Old River Rd., Cleveland, OH .... (216) 621-1771
See our ad on page 77
Sherman, Harriet/ 55 W. 95th Street, New York, NY .... (212) 222-6088
Sherman, Oren/ 30 Ipswich Street Studio 209, Boston, MA .... (617) 437-7368
Sherman, Otto David/ 295 Madison Ave Suite 926,
New York, NY.. (212) 684-7020
Shore, Robert/ 41 Union Square, New York, NY .... (212) 989-2396
Shub, Steve/ 114 E. 32nd St., New York, NY .... (212) 685-2770
SHURTLEFF, GINI/ 43 E. 19th St., New York, NY .... (212) 254-4996
See our ad on page 164
Sidney, Douglas Graphic Design/ 90 Painters Mill Rd. Suite I,
Owings Mills, MD .... (301) 363-6555
Silber, Maurice/ 183-07 69th Ave, Fresh Meadows, NY .... (212) 969-7744
Silbert, Bill/ 1714 E. 23rd Street, Brooklyn, NY .... (212) 627-0452
Silverman, Burt/ 324 W. 71st Street, New York, NY .... (212) 799-3399
Silvestri, Marco Assoc/ 2713 Rt 23, Newfoundland, NJ .... (201) 697-0018
Silvey, W.H./ 3442 90th St, Jackson Heights, NY..................... (212) 426-7286
Simeone, Lauren E./ 931 N. Lawrence Street,
Philadelphia, PA .... (215) 925-8181
Simmons, Ray/ 119-21 222nd St, Cambria Heights, NY .... (212) 528-9272
Sims, Blanche/ 185 Goodhill Road, Weston, CT .... (203) 226-7674
Sinagra, Attilio/ 2305 Arctic Avenue, Atlantic City, NJ .... (609) 344-9160
Singer, Paul Design/ 494 14th St., New York, NY .... (212) 499-8172
Siracusa, Catherine/ 112 West 74th Street, New York, NY .... (212) 580-8084
Skardinski, Stan/ 201 East 28th Street, New York, NY .... (212) 532-0928
Sketch Pad Studio, The/ 6 Jane Street, New York, NY .... (212) 989-7074
Skibinski, Ray/ 694 Harrell Avenue, Woodbridge, NJ .... (201) 634-3074
Skolsky, Mark/ 429 E 82 St, New York, NY .... (212) 288-4262
Slackman, Chas. B./ 320 E 57th, New York, NY .... (212) 758-8233
Slater, John H/ 93 1/2 E 7th St, New York, NY .... (212) 669-7301
Sloan, Lois/ 3133 Connecticut Avenue, Washington, DC .... (202) 387-3305
Sloan, William/ 444 E. 82nd Street #12C, New York, NY .... (212) 988-6643
Smallwood, Steve/ 50 W. 34th St. Apt. 6c1, New York, NY .... (212) 564-7923
Smith, Cornelia/ New York, NY .... (212) 689-3902
Smith, Douglas T./ 405 Washington Street #2, Brookline, MA....... (617) 566-3816
Smith, Ellen/ 140-150 Huyshope Ave 5th Fl, Hartford, CT........... (203) 525-5117
Smith, Elwood H/ 67 Irving Place, New York, NY .... (212) 674-8080
SMITH, JAMES NOEL/ 1011 N. Clinton, Dallas, TX .... (214) 946-4255
See our ad on page 165
Smith, Jolyn/ 430 West 24th Street Apt 2A, New York, NY .... (212) 989-0045
Smith, Jos A/ 159 John Street 6 Floor, New York, NY .... (203) 746-1858
Smith, Laura/ 61 Lexington Ave., New York, NY .... (212) 889-0490
Smith, Robert/ 126 E. 10th Street, New York, NY.................... (212) 677-3059
Smith, Tyler Art Direction/ 127 Dorrance St, Providence, RI .... (401) 751-1220
Smith, William/ PO Box 227 Windy Bush Road, Pineville, PA....... (215) 598-7377
Smollin, Michael/ 15 Reichert Circle, Westport, CT .... (203) 227-3114
SMP Graphic Service Center/ 26 E 22nd St, New York, NY .... (212) 254-2282
Smythe, Danny/ 420 Madison Ave. #401, New York, NY .... (212) 980-3501
Snyder, Nancy/ 760 George Street Apt. 2, Norristown, PA .... (215) 272-6432
Society of Illustrators/ 128 E 63rd, New York, NY .... (212) 838-2560
Soderlind, Kirsten/ 111 Wooster St. PHC, New York, NY .... (212) 925-0491
Sofka, Ross/ 621 Myrtle Avenue, Roselle Park, NJ .... (201) 245-3453
Soileau, Hodges/ 350 Flax Hill Rd., Norwalk, CT .... (203) 852-0751
Solomon, Debra/ 536 W. 111th St. #55, New York, NY .... (212) 662-5619
Soloski, Tommy/ 106 East 19th St #1201, New York, NY........... (212) 674-1461
Sopin, Nan Grover/ 150 Stokes St, Freehold, NJ .... (201) 462-7154
Sottung, George/ 111 Tower Rd, Brookfield Ctr, CT.................. (203) 775-6708
SOUTH, RANDY/ 48 2nd St. 5th Fl., San Francisco, CA .... (415) 543-1170
See our ad on page 166
SOYKA, ED/ 231 Lafayette Ave., Peekskill, NY .... (914) 737-2230
See our ad on page 167
Spanfeller, Jim/ Mustato Road, Katonah, NY .... (914) 232-3546
Sparks, Barbara/ 2 West Rocks Road, Norwalk, CT................... (203) 866-2002
Sparks, Richard/ 2 West Rocks Road, Norwalk, CT .... (203) 866-2002
Spector, Joel/ Graybar Bld. 420 Lexington Av., New York, NY ...... (212) 986-5680
SPENCER, JOE/ 11201 Valley Spring Ln.,
Studio City, CA... (818) 760-0216
See our ad on pages 168, 169
Spencer, Richard/ 127 Mt. Auburn Street, Cambridge, MA........... (617) 492-5618
Spina, Paul/ 94 Bowery, New York, NY................................. (212) 966-7244

Spohn, Cliff/ Graybar Bld. 420 Lexington Av., New York, NY .... (212) 986-5680
Spollen, Chris/Moonlight Press/ 203 Center Street,
   Staten Island, NY .... (212) 979-9695
Sposato, John/ 43 E 22 St, New York, NY .... (212) 477-3909
Sprague, Andrew/ 210 E. 84th Street, New York, NY .... (212) 744-2646
Springer, Sally/ 185 Goodhill Road, Weston, CT .... (203) 226-7674
Stabin, Victor/ 100 W 15th Str, New York, NY .... (212) 243-7688
Stahl, Benjamin F./ Litchfield, CT .... (203) 567-8005
Stahl, Nancy/ 194 Third Ave., New York, NY .... (212) 475-0440
Staico, Kathy/ 353 West 53rd Street, New York, NY .... (212) 582-0023
Stalland, Christiane/ 126 E. 30th Street, New York, NY .... (212) 679-2569
Stamaty, Mark Alan/ 118 Mac Dougal Street, New York, NY .... (212) 475-1626
Stankiewicz, Steve/ 335 1st Avenue, New York, NY .... (212) 477-4229
Stark, Bruce/ 161 Chestnut, Emerson, NJ .... (201) 262-8975
Stavrinos, George/ 76 W 86th, New York, NY .... (212) 724-1557
Steadman, Barbara/ 330 E. 33rd Street #10-A, New York, NY ...... (212) 684-6326
Steadman, E. T./ 470 W. 23rd St., New York, NY .... (212) 242-6367
STEARNEY, MARK/ 405 N. Wabash, Chicago, IL .... (312) 644-6669
   See our ad on page 170
STEELE, ROBERT GANTT/ 14 Wilmot St.,
   San Francisco, CA.. (415) 885-2611
   See our ad on page 171
Steinberg, Claudia/ 21 E. 10th Street, New York, NY .... (212) 533-6344
Steiner, Frank/ 310 Madison Ave. #1225, New York, NY .... (212) 867-8092
Sternglass, Arno/ 6 Jane St, New York, NY .... (212) 989-7074
Sterrett, Jane/ 160 Fifth Ave., New York, NY .... (212) 929-2566
Stevens, Phyllis/ 112 E Tenth St, New York, NY .... (212) 674-0496
STEWART, JONATHAN/ 113 S. 20th St.,
   Philadelphia, PA... (215) 561-0805
   See our ad on page 172
Stewart, Pat/ 201 East 28th Street, New York, NY .... (212) 532-0928
St. George, Bill/ 286 Summer St, Boston, MA .... (617) 338-6788
Stiles, Fran/ 161 W. 54th Street #804, New York, NY .... (212) 757-4278
Stillman, Susan/ 126 W 71 St, New York, NY .... (212) 724-5634
Stinson, Paul/ 1320 H Street, Belmar, NJ .... (201) 681-4623
Stirnweis, Shannon/ 31 Fawn Pl., Wilton, CT .... (203) 762-7058
Stivers, Don/ 71 Musket Ridge Road, Wilton, CT .... (203) 762-8480
Stokes, Linda/ 10 Phillene Dr, Norwalk, CT.......................... (203) 866-2735
Stone Associates/ 1133 Broadway, New York, NY .... (212) 675-0226
Stone, D.K./ 6 Farmview Rd., Port Washington, NY .... (516) 627-7040
Stone, Gilbert L/ Box 216, Patterson, NY .... (914) 878-9422
Stone, Hal/ 105 Manchester Drive, Mount Kisco, NY .... (914) 666-6811
Stone, Sylvia/ 24 Prudence Drive, Stamford, CT .... (203) 322-2634
Storey, Barron/ 333 E 30 St, New York, NY .... (212) 679-1358
Stott, Dot/ 201 East 28th Street, New York, NY .... (212) 532-0928
Strandquest, Dominique Mich/ 70 W. 71st Street,
   New York, NY .... (212) 580-3796
Strimban, Robert/ 349 W. 20th Street, New York, NY .... (212) 243-6965
Studio Six/ 55 Bethune St, New York, NY .... (212) 242-1407
Studio 23/ 6 West 20 Street, New York, NY .... (212) 243-7362
Studio 900/ 900 Newbridge Ave, N Bellmore, NY .... (516) 221-8076
Suares, J C/ New York, NY .... (212) 734-6989
Sullivan, Suzanne Hughes/ 1960 Broadway Ste. 2e,
   New York, NY .... (212) 873-3797
SUMICHRAST, JOZEF STUDIO/ 860 N. Northwoods Dr.,
   Deerfield, IL... (312) 945-6353
   See our ad on page 173
Sunlight Pictures Corp./ 322 E. 39th Street, New York, NY .... (212) 686-5000
Sutton, Judith/ 152 W. 76th Street Apt. 3B, New York, NY .... (212) 496-8314
Swan,Susan Illustration/Design/ 10 Sylvan Rd, South,
   Westport, CT .... (203) 226-9104
Swatek Romanoff Design/ 156 Fifth Ave, New York, NY .... (212) 807-0236
Taback, Simms/ 38 East 21st Street, New York, NY .... (212) 674-8150
Tafuri, Thomas/ 105 W 55, New York, NY .... (212) 757-2431
Takakjian, Asdur/ 17 Merlin Avenue, North Tarrytown, NY .... (914) 631-5553
Tallarico, Tony/ 26 Payan Avenue, Valley Stream, NY .... (516) 561-7822
Tamburine, Jean/ 73 Renolds Drive, Meriden, CT .... (203) 235-1800
Tamura, David/ 153 E 26th St, New York, NY .... (212) 686-4559
Tandem Graphics/ 5313 Waneta Road, Bethesda, MD .... (301) 320-5008
Tankersley, Paul/ 29 Bethune Street, New York, NY .... (212) 924-0015
Tanner, Bert/ 225 E 46 St, New York, NY .... (212) 752-8571
Tapa-Graphics/ 174 5th Avenue, New York, NY .... (212) 243-0176
Tauss, Herb/ S. Mountain Pass, Garrison, NY .... (914) 424-3765
Taylor, Anique/ 322 E. 11th Street, New York, NY .... (212) 477-5245
Taylor, Heather/ 183 Sterling S, Greenport, NY .... (516) 477-2447

Taylor, Jody/ 201 East 28th Street, New York, NY .... (212) 532-0928
Taylor, Katrina/ 553 Woodbury Rd, Huntington, NY .... (516) 367-4026
Teddy Studio/ 41 Union Sq W, New York, NY .... (212) 929-4426
Tennant, Craig/ 54 Clevland St, Ramsey, NJ .... (201) 825-7661
TENNISON, JAMES E./ 713 Highland Dr., Arlington, TX .... (817) 861-1550
   See our ad on page 174
Tercovich, Douglas Assoc/ 575 Madison Ave, New York, NY........ (212) 838-4800
Terreson, Jeffrey/ Graybar Bld. 420 Lexington Av.,
   New York, NY .... (212) 986-5680
Thaler, Mike/ PO Box 223 Rd 1, Stone Ridge, NY .... (914) 687-7453
Thom, Allison/ 540 W. 55th Street, New York, NY .... (212) 582-5667
Thompson Asso Inc/ 752 Bloomfield Ave, Windsor, CT .... (203) 688-7281
Thompson, Ken/ 20 W. 11th Street, New York, NY .... (212) 477-0608
Thompson, Sue/ R 1 Box 131B, Pomfret Center, CT .... (203) 974-2030
Thorpe, Peter/ 254 Park Ave S, New York, NY .... (212) 477-0131
TIGERFLY, INC./ 225 Santa Monica Blvd. Rm. 404, Santa Monica, CA ....
Timm, Clifford/ 138 Dean Street, Brooklyn, NY .... (212) 522-6588
Timm, Clifford/ 185 Goodhill Road, Weston, CT .... (203) 226-7674
Timmins, Jim/ 226 Greenwood Ave, Bethel, CT...................... (203) 743-3357
Tinkelman, Murray/ 60 East 42nd Street, New York, NY .... (212) 682-1490
Tise, Katherine/ 200 E 78th St #8C, New York, NY .... (212) 570-9069
Tomlinson, Richard/ 319 E. 24th St., New York, NY .... (212) 685-0552
Toulmin-Rothe, Ann/ Studio 2 49 Richmondville Ave,
   Westport, CT .... (203) 226-5008
Travers, Bob/ 310 Madison Ave. #1225, New York, NY .... (212) 867-8092
Trevor, Emily/ 116 Pinehurst Avenue, New York, NY .... (212) 781-6868
Tritchonis, Anestos/ 38 Stone Henge Road, Weston, CT .... (203) 227-4385
Trull, John/ 1573 York Avenue, New York, NY .... (212) 535-5383
Tsui, George/ 2250 Elliot St., Merrick, NY .... (516) 223-8474
TUCKER, EZRA/ 1295 Old River Rd., Cleveland, OH................ (216) 621-1771
   See our ad on page 72
Tucker, Tom/ 2014 W 8th St, Erie, PA .... (814) 459-2683
Tughan, James/ New York, NY .... (212) 684-4255
Tuke, Joni & Associates, Inc./ 368 W. Huron Street,
   Chicago, IL .... (312) 787-6826
Tulka, Richard/ 19 Fiske Place Apt. C3, Brooklyn, NY .... (212) 636-1761
Tunstull, Glen/ 120 E. 32nd Street, New York, NY .... (212) 689-3233
Uram, Lauren/ 251 Washington Ave., New York, NY .... (212) 789-7717
VACCARELLO, PAUL/ 1749 N. Wells St., Chicago, IL................ (312) 664-2233
   See our ad on page 175
Valeho, Boris/ 24 St. Andrews Place, Yonkers, NY.................. (914) 423-8694
Valen Associates/ Box 8, Westport, CT .... (203) 227-7806
Valen Assoc/Modell, Frank/ Box 8, Westport, CT .... (203) 227-7806
Valla, Victor R/ Box 214 Lyons Place, Basking Ridge, NJ .... (201) 221-9034
Van Horn, Michael/ 425 W 23rd St Rm 17A, New York, NY......... (212) 243-2750
Van Ryzin, Peter/ 32 Edge Water Drive, Old Greenledge, CT........ (203) 637-8076
VARGO, KURT/ 111 E. 12th St., New York, NY .... (212) 982-6098
   See our ad on page 176
Veno, Joe/ 20 Cutler Rd., Hamilton, MA .... (617) 468-3165
Ventilla Istvan/ 715 Park Ave, New York, NY........................ (212) 226-3866
Vermont, Hillary/ 218 E. 17th Street, New York, NY .... (212) 674-3845
Vernaglia, Michael/ 1251 Bloomfield St, Hoboken, NJ .... (201) 659-7750
Vetromile, Alfred/ 137 Cutler Rd, Greenwich, CT .... (203) 869-6506
Victor, Joan Berg/ 863 Park Ave, New York, NY .... (212) 988-2773
Viewpoint Graphics Inc/ 10 Park Ave, New York, NY .... (212) 685-0560
Vignelli, Massimo/ 410 E 62nd, New York, NY .... (212) 593-1416
Virgona, Hank/ 41 Union Square, New York, NY .... (212) 243-5874
Visible Studio/ 99 Lexington Ave, New York, NY .... (212) 683-8530
Viskupic, Gary/ 7 Westfield Dr., Center Port, NY .... (516) 757-9021
Visu Com Inc/ 1207 Bernard, Baltimore, MD .... (301) 947-6400
VITSKY, SALLY/ 157 W. 57th St., New York, NY.................... (212) 247-1130
   See our ad on pages 64, 65
Viviano, Sam/ 25 West 13th Street, New York, NY .... (212) 242-1471
Vogt, Elaine/ 242 E. 83rd Street #4D, New York, NY .... (212) 988-6430
Voth, Gregory E/ 231 West 20, New York City, NY.................. (212) 807-9766
Waitzman, William/ 265 Riverside Dr., New York, NY .... (212) 662-2645
Wajdowicz, Jurek/ 1123 Broadway, New York, NY .... (212) 807-8144
Wald, Carol/ 57 E 78th St, New York, NY .... (212) 737-4559
Waldman, Michael/ 506 W 42nd St, New York, NY .... (212) 239-8245
Waldman, Neil/ 12 Turner Road, Pearl River, NY .... (914) 735-8131
Waldman, Veronica/ 115 E Ninth Street, New York, NY............. (212) 260-3552
Walker, Bob/ 420 Lexington Ave Rm 2743, New York, NY.......... (212) 688-4555
Walker, Charles W/ 18 Paul Pl, Roosevelt, NY .... (516) 379-3039
Walker, Jim/ New York, NY .... (212) 737-5062
WALKER, JOHN S. P./ 47 Jane St., New York, NY.................. (212) 242-3435
   See our ad on page 177

ILLUSTRATION/East

Walker, Norman/ 37 Stone Henge Road, Weston, CT.................. (203) 226-5812
Waller, Charles/ New York, NY .... (212) 752-4392
WALTON, STUART C./ 1295 Old River Rd.,
   Cleveland, OH... (216) 621-1771
   See our ad on page 76
Walz, Richard/ New York, NY .... (212) 929-5840
Wanamaker, JoAnn/ 225 W. 86th Street, New York, NY.............. (212) 724-1786
Wanke, Mike/ 8 Bonny Road, Brookfield, CT............................ (203) 775-4609
Ward, Wendy Freelance Finder/ 200 Madison Ave, New York, NY... (212) 684-0590
WARNER, MICHELE/ 1011 N. Clinton, Dallas, TX.................... (214) 946-1430
   See our ad on page 178
Wartik, Hersch/ 141 E. 33rd Street, New York, NY .... (212) 685-4250
Wasserman, Myron Studio/ 113 Arch Street, Philadelphia, PA .... (215) 922-4545
Wasson, Cameron/ 4 S. Portland Ave. #3, New York, NY............ (212) 875-8277
Watson, Karen/ 100 Churchill Avenue, Arlington, MA .... (617) 641-1420
Watts, Mark/ Graybar Bld. 420 Lexington Av., New York, NY .... (212) 986-5680
Wax, Amy Illustrators/ 310 E Ninth St, New York, NY .... (212) 982-8341
Waxberg & Associates/ 8-10 Broad St, Redbank, NJ.................. (212) 567-3121
Weaver/ 129 W 22nd St, New York, NY .... (212) 242-8215
Weaver, Jack/ 70 Canal St, Yardley, PA................................... (215) 493-6572
Weaver, Robert/ 42 E. 12th Street, New York, NY..................... (212) 254-4289
Weiman, Jonathan/ 147 W. 85th Street Apt. 3F, New York, NY ..... (212) 787-3184
Weissman, Sam Q./ 2510 Fenton Avenue, Bronx, NY .... (212) 840-3300
Weller, Linda Boehm/ 185 Goodhill Road, Weston, CT................ (203) 226-7674
Wells, Skip/ 244 W. 10th Street, New York, NY .... (212) 242-5563
WELLS, SUSAN/ 5134 Timber Trail N.E., Atlanta, GA .... (404) 255-1430
   See our ad on page 179
Weymouth Design/ 234 Congress St, Boston, MA...................... (617) 542-2647
Whelan, Michael/ 172 Candlewood Lake Road, Brookfield, CT .... (203) 775-6679
Whistl'n Dixie/ 200 E. 58th Street, New York, NY..................... (212) 935-9522
White, Charlie III/ 194 Third Avenue, New York, NY.................. (212) 475-0440
Whitehouse, Debora/ 55 Bethune St., New York, NY.................. (212) 242-1407
Whitesides, Kim/ New York, NY .... (212) 490-2450
White, Willardson Studio/ 194 Third Ave, New York, NY............. (212) 475-0440
Whitman Studio Inc/ 2 Market St, Paterson, NJ .... (201) 684-7511
Whittingham, William/ 19 Timberridge Road, Madison, CT........... (203) 245-0057
WILCOX, DAVID/ 135 E. 54th St., New York, NY .... (201) 832-7368
   See our ad on page 180
Wilkinson, Bill/ 155 E. 38th Street, New York, NY .... (212) 697-6170
Wilkinson, Chuck/ 60 E. 42nd St. #505, New York, NY............... (212) 682-1490
Willardson & White/ 194 Third Ave., New York, NY .... (212) 475-0440
Williams, Frank/ Philadelphia, PA .... (215) 928-0918
Williams, Oliver/ 141 5th Avenue, New York, NY .... (212) 674-1903
Williams, Paul/ PO Box 1203, Weston, CT .... (203) 986-5680

Williams, Richard/ 112 Ruskin Ave, Syracuse, NY .... (212) 741-2539
Williams, Richard/ 58 West 15th Street, New York, NY .... (212) 741-2539
Wilson, Gahan/ New York, NY .... (212) 772-2363
Wimmer, Chuck/ 185 Goodhill Rd., Weston, CT .... (203) 226-7674
Wimmer, Donald E./ 10 Nyma Way, Succasunna, NJ.................. (201) 584-6904
Winborg, Larry/ 120 E. 32nd Street, New York, NY .... (212) 689-3233
Winsten, M. W./ 267 Fifth Ave., New York, NY .... (212) 686-5576
Witzig, Fred/ 9 W Ivy Ln, Tenafly, NJ .... (201) 567-1834
Wohlberg, Ben/ 43 Great Jones St., New York, NY .... (212) 254-9663
Wolff, Punz/ 151 E. 20th St. #5G, New York, NY .... (212) 254-5705
WOLF, LESLIE/ 3 E. Ontario #25, Chicago, IL........................ (312) 935-1707
   See our ad on page 155
Wolkcas Advertising Inc/ 8 Wade Rd, Latham, NY .... (518) 783-5151
Wood, Alan Graphic Design Inc/ 274 Madison Avenue,
   New York, NY.. (212) 889-5195
Woodend, Jim/ 342 Madison Avenue, New York, NY .... (212) 697-8525
Wood, Muriel/ New York, NY .... (212) 737-5062
Wood, Page/ 114 E. 32nd St., New York, NY............................ (212) 685-2770
Words & Company Inc/ 3312 M St NW, Washington, DC .... (202) 337-5850
Worldling Designs Inc/ 320 É 22 St, New York, NY .... (212) 505-7732
Wright, Bob Creative Group/ 247 North Goodman St,
   Rochester, NY... (716) 271-2280
Wright, Walter/ 225 Lafayette St., New York, NY..................... (212) 334-9310
Write, Walter/ New York, NY .... (212) 929-5840
Wronker, Eytan/ 144-44 Village Road, Jamaica, NY .... (212) 380-3990
Wynne, Patricia/ 446 Central Park W, New York, NY .... (212) 865-1059
Yerkes, Lane/ 85 E. Plumstead Avenue, Lansdowne, PA .... (215) 623-0623
Yoshi, Miyake/ 185 Goodhill Rd, Weston, CT .... (203) 226-7674
Young, Robert Assoc./ 78 N. Union St., Rochester, NY .... (716) 546-1973
Yule, Susan Hunt/ 176 Elizabeth, New York, NY....................... (212) 226-0439
Zagorski, Stanislaw/ 142 E. 35th Street, New York, NY .... (212) 532-2348
Zaid, Barry/ New York, NY .... (212) 751-4656
Zalben, Jane Breskin/ Port Washington, NY .... (516) 944-8590
Zallinger, Jean Day/ 5060 Ridge Road, New Haven, CT .... (203) 288-0384
Zander, Hans/ New York, NY .... (212) 737-5062
Zann, Nicky/ 210 E. 29th St., New York, NY .... (212) 684-6144
Zapatka, Barbara/ 111 Bank Street, New York, NY .... (212) 243-2691
Zdinak, William/ 2 Indian Dr, Old Greenwich, CT .... (203) 637-9588
Zelinsky, Paul O./ 142 Montaque Street, Brooklyn, NY .... (212) 855-1841
Zick, Brian/ 194 Third Avenue, New York, NY .... (212) 475-0440
Ziemienski, Dennis/ 121 West 3rd Street #D, New York, NY .... (415) 441-4384
ZIERING, BOB/ 107 E. 38th St., New York, NY...................... (212) 689-5886
   See our ad on pages 14, 15
Zimmerman, Jerry/ 287 Frances Street, Teaneck, NJ .... (201) 836-6469
Zimmerman, Robert/ 191 Stadley Rough Road, Danbury, CT .... (203) 792-0783
Zuckerberg, Stanley/ 21 Old Farm Rd, Levittown, NY................. (516) 735-8862

DESIGN, ART DIRECTION, CREATIVE SERVICES

Aarons, Lawrence Crea Svcs/ 360 Lexington Avenue,
New York, NY .... (212) 247-2777
Abacrome Inc/Custom Banners/ 18 East 16 St, New York, NY ...... (212) 989-1190
Abbe, Dennis/ 246 West End Ave, New York, NY .... (212) 787-3851
Aber, Linda/ 9905 Doubletree Court, Potomac, MD .... (914) 268-7455
Accurate Paste-Ups/ 299 Madison Ave, New York, NY .... (212) 682-4979
Adams Darcy Art Inc/ 1995 Linden Blvd., Elmont, NY .... (516) 825-0022
Ad-Art & Design/ 178 Riverside Ave, Riverside, CT .... (203) 637-9357
Ad Design Concepts/ 226 E 27 #3A, New York, NY .... (212) 685-6353
Addpix Studios/ 54 W. 39, New York, NY .... (212) 398-9470
Adfinity Plus Inc/ 3918 Carrell Blvd, Oceanside, NY .... (516) 536-3236
Adler, Kermit/ Ten Park Avenue 27J, New York, NY .... (212) 391-3516
Adler-Schwartz Graphics, Inc/ 203 E Quadrangle Cross Keys,
Baltimore, MD .... (301) 433-4400
Advertir, Ltd./ 80 West 40th Street, New York, NY .... (212) 840-2710
Advertising Consultants Inc/ Rt 121A, Chester, NH .... (603) 887-4406
Agnew Moyer Smith Inc/ 850 Ridge Ave, Pittsburgh, PA .... (412) 322-6333
Aliman, Elie Graphic Design In/ 134 Spring Street,
New York, NY .... (212) 925-9621
Allen, Carole S./ 4 Hemlock Road, Wayland, MA .... (617) 653-1902
Allerton & Ranick Mktg Commun/ 1101 Clark Bldg,
Pittsburgh, PA .... (412) 261-3816
Alpha Design/ P O Box 1108, Frederick, MD .... (301) 662-3363
Altman, Donna/ 64 N. Moore Street, New York, NY .... (212) 925-5663
Alvine Advertisng Graphics Inc/ 324 Passaic Avenue,
Nutley, NJ .... (201) 235-0734
Amberger, Michael/Design Group/ p.O. Box 164, Hanover, NH ...... (603) 643-8283
American Art Studio/ 228 E 22nd St, New York, NY .... (212) 475-4878
Anastasi, Robert/ John Hancock Tower C/O HHCC, Boston, MA ..... (617) 437-1600
Ancona Design Atelier/ 524 W 43rd, New York, NY .... (212) 947-8287
Andrietta, Marie/ 111 Third Avenue #15E, New York, NY .... (212) 260-3234
Antler & Baldwin Inc/ 7 E 47th St, New York, NY .... (212) 751-2031
A P F Showroom Inc - Frames/ 783 Madison Avenue,
New York, NY .... (212) 988-1090
Appelbaum & Curtis Inc/ 333 E. 49th Street, New York, NY ...... (212) 752-0679
Apteryx, Ltd/ 71 Vanderbilt Ave. Rm. 346, New York, NY .... (212) 838-9483
Art and Design/ 9 Stonecrop Road, Norwalk, CT .... (203) 847-7190
Art Board/ 246 E 44th, New York, NY .... (212) 867-5930
Art Directors Club of Boston/ 214 Beacon Street, Boston, MA ... (617) 536-8999
ARTFILE/ P.O. Box 1024, Cary, NC .... (919) 781-5087
See our ad on page 183
Artifax/ 14 Cogswell Place, New Brunswick, NJ .... (201) 828-0104
Art Pro Graphics/ 7 W. 36th Street, New York, NY .... (212) 594-3031
Art Service Assoc Inc/ 717 Liberty Ave Clark Bldg,
Pittsburgh, PA .... (412) 391-0902
Artstyles Inc./ 701 Smithfield Street, Pittsburgh, PA .... (412) 261-1601
August, Ray/ 149-41 Elm Ave, Flushing, NY .... (212) 445-1792
Bakacs, George/ 33-09 Parsons Blvd., Flushing, NY .... (212) 539-1778
Baker, Fred Productions/ 35 West 92nd Street, New York, NY .... (212) 865-1975
Balasas, Cora/ 651 Vanderbilt St, Brooklyn, NY .... (212) 633-7753
Balukas & William Graphic Dsgn/ 179 Duane Street,
New York, NY .... (212) 226-3664
Bandoian, Catherine/ 132 Bayberry Lane, Westport, CT .... (203) 226-5681
Banks and Company/ 729 Boylston Street, Boston, MA .... (617) 262-0020
Barnard Design/ 3 W 18th St, New York, NY .... (212) 675-1070
Barnes, S Design Ltd/ 1200 Broadway, New York, NY .... (212) 679-0086
Barton Denmarsh Esteban Inc/ 524 Penn Ave, Pittsburgh, PA .... (412) 261-5220
Bauch Design, Jon/ 920 Broadway, New York, NY .... (212) 473-7637
Beaudoin, Rayne A Design/ 310 W 89th St #1F, New York, NY .... (212) 873-9470
BEC Design/ 59 Hillcrest Road, Reading, MA .... (617) 942-0577
Becker/Hockfield Design Assoc/ 106 E 19th St, New York, NY .... (212) 505-7050
Beckerman, Ann/ 50 W. 29th Street, New York, NY .... (212) 684-0496
Beckles, Ken/ 126 Fifth Avenue, New York, NY .... (212) 691-2641
Bedford Photo-Graphic Studio/ Rt. 22 P.O. Box 64,
Bedford, NY .... (914) 234-3123
Beeko Artists Materials/ 150 East 43 Street, New York, NY .... (212) 682-4224
Behar Enterprises Inc/ 219 Stewart Ave, Garden City, NY ...... (516) 294-0630
Bel-Aire Associates/ 745 Fifth Ave, New York, NY .... (212) 838-1060
Bell Graphic Design, James/ 119 West 23rd St, New York, NY .... (212) 929-8855
Bender, Don/ 32 W. Hobart Gap Road, Livingston, NJ .... (201) 992-1342
Maybender Design Assoc., Inc./ 247 W 30th St, New York, NY .... (212) 695-7107
Benetos, F John/ 37-09 222 Street, Bayside, NY .... (212) 229-0608
Berger, Jack/ 41 W 53rd St, New York, NY .... (212) 245-5705
Bernard Design International/ Waldorf Astoria 301 Park Ave,
New York, NY .... (212) 753-4728

Bernath, Karen/ 117 W. 74th Street, New York, NY .... (212) 873-3176
Bernstein, Irving/ 2035 Legion Street, Bellmore, NY .... (516) 785-5365
Besalel, Ely/ 235 E. 49th Street, New York, NY .... (212) 759-7820
Bessen and Tully Inc./ 880 3rd Avenue, New York, NY .... (212) 838-6406
Bevil, Serge Designs/ 156 5th Avenue, New York, NY .... (212) 242-1900
Bevington Design Inc/ 9-01 44th Drive, Long Island Cty, NY .... (212) 786-3680
Biehorst, Jane Byers/ P.O. Box 566, West Shokan, NY .... (914) 657-6707
Bivans, W S Inc/ 303 Park Ave. S. Studio 308, New York, NY ... (212) 254-7569
Blake, Amy Jo/ 1919 Panama St, Philadelphia, PA .... (215) 893-9149
Blue Hen Graphics/ 3 Great Jones Street, New York, NY .... (212) 260-2423
Boehning, Genevieve R./ 60 East 42nd St Suite 631,
New York, NY .... (212) 687-6696
Bogen, Irving/ 274 Madison Avenue, New York, NY .... (212) 686-1364
Bogorad, Alan/ 320 E. 42nd Street, New York, NY .... (212) 661-3340
Bolger & Galenas Advertising/ 217 Mt Horeb Rd Box 4560,
Warren, NJ .... (201) 560-9500
Bolognese, Leon/ 135 Connecticut Avenue, Freeport, NY .... (516) 379-3405
Bomzer Associates, Barry/ 66 Canal Street, Boston, MA .... (617) 227-5151
Bonder, Ronne Studio/ 318 E. 53rd Street, New York, NY .... (212) 759-4624
Bonnett, Niki/ 223 Byram Shore Rd, Greenwich, CT .... (203) 531-6609
Bordnick and Associates/ 151 W 28th St, New York, NY .... (212) 777-1860
Box Productions Inc/ 32 W 46th St, New York, NY .... (212) 730-8108
Bradbury, Heston, Ward Inc/ 7 E 47th St, New York, NY .... (212) 308-4800
Brainin, Max/ 135 Fifth Avenue, New York, NY .... (212) 254-9608
Braswell, Lynn/ 320 Riveside Dr #15F, New York, NY .... (212) 222-8761
Bratnober, Sarah/ 65 2nd Avenue #4C, New York, NY .... (212) 751-3122
Breinberg, Aaron/ 66-15 Thornton Pl., Forest Hills, NY .... (212) 261-2544
Breton Agency, Inc/ 543 Tarrytown Road, White Plains, NY ..... (914) 682-8822
Brinkman Design Associates/ 33 Shawnee Avenue, Rockaway, NJ ... (201) 625-8014
Brissette, David/ 5 Sheridan Street, Fitchburg, MA .... (617) 342-9479
Brooks, Hal/ 62 W. 45th St., New York, NY .... (212) 398-9540
Brown, Alastair Assocs/ 500 Fifth Ave, New York, NY .... (212) 221-3166
Brown, Kirk Q Designs/ 1092 Blake Avenue, Brooklyn, NY ...... (212) 434-4638
Bulldog/ 156 5th St Suite 322, New York, NY .... (212) 206-7853
Burgess Associates/ 45 Newbury, Boston, MA .... (617) 262-0114
Burnett, Steve, Inc/ 330 West 42nd St, New York, NY .... (212) 594-7122
Burroughs, Miggs/ Box 6, Westport, CT .... (203) 227-9667
Byars, Mel Design/ 95 Christopher St, New York, NY .... (212) 242-3851
Byrne Design/ 250 Fifth Avenue, New York, NY .... (212) 889-0502
Byrne, Patricia/ 137 W. 77th Street, New York, NY .... (212) 877-0078
Calderon, Jack Studios Ltd/ 119 W 57th St, New York, NY ..... (212) 541-4848
Caldersead and Phin/ 101 5th Ave, New York, NY .... (212) 807-6680
Callahan, Grady/ 2301 N Calvert Street, Baltimore, MD .... (301) 366-3841
Calles, Dona/ One Sipperleys Hill, Westport, CT .... (203) 226-3976
Calogero, Eugenia/ 35 W. 82nd Street, New York, NY .... (212) 873-3297
Camera, Marsha/ 159 W. 75th Street, New York, NY .... (212) 799-9519
Canon Graphics Inc/ 16 East 52 Street, New York, NY .... (212) 832-0397
Canzani, Cathleen/ 310 E. 46th Street, New York, NY .... (212) 697-8729
Captain Graphics/ 79A Chestnut Street, Boston, MA .... (617) 367-1008
Caravello Studios Inc/ 104 E 40th St, New York, NY .... (212) 661-5540
Carmel, Abraham P. I.D.S.A./ 7 Peter Beet Drive,
Peekskill, NY .... (914) 737-1439
Carnase, Inc./ 30 East 21st Street, New York, NY .... (212) 777-1500
Castenir, Ralph RC Graphics/ 157 E. 57th Street,
New York, NY .... (212) 755-1383
Tobol Group, Inc./ 260 Northern Blvd., Great Neck, NY .... (516) 437-3229
Catalogue Productions/ 544 W 38th, New York, NY .... (212) 564-2758
Cato-Johnson/ 100 Park Ave, New York, NY .... (212) 210-5595
Celedonia, Arthur/ 150 E. 35th Avenue, New York, NY .... (212) 689-5027
Cello-Tak Mfg Co/ 35 Alabama Ave, Island Park, NY .... (516) 431-7733
Chameleon Graphics Inc/ PO Box 868, Woodbury, CT .... (203) 263-0268
Charrette/ 215 Lexington Ave, New York, NY .... (212) 683-8822
Chasin & Russo Inc/ 1140 Ave of the Americas, New York, NY ... (212) 575-1250
Chelius, Scott/ 2315 Broadway Rm 402, New York, NY .... (212) 595-7874
Chevannes Design/ 770 Lexington Avenue 9th Floor,
New York, NY .... (718) 788-3550
Chu, H L & Company Ltd/ 39 West 29 Street 11 Floor,
New York, NY .... (212) 889-4818
Church, Wallace Associates/ 305 E 46th St, New York, NY ..... (212) 755-2903
Cioaba, Adrian/ 730 Newark Ave, Jersey City, NJ .... (201) 659-3409
Cluen, Jack/Graphic Design/ PO Box 333, Naugatuck, CT .... (203) 729-8358
Cochetti, Anne Todd/ 1232 Wolf St, Philadelphia, PA .... (215) 271-7021
Cohen, Michael Graphic Design/ 155 E 55th Street, New York, NY ... (212) 838-4861
Colangelo, Ted Associates/ the Mill 340 Pemberwiek Rd.,
Greenwich, CT .... (203) 531-3600

Creative Solutions!

Electronic Imaging Services from G.S. Lithographers

Realize your creative power with G.S.'s Electronic Imaging

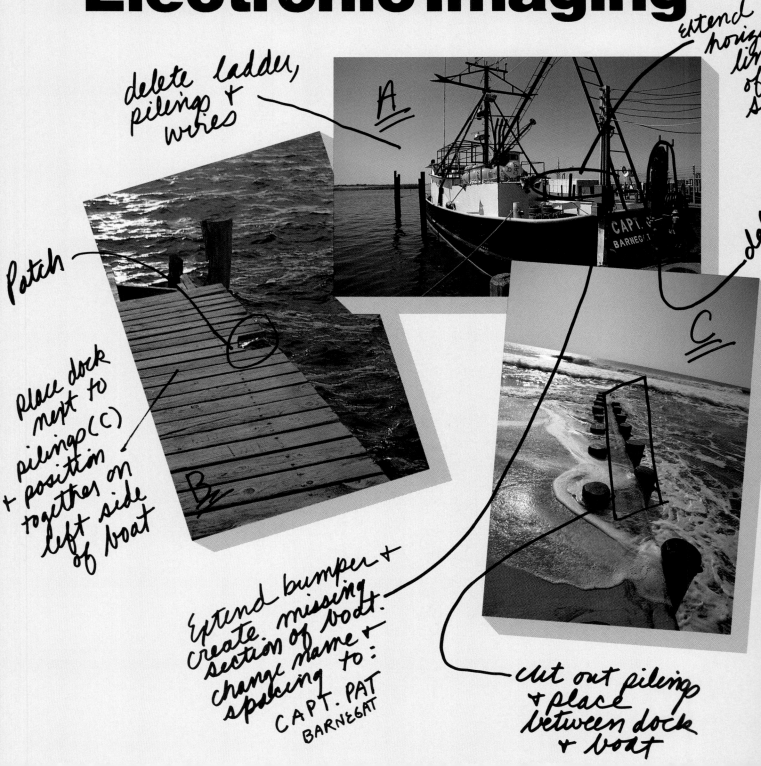

You've got a unique concept, but the execution seems impossible. So many changes have to be made that everyone says it can't be done.

It *can* be done! As specialists in turning creative problems into creative solutions, G.S. Lithographers *can* execute any idea your imagination dreams up. Now your possibilities are endless.

 G.S. Lithographers*
Advertising Preparatory Specialists

Use our toll-free number: 800/CALL4GS
(In New Jersey, call: 201/933-8585)

*A Techtron Graphic Arts Company

The G.S. Commitment

The Best People

We are a house of skilled craftsmen: artists and technicians who derive tremendous pride from producing top quality jobs.

The Best Equipment

G.S., a member of the Techtron Graphic Arts Company, utilizes state-of-the-art equipment in all departments.

The Best Location

We're in the Meadowlands of New Jersey, a few minutes from the Lincoln Tunnel and midtown Manhattan. Out-of-town clients are pleased to find us around the corner from Teterboro Airport and less than a half hour from Newark and LaGuardia Airports.

Our New York City Sales/Service Office is located at 200 W. 51st St., and our delivery staff leaves the plant on the hour for points throughout the metropolitan area.

The Best Hours

24 hours a day, seven days a week.

The Best Sales Force

We've left the song-and-dance men on Broadway. Our representatives all have extensive production experience, and they stay personally involved with each job until it leaves the plant— and beyond.

The Best Customers

Some of the world's most prestigious advertising agencies and magazines make us their headquarters for pre-press work. Whether you're large or small we'll treat you as one of our best customers. The way we stand behind our clients is legendary in the industry. That's why they keep coming back for more.

Our History

From our first account in 1945, which required the solving of difficult technical problems, we have built, maintained and enhanced our reputation as one of the most dependable, innovative, and quality-oriented pre-press houses in the industry.

In 1969 we moved to our present custom-designed plant in Carlstadt, New Jersey, which houses the latest state-of-the-art equipment. The expertise of our technicians and artists allows us to utilize modern-day technology in a most far-reaching and creative manner. And in the 1980's we continue to flourish as pioneers and problem solvers.

Now, nearly 40 years after our inception, we proudly maintain our position as the prime source for typography, separations, film and specialty printing services for the major advertising agencies, publications and corporations in the New York-New Jersey-Pennsylvania metropolitan area.

Our Services:

- Electronic Imaging
- Color Separations
- Complete Film Services
- Production Press Proofing
- Quality Typography
- Full Page Make-Up
- Ad Management
- Short Run Color Printing

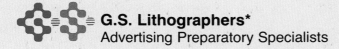 **G.S. Lithographers***
Advertising Preparatory Specialists

Manufacturing Facilities:
1 Kero Road, Carlstadt, NJ 07072
701 Ashland Avenue, Folcroft, PA 19032

Sales Offices:
New York   —212/736-4888
New Jersey—201/933-8585
Folcroft, PA—215/532-2170
Toll-free   —800/CALL4GS

*G.S. Lithographers is a member of the Techtron Graphic Arts Company

Colavecchio, Alan S/ 906 Torringford West St,
Torrington, CT .... (203) 482-7063
Comp Art Plus/ 12 W. 27 St., New York, NY .... (212) 689-8670
Continuity Graphic Assc., Inc./ 62 W. 45th St.,
New York, NY.. (212) 869-4170
Cook & Shanosky Assoc Inc/ 221 Nassau St, Princeton, NJ .... (609) 921-0200
Corchia Woliner Associates/ 130 W 56th Street, New York, NY ..... (212) 977-9778
Corporate Graphic Design Inc/ 49 West 45th Street,
New York, NY.. (212) 382-2822
Cosgrove Associates Inc./ 223 East 31st Street,
New York, NY.. (212) 889-7202
Costich & McConnell Inc/ 225 Marcus Blvd, Hauppauge, NY .... (516) 231-4160
Cousins,Morison S & Associates/ 964 Third Ave, New York, NY ..... (212) 751-3390
Cowley, Paul J. & Associates/ 315 North Clinton St.,
Syracuse, NY .... (315) 475-8453
Crawford, Phyllis/ 201 E. 17th Street, New York, NY .... (212) 674-5230
Creative Freelancers/ 62 West 45th Street, New York, NY .... (212) 398-9540
Creative Graphics/ 153 Main Parkway West, Plainview, NY .... (516) 433-5147
Creative Services & Design/ 1529 Wisconsin Ave NW,
Washington, DC .... (202) 333-3560
CRONAN, MICHAEL PATRICK/ One Zoe St.,
San Francisco, CA.. (415) 543-6745
See our ad on pages 184, 185
Crooks, Sue/ 156 W. 10th Street, New York, NY .... (212) 924-5668
Crozier, Bob & Associates Inc/ 1201 Pennsylvania Ave Ste 700,
Washington, DC .... (202) 638-7134
Csoka/Benato/Fleurant Inc/ 79 Madison Ave, New York, NY .... (212) 686-6741
Cuevas, Robert/ 230 E. 44th Street, New York, NY .... (212) 661-7149
Cutro Associates, Inc/ 47 Jewett Avenue, Tenafly, NJ .... (201) 569-5548
Cybulska, Cynthia/ 3191 Emmons Avenue, Brooklyn, NY............. (212) 934-2757
Dakota Design Inc/ Rte 363 Leighton Bldg,
King of Prussia, PA .... (215) 265-1255
D'Amico, James/ 1123 Broadway, New York, NY .... (212) 620-0369
Dane, Norman Art Studio/ 19 W 44th St, New York, NY.............. (212) 840-1924
Danielsdesign Inc/ 150 E 35th St, New York, NY .... (212) 889-0071
Darden, Howard/ 62 W. 45th St., New York, NY .... (212) 398-9540
Darras-Maxwell, Penny/ 24 Bates Street, Cambridge, MA........... (617) 876-0361
D & D Headlines & Graphics/ 969 First Avenue, New York, NY ..... (212) 751-8994
De Blass, Diana Marketing Inc/ 55 Park Ave, New York, NY .... (212) 685-1724
De Harak Assoc/ 320 W 13th St, New York, NY .... (212) 929-5445
De La Houssaye Design/ 417 Lafayette St, New York, NY .... (212) 460-5701
Del Gaudio, Joseph Design Grp/ 215 W. 98th Street,
New York, NY.. (212) 222-7432
Demarco, Frank/ 208 Fifth Avenue, New York, NY .... (212) 725-0658
Demario, John Advertising/ PO Box 233, Absecon, NJ .... (609) 646-3647
Design Alliance Inc/ 353 Lexington Ave, New York, NY............... (212) 689-3503
Design Center Incorporated/ 29 Commonwealth Ave, Boston, MA... (617) 536-6846
Design Consortium/ 413 Walnut St, Harrisburg, PA.................... (717) 234-6414
Designed To Print Inc/ 270 West 73rd Street,
New York City, NY.. (212) 362-2376
Designers 3 Inc/ 25 West 43rd Street, New York, NY .... (212) 221-5900
Design Four/ 1466 Broadway, New York, NY .... (212) 921-1919
Design Group of Boston/ 437 Boylston St, Boston, MA .... (617) 437-1084
Design Intrigue/ 3 Holden Street Studio 222, Providence, RI .... (401) 331-6336
Designworks Inc/ 127 Mt. Auburn Street, Cambridge, MA .... (617) 876-7035
Design-X Communications, Inc./ 25 Broadway, Kingston, NY........ (914) 331-4620
Diamond Art Studio/ 515 Madison Ave, New York, NY .... (212) 355-5444
DiFranza-Williamson/ 1414 6th Avenue, New York, NY .... (212) 832-2343
Dill Graphic Studio/ 98 Grand Ave, Englewood, NJ.................... (201) 568-3111
Dispigna, Tony/ 67 Irving Place, New York, NY .... (212) 674-2647
D K Graphics/ 56 W 45 St Ste 1600, New York, NY .... (212) 944-1885
DK Graphics Inc/ 56 W 45th St, New York, NY .... (212) 944-1885
DMCD/ 911 Washington Street, Wilmington, DE........................ (302) 654-5277
DockxDesign/ Two Park Square, Boston, MA .... (617) 542-7438
Doherty & Doherty Creative (Se/ 74 Greenwich Avenue,
Greenwich, CT .... (203) 629-2600
Donato and Krutick/ 56 W 45 St Ste 1600, New York, NY .... (212) 944-1885
Donato & Berkley Inc/ 386 Park Ave South, New York, NY........... (212) 532-3884
Donnelly, Ellis Design/ 294 Elizabeth Street, New York, NY......... (212) 473-8559
Donovan and Green Designers/ 1 Madison Ave, New York, NY ..... (212) 725-2233
Doret, Michael/ 12 E. 14 St. #4d, New York, NY .... (212) 929-1688
Double Check Studio/ 120 East 57th Street, New York, NY .... (212) 758-3830
Draper Shreeve Design/ 28 Perry Street, New York, NY.............. (212) 675-7534
Drate Design Inc/ 160 5th Ave Rm 613, New York, NY .... (212) 620-4672
Dugoff, Sharen F./ 4212 Wilder, Bronx, NY .... (212) 994-7051

Dwyer, Tom/ 420 Lexington Ave, New York, NY .... (212) 986-7108
Dyographics Inc/ 79 Walnut St, Belmont, MA .... (617) 489-3505
East Coast Advtsng& Typography/ 318 E Main St P O Box 694,
Salisbury, MD... (301) 546-3728
East Coast Video Systems/ 548 Broadway, New York, NY .... (212) 431-7453
E B Design/ 127 East 59th Street, New York, NY .... (212) 421-1950
Echolight Corporation/ 151 Kentucky Ave SE, Washington, DC ...... (202) 546-1220
Edge, Dennis Design/ 36 East 38 Street, New York, NY.............. (212) 679-0927
Eisenhart, Richard E/ 81 Westmont Ave, Elmira, NY .... (607) 733-6434
Eisenman & Enock Inc/ 25 Hudson St, New York, NY .... (212) 431-1000
Eisenman-Todd Inc/ 222 Cedar Lane, Teaneck, NJ .... (201) 836-5900
Emerson-Wajdowicz Studios Inc./ 1123 Broadway, New York, NY... (212) 807-8144
Ericksen Adv. & Design, Ltd./ 310 Madison Ave, New York, NY ..... (212) 599-0553
Eskil Ohlsson Assoc. Inc./ 625 Madison Avenue, New York, NY ..... (212) 758-4412
Etc Graphics, Inc./ 386 Park Ave S, New York, NY .... (212) 889-8777
Eurografica Adv Design/ 655 Boylston Street, Boston, MA .... (617) 266-6566
Fannell Studio/ 8 Newbury Street, Boston, MA .... (617) 267-0895
Farber, Ronald/ 215 W. 92nd Street, New York, NY .... (212) 877-4689
Farmakis, Andreas/ 835 3rd Avenue, New York, NY .... (212) 758-5280
Feinen, Jeff/ 333 E 49th St Suite 7H, New York, NY .... (212) 734-4533
Ferris & Levine-Great Design/ 144 Marne Avenue,
Fairfield, CT .... (203) 367-7559
Filicori Visual Communications/ 4 Gramercy Park,
New York, NY.. (212) 677-0065
Filippo, Adam & Moran Inc/ 1206 Fifth Avenue,
Pittsburgh, PA .... (412) 261-3720
Finn/ 154 E 64th St, New York, NY .... (212) 838-1212
Fitzgerald, Roderick/ PO Box 6039, Peabody, MA .... (617) 532-5880
Flagg, Holley/ 103 E. 84th Street, New York, NY .... (212) 734-5790
Flagler Advertising/ P.O. Box 1317, Brookline, MA .... (617) 566-6971
Flahive/Prospero/ 585 West End Ave, New York, NY .... (212) 787-5247
Fleishman, Jill/ 333 E. 6th Street, New York, NY .... (212) 260-3046
Forbes & Catoggio Adv/ 114 E 32nd St, New York, NY.............. (212) 889-0202
Foreplay Studios/ 33 Greene St, New York, NY .... (212) 226-0188
Forzaglia, John Inc-Art Studio/ 211 East 43 St,
New York, NY.. (212) 661-4370
Fossella, Gregory Assoc/ 479 Commonwealth Ave, Boston, MA ...... (617) 267-4940
Frattolillo, Rinaldo/ 527 Madison Ave, New York, NY .... (212) 486-1901
Free Lance Exchange, Inc./ 342 Madison Ave., New York, NY....... (212) 682-3042
Freelance Finders/ 200 Madison Ave Suite 2402, New York, NY .... (212) 684-0590
Friday Saturday Sunday, Inc./ 210 East 15th St,
New York, NY.. (212) 260-8479
Friedman, Irene/ 225 W. 12th Street, New York, NY.................. (212) 243-4882
Frissora, Bob Design Co Inc/ 310 Madison Avenue,
New York, NY.. (212) 599-1727
Froom, Georgia/ 62 W 39th Rm 803, New York, NY .... (212) 944-0330
Gadman, Vera/ 9 W. 69th Street, New York, NY .... (212) 877-2053
Gale, Cynthia/ 229 E. 88th St., New York, NY .... (212) 860-5429
Gale, Robert A Inc/ 970 Park Ave, New York, NY..................... (212) 535-4791
Ganton, Brian J ASMP/ 205 E 42nd St, New York, NY .... (212) 221-7318
Garland, Nathan/ 412 Orange Street, New Haven, CT .... (203) 562-9539
Gasser, Gene/ 300 Main Street, Chatham, NJ .... (201) 635-6020
Gateway Studios/ 225 Ross St, Pittsburgh, PA.......................... (412) 471-7224
Gatter Inc/ 342 Madison Avenue, New York, NY....................... (212) 687-4821
Gatti/ 114 East Thirty Second Street, New York, NY .... (212) 689-0133
Gerald, Ken Associates/ 200 W 57 St Suite 1405,
New York, NY.. (212) 247-5847
Gersin Associates, Robert P/ 11 E. 22nd Street,
New York, NY.. (212) 777-9500
Gerstman & Meyers Inc./ 60 West 55th Street, New York, NY....... (212) 586-2535
Geyer, Dale/ 64-85 Saunders St., Rego Park, NY...................... (212) 896-4299
Giambarba, Paul/ P O Box 10, Centerville, MA......................... (617) 775-7745
Gianakos, Cristos/ 93 Mercer St, New York, NY .... (212) 925-0560
Gill, Bob/ 1200 Broadway, New York, NY .... (212) 689-3229
Giordano, Ciro Design Assoc/ 214 Derby Street, Salem, MA......... (617) 745-6000
GIRVIN, TIM DESIGN, INC./ 911 Western Ave. #408,
Seattle, WA .... (206) 623-7808
See our ad on page 186
Glaser, Milton/ 207 E 32 St, New York, NY .... (212) 889-3161
Glasheen Advertising Inc/ 300 E 34th St, New York, NY .... (212) 889-3188
Glasser, Roberta Graphic Dsgn/ 205 E 42nd St, New York, NY...... (212) 599-0988
Glassman, Kramer Miller Lomden/ 1528 Waverly Street,
Philadelphia, PA .... (215) 545-7077
Glick, Barry/ Almost Heaven Hot Tubs Ltd, Renick, WV .... (304) 497-3163
Glover, J. P. Design Assoc./ 5001 Baum Blvd, Pittsburgh, PA .... (412) 621-5533

Glusker, Irwin/ 154 W 57th, New York, NY .... (212) 757-4438
Glynn/Palmer Associates, Inc/ 1457 Broadway, New York, NY ...... (212) 719-5077
G.N.V.C. Visual Communictns/ 409 One Tenn Center West,
   Pittsburgh, PA .... (412) 787-9870
Goetz Graphics/ 23 E 26th St, New York, NY .... (212) 679-4250
Gola, Sandra/ 466 Boulevard, Garfield, NJ .... (201) 772-2152
Golden, Nancy L./ 3800 Fords Ln., Baltimore, MD .... (301) 358-9104
Goldstein, Stan Graphics Inc/ 5 Beekman St, New York, NY .... (212) 962-2845
Goodwin, John C./ 28 Meadow Street, Demarest, NJ .... (201) 768-0777
Gordon, Joel/ 5 E. 16th St., New York, NY .... (212) 989-9207
Gorelick Inc./Mkt.-Comm. Dsgn./ 999 Raritan Road, Clark, NJ ...... (201) 382-4141
Gorman, Chris Associates, Inc./ 12 East 41st Street,
   New York, NY... (212) 696-9377
Goslin, Charles/ 264 Garfield Place, Brooklyn, NY................... (212) 499-6728
Grafx Multi Media Inc/ 137 W 28th St, New York City, NY .... (212) 239-0254
Graham Associates, Inc/ 1899 L St, Lower Lobby,
   Washington, DC.. (202) 833-9657
Graham, L J Co Inc/ 510 Madison Ave, New York, NY .... (212) 752-1933
Grand Design/ 368 Congress St - 5th Fl, Boston, MA.............. (617) 451-0596
Graphic Artists Associates/ E Burke, VT .... (802) 626-5808
Graphic Artists Guild/ 30 E 20th, New York, NY...................... (212) 777-7353
Graphic Art Resource Assoc/ 257 West Tenth Street Suite 5E,
   New York, NY... (212) 929-0017
Graphic Horizons Inc/ 10 Hubert Street, New York, NY .... (212) 219-2040
Graphic Ink/ 33 Commonwealth Rd, Watertown, MA................. (617) 923-9418
Graphicreations Ad Agency/ 37 Fulton Street,
   White Plains, NY .... (914) 428-7571
Graphics By Nostradamus/ 250 West 57th Street Suite 112,
   New York, NY... (212) 581-1362
G-Raphics Design Studio, Inc./ 173 Congress Street,
   Brooklyn Hts, NY .... (212) 625-0417
Graphics for Industry, Inc./ 8 W. 30th St., New York, NY .... (212) 889-6202
Graphics Forum/ 607 Investment Bldg, Pittsburgh, PA .... (412) 566-2232
Graphics Institute/ 1633 Broadway, New York, NY .... (212) 887-8670
Graphic Suite, The/ 235 Shady Avenue, Pittsburgh, PA............. (412) 661-6699
Graphis Magazine/ PO Box 427, Woodside, NY .... (212) 565-0004
Grear, Malcolm Designers/ 391 Eddy Street, Providence, RI......... (401) 331-5656
Greco, Tony and Associates Inc/ 232 Madison Avenue,
   New York, NY... (212) 683-5410
Greenebaum Graphic Design/ 86 Walnut Street, Natick, MA....... (617) 655-8146
Greenfield, Joan/ 1026 6th Avenue, New York, NY .... (212) 354-0409
Green, Mel Design/ 50 Moraine Street, Belmont, MA .... (617) 484-0164
Greig Advertising/Design/ 68 East Hartsdale Avenue,
   Hartsdale, NY... (914) 681-0508
Grien, Anita/ 155 E. 38th St., New York, NY........................... (212) 697-6170
Griffiths, Ed/ 62 Fairview Avenue, Tarrytown, NY .... (914) 631-2911
Grob Design Inc/ 70 Washington St, Salem, MA...................... (617) 741-1704
Groff-Long Assoc/ 4421 East-West Hwy, Washington, DC .... (301) 654-0279
Gross, Stu Advertising/Design/ 223 E. 10th Street #3,
   New York, NY... (212) 460-9181
Group Four Design/ 147 Simsbury Rd., Avon, CT .... (203) 678-1570
Group 4 Graphics/ 310 Madison Ave, New York, NY .... (212) 687-8310
Grunfeld Graphics Ltd/ 80 Varick Street, New York, NY .... (212) 431-8700
Gulotta, Gerald/ Hemlock Trail, New City, NY .... (914) 634-3320
Haber, Vera/ 333 E 49th St Suite 7H, New York, NY .... (212) 734-4533
Hagle, Bob/Lord Corp./ 2000 W. Grandview Blvd., Erie, PA....... (814) 868-3611
Haines, John Design Inc/ 53 East Tenth Street, New York, NY ...... (212) 254-2326
Hainline, Wallace F Assocs/ 45 Kensico Dr, Mt Kisco, NY............ (914) 666-8070
Hall, Barbara/ 150 W. 87th Street #6D, New York, NY.............. (212) 595-6289
Halverson, Janet/ 320 E. 53rd Street, New York, NY .... (212) 688-2864
Halvorsen, Everett/ 874 58th Street, Brooklyn, NY................... (212) 871-5846
Halyard Group Advertising, The/ 214 Derby Street, Salem, MA .... (617) 745-6800
Hammond/Keehn Inc/ 415 Lexington Ave, New York, NY........... (212) 682-6181
Hansen, Gordon & Zaritsky Inc/ 97 South St, Northampton, MA.... (413) 586-8884
Harmon Kemp Inc/ 95 5th Ave, New York, NY .... (212) 929-0226
Harrington-Jackson/ 10 Newbury, Boston, MA .... (617) 536-6164
Harris, Karolina/ 240 E. Palisade Avenue, Englewood, NJ.......... (201) 567-9241
Harris, Levey/ 555 North Ave, Fort Lee, NJ............................ (201) 947-3886
Hartman, Harry Studio & Design/ 61 W. 23rd Street,
   New York, NY... (212) 675-5454
Hartwell, Alan/ 134 E 70th St, New York, NY .... (212) 734-4000
Harvard Sq Art Centre/ 14 Holyoke Str, Cambridge, MA .... (617) 491-3883
Hassold, Eugene Design Assoc/ 717 Market St #523,
   San Francisco, CA .... (415) 974-1211
Hayes, Daniel/ 1435 Lexington Avenue #7C, New York, NY......... (212) 289-5073

Hecker, Mark Studio Inc/ 920 Broadway Ste. 1501,
   New York, NY.. (212) 505-1234
Heffner/Graphics/ 30 Clinton Street, Brooklyn, NY .... (212) 875-1126
Heiney, John/ 200 E. 33rd Street, New York, NY....................... (212) 686-1121
Heinsen, Else/Design Consultnt/ 215 E 89th St,
   New York City, NY... (212) 289-2447
H G Associates Inc/ 8 W. 40th Street, New York, NY .... (212) 221-3070
Highland Design Associates Inc/ 350 Rabro Drive,
   Hauppauge, NY .... (516) 348-0282
Hillman, Thomas, Design/ 130 Nonantum Road, Newton, MA ...... (617) 527-8302
Hirsch, Diane L/ ITT Corp 9th Fl 320 Park Ave, New York, NY...... (212) 940-2264
Holland, Barry K/ 6 Windham Crescent, Kings Park, NY .... (516) 979-7043
Hooper, Ray/ 1123 Broadway #802, New York, NY .... (212) 924-5480
Hora Design/ 853 Broadway, New York, NY .... (212) 473-4181
Horizon Design/ 138 Chatsworth Ave, Larchmont, NY .... (914) 834-2388
Horton, Roy Studios, Inc./ 119 West 57 Street, New York, NY ...... (212) 246-0040
Hot Flash Creative Svcs. Inc./ 16 East 42nd St.,
   New York, NY.. (212) 986-3820
Hub Graphics Corp/ 16 E. 52nd Street, New York, NY .... (212) 421-5807
Hudson, Ross Design/ 107 E 89th St, New York, NY .... (212) 876-8878
IGC Graphics/ 433 Park Ave. S., New York, NY .... (212) 689-5148
Image Communications Inc/ 85 Fifth Avenue, New York, NY........ (212) 807-9677
Image Network Inc/ 645 West End Ave, New York City, NY.......... (212) 877-1734
Impact Designs/ 200 Eagle Road Suite 2, Wayne, PA .... (215) 688-0540
Inforgraphics/ 30 E 42nd St, New York, NY .... (212) 682-2562
Ingersoll, W. Eugene/ 299 Madison Ave., New York, NY............. (212) 986-4334
Inghram, Dan Inc/ 805 Hooper Avenue, Toms River, NJ .... (201) 341-0200
Clarke & Corcillo, Inc./ 530 Westport Avenue, Norwalk, CT .... (203) 846-1617
James, Mai/ 200 E 78th St, New York, NY.............................. (212) 628-7682
Jarrin Design/ PO Box 421 Fancher Rd, Pound Ridge, NY .... (914) 764-4625
Jastram, Ed Studio/ 299 Madison Ave, New York, NY .... (212) 682-5048
Jefferson, Affrekka/ 140-09 158th Street,
   Jamaica Queens, NY .... (212) 528-6907
Jenkins & Page/ 65 Fourth Ave, New York, NY........................ (212) 982-8266
Johnson Design Associates/ 403 Massachusetts Avenue,
   Acton, MA .... (617) 263-5345
Johnson & Simpson/ 49 Bleeker St, Newark, NJ .... (201) 624-7788
Jones, Dick Design Inc/ 826 Public Ledger Bldg,
   Philadelphia, PA .... (215) 625-0111
Julian, David/ 55 Eighth Ave, Brooklyn, NY .... (212) 638-0974
Kaeser & Wilson Design Ltd/ 330 Seventh Ave, New York, NY...... (212) 563-2455
Kaplan, Mr. & Mrs. C./ 14 Wagnor Road, Westport, CT .... (203) 227-5466
Karlin, Bernard/ 41 E. 42nd Street, New York, NY .... (212) 687-7636
Kass Associates Inc/ 1966 Broadway, New York, NY .... (212) 874-0418
Kass Communications/ 505 8th Avenue, New York, NY .... (212) 868-3133
K A S T Communications Inc/ 22 East 36 St, New York, NY .... (212) 889-7993
Katz, Harold Adv. & Packaging/ 150 Great Neck Rd.,
   Great Neck, NY .... (516) 466-8610
Katz Wheeler Design/ 37 S 20th St, Philadelphia, PA............... (215) 567-5668
Keene, Sylvia Colard/ 9 Hunting Lane, Lynnfield, MA................. (617) 334-5097
Kell and Chadick, Inc/ 1110 Fidler Lane #1400,
   Silver Spring, MD .... (301) 585-4000
Kennedy, Susan/ 337 Florida Hill Rd, Ridgefield, CT................. (203) 431-3030
Kimmins/Anderson Assoc/ 381 Park Ave S, New York, NY .... (212) 689-2855
KINETICS/ 444 N. Wabash Ave., Chicago, IL .... (312) 644-2767
See our ad on pages 3rd Cover
King, Jean Callan/ 315 Riverside Drive, New York, NY .... (212) 866-8488
Klaboe, David/ 150 East 30th Street, New York, NY .... (212) 683-6192
Kleb Assoc/ 25 W 45th, New York, NY.................................. (212) 246-2847
Klim, Matt & Assoc Inc/ Avon Park N, Avon, CT...................... (203) 678-1222
Klitsch, Libby Johnson/ 1719 Delancey Pl, Philadelphia, PA .... (215) 735-5985
Knapp, R S Co Inc/ 725 Valley Brook Ave, Lyndhurst, NJ .... (201) 438-1500
Knigin, Michael/ 832 Broadway, New York, NY .... (212) 473-0322
Kops, Debi/ 88 Lexington Ave, New York City, NY.................... (212) 683-6249
Korn, Bob/ 370 1/2 Pacific Street, Brooklyn, NY...................... (212) 858-8851
Kovanen, Erik/ 102 Twin Oak Ln, Wilton, CT .... (203) 762-8961
Kovar,Constance Graphic Design/ 300 Woodbury Rd,
   Woodbury, NY .... (516) 692-5500
Krackehl, Gene/ 55 Lily Pond Lane, Katonah, NY .... (914) 232-4409
Krauss, Gerald/ Creamer, Inc,. New York, NY .... (212) 887-8242
Krawciw, Tanya/ 429 E. 52nd Street #22F, New York, NY........... (212) 753-7748
Laccone, Lorna Design/ 575 Madison Avenue Suite 401,
   New York, NY.. (212) 688-4583
Lindgren Design Associates/ 127 Mt. Auburn, Cambridge, MA .... (617) 547-7515
Langdon, John/ 106 S. Marion Ave, Wenonah, NJ.................... (609) 468-7868

DESIGN, ART DIRECTION, CREATIVE SERVICES/East

Latham Brefka Assocs/ 883 Boylston Street, Boston, MA............. (617) 227-3900
Laughlin, R Bruce Heady Graphi/ 156 W 44th St, New York, NY.... (212) 921-9732
Lausch, David Graphics/ 2613 Maryland Ave, Baltimore, MD........ (301) 235-7453
Lawrence Studio Inc./ 509 Madison Avenue, New York, NY.......... (212) 758-3140
LDR, International/ 4121 Wilshire Blvd. Ste. A-4,
Los Angeles, CA.. (213) 382-4065
Lebowitz, Moe/ 2599 Phyllis Drive, North Bellmore, NY.............. (516) 826-3397
Le Brun Associates Inc/ 276 Fifth Avenue, New York, NY........... (212) 689-0599
Lee, Barry Communications/ 60 Broad Hollow Road,
Melville, NY.. (516) 351-6060
Leeds, Judith K./ 14 Rosemont Ct, North Caldwell, NJ................ (201) 226-3552
Lee-Myles Assocs/ 160 E 56th St, New York, NY......................... (212) 758-3232
Leichman, Seymour/ 276 Riverside Drive, New York, NY.............. (212) 749-7770
Leigh, Anne/ 45 E 19th St, New York, NY................................... (212) 260-1880
Lempert Design & Marketing/ 202 Belleville Avenue,
Belleville, NJ... (201) 759-2927
Lento, Julia/ 267 Fifth Avenue, New York, NY............................ (212) 233-8989
Leone Design Group/ 160 Fifth Avenue, New York, NY................ (212) 989-8838
Leong, Donald/ 7221 Bryan Street, Philadelphia, PA................... (215) 247-9396
Lerner, Jerry/ 11 Lincoln Ave, West Orange, NJ......................... (212) 265-4300
Lesley-Hille Inc./ 32 East 21st Street, New York, NY.................. (212) 677-7570
Letvin Design/ 19 Hall Street, Boston, MA................................ (617) 524-6248
Leung, Richard/ 51 E 42 St Room 1410, New York, NY................ (212) 986-4604
Leutwyler Associates Inc./ 95 Madison Avenue, New York, NY...... (212) 689-0480
Lewinter, Renee/ 41 Sewall Street, Somerville, MA..................... (617) 628-5695
Lichtenberg, Al Graphic Art/ 10 E 40th St, New York, NY............ (212) 865-4312
Lieberman, Ron/ 109 W. 28th St., New York, NY......................... (212) 947-0653
Liebert Studios Inc/ 6 E 39th St, New York, NY.......................... (212) 686-4520
Lika Associates Inc/ 160 E 38th Street, New York, NY................. (212) 490-3660
Lisandro, Pina Design and Prod/ 142-41 41 Ave Apt 514,
Flushing, NY... (718) 463-0724
Lister Butler Inc/ 437 Fifth Ave, New York, NY........................... (212) 889-0578
Logowitz & Moore Design Assoc/ 85 Chestnut St, Boston, MA....... (617) 227-2210
Lopez, Dick Inc/ 355 Lexington Ave, New York, NY...................... (212) 599-2327
Lord, Cile/ 42 E. 12th Street, New York, NY............................... (212) 228-6030
Lubliner/Saltz Inc/ 183 Madison Ave, New York, NY.................... (212) 679-9810
Luckett & Associates/ 18 W 23rd St, New York, NY..................... (212) 620-9770
Lynch, Sheila/ 365 W. 20th Street, New York, NY....................... (212) 255-3222
Macagnone, V/ 211 E 43rd St, New York, NY.............................. (212) 221-5729
Macey Noyes Associates Inc/ 10 Signal Road, Stamford, CT......... (203) 324-1142
Magalos, Christopher & Company/ 3308 Church Road,
Cherry Hill, NJ... (609) 667-7433
Manhattan Design/ 47 West 13th Street, New York, NY............... (212) 620-0506
Manzo/Finalboro/ 301 E 45 St, New York, NY.............................. (212) 986-3342
Marchese, Frank/ 444 E. 82nd Street, New York, NY.................... (212) 988-6267
Marciuliano, Frank Inc/ 300 E 42nd, New York, NY...................... (212) 697-0740
Markel Freda/ 1060 Park Avenue, New York, NY.......................... (212) 534-7521
Marketing East/ 520 West Ave, Norwalk, CT................................ (203) 866-2234
Marsh, Susan/ 1698 Mass Ave, Cambridge, MA............................ (617) 492-5618
Martinot, Claude/ 145 2nd Avenue Apt. 20, New York, NY............ (212) 473-3137
Martin's, Bruce Rough Riders/ New York, NY.............................. (212) 620-0539
Martucci Studio/ 250 Boylston St, Boston, MA............................ (617) 266-6960
Marzulli Assoc Inc/ 303 E 53rd St, New York, NY........................ (212) 371-0670
Max, Peter/ 118 Riverside Dr, New York, NY................................ (212) 873-9800
Maxwell, Madeleine/ 28 Fletcher Street, Winchester, MA.............. (617) 729-7889
McBride International/ 157 Sisson Ave, Hartford, CT.................... (203) 523-7707
McCaffery, Janet/ 1 W. 67th Street, New York, NY....................... (212) 874-4238
McCallum, Roberta G./ 411 E. 81st Street, New York, NY............. (212) 472-9537
McCloskey, Linda/ 14 Paddock Road, Port Chester, NY................. (914) 939-6624
McDade, William C Inc/ 24 Elm Street, Morristown, NJ................. (201) 538-8133
McLaughlin & Schilling/ 53 East 64 Street, New York, NY............ (212) 988-2910
McNamara Associates Inc/ 211 E 51st St, New York, NY............... (212) 759-5910
McNeill & Company/ PO Box 19373, Washington, DC..................... (301) 864-6165
M & Co/ 157 W 57th St, New York, NY... (212) 582-7050
Meier Advertising Inc/ 37 W 57th St, New York, NY..................... (212) 355-6460
Melanson, Donya & Associates/ 130 Oliver Street, Boston, MA...... (617) 482-0421
Mentken, Ed/ 165 West 91 Street, New York, NY.......................... (212) 595-9489
Mentzer, Jerry/ 725 Liberty Ave 4th Floor, Pittsburgh, PA............. (412) 642-2868
Mercer St. Design Works/ 119 Mercer St., Jersey City, NJ............ (201) 434-3535
Metz Designs Inc/ 26 E 63rd St Suite 9-F, New York, NY.............. (212) 758-9871
Meyers, Herman/ 209 Hillside Dr, Neptune, NJ............................ (201) 774-5694
Michaelis/Carpelis Design/ 17 E 45th St, New York, NY................ (212) 867-8190
Midnight Oil Design Studio/ 309 W. 57th Street,
New York, NY.. (212) 582-9071
Miho, James/ 46 Chalburn Rd, Redding, CT................................ (203) 938-3214
Miller, Irving/ 641 Lexington Ave., New York, NY......................... (212) 755-4040
Miller,Richard P Creative Serv/ 202 E 35th St, New York, NY....... (212) 686-8555
Miller, Sonda/ 585 West End Ave, New York, NY........................... (212) 880-8300
Miranda, Arthur Graphics/ 60 E Ninth St, New York, NY................ (212) 254-6373
Mirenburg, Barry L.S., Design/ 413 City Island Avenue,
New York, NY.. (212) 885-0835
Mitchell & Company/ 1627 Connecticut Ave. N.W.,
Washington, DC... (202) 483-1301
Mizerek Design Inc/ 48 East 43 St, New York, NY......................... (212) 986-5702
M-ME Graphics Designs/ 19 Harwood Terrace, Leominster, MA..... (617) 537-8785
Modi & Beckler Design/ 271 Madison Avenue, New York, NY........ (212) 683-6592
Modular Marketing Inc/ 1841 Broadway, New York, NY................. (212) 581-4690
Moeckli, Erich Visual Concepts/ 444 E 82nd Street,
New York, NY.. (212) 794-9450
Monderer, Stewart Design/ 9 Gardner Terrace, Allston, MA........... (617) 782-3641
Montgomery, Barbara/ 527 Madison Ave, New York, NY................. (212) 753-1732
Moore, Allen Graphics Photogra/ 525 Main St,
Poughkeepsie, NY.. (914) 485-5368
Morris, Ann/ 140 E 56th St, New York, NY................................... (212) 355-1603
Mosberg, Stewart Design Assocs/ 11 West 73rd Street,
New York, NY.. (212) 873-6130
Moseley, Richie/ 409 Sixth Ave., Brooklyn, NY............................ (212) 499-7045
Moshier, Harry Assoc Inc/ 18 E 53 St, New York, NY.................... (212) 980-9744
Mueller & Wister Studio/ 1211 Chestnut Street,
Philadelphia, PA.. (215) 568-7260
Munich,Mildred Advertising Art/ 69 Ontario Road,
Bellerose, NY.. (212) 343-0363
Munson, Valerie Gale/ 79 2nd Place, Brooklyn, NY...................... (212) 855-3152
Murello, John/ 17 E. Carpenter Street, Valley Stream, NY............ (516) 825-0417
Murphy, Erik/ 70 Main Street, Peterborough, NH......................... (603) 924-9281
Murtha,DeSola,Finsilver,Fiore/ 800 Third Avenue,
New York, NY.. (212) 832-4770
My Own Color Lab/ 45 W 45th St, New York, NY.......................... (212) 391-8638
National Advertising Brokers/ P.O. Box 337, Albany, NY............... (518) 785-3422
Navratil, Sid/ 1305 Clark Bldg, Pittsburgh, PA.............................. (412) 471-4322
Needlepoint Creations/ 1031-40th Street, Brooklyn, NY................ (212) 854-3490
Neider, Allan/ 333 E 49th St Suite 7H, New York, NY.................. (212) 734-4533
Neisworth, Robert T./ 12 Harper Road, Aliquippa, PA.................. (412) 457-7993
Nelson, Dorothy/ 242 E. 83rd Street #4D, New York, NY.............. (212) 988-6430
Nemser, Robert S/ 635 Madison Avenue, New York, NY................. (212) 832-9595
New American Graphics/ 240 Madison Ave, New York, NY............ (212) 532-3551
Newdorf, Steven/ 7-04 5th St., Fair Lawn, NJ.............................. (201) 797-4632
Newton Associates Inc/ 413 E Lancaster Ave PO Box 50,
St Davids, PA.. (215) 964-9300
Nimeck Graphic Dsgn. & Lttrng./ Rd 4 Riva Avenue #358A,
North Brunswick, NJ... (201) 821-8741
Norrie Gordon Assoc Inc/ 122 East 25th St, New York, NY........... (212) 598-6900
Novak, Karen/ 1123 Broadway, New York, NY.............................. (212) 206-1568
Novellino, Nino/ Shore Rd PO Box 325, Cornwall-Hudson, NY...... (914) 534-9120
Oak Tree Graphics/ 1450 Broadway, New York, NY....................... (212) 398-9357
Olbrys, Anthony/ 41 Pepper Ridge Road, Stamford, CT.................. (203) 322-9422
Ollio Studios/ 1235 Fulton Bldg, Pittsburgh, PA........................... (412) 281-4483
Ong & Assocs/ 485 Madison Ave, New York, NY............................ (212) 355-4343
On Target Graphic Svcs Inc/ 1185 E. Putnam Ave.,
Riverside, CT... (203) 637-8300
O'Shea, Denise E/ 13 Hickam Lane, Bedford, MA........................ (617) 274-6863
Pace Communications Inc/ 310 E 46th St, New York, NY.............. (212) 687-8105
Pacella, Laura/ 40 Cross St PO Box 695, Norwell, MA.................. (617) 659-7521
Page Arbitrio & Resen Ltd/ 305 E 46th St, New York, NY.............. (212) 421-8190
Paine/Bluett/Paine Inc./ 4617 Edgefield Road, Bethesda, MD....... (301) 493-8445
Paino Promotions/ 31 E 28th St, New York, NY.............................. (212) 689-7471
Parise, Lee/ 3537 W Main St, Mt Kisco, NY................................. (914) 241-7291
Parks, Sabina/ 1234 Mass. Ave. N.W., Washington, DC................ (202) 737-8255
Parry, Ivor A./ 4 Lorraine Dr., Eastchester, NY............................. (914) 961-7338
Passy, Marc-Albert/ 329 E 63rd St, New York, NY........................ (212) 826-6172
Pavone, Joseph/ 76 Bay 26th Street, Brooklyn, NY....................... (212) 946-4998
Pearson, Nancy/ 150 W 55th St, New York, NY............................ (212) 245-1491
Pellegrini & Associates Inc/ 16 E. 40th Street,
New York, NY.. (212) 686-4481
Penn Art Associates/ 307 4th Ave Bank Tower 705,
Pittsburgh, PA... (412) 471-4664
Penn, Tom Limited/ 243 East 58th Street, New York, NY............. (212) 888-6590
Perceptive Marketers Agcy Ltd/ 1920 Chestnut St,
Philadelphia, PA.. (215) 665-8736
Perlman Withers Inc/ 236 E 46th St, New York, NY...................... (212) 599-2380

Perl, Susan Design/ PO Box 971, Providence, RI .... (401) 232-3588
Personal Touch, The/ 10 Columbus Circle, New York, NY............ (212) 752-2345
Peters, Stan Assoc Inc/ 236 E 36th St, New York, NY................. (212) 684-0315
Pettis, Valerie/ 88 Lexington Av #17G, New York, NY .... (212) 683-7382
Petti, William Design, Inc/ 34 Oxford Rd, White Plains, NY......... (914) 682-0696
PFC Advertising Service Co/ 299 Madison Ave, New York, NY...... (212) 391-8030
Picker, Marsha/ 314 W. 19th Street, New York, NY.................... (212) 242-0852
Picone, Robert Advertising/ 289CC Ridge Road,
     Whitehouse Sta., NJ .... (201) 534-6346
Pilallis, Joan/ 1750 Jennings Way, Paoli, PA........................... (215) 296-4039
Pinwheel Graphic Arts Services/ 404 Park Avenue South,
     New York, NY... (212) 684-5140
Plataz, George/ Martin Bldg, Pittsburgh, PA .... (412) 322-3177
Polito, Bill/ 305 W 86th St, New York City, NY .... (212) 877-0714
Pollicino, A. J. Agency Svcs./ 17 Elmwood Court,
     Plainview, NY .... (516) 938-7040
Polson, Saul/ 40 E 84th St, New York, NY............................... (212) 861-6957
Popshots Inc/ 71 W 23rd Street, New York, NY .... (212) 243-7885
Port Miolla Assocs Inc/ 400 Main St, Stamford, CT................... (203) 348-4281
Poverty Hollow Studios/ Box 177, Redding Ridge, CT .... (203) 938-2894
Premedia Inc/ 15 West 44th St, New York, NY .... (212) 921-2470
Prestype/ 194 Veterans Blvd, Carlstadt, NJ .... (201) 933-6011
Priestley, Russell T/ 344 Boylston, Boston, MA .... (617) 267-2088
Primary Design Group Inc/ 138 Spring Street, New York, NY....... (212) 219-1000
Profile Press Inc./ 245 7th Avenue, New York, NY.................... (212) 675-4188
Promotion Solutions, Inc./ 23 E 22nd St, New York, NY............. (212) 505-6616
PRonedeus Arts Inc/ 1776 Broadway, New York, NY .... (212) 586-3770
PUSHPIN LUBALIN PECKOLICK/ 67 Irving Pl.,
     New York, NY .... (212) 674-8080
     See our ad on pages 188, 189
Quon, Mike Design Office/ 53 Spring St., New York, NY .... (212) 226-6024
Rachlin, Yale M/ 715 Boylston St, Boston, MA......................... (617) 267-0804
Racz, Michael/ New York, NY.. (212) 477-0401
Rahl Studio/ 17 W 45th Street, New York, NY .... (212) 840-8516
Ratzkin, Lawrence/ 392 Fifth Avenue, New York, NY .... (212) 279-1314
Raustiala, George/ 154 W. 57th Street, New York, NY .... (212) 541-7376
Raymond, Arthur S, Advertising/ 19 W 44th St, New York, NY...... (212) 840-2352
Raynes Graphics, Coco/ 11 Remington Street, Cambridge, MA...... (617) 354-2526
R C Graphics/ 157 E 57th, New York, NY................................. (212) 755-1383
R D Graphics/ 51 East 42nd Street, New York, NY .... (212) 682-6734
Reese, Tomases and Ellick Inc/ 604 W 10 St, Wilmington, DE ...... (302) 652-3211
Regn/Califano, Inc/ 330 W. 42nd Street, New York, NY .... (212) 239-0380
Reimers, Edith L./ 36 E. 38th Street, New York, NY .... (212) 286-9292
Reinhardt Design Inc/ 175 Main St, White Plains, NY .... (914) 761-4450
Renaissance Communications Inc/ 7835 Eastern Avenue,
     Silver Spring, MD .... (301) 587-1505
Resource Manhattan/ 38 East 57 Street, New York, NY .... (212) 644-3850
Rhaco Advertising/ 549 W. Market St., York, PA....................... (717) 846-0653
Ritta & Associates/ 568 Grand Avenue, Englewood, NJ .... (201) 567-4400
RJ&A/ PO Drawer 21150, Baltimore, MD.................................. (301) 465-8870
Robbins, Ira/ 157 Luquer Street, Brooklyn, NY......................... (212) 624-5194
Rockett & Associates/ 31 Hillside Rd, So. Deerfield, MA .... (413) 665-3064
Rogalski Associates/ 186 Lincoln Str, Boston, MA..................... (617) 451-2111
Rolon De Clet, Rachel/ 5-34 50 Ave., Long Island Cy., NY........... (718) 729-9146
Rosenberg, Jessica Krueger/ 515 W 59th St #31N,
     New York, NY... (212) 757-0785
Rosen, David Michael/ 238 E 24 Street, New York, NY............... (212) 684-5193
Rosenwald, Laurie/ 45 Lispenard St, New York, NY.................. (212) 966-6896
Rose, Sheldon S./ 64-90 99th Street, Forest Hills, NY................ (212) 830-0772
Ross, Andrew Studio/ 148 W 28 St, New York, NY .... (212) 807-6699
ROSS DESIGN ASSOCIATES, INC./ 27 W. 20th St.,
     New York, NY .... (212) 206-0044
     See our ad on pages 190, 191
Rossin Creative Group, The/ 1 E 42nd, New York, NY .... (212) 599-0173
Roston & Co/ 102 Station Road, Great Neck, NY...................... (516) 487-8735
RSV & Associates Inc/ 437 Boylston St, Boston, MA.................. (617) 262-9450
RSW Concept & Design/ 234 5th Ave, New York, NY .... (212) 684-1752
Sadowsky, Horace & Associates/ 20 Jerusalem Avenue,
     Hicksville, NY .... (516) 681-6550
Saiki Design Inc./ 185 Madison Avenue, New York, NY .... (212) 679-3523
Saks, Arnold/ 16 E 79th, New York, NY .... (212) 861-4300
Salesplan Group Ltd/ 42 West 39 Street, New York, NY .... (212) 840-3100
Salpeter-Paganucci, Inc/ 142 East 37 Street, New York, NY .... (212) 683-3310
Saltzman, Mike Group Inc/ 27 W 20th St, New York, NY........... (212) 929-4655
Salvatori, Sarah/ 5 Tudor City Pl, New York City, NY .... (212) 661-3651

Samerjan, George/ 45 Cantitoe St, Katonah, NY .... (914) 232-3725
Sanborn, George/ 299 Madison Ave. Ste. 1200, New York, NY ...... (212) 949-1279
Sandage Advertising&Marketing/ 215 College St,
     Burlington, VT .... (802) 658-4800
Sandgren Assoc/ 60 E 42nd, New York, NY.............................. (212) 687-5060
Santoro Design Consultants/ 503 W 27 St 3rd Floor,
     New York, NY... (212) 651-5126
Saunier, Fredric/ 295 Park Ave So, New York, NY .... (212) 420-4797
Sawyer, Arnie Studios, Inc/ 15 West 28th Street,
     New York, NY... (212) 685-4927
Saxton Communication Group Ltd/ 605 Third Avenue,
     New York, NY... (212) 953-1300
Scerra, Peter/ 342 Madison Ave, New York, NY........................ (212) 490-1610
Schechter Group, The/ 212 East 49th Street, New York, NY .... (212) 752-4400
Schecterson and Schecterson/ 6 East 39 Street Suite 1101,
     New York, NY... (212) 889-3950
Schenck-Row, Kathleen/ 476 Broadway, New York, NY............. (212) 777-1126
Schoenfeld Design Assoc./ 387 Passaic Ave., Fairfield, NJ .... (201) 334-6257
Schuman, Harold Studio/ 359 Boylston Street, Boston, MA .... (617) 266-0911
SCHWAB, MICHAEL DESIGN/ 118 King St.,
     San Francisco, CA.. (415) 546-7559
     See our ad on page 187
Schwartz, Judith/ 667 Madison Avenue, New York, NY .... (212) 750-9720
Scott-Jeffery Group, Inc/ 186 Franklin St, New York, NY .... (212) 431-5841
Seagull, Sara/ 107 W. 28th Street, New York, NY .... (212) 564-5477
Seid, Eva Design/ 85 South Street, New York, NY..................... (212) 825-1984
Seidler, Sheldon/ 244 E 58th St, New York, NY .... (212) 421-5499
SEKIGUCHI, YOSHI/ 437 Marshman St.,
     Highland Park, IL... (312) 433-4140
     See our ad on page 194
Selak, James L./ 14 Brandywine Lane, Fairport, NY .... (716) 223-0150
Seman Graphics/ 12 Eighth St, Pittsburgh, PA .... (412) 261-3511
Sendor, Morris/ 7 Stonehurst Court, Pomona, NY .... (914) 354-8407
Shafer, Rik & Assoc, Inc/ 260 Main St., Northport L.I., NY .... (516) 754-1750
Shafer Studio/ 141 East 44th Str., New York, NY...................... (212) 986-3030
Shanner & Pappas/ 528 Clinton Ave, Bridgeport, CT................. (203) 576-1516
Shapiro, Deborah Designs/ 150 Bentley Ave, Jersey City, NJ .... (201) 432-5198
Shapiro Design Associates Inc/ 55 West 45th Street,
     New York, NY... (212) 221-2625
Siegel, Joel A/ 74 Laurel Hollow Court, Edison, NJ................... (914) 643-1624
Sikorski, Tony/ 2304 Clark Building, Pittsburg, PA................... (412) 391-8366
Silvia, Ken Design Group/ 103 Broad Street, Boston, MA........... (617) 451-1995
Simon, A. Christopher/ 5 Colony Court, Stamford, CT .... (203) 322-6814
Singer, Paul Design/ 494 14th St., New York, NY .... (212) 499-8172
Skolnick, Arnold Imago Design/ 150 5th Avenue, New York, NY..... (212) 620-3140
Stolt, Jill Associates/ 1239 University Ave, Rochester, NY .... (716) 461-2594
Slome, Dorothy/ Box 302, Teaneck, NJ .... (201) 836-1388
Smallkaps Assoc Inc/ 40 E 34th St, New York, NY .... (212) 683-0339
Small, Sherry Associates/ 301 E 79th St, New York, NY .... (212) 794-2180
Smith & Smith/ 150 Lincoln Pl, Brooklyn, NY........................... (212) 636-0050
Snibbe, Patricia/ 139 E. 18th Street, New York, NY .... (212) 475-1730
Sobel, Phillip E., Artist/ 100-26 67th Drive,
     Forest Hills, NY .... (718) 476-3841
Sochynsky, Ilona Associates/ 200 E 36th St, New York, NY .... (212) 686-1275
Solay & Hunt/ 28 W 44th St, New York, NY............................. (212) 840-3313
Sound Graphics/ 300 Henry Street, Brooklyn, NY .... (718) 852-2971
Spier, Carol L/Design/Logos/Pk/ 488 Madison Ave 5th Fl %EJL,
     New York, NY... (212) 751-5185
Spinac, Susan B./ 29 E. 22nd Street, New York, NY .... (212) 677-1499
Stanger Graphics, Linda/ 310 Madison Avenue, New York, NY....... (212) 953-1055
Starr Thomas & Associates Inc/ 23 E 37th St, New York, NY .... (212) 532-6506
Stastny/Fashion Art Direction/ 46 West 83rd St #3A,
     New York, NY... (212) 877-8908
Stefl, Jerry Graphic Design/ 222 W. Palisade Blvd.,
     Palisades Park, NJ .... (201) 947-1292
Stern, Elliot Joel/ 310 East 23 Street, New York, NY .... (212) 473-1923
Stern, Jerry/ 37 W. 46th Street, New York, NY .... (212) 575-7875
Stevens, Monroe/ Route 1 Box 340, Slatington, PA .... (215) 767-6812
Stillman, Linda Graphic Design/ 115 East 90th St,
     New York, NY... (212) 410-3225
Stone Reprographics/ 44 Brattle St, Cambridge, MA .... (617) 495-0200
Strohbach, Hermann/ 435 E. 57th Street, New York, NY .... (212) 755-4819
Structural Graphics Inc/ Plains Rd, Essex, CT .... (203) 767-2661
Structures Creative/ 201 East 69th Street Apt 6-I,
     New York City, NY.. (212) 734-0944

Stuart, Preston Art Services/ 12 East 97 Street,
New York, NY... (212) 722-6637
Studio Cygnus Inc/ 1114 Ave of the Americas, New York, NY .... (212) 391-1099
Success Advertising Agency/ 1426 54th Street, Brooklyn, NY .... (212) 851-6965
Sugar, Robert/ 162 Bennett Avenue, New York, NY .... (212) 207-7335
Sunshine Design, Ltd./ 124 East King Street, York, PA .... (717) 848-4474
Swan, Jim/ 272 Riverside Avenue, Riverside, CT .... (203) 637-5139
Swanson, Martha Lethola/ 14 Wyman Road, Cambridge, MA......... (617) 492-5231
Sweet, Elizabeth Barry/ 3 Fruit Street, Newburyport, MA............. (617) 465-5875
Tactype/ 127 W 26th St, New York, NY .... (212) 924-1800
Talarczyk, Robert Communicatio/ PO Box 55, Fair Haven, NJ....... (201) 747-2205
Talone & Labrasca/ 1920 Sanson St, Philadelphia, PA .... (215) 352-8924
Tamiz-Graphics/ 16 Oakridge Street, Mattapan-Boston, MA.......... (617) 296-7320
Tavkar, Suhas Mechanical Art/ 222 E 46th St Rm 403,
New York, NY... (212) 682-6367
Taylor, Deborah/ 29 Commonwealth Avenue, Boston, MA............ (617) 236-4791
Taylor, Stan/ 6 E 39th, New York, NY .... (212) 685-4741
TECHNO N Y/ 66 Madison Avenue #2A, New York, NY .... (212) 689-3411
Terk, Neil & Co/ 412 E 59 St, New York, NY .... (212) 838-1922
Thomson, Paula/ 326 E. 34th Street, New York, NY .... (212) 689-1396
Thorp Bros/ 410 E 62nd, New York, NY .... (212) 752-4232
Tiani, Alex/ New York, NY .... (212) 683-3310
Timely Advertising/ 542 Somerset St, N Plainfield, NJ .... (201) 561-0988
Tinkel, Kathleen Cronin/ 12 Burr Road, Westport, CT.................. (203) 227-2357
T M P Inc Art Services/ 1633 Broadway 33rd Floor,
New York, NY... (212) 940-7955
Todd, Michael/ 164 E 56th St, New York, NY .... (212) 371-3896
Topart, Inc/ 119 W 57th St, New York, NY .... (212) 489-8623
Tortora, Dominique/ 223 E 89th St, New York, NY .... (212) 534-6468
Tourin, David/ 682 Tuckahoe Road, Yonkers, NY .... (914) 337-7892
Tower Graphic Arts Corp/ 575 Lexington Ave, New York, NY .... (212) 421-0850
Triangle/Vogue Graphic Comms/ 109 Union St,
Palisades Park, NJ .... (201) 947-3302
Tribich Design Associates Inc/ 150 East 35th Street,
New York, NY... (212) 679-6016
Tripack POP Display Mfgs/ 53 Montauk Drive - Suite 101,
Vernon, CT.. (203) 647-1723
Troller, Fred & Associates/ 12 Harbor Lane, Rye, NY .... (914) 698-1405
Trovato, Charles S/ 278 Bay Ridge Pkwy, Brooklyn, NY.............. (212) 238-7601
Tscherny, George Inc/ 238 E 72nd St, New York, NY .... (212) 734-3277
Tull, David Communicat Design/ 38 S Paca St, Baltimore, MD ...... (301) 752-7070
Turzio's Table/ 18 E 48th St, New York, NY .... (212) 751-9350
Tuxedo Park Graphics Inc/ 333 DeMartino, Yonkers, NY .... (914) 965-5410
Two Heads-The Art & Copy Team/ 401 East 81st Street,
New York, NY... (212) 861-0269
Cruz, Ray Graphics/ 246 W. 38 St., New York, NY .... (212) 260-6870
Univers Design/ 143 West 69th Street, New York, NY................. (212) 362-4628
UNLIMITED SWAN, INC./ 272 Riverside Ave.,
Riverside, CT.. (203) 637-4840
See our ad on pages 192, 193

Valentin Associates Inc./ 45 E. 20th St., New York, NY .... (212) 228-1733
Vanzee Associates/ 50 Sound Beach Avenue, Old Greenwich, CT..... (203) 637-0699
Vila, Doris/ 157 E 33 St, New York, NY .... (212) 686-5387
Vlad, George/ PO Box 515, Tuckahoe, NY .... (914) 779-6698
Vladimir Art Studio/ 392 Fifth Ave, New York, NY .... (212) 947-0464
Voutas, Martha Productions/ 1181 Broadway, New York, NY........ (212) 889-7887
Waks, Albert/ 430 E. 11th Street, New York, NY .... (212) 228-1287
Wald, Susan Assoc Inc/ 157 E 72nd St, New York, NY .... (212) 570-2386
Walker Graphic Design/ 5800 Arlington Avenue, Riverdale, NY ..... (212) 884-9117
Wasserman & Associates/ 863 Broadway, New York, NY............. (212) 989-8844
Waters, John Associates, Inc/ 3 W. 18th Street,
New York, NY... (212) 807-0717
Waxberg & Associates/ 8-10 Broad Street, Red Bank, NJ .... (201) 530-0085
Weaver, Nlee/ 129 W 22nd St #9A, New York City, NY .... (212) 242-8215
Weed, Eunice Associates Inc./ 370 Lexington Avenue,
New York, NY... (212) 725-4933
Weems, Samuel/ 119 College Avenue, West Somerville, MA .... (617) 666-4666
Weil, Susan/ 25 Lake Street, White Plains, NY .... (914) 428-6841
Weinstein, Iris/ 39 E. 12th Street, New York, NY...................... (212) 228-1673
Weiss, Helene J/ 233 E. 21st Street, New York, NY .... (212) 254-1365
Wharton Marketing Group Ltd/ 155 East 23rd Street Suite 209,
New York, NY... (212) 260-0320
Whelan Design Office Inc, The/ 144 West 27 Street,
New York, NY... (212) 691-4404
Whitehouse & Katz/ 18 East 16th St, New York, NY.................. (212) 398-0879
Wilks, Ron/ 301 E. 22 Street, New York, NY .... (212) 260-0153
Wille, Robert Art Director/ Landmark Adv & PR, 20 Troy Rd,
Whippany, NJ .... (201) 887-1200
Willing Group, The/ 635 Center Avenue, Mamaroneck, NY .... (914) 381-4700
Wintering Communications/ 14 W. 55th Street, New York, NY ...... (212) 246-9887
Winters, Joan/ 236 E 5th Street #3D, New York, NY.................. (212) 475-6605
Wintner, Leslie/ 393 Beacon Street, Boston, MA....................... (617) 353-1010
Woll, Elizabeth Ann/ 120 W. Main Street, Mt. Kisco, NY............. (914) 241-3274
Wood, Alan/ 274 Madison Avenue, New York, NY .... (212) 889-5195
Word-Wise Advertising/ 325 West 45 Street, New York, NY .... (212) 247-0124
Working Graphics/ 135 E 56th St, New York, NY...................... (212) 752-9415
WPR Advertising/ 4 Lakeside Office Park, Wakefield, MA .... (617) 245-1515
Wright, Kent M Associates Inc/ 22 Union Avenue, Sudbury, MA..... (617) 443-9909
Yamashita, Taro Hiroshi/ 211 E 53rd St, New York, NY.............. (212) 753-3242
Youner, Herb/Design/ 21 Jordan Rd, Hastings on Hud, NY .... (914) 478-2592
Young and Thomas/ 8 Steephill Road, Weston, CT.................... (203) 227-5672
Your Corporate Look/ 60 E 42nd Street Room 648,
New York, NY... (212) 682-2555
Zahor Design Incorporated/ 150 East 35th Street,
New York, NY... (212) 532-7475
Zalkind-Schur, Margot/ 15 Sleeper Street, Boston, MA .... (617) 423-0729
Zavada, Barbara J. Associates/ 58 Dannell Drive,
Stamford, CT... (203) 322-4048
Zmiejko Associates Design/ PO Box 126, Freeland, PA .... (717) 636-2304

PHOTOGRAPHY

PHOTOGRAPHERS

AAA Perluck, David/ 270 Broadway, Providence, RI .... (401) 831-5796
Aaron, Peter/ 222 Valley Place, Mamaroneck, NY.................... (914) 698-4060
Abarno, Richard/ #4 Red Cross Ave, Newport, RI.................... (401) 846-5820
Abatelli, Gary/ 80 Charles St., New York, NY.................... (212) 243-1034
Abbe, Kathryn/ Brookville Road, Jericho, NY.................... (516) 921-2379
Abbey Photographers Inc/ 268 Broad Avenue,
    Palisades Park, NJ .... (201) 947-1221
Abbott, Berenice/ Rd 1, Abbott Village, ME.................... (207) 997-3763
Abbott, Waring/ 78 Franklin Street, New York, NY.................... (212) 925-6082
Abraham, Jack/ 48 E. 29th Street, New York, NY.................... (212) 889-1063
Abramowitz, Jerry/ 680 Broadway, New York, NY.................... (212) 420-9500
Abrams, Larry/ 7 River St., Milford, CT.................... (203) 878-5090
Abramson, Michael/ 84 University Pl., New York, NY.................... (212) 691-2601
Abrams, Paul/ 230 Central Park W, New York, NY.................... (212) 787-6646
Acs, Sandor/ 39 W. 67th Street, New York, NY.................... (212) 787-0868
Adams, George/ 15 W 38th, New York, NY .... (212) 391-1345
Adams, Molly/ Kennedy Road, Mendham, NJ.................... (201) 543-4521
Adams Studio Inc/ 1523 22st NW Courtyard, Washington, DC ...... (202) 785-2188
Adkins, Bill/ 1501 Taney Ave., Frederick, MD .... (301) 663-6988
Adler, Arnold/ 214 E. 26 St., New York, NY.................... (212) 532-2584
Aerograhics/ 514 W. 24th Street, New York, NY.................... (212) 807-0816
Aguiar, Walter/ Old Chelsea Station, New York, NY.................... (212) 929-9045
Aharoni, Oudi/ 325 the Bowery, New York, NY .... (212) 777-0847
Aich, Clara/ 218 E 25th, New York, NY.................... (212) 686-4220
Aiello, Frank/ 2072 E. 19th St., Brooklyn, NY.................... (212) 339-3787
Aiosa, Vincent C./ 5 West 31 Street, New York, NY.................... (212) 563-1859
AJ Photoproductions/ 198-25 Dunton Ave, Hollis, NY.................... (212) 776-6983
Akis, Emanuel Photography/ 6 W. 18th Street, New York, NY .... (212) 620-0299
Alastair Finlay/ 38 E 21st, New York, NY.................... (212) 260-4297
Albert, Jade/ 636 Avenue of the Americas, New York, NY.................... (212) 288-9653
Alberts, Andrea/ 100 Fifth Avenue, New York, NY.................... (212) 242-5794
Albert's Photo/ 409 Moody St., Waltham, MA.................... (617) 894-0082
Alcindor's Studio/ 682 Sixth Ave, New York, NY.................... (212) 243-0351
Alcorn, Richard/ 160 W 95th, New York, NY.................... (212) 866-1161
Alexander, Jules/ 126 Madison Ave., New York, NY.................... (212) 686-7752
Alexander, Jules/ 9 Belmont Ave., Rye, NY.................... (914) 967-8985
Alexander, Robert J./ 50 W. 29th Street, New York, NY.................... (212) 684-0180
Alexanders, John/ 308 E. 73rd Street, New York, NY.................... (212) 734-9166
Alexanian, Nubar:Photographer/ One Thompson Sq Box 311,
    Charlestown, MA .... (617) 242-4312
Allen, Jim/ 21 E. 22nd St., New York, NY.................... (212) 473-8020
Allied Photo Studios Inc/ 121 Pleasant Ave,
    Upper Saddle Rv, NJ .... (201) 327-6688
All-Photography Studio/ 1529 Wisconsin Avenue NW,
    Washington, DC .... (202) 333-3560
Alonso Associates/ 425 Fairfield Avenue, Stamford, CT.................... (203) 359-2838
Alosa, Vincent/ 5 W 31st, New York, NY.................... (212) 563-1859
Alpha Commercial Studio/ 36 E. 20th Street, New York, NY.................... (212) 674-2350
Alt, Howard/ 24 West 31 St, New York, NY.................... (212) 594-3300
Altman, Steve/ 79 Grand St., Jersey City, NJ.................... (201) 434-0022
Aly, Bob/ 91 Teneyck Walk, Brooklyn, NY.................... (212) 387-6819
Amabile, Mark/ 381 Park Avenue S. Rm 621, New York, NY.................... (212) 683-2896
Amato, Paul/ 88 Lexington Ave, New York, NY.................... (212) 725-0904
Ambrose, Ken/ 44 E. 23rd Street, New York, NY.................... (212) 260-4848
American Artists Rep. Inc./ 353 W 53 St., New York, NY.................... (212) 682-2462
American Audio Visual Inc./ 216 East 45 St, New York, NY.................... (212) 661-6100
Ames, Thomas, Jr./ 404 Third St, Hoboken, NJ.................... (201) 656-2941
Amrine, Jamie Studio/ 30 W 22 St, New York, NY.................... (212) 243-2178
Ancona, George/ Crickettown Rd, Stony Point, NY.................... (914) 786-3043
Anderson, Dick/ Mooreland Road, Greenwich, CT.................... (203) 661-4197
Anderson, Earl Andre/ Bronx, NY.................... (212) 519-7062
Anderson, Jean/ One Lexington Ave, New York City, NY.................... (212) 673-8569
Anderson, Jim/ 188-190 Grand St, Brooklyn, NY.................... (212) 388-1083
Anderson, Richard/ 2523 N Calvert St, Baltimore, MD.................... (301) 889-0585
Anderson, Stephen/ 251 W 19th, New York, NY.................... (212) 255-5256
Anderson, Wayne A./ 951 S. Plymouth Ave., Rochester, NY.................... (716) 328-2675
Andrews, Bert/ 750 Eighth Avenue, New York, NY.................... (212) 354-5430
Angelakis, Manos/ 114 E 32nd St Suite 902, New York, NY.................... (212) 685-2770
Ansin, Mikki/ 2 Ellery Square, Cambridge, MA.................... (617) 661-1640
Antonio-Stephen Studio/ 36 E 20th St, New York, NY.................... (212) 674-2350
Anyon, Benjamin/ 206 Spring Run Lane, Downingtown, PA.................... (215) 363-0744
APA / NY/ 118 E. 25th Street, New York, NY.................... (212) 254-5500

Appelbaum, Stephen/ 1551 Stuyvesant Avenue, Union, NJ.................... (201) 687-7727
Apple, Richard/ 80 Varick Street, New York, NY.................... (212) 966-6782
Apple Studios/ 1551 Stuyvesant Ave, Union, NJ.................... (201) 687-7727
Arakawa, Nobu/ 40 E. 21st Street, New York, NY.................... (212) 475-0206
Aranita, Jeffrey/ 60 Pineapple St, Brooklyn, NY.................... (212) 625-7672
Arcieri, Tremont/ 320 E 39th, New York, NY.................... (212) 689-3399
Ardai, Tibor/ 350 E. 52 St., New York, NY.................... (212) 758-0203
Arky, David/ 3 West 18th Street, New York, NY.................... (212) 242-4760
Arma, Thomas/ 38 W. 26th Street, New York, NY.................... (212) 243-7904
Arnold, Peter, Inc./ 1466 Broadway, New York, NY.................... (212) 840-6928
Arpadi, Allen G./ 450 Broome Street, New York, NY.................... (212) 966-4185
Ashe, Bill Studio/ 534 W 35th, New York, NY.................... (212) 695-6473
Ashe, Terry/ 315 W. 86th Street Apt. 7F, New York, NY.................... (212) 580-8921
A S M Hq/ 205 Lexington Ave 19th Floor, Farmingdale, NY.................... (212) 889-9144
Atkin, Jonathan/ 23 E. 17 St., New York, NY.................... (212) 242-5218
Atlantic Photo Svc/ 669 Boylston, Boston, MA.................... (617) 267-7480
Aubrey, Daniel/ 365 First Ave, New York City, NY.................... (212) 598-4191
Aucoin, Stephen/ 38 W 26th, New York, NY.................... (212) 243-3015
Audio Visual Group/ 1107 Walnut St, Philadelphia, PA.................... (215) 923-0348
Auerbach, Scott/ 32 Country Rd, Mamaroneck, NY.................... (914) 698-9073
August, Ray/ 149-41 Elm Ave., Flushing, NY.................... (718) 445-1792
Avedis Studio/ 381 Park Avenue S., New York, NY.................... (212) 685-5888
Avedon, Richard/ 407 E 75th St, New York, NY.................... (212) 879-6325
Avis, Paul/ 142 Main St, Nashua, NH.................... (603) 886-1757
Azzi, Robert/ 415 Madison Avenue, New York, NY.................... (212) 750-1020
Babushkin, Mark/ 110 W. 31st Street, New York, NY.................... (212) 239-6630
Baghsarian Studio, Avedis/ 381 Park Avenue S., New York, NY.................... (212) 685-5387
Bahrt, Irving/ 305 E 46th, New York, NY.................... (212) 759-1750
Baker, Bill Photojournalism/ 1045 Pebble Hill Road,
    Doylestown, PA.................... (215) 348-9743
Baker, Christopher/ 160 Fifth Ave, New York, NY.................... (212) 924-6760
Baker, Gloria S./ 22 W. 75th Street, New York, NY.................... (212) 877-1416
Baker, Joe/ 156 Fifth Avenue, New York, NY.................... (212) 924-3440
Bakerman, Nelson/ 342 W. 56th St. #1d, New York, NY.................... (212) 489-1647
Bakit Bath/ 32 E 30th, New York, NY.................... (212) 683-6093
Baldwin, Joel/ 20 E. 20th Street, New York, NY.................... (212) 533-7470
Bale, Jr./ 110 W. 40th St. Rm. 607, New York, NY.................... (212) 431-6539
Ballantyne, Thomas C./ 270 Westford Road, Concord, MA.................... (617) 369-7599
Bank, Bobby/ 3025 Ocean Ave, Brooklyn, NY.................... (212) 332-5563
Banks, Don/ 10 Waterside Plz, New York, NY.................... (212) 684-4139
Bantry, Bryan/ 105 West 55 Street, New York, NY.................... (212) 245-0200
Barba, Dan/ 201 E. 16th St., New York, NY.................... (212) 420-8611
Barber, Jim/ 873 Broadway, New York, NY.................... (212) 598-4500
Barboza, Anthony/ 108 E. 16th Street, New York, NY.................... (212) 674-5759
Barclay Studios, Robert W./ 5 W. 19th Street, New York, NY.................... (212) 255-3440
Bardes, Harold/ 1812 Kennedy Blvd., Union City, NJ.................... (201) 867-7808
Barkentin, George/ 15 W 18th Street, New York, NY.................... (212) 243-2174
BARKER, KENT PHOTOGRAPHY/ 2039 Farrington,
    Dallas, TX .... (214) 760-7470
    See our ad on page 198
Barksdale, William E Agri Phot/ PO Box 17726, Memphis, TN.................... (901) 767-9540
Barnell, J D/ 164 Madison Ave, New York, NY.................... (212) 686-8850
Barnett, Peggy and Ronald/ 26 E. 22nd Street, New York, NY.................... (212) 673-0500
Barone, Christopher/ 381 Wright Avenue, Kingston, PA.................... (717) 287-4680
Barrett, Albert F/ 333 W. 52nd Street, New York, NY.................... (212) 582-9444
Barrett Gallagher/ 222 Central Park S., New York, NY.................... (212) 246-3127
Barrick, Rick/ 12 E. 18th Street, New York, NY.................... (212) 741-2304
Barr, Neal/ 222 Central Park S, New York, NY.................... (212) 765-5760
Barrow, Scott/ 214 W. 30th Street, New York, NY.................... (212) 736-4567
Barrows, Wendy/ 205 East 22 St, New York, NY.................... (212) 685-0799
Bartay Studio/ 15 East 31st St. - 5th Fl., New York, NY.................... (212) 725-1359
Bartlett, Linda/ 3316 Runnymede Place N.W., Washington, DC .... (202) 362-4777
Bartone, Laurence/ 20 E. 20th Street, New York, NY.................... (212) 254-6430
Barton, Paul/ 101 W 18th Street, New York, NY.................... (212) 533-1422
Baruffi, Andrea/ 72 Barrows Street Apt. 6G, New York, NY.................... (212) 989-8357
Baskin, Gerry/ 12 Union Park Street, Boston, MA.................... (617) 482-3316
Bassman, Lillian/ 117 E. 83rd Street, New York, NY.................... (212) 737-4737
Bates, Carolyn/ Burlington, VT.................... (802) 862-5386
Bates, Ray/ West Street, Newfane, VT.................... (802) 365-7770
Batlin Inc., Lee/ 37 E. 28th Street, New York, NY.................... (212) 685-9492
Battaglia, Nancy/ P.O. Box 229, Lake Placid, NY.................... (518) 523-3440
Baumann, Barbara/ 156 W. 73rd Street, New York, NY.................... (212) 724-9855
Bean, Jeremiah/ 96 North Avenue, Garwood, NJ.................... (201) 789-2200
Bean, John/ 5 W. 19th St., New York, NY.................... (212) 242-8106
Beard, Peter/ 136 E 57th, New York, NY.................... (212) 246-0679

Beauchamp, Jacques/ 42 E. 23rd Street, New York, NY .... (212) 475-7787
Beaudin, Ted/ 6 W. 37th Street, New York, NY .... (212) 594-4082
Bebirian/ 70-02 Nansen Street, Forest Hills, NY .... (212) 268-6957
Bechtold, John/ 117 E 31st, New York, NY .... (212) 679-7630
Beck, Arthur/ 119 W. 22nd Street, New York, NY .... (212) 691-8330
Becker, Donald A./ 13115 Dauphine St., Silver Spring, MD .... (301) 949-0473
Beckerman, Arnold/ 153 E 32nd St, New York, NY .... (212) 889-6070
Beckman, Janette/ 59 Franklin St, New York, NY .... (212) 431-5853
Beck-Odette, Alice/ 209 E. 23rd Street, New York, NY .... (212) 679-7350
Bedford Photo-Graphic Studio/ P.O. Box 64 Rt. 22,
    Bedford Village, NY .... (914) 234-3123
Beigel, Dan/ 2024 Chesapeake Rd., Annapolis, MD .... (301) 757-0635
Bellak Richard/ 127 Remsen Street, Brooklyn, NY .... (212) 858-2417
Bell, Chuck/ 818 Liberty Avenue, Pittsburgh, PA .... (412) 261-2022
Beller, Janet/ 48 W. 21 St., New York, NY .... (212) 741-2776
Bell, Hugh/ 873 Broadway, New York, NY .... (212) 260-2260
Belmonte Camera/ 43 Homestead Ave, Greenfield, MA .... (413) 773-7744
Bender, Rhoda/ 29 Arista Drive, Dix Hills, NY .... (516) 549-9158
Benedict, William/ 5 Tudor City Place, New York, NY .... (212) 697-4460
Bennett, Bruce Photography/ 35 Meadow Lane, Hicksville, NY ...... (516) 681-2850
Bennett, Ed/ 64 E 55th St, New York City, NY .... (212) 371-8541
Bennett, Jerre L./ 214 Sullivan St. 5th Fl. D,
    New York City, NY .... (212) 677-2345
Bennett, Philip/ 1181 Broadway, New York, NY .... (212) 683-3906
Benn, Nathan/ 925 1/2 F Street N.W., Washington, DC .... (202) 638-5705
BENSON, HANK PHOTOGRAPHY/ 653 Bryant St.,
    San Francisco, CA .... (415) 543-8153
      See our ad on pages 200, 201
Benson, Harry/ 181 E 73rd, New York, NY .... (212) 249-0284
Benson, Richard Photography/ 156 Fifth Avenue Room 410,
    New York, NY .... (212) 242-3126
Benveniste, Kathleen/ 104 W 17th, New York, NY .... (212) 242-4153
BERENHOLTZ, RICHARD/ 600 W. 111th St., New York, NY ...... (212) 222-1302
      See our ad on page 199
Berger, Eduard/ 42 W 29th New York, NY .... (212) 686-4445
Berger, Vivian/ 441 Kimball Avenue, Yonkers, NY .... (914) 237-5914
Berg, Hal/ 67 Hillary Circle, New Rochelle, NY .... (914) 235-9356
Bergier, Barbara Studio/ 55 W. 21st Street, New York, NY .... (212) 242-8308
BERGMAN, ALAN/ 8241 W. 4th St., Los Angeles, CA .... (213) 852-1408
      See our ad on page 202
Berkun, Phillip/ 119 Fifth Ave., New York, NY .... (212) 254-7358
Berkwit Lane/ 262 Fifth Ave, New York, NY .... (212) 889-5911
Berman, Howard/ 5 E. 19th Street, New York, NY .... (212) 473-3366
Berman, Malcolm/ 253 N Third St, Philadelphia, PA .... (215) 928-1061
Bernard, Michel G/ 150 E. 58th Street, New York, NY .... (212) 888-7272
Bernson, Carol/ 119 Fifth Avenue, Rm 806, New York, NY .... (212) 473-3884
Bernstein, Alan/ 365 First Ave, New York, NY .... (212) 254-1355
Bernstein & Andriulli, Inc/ 60 E 42 St, New York, NY .... (212) 741-3104
Bernstein, Daniel/ 7 Fuller Street, Waltham, MA .... (617) 894-0473
Bernstein, David M./ 67 Columbia Street, New York, NY .... (212) 477-1983
Berry & Homer Photgrphcs, Inc./ 1210 Race St.,
    Philadelphia, PA .... (215) 563-0888
Bersell, Barbara/ 12 E. 86 St., New York, NY .... (212) 734-9049
Bester, Roger Inc./ 119 Fifth Ave., New York, NY .... (212) 254-0108
Betz, Charles/ 50 West 17 Street, New York, NY .... (212) 807-0457
Bevilacqua Studio/ 202 East 42nd Street, New York, NY .... (212) 490-0355
Bezahler, Alysse/ 598 Broadway 11th Floor,
    New York City, NY .... (415) 621-7589
Bezushko, Bob & George/ 1311 Irving St, Philadelphia, PA .... (215) 735-7771
Bibikow, Walter/ 76 Batterymarch St, Boston, MA .... (617) 451-3464
Biddle, Geoffrey/ 5 E. 3rd Street, New York, NY .... (212) 228-6165
Big City Productions/ 5 East 19 Street, New York, NY .... (212) 473-3366
Bindas Studios/ 205 A Street, Boston, MA .... (617) 268-3050
Bingham and Hagenbuch/ 8 Abbott Street, East Rochester, NH ..... (603) 332-5266
Binzen, Bill/ Indian Mountain Road, Lakeville, CT .... (203) 435-2485
Biondo, Tom C/O Brennan/ 32 E 38th St, New York, NY .... (212) 889-6555
Bisbee, Terry/ 290 W. 12th Street, New York, NY .... (212) 242-4762
Bishop, David/ 251 W 19th Street #2C, New York, NY .... (212) 929-4355
Bishop, Edward/ 186 Lincoln Street, Boston, MA .... (617) 536-7465
Bishop, Randa/ 59 W 12th, New York, NY .... (212) 206-1122
Bittner, Peter Studio/ 36 E. 20th Street, New York, NY .... (212) 242-4150
BLACK BOX STUDIOS, INC./ 824 Exposition #215,
    Dallas, TX .... (214) 826-3348
      See our ad on page 203
Black Box, The/ 126 5th Avenue, New York, NY .... (212) 255-4164

Blackman, Barry/ 115 E 23rd Street 10th Floor, New York, NY ..... (212) 473-3100
Blackman, Jeffrey/ 23-23 E. 12th Street, Brooklyn, NY .... (212) 769-0986
Blackstock, Ann/ 400 W. 43 St. #4e, New York, NY .... (212) 695-2525
Blaine Waller/ 202 E 35th, New York, NY .... (212) 686-8555
Blakeley, Jim Photographer,Inc/ 1061 Folsom Street,
    San Francisco, CA .... (415) 558-9300
Blake, Mike Photography/ 107 South Street, Boston, MA .... (617) 451-0660
Blakeslee Lane Inc/ 916 N Charles St, Baltimore, MD .... (301) 727-8800
Blanch, Andrea/ 434 E. 52nd Street, New York, NY .... (212) 888-7912
Blank, Bruce/ 228 Clearfield Ave., Norristown, PA .... (215) 539-6166
Blate, Samuel R Assocs/ 10331 Watkins Mill Dr,
    Gaithersburg, MD .... (301) 840-2248
Bleiman, Jack/ 23 Main St, Phoenixville, PA .... (215) 933-4561
Bleiweiss, Herb/ 959 Eighth Avenue, New York, NY .... (212) 262-3318
Blevins, Burgess/ 103 E. Read Street, Baltimore, MD .... (301) 685-0740
Blinkoff, Richard/ 147 W. 15th Street, New York, NY .... (212) 620-7883
Blizzard, William C./ Box 11 Riv. Mobile H, Winfield, WV .... (304) 755-0094
Block, Ira/ 512 E. 82 St., New York, NY .... (212) 879-4697
Block, Ray/ 458 W. 20th Street, New York, NY .... (212) 691-9375
Bloom, Mary/ 178 Fifth Avenue, New York, NY .... (212) 255-1896
Bobbe, Leland/ 51 West 28th St, New York City, NY .... (212) 685-5238
Bobrow, Andy/ 320 W 89th, New York, NY .... (212) 874-7330
Bodi Studios/ 340 W 39 Street, New York, NY .... (212) 947-7883
Bogertman Inc/ 34 W 28 St, New York, NY .... (212) 889-8871
Bohmark Ltd./ 43 E. 30th Street, New York, NY .... (212) 889-9670
Bohm, L D Studios/ 7 Park St, Montclair, NJ .... (201) 746-3434
Bolesta, Alan/ 11 Riverside Dr., New York, NY .... (212) 873-1932
Bolster, Mark/ 1736 Second Ave., New York, NY .... (212) 348-0965
Boman, Eric/ 425 W 23rd St Suite 17A, New York, NY .... (212) 243-2750
Bookbinder, Sigmund/ Box 833 Jeremy Swamp Rd.,
    Southbury, CT .... (203) 264-5137
Bordnick, Barbara/ 39 E. 19th Street, New York, NY .... (212) 533-1180
BORDNICK, BARBARA/ 39 E. 19th St., New York, NY .... (212) 533-1180
      See our ad on page 204
Borst, Richard/ 193 Prince St, New York, NY .... (212) 254-9511
Boscarino, John/ 257 Park Ave S, New York, NY .... (212) 777-2800
Bosch, Peter/ 477 Broome St, New York City, NY .... (212) 925-0707
Boston Photocopy Inc/ 217 Stuart Street, Boston, MA .... (617) 542-1125
Bosworth & Daughter/ 350 Beacon, Boston, MA .... (617) 262-1247
Boszko, Ron Photographer/ 140 W 57th, New York, NY .... (212) 541-5504
Bowden, John/ 1007 E Street SE, Washington, DC .... (202) 543-3526
Bower, Holly/ 61 E. 11th Street, New York, NY .... (212) 228-3198
Bowman, Michael/ 317 West 98th Street, New York, NY .... (212) 662-5893
Bowman, Ron/ PO Box 7071, Lancaster, PA .... (717) 898-7716
Bowman, Thomas/ 4 Judy Dr. Rd. #3, Annville, PA .... (717) 838-3136
Bowron, Scott/ 114 West 29th Street, New York, NY .... (212) 594-0293
Boxer, Jeff/ 14 Newbury St, Boston, MA .... (617) 266-4037
BOYD, BILL PHOTOGRAPHY/ 614 Santa Barbara St.,
    Santa Barbara, CA .... (805) 962-9193
      See our ad on page 205
Boyd, Gus/ 130 E. 75th Street, New York, NY .... (212) 988-5095
Bracco, Bob/ 43 E. 19th Street, New York, NY .... (212) 228-0230
Brady, Mathew B./ 31 W. 27th St. 12th Floor, New York, NY ...... (212) 683-6060
Branco, Tony/ 32 Bella Vista St, Locust Valley, NY .... (516) 674-3480
Brandenburg, Jim/ 1145 17th St NW, Washington, DC .... (202) 857-7643
Brandt, Peter/ 73 Fifth Ave. #6b, New York, NY .... (212) 242-4289
Branovan-Harting Studio/ 327 Summer St, Boston, MA .... (617) 451-6330
Braune, Peter/ 134 West 32 St Room 602, New York City, NY ...... (212) 219-2489
Braun, Yenachem/ 35 W 31st St, New York City, NY .... (212) 736-2254
Braveman, Alan-Michael Studios/ 485 Fifth Ave, New York, NY ..... (212) 682-1794
Braverman, Ed Strobo/Motion/ 337 Summer St, Boston, MA ...... (617) 423-3373
Bredel, Walter/ 21 E. 10th Street, New York, NY .... (212) 228-8565
Brenner, Jay/ 18 E. 17th Street, New York, NY .... (212) 741-2244
Breskin/Emberling Studio/ 324 Lafayette Street,
    New York, NY .... (212) 925-2271
Breskin, Michael/ 324 Lafayette St., New York, NY .... (212) 925-2271
Brewster, Don/ 235 West End Avenue, New York, NY .... (212) 874-0548
Bridges, Kiki/ 147 W. 26th St., New York, NY .... (212) 807-6563
Brignolo, Joseph B/ Oxford Springs Rd, Chester, NY .... (914) 496-4453
Brill, James/ 237 E. 79 St., New York, NY .... (212) 744-4583
Britton, Peter/ 315 E. 68th Street, New York, NY .... (212) 737-1664
Britz Fotograf/ 2619 Lovegrove Street, Baltimore, MD .... (301) 338-1820
Brizzi, Andrea/ 175 Washington Park, Brooklyn, NY .... (212) 522-0836
Brodsky, Joel/ 276 5th Ave Room 1103, New York, NY .... (212) 696-1280
Brody, Bob/ 5 W. 19 St., New York, NY .... (212) 741-0013

Brody, Robert/ 5 W. 19th Street, New York, NY .... (212) 741-0013
Bronson, Emerick/ Box 1500, Sag Harbor, NY .... (516) 725-2266
Bronstein, Steve/ 5 E 19th, New York, NY .... (212) 473-3366
Brooks, Charlotte/ Milltown Road, Holmes, NY .... (914) 878-9376
Brosan/ 873 Broadway, New York, NY .... (212) 473-1471
Brown, Blain/ 32 W. 31st Street, New York, NY .... (212) 279-0162
Brown, Curtis/ 130 W 20th St, New York City, NY .... (212) 807-1511
Brown, Ed/ 146 W 29th Street, New York, NY .... (212) 580-2483
Brownell, David/ Box 97, Hamilton, MA .... (617) 468-4284
Brown, Jim/ 286 Summer St, Boston, MA .... (617) 423-6484
Brown, Nancy & David/ 6 W. 20th Street, New York, NY .... (212) 675-8067
Brown, Stephen R./ 1882 Columbia Road NW, Washington, DC ..... (202) 667-1965
Brown, Steven/ 465 W. 23rd Street, New York, NY .... (212) 243-2474
Brown Studio, Owen/ 134 W. 29th Street, New York, NY .... (212) 947-9470
BRT Photographic Illustrations/ 911 State St.,
 Lancaster, PA .... (717) 393-0918
Bruderer, Rolf/ 443 Park Avenue S., New York, NY .... (212) 684-4890
Brummett, Richard/ 117 W. 13th Street, New York, NY .... (212) 989-2313
BRUNO/HOLLY KAPLAN/ 35 W. 36th St., New York, NY .... **(212) 563-2730**
 See our ad on page 216
Bryan, Bob/ 10 W. 18th Street, New York, NY .... (212) 989-2595
Bryson, John/ 12 E. 62nd Street, New York, NY .... (212) 755-1321
Buceta, Jaimey/ 300 Park Ave. S., New York, NY .... (212) 254-2160
Buchanan, Robert Photog/ 12 Cleveland Street, Valhalla, NY .... (914) 997-1944
Buck, Bruce/ 171 First Ave, New York, NY .... (212) 777-8309
Buck, Ken Photography/ 23 Oxford Cir., Belmont, MA .... (617) 484-3829
Buckler, Susanne/ 344 West 38th Street, New York, NY .... (212) 279-0043
Buckley, Peter/ 140 E. 83rd Street Apt. 10, New York, NY ..... (212) 744-0658
Buckner, Bill/ 37 W. 20 St., New York, NY .... (212) 242-5129
Buckner, Ray/ 119 W. 23. St., New York, NY .... (212) 924-4620
Budde John/ 211 East 17th Street, New York, NY .... (212) 533-3138
Budin, Elbert Suarez Santiago/ 424 W. 33rd Street,
 New York, NY .... (212) 564-9050
Buice, Brad/ 132 West 21 St, New York, NY .... (212) 206-0966
Bulkin, Susan/ 1700 Pine Street, Philadelphia, PA .... (215) 985-9090
Bullaty, Sonja/ 336 Central Park W., New York, NY .... (212) 663-2122
Bungarz, Jack/ 228 Penny Ave., Wilmington, DE .... (302) 764-1318
Buonanno, Ray/ 237 W. 26 St., New York City, NY .... (212) 675-7680
Burke, John Hamilton/ 31 Stanhope Street, Boston, MA .... (617) 536-4912
Burklin, Bruno/ 873 Broadway, New York, NY .... (212) 420-0208
Burnes/Von Koschembahr/ 12 Fitch St, East Norwalk, CT .... (203) 866-0032
Burpee, Liz/ 249 E. 48th Street, New York, NY .... (212) 752-2967
Burrell, Fred/ 16 W. 22nd Street, New York, NY .... (212) 691-0808
Buschner Studios Inc/ 77 Saginaw Dr, Rochester, NY .... (716) 473-0010
BUSH, CHARLES WILLIAM/ 7623 Beverly Blvd.,
 Los Angeles, CA.. **(213) 937-8246**
 See our ad on pages 206, 207
Bushnell, Catharine/ 300 E. 40th Street #24W, New York, NY ...... (212) 697-9746
Butwick, Roslyn/ 360 W 28th Street, New York, NY .... (212) 603-9144
Byers, Bruce/ 11 W. 20th Street, New York, NY .... (212) 242-5846
Cable, Wayne Photography/ 1302 W. Waveland Ave.,
 Chicago, IL .... (312) 248-2959
CACITTI, STAN/ 589 Howard St., San Francisco, CA .... **(415) 974-5668**
 See our ad on page 209
Cadge Productions/ 15 W 28th, New York, NY .... (212) 685-2435
Cahill, Bill/ 37 E. 28th Street, New York, NY .... (212) 725-8178
Cahill, Steve/ 175 Wyman St, Waltham, MA .... (617) 890-6300
Cailor/Resnick/ 237 W. 54th Street, New York, NY .... (212) 977-4300
Calderwood, Gary/ 4433 Spruce Street, Philadelphia, PA .... (215) 386-0654
Callis Studio, Chris/ 91 Fifth Avenue, New York, NY .... (212) 243-0231
Cal, Mario/ 27 West 20th Street, New York, NY .... (212) 807-7926
Camart Studio/ 6 W 20th, New York, NY .... (212) 691-8840
Camera Communications/ 39 W. 38th Street, New York, NY .... (212) 391-1373
Camera Five Inc./ 6 W. 20th Street, New York, NY .... (212) 989-2004
Campbell, Barbara/ 147 W. 22 St., New York, NY .... (212) 929-5620
Campbell Photos, Inc./ 86 University Ave., Rochester, NY .... (716) 454-1724
Camp, Don/ 4511 Spruce Street, Philadelphia, PA .... (215) 387-9528
Campos, John/ 18 W. 27 St., New York, NY .... (212) 889-4018
Camp, Woodfin/ 415 Madison Ave., New York, NY .... (212) 750-1024
C & I PHOTOGRAPHY, INC./ 3523 Ryder St.,
 Santa Clara, CA.. **(408) 733-5855**
 See our ad on page 208
Cannareila, Bud/ 156 Fifth Avenue Rm 308, New York, NY .... (212) 691-1750
Cannon, Gregory/ 44 W. 17th St., New York, NY .... (212) 243-2798
Cantor, Mark S Studio/ 156 Fifth Ave, New York City, NY .... (212) 924-1764

Cantor, Phil/ 75 Ninth Ave., New York, NY .... (212) 243-1143
Capa, Cornell/ 275 Fifth Avenue, New York, NY .... (212) 860-1772
Caravaglia, Tom/ 830 Broadway, New York, NY .... (212) 260-4840
Cardacino, Michael/ 123 West 28th St, New York, NY .... (212) 947-9307
Carrier, John/ 601 Newbury St, Boston, MA .... (617) 262-4440
Carrino, John Studio/ 160 Fifth Avenue, New York, NY .... (212) 243-3623
Carroll, Don/ 188 Grand St, New York, NY .... (212) 219-2824
Carroll, Hanson/ New Boston Rd, Norwich, VT .... (802) 649-1094
Carstens, Don/ 19 E. 22nd Street, Baltimore, MD .... (301) 385-3049
Carter, Bill/ 39 East 12th St, New York, NY .... (212) 505-6088
Carter, Dwight/ 120 W. 97th Street, New York, NY .... (212) 662-8116
Carter, Fred/ 212 Race St Suite 3A, Philadelphia, PA .... (215) 925-6766
Carver, Douglas/ 441 Third Ave., New York, NY .... (212) 686-4886
Casanova, Patrice/ 1160 Broadway, New York, NY .... (212) 725-1055
Cashin, Art/ 5 W 19th, New York, NY .... (212) 255-3440
CASLER, CHRISTOPHER/ 1600 Viewmont Dr.,
 Los Angeles, CA.. **(213) 854-7733**
 See our ad on page 210
Castle, Ed/ 5057 Bradley Blvd. #5, Chevy Chase, MD .... (301) 652-6139
CAULFIELD, JAMES/ 114 W. Kinzie St., Chicago, IL................. **(312) 828-0004**
 See our ad on page 211
Cavallo, Robert/ 1065 Park Avenue, New York, NY .... (212) 838-0260
Cavanagh, John P./ 524 E. 5 St. #4, New York, NY .... (212) 673-2164
Caverly Studio Kat/ 149 W 24th St, New York City, NY .... (212) 757-8388
Cayman Gallery/ 381 W. Broadway, New York, NY .... (212) 966-6699
Cearley, Guy/ 156 5th Avenue Apt. 600, New York City, NY ...... (212) 243-6629
Cenicola, Tony/ 32 Union Sq. E. #613, New York, NY .... (212) 420-9798
Center Photo Svc/ 719 Boylston Street, Boston, MA .... (617) 267-7710
Certo, Rosemarie/ 2519 Parrish St., Philadelphia, PA .... (215) 232-2814
Chadman Studios/ 601 Newberry Street, Boston, MA .... (617) 262-3800
Chalifour, Benoit/ New York, NY .... (212) 684-4255
Chalkin, Dennis Studio, Inc./ 5 E. 16. St., New York, NY .... (212) 929-1036
Chamberlain, Dean/ 515 Broadway, New York, NY .... (212) 925-6686
Chan, Amos/ 174 Duane St, New York, NY .... (212) 219-0574
Chandoha, Walter/ Annandale, NJ .... (201) 782-3666
Chanteau, Pierre/ 209 W. 38th Street, New York, NY .... (212) 221-5860
Chapple, Ross/ 5025 Bradley Blvd, Chevy Chase, MD .... (703) 347-0407
Charlas, Jacques/ 774 Lincoln Ave., Bridgeport, CT .... (203) 335-5859
Charles, Bill/ 265 W 37th St Penthouse D, New York, NY .... (212) 719-9156
Charles, Janet/ 255 W 14th St, New York City, NY .... (212) 243-4251
Charrier, Michael Edward/ 164 Lexington Ave,
 New York City, NY .... (212) 532-0516
Chatelain, Alex/ 636 Sixth Ave, New York, NY .... (212) 675-0501
Chauhan, Dilip K/ 226 Nevada St, Newtonville, MA .... (617) 969-1375
CHAUNCEY, PAUL PHOTOGRAPHY/ 388 N. Hydraulic,
 Wichita, KS.. **(316) 262-6733**
 See our ad on pages 212, 213
Chaz/ 61 Crosby Street, New York, NY .... (212) 925-6706
Checani, Richard/ 31 East 32nd Street, New York, NY .... (212) 889-2049
Chen, Paul C. Studios Inc./ 133 Fifth Avenue, New York, NY ..... (212) 674-4100
Cherin, Alan/ 955 Liberty Ave, Pittsburgh, PA .... (412) 261-2717
Chernin, Bruce/ 330 W. 86th Street, New York, NY .... (212) 496-0266
Chesser, Vickie/ 211 East 70th St. Suite 17-C, New York, NY ...... (212) 570-6876
Chiappinelli, Don/ 122 W. 20 St. #2f, New York, NY .... (212) 691-4291
Chinsee, George/ 100 Fifth Ave Rm 809, New York, NY .... (212) 929-8017
Choroszewski, Walter J./ 45-15 Auburndale Ln., New York, NY ..... (212) 463-5439
Christensen, Paul/ 286 Fifth Avenue, New York, NY .... (212) 279-2838
Christian, Dan/ 38 W 26th St, New York, NY .... (212) 255-1532
CHRYNWSKI, WALTER/ 154 W. 18th St., New York, NY........... **(212) 675-1906**
 See our ad on page 214
Church, Diana/ 31 W. 31st Street, New York, NY .... (212) 736-4116
Chwatsky, Ann/ 85 Andover Road, Rockville, NY .... (516) 766-2417
Cicero, Ray/ 601 Riverside Avenue, Westport, CT .... (203) 226-4723
Cirone, Bettina/ 57 W. 58th Street, New York, NY .... (212) 888-7649
Clarke, Grier/ 255 W. 84th Street, New York, NY .... (212) 580-3698
Clark Quin Studio/ 332 A St., Boston, MA .... (617) 451-2686
Eggers, Claus/ 900 Broadway, New York, NY .... (212) 473-0064
Claxton, William/ 275 7th Avenue, New York, NY .... (212) 689-1340
Claycomb, Edward/ 17 E. 31 St., New York, NY .... (212) 246-4329
Clay, Langdon/ 42 W. 28th Street, New York, NY .... (212) 689-2613
Clayton, Tom (Rep Linda Badd)/ 1591 2nd Ave, New York, NY ..... (212) 744-1933
Cleff, Bernie/ 715 Pine Street, Philadelphia, PA .... (215) 922-4246
Clemens, Clint/ 346 Newbury Street, Boston, MA .... (617) 437-1309
Clemens, Peter/ 153 Sidney Street, Oyster Bay, NY .... (516) 922-1759
Clementi, Joe/ 263 W. 30 St., New York, NY .... (212) 736-1076

Clifford, Geoffrey C/ Craggle Ridge, Reading, VT........................ (802) 484-5047
Clough, Terry/ 147 West 25th Street, New York, NY.................. (212) 255-3040
COBB, LISA & ASSOCIATES/ 2200 N. Lamar #202,
Dallas, TX.. (214) 939-0032
See our ad on pages 32, 37, 122, 139, 165, 174, 178
Cobb Photography Ltd., Jan/ 381 Park Avenue South,
New York, NY.. (212) 889-2257
Cobin, Marty/ 145 E. 49th Street, New York, NY..................... (212) 758-5742
Cochran, George/ 381 Park Ave S, New York, NY...................... (212) 689-9054
Cockrell, Jere/ 140 Fifth Avenue, New York, NY........................ (212) 242-1356
Coggin, Roy/ 64 W. 21st Street, New York, NY......................... (212) 929-6262
Cohen-Davis Assoc Inc/ 151 W 19th Str, New York, NY.............. (212) 206-9333
Cohen, Ken/ 200 E. 17 St., New York, NY.................................. (212) 674-1831
Cohen, Lawrence E./ 277 E. 10 St. 1W, New York, NY................. (212) 777-3346
Cohen, Leonard Studio Inc/ 326 Kater St, Philadelphia, PA.......... (215) 922-6655
Cohen, Marc David/ 5 W. 19th Street, New York, NY.................. (212) 741-0015
COHN, RIC/ 156 5th Ave., New York, NY............................. (212) 924-6749
See our ad on page 215
Colabella, Vinnie/ , NY... (212) 949-7456
Colburn, Jim/ 234 E. 52nd Street, New York, NY........................ (212) 753-3677
Colby, Ron/ 140 E. 28th Street, New York, NY........................... (212) 684-3084
Coleman, Gene/ 250 West 27, New York, NY.............................. (212) 691-4752
Coleman, Ms Alix/ Box 23 907 Weldon Ln, Bryn Mawr, PA.......... (215) 525-6482
Collette, Roger/ 39 Pinehurst Rd, East Providence, RI................. (401) 433-2143
Collins, Chris/ 381 Park Ave. S., New York, NY......................... (212) 725-0237
Collins, Fred Studio Inc/ 186 South St, Boston, MA..................... (617) 426-5731
Collins, Sheldan/ 27 W 24th St, New York, NY........................... (201) 867-6297
Collins, William Auth/ P.O. Box 1190, Washington, DC................ (202) 625-4441
Collum, Charles/ 49 Crosby St, New York, NY............................ (212) 219-0244
Colodzin, Bonnie/ #2 Tudor City Place, New York, NY................. (212) 661-7594
Coloratura/ P.O. Box 1749 67 Brookside, Boston, MA.................. (617) 522-5132
Colton, Robert/ 1700 York Av, New York, NY............................ (212) 831-3953
Commercial Studios/ 257 Park Ave S, New York, NY.................... (212) 777-2800
Comte, Michel/ 160 Fifth Ave., New York, NY............................ (212) 924-6760
Conaty, Jim Photography/ One Winthrop Square, Boston, MA....... (617) 482-0660
Conboy, John/ 1225 State St., Schenectady, NY......................... (518) 346-2346
Condax, John/ 1320 Nectarine Street, Philadelphia, PA............... (215) 923-7790
Confer, Holt/ 2016 Franklin Place, Wyomissing, PA..................... (215) 678-0131
Connelly, Hank/ 6 West 37th Street, New York, NY..................... (212) 563-9109
Connors, Bill Studio/ 310 E 46th, New York, NY......................... (212) 490-3801
Conrad N' Jacqueline/ 169-15 Jamaica Ave., Jamaica, NY............ (212) 877-7240
Conte, Margot/ 165 Old Mamaroneck Road, White Plains, NY....... (914) 997-1322
Cooke, Colin/ 380 Lafayette St, New York City, NY...................... (212) 254-5090
Cooke, Jerry/ 161 E. 82nd Street, New York, NY........................ (212) 288-2045
Cook, Irvin/ 69 Mercer St., New York, NY................................ (212) 925-6216
Cook, Rod/ 108 W. 25th Street, New York, NY........................... (212) 242-4463
Cooney, Sally/ 145 E 27th St, New York City, NY........................ (212) 532-0353
Cooper & Coughlin/ Main Street, New London, NH...................... (603) 526-4645
Cooper, John F/ 95 Summit Avenue, Summit, NJ......................... (201) 273-0368
Cooper, Steve/ 5 W 31st, New York, NY.................................. (212) 279-4543
COPE, GIL/ 50 W. 17th St., New York, NY............................ (212) 206-0436
See our ad on page 295
Copeland, Cathy/ 305 Newbury #42, Boston, MA......................... (617) 262-4677
Copier, Jaques/ 104 Fifth Ave, New York City, NY...................... (212) 989-0761
Copy Line/ 40 W 37th St, New York, NY................................... (212) 563-3535
Cornell Photography/ 6 Wall Street, Wellesley Hills, MA............. (617) 431-1603
Cornicello, John/ 245 W 29th St, New York, NY......................... (212) 564-0874
Corona Color Studios/ 10 W 33rd St, New York, NY..................... (212) 239-4990
Corporate Photographers Inc/ 45 John St Room 1109,
New York, NY.. (212) 964-6515
COSIMO/HOLLY KAPLAN/ 35 W. 36th St., New York, NY......... (212) 563-2730
See our ad on page 217
Cottrell, William/ 36 W. 20th Street, New York, NY................... (212) 929-2141
Coupon, William/ 237 Lafayette Street, New York, NY.................. (212) 431-4956
Courbet, Elizabeth/ 856 West End Ave., New York, NY................. (212) 222-1215
Couzens, Larry/ 16 E. 17th Street, New York, NY....................... (212) 620-9790
Covello, Joe/ 54 W. 16th Street, New York, NY.......................... (212) 691-2656
COWAN, FRANK STUDIO, INC./ 5 E. 16th St.,
New York, NY.. (212) 675-5960
See our ad on page 218
Cox, David/ 25 Mercer St, New York City, NY............................ (212) 925-0734
Craig, Michel Photo/ 25 Fifth Avenue, New York, NY................... (212) 477-2956
Craig, Stuart L Jr/ 381 5th Avenue 2nd Floor, New York, NY........ (212) 683-5227
Crampton, Nancy/ 35 W. 9th Street, New York, NY..................... (212) 254-1135
Crane, Tom/ 113 Cumberland Place, Bryn Mawr, PA.................... (215) 525-2444
Creative Image Photography/ 325 Valley Rd., West Orange, NJ...... (201) 325-2352
Cronin, Casey/ 115 Wooster St., New York, NY.......................... (212) 334-9253
Cserna, George/ 80 2nd Avenue, New York, NY........................... (212) 477-3472
Cucinotta, Ambrose/ 1525 W. 4th Street, Brooklyn, NY................ (212) 645-0856
Cuington, Phyllis/ 38 E 19th 8th Floor, New York, NY................. (212) 477-5107
Culver, Gene/ 160 Anstice Street, Oyster Bay, NY...................... (516) 922-1708
Cunningham, Peter/ 214 Sullivan Street, New York, NY............... (212) 475-4866
CURATOLA, TONY/ 18 E. 17th St., New York, NY.................... (212) 243-5478
See our ad on page 219
Curtis, Jackie/ 19 Alewives Road, Norwalk, CT.......................... (203) 866-9198
Curtis, John/ New York, NY.. (212) 509-2550
Curtis, John Photography/ 50 Melcher St, Boston, MA................ (617) 451-9117
Daley, James Dee/ 105 Fifth Avenue Suite 9C, New York, NY....... (212) 675-7953
Daniels, Marc/ 20 N. Third Street, Philadelphia, PA.................. (215) 592-0333
Dantuono, Paul/ 433 Park Avenue South, New York, NY................ (212) 683-5778
Dantzic, Jerry/ 910 President Street, Brooklyn, NY.................... (212) 789-7478
D'Arazien, Arthur/ 92 Westhills Road, New Canaan, CT................ (203) 966-2811
Daryl, George/ 581 6th Avenue, New York, NY........................... (212) 675-8590
Datoli, Michael/ 121 West 17th Street #4C, New York, NY............ (212) 243-2750
Dauman, Henri/ 4 East 88th, New York, NY............................... (212) 860-3804
Davidson, Cameron/ 2311 Calvert Street N.W., Washington, DC.... (202) 328-3344
Davidson, Darwin K./ 32 Bank Street, New York, NY................... (212) 242-0095
Davidson, Erika/ 30 W. 60th Street, New York, NY..................... (212) 246-5066
Davies, Nora/ 370 E 76th, New York, NY.................................. (212) 628-6657
Davis, Dick/ 400 E. 59th Street, New York, NY.......................... (212) 751-3276
Davis, Hal Studio/ 220 E. 23rd Street, New York, NY.................. (212) 245-3192
Davis, Harold/ 874 Broadway, New York, NY.............................. (212) 228-0866
Davis, Richard/ 17 E. 16th Street, New York, NY........................ (212) 675-2428
Davis, Rick/ 18 North New St., West Chester, PA........................ (215) 436-6050
Day, Bob/ 29 East 19 Street, New York, NY............................... (212) 475-7387
Day, Olita/ 29 E 19th St, New York, NY.................................... (212) 673-9354
DEAHL, DAVID PHOTOGRAPHY, INC./ 70 W. Hubbard St.,
Chicago, IL.. (312) 644-3187
See our ad on pages 220, 221
Deane, John/ 529 W. 42 St. #4f, New York, NY........................... (212) 563-3054
DeCamp, Michael A./ 265 James Street, Morristown, NJ................ (201) 538-1693
De Cesare, John/ 135-25 Hoover Ave. #5n, Jamaica, NY................ (718) 263-8384
DeFever, Kit/ 156 Fifth Ave, New York, NY................................ (212) 989-5910
DeFrancis, Peter/ 424 Broome St., New York, NY........................ (212) 966-1357
De Jesus, Carmen L/ 606 W 113th St, New York City, NY............. (212) 666-3597
DELESSIO, LEN/ 7 E. 17th St., New York, NY.......................... (212) 206-8725
See our ad on page 222
Delsol, Michel/ 100 5th Av, New York, NY................................ (212) 807-8370
DeLucia, Ralph/ 120 E. Hartsdale Avenue, Hartsdale, NY............. (914) 472-2253
De Maid, Joe/ 20 Vernon St., Somerville, MA............................ (617) 628-9200
Demarchelier, Patrick (Photog)/ 162 West 21 Street,
New York, NY.. (212) 245-0200
Demenil, Adelaide/ 222 Central Park South, New York, NY........... (212) 541-8265
Demetriad, Dan/ 200 W 57th St Suite 200, New York, NY............ (212) 245-1720
Demichele, Bill/ 113 State St., Albany, NY................................. (518) 436-4927
DeMilt, Ronald Studios, Inc./ 873 Broadway, New York, NY.......... (212) 228-5321
Denison, William/ 1219 Roundhill Road, Baltimore, MD.............. (301) 889-5271
Denner, Manuel/ 249 W. 29 St., New York, NY........................... (212) 547-6220
Derex, David/ 247 W 35th St, New York, NY.............................. (212) 947-9302
Derr, Stephen/ 418 West 46th Street, New York, NY................... (212) 246-5920
Desanto, Thom/ 134 Fifth Ave., New York, NY........................... (212) 989-5622
De Scoise, Nicholas/ New York, NY.. (212) 757-6454
Design Photographers Int'l/ 521 Madison Avenue,
New York, NY.. (212) 752-3930
DeToy Ted/ 205 W. 19th Street, New York, NY.......................... (212) 675-6744
DeVito, Bart/ 43 E. 30th Street, New York, NY.......................... (212) 889-9670
De Vito, Michael J Jr/ 48 West 25th Street, New York, NY............ (212) 243-5267
De Voe, Marcus E./ 34 E. 81 St., New York, NY......................... (212) 737-9073
De Wys, Leo/Leo Dewys Inc./ 200 Madison Ave. 2225,
New York, NY.. (212) 689-5580
DeZanger, Arie/ 80 W 40th St, New York City, NY...................... (212) 354-7327
Dhimitra Tassi/ 160 East 48th Street, New York City, NY............. (212) 753-5149
Diamond, Herbert/ 8 Mayflower Rd., Framingham, MA................. (617) 877-2752
Diamond, Joe Photography/ 142 W 26 St, New York, NY............. (212) 807-0138
Dibue, Robert Studio, Inc/ 40 West 20th Str, New York, NY......... (212) 206-0860
DiCamillo, John/ 4220 Kelway Road, Baltimore, MD................... (301) 467-0749
Dicarlo, Barbara/ 500 E. 85th Street, New York, NY.................... (212) 734-2509
Dick, David/ 15 W. 28th Street, New York, NY........................... (212) 889-8620
Dickstein, Bob/ 101 Hillturn Ln, Rosyln Heights, NY.................. (516) 621-2413
Diebold, George/ 416 Bloomfield Ave, Montclair, NJ................... (201) 744-5789

Digiacomo, Mel/ 32 Norma Road, Harrington Park, NJ .... (201) 767-0870
Dillon, George/ 275 Tremont, Boston, MA .... (617) 482-6154
DiMaggio, Joe/Kalish, Joanne/ 512 Adams Street,
    Centerport, NY .... (516) 271-6133
DiMarco, Salvatore C., Jr./ 1002 Cobbs Street,
    Drexel Hill, PA .... (215) 789-3239
Dimensional Images/ 791 Tremont Street, Boston, MA .... (617) 266-9336
D'Innocenzo Studios, Ltd./ 91 Fifth Ave., New York, NY .... (212) 620-0610
Dishman, Leon/ 12001-807 Old Columbia Pike,
    Silver Spring, MD .... (301) 622-1812
Dixon Mel Studio/ 29 E. 19th Street, New York, NY .... (212) 677-5450
Dockery, Lawrence/ 175 5th Ave Suite 3279, New York, NY .... (212) 477-5107
Dolce, Steven/ 135 Fifth Avenue, New York, NY .... (212) 777-3350
Dole, J.J./ 145 E 22nd St Suite 3H, New York City, NY .... (212) 473-0108
Dolgins, Alan/ New York, NY .... (212) 532-5083
Dolin, Penny Ann/ 107 Briar Brae Rd., Stamford, CT .... (203) 322-7499
Domke, J.G./ 543 Industrial, Yeadon, PA .... (215) 622-1130
Donato Leo/ 170 Fifth Ave, New York, NY .... (212) 989-4200
Dorf, Myron J/ 205 W 19th, New York, NY .... (212) 255-2020
Dorin, Jay/ 220 Cabrini Blvd., New York, NY .... (212) 781-7378
Dorno Studio Photog./ 215 A Central Ave., Farmingdale, NY .... (516) 293-4171
Doster, Michael/ 154 W 57th St, New York, NY .... (212) 757-1196
Doubilet, David/ 1040 Park Avenue Apt. 6J, New York, NY .... (212) 348-5011
Douglass Assoc Studios/ 3 Cove of Cork Lane, Annapolis, MD .... (301) 266-5060
Douglass, James S / Photogroup/ 5161 River Rd Bldg 2B,
    Bethesda, MD .... (301) 652-1303
DPI/ 521 Madison Ave., New York, NY .... (212) 752-3930
Drabkin, Si Studios/ 25 W. 39th Street, New York, NY .... (212) 398-0050
Drake, James A./ 635 Spruce Street, Philadelphia, PA .... (215) 925-8927
Dresner, Harvey Studios Inc./ 202-26 45th Avenue,
    Bayside, NY .... (212) 225-2332
Drew, Rue Faris/ 177 E. 77th Street, New York, NY .... (212) 794-8994
Dreyer, Peter H./ 166 Burgess Ave, Westwood, MA .... (617) 762-8550
DUBIEL, DENNIS/ 1313 W. Randolph St., Chicago, IL .... (312) 666-0136
    See our ad on pages 224, 225
DUBLER, DOUGLAS PHOTOGRAPHY/ 162 E. 92nd St.,
    New York, NY .... (212) 410-6300
    See our ad on page 223
Duckworth, Paul/ 124 W. 23 St., New York, NY .... (212) 242-6252
Dudek, Kathryn/Photography/ P O Box 478, Floral Park, NY .... (212) 343-4140
Duffy, John/ 73 Central Street, Woburn, MA .... (617) 933-3482
Duke, Dana/ 620 Broadway, New York, NY .... (212) 260-3334
Dunas, Jeff/ 121 West 17th Street, New York, NY .... (212) 242-1266
Duncan Ltd., Kenn/ 853 Seventh Avenue, New York, NY .... (212) 582-7080
Dunning, Hank/ 50 W 22nd, New York, NY .... (212) 675-6040
Dunning Inc., R & D/ 57 W. 58th Street, New York, NY .... (212) 688-0788
Dunn, Paul Studio/ 239 A Street, Boston, MA .... (617) 542-9554
Dunn, Phoebe Photographers/ 20 Silvermine Road,
    New Canaan, CT .... (203) 966-9791
Dunoff, Rich/ 407 Bowman Ave, Merion Station, PA .... (215) 627-3690
Dunwell, Steve/ 20 Winchester Street, Boston, MA .... (617) 423-4916
Durrance, Dick, II/ Rockport, ME .... (207) 236-3990
Dwiggins, Gene/ 204 Westminster Mall, Providence, RI .... (401) 421-6466
Eagan, Timothy/ 319 E 75 St #2D, New York, NY .... (212) 517-7665
Eager, Sean/ 15 W 18th St 3rd Fl, New York City, NY .... (212) 243-2174
Earle, John/ P.O. Box 63, Cambridge, MA .... (617) 628-1454
Eastep, Wayne/ 443 Park Ave. S. #1006, New York, NY .... (212) 686-8404
Eastern Photo Service/ 200 Madison Ave., New York, NY .... (212) 689-5580
East West Photo Group/ 112 Fourth Avenue, New York, NY .... (212) 460-5923
Eckstein, Ed/ 234 5th Avenue, New York, NY .... (212) 685-9342
Edahl/ 236 W 27th St, New York, NY .... (212) 929-2002
Edelman IV, Harry R./ 1335 Brinton Road, Pittsburgh, PA .... (412) 371-6865
Edelman, Richard/ 361 W. 36th Street, New York, NY .... (212) 736-7558
Edgeworth, Anthony/ 333 Fifth Avenue, New York, NY .... (212) 679-6031
Edwards, Gregory/ 30 East End Avenue, New York, NY .... (212) 879-4339
Edwards, Robin/ 139 E. 57th Street, New York, NY .... (212) 888-6732
Egan, Jim/ 220 W Exchange St, Providence, RI .... (401) 521-7052
Egan Photographics/ 62 Washington St., Middletown, CT .... (203) 346-9008
Eguiguren, Carlos/ 139 E. 57th Street, New York, NY .... (212) 888-6732
Ehrenpreis, David Studio/ 156 5th Avenue, New York, NY .... (212) 242-1976
Ehrlich, George/ P.O. Box 186, New Hampton, NY .... (914) 355-1757
Eindhoven, Jurriaan/ New York, NY .... (212) 684-4255
Eisenberg, Steve/ 448 W. 37th Pha, New York, NY .... (212) 563-2061
Eisendrath, David B./ 37 Garden Place, Brooklyn, NY .... (212) 624-3222
Ekstrom, Niki/ 419 E. 75th Street, New York, NY .... (212) 744-2972

Elbers, Johan/ 18 E. 18 St., New York, NY .... (212) 929-5783
Elgort, Arthur/ 300 Central Park West, New York, NY .... (212) 724-6557
Elkin, Irving/ 12 E. 37th Street, New York, NY .... (212) 686-2980
Elkins, Joel Studio/ 5 E 16 St, New York, NY .... (212) 989-4500
Elkus Studio/ 5 Union Square, New York, NY .... (212) 255-0907
ELLE/ 3719 Gilbert Ave., Dallas, TX .... (214) 526-6712
    See our ad on pages 226, 227
Elliott, Jon/ 329 W. 85th Street Apt. 3B, New York, NY .... (212) 799-8828
Ellis, Ray/ 176 Westminster Road, Brooklyn, NY .... (718) 282-6449
Ellman, Faye/ 270 W. 25th Street, New York, NY .... (212) 243-3759
Elmer, Joe Studio/ 200 E 87th, New York, NY .... (212) 369-7077
Elmi, Ross/ 12 E 32nd, New York, NY .... (212) 686-1417
Elmore, Steve/ 1640 York Avenue, New York, NY .... (212) 472-2463
Elness Studio/ 61 W 23rd, New York, NY .... (212) 242-5045
Elson, Paul/ 8200 Blvd. E., N. Burgen, NJ .... (201) 662-2882
Emberling, David/ 38 W. 26 St., New York, NY .... (212) 242-7455
Emmet, Herman/ 36 W. 62 St., New York, NY .... (212) 307-1450
ENDRESS, JOHN PAUL/ 254 W. 31st St., New York, NY .... (212) 736-7800
    See our ad on pages 228, 229
Engel, Mort/ 260 Fifth Avenue, New York, NY .... (212) 889-8466
Englander, Maury/ 43 Fifth Avenue, New York, NY .... (212) 242-9777
Epstein Photography/ 694 Center St., Chicopee, MA .... (413) 736-8532
Epstein, Robert H/ 31 Union Sq W, New York, NY .... (212) 243-2165
Epstein, S Karin/ 233 E 70th Street, New York, NY .... (212) 472-0771
Ericksen, Klye/ 250 Mercer, New York, NY .... (212) 475-1602
Erwitt, Elliot/ 88 Central Park W, New York, NY .... (212) 799-6767
Essel, Robert/ 39 West 71st Apt 6, New York, NY .... (212) 877-5228
ESTEL, SUZANNE STUDIOS/ 2325 Third St.,
    San Francisco, CA .... (415) 864-3661
    See our ad on page 230
Estenssoro, Hugo/ 117 MacDougal Street Apt. 4, New York, NY .... (212) 777-2912
Estevez, Herman/ 19 West 24 St, New York, NY .... (212) 807-9614
Esto Photographics/ 222 Valley Place, Mamaroneck, NY .... (914) 698-4060
Estrada, Sigrid/ 902 Broadway, New York, NY .... (212) 673-4300
Evans, Bob/ 1466 Broadway, New York, NY .... (212) 840-6928
Everett Profit/ 533 Mass Ave, Boston, MA .... (617) 267-5840
Excalibur Photo Graphics/ 444 Madison Ave, New York, NY .... (212) 759-8280
Eyle, Nicolas/ 304 Oak, Syracuse, NY .... (315) 422-6231
Ezra, Martin & Associates/ 48 Garrett Road, Upper Darby, PA ...... (215) 352-9595
Falkensteen & Gershman/ 114 E. 32nd Street, New York, NY .... (212) 686-0551
Fantasy Photography by Daphne/ 282 Newbury St, Boston, MA ...... (617) 536-1633
Faraghan, George/ 1621 Wood Street, Philadelphia, PA .... (215) 564-5711
Farber, Robert/ 35 W 31st, New York, NY .... (212) 564-0031
Farrell, John William/ 611 Broadway Penthouse 905,
    New York, NY .... (212) 460-9001
Faulkner, Douglas/ 5 W. 8th Street, New York, NY .... (212) 260-4758
Fay Photo/ 201 South Street, Boston, MA .... (617) 267-2000
Fay Studios, Stephen/ 154 W 57th 8th Fl Studio 832,
    New York, NY .... (212) 757-3717
Feil, Charles W., III/ 402 Grove Ave. Box 201,
    Washington Grv., MD .... (301) 258-8328
Feinstein, Gary/ 19 E. 17th Street, New York, NY .... (212) 242-3373
Feirstein, Joyce/ 215 E. 81 St. #7b, New York, NY .... (212) 472-3753
Feldman, Martin/ 77 College Street, Burlington, VT .... (802) 658-6815
Fellerman, Stan/ 152 W. 25th Street, New York, NY .... (212) 243-0027
Fellman, Sandy/ 548 Broadway, New York, NY .... (212) 925-5187
Fennell, Mary/ 57 Maple Ave., Hastings-Hdsn., NY .... (914) 478-3627
Ferorelli, Enrico/ 50 W 29th, New York, NY .... (212) 685-8181
Ferreira, Al Photography/ 237 Naubuc Avenue,
    East Hartford, CT .... (203) 569-8812
Ferrer, Linda/ 60 W. 15th Street, New York, NY .... (212) 691-6615
Fetter, Frank/ 400 E. 78th Street, New York, NY .... (212) 249-3138
Field, Pat/ 16 E. 23 St., New York, NY .... (212) 477-9016
Fields, Bruce/ 71 Greene St, New York, NY .... (212) 431-8852
Figliozzi, Stephen M/ 930 F St NW, Washington, DC .... (202) 393-0730
Fincher, Les/ 902 Broadway, New York City, NY .... (212) 475-3258
FINDEL, STEFAN, INC./ 1133 Spring St. N.W.,
    Atlanta, GA .... (404) 872-8103
    See our ad on page 231
Fine, Peter M./ 115 Crosby Street, New York, NY .... (212) 431-9776
Fine, Ron Photographer/ 2307 18th Street N.W.,
    Washington, DC .... (202) 462-2211
Fink, Peter/ 1 W 72nd, New York, NY .... (212) 873-7286
Finlay, Alastair/ 38 E. 21st Street 9th Floor, New York, NY .... (212) 260-4297
Finn, David/ 110 E. 59th Street, New York, NY .... (212) 593-6400

FINZI STUDIO LTD./ 36 W. 20th St., New York, NY .... (212) 255-2110
  See our ad on page 232
Firman, John/ 434 E. 75th Street, New York, NY .... (212) 794-2794
First Impressions/ PO Box 323, Morgantown, PA .... (215) 286-6500
Fischer, Bob/ 135 E 54th St, New York City, NY .... (212) 755-2131
Fischer, Carl Photog./ 121 E. 83 St., New York, NY .... (212) 794-0400
Fischer, Robert E Jr/ 317 Ruskin Rd, Buffalo, NY .... (716) 834-3334
Fishbein, Chuck/ 49 W. 27th Street, New York, NY .... (212) 532-4452
Fish, Dick/ 40 Center Street, Northampton, MA .... (413) 584-6500
Fisher, Al/ 601 Newbury St., Boston, MA .... (617) 536-7126
Fishman, Chuck/ 69 1/2 Morton St., New York, NY .... (212) 242-3987
Fish, Vinnie/ PO Box 794, Stony Brook, NY .... (516) 689-9672
Fitch, Charles Marden/ 1120 Cove Rd., Mamaroneck, NY .... (914) 698-6631
Fiterman Studio/ 208 S. Pulaski Street, Baltimore, MD .... (301) 566-2750
Fitzhugh, Susie/ 3809 Beech Avenue, Baltimore, MD .... (301) 243-6112
Fiur, Lola Troy/ 360 E. 65 St., New York, NY .... (212) 861-1911
Fland, Peter/ 28 Fairlawn Drive, Deer Park, NY .... (516) 667-4436
Flanigan, Jim/ 2302 Lombard Street, Philadelphia, PA .... (215) 546-5545
Flatow, Carl/ 20 E. 30th Street, New York, NY .... (212) 683-8688
Flatow, Herbert Jerome/ 70 E 10th Street Apt 8B,
  New York, NY .... (212) 228-1707
Flax, Jeff/ 156 Fifth Ave, New York, NY .... (212) 242-0917
Fleming, Peter/ 303 Park Avenue S., New York, NY .... (212) 777-5419
Fleshner Photography/ 1122 Washington Avenue, Portland, ME ..... (207) 797-5982
Flint, Simpson/ 60 E 42nd St, New York, NY .... (212) 682-1490
Floret, Evelyn/ 3 E. 80th Street, New York, NY .... (212) 472-3179
Flowers, Adrian/ New York, NY .... (212) 684-4255
F-90 Inc./ 60 Sindle Avenue, Little Falls, NJ .... (201) 785-9090
Focus On Sports, Inc./ 222 E. 46th St., New York, NY .... (212) 661-6860
Folkenstein and Gershman/ 114 E 32nd, New York, NY .... (212) 686-0551
Foote, James A/ 22 Tomac Avenue, Old Greenwich, CT .... (203) 637-3228
Forastien, Marili/ 156 Fifth Ave, New York, NY .... (212) 924-9412
Forbes, Angus/ New York, NY .... (212) 832-6900
Forbes, Deirdre Drohan/ 3001 Henry Hudson Pkwy, Bronx, NY ..... (212) 548-7092
Ford, Charles/ 32 E 22nd St, New York City, NY .... (212) 533-9760
Forelli, Chip/ 316 Fifth Ave., New York, NY .... (212) 564-1835
Forrest, Bob/ 273 Fifth Ave, New York City, NY .... (212) 288-4458
Forsyth, Al DPI/ 521 Madison Ave., New York, NY .... (212) 752-3930
Forte, John Studio/ 162 W 21st, New York, NY .... (212) 620-0584
Foster, Frank/ 323 Newbury Street, Boston, MA .... (617) 536-6600
Foster, Nicholas/ 143 Claremont Road, Bernardsville, NJ .... (201) 234-1570
Fox, Flo/ 30 Perry St., New York, NY .... (212) 255-1260
Fox, Jeffrey Photography/ 6 West 20th St, New York, NY .... (212) 620-0147
Fox, Peggy/ 371 Padonia Rd., Cockeysville, MD .... (301) 252-0003
FPG Intl Corp/ 251 Park Ave S, New York, NY .... (212) 777-4210
Francekevich, Al/ 73 Fifth Avenue, New York, NY .... (212) 691-7456
Francisco, Gus & Bellie A./ 220 E. 23rd Street,
  New York, NY .... (212) 683-0418
Francki, Jo/ 31 Union Sq W, New York City, NY .... (212) 242-7716
Frank, Dick/ 11 W 25th St, New York, NY .... (212) 242-4648
Frankel, Tracy/ 41 Union Square, New York, NY .... (212) 243-5687
Franzos, Stan Photography/ 5261 Forbes Ave, Pittsburgh, PA ...... (412) 687-8850
Fraser, Douglas/ 9 E 19th St, New York City, NY .... (212) 777-8404
Fraser, Renee/ 1167 Massachusetts Ave., Arlington, MA .... (617) 646-4296
Fredric Studios Inc./ 46 East 21 Street, New York, NY .... (212) 673-3070
Freedman, Lionel-Camera 73 Inc/ 325 East 73rd Street,
  New York, NY .... (212) 737-8540
Freeman, Bill/ 415 Farms Rd, Greenwich, CT .... (212) 686-3195
**FREEMAN, CHARLIE PHOTOGRAPHY/ 3333 Elm St.,
  Dallas, TX** .... (214) 742-1446
  See our ad on page 233
Freeze Frame Studios, Inc./ 255 Leona Ave., Bogota, NJ .... (201) 343-1233
Freid, Joel Carl/ 812 Loxford Terrace, Silver Spring, MD .... (301) 681-7211
Frerking, Erich Photog., Inc./ 1 Bridge St., Irvington, NY ...... (914) 591-6047
Freson, Robert Studios/ 154 W 57th, New York, NY .... (212) 246-0679
Friedman, Benno/ 26 W. 20th Street, New York, NY .... (212) 255-6038
Friedman, Bill/ PO Box 3613, Stamford, CT .... (203) 348-8114
Friedman, Carol/ 60 Grand St, New York City, NY .... (212) 925-4951
Friedman, Jerry/ 873 Broadway, New York, NY .... (212) 505-5600
Friedman, Steve/ 545 W. 111th Street, New York, NY .... (212) 864-2662
Friedman, Stuart/ 27 East 62nd Street, New York, NY .... (212) 751-1658
Friedman, Walter/ 58 W 68th, New York, NY .... (212) 874-5287
Frye, Vincent/ 257 W 55th, New York, NY .... (212) 765-1738
Fuhring, Jane/ 19 Wyatt St, Somerville, MA .... (617) 628-4792
Fundamental Photographs/ 210 Forsyth Street, New York, NY ...... (212) 473-5770

Funk, Mitchell/ 500 E 77th, New York, NY .... (212) 988-2886
Funt, David W/ 220 E 23rd, New York, NY .... (212) 686-4111
FURMAN, MICHAEL/ 115 Arch St., Philadelphia, PA .... (215) 925-4233
  See our ad on page 234
Furones, Claude E./ 40 Waterside Plaza, New York, NY .... (212) 683-0622
Furst, Franz E Photography/ 420 E. 55th Street,
  New York, NY .... (212) 753-3148
Furst, Ina/ 4670 Waldo Ave, Riverdale, NY .... (212) 548-6464
Gage, Rob/ 353 W 53 St, New York, NY .... (212) 682-2462
Gairy, John/ 11 W. 17th Street, New York, NY .... (212) 242-5805
Galante, James T./ 145 E 37 St Apt 2R, New York, NY .... (212) 696-0388
Galante Photography/ 9 West 31st Street, New York, NY .... (212) 239-0412
Galella, Ron Limited/ 17 Glover Avenue, Yonkers, NY .... (914) 237-2988
Gallagher, Barrett/ 222 Central Park S, New York, NY .... (212) 246-3127
Gallery, Bill/ 86 South St, Boston, MA .... (617) 542-0499
Gallob, Edward/ 2219 Delancy Place, Philadelphia, PA .... (215) 567-1806
Gallucci, Ed/ 381 Park Ave. S., New York, NY .... (212) 532-2720
Galluzzi, John/ 8 E. 12th Street, New York, NY .... (212) 243-6238
GALTON, BETH/ 130 W. 25th St., New York, NY .... (212) 242-2266
  See our ad on page 235
Galton, Beth/ 91 Fifth Ave. 4 Fl., New York, NY .... (212) 242-2266
Galvin, Kevin/ PO Box 30, Hanover, MA .... (617) 826-4795
Ganton, Brian/ PO Box 103, Verona, NJ .... (201) 239-8824
Garber, Bette S/ 2110 Valley Drive, West Chester, PA .... (215) 436-5400
Garber, Ira/ 150 Chestnut St., Providence, RI .... (401) 274-3723
Garcia, Rafael/ 18 Martin Lane, Westbury, NY .... (516) 333-8166
Garcia, Ray/ 60 E. 11th Street, New York, NY .... (212) 674-5494
Garcia, Sam/ PO Box 1109, Port Washington, NY .... (516) 883-0872
Garetti, John/ 140 W. 22nd Street, New York, NY .... (212) 242-1154
Garfield, Peter/ 3401 K St NW, Washington, DC .... (202) 333-1379
Garik, Alice J./ 275 Clinton Ave., Brooklyn, NY .... (212) 783-1065
Garret, William/ 315 W. 54th St. #12, New York, NY .... (212) 245-6584
Garrison, G. E. Photography/ 52 O St. N.W., Washington, DC ......
Gates, Ralph/ 364 Hartshorn Dr, Short Hills, NJ .... (201) 379-4456
GATZ, LARRY/ 8610 Sunny Ridge Dr., Houston, TX .... (713) 550-8455
  See our ad on page 236
Gee, Elizabeth/ 280 Madison Avenue, New York, NY .... (212) 683-6924
Geer, Garry/ 77 Bleecker St. #823, New York, NY .... (212) 533-8467
Geer, Richard/ 611 Cathedral St., Baltimore, MD .... (301) 244-0292
Geller, Bonnie/ 57 W. 93rd Street, New York, NY .... (212) 864-5922
Geneletti, Ezio/ New York, NY .... (212) 684-4255
Germer, Michael/ 839 Beacon St, Boston, MA .... (617) 262-0170
Gesar, Aram/ 417 Lafayette St, New York, NY .... (212) 228-1852
Gescheidt, Alfred/ 175 Lexington Avenue, New York, NY .... (212) 889-4023
Getlen, David/ 60 Gramercy Park, New York, NY .... (212) 475-6940
Giammatteo, John/ 343 Jackson Hill Rd., Middlefield, CT .... (203) 349-3743
Giandomenico, Bob/ 13 Fern Ave., Collingswood, NJ .... (609) 854-4915
GIBSON, MARK E./ P.O. Box 14542, San Francisco, CA .... (415) 431-5411
  See our ad on page 237
Gidion, Inc./ 119 Fifth Ave., New York, NY .... (212) 677-8600
Giese, Al/ 156 Fifth Avenue, New York, NY .... (212) 675-2727
Giglio, Harry Photography/ 925 Penn Ave, Pittsburgh, PA .... (412) 261-3338
Gigli, Ormand/ 327 E. 58th Street, New York, NY .... (212) 758-2860
**GILBERT, ELLIOT/ 311 N. Curson Ave.,
  Los Angeles, CA** .... (213) 939-1846
  See our ad on page 238
Gilbert, Thom/ 50 W 67th St, New York, NY .... (212) 580-4769
Gillardin, A Studios/ 6 West 20 6th Floor, New York, NY .... (212) 675-2950
Gillette, Guy/ 133 Mountain Dale Road, Yonkers, NY .... (914) 779-4684
Gilmour, James/ 377 Park Avenue S., New York, NY .... (212) 532-8288
Ginsburg, Mike/ 245 E 19th, New York, NY .... (212) 677-0167
Ginter, Marty/ 2812 Boas St, Harrisburg, PA .... (717) 232-2905
Giovanni, Raeanne/ 156 5th Avenue, New York, NY .... (212) 254-6406
Giraldi Photography Studio/ 54 West 39th Street 2nd Floor,
  New York, NY .... (212) 840-8225
Gladstone, Gary/ 237 E 20th St, New York, NY .... (212) 777-7772
Glancz, Jeff/ 38 W. 21 St. 12 Fl., New York, NY .... (212) 741-2504
Glaser, Harold/ 143-30 Roosevelt Avenue, Flushing, NY .... (212) 939-1829
Glassman, Carl/ 80 N. Moore Street Apt. 37G, New York, NY .... (212) 732-2458
Glattauer, Ned/ 343 E 30th, New York, NY .... (212) 686-6927
Glaviano, Marco/ 40 W. 27th Street, New York, NY .... (212) 683-8680
Glinn, Burt/ 41 Central Park W., New York, NY .... (212) 877-2210
Globus Brothers, the/ 44 W. 24 St., New York, NY .... (212) 243-1000
Gneiting, Robin/ 448 W. 37th Street, New York, NY .... (212) 687-8526
Goell, Jonathan/ 109 Broad St, Boston, MA .... (617) 423-2057

Goff, Lee/ 32 E. 64th Street, New York, NY .... (212) 223-0716
Goldberg, Ken/ 19 West 24th Street, New York, NY .... (212) 807-8244
Goldberg, Les/ 330 E. 59th Street, New York, NY .... (212) 751-2772
Gold, Bernie/ 873 Broadway, New York, NY .... (212) 677-0311
Goldblatt, Steven/ 32 S. Strawberry Street,
    Philadelphia, PA... (215) 925-3825
Gold, Charles/ 170 Fifth Ave., New York, NY .... (212) 242-2600
Goldfarb, Ed/ 428 E. 84th Street, New York, NY .... (212) 543-6183
Gold, Gary/ 1 Madison Pl., Albany, NY .... (518) 434-4887
Gold Inc., Charles/ 170 Fifth Avenue, New York, NY .... (212) 242-2600
Goldman, Mel Studios/ 329 Newbury, Boston, MA .... (617) 536-0539
Goldman, Richard/ 36 W. 20th Street, New York, NY .... (212) 675-3021
Goldman, Tony/ 101 Greene St, New York, NY .... (212) 925-2415
Goldsmith, Alan/ P.O. Box 688, Woodbury, CT .... (203) 263-3841
Goldsmith, Lynn Inc/ 241 W 36th Street Loft 7, New York, NY ..... (212) 736-4602
Goldstein, Arthur/ 253 W. 28th Street, New York, NY .... (212) 695-7246
Goldstein, Robert/ PO Box 310, New Milford, NJ .... (201) 262-5959
Goll, Charles R./ 404 E. 83 St., New York, NY .... (212) 628-4881
Golob, Stanford/ 40 Waterside Plz, New York, NY.............. (212) 532-7166
Goltzer, Seth/ P.O. Box 5092, Westport, CT .... (203) 222-0462
Gonzalez, Gustavo/ 13 West 17 Street, New York, NY .... (212) 206-1043
Gonzalez Studio, Manuel/ 119 Fifth Avenue, New York, NY .... (212) 254-2200
Goodman, John/ 337 Summer St, Boston, MA.................... (617) 482-8061
Goodman, Lou/ 322 Summer, Boston, MA........................ (617) 542-8254
Gorchev & Gorchev Inc./ 11 Cabot Road, Woburn, MA .... (617) 933-8090
Gordon, Joel/ 112 Fourth Ave., New York, NY .... (212) 254-1688
Gorin, Bart/ 1160 Broadway, New York, NY .... (212) 683-3743
Gorodnitzki, Diane/ 160 W. 71st Street, New York, NY .... (212) 724-6259
Goro, Fritz Science Photogrphr/ 324 N. Bedford Rd.,
    Chappaqua, NY .... (914) 238-8788
Gorrill, Robert B./ 70 Gladstone Street, Squantum, MA .... (617) 328-4012
Gotfryd, Bernard/ 46 Wendover Road, Forest Hills, NY .... (212) 261-8039
Gotman, John/ 111 W. 24th Street, New York, NY .... (212) 255-0569
Gottfried, Arlene/ 240 E. 23rd Street, New York, NY .... (212) 685-4212
Gottheil, Philip/ 249 W 29 St, New York, NY .... (212) 564-0971
Gottlieb, Dennis/ 5 Union Square W., New York, NY............ (212) 620-7050
GOULD, CHRISTOPHER PHOTOGRAPHY/ 224 W. Huron,
    Chicago, IL.. (312) 944-5545
    See our ad on pages 240, 241
Gould, Peter L/ 7 E 17th, New York, NY .... (212) 741-2529
Gove, Geoffrey/ 117 Waverly Pl, New York, NY .... (212) 260-6051
Graff, Randolph/ 160 Bleecker Street, New York, NY .... (212) 254-0412
Granel, Renaud/ 1641-13G Third Ave, New York, NY .... (212) 722-1942
Grant, Ed/ 119 W. 57th Street, New York, NY .... (212) 757-7462
Grant, Robert/ 91 Fifth Avenue, New York, NY .... (212) 255-2323
Graphic Accent/ Box 243 - 446 Main St., Wilmington, MA.......... (617) 658-7602
Graphics 55/ 39 W 19th St, New York, NY .... (212) 686-6111
Graves, Tom/ 136 E. 36 St., New York, NY .... (212) 683-0241
Gray, Bernard/ 225 E. 67th Street, New York, NY.............. (212) 249-4446
Gray, Budd/ 511 N. Highland Street, Arlington, WV.............. (703) 527-1298
Gray, Mitchel/ 169 E 86th, New York, NY .... (212) 427-2287
Grayson, Jay Photography/ 230 Park Ave. Ste. 923,
    New York, NY... (212) 490-6490
Gray, Stuart/ PO Box 197, Mt Tremper, NY .... (914) 688-5914
Gray, Susan Photographer/ 240 East 74th Street,
    New York, NY... (212) 472-3749
Grebinar, Paul/ 239 Park Avenue S., New York, NY.............. (212) 777-6045
Green-Armytage, Stephen/ 171 W. 57th Street, New York, NY .... (212) 247-6314
Greenberg, David/ 54 King St, New York, NY .... (212) 243-7351
Green, Beth/ 60 Riverside Drive, New York, NY .... (212) 350-1928
Greene, Joshua/ 448 West 37 St Suite 8D, New York City, NY ..... (212) 239-1394
GREENFIELD, LOIS/ 35 W. 31st St., New York, NY................ (212) 947-0898
    See our ad on page 239
Greenfield-Sanders, Timothy/ 135 E. 2nd Street,
    New York, NY... (212) 674-7888
Gregory, John/ 105 Fifth Ave, New York, NY .... (212) 691-1797
Greniers Inc., the/ 284 Pine St., Holyoke, MA.................. (413) 532-9406
Griebsch, John/ 183 St. Paul St., Rochester, NY.............. (716) 546-1303
Griffin, Arthur L./ 22 Euclid Avenue, Winchester, MA.......... (617) 729-2690
Griffing, Fred/ Ferris Lane, Upper Grandview, NY .... (914) 353-0619
Griffin, Marti/ 1200 Foster St NW, Atlanta, GA .... (404) 351-8493
Grill, Tom/ 301 E. 47th Street, New York, NY .... (212) 889-9700
Grodman, Robert/ 18 E. 18th Street 4 West, New York, NY .... (212) 929-0424
Groskinsky, Henry/ 5 Woodcleft Avenue, Port Washington, NY ..... (516) 883-3294
Gross, Cy/ 59 W 19, New York, NY............................. (212) 243-2556

Gross, David/ 922 Third Ave., New York, NY .... (212) 688-4729
Gross, Garry/ 235 W 4th Street, New York, NY .... (212) 807-7141
Gross, Geoffrey/ 39 West 29 St, New York City, NY .... (212) 685-8850
Gross, Lance/ Hartford Plaza, Hartford, CT .... (203) 528-0100
Grossman, Eugene/ 80 N. Moore Street Suite 14J,
    New York, NY... (212) 962-6795
Grossman, Henry/ 37 Riverside Drive, New York, NY............ (212) 580-7751
Grossman, Mildred/ 35-24 78th St, Jackson Heights, NY........ (212) 426-0740
Gross, Stuart M. Photography/ 32 Union Sq. E., New York, NY ..... (212) 674-6513
Group Four/ 225 E. 67th Street, New York, NY................ (212) 249-4446
Group Four Photography Inc./ 314 West 53rd Street,
    New York, NY... (212) 621-9295
Grubb, Erle/ 638 W End Ave, New York, NY .... (212) 799-7084
Gruber, Terry/ 885 West End Avenue, New York, NY............ (212) 749-2840
Grumbles, Robert/ 333 East 49th Street, New York, NY........ (212) 734-4533
Grundy, Jane/ 150 W. 82 St. #8b, New York, NY .... (212) 787-8454
Gruol, David/ 92 Western Ave, Morristown, NJ .... (201) 267-2847
Gscheidle, Gerhard/ 381 Park Ave S, New York, NY............ (212) 532-1374
Guarinello, Greg/ 252 Highwood St., Teaneck, NJ .... (201) 836-2333
Gudnason, Torkil/ 58 W. 15th Street, New York, NY .... (212) 929-6680
Gummerson, Anne/ 1506 Park Ave., Baltimore, MD .... (301) 383-1209
Gunzel, Chris Photography/ 135 W. 36 St., New York, NY........ (212) 695-1595
Gurovitz, Judy/ 207 E 74th, New York, NY .... (212) 988-8685
Gustavo Gonzalez/ 13 W 17th, New York, NY .... (212) 206-1043
Guyaux, Jean-Marie/ 29 E 19th, New York, NY .... (212) 677-1224
Haak, Ken/ 122 E 30th, New York, NY .... (212) 679-6284
Haas, Ernst/ 853 Seventh Avenue, New York, NY .... (212) 247-4543
Haas, Ken/ 15 Sheridan Square, New York, NY .... (212) 255-0707
Hadjolian, Serge Ph D, Analyst/ 30 Central Park South,
    New York, NY... (212) 371-9696
Hagen, Boyd B./ 680 Broadway, New York, NY .... (212) 473-2008
Hagerman, Ron/ 51 Clearview Ave, Somerset, MA .... (617) 676-9017
Haggerty, David/ 126 Fifth Avenue, New York, NY............ (212) 989-0600
Hagle, Robert/ 4642 W. Lake Rd., Erie, PA .... (814) 838-6640
Halebian, Carol/ 56 W. 65 St. #6h, New York, NY............ (212) 877-8271
Haling, George Productions/ 231 West 29th Street,
    New York, NY... (212) 736-6822
Hall, Clayton Photo Studios/ 247 W 35th St, New York, NY........ (212) 947-8160
Halsband, Michael/ 1200 Broadway, New York, NY.............. (212) 889-2994
Hamlin, Elizabeth/ PO Box 177, Dorchester, MA................ (617) 265-3436
Hamilton, David William/ 47 Walker Street Loft 2,
    New York, NY... (212) 226-1271
Hammond, Lydia/ 449 E. 14th Street, New York, NY............ (212) 254-0647
Hammond, Maury/ 9 E 19th St, New York, NY .... (212) 460-9990
Hampton Photography/ 27 East 21st Street, New York, NY .... (212) 598-4200
Hankin, Jeff/ 1003 Riverside Avenue, Baltimore, MD .... (301) 889-8770
Hanlon, Gary/ 40 W. 20 St., New York, NY .... (212) 206-9144
Hansen, Constance/ 78 5th Ave, New York, NY .... (212) 691-5162
Hansen, James/ PO Box 721, Setauket, NY .... (516) 941-4179
Hansen, Steve/ 40 Winchester Street, Boston, MA.............. (617) 426-6858
Hansen, Wendy/ 200 Park Ave South, New York, NY............ (212) 477-0649
Harbutt, Charles/ 1 5th Ave, New York, NY .... (212) 431-1610
Hardin, Edward/ 156 5th Avenue, New York, NY .... (212) 242-2958
Hardin, G. Paul/ 310 E. 46th, New York, NY .... (212) 490-3801
Harmon, Rodd/ 130 West 57th Street, New York City, NY .... (212) 582-1501
Harrington, Grace/ 300 W. 49th Street, New York, NY .... (212) 246-1749
Harrington, Phillip/ 91 Rugby Road, Brooklyn, NY............ (212) 284-0212
HARRIS, BART/ 70 W. Hubbard, Chicago, IL .... (312) 751-2977
    See our ad on page 242
Harris, Brownie/ 459 W. 21st Street, New York, NY............ (212) 929-1796
Harris, Michael/ 18 W. 21st Street, New York, NY............ (212) 255-3377
Harrison, Howard Studios/ 20 W 20th, New York, NY............ (212) 989-9233
Harris, Ronald G./ 119 West 22nd Street, New York, NY .... (212) 255-2330
Hart, John/ 344 W 72nd, New York, NY........................ (212) 873-6585
Hartmann, Erich/ 251 Park Avenue S., New York, NY .... (212) 475-7600
Harvey, Ned/ 129 W. 22nd St., New York, NY .... (212) 807-7043
Hashi Studio/ 49 W. 23rd Street, New York, NY .... (212) 675-6902
Haskins, Sam/ 200 E. 62nd Street, New York, NY .... (212) 935-5027
Hausman, George/ 1181 Broadway, New York, NY .... (212) 686-4810
Haviland, Brian&Richard Lerner/ 34 E 23rd Street,
    New York, NY... (212) 598-0070
Hawkes, Michael/ 78 5th Ave, New York, NY .... (212) 254-6281
Hayes, Dannielle/ 156 2 Ave., New York, NY .... (212) 473-7826
Haynes, G Paul/ 119 West 23 St, New York, NY .... (212) 675-7666
Haynes, Michael/ 420 Madison Ave, New York, NY .... (212) 980-3510

Hayward, Bill/ 215 Park Ave S, New York City, NY .... (212) 228-6206
Heayn, Mark Studio/ 17 W. 24th Street, Baltimore, MD .... (301) 235-1608
Hedrich, David/ 7 E. 17th Street, New York, NY .... (212) 924-3324
HEDRICH, SANDI/ 11 W. Illinois St., Chicago, IL .... (312) 321-1151
See our ad on page 243
Heilman, Grant/ Box 317, Lititz, PA .... (717) 626-0296
Heintze, Steve/ 3 Midline Rd., Gaithersburg, MD .... (301) 977-1051
Heir, Stuart/ 20 W. 20th St., New York, NY .... (212) 620-0754
Heisler, Gregory/ 611 Broadway Studio 900, New York, NY .... (212) 777-8100
Heist, H. Scott/ 616 Walnut St., Emmaus, PA .... (215) 965-5479
Helburn, William Inc/ 161 E 35 St, New York, NY .... (212) 683-4980
Heller, Brian C./ 78 S. Courtland, East Stroudsbur, PA .... (717) 421-3175
Helmar, Dennis/ 134 Beach Street Suite 1016, Boston, MA .... (617) 451-1496
Helms, Bill, Inc/ 1175 York Avenue, New York, NY .... (212) 532-4010
Henke, Robert/ 75 Park Terrace E., New York, NY .... (212) 567-4564
Heron, Michael/ 28 W. 71st Street, New York, NY .... (212) 787-1272
Herr, H. Buff/ 56 W. 82nd Street, New York, NY .... (212) 595-4783
Herr, R. Timothy/ 433 E. 51st Street, New York, NY .... (212) 371-0076
Hess, Brad/ 485 5th Avenue, New York, NY .... (212) 599-1500
Hess, Trudee/ 333 E. 49th Street, New York, NY .... (212) 755-0532
Heyert, Elizabeth/ 251 W 30th St, New York City, NY .... (212) 564-3257
Heyman, Abigail/ 40 W. 12th Street, New York, NY .... (212) 989-2010
Heyman, Ken/ 3 E 76th St, New York, NY .... (212) 879-8377
Heymann, John/ 13A Roberts Rd, Cambridge, MA .... (617) 661-1840
Hickman, Louis/ 1601 Watchung, Plainfield, NJ .... (201) 561-2696
Hideoki Studio/ 236 W 26th, New York, NY .... (212) 255-1532
Hill, Fred G/ 165 Cherry St., Burlington, VT .... (802) 864-4385
Hilliard, Henry Photographer/ 59 Summer St., Somerville, MA ...... (617) 776-7995
Hilliard, Mary/ 120 E 85th St, New York, NY .... (212) 879-7839
Hill, John T/ 388 Amity Road, Bethany, CT .... (203) 393-0035
HILL, PAT/ 37 W. 20th St., New York, NY .... (212) 679-0884
See our ad on page 244
Hillside Photo/ 4 Ridgeway Ave., Hillside, NJ .... (201) 352-2137
Himmel, Liza/ 117 E 83rd, New York, NY .... (212) 737-4737
Hines, Bernard/ 31 E 20th St, New York City, NY .... (212) 475-4547
Hine, Skip/ 34 W. 17th Street, New York, NY .... (212) 691-5903
Hiro/ 50 Central Park W., New York, NY .... (212) 580-8000
Hirshfeld, Max/ 923 F Street N.W., Washington, DC .... (202) 638-3131
Hirst, Michael/ 300 E. 33rd Street, New York, NY .... (212) 982-4062
Hoban, Tana/ 105 E. 16th Street #6N, New York, NY .... (212) 477-6071
Hochman, Richard/ 210 Fifth Ave, New York, NY .... (212) 532-7766
Hocker III, John W./ PO Box 341, Cape May Ct Hse, NJ .... (609) 886-1791
Hoebermann Studio/ 49 W 44th, New York, NY .... (212) 840-2678
Hoedt Studios/ 125 South 9th St, Philadelphia, PA .... (215) 922-2448
Hofer, Evelyn/ 55 Bethune Street, New York, NY .... (212) 691-0084
Holden Ltd., Chris/ 118 E. 28th Street, New York, NY .... (212) 685-4655
Holland, Chris/ New York, NY .... (212) 684-4255
Hollander, David/ PO Box 443, Springfield, NJ .... (201) 467-0870
Hollyman, Tom/ 300 E 40th, New York, NY .... (212) 867-2383
Holt, John Studios/ The Penthouse 145 South St, Boston, MA .... (617) 426-7262
Holt, Tim/ 308 E. 73rd Street, New York City, NY .... (212) 737-5103
Hookailo, Melvin F Photog CPP/ At The Brook House 44 Wash St,
Brookline, MA .... (617) 738-4960
Hooper, Thomas/ 126 Fifth Avenue, New York, NY .... (212) 691-0122
Hopker, Thomas/ 250 E. 63rd Street, New York, NY .... (212) 832-0163
Hopkins, Douglas/ 636 Ave of the Americas, New York, NY .... (212) 243-1774
Hopkins, Steven/ 475 Carlton Avenue, Brooklyn, NY .... (212) 783-6461
Hopson, Gareth Photography/ 22 East 21st, New York, NY .... (212) 535-3800
Hornick/Rivlin Studio/ 368 Congress St, Boston, MA .... (617) 482-8614
Horowitz, Irwin/ 485 Fifth Ave, New York, NY .... (212) 697-0513
HOROWITZ, RYSZARD/ 103 Fifth Ave., New York, NY .... (212) 243-6440
See our ad on page 245
Horowitz, Ryszard/ 103 Fifth Ave., New York, NY .... (212) 243-6440
Horowitz, Ted/ 465 West End Ave, New York, NY .... (212) 595-0040
Horst/ 166 E 63rd, New York, NY .... (212) 751-4937
Horvath & Assoc Studios Ltd/ 95 Charles Street,
New York, NY .... (212) 741-0300
Hotshots Advertising Photog./ 35 Congress St./P.O. Box 896,
Salem, MA .... (617) 744-1557
Houghton, Jim Photographer/ 170 West 23 St #4V,
New York, NY .... (212) 889-3920
Hourigan, Terry/ 9 Murray St, New York, NY .... (212) 608-5775
Howard, Carl/ 27 Huckleberry Lane, Jonesville, NY .... (518) 877-7615
Howard, Ken/ 130 W. 17th Street 9th Floor, New York, NY .... (212) 691-3445
Howard, Leslie/ 69 Wood Avenue, Monticello, NY .... (914) 794-3389
Howard, Richard/ 144 Holworthy St, Cambridge, MA .... (617) 576-6968
Howard, Rosemary/ 902 Broadway, New York, NY .... (212) 473-5552
Hubbell, William/ 99 East Elm Street, Greenwich, CT .... (203) 629-9629
Hugelmeyer, John/ 6 E 39th, New York, NY .... (212) 889-1189
Hungaski, Andrew/ Meriebrooke Lane, Stamford, CT .... (203) 327-6763
Huntzinger, Robert/ 514 W 37, New York, NY .... (212) 947-4177
Huss, Robert A Assoc/ 56 Hillcrest Blvd., Warren, NJ .... (201) 754-3742
Huston, Larry/ 40 E. 21st Street, New York, NY .... (212) 777-7541
HUSZAR/ 156 Fifth Avenue, New York, NY .... (212) 929-2593
Huszar, Steven/ 156 Fifth Ave, New York, NY .... (212) 929-2593
Hutchings, Richard/ 174 Rochelle Street, City Island, NY .... (212) 885-0846
Hutchinson, Gardiner Photog/ 280 Friend Street, Boston, MA .... (617) 523-5180
Hutzler, Jacques/ 201 E. 36th Street, New York, NY .... (212) 532-7363
Hyatt, Morton/ 352 Park Avenue South 2N Floor, New York, NY ... (212) 889-2955
Hyde, Scott/ 330 East 19th St, New York, NY .... (212) 677-4830
Hyman, Paul/ 236 West 26th St, New York, NY .... (212) 255-1532
Iannazzi, Robert F/ 450 Smith Road, Pittsford, NY .... (716) 624-1285
Ichi Studio/ 303 Park Ave South, New York, NY .... ( ) 254-4810
Ideas and Images/ 294 City Island Avenue, Bronx, NY .... (212) 885-0769
Iger, Martin/ 349 E. 49th Street, New York, NY .... (212) 755-7226
Iglarsh, Gary/ 2229 N. Charles Street, Baltimore, MD .... (301) 235-3385
Ihara, Yasuhiro/ 5 Union Sq., New York, NY .... (212) 243-4862
Ikeda, Shig/ 636 Ave of Americas 4-C, New York, NY .... (212) 924-4744
Image Bank, The/ 633 Third Ave., New York, NY .... (212) 953-0303
Image Factory, Inc/ 2229 N. Charles Street, Baltimore, MD .... (301) 235-2226
Image Photographic Lab/ 507 Fifth Ave, New York, NY .... (212) 867-4747
Images/ 1119 Arnold Dr., Endicott, NY .... (607) 748-9329
Images Commercial Photography/ 110 Grand Ave, Englewood, NJ .. (201) 871-4406
Images Unltd / Ed Snider/ 106 E. 19th Street, New York, NY .... (212) 673-3652
IMBROGNO/ 411 N. Lasalle St., Chicago, IL .... (312) 644-7333
See our ad on pages 246, 247
Impact Multi Image, Inc./ 53 Laurel Dr., Somers Point, NJ .... (609) 927-8100
Incredible AfterImages Inc/ New York, NY .... (212) 563-5000
Ing, Francis/ 112 W. 31st Street, New York, NY .... (212) 279-5022
Int'l. Stock Photography, Ltd./ 113 E. 31 St., New York, NY .... (212) 696-4666
Ishimuro Studio/ 170 Fifth Avenue, New York, NY .... (212) 255-9198
Isoldi, Anthony T/ 3770 Richmond Ave, Staten Island, NY .... (212) 984-4256
Jackson, Martin/ 181 E. 78th Street, New York City, NY .... (212) 288-3875
Jackson, Reggie/ 135 Sheldon Terrace, New Haven, CT .... (203) 787-5191
Jackson, Walter/ 105 East 16 Street, New York, NY .... (212) 673-1358
Jacobsen, Paul/ 150 Fifth Avenue, New York, NY .... (212) 243-4732
Jacobs, Martin/ 34 E. 23rd Street, New York, NY .... (212) 475-1160
Jacobson, Alan J. Photography/ 250 W. 49th St.,
New York, NY .... (212) 265-0170
Jacobs, Richard B./ 138 Chatsworth Avenue, Larchmont, NY .... (914) 834-0722
Janapa Photo Ltd./ 303 W. 13 St., New York, NY .... (212) 206-6579
Janeart Ltd/ 161 West 15th St Studio 1C, New York, NY .... (212) 691-9701
Jann, Gayle/ 352 E. 85 St., New York, NY .... (212) 861-4335
Janoff, Dean/ 514 W 24th, New York, NY .... (212) 362-9546
Jay, Louis Studio/ 139 West 22nd Street, New York, NY .... (212) 675-1424
Jeffrey, Lance/ 30 E. 21st Street, New York, NY .... (212) 674-0595
Jeffrey, Richard/ 119 W. 22nd Street, New York, NY .... (212) 255-2330
Jeffry, Alix/ 71 W. 10th Street, New York, NY .... (212) 982-1835
Jensen, Peter M./ 22 E. 31 St., New York, NY .... (212) 689-5026
Jervas, George/ 600 Old Country Rd, Garden City, NY .... (516) 294-8750
Jim, Billy/ 54 Catherine St, New York, NY .... (212) 233-8157
Joachim, Bruno/ 326 A St, Boston, MA .... (617) 451-6156
Joel, Seth/ 440 Park Avenue S., New York, NY .... (212) 685-3179
Joern, James/ 125 Fifth Avenue, New York City, NY .... (212) 260-8025
Johansky, Peter/ 108 E. 16th St. 6th Fl., New York, NY .... (212) 260-4301
Johns, David/ 5615 Phillips Ave. #9, Pittsburgh, PA .... (412) 521-6852
Johnson, Eric Glenn/ 889 Broadway, New York, NY .... (212) 383-4161
Johnson, Frederick/ 66 Woodport Rd., Sparta, NJ .... (201) 729-4277
JOHNSON, MARK PHOTOGRAPHER/ P.O. Box 57561,
Dallas, TX .... (214) 939-0213
See our ad on page 248
JOHNSON, RON/ 2460 Eliot St., Denver, CO .... (303) 458-0288
See our ad on page 249
Jones, Chris/ 220 Park Ave S #6B, New York City, NY .... (212) 777-5361
Jones, Jerry Photographer/ 6207 Edloe, Houston, TX .... (713) 668-4328
Jones, J Wesley/ 114 E 25th, New York, NY .... (212) 260-5700
Jones, Lou/ 22 Randolph Street, Boston, MA .... (617) 426-6335
Jones, Marvin/ 3900 16th St. N.W. #511, Washington, DC .... (202) 726-9361
Jones, Peter/ 139 Main Street, Cambridge, MA .... (617) 492-3545
Jongen, Antoinette/ 27 Alewive Brook Road, East Hampton, NY ..... (516) 324-2786

Jook Leung Photography/ 110 East 23rd Street, New York, NY...... (212) 254-8334
Joseph, George E./ 19 Barnun Road, Larchmont, NY................... (914) 834-1425
Joseph, Helene/ 4 W 90th, New York, NY............................... (212) 580-0640
Judy/ 13 Karsten Drive, Suffern, NY .... (914) 357-7494
Jurado, Luis/ 119 Fifth Ave, New York City, NY .... (212) 677-3100
Juschkus, Raymond/ 45 John Street Room 1109, New York, NY .... (212) 964-6515
Kachaturian, Armen/ 10 E. 23rd Street, New York, NY .... (212) 533-3550
Kage, Manfred/ New York, NY.. (212) 840-6928
Kahn, R.T./ 156 E. 79th Street, New York, NY .... (212) 988-1423
Kakizaki, Seiji/ 359 Canal Street, New York, NY .... (212) 966-2360
Kalan, Mark R./ 922 President Street, Brooklyn, NY................. (212) 857-3677
Kalfus, Lonny/ 36 Myrtle Ave., Edgewater, NJ .... (212) 868-3370
Kalinsky, George/ 4 Pennsylvania Plaza, New York, NY .... (212) 563-8095
Kalisher, Simpson/ Roxbury, CT .... (203) 354-8893
Kaliski, Arthur/ PO Box 54 Route 25-A, Northport, NY .... (516) 757-0745
Kaltman, Naomi/ 79 Mercer Street, New York, NY .... (212) 431-6194
Kamper, George/ 62 N Union St, Rochester, NY .... (716) 454-7006
Kamp, Eric/ 98-120 Queens Blvd, Forest Hills, NY .... (212) 896-7780
Kamsler, Leonard/ 140 Seventh Avenue, New York, NY .... (212) 242-4678
Kane, Art/ 1181 Broadway, New York, NY .... (212) 679-2016
Kane, Peter T./ 342 Madison Avenue, New York, NY.................. (212) 687-5848
Kan Photography/ 122 W 26 St 12th Flr, New York, NY .... (212) 989-1083
Kaplan, Alan/ 7 E 20th, New York, NY................................. (212) 982-9500
Kaplan, Barry/ 323 Park Avenue S., New York, NY .... (212) 254-8461
Kaplan, Carol/ 20 Beacon Street, Boston, MA .... (617) 720-4400
Kaplan, Morris/ 218 W 47th St, New York City, NY .... (212) 764-1130
Kaplan, Peter B./ 126 W. 23. St., New York, NY .... (212) 989-5215
Kaplan, Peter J./ 924 West End Avenue, New York, NY .... (212) 222-1193
Karales, James H./ 147 W. 79th Street, New York, NY .... (212) 799-2483
Karia, Bhupendra/ 9 E. 96th Street #15B, New York, NY .... (212) 860-5479
Karlson, Norman/ 300 E. 61st Street, New York, NY .... (212) 753-3155
Karp, Ken/ 34 West 17 St, New York, NY .... (212) 807-0481
Karsten, Dirk Photography/ New York, NY .... (212) 684-4255
Karsten, Ken/ 69 Ledgebrook Drive, Norwalk, CT .... (203) 866-7119
Karzen, Marc/ 511 East 80th Street, New York, NY .... (212) 744-1479
Kassabian, Ashod/ 127 E. 59 St., New York, NY .... (212) 421-1950
Katchian, Sonia/ 47 Greene St., New York, NY .... (212) 966-9641
Katz, Baruch/ 252 W. 37th Street 15th Floor, New York, NY .... (212) 947-8074
Katz, Marty/ 1308 Pine Ridge Ln., Baltimore, MD .... (301) 484-3500
Katz, Paul/ 381 Park Ave. S., New York, NY .... (212) 684-4395
Kaufman, Curt/ 320 E. 58th Street, New York, NY .... (212) 759-2763
Kaufman, Mickey/ 144 W. 27th Street Apt. 7F, New York, NY ...... (212) 255-1976
Kaufman, Ted/ 121 Madison Avenue, New York, NY .... (212) 685-0349
Kawalerski, Ted/ 52 San Gabriel Drive, Rochester, NY .... (716) 244-4656
Kaz Studio/ 44 W. 37th Street, New York, NY .... (212) 563-1167
Keaveny, Francis/ 260 Fifth Ave, New York, NY .... (212) 683-1033
Keith H Vm Hamilton/ 749 F D R Dr, New York, NY .... (212) 982-3375
Keller, Tom/ 440 E 78th St, New York City, NY .... (212) 472-3667
Kelley, Charles W Jr/ 649 Second Ave, New York City, NY .... (212) 686-3879
Kelley, Tom Studios/ 8525 Santa Monica Blvd,
    Los Angeles, CA... (213) 657-1786
Kellman, Ray/ Menemsha, MA .... (617) 645-9446
Kellner, Jeff/ 16 Waverly Pl, New York City, NY .... (212) 475-3719
Kelly, Bill/ 140 Seventh Avenue, New York, NY .... (212) 989-2794
Kelly/Mooney Photog./ 87 Willow Ave., N. Plainfield, NJ.......... (212) 360-2576
Kelly, Thomas A./ 87 Willow Ave., N. Plainfield, NJ .... (201) 757-5924
Kemper, Charles/ 97 Perry Street Apt 13, New York City, NY ...... (212) 807-0323
Kendalton, David/ 532 Lafayette Avenue, Toms River, NJ........... (201) 244-1974
Kennedy, David M./ 10 W 18th, New York, NY .... (212) 255-9212
Kennedy, Donald/ 160 Fifth Ave, New York, NY .... (212) 924-6760
Kenro Izu/ 156 Fifth Ave, New York, NY .... (212) 254-1002
Kent, Karen/ 29 John St., New York, NY .... (212) 962-6793
Kentz, Mike/ 26 W. 38 St., New York, NY .... (212) 869-1171
Kern, Karen M./ 17 Park Ave, New York, NY .... (212) 683-9216
Kerr, Barbara & Justin/ 14 W 17th, New York, NY .... (212) 741-1731
Kertesz, Andre/ 2 Fifth Avenue, New York, NY .... (212) 477-5737
Khornak, Lucille/ 425 E 58th, New York, NY .... (212) 593-0933
Kiehl, Stuart/ 365 First Avenue, New York, NY .... (213) 556-2182
Kiernan, Jim/ 34 W. 17th Street, New York, NY .... (212) 243-3547
King, Bill/ 100 Fifth Avenue, New York, NY .... (212) 675-7575
King, Kathleen/ 105 5th Avenue #9C, New York, NY .... (212) 691-1797
King, Ralph J./ 103 Broad Street, Boston, MA .... (617) 426-3565
King, William Douglas/ 1519 50th Street, Brooklyn, NY .... (212) 851-0332
Kirk, Barbara E./ 447 E. 65th Street, New York, NY .... (212) 734-3233
Kirk, Charles/ 333 Park Ave. S., New York, NY .... (212) 677-3770

Kirkland, Douglas/ 200 E. 62nd Street, New York, NY .... (212) 935-5027
Kirk, Malcolm/ 12 E 72nd St, New York City, NY .... (212) 744-3642
Kirk, Russell/ 31 W 21st St, New York, NY .... (212) 691-0014
Kirksey, Gary/ 107 E. 6 St., Hoboken, NJ .... (201) 435-2794
Kirk Studios, Charles/ 333 Park Avenue S., New York, NY .... (212) 677-3770
Kirschner, Stan Photo Fabric./ 8 Scotsdale Rd.,
    S. Burlington, VT... (802) 862-3768
Kisch, John/ 11 W 30th, New York, NY................................. (212) 947-3178
Kiss, Robert/ 29 E. 19 St., New York, NY .... (212) 505-6650
Kitman, Carol/ 147 Crescent Avenue, Leonia, NJ .... (201) 947-2969
Klansky, Arthur J/Jane Sobel/ 154 W 57, New York, NY .... (212) 691-9701
KLEINMAN, KATHRYN/ 542 Natoma St.,
    San Francisco, CA... (415) 864-2406
    See our ad on page 252
Klein, Matthew/ 15 W. 18th St., New York, NY .... (212) 255-6400
Klein, Rudi/ 873 Broadway, New York, NY............................. (212) 460-8245
Kligge, Robert/ 5 W 30th St, New York, NY .... (212) 736-0119
Kligman, Fred/ 4733 Elm St, Bethesda, MD .... (301) 652-6333
Kline Photography/ 206 Munsee Way, Westfield, NJ .... (201) 654-8515
Knapp, Stephen/ 74 Commodore Road, Worcester, MA .... (617) 757-2507
Kobrin, Harold/ P.O. Box 115, Newton, MA .... (617) 527-3302
KOEHLER, RICK STUDIOS/ 1622 Moulton Pky. Ste. A,
    Tustin, CA... (714) 730-5982
    See our ad on page 253
Koenig, Gea/ 463 West Street, New York, NY .... (212) 243-3248
Koenig, Phil/ 49 Market, New York, NY .... (212) 964-1590
KOHANIM, PARISH/ 1130 W. Peach Tree St. N.W.,
    Atlanta, GA.. (404) 892-0099
    See our ad on page 254
Kolansky, Palma/ 155 W. 13th Street, New York, NY................. (212) 243-4077
Kopelow, Paul/ 135 Madison Avenue, New York, NY .... (212) 689-0685
Korsh, Ken/ 118 East 28 Street, New York, NY .... (212) 685-8864
Kosoff, Brian/ 40 W. 24th Street, New York, NY .... (212) 243-4880
Koudis, Nick Studios/ 40 East 23 St, New York, NY .... (212) 475-2802
Kouirinis, Bill/ 381 Park Ave S, New York City, NY .... (212) 696-5674
Kovach, Ivan/ 3725 Lyme Ave., Brooklyn, NY .... (718) 373-7512
KOZAN, DAN/ 32 W. 22nd St., New York, NY .... (212) 691-2288
    See our ad on page 255
Kozan, Dan Studio/ 32 W 22nd Str, New York, NY .... (212) 691-2288
KOZLOWSKI, MARK PHOTOGRAPHY/ 39 W. 28th St.,
    New York, NY .... (212) 684-7487
    See our ad on pages 256, 257
Kralochuil, Antonin/ 237 E. 31st Street, New York, NY .... (212) 686-6883
Kramer & Associates, Joan/ 720 Fifth Avenue 15th Floor,
    New York, NY... (212) 224-1758
Kramer, Daniel Studio/ 110 West 86 Street, New York, NY .... (212) 873-7777
Kramer, Joan/ New York, NY .... (212) 224-1758
Kranzler, Dick/ 162 W 21st St, New York City, NY .... (212) 242-4167
Krasemann, Stephen J/ 1466 Broadway, New York, NY .... (212) 840-6928
Kraus, Gerald/ 46 Janet St, Pt Jeffersn Sta, NY.................. (516) 473-9105
Krejci, Donald J./ New York, NY .... (212) 242-3900
Krementz, Jill/ 228 E. 48th Street, New York, NY .... (212) 688-0480
Kresge, C. Dennis/ 206 E. Main Street, Palmyra, PA .... (717) 838-5603
Krevansky, Barry/ 234 W. 20 St., New York, NY .... (212) 691-1593
Krieger, Harold Studios/ 225 E. 31st Street, New York, NY .... (212) 686-1690
Krist, Bob/ 220 Overlook Ave, Leonia, NJ .... (201) 943-8874
Krongard, Steve/ 212a E. 26th Street, New York, NY .... (212) 689-5634
Kruger Jr., Alexander/ 518 Miner Terrace, Linden, NJ .... (201) 862-2910
Kugler, Dennis/ 43 Bond St., New York, NY .... (212) 677-3826
Kuhn, Ann Spanos/ 1155 Broadway, New York, NY .... (212) 685-1774
Kuklin, Susan/ 436 West 23 St, New York, NY .... (212) 620-8125
KURISU, KAZ/ 819 1/2 N. Fairfax Ave.,
    Los Angeles, CA... (213) 655-7287
    See our ad on page 258
Kuzmanoff, Leon/ 508 La Guardia Place, New York, NY .... (212) 673-0169
Labua, Frank/ 37 N. Mountain Ave., Montclair, NJ .... (201) 783-6318
Ladner, Stephen/ 206 E. 63rd Street, New York, NY .... (212) 753-6095
Laffitte, Frank/ 145 E 16th, New York, NY .... (212) 533-8643
Lai, Chun Y./ 428 Broome St., New York, NY .... (212) 966-5025
Lambray, Maureen/ New York, NY .... (212) 879-3960
Lamonica, Chuck/ 16 W. 22nd Street, New York, NY .... (212) 243-4400
LaMonica Chuck/ 16 West 22 Street, New York, NY .... (212) 243-4400
La Monica, Chuck/ 16 W. 22. St., New York, NY .... (212) 243-4400
Landsberg, Erik/ 1018 Garden St., Hoboken, NJ .... (201) 659-7491
Landsman, Gary D & Associates/ 12011 Nebel Street,
    Rockville, MD.. (301) 468-2588

**LANE, BOBBI/ 7213 Santa Monica Blvd.,
Los Angeles, CA**.. (213) 874-0557
See our ad on page 259
Lane, Jonathan/ 48-50 37th St Apt 1-G, Long Island Cty, NY........ (212) 729-4975
Lane, Judy/ 444 East 82 Street, New York City, NY .... (212) 861-7225
Lane, Whitney/ 109 Somerstown Road, Ossining, NY .... (914) 762-5335
Lange, George/ 817 West End Avenue, New York, NY .... (212) 666-1414
Lange, Paul/ 156 5th Avenue, New York, NY .... (212) 242-1680
Langerman, Steven/ 16 W. 22nd Street, New York, NY .... (212) 691-9322
LANGLEY, DAVID/ 536 W. 50th St., New York, NY .... (212) 581-3930
See our ad on pages 260, 261
Langley Productions/ 212 East 16th Street, New York, NY .... (212) 777-1853
Lanman, Jonathan Photographers/ 41 Bristol St., Boston, MA....... (617) 574-9420
Lanzano, Louis/ 49 W 19th St, New York City, NY .... (212) 929-7668
Lapides, Susan/ 60 Chilton Street, Cambridge, MA .... (617) 864-7793
La Placa Productions/ 1155 Broadway, New York City, NY .... (212) 725-4949
Lariche, Michael/ 30 S. Bank St., Philadelphia, PA .... (215) 922-0447
La Riche, Michael Studios/ 30 South Bank Street,
Philadelphia, PA.. (215) 922-0447
Lari, Giorgio/ 160 Fifth Ave., New York, NY .... (212) 924-6760
Laron, Peter Allen/Esto/ 677 Madison Ave, New York, NY .... (212) 486-0019
LARRAIN, GILLES/ 95 Grand St., New York, NY .... (212) 925-8494
See our ad on pages 262, 263
Laszlo Studio, Inc./ 28 W. 39 St., New York, NY .... (212) 575-0314
Lategan, Barry/ 502 LaGuardia Place, New York, NY .... (212) 228-6850
Lattari, Antony/ 448 West 37th St, New York City, NY .... (212) 947-7488
Laurance, Bruce/ 253 West 28th Street, New York, NY .... (212) 947-3451
Laure, Jason/8 W 13th, New York, NY .... (212) 691-7466
Lautman, Robert C./ 4906 41st Street N.W., Washington, DC .... (202) 966-2800
Lavine, Arthur/ 1361 Madison Ave, New York, NY .... (212) 348-2642
Lawlor, John/ 310 E. 46 St., New York, NY............................ (212) 490-1034
Lawne, Judy/ 7 East 17 Street, New York, NY .... (212) 929-7408
Lawrence, Bernard/ 36 E 20th, New York, NY .... (212) 475-6050
Lawrence, Christopher/ 12 E 18th St, New York City, NY .... (212) 807-8028
Laxman, Glenn/ 40 E 21st St, New York City, NY .... (212) 673-4879
Layman, Alex/ 6 West 18 St, New York, NY .... (212) 989-5845
Layman Newman Studio Inc/ 6 W 18th St, New York, NY........... (212) 989-5845
Leaman Photography, Chris/ 105 Plant Avenue, Wayne, PA .... (215) 688-3290
Le Baube, Guy/ 310 E 46th, New York, NY .... (212) 986-6981
Leduc, Lyle/ 320 E. 42 St. #1014, New York, NY .... (212) 697-9216
Lee, Carol/ 214 Beacon Street, Boston, MA........................... (617) 523-5930
Lee, Daniel Studio/ 550 W 43rd Street, New York, NY .... (212) 239-4646
Leeds, Karen/ 119 W. 23rd St., New York, NY .... (212) 243-4546
Lee, Richard/ 1524 Virginia St. E., Charleston, WV .... (304) 343-8126
Lee, Vincent/ 5 Union Square Room 301, New York, NY .... (212) 620-7080
Lefler, David/ 226 W 25 St, New York, NY .... (212) 242-2342
LEGNAME, RUDI/ 389 Clementina, San Francisco, CA .... (415) 777-9569
See our ad on pages 264, 265
Leighton, Tom - Penthouse 12/ 321 E 43rd St, New York, NY....... (212) 370-1835
Lei, John/ 222 Park Ave S, New York City, NY .... (212) 674-7695
Leinwand, Freda/ 463 West St, New York City, NY .... (212) 691-0997
Leipzig, Arthur/ 378 Glen Avenue, Sea Cliff, NY .... (516) 676-6016
Lemieux, Charles P., III/ Fairfield, CT .... (203) 259-4987
LENG, BRIAN/ 1021 1/2 N. La Brea, Los Angeles, CA .... (213) 850-0995
See our ad on page 268
Lennard, Erica/ 519 W 26th St, New York City, NY .... (212) 947-9019
Lens 14 Inc./ 234 Forbes Ave, Pittsburgh, PA........................ (412) 471-1445
Leo, Donato/ 170 5th Avenue, New York, NY .... (212) 989-4200
Leonian, Phillip/ 220 E 23rd, New York, NY .... (212) 685-2310
Lerner, Richard/ 34 E. 23rd Street, New York, NY .... (212) 598-0070
Lesnick, John M/ 149 W 24th St, New York City, NY .... (212) 675-3168
Lester/ 167 N Riverside, Croton Hudson, NY .... (914) 271-5436
Lettau, Ed/ 61 Cleveland St, Orange, NJ .... (201) 673-5841
Leung, Jook/ 110 E. 23rd Street, New York, NY .... (212) 254-8334
Leuthold, Catherine/ 300 E. 70th Street, New York, NY............ (212) 570-9019
Levart, Herb/ 566 Secor Road, Hartsdale, NY .... (914) 946-2060
Leveille, David J/ 27-31 St Bridget's Drive, Rochester, NY......... (716) 423-9474
Levin, Aaron/ 200 N. Pearl St., Baltimore, MD....................... (301) 528-1444
Levinson, Ken/ 35 E 10th, New York, NY .... (212) 254-6180
Levitt, Ray/ 285 Madison Avenue, New York, NY.................... (212) 532-2424
Levy, Peter/ 119 W 22nd, New York, NY .... (212) 691-6600
Levy, Richard/ 5 W. 19th Street, New York, NY .... (212) 243-4220
Lewin, Gideon/ 25 West 39th St, New York, NY .... (212) 921-5558
Lewis, Constance/ 306 E. 78 St., New York, NY .... (212) 734-4147
Lewis, John Stage/ Iron Mountain Rd, New Milford, NY .... (914) 986-1620

Lewis, Robert/ 333 Park Ave S, New York City, NY .... (212) 475-6564
Lewis, Ross/ 460 W. 24th Street, New York, NY....................... (212) 691-6878
Lewis Studios Inc/ 344 Kaplan Dr, Fairfield, NJ .... (201) 227-1234
Lexington Labs Inc/ 17 W 45th St, New York, NY .... (212) 382-0920
Ley, Russell/ 14 Hawk St., Scotia, NY .... (518) 370-1802
Liberatore, Virginia/ 552 Broadway #6n, New York, NY .... (212) 925-0723
Lieberman, Allen/ 5 Union Square West, New York, NY .... (212) 255-4646
Lieberman Photography/ 2426 Linden Lane, Silver Springs, MD..... (301) 565-0644
Liebman, Larry/ 45 F Dunes Lane, Port Washington, NY .... (212) 354-8737
Lilley, Weaver/ 125 S. 18th Street, Philadelphia, PA................. (215) 567-2881
Lillibridge, David/ Route 4 PO Box 1172, Burlington, CT .... (203) 673-9786
Limagerie Studio/ 9219 Baltimore Blvd., College Park, MD......... (301) 441-9200
Limont, Alexander/ 137 W. Harvey Street, Philadelphia, PA .... (215) 438-7259
Linck, Tony/ 2100 Linwood Avenue, Fort Lee, NJ .... (201) 944-5454
Lindley, Thomas/ 133 5th Avenue, New York, NY .... (212) 505-0966
Lindsay, Guy/ 392 Central Pk West, New York, NY .... (212) 666-9226
Lipton, E Trina/ 60 E. 8th Street, New York, NY...................... (212) 533-3148
Lisi-Hoeltzell/ 119 Fifth Ave, New York, NY .... (212) 228-1741
Lisi-Hoeltzell Photog., Ltd./ 119 Fifth Ave., New York, NY .... (212) 674-5350
Little, Christopher/ 4 W 22nd Street 10th Floor,
New York, NY.. (212) 691-1024
Little, Stephen G/Photogroup/ 5161 River Rd, Bldg 2B,
Bethesda, MD .... (301) 652-1303
Littlewood, John/ PO Box 141, Woodville, MA .... (617) 435-4262
Litwin, Richard/ 23 E 11th St, New York, NY .... (212) 620-7144
Lloyd, Harvey/ 310 E. 23rd Street, New York, NY .... (212) 533-4498
Lobell, Richard/ 25-12 Union St., Flushing, NY .... (212) 445-6864
Lockwood, Lee Photography/ 27 Howland Rd, W Newton, MA...... (617) 965-6343
Loew, Anthony/ 32 E 22nd St, New York City, NY .... (212) 777-2220
Lokmer, John/ 925 Penn Ave, Pittsburgh, PA .... (412) 765-3565
Lombardi, Frederick/ 180 Pinehurst Avenue, New York, NY .... (212) 568-0740
Lomeo, Angelo & S. Bullaty/ 336 Central Park West,
New York, NY.. (212) 663-2122
Londoner, Hank/ 18 W. 38th Street, New York, NY .... (212) 354-0293
Longcore, Bill/ Riley Rd, New Windsor, NY .... (914) 564-6972
Longcor, William K./ Rd 2 Box 381, Andover, NJ .... (201) 398-2225
Long, Joe/ 225 E 67th, New York, NY .... (212) 249-4446
Longley, Steve/ 2224 N Charles St, Baltimore, MD .... (301) 467-4185
Longshots/ 4421 East West Highway, Washington, DC .... (301) 654-0279
Lonninge Lars, Photography Inc/ 244 Fifth Avenue,
New York, NY.. (212) 532-7272
Loven, Paul Photography/ 2301 N 16th St The Studio,
Phoenix, AZ.. (602) 253-0335
Lucas, W.Frederick/ 5 Vesta Street, Nantucket, MA .... (617) 228-1236
Lucka, Klaus/ 35 W. 31st Street, New York, NY .... (212) 594-5910
Lukas, Neil/ 93 Nassau St. #410, New York, NY .... (212) 619-4084
Lukowicz, Jerome/ 122 Arch St., Philadelphia, PA .... (215) 922-7122
Lulow, William/ 302 W. 86th Street, New York, NY.................. (212) 873-5380
Luria, Dick Photographers Inc/ 5 E 16th, New York, NY .... (212) 929-7575
**LURIA, DICK PHOTOGRAPHY, INC./ 5 E. 16th St.,
New York, NY** .... (212) 929-7575
See our ad on pages 266, 267
Lusk, Frank/ 25 E. 37 St., New York, NY.............................. (212) 679-1441
Lustica, Tee/ 156 Fifth Avenue #925, New York, NY .... (212) 924-3440
Lynch, Ron/ 124 Bloomfield St, Hoboken, NJ .... (201) 963-3476
Lynn, Don/ 31 W. 31st St, New York, NY .... (212) 239-6969
Macedonia, Carmine/ 6 W. 20th Street, New York, NY .... (212) 255-7910
Macia, Rafael/ 55 W 82nd, New York, NY .... (212) 799-4441
Mack, Donald/ 69 W 55th, New York, NY.............................. (212) 246-6086
Mackenzie, Maxwell/ 2321 37th St. N.W., Washington, DC.......... (202) 342-8266
Macweeney, Alen/ 171 First Ave, New York, NY .... (212) 473-2500
Maglott, Larry/ 249 A St. #22, Boston, MA .... (617) 492-4288
Magnet, Jeffrey C/ 628b-1620 Worcester Rd, Framingham, MA..... (617) 875-4227
Magnum Photos, Inc/ 251 Park Avenue S., New York, NY .... (212) 475-7600
Mahaffey, Kathleen/ 84 Monsey Hts. Rd., Monsey, NY .... (914) 356-1654
Maione, Don/ 34 W 17th St, New York, NY............................ (212) 741-2929
Maione, Michael P/ 78 Clark Drive, East Northport, NY .... (516) 423-1593
MAISEL, JAY/ 190 Bowery, New York, NY .... (212) 431-5013
See our ad on pages 270, 271
Malignon, Jacques/ 34 W. 28th Street, New York, NY .... (212) 532-7727
MANARCHY, DENNIS/ 229 W. Illinois St., Chicago, IL .... (312) 828-9272
See our ad on pages 272, 273
Mandarino, Tony/ 114 E 32nd St, New York City, NY .... (212) 686-2866
Manheim, Michael Philip/ PO Box 35, Marblehead, MA .... (617) 631-3560
Manis/Photo/ 59 E 3rd Street Apt 5B, New York, NY................ (212) 674-1809

Manna, Lou Studio/ 20 E. 30th Street, New York, NY .... (212) 683-8689
MANNO, JOHN/ 20 W. 22nd St., New York, NY .... (212) 243-7353
    See our ad on page 269
Manno, John/ 20 W. 22 St., New York, NY .... (212) 243-7353
Manos, Constantine/ 251 Park Avenue S., New York, NY .... (212) 475-7600
Mansour, Gozo/ 40 W. 17th St., New York, NY .... (212) 620-8115
Manuel-Denner/ 249 W 29th, New York, NY .... (212) 947-6220
Manza, Don/ 15 W 24th, New York, NY .... (212) 242-6559
Marchael, John/ 100 West 38th St, New York, NY .... (212) 921-0008
Marchese, Frank/ 56 Arbor Street, Hartford, CT .... (203) 232-4417
MARCHESE, JIM/ 200 W. 20th St., New York, NY .... (212) 242-1087
    See our ad on page 274
Marco, Phil Productions/ 104 Fifth Ave, New York, NY .... (212) 929-8082
Marcus, Helen/ 120 E 75th, New York, NY .... (212) 879-6903
MARESCA, FRANK/ 236 W. 26th St. #903, New York, NY .... (212) 620-0955
    See our ad on page 275
Margerin, Bill/ 251 Park Ave S, New York, NY .... (212) 473-7945
Marinelli, Jack/ 673 Willow Street, Waterbury, CT.................... (206) 756-3273
Mario, Cal Studio/ 27 West 20th Street, New York, NY .... (212) 807-7926
Mark, Mary Ellen/ 251 Park Avenue S., New York, NY .... (212) 431-1610
Marmaras, John/ 22 West 21 Street, New York, NY .... (212) 741-0212
Maroon, Fred J./ 2725 P Street N.W., Washington, DC............... (202) 337-0337
Marshall,John Photography,ASMP/ 344 Boylston Street,
    Boston, MA... (617) 536-2988
Marshall, Lee/ 201 W. 89th Street, New York, NY .... (212) 799-9717
Marsico, Dennis/ 110 Fahnestock Rd, Pittsburgh, PA .... (412) 781-6349
Marsi, Frank/ 34 East 29th Street, New York, NY .... (212) 696-0688
Martel, Maria/ 184 E. 64th Street, New York, NY .... (212) 246-1910
Martens, Wayne/ 112 West 31st Street, New York, NY .... (212) 239-0283
Martin, Bard/ 142 W. 26th Street, New York, NY .... (212) 929-6712
Martin, Bill/ 110 W 17th St, New York City, NY .... (212) 929-2071
Martin, Butch/ 344 W. 38th St. #10e, New York, NY .... (212) 370-4959
Martin, Dennis/ 11 West 25th Street, New York, NY .... (212) 929-2221
MARTINEZ, DAVID/ 2325 Third St. #433,
    San Francisco, CA .... (415) 558-8088
    See our ad on page 276
Martin, Jeff/ 8 Monmouth St., Redbank, NJ .... (201) 747-0269
Martin, Kenneth Photography/ 85 Fayerweather St.,
    Cambridge, MA .... (617) 497-6713
Martin, Marilyn/ 560 Harrison Ave., Boston, MA .... (617) 426-0064
Martin, Miguel/ 5 W. 31st Street, New York, NY .... (212) 564-3677
Marx, Richard/ 8 W 19th, New York, NY .... (212) 929-8880
Mason, Donald/ 101 W. 18th Street 4th Floor, New York, NY....... (212) 675-3809
Massar, Ivan/ 296 Bedford Street, Concord, MA...................... (617) 369-4090
Masser, Randy/ 953 President St., Brooklyn, NY .... (212) 783-2250
Massie, Kim/ Old Mill Rd, Lionsville, NY .... (914) 687-7744
Masters, Hilary/ Ancramdale, NY...................................... (518) 329-1522
MASTERSON, ED/ 11211 Sorrento Vly. Rd. Ste. S,
    san Diego, CA .... (619) 457-3251
    See our ad on page 277
Masucci, Myrna/ 141 E 33 St, New York, NY .... (212) 532-9311
Mats CH Nordstrom/ 125 St. Paul Street, Brookline, MA............. (617) 739-6795
Matsumoto, Tosh Inc/ 5 West 19th Street, New York, NY .... (212) 989-5663
Matthews, Cynthia/ 200 E. 78th Street, New York, NY .... (212) 288-7349
MATT, PHIL/ P.O. Box 10406, Rochester, NY .... (716) 461-5977
    See our ad on page 278
Maucher, Arnold/ 527 Third St, Brooklyn, NY .... (212) 206-1535
MAXHAM, ROBERT/ 319 E. Huisache, San Antonio, TX........... (512) 735-3537
    See our ad on page 279
Mayer, Seth L Photography/ 10 Pheasant Lane, Bloomfield, CT ..... (203) 243-0130
Mazzurco, Phil/ 150 Fifth Avenue, New York, NY.................... (212) 989-1220
McCabe, David Studio/ 39 West 67th Street, New York, NY .... (212) 874-7480
McCabe, Inger/ 10 Gracie Square, New York, NY .... (212) 420-1170
McCabe, Robert Photography Inc/ 117 East 24th St,
    New York, NY.. (212) 677-1910
McCants, Solomon D III/ 120-11 178 Place, Jamaica, NY .... (212) 776-3673
McCarthy, Margaret/ 31 East 31st Street Suite 11A,
    New York, NY.. (212) 696-5971
McCartney, Susan/ 902 Broadway Room 1608, New York, NY....... (212) 533-0660
McCash and Wheat Photography/ 225 W 25th St, Baltimore, MD .. (301) 889-1780
McConnell, Jack/ 182 Broad St, Wethersfield, CT..................... (203) 563-6154
McCormick and Nelson/ 34 Piave Street, Stamford, CT .... (203) 348-5062
McCormick, Ed/ 179 South Street, Boston, MA .... (617) 542-7229
McCoy, Dan J./ Main Street, Housatonic, MA .... (413) 274-6211
McCurdy, J Chang/ 156 Fifth Ave, New York, NY..................... (212) 243-6949

McDaniel, Jerry/ 155 E. 38th Street, New York, NY .... (212) 697-6170
McDarrah, Fred W./ 505 La Guardia Place, New York, NY........... (212) 777-1236
McDermott, Brian P/ 14 Sherwood Ave, Ossining, NY............... (914) 941-6012
McDonald, Kevin R./ 1185 Linden Ave., Stratford, CT .... (203) 378-2999
McElroy, Robert R./ 245 W. 107th Street, New York, NY .... (212) 866-1877
McFarland, Lowell & Nancy/ 115 West 27 St, New York, NY .... (212) 691-2600
McGinty, Kathie A/ 377 W 11th St, New York City, NY .... (212) 620-0596
McGowan, Kenneth/ 504 La Guardia Place, New York, NY .... (212) 674-6026
McGrail, John/ 522 E. 20th St., New York, NY........................ (212) 475-4927
McGrath, Norman/ 164 W. 79th Street, New York, NY.............. (212) 799-6422
McKean, Tom/ 1113 Arch St., Philadelphia, PA .... (215) 569-9221
McKee, Sandy/ 4264 Westroads Dr, W Palm Beach, FL.............. (305) 844-4667
McKenna, Rollie/ 1 Hancox Street, Stonington, CT .... (203) 535-0110
McKiernan, Scott/ 129 Front Street, New York, NY .... (212) 825-0073
McKinley, Barry/ 277 W 10th, New York, NY .... (212) 243-1102
McLaughlin-Gill, Frances/ 454 W 46th St, New York, NY .... (212) 664-7637
McLaughlin Studios Ltd/ 1239 Broadway, New York, NY .... (212) 889-4304
McLean, Cyril/ 920 Broadway Rm. 902, New York, NY .... (212) 777-4990
MCLOUGHLIN, JAMES/ 148 W. 24th St., New York, NY .... (212) 206-8207
    See our ad on pages 280, 281
McLouth, Meredith Photography/ 111 West 24th St.,
    New York, NY.. (212) 691-1211
McQueen, Ann/ 791 Tremont Street, Boston, MA..................... (617) 267-6258
McQueen, Hamilton/ 126 Fifth Avenue, New York, NY .... (212) 924-1393
Mead, Chris/ 215 Park Avenue South, New York, NY .... (212) 475-0448
MediaConcepts Corporation/ 14 Newbury Street, Boston, MA ...... (617) 437-1382
Media Graphics/ 378 Third Ave, New York, NY .... (212) 686-2113
Medichrome/ 271 Madison Ave., New York, NY .... (212) 679-8480
Mednick, Seymour/ 316 S. Camac, Philadelphia, PA .... (215) 735-6100
Medvec, Emily-Echolight Corp/ 151 Kentucky Av SE,
    Washington, DC .... (202) 546-1220
Meek, Richard/ 8 Skyline Drive, Huntington, NY...................... (516) 271-0072
Meiller, Henry/ 1026 Wood Street, Philadelphia, PA .... (215) 922-1525
Meiselas, Susan/ 251 Park Avenue South, New York, NY .... (212) 475-7600
Melford, Michael/ 32 E. 22nd Street, New York, NY .... (212) 473-3095
Melillo, Nick/ 118 W. 27th Street #3R, New York, NY .... (212) 691-7612
Mellor, Doug/ Darby & Maple Roads, Haverford, PA .... (215) 649-6087
Melo, Michael/ Box 20, Winterport, ME .... (207) 223-8894
Meltzer, Peter/ 15 W 11th Street, New York City, NY .... (212) 675-6630
Meluso, George/ 15 W 28th, New York, NY .... (212) 685-5544
Memory Shop Inc./ 109 E. 12th Street, New York, NY .... (214) 473-2404
Memo Studio/ 39 W. 67th Street, New York, NY .... (212) 787-1658
Menashe, Abraham/ 900 West End Avenue Apt. 7C, New York, NY . (212) 254-2754
Menda, George, Inc./ 907 Broadway, New York, NY .... (212) 674-1590
Mendelsohn, David/ Sky Farm Rd., Northwood, NH.................. (603) 942-7622
Mendlowitz, Benjamin/ 41 Walnut St, Somerville, MA .... (617) 776-2297
Menkin Studios/ 119 W. 22nd Street, New York, NY .... (212) 924-4240
Menschenfreund, Joan/ 168 W. 86th Street Apt. 14A,
    New York, NY.. (212) 362-8234
Meola, Eric/ 535 Greenwich Street, New York, NY .... (212) 255-5150
Mercer, Ralph Photographer/ 369 W. Union Street,
    E. Bridgewater, MA... (617) 378-7512
Merle, Michael G/ 5 Union Sq West, New York, NY.................. (212) 741-3801
Merrim, Lewis/ 31 E. 28th Street, New York, NY..................... (212) 889-3124
Mervar Studio/ 29 W 38th, New York, NY .... (212) 354-8024
Meshekoff, Matthew/ 170 Fifth Ave, New York City, NY............ (212) 243-4369
Messer, Helaine/ 535 W. 113th Street, New York, NY .... (212) 864-0765
Meyerowitz, Joel/ 151 W. 19th St., New York, NY .... (212) 666-6505
Michael, Lee/ 200 Henry Street, Stamford, CT .... (203) 327-3270
Michals, Duane/ 109 E. 19th Street, New York, NY .... (212) 473-1563
Mikoleski, Pete/ 86-13 55th Rd, Elmhurst, NY........................ (212) 478-4133
Milbauer, Dennis/ 15 W. 28 St. 10 Flr., New York, NY............... (212) 532-3702
Miles, Ian/ 313 E 61st, New York, NY.................................. (212) 688-1360
MILES, REID/ 1136 N. Las Palmas, Hollywood, CA.................. (213) 462-6106
    See our ad on pages 282, 283
Miljakovich, Helen/ 114 Seventh Avenue Apt. 3C,
    New York, NY.. (212) 242-0646
Millard, Howard/ 220 Sixth Ave., Pelham, NY....................... (914) 738-3689
Miller, Bert/ 30 Dongan Place, New York, NY .... (212) 567-7947
Miller, Bill/ 36 E. 20th Street, New York, NY .... (212) 674-8026
Miller, Donald L/ 485 Fifth Ave, New York, NY .... (212) 986-9783
Miller, Eileen/ 28 W. 38th Street, New York, NY .... (212) 944-1507
Miller, Josh/ 126 W 22nd, New York, NY .... (212) 255-0710
Miller Photography, Gary/ 16 Bedford Road, Katonah, NY.......... (914) 232-8279
Miller, Robin/ 1700 Pine St, Philadelphia, PA........................ (215) 985-9090

Miller, Roger/ 1411 Hollins Street, Baltimore, MD .... (301) 566-1222
Miller, Sue Ann/ 16 W 22nd St, New York City, NY .... (212) 691-2325
Millman, Lester J./ 23 Court St, White Plains, NY................... (914) 967-0486
Mims, Allen/ 107 Madison Avenue, Memphis, TN..................... (901) 527-4040
Mindell, Doug/ 811 Boylston St., Boston, MA........................ (617) 262-3968
Minh Studio/ 200 Park Avenue S. #1507, New York, NY .... (212) 477-0649
Misof, Gunther Studio/ New York, NY .... (212) 684-4255
Mistretta, Martin/ 91 5th Avenue, New York, NY.................... (212) 675-1547
Mitchell, Benn Photographer/ 103 Fifth Avenue, New York, NY .... (212) 255-8686
Mitchell, Jack/ 356 E 74th Street, New York, NY.................... (212) 737-8940
Mitchell, Lewis/ 18 E 17th, New York, NY .... (212) 243-6599
Mitchell, Mike/ 930 F St #800, Washington, DC .... (202) 347-3223
Moerder, Dan/ 2115 Wallace St, Philadelphia, PA .... (215) 978-7414
Mogeriey, Jean/ 220 E. 65 St. #8d, New York, NY .... (212) 758-4068
Molinaro, Neil R./ 46 Lindsley Avenue, Irvington, NJ .... (201) 399-7735
Molofsky, Howard/ 156 Fifth Ave, New York City, NY............... (212) 929-3338
Monroe, Robert/ 255 W. 90th Street, Cuddlebackville, NY........... (914) 754-8329
Mooney, Gail/ 87 Willow Ave., N. Plainfield, NJ .... (201) 757-5924
Mooney, Kelly Photo./ 87 Willow Ave., N. Plainfield, NJ .... (212) 360-2576
Moon, Sarah/ 67 Irving Place, New York, NY........................ (212) 674-8080
MOORE, CHRIS/ 20 W. 22nd St. #810, New York, NY .... (212) 242-0553
   See our ad on page 284
Moore, Cliff/ Box 365, Rocky Hill, NJ .... (609) 921-3754
MOORE, GARY R./ 1125 E. Orange Ave., Monrovia, CA .... (818) 359-9414
   See our ad on page 284
Moore, James/ 38 E. 19th Street, New York, NY .... (212) 674-7150
Moore, Marvin/ 234 Fifth Ave. 5 Flr., New York, NY .... (212) 696-4001
Moore, Peter/ 351 W 30th, New York, NY .... (212) 564-5989
Moore, Truman/ 873 Broadway, New York, NY .... (212) 533-3655
Mopsik, Eugene H/ 419 S Perth St, Philadelphia, PA .... (215) 922-3489
MORAN, NANCY/ 143 Green St., New York, NY .... (212) 505-9620
   See our ad on page 286
Morath, Inge/ 251 Park Avenue South, New York, NY............... (212) 475-7600
Morello, Joe Photography/ 40 W. 28th Street, New York, NY....... (212) 684-2340
Morely, Bob/ 15 East Street, Boston, MA .... (617) 482-7279
Moretz, Charles/ 141 Wooster St, New York, NY .... (212) 254-3766
Morgan, Jeff/ 27 W. 20th St., New York, NY .... (212) 924-4000
Morley, Bob/ 15 East Street, Boston, MA .... (617) 482-7279
Morrin, John/ 140 W. 57th Street, New York, NY .... (212) 245-8435
Morris, Bill/ 34 E 29th St, New York, NY .... (212) 685-7354
Morris, Leonard/ 200 Park Avenue South, New York, NY .... (212) 473-8485
Morrison, Ted/ 286 Fifth Ave, New York, NY .... (212) 279-2838
Morrow, Christopher Photog/ 163 Pleasant Street,
   Arlington, MA .... (617) 648-6770
Morsch, Roy/ 1200 Broadway, New York, NY .... (212) 679-5537
Morsillo, Les/ 20 St Marks Place, New York, NY .... (212) 674-3124
Moscati, Frank/ 139 Fifth Ave, New York, NY .... (212) 228-4000
Mougin, Claude/ 227 W 17th Street, New York, NY .... (212) 691-7895
Moyer, Robin/ 394 Fairville Road, Chadds Ford, PA .... (215) 388-7598
Mozo-Saravia, Carlos/ 74 Oakland Street, Stratford, CT .... (203) 377-0500
Mucci, Tina/ 59 West 73rd St, New York, NY .... (212) 877-4017
Muhlstock, Chuck/ 305 E. 86th Street, New York, NY .... (212) 369-5916
Mulaire, Douglas/ 135 Hudson St., New York, NY .... (212) 334-9863
Mullen, Dan Studio/ 110 Madison Ave, New York, NY .... (212) 725-8753
Muller, Rudy/ 318 E. 39th Street, New York, NY .... (212) 679-8124
Mulligan, Bob/ 109 Broad St, Boston, MA .... (617) 426-3221
Mulligan, Joseph/ 239 Chestnut St., Philadelphia, PA .... (215) 592-1359
Mulvehill, Larry/ P.O. Box 100, Slate Hill, NY .... (914) 355-1222
Munro, Gordon/ 381 Park Avenue South, New York, NY .... (212) 889-1610
Munson, Russell/ 6 E. 39th Street, New York, NY .... (212) 689-7672
Munster, Joseph/ Old Route 28, Phoenicia, NY .... (914) 688-5347
Muresan, Jon/ 907 Broadway, New York, NY .... (212) 505-8514
Murray, Bob Studio/ 149 Franklin Street, New York City, NY ..... (212) 226-6860
Murrell, Gerard/ 93 East 7th Street #4, New York, NY .... (212) 475-0537
Murro, Anthony/ 152 W 25th, New York, NY .... (212) 691-4220
Musto, Tom/ 225 South Main Street, Wilkes-Barre, PA .... (717) 822-5798
Mydans, Carl/ 212 Hommocks Road, Larchmont, NY .... (914) 834-9206
Myers, Steve/ 110 S. Main St., Almond, NY .... (607) 276-6400
Myers Studios, Inc./ 21 Princeton Pl., Orchard Park, NY .... (716) 662-6002
Myron/ 127 Dorrance St, Providence, RI .... (401) 421-1946
Naar, Jon/ 230 E. 50th Street, New York, NY .... (212) 752-4625
Nadelson, Jay/ 116 Mercer St, New York, NY .... (212) 226-4266
Nahoum, Ken/ 55 Northmore St. #2a, New York, NY .... (212) 219-0592
Naideau, Harold Photography/ 233 W 26th St, New York, NY...... (212) 691-2942
Nakamura, Tohru/ 112 Greene Street, New York, NY .... (212) 334-8011

Nakano, George/ 119 W. 22nd Street, New York, NY .... (212) 228-9370
Nalewajk, Jerome/ 2454 Broadbridge Ave., Stratford, CT .... (203) 375-0207
Namoum, Ken/ 55 N. Moore St., New York, NY .... (212) 219-0592
Namuth, Hans/ 157 W. 54th Street, New York, NY .... (212) 245-2811
Nanfra, Vincent/ 62 Preston Avenue, Staten Island, NY .... (212) 687-8920
Nardelli, Will/ PO Box 2913, New York, NY .... (212) 683-6930
Nathans, Rhoda/ 141 E 89th St, New York, NY .... (212) 831-5883
Nat'l Conf Pro Photographers/ C/O Conference Mgmt PO Bx 4990,
   Norwalk, CT .... (203) 852-0500
Neal, Steven/ 3114 Nash Pl. S.E., Washington, DC.................. (202) 584-4957
Nealy, Keith/ 12 E. 22nd Street, New York, NY .... (212) 673-9870
Nedlin, Radie/ 14 Melbourne Road, Great Neck, NY .... (516) 482-6073
Nehr, Adam Photographic Illus./ 1028 W. 22 St., Erie, PA .... (814) 459-3946
Neil, Joseph/ 27 W. 20th St., New York, NY .... (212) 255-5700
Nelken, Dan/ 43 W. 27th Street, New York, NY .... (212) 532-7471
Nelson, Laurence/ 535 Worcester St, Wellesley, MA................ (617) 235-0891
Nemeth Studio, Bruce/ 220 E. 23rd Street, New York, NY .... (212) 686-3272
Nerney, Dan/ 137 Rowayton Ave., Rowayton, CT .... (203) 853-2782
Neste, Anthony/ P.O. Box 602, Deer Park, NY .... (516) 667-3453
Nettis, Joseph/ 1717 Walnut Street, Philadelphia, PA .... (215) 563-5444
Neumayer, Joseph W/ 118 East 28th Street Room 808,
   New York City, NY... (212) 685-0285
Neurath, Eric/ 275 Washington St., Cambridge, MA................. (617) 497-1595
NEWBY, STEVE PHOTOGRAPHY/ 4501 Swiss Ave.,
   Dallas, TX .... (214) 821-0231
   See our ad on page 287
New England Photo Craft/ 1 Mckee St., East Hartford, CT .... (203) 528-0100
New Horizon Photo/ Chili Paul Plaza 3240 Chili Av,
   Rochester, NY... (716) 889-4180
Newirth, Scott/ 104 W 17th St, New York City, NY .... (212) 242-7303
Newler, Michael/ 201 E 83rd St, New York City, NY .... (212) 628-2382
Newman, Arnold/ 39 W. 67th Street, New York, NY .... (212) 877-4510
Newman, Irving/ 900 Broadway, New York, NY..................... (212) 228-2760
Newman, Marvin/ 227 Central Park W, New York, NY .... (212) 362-2044
Ney, Nancy/ 108 E 16th St, New York, NY .... (212) 260-4300
Ng, Kaimen Norman/ 36 E 20th, New York, NY .... (212) 982-3230
Niccolini, Dianora/ 356 E. 78th Street, New York, NY.............. (212) 288-1698
Nicholas, Peter/ 25 W. 39th Street, New York, NY .... (212) 354-4681
Nichols, Don/ 1241 University Avenue, Rochester, NY .... (716) 461-9666
Nicholson, Nick/ 121 W. 72nd Street Apt. 2E, New York, NY........ (212) 362-8418
Nicolaysen, Ron/ 448 W 37th Street, New York City, NY .... (212) 947-5167
Nicotera, Doug/ 8 Roller Dr, Harrisburg, PA .... (717) 939-8845
Niefield, Terry/ 210 Fifth Avenue, New York, NY .... (212) 686-8722
Nighswander, Tim/ 315 Peck St, New Haven, CT .... (203) 789-8529
Nikas, Basil W/ 710 Park Ave, New York City, NY .... (212) 472-1570
Nisnevich, Lev/ 133 Mulberry Street, New York, NY .... (212) 219-0535
Nivelle, Serge/ 36 Gramercy Park East, New York, NY .... (212) 473-2802
Niwa-Ogrudek Ltd./ 30 E. 23rd Street, New York, NY .... (212) 982-7120
Nobart NY Inc/ 33 E. 18th Street, New York, NY .... (212) 475-5522
Noble, Inc./ 611 Cathedral St., Baltimore, MD..................... (301) 244-0292
Nobu Arakawa Studio/ 40 East 21st Street, New York, NY .... (212) 475-0206
Nobu Studio/ 156 Fifth Ave, New York, NY......................... (212) 924-7840
Nocella, Sam/ 2030 Richard Road, Willow Grove, PA .... (215) 659-2171
Nochton, Jack/ 1238 W. Broad Street, Bethlehem, PA.............. (215) 691-2223
Nones, Leonard/ 5 Union Sq, New York, NY .... (212) 741-3990
North Light Photography/ 931 Penn Ave., Reading, PA............. (215) 373-5553
Northlight Visual Comm.Group/ 45 Academy Street, Newark, NJ.... (201) 624-3990
Northlight Visual Comm Group/ 21 Quine St, Cramford, NJ......... (201) 272-1155
Norton, C Dick/ 172 Newbury Street, Boston, MA .... (617) 266-1065
Novack, Ed/ 28 Liberty St, Deer Park, NY .... (516) 242-0390
Oasis Studios-Susan Flaherty/ 205 Fifth Avenue,
   Bradley Beach, NJ .... (201) 988-8362
Obremski, George/ 1200 Broadway, New York, NY .... (212) 684-2933
O'Brien, Michael/ 22 W. 85th Street, New York, NY .... (212) 787-2697
O'Brien, Michael/ 33 W 17th St, New York City, NY .... (212) 242-7635
Ochi-Photography/ 636 6th Avenue, New York City, NY............. (212) 807-7711
Ogilvy, Stephen/ 876 Broadway, New York City, NY .... (212) 505-9005
Ohringer, Frederick/ 130 E 18th St, New York, NY .... (212) 473-6701
Ohta Studio/ 15 East 11th St, New York, NY .... (212) 243-2353
Okada, Tom/ 45 W. 18th St, New York, NY .... (212) 989-6595
O'Kino, Fuji/ 18 Banks St, Somerville, MA .... (617) 776-8496
Olivo, John/ 545 W. 45th Street, New York, NY .... (212) 765-8812
Olman, Bradley/ 15 W 24th, New York, NY .... (212) 243-0649
Olson, John Productions/ Pier 61 23rd at 12th Ave,
   New York, NY... (212) 243-5800

PHOTOGRAPHERS/East

OLVERA, JIM/ 2700 Commerce St., Dallas, TX .... (214) 939-0550
See our ad on page 288
O'Neal, Charles T/ 416 W 20th St, New York City, NY .... (212) 691-7768
O'Neill, Michael/ 134 10th Avenue, New York City, NY .... (212) 807-8777
Oppersdorff, Mathias/ 1220 Park Avenue, New York, NY .... (212) 860-4778
Oransky, Alan/ 262 Upland Road, Cambridge, MA .... (617) 354-5887
O'Reilly, Robert J./ 311 E. 50th Street, New York, NY .... (212) 832-8992
Orel Photography/ 140 Broadway, Hawthorne, NY .... (914) 271-5542
Orenstein, Ronn/ 55 W. 26th St., New York, NY .... (212) 685-0563
Oringer, Hal Inc/ 32 W 31st, New York, NY .... (212) 564-7544
Oristaglio, Susan/ 155 West 81 St, New York, NY .... (212) 877-8495
Orkin, Ruth/ 65 Central Park West, New York, NY .... (212) 362-1658
Orling, Alan S./ 53 E. 10th Street, New York, NY .... (212) 473-8363
O'Rourke, J. Barry/ 1181 Broadway, New York, NY .... (212) 686-4224
O'Rourke, Randy/ 339 E 21st St, New York City, NY .... (212) 674-3878
Orrico, Charles J./ 72 Barry Lane, Syosset, NY .... (516) 364-2257
Ortiz, Gilbert/ 249 W 29th St, New York City, NY .... (212) 736-8770
Ortner, Jon/ 64 W. 87th Street, New York, NY .... (212) 873-1950
Ortoli, Fred/ 15 Garden St., Seymour, CT .... (203) 888-7861
Osborn, Jim/ 3330 Emerson Ave, Parkersburg, WV .... (304) 428-1631
O'Shaughnessy, Bob/ 50 Melcher St., Boston, MA .... (617) 542-7122
Osonitsch, Robert/ 112 Fourth Ave, New York, NY .... (212) 533-1920
Otsuki, Toshi/ 241 W 36th St, New York City, NY .... (212) 594-1939
Oudi/ 704 Broadway, New York, NY .... (212) 777-0847
Owens, Frank Studios Inc/ 11 W 29th St, New York City, NY .... (212) 686-7814
Owen, Sigrid/ 221 E 31st, New York, NY .... (212) 686-5190
Ozgen, Nebil/ 6 W. 20th Street, New York, NY .... (212) 924-1719
Paccione, Onofrio/ 73 5th Avenue, New York, NY .... (212) 691-8674
Page, Lee/ 310 E. 46th St., New York, NY .... (212) 286-9159
Page, R. F./ 701 1/2 Walnut Ave., Syracuse, NY .... (315) 472-8046
Pagliuso, Jean/ 12 E. 20th Street, New York, NY .... (212) 674-0370
Pagnano, Patrick/ 217 Thompson Street, New York, NY .... (212) 475-2566
Palmer, Gabe/ 30 Rock Ledge, W Redding, CT .... (203) 227-1477
Palmer, Gabe/ 269 Lyons Plains Rd., Weston, CT .... (203) 227-1477
Palmer/Kane/ 30 Rockledge Road, W Redding, CT .... (203) 938-3227
Palubniak, Jerry & Nancy/ 143 West 27 St, New York, NY .... (212) 924-1512
Panopoulos, Gerald/ 20 W 22nd St, New York City, NY .... (212) 242-3132
Pantages, Tom/ 7 Linden Avenue, Gloucester, MA .... (617) 525-3678
Papadopolous Peter/ 78 Fifth Ave, New York, NY .... (212) 675-8830
Pappas, Tony/ 110 West 31st Street, New York, NY .... (212) 868-2032
Paradigm Productions/ 6437 Ridge Avenue, Philadelphia, PA .... (215) 482-8404
Paras, Michael N./ 236 Elizabeth St., New York, NY .... (212) 278-6768
Parik, Jan/ 165 E. 32nd St., New York, NY .... (212) 686-3514
Parker, Phillip M/ 202 Dudley St, Memphis, TN .... (901) 529-9200
Parker, Robert B./ PO Box 102, Corning, NY .... (607) 962-4104
Parraga, Alfredo/ 545 W. 45th Street, New York, NY .... (212) 765-8812
Parsons, Bill/ 518 West 9th Street, Little Rock, AR .... (501) 372-5892
Pastner, Robert/ 166 E. 63rd Street, New York, NY .... (212) 838-8335
Pateman, Michael/ 155 E 35th St, New York, NY .... (212) 685-6584
Paul Ltd., Martin/ 247 Newbury Street, Boston, MA .... (617) 536-1644
Paul, Tina/ 300 Mercer St. #17m, New York, NY .... (212) 473-2922
Paz, Peter/ 41 Union Sq. W. #1123, New York, NY .... (212) 206-8466
Peacock, Christian/ 28 W 86th Street, New York, NY .... (212) 580-1422
Pease, Greg Photography/ 23 East 22nd Street, Baltimore, MD ..... (301) 332-0583
Peck, Joseph/ 878 Lexington Ave, New York, NY .... (212) 472-1929
Peden, John/ 168 Fifth Avenue, New York, NY .... (212) 255-2674
Pederson, Erwin Inc/ 924 Broadway, New York, NY .... (212) 677-0044
Pehlman, Barry Photography/ 806 King Road, Malvern, PA .... (215) 644-8662
Peirce, Michael/ 82 Avon Hill St, Cambridge, MA .... (617) 491-0643
Pellegrini Frances/ 113 E 22nd Street, New York, NY .... (212) 228-1010
Peltz, Stuart/ 6 W. 18th Street, New York, NY .... (212) 929-4600
Pemberton, John/ 37 E. 28th Street, New York, NY .... (212) 532-9285
Pendleton, Bruce/ 485 Fifth Avenue, New York, NY .... (212) 986-7381
Penneys, Robert/ 147 N. 12th Street, Philadelphia, PA .... (215) 925-6699
Penn, Irving/ Box 934 FDR Station, New York, NY .... (212) 246-0679
Peress, Gilles/ 251 Park Avenue S., New York, NY .... (212) 475-7600
Perkell, Jeff/ 110 Madison Ave, New York, NY .... (212) 684-3988
Perla, Dario/ 117 Bank St, New York, NY .... (212) 242-7470
Perlmutter, Steven/ 7 River St., Milford, CT .... (203) 878-5090
Perluck, David/ 270 Broadway, Providence, RI .... (401) 273-7586
Perron, Robert/ 104 E. 40th Street, New York, NY .... (212) 661-8796
Perry, Paul Robert/ 476 Clinton Avenue Suite 4F,
Brooklyn, NY .... (212) 638-3624
PERWEILER, GARY/ 873 Broadway, New York, NY .... (212) 254-7247
See our ad on page 289
Peters, Barbara/ 1 5th Ave, New York, NY .... (212) 777-6384
Petersen, Brent/ 750 3rd Avenue, New York, NY .... (212) 573-7195
Peterson, Gosta Inc./ 200 East 87 Street, New York, NY .... (212) 876-0560
Petoe, Denes/ 39 E 29th, New York, NY .... (212) 689-1528
Pfizenmaier, Ed/ 42 E 23 St 6 Floor, New York, NY .... (212) 475-0910
Pfletschinger, Hans/ 1466 Broadway, New York, NY .... (212) 840-6928
Philiba, Allan A./ 3408 Bertha Dr., Baldwin, NY .... (212) 286-0948
Phillips, John/ 100 W. 57th Street, New York, NY .... (212) 246-1579
Phillips, Ned/ 1 Union Sq W, New York, NY .... (212) 691-9890
Phillips, Robert/ 101 W. 57th Street, New York, NY .... (212) 757-5190
Phillips Studio, Randall/ 40 W. 22nd Street, New York, NY .... (212) 243-6408
PHOTO 85/ 17 Washington St./P.O.Box 4990,
norwalk, CT .... (203) 852-0500
PHOTO DISTRICT NEWS/ 167 Third Ave., New York, NY .... (212) 677-8418
Photofile Intl. Ltd./ 32 E. 31st, New York, NY .... (212) 989-0500
Photo Forum/ 110 W. 17th Street, New York, NY .... (212) 924-9460
Photographic Associates/ 8 Monmouth St, Red Bank, NJ .... (201) 747-0269
PHOTOGRAPHIC COMMUNICATIONS/ 2004 Martin Ave.,
Santa Clara, CA .... (408) 727-2233
See our ad on page 290
Photographic Concepts/ 352 Park Ave S, New York, NY .... (212) 689-3201
Photographic House Inc/ 8 Gloria Ln, Fairfield, NJ .... (201) 575-1932
Photographic Illustrations Ltd/ 7th and Ranstead Sts.,
Philadelphia, PA .... (215) 925-7073
Photographic Images/ 39 Westmoreland Ave, White Plains, NY ...... (914) 761-8885
Photography Associates/ 140-150 Huyshope Ave, Hartford, CT ...... (203) 249-1105
Photography By Art Salander/ 11 Delaware Ave, Commack, NY ..... (516) 462-5054
Photography for Industry/ 230 W. 54th Street, New York, NY .... (212) 757-9255
Photography Inc/ 125 Kingston, Boston, MA .... (617) 426-8581
Photoquest International, Inc./ 521 Madison Ave.,
New York, NY .... (212) 986-1224
Photo Researchers/ 60 E. 56th Street, New York, NY .... (212) 758-3420
Photoscope, Inc./ 12 W. 27th St., New York, NY .... (212) 696-0880
Photo Take/ 4523 Broadway, New York, NY .... (212) 942-8185
Photo Trends/ PO Box 650, Freeport, NY .... (212) 279-2130
Photri/Photo Research Int'L./ New York, NY .... (212) 926-0682
Pickerell, James H./ 8104 Cindy Lane, Bethesda, MD .... (301) 365-1126
Picture Group Inc./ 5 Steeple Street, Providence, RI .... (401) 273-5473
Piel, Denis C/O Xavier Moreau/ 111 West 57, New York, NY .... (212) 582-9805
Pignataro, Philip F/ 130 C Jefryn Blvd East, Deer Park, NY .... (516) 595-1616
Pilgreen, John/ 91 Fifth Ave 3rd Floor, New York, NY .... (212) 243-7516
Pilling, Richard/ 13-25 Burbank St, Fair Lawn, NJ .... (201) 791-2282
Pilossof, Judd/ 142 W 26th St, New York City, NY .... (212) 989-8971
Pinderhughes/ 536 W 111th St, New York City, NY .... (212) 662-5105
Pinsley, Jules/ 84-21 Smedley Street, Jamaica, NY .... (212) 291-2871
Pioppo Assocs/ 50 W 17th Street, New York City, NY .... (212) 243-0661
Pippin, Wilbur/ 106 Fifth Avenue, New York, NY .... (212) 675-5514
Piscioneri, Joseph/ 333 Park Avenue South, New York, NY .... (212) 533-7982
Pite, Jonathan E./ 430 W. 14 St. #502, New York, NY .... (212) 206-7377
Plank Photography/ 981 River Road, Reading, PA .... (215) 376-3461
Platt, Mark/ 41 E 20th, New York, NY .... (212) 475-1481
Plotkin, Bruce/ 3 West 18th Street, New York, NY .... (212) 691-6185
Pobereskin, Joseph/ 70 8th Ave, New York, NY .... (212) 783-7079
Pobiner, Ted Studios Inc/ 381 Park Ave S, New York, NY .... (212) 679-5911
Podesser, Victor/ 17 W 20th St, New York City, NY .... (212) 929-6912
Poggenpohl, Eric/ 1816 S Street N.W., Washington, DC .... (202) 387-0826
Pohuski, Michael/ 36 S Paca St, Baltimore, MD .... (301) 962-5404
Polansky, Allen/ 1431 Park Avenue, Baltimore, MD .... (301) 383-9021
POLASKI, JIM/ 215 W. Superior 6th, Chicago, IL .... (312) 751-2526
See our ad on pages 292, 293
Policastro, Anthony/ 117 Isabelle Street, Metuchen, NJ .... (201) 494-2990
Pollard, Pat Photography/ 75 Pratt Street, Hartford, CT .... (203) 549-5085
Polsky, Herb/ 1024 Sixth Ave, New York, NY .... (212) 730-0508
Polumbaum, Ted/ 326 Harvard Street, Cambridge, MA .... (617) 491-4947
POMERANTZ, RON/ 325 W. Huron St., Chicago, IL .... (312) 787-6407
See our ad on page 291
Poole, Frank/ 85 Willow St., New Haven, CT .... (203) 787-1074
Popper, Andrew/ 330 First Avenue, New York, NY .... (212) 982-9713
Porcella, Phil/ 109 Broad Street, Boston, MA .... (617) 426-3222
Porter, Charles/ Georgetown Square C-4, Poughkeepsie, NY .... (914) 454-7033
Porter Photographer, Art/ 29 E. 32nd Street, New York, NY .... (212) 685-1555
Portogolio Photo Serv./ 72 W. 45 St., New York, NY .... (212) 840-2636
Postal, Jonathan/ 280 Mulberry St, New York City, NY .... (212) 226-2799
Poster, James S/ 210 Fifth Ave, New York City, NY .... (212) 349-3720
Pottle, Jock/ 301 W. 89th St. #15, New York, NY .... (212) 874-0216

Powers, Guy/ 69 Mercer Street, New York, NY (212) 925-6216
Praus, Edgar G./ 176 Anderson Ave., Rochester, NY (716) 442-4820
Prengle, Robert Photography/ 2132 N. Market St., Wilmington, DE (302) 656-8009
Pressman, Herb/ 118 East 28th Suite 908, New York City, NY (212) 683-5055
Pretzer, Ron/Luxe/ 34 Oak St., Geneseo, NY (716) 243-5291
Prezant Photography, Steve/ 1181 Broadway, New York, NY (212) 684-0822
Pribula, Barry/ 62 Second Avenue, New York, NY (212) 777-7612
Price, Clayton J./ 205 W. 19 St., New York, NY (212) 929-7721
Price, David/ 4 E 78th, New York, NY (212) 794-9040
Prigent, Roger/ 253 E 74th, New York, NY (212) 288-7569
Priggen, Leslie/ 144 W. 27th Street, New York, NY (212) 243-4800
Prince, Len/ 141 Fifth Ave, New York, NY (212) 533-6460
Pro Color/ 940 Federal Rd., Brookfield, CT (203) 792-2374
Proctor, Keith Studio/ 78 Fifth Avenue, New York, NY (212) 807-1044
Proscenium/ 845 3rd Ave, New York, NY (212) 421-6500
Pruitt, David/ 156 Fifth Avenue, New York, NY (212) 807-0767
Pruzan, Michael/ 1181 Broadway, New York, NY (212) 686-5505
Puhlmann, Rico/ 156 Fifth Ave Rm 1218, New York, NY (212) 620-4211
Purring, A James/ Swiss Lane Rd, Malvern, PA (215) 933-8393
Purse, Dennis/ 36 W. 25th Street, New York, NY (212) 807-7833
Puzzutelli, Thomas/ 130 West 25th Street, New York City, NY (212) 807-6099
Quality Images/ 7 River St., Milford, CT (203) 878-5090
Quartuccio, Dom/ 5 Tudor City Pl, New York, NY (212) 661-1173
Quat, Daniel Photography Inc/ 156 5th Avenue 2nd Floor, New York, NY (212) 807-0588
Quintero, Antonio/ 205 Clift St., Central Islip, NY (516) 234-4625
Raab, Michael/ 831 Broadway, New York, NY (212) 533-0030
Rabanne, Roberto/ 1560 Broadway, New York City, NY (212) 869-3530
Raboy, Marc Photography/ 205 W 19th, New York, NY (212) 242-4616
Rachum Studios/ 31 Peoples Arcade, Bridgeport, CT (203) 333-0909
Racioppo, Bob/ 10 Ocean Pky., Brooklyn, NY (212) 853-0225
Rainbow/ Box 573, Housatonic, MA (413) 274-6211
Rajs, Jake J./ 36 West 20th St, New York, NY (212) 675-3666
Ranck, Rosemary/ 323 W. Mermaid Ln., Philadelphia, PA (215) 242-3718
Randolph, Bob/ 514 Tenth St NW Suite 902, Washington, DC (202) 783-2255
Raso, Peter V I P Studios/ 1940 Mayflower Avenue, Bronx, NY (212) 829-4992
Ratigan, William P./ 189 Second St., Troy, NY (518) 272-2626
Ratkai, George/ 404 Park Avenue S., New York, NY (212) 725-2505
Rattner, Robert/ 106-15 Jamaica Avenue, Richmond Hill, NY (212) 441-0826
Ray, Bill/ 350 Central Park West, New York, NY (212) 222-7680
Redmond, Calvin/ 5 W 20th St, New York City, NY (212) 675-4946
REESE, DONOVAN/ 4801 Lemmon Ave., Dallas, TX (214) 526-5851
See our ad on page 294
Reichenthal, Martin/ 27 W. 24th Street, New York, NY (212) 242-0076
Reiher, Jim/ 31 W 31st St, New York City, NY (212) 736-4571
Reinhardt, Mike/ 154 W. 57th Street, New York, NY (212) 541-4787
Reinmiller, Mary Ann/ 163 W. 17th Street, New York, NY (212) 243-4302
Renaissance Productions/ 50 W 17th Street, New York, NY (212) 206-0436
Renard, Jean/ 304 Boylston, Boston, MA (617) 266-8673
Renckly, Joe/ 725 Liberty Avenue, Pittsburgh, PA (412) 261-4029
Revis, William/ 28 Rutgers Dr., Oakland, NJ (201) 337-7009
Reznicki, Jack Studio/ 119 Fifth Ave, New York, NY (212) 473-0943
Rezny, Aaron/ 119 W. 23rd Street, New York, NY (212) 691-1894
Rezny, Abe/ 28 Cadman Plaza W Studio 7F, Brooklyn Height, NY (212) 226-7747
Rice Studio Inc., Neil/ 91 Fifth Avenue, New York, NY (212) 924-6096
Richman, Mel Inc/ 15 N. Presidential Blvd., Bala-Cynwyd, PA (215) 667-8900
Richmond, Jack/ 12 Farnsworth St., Boston, MA (617) 482-7158
Riemer, Ken/ 183 St. Paul Street, Rochester, NY (716) 232-5450
Ries, Henry/ 204 E 35th, New York, NY (212) 689-3794
Ries, Stan/ 48-52 Great Jones Street, New York, NY (212) 533-1852
Riley, Catherine/ 12 E. 37th Street, New York, NY (212) 532-8326
Riley, David-Carin/Photography/ 152 West 25th St, New York, NY (212) 741-3662
Riley, George Photographer/ Sisquisic Trail PO Box 840, Yarmouth, ME (207) 846-5787
Riley, Jon/ 12 E. 37th Street, New York, NY (212) 532-8326
Rinaldi, Cecilia/ 53 N. Long Beach Ave., Freeport, NY (516) 623-7555
Ritta, Bob Studio/ 41 W 24th, New York, NY (212) 255-8333
Ritter, Frank/ 127 E. 90th Street, New York, NY (212) 427-0965
Rivelli, William/ 303 Park Avenue S., New York, NY (212) 254-0990
Rizzi, Leonard/ 5161 River Rd. Bg 20b, Bethesda, MD (301) 652-1303
Rizzo, Alberto/ 330 E 23rd St, New York, NY (212) 684-7440
Rizzuto, Dennis/ 2930 161st Street, Flushing, NY (212) 261-4740
Roberts, Ebet/ 245 W. 107 St. #10c, New York, NY (212) 316-3696
Roberts, Grant/ 11 W. 20 St., New York, NY (212) 620-7921
Roberts,Stefan K. Assoc., Inc./ 155 East 47th Street, New York, NY (212) 688-9798
ROBINS, LAWRENCE/ 50 W. 17th St., New York, NY (212) 206-0436
See our ad on page 295
Robinson, Cervin/ 251 W. 92nd Street, New York, NY (212) 873-0464
Robinson, George A./ Box 377 Old Pump Rd., Jericho, VT (802) 899-3703
Robins, Susan/ 124 N. 3rd St., Philadelphia, PA (609) 795-8386
Rockfield, Bert Studio/ 31 E 32nd St, New York, NY (212) 689-3900
Rockhill, Morgan/ 204 Westminster Mall, Providence, RI (401) 274-3472
Rodan, Don/ 23 W 12th St, New York City, NY (212) 242-2458
Roderick, Jim Stock Index/Ston/ 76 Irving Pl, New York, NY (212) 777-7909
Rode, Robert/ 2670 Arleigh Road, East Meadow, NY (516) 579-9462
Rodriguez, Manuel A/ 19 Cleveland Pl, New York, NY (212) 966-6853
Rogers, Bruce/ 37 W 20th St, New York City, NY (212) 620-9025
Rohner, Patrick/ New York, NY (212) 684-4255
Rokach, Alan/ Ny Botanical Gardens, Bronx, NY (212) 220-8698
Rolf Dehaan/ 97 East 7th Street, New York, NY (212) 475-4850
Romano, R. E./ 1155 Broadway, New York, NY (212) 696-0264
Romanski, John C/ 210 Monitor St, Brooklyn, NY (212) 389-4774
Roseman, Shelly/ 723 Chestnut Street, Philadelphia, PA (215) 922-1430
Rosenberg, Arnold Studio/ PO Box 1034, E Hampton, NY (516) 324-1227
Rosenberg, Ken Photography/ 514 West End Avenue, New York, NY (212) 362-3149
Rosenberg, Len/ 2077 Clinton Avenue South, Rochester, NY (716) 244-6910
Rosenfeld, Stanley/ 175 Riverside Drive, New York, NY (212) 787-6653
Rosengarten, Geoff/ 36 W 25th St 4th Fl, New York, NY (212) 807-7833
Rosenthal, Barry Studio/ 1155 Broadway, New York, NY (212) 889-5840
Rosenthal, Ben/ 20 E 17th St, New York City, NY (212) 807-7737
Rosenthal, Marshal M/ 231 W 18th St, New York City, NY (212) 807-1247
Rosenthal, Steve/ 59 Maple Street, Auburndale, MA (617) 244-2986
Rose, Uli/ 119 5th Ave, New York, NY (212) 505-5234
Rosner, Eric/ 1133 Arch St., Philadelphia, PA (215) 567-2758
Ross, Ben/ 488 Clinton Street, Brooklyn, NY (212) 858-4067
Ross, Douglas Studios/ 610 8th Ave., E. Northport, NY (516) 754-2023
Ross, Leonard/ Pine Top Trail, Bethlehem, PA (215) 868-8225
Ross, Mark/ 345 E. 80th Street, New York, NY (212) 744-7258
Ross, Robert L/ 98 Riverside Drive, New York, NY (212) 799-1040
Rossum, Cheryl/ 310 E. 75th Street, New York, NY (212) 628-3173
Rost, John N./ 1268 76 St., Brooklyn, NY ( ) 680-0887
Rothaus, Ede/ 34 Morton Street, New York, NY (212) 989-8277
Roth, Joan/ 215 E 80th St, New York City, NY (212) 628-8160
Roth, Peter/ 8 W 19th, New York, NY (212) 242-4853
Rothstein, Arthur/ 122 Sutton Manor, New Rochelle, NY (914) 636-4590
Rotman, Jeff/ 14 Cottage Ave., Somerville, MA (617) 666-0874
Rousseau, Will/ 1068 Second Avenue, New York, NY (212) 755-5330
Royal Communications Inc/ 112 Main Road, Route 202, Montville, NJ (201) 335-0300
R S Photo Service Ltd/ 86 Weybosset St, Providence, RI (401) 521-9653
R T and Company/ 298a Ocean St, Hyannis, MA (617) 775-0708
Rubenstein, Raeanne/ 8 Thomas Street, New York, NY (212) 964-8426
Rubin, Al/ 250 Mercer St, New York, NY (212) 674-4535
Rubin, Daniel/ 126 West 22nd St, New York, NY (212) 989-2400
Rubin, Steffany/ 145 E. 30th St., New York, NY (212) 685-2757
Rubinstein, Eva/ 145 W. 27th Street, New York, NY (212) 243-4115
Rudnick, Michael/ 1 Bank St. #2I, New York, NY (212) 924-7883
Rudolph, Nancy/ 35 W. 11th Street, New York, NY (212) 989-0392
Rugen-Kory Photography/ 27 W. 20, New York City, NY (212) 777-3889
Ruggeri, Lawrence Photography/ 10 Post Office Rd, Silver Spring, MD (301) 588-3131
Russell, Kirk/ 31 West 21st Street, New York, NY (212) 206-1446
Russell, Rae/ 75 Byram Lake Road, Mount Kisco, NY (914) 241-0057
Russell, Ted/ 37 E. 28th Street, New York, NY (212) 532-4150
Russo, Rich Inc/ 97 Chestnut St, Newark, NJ (201) 465-7851
Rutledge, Don/ 450 Park Ave S 4th Floor, New York, NY (212) 679-3288
RYAN, TOM PHOTOGRAPHY/ 1821 Levee, Dallas, TX (214) 651-7085
See our ad on page 296
Ryan, Will/ 16 E. 17th Street, New York, NY (212) 242-6270
Rysinski, Edward/ 636 Ave. of the Americas, New York, NY (212) 807-7301
Ryuzo/ New York, NY (212) 254-5443
Sa-Adah, Jonathan/ PO Box 247, Hartford, VT (802) 295-5327
Sachs, Arthur/ 200 Park Ave S, New York City, NY (212) 777-6993
Sacks, Ron/ 12612 Nw Barnes Rd, Portland, OR (503) 641-4051
Sagala Studio, Steve/ 60 Main Street, Madison, NJ (201) 377-1418

Sagarin, Dave/ 425 Riverside Drive, New York, NY .... (212) 663-1439
Sager, Anne/ 35 E 75th, New York, NY .... (212) 535-5593
Sahula, Peter/ 45 E. 19th Street, New York, NY .... (212) 982-4340
Sakmanoff, George/ 179 Massachusetts Avenue, Boston, MA .... (617) 262-7227
Salaff, Fred/ 322 West 57 St, New York, NY .... (212) 246-3699
Salas, Ricardo/ 126 Fifth Ave, New York City, NY .... (212) 929-6995
Salgado, Robert/ River Road Rd #3, New Hope, PA .... (215) 862-2895
Salmieri, Steve/ 325 Broome Street, New York, NY .... (212) 431-7606
Salomone, Frank/ 296 Brick Blvd., Bricktown, NJ .... (201) 920-1525
Salsbery, Lee/ 14 7th Street N.E., Washington, DC .... (202) 543-1222
Saltzman, Nolan/ 440 Park Avenue S., New York, NY .... (212) 685-3179
Salvati, Jerry/ 206 E 26th St, New York, NY .... (212) 696-0454
Salzano, James/ 91 5th Avenue, New York, NY .... (212) 242-4820
Samardge, Nick/ 220 E 23rd, New York, NY .... (212) 679-2526
Samuels Studio Inc/ Box 201 8 Waltham St, Maynard, MA .... (617) 897-7901
Sand/ 641 Lexington Avenue, New York, NY .... (212) 421-6249
Sandbank, Henry/ 105 E. 16th Street, New York, NY .... (212) 674-1151
Sanders, Chris/ 133 8 Ave., New York, NY .... (212) 206-0352
Sanders Printing Corp/ 350 Hudson Street, New York, NY .... (212) 691-1070
S and J Studio/ 888 7th Avenue, New York, NY .... (212) 582-6715
Sandone, A. J./ 91 Fifth Ave., New York, NY .... (212) 807-6472
Sandrow, Hope/ 100 5th Avenue Room 800, New York, NY .... (212) 255-7536
Santoro, Carl J Photography/ 210 Fairfield Avenue,
Carle Place, NY .... (516) 746-4468
Santoro Studio, G./ 853 Seventh Avenue, New York, NY .... (212) 581-5545
Saraceno, Paul Photography/ 46 Waltham St., Boston, MA .... (617) 542-2779
Sarapochiello Studio/ 106 Fifth Avenue, New York, NY .... (212) 242-0413
Sarich, David/ 11 Cabot Road, Boston, MA .... (617) 933-8090
Sartor, Vittorio/ 32 Union Square East, New York, NY .... (212) 674-2994
Sasson, Robert/ 352 W. 15 St. #106, New York, NY .... (212) 675-0973
SATO PHOTOGRAPHY, INC./ 152 W. 26th St.,
New York, NY .... (212) 741-0688
See our ad on page 297
Satterwhite, Al/ 515 Broadway, New York, NY .... (212) 219-0808
Satterwhite, Steve/ 13 Avenue A, New York, NY .... (212) 677-0820
Sauter, Ron/ 183 St. Paul St., Rochester, NY .... (716) 232-1361
SAVAS, JAMES/ 37 W. 20th St. #1105, New York, NY .... (212) 620-0067
See our ad on pages 298, 299
Sawchuk, Michael/ 18 West 27th Street, New York, NY .... (212) 685-1725
Sawicki, Dick/ 135 Madison Ave N Penthouse, New York, NY .... (212) 679-7471
Saylor, H Durston/ 219 W 16th St, New York City, NY .... (212) 620-7122
Scarlett, Nora/ 37 West 20th St, New York, NY .... (212) 741-2620
Scavullo, Francesco/ 212 E. 63rd Street, New York, NY .... (212) 838-2450
Scharf, David/ New York, NY .... (212) 840-6928
Schaub, Bernard/ 260 Riverside Dr, New York, NY .... (212) 662-3281
Schein, Barry/ 118-60 Metropolitan Ave, Kew Gardens, NY .... (212) 849-7808
Schenk, Fred/ 112 Fourth Avenue, New York, NY .... (212) 677-1250
Scher, Dorothea/ 235 E 22nd, New York, NY .... (212) 841-2343
Scherzi,James Photography,Inc./ 116 Townline Road,
Syracuse, NY .... (315) 455-7961
SCHEWE, JEFF/ 624 W. Willow, Chicago, IL .... (312) 951-6334
See our ad on pages 300, 301
Schiavone, Carmen/ 271 Central Park W, New York City, NY .... (212) 496-6016
Schiff, Nancy Rica/ 24 W. 30th Street, New York, NY .... (212) 679-9444
Schill, Bill/ 29 Trinity Pl, Barrington, NJ .... (609) 547-0148
Schiller, Leif/ 244 5th Ave, New York, NY .... (212) 532-7272
Schilling, Richard/ 53 E. 64 St., New York, NY .... (212) 988-2910
Schlachter, Trudy/ 160 5th Ave., New York, NY .... (212) 741-3128
Schleipman, Russell F./ Zero Nearen Row, Charlestown, MA .... (617) 242-9298
Schlivek, Louis/ 229 Heights Road, Ridgewood, NJ .... (201) 444-6544
Schlowsky Studios/ 145 South St, Boston, MA .... (617) 338-4664
Schmitt, Steve/ 337 Summer St, Boston, MA .... (617) 482-5482
Schneider, Josef A./ 119 W. 57th Street, New York, NY .... (212) 265-1223
Schneider, Peter/ 902 Broadway, New York, NY .... (212) 982-9040
Schneider Studio/ 59 W 19th Street, New York, NY .... (212) 691-9588
Schneider Studio Assocs Inc/ 135 W 36th St,
New York City, NY .... (212) 695-3620
Schoen, Robert Photography/ 241 Crescent St., Waltham, MA .... (617) 647-5546
Schoon, Tim/ PO Box 7446, Lancaster, PA .... (717) 291-9483
Schreck, Bruno/ 873 Broadway, New York, NY .... (212) 420-0208
Schreyer, Mark/ One S Portland Ave, Brooklyn, NY .... (212) 596-7745
Schroers, Kenneth W., Studio/ 811 Main St., Hackensack, NJ .... (201) 646-9277
Schub and Bear/ 136 E 57th St, New York, NY .... (212) 246-0679
Schulze, Fred/ 38 W 21st St, New York, NY .... (212) 242-0930
Schulz, Herbert/ 150 Thompson St, New York City, NY .... (212) 460-5536
Schuster, Sharon/ 320 W 90th St, New York City, NY .... (212) 877-1559
Schwartzberg, Stuart/ 40 E 23rd, New York, NY .... (212) 254-2988
Schwartz, Lise/ 250 Mercer St, New York, NY .... (212) 475-1602
Schwartz, Marvin W./ 223 W. 10th Street, New York, NY .... (212) 929-8916
Schwartz, Robin/ 255 West 95th St Apt 5E, New York City, NY .... (212) 316-1854
Schwartz, Sing-Si/ 39 W. 38th Street, New York, NY .... (212) 354-6788
Schweikardt, Eric/ PO Box 56, Southport, CT .... (203) 375-8181
Schweitzer, Andrew/ 333 Park Ave. South, New York, NY .... (212) 473-2395
Schwerin, Ron/ 889 Broadway, New York, NY .... (212) 228-0340
Science Photo Library Int'L./ 118 E. 28th St., New York, NY .... (212) 683-4028
Sclight, Greg/ 146 W. 29th Street, New York, NY .... (212) 736-2957
Scocozza, Victor/ 117 E. 30th Street, New York, NY .... (212) 686-9440
Sculnick, Herb/ 7th 2nd Street, Athens, NY .... (518) 945-1598
Seabury, Thomas/ 40 Queensberry St, Boston, MA .... (617) 262-9642
Search, Howard/ P.O. Box 265, Bradford, VT .... (802) 222-4529
Seaton, Tom/ 91 Fifth Avenue, New York, NY .... (212) 989-3550
Secunda, Sheldon/ 112 Fourth Ave, New York, NY .... (212) 477-0241
Sedik, Joe Photography/ 342 Perkiomen Ave., Lansdale, PA .... (215) 368-6832
Seesehahn, Charles/ 249 W 29th St, New York, NY .... (212) 563-6612
Segal, Mark/ 115 Crescent Ln., Stelle, IL .... (815) 256-2240
Segal, Mark/ 2141 Newport Pl. N.W., Washington, DC .... (202) 223-2618
Seger, Toby/ 5808 Holden St., Pittsburgh, PA .... (412) 487-6474
Seghers II, Carroll/ 441 Park Ave S, New York, NY .... (212) 679-4582
SEGREST, JERRY PHOTOG., INC./ 1707 S. Ervay,
Dallas, TX .... (214) 426-6360
See our ad on page 302
Seibert, Elena/ 277 Water St., New York, NY .... (212) 766-1345
Seidel Associates, Inc/ 21 Solebury Mountain Road,
New Hope, PA .... (215) 862-9840
Seidman, Amy/ 17 E. 97th Street, New York, NY .... (212) 534-0085
Seidman, Barry/ 119 Fifth Ave, New York, NY .... (212) 477-6600
Seiji Kakizaki/ 359 Canal St, New York, NY .... (212) 966-2360
Seitz, Sepp/ 381 Park Avenue South, New York, NY .... (212) 683-5588
Seitz, William/ Bee Brook Rd., New Preston, CT .... (203) 868-2095
Selby, Richard/ 113 Greene Street, New York, NY .... (212) 431-1719
Seligman, Paul/ 163 W. 17th Street, New York, NY .... (212) 242-5688
Seligson, Stanley/ 468 Park Ave South Room 1402,
New York, NY .... (212) 679-9616
Selkirk, Neil, Inc.Photography/ 515 W 19 St,
New York City, NY .... (212) 243-6778
SELLERS, DAN PHOTOGRAPHY/ 2258 Vantage St.,
Dallas, TX .... (214) 631-4705
See our ad on page 303
SELTZER, ABE STUDIOS, INC./ 524 W. 23rd St.,
New York, NY .... (212) 807-0660
See our ad on page 304
Senty, George L/ 25 Tudor City Pl #219, New York, NY .... (212) 557-2787
Serbin, Vincent/ 19 Primrose Lane, Bricktown, NJ .... (201) 458-4647
Set Shop, The/ 3 W 20th, New York, NY .... (212) 929-4845
Sewell, Jim/ 720 W. 181 St. #46, New York, NY .... (212) 795-0537
Shacter, Susan/ 7 E 17th St, New York City, NY .... (212) 741-1476
Shaefer, Richard/ 71 West 23rd Street, New York, NY .... (212) 684-7252
Shafer, Robert/ 3554 Quebec Street N.W., Washington, DC .... (202) 362-0630
Shaffer, Stan/ 59 W 19th St 5B, New York, NY .... (212) 807-7700
Shaman, Harvey/ 109 81st Avenue, Kew Gardens, NY .... (212) 793-0434
Shames, Martin Photography/ 23 Amity Road, Bethany, CT .... (203) 393-0211
Shames, Stephen/ Black Star 450 Park Avenue So,
New York, NY .... (212) 777-1627
Sharron Photographics/ 260 W 36th, New York, NY .... (212) 239-4980
Shawn, John/ 718 Bay Ave, Toms River, NJ .... (201) 244-5824
Shelley, George/ 873 Broadway, New York, NY .... (212) 473-0519
Shelton, Sybil/ 416 Valley View Road, Englewood, NJ .... (201) 568-8684
Sheriff, Bob/ 963 Humphrey Street, Swampscott, MA .... (617) 599-6955
Sherman, Guy/ 277 W. 10th Street, New York, NY .... (212) 675-4983
Sheryll, Leslie/ 698 West End Avenue, New York, NY .... (212) 866-7765
Shiansky Studio, Harry/ 118 E. 28th Street, New York, NY .... (212) 889-5489
Shig Ikeda/ 636 6th Ave, New York, NY .... (212) 751-0529
Shiraishi, Carl/ 137 E. 25th Street, New York, NY .... (212) 679-5628
Shore, Stephen/ Rd. 3 Box 280, Rhinebeck, NY .... (914) 876-4450
Shostal Associates/ 164 Madison Ave., New York, NY .... (212) 686-8850
Shotwell, John/ 348 Congress St., Boston, MA .... (617) 542-5077
Shull, Hank/ 58 Mansfield Ave, Darien, CT .... (203) 655-6536
Shung, Ken/ 220 E 49th St, New York, NY .... (212) 759-5317
Sidney, Rhoda F/ 60 Franklin Street, Englewood, NJ .... (201) 568-3919
SIEGEL, DAVID M./ 224 N. 5th Ave., Phoenix, AZ .... (602) 257-9509
See our ad on page 305

PHOTOGRAPHERS/East

Siegel Hyam Photography/ PO Box 356, Brattleboro, VT .... (802) 257-0691
Siegler Photography Studios/ 38 Orange Avenue, Walden, NY........ (914) 778-7300
Silano, Bill/ 138 E. 27th Street, New York, NY .... (212) 889-0505
Silberstein, Jacques Dominique/ 220 E 23rd Street,
New York, NY.. (212) 684-1050
Silbert, Layle/ 505 La Guardia Pl, New York, NY .... (212) 677-0947
Silk, Georgiana/ 190 Godfrey Road E., Weston, CT .... (203) 226-0408
Silver, Larry/ 236 West 26th Street, New York, NY .... (212) 807-9560
Silverman, Paul/ 49 Ronald Dr., Clifton, NJ .... (212) 472-4339
Silver, Marvin/ 260 W 36th, New York, NY .... (212) 279-0900
Silver, Stan/ 113 E 31st St, New York, NY .... (212) 683-8280
SIMKO, ROBERT/ 375 S. End Ave. #30L, New York, NY .... (212) 912-1192
See our ad on page 306
Simmons, Erik Leigh/ 259 A Street, Boston, MA .... (617) 482-5325
Simon, Peter Angelo/ 504 La Guardia Place, New York, NY .... (212) 473-8340
Simon, Peter R./ RFD 136 State Road, Gayhead, MA .... (617) 645-9575
Simpson/Flint/ 2133 Maryland Avenue, Baltimore, MD .... (301) 837-9923
Simpson, Jerry/ 28 W. 27th St., New York, NY .... (212) 696-9738
Sims, Jennifer/ 1150 5th Ave, New York, NY.............................. (212) 860-3005
Sinclair, D C Photography/ 148 Middle St Suite 404,
Portland, ME.. (207) 772-6161
Singer, Barry/ 346 E. 51st Street, New York, NY .... (212) 935-0532
Singer, Stuart M/ Southside Stringtown Rd, Sparks, MD.............. (301) 771-4609
Sing-Si Schwartz Photography/ 39 West 38th Street,
New York, NY.. (212) 354-6788
Sint, Steven/ 6 Second Road, Great Neck, NY .... (516) 487-4918
Siteman, Frank/ 136 Pond Street, Winchester, MA .... (617) 729-3747
Skalski, Ken/ 866 Broadway, New York City, NY .... (212) 777-6207
Skelley, Ariel/ 249 W 29th St, New York City, NY........................ (212) 868-1179
Skogsbergh, Ulf/ 100 Fifth Ave, New York, NY .... (212) 255-7536
Skolnick-Chany Inc/ 468 Park Avenue S., New York, NY .... (212) 889-2824
Skolnik, Lewis Photography/ 135 West 29th St,
New York City, NY.. (212) 239-1455
Merrell Wood Studio/ 244 5th Ave. Ph., New York, NY .... (212) 686-4807
Slade, Chuck/ 12 E. 14th #413, New York, NY .... (212) 807-1153
Slavin, Neal/ 62 Greene Street, New York, NY .... (212) 925-8167
Sloane-White, Barbara/ 234 Fifth Avenue Room 311,
New York City, NY.. (212) 730-1188
Slotnick, Jeff/ 63 St. Marks Pl. #1b, New York, NY .... (212) 420-9643
Smilow, Stanford/ 5 Union Sq W, New York, NY .... (212) 255-0310
Smith and Warren Photographers/ PO Box 205, Pittsburgh, PA ..... (412) 687-7500
Smith, Benjamin Franklin/ 145 Nassau, New York, NY.................. (212) 349-0125
Smith, Beuford/ 141 Clinton Ave, Brooklyn, NY........................... (212) 624-7670
Smith, Camilla/ 96 Grand St, New York, NY............................... (212) 868-3330
Smith, Chris Photography/ 19 E. 22nd St., Baltimore, MD .... (301) 659-0986
Smith, George/ 366 W 23rd St, New York, NY .... (212) 989-4336
Smith, Gordon E/ 36 West 25 St, New York City, NY.................... (212) 807-7840
Smith, Hugh R./ 2515 Burr Street, Fairfield, CT .... (203) 259-6262
Smith, Jeff/ 30 E. 21st Street, New York, NY .... (212) 674-8383
Smith, J Frederick/ 400 E 52nd St, New York City, NY .... (212) 838-9797
Smith, Phillip W./ P.O. Box 400, Pennington, NJ .... (609) 737-3370
Smith, Sam/ 3409 Fish Hatchery Road, Allentown, PA .... (215) 433-6707
Smith, Stuart/ 68 Raymond Ln., Wilton, CT................................ (203) 762-3158
Smith, William E./ 498 West End Ave., New York, NY .... (212) 877-8456
Smith, W Michael/ 14 Woodlawn Avenue, South Norwalk, CT........ (203) 838-8534
Smyth, Kevin T./ 604 Main Street, Belmar, NJ............................ (201) 681-2602
Snedeker, Katherine/ 16 E. 30th Street, New York, NY................. (212) 684-0788
Snyder, Clarence/ 717 Porter Street, Easton, PA......................... (215) 252-2109
Snyder, Norman/ 514 Broadway, New York, NY .... (212) 219-0094
Sochurek, Howard/ 680 Fifth Avenue, New York, NY .... (212) 582-1860
Solomon, Paul/ 440 W. 34 St., New York City, NY........................ (212) 760-1203
Solomon, Ron/ 424 East 25, Baltimore, MD .... (301) 366-6118
Solowinski, Ray/ 154 W 57, New York, NY .... (212) 757-7940
SOORENKO, BARRY A./ 5161 River Rd. Bldg. 2-B,
Washington, DC .... (301) 652-1303
See our ad on page 307
Soot, Olaf/ 419 Park Ave. S., New York, NY................................ (212) 686-4565
Sorce, Wayne/ 20 Henry St, Brooklyn Hts, NY .... (212) 237-0497
Sorel, Ed/ 156 Franklin St, New York, NY................................... (212) 966-3949
Sorel,Elaine Career Consultant/ 640 West End Ave,
New York, NY.. (212) 873-4417
Sorensen, Chris/ P O Box 1760 Murray Hill Sta, New York, NY..... (212) 684-0551
Spagnolo, David/ 144 Reade St, New York, NY .... (212) 226-4392
Spahn, David B/ 381 Park Ave S, New York City, NY.................... (212) 689-6120
Spartana, Stephen/ 1802 E. Lombard St., Baltimore, MD .... (301) 327-1918

Spatz, Gene/ 264 Sixth Ave, New York, NY .... (212) 777-6793
Speier, Leonard/ 190 Riverside Drive, New York, NY .... (212) 595-5480
Spencer Associates/ P.O. Box 67, Lexington, MA .... (617) 861-0622
Spiegel, Ted/ Rd 3 Box 173, South Salem, NY .... (914) 763-3668
Spindel, David M/ 18 E 17th St, New York City, NY..................... (212) 989-4984
Spinelli, Frank/ 12 West 21st Street, New York, NY .... (212) 243-8318
Spiro, Don/ 52 Asbury Avenue, Atlantic Hghlnd, NJ.................... (201) 872-9196
Spiro, Edward/ 82-01 Britten Avenue, Elmhurst, NY .... (212) 424-7162
Sports Illustrated Picture Agy/ Time Life Building Room 1919,
New York, NY.. (212) 841-3663
Spratt, Jack Photographer/ P.O. Box 199, N. Kingstown, RI .... (401) 295-0606
Spreitzer, Andy/ 50 W 17th St, New York City, NY .... (212) 675-9221
Staedler, Lance/ 154 W 27th St, New York City, NY..................... (212) 243-0935
Stafford, Rick/ 26 Wadsworth, Allston, MA .... (617) 495-2389
STAFFORD, VERN/ P.O. Box 1971 222 Commerce St.,
Kingsport, TN .... (615) 246-9578
See our ad on page 311
Stage, John Lewis/ Iron Mountain Road, New Milford, NY .... (914) 986-1620
Stahl, Bill/ 87 Mulberry Ave., Garden City, NY............................ (516) 741-5709
Stahman, Robert/ 1200 Broadway, New York, NY .... (212) 679-1484
Staller, Jan/ 37 Walker Street, New York, NY .... (212) 966-7043
Standart, Joe/ 5 West 19th Street, New York, NY .... (212) 924-4545
Stanton, William/ 160 W. 95th Street Apt. 9D, New York, NY....... (212) 662-3571
Star, Scott/ 135 Spring St., New York, NY.................................. (212) 966-7138
States, Randall/ 406 Sackett St., Brooklyn, NY .... (212) 852-8674
Stearns, Philip O./ 21 W. 58th Street Apt. 6C,
New York, NY.. (212) 751-5406
Stearns, Stan/ 121 Main Street, Annapolis, MD........................... (301) 268-5777
Stechow, Kirsten/ 249 W. 29th St., New York, NY .... (212) 947-6220
Steedman, Richard/ 214 E 26 St, New York, NY........................... (212) 679-6684
Steer, John/ 37 King St, Norwalk, CT .... (203) 838-3052
Stefel, Tobi/ 166 W 22nd St, New York City, NY.......................... (212) 243-6815
Stegemeyer, Werner/ 377 Park Avenue S., New York, NY .... (212) 686-2247
Steigelman, Glenn Inc/ 873 Broadway, New York, NY .... (212) 533-6080
Steigman, Steve/ 5 E. 19th Street, New York, NY .... (212) 473-3366
Steinbrenner, Karl Eric/ 140 W. 22 St., New York, NY .... (212) 807-8936
Steiner, Charles/ 61 Second Avenue, New York, NY..................... (212) 777-0813
Steiner, Christian/ 300 Central Park West, New York, NY .... (212) 799-4522
Steiner, Karel/ 22 E 21 Street, New York, NY............................. (212) 460-8254
Steiner, Lisl/ Trinity Pass, Pound Ridge, NY.............................. (914) 764-5538
Steiner, Peter/ 183 St. Paul St., Rochester, NY .... (716) 454-1012
Steiner, Roland/ New York, NY.. (212) 684-4255
Stein, Geoffrey R./ 348 Newbury Street, Boston, MA .... (617) 267-1675
Stein, Larry/ 5 W. 30th St., New York, NY.................................. (212) 239-7264
Stein, Lisa/ 321 E 12 St #20, New York, NY................................ (212) 777-4483
Stein-Mason Studio Inc/ 348 Newbury, Boston, MA .... (617) 536-8227
Stember, John/Daylight Studio/ 154 W. 57th Street,
New York, NY.. (212) 757-0067
Sterenberg, Hilarie/ 183 Webster St. #2, E. Boston, MA............... (617) 567-5204
Stern, Anna/ 261 Broadway #3c, New York, NY........................... (212) 349-1134
Stern, Bert/ 420 E 64th St, New York, NY .... (212) 832-7589
Stern, Bob/ 12 W. 27th St., New York, NY .... (212) 889-0860
Stern, Irene/ 117 E 24 Street, New York, NY.............................. (212) 475-7464
Stern, John Studio/ 451 W Broadway, New York, NY.................... (212) 477-0656
Stern, Laszlo/ 157 W. 54th Street, New York, NY .... (212) 757-5098
STETTNER, BILL/ 118 E. 25th St., New York, NY .... (212) 460-8180
See our ad on pages 308-310
STEVENS, BOB/ 9048 Santa Monica Blvd.,
Los Angeles, CA.. (213) 271-8123
See our ad on pages 312, 313
Stevenson, Terry/ 118 W 27th, New York, NY............................. (212) 620-9066
Sticht, Martin F./ 217 Dean Street, Brooklyn, NY .... (212) 643-0857
Stierer, Dennis/ 34 Plympton St Loft 3, Boston, MA.................... (617) 357-9488
Stier, Kurt Studios/ 93 Mass Ave Suite 402, Boston, MA .... (617) 247-3822
Stiles, James/ 235 Berkeley Pl., Brooklyn, NY............................. (212) 857-3075
St. John, Lynn/ 308 East 59th Street, New York, NY.................... (212) 308-7744
Stock, Dennis/ 251 Park Avenue S., New York, NY....................... (212) 475-7600
Stock Market, The/ 1181 Broadway, New York, NY....................... (212) 684-7878
Stockmarket, the/ 1181 Broadway, New York, NY......................... (212) 684-7878
Stock Shop, The/ 271 Madison Ave., New York, NY...................... (212) 679-8480
STOECKLEIN, DAVID R./ Ketchum, ID .... (208) 726-5191
See our ad on pages 314, 315
Stogo, Don/ 310 E 46th St, New York, NY.................................. (212) 490-1034
Stokes, Stephanie/ 40 E. 68th Street, New York, NY.................... (212) 744-0655
STOLK, ROBERT PHOTOGRAPHY/ 1970 Harrison St.,
San Francisco, CA... (415) 621-4649
See our ad on page 316

Stoller, Ezra/ 222 Valley Place, Mamaroneck, NY .... (914) 698-4060
Stone, Erika/ 327 East 82 Street, New York, NY .... (212) 737-6435
Stone, Steven/ 40R Rugg Rd, Allston, MA .... (617) 782-1247
Stoppee Photographic Group/ 13 W Main St, Richmond, VA .... (804) 644-0266
Storch, Otto/ 22 Pondview Lane Box 712, East Hampton, NY .... (516) 324-5031
Stratos, Jim/ 176 Madison Ave, New York City, NY .... (212) 696-1133
Strauss, Steve/ 43 W 39th, New York, NY .... (212) 354-7828
Streiff, Eric/ 236 West 27 Street, New York City, NY .... (212) 691-4186
Strobe Studio, The/ 1155 Broadway, New York, NY .... (212) 532-1977
Strobe Studio, The/ 91 5th Avenue, New York, NY .... (212) 675-2345
Strode Eckert Photographic/ 1407 S.E. Belmont St.,
    Portland, OR .... (503) 234-2344
Strohmeyer, Pamela Thomas/ 18 Hillandale Road, Ryebrook, NY.... (914) 939-5920
Stromberg, Bruce/ 1818 Spruce St., Philadelphia, PA .... (215) 545-0842
Strongin, James W./ 11 Henhawk Lane, Huntington, NY .... (516) 271-0860
Strongin, Jeanne/ 61 Irving Pl, New York City, NY .... (212) 473-3718
Strongwater, Peter/ 88 Lexington Ave, New York, NY .... (212) 475-4537
Stuart, John/ 80 Varick St. #4b, New York, NY .... (212) 966-6783
Stuart, Stephen Photography/ 9 Legion Drive, Valhalla, NY .... (914) 682-1418
Studio Associates/ 30-6 Plymouth St., Fairfield, NJ .... (201) 575-2640
Studio, Inc., The/ 818 Liberty Ave., Pittsburgh, PA .... (412) 261-2022
Studio 1209-Kurt Frank/ 1209 St. Paul St. #100,
    Baltimore, MD .... (301) 244-0092
Studio L'Image/ 19 W 34 Street Suite 603, New York, NY .... (212) 771-7464
Studio 8 Photographers/ 246-17 Jamaica Ave, Bellrose, NY .... (212) 347-8887
Stupakoff, Otto/ 80 Varick Street, New York, NY .... (212) 334-8032
Styrkowicz, Tom/ 305 W. 55th Street, New York, NY .... (212) 582-2978
Success-O-Matic/ 1030 Avenue of the Americas, New York, NY..... (212) 221-0887
Sun, Edward/ 19 East 21 Street, New York, NY .... (212) 505-9585
Susoeff, William/ 1063 Elizabeth Drive, Bridgeville, PA .... (412) 941-5241
Sussman, David/ 115 E. 23rd Street, New York, NY .... (212) 254-9380
Sussman, Jodi/ 108 Penarth Road, Bala Cynwyd, PA .... (215) 667-3979
Sutphen, Chazz Photographer/ 22 Crescent Beach Dr.,
    Burlington, VT .... (802) 862-5912
Sutton, Humphrey/ 18 E. 18th Street, New York, NY .... (212) 989-9128
Svensson, Steen/ 52 Grove St, New York, NY .... (212) 242-7272
Swann/Niemann/ 1618 A 14 St. N.W., Washington, DC .... (202) 328-1800
Swedowsky, Ben/ 381 Park Ave S, New York, NY .... (212) 684-1454
Sweet, Ozzie/ PO Box 223, Francestown, NH .... (603) 547-6611
Swoger, Arthur/ 18 Medway St. #3, Providence, RI .... (401) 331-0440
Szabo, Art/ 156 Depot Rd. #A, Huntington Sta., NY .... (516) 549-1699
Szasz, Suzanne/ 15 W. 46th Street, New York, NY .... (212) 832-9387
Tadder, Morton/ 1010 Morton St, Baltimore, MD .... (301) 837-7427
Taka/ 636 6th Ave 5A, New York, NY .... (212) 807-7711
Tamin Production Inc/ 144 W 27th St 2nd Fl, New York, NY....... (212) 807-6691
Tanaka, Victor/ 156 Fifth Avenue, New York, NY .... (212) 675-3445
Tannenbaum, Ken Inc./ 16 West 21 Street, New York, NY .... (212) 675-2345
Tanous, Dorothy/ 12 W 27th St, New York City, NY .... (212) 947-5031
Taranto, Frank/ 22 B University Cir, Linden, NJ .... (201) 925-3115
Tara Universal Studios/ 34 E 23rd St, New York City, NY .... (212) 260-8280
Tardi, Joseph/ 100 7th Avenue, Troy, NY .... (518) 235-1984
Tassi, Dhimitra/ 160 E 48th St, New York, NY .... (212) 753-5149
Taylor, Jonathan/ 5 W. 20th Street, New York, NY .... (212) 741-2805
Tcherevkoff Studio, Michel/ 873 Broadway, New York, NY .... (212) 228-0540
Teatum, Marc/ 12 Hancock St. 1 Flr., Salem, MA .... (617) 745-4533
Tedeschi, Joan/ 137 E. 38 St., New York, NY .... (212) 725-1478
Teicholz, Leslie/ 450 W 20th St, New York, NY .... (212) 243-5088
Telion, Serch/ 134 W. 32 St. #602, New York, NY .... (212) 279-3870
Tenin, Barry/ PO Box 2660 111 Hills Point Rd, Westport, CT .... (203) 226-9396
Tepper, Peter/ 195 Tunxis Hill Road, Fairfield, CT .... (203) 367-6172
Tercasio/ 35 Union Square W, New York, NY .... (212) 929-0058
Terk, Harold/ 170 Quarry Rd, Stamford, CT .... (212) 838-1922
Terry, Karen/ 131 Boxwood Dr., Kings Park, NY .... (516) 724-3964
Tesa, Rudolph/ 119 W. 23 St. #505, New York, NY .... (212) 620-4514
Tesi, Mike Photography/ 12 Kulick Road, Fairfield, NJ .... (201) 575-7780
Tessler, Stefan/ 115 W. 23 St., New York, NY .... (212) 924-9768
Thomas, Ed/ 138 S. Highland St., W. Hartford, CT .... (203) 232-9054
Thomas, Wes/ 173 Wooster St, New Haven, CT .... (203) 624-1996
Thompson, Eleanor/ 147 West 25th St, New York, NY .... (212) 925-0902
Thornton Studio, Inc/ 18 West 27th St, New York, NY .... (212) 685-1725
Thuy Vuong & Associates/ 51 East 42nd Street, New York, NY..... (212) 697-1806
Tillman, Denny/ 39 E. 20th Street, New York, NY .... (212) 674-7160
Tito Barberis/ 333 Park Ave S, New York, NY .... (212) 473-1693
Togashi/ 100 Fifth Avenue, New York, NY .... (212) 929-2290
Tolbert, Brian R/ 911 State Street, Lancaster, PA .... (717) 393-0918

Tomalin, Norman Owen/ 381 Fifth Avenue, New York, NY........... (212) 683-5227
Tomo Studio/ 112 Fourth Avenue, New York, NY .... (212) 982-2392
Topple, Edward C/ 11 Wall Street, New York, NY .... (212) 623-6192
Topp Studio/ 21 East 26 Street, New York, NY .... (212) 532-4412
Torkil Gudnason/ 58 W 15th, New York, NY .... (212) 929-6680
Tornallyay, Martin Assoc Inc/ 63 Taff Avenue, Stamford, CT .... (203) 357-1777
Tornberg, Ralph/ 6 E. 39th Street, New York, NY .... (212) 685-7333
Toshi Studio/ 135 Fifth Avenue, New York, NY .... (212) 260-2556
Tosh Matsumoto/ 5 W 19 St, New York, NY .... (212) 989-5663
Total Picture/Peter Schneider/ 902 Broadway, New York, NY....... (212) 982-9040
TOTO, JOE/ 148 W. 24th St., New York, NY .... (212) 620-0755
    See our ad on pages 317-319
Townsend, Wendy/ 301 E. 78th Street, New York, NY .... (212) 744-5753
Tress, Arthur/ 2 Riverside Dr, New York, NY .... (212) 877-1305
Triggs Color Printing Corp/ 216 W 18th St, New York, NY .... (212) 243-9004
Troia, Bob/ 112 N. 12th Street, Philadelphia, PA .... (215) 925-4322
Trost, Del/ 117 Tanglewood Est, Keene, NH .... (603) 352-3661
Trueworthy, Nance/ P.O. Box 8353, Portland, ME .... (207) 774-6181
Truman, Gary T./ P.O. Box 7144, Charleston, WV .... (304) 755-3078
Trumbo, Keith/ 275 West 96 #18A, New York, NY .... (212) 662-9355
Truran, Bill/ 31 W 21st St, New York, NY .... (212) 741-2285
Trzoniec, Stanley/ 16 Sanders Dr, Shrewsbury, MA .... (617) 842-6721
Tsufura, Satoru/ 48 Bentley Road, Cedar Grove, NJ .... (201) 239-4641
Tuckerman, John/ PO Box 301, Springhouse, PA .... (215) 643-6663
Tucker, William L. Uniphoto/ P.O. Box 3678, Washington, DC....... (202) 333-0500
Tuke, Joni & Associates, Inc./ 368 W. Huron Street,
    Chicago, IL .... (312) 787-6826
Tully, Roger/ 344 W 38th Street #100, New York, NY .... (212) 947-3961
Turbeville, Deborah/ 160 Fifth Ave, New York, NY .... (212) 924-6760
TURNER, PETE/ 154 W. 57th St., New York, NY .... (212) 765-1733
    See our ad on pages 320, 321
Turner, Sam/ 321 E. 21 St., New York, NY .... (212) 777-8715
Turpan, Dennis P./ 25 Amsterdam Avenue, Teaneck, NJ .... (201) 837-4242
Tur, Stefan/ 30 E. 20th Street, New York, NY .... (212) 475-1699
Tweel, Ron Photography/ 241 W. 36th St., New York, NY .... (212) 563-3452
Tyrell, Mellon/ 69 Perry Street, New York, NY .... (212) 242-3472
Ultra Photo Works/ 468 Commercial Ave, Palisades Park, NJ....... (201) 592-7730
Umans, Marty Photography/ 110 West 25th Street,
    New York, NY.. (212) 242-4463
UNANGST, ANDREW/ 381 Park Ave. S., New York, NY .... (212) 889-4888
    See our ad on page 322
Uncle Sam's Umbrella/ 161 W 57th St, New York City, NY .... (212) 582-1976
Underhill, Les/ 10 W 18th, New York, NY .... (212) 691-9920
Uniphoto/ 1071 Wisc. N.W. P.O. Box 3678, Washington, DC .... (202) 333-0500
Unitas, Joseph C/ 314 E McMurray Rd, McMurray, PA .... (412) 941-9009
Urban, John/ 1424 Canton Avenue, Milton, MA .... (617) 333-0343
Urbina, Walt/ 7208 Thomas Blvd, Pittsburgh, PA .... (412) 242-5070
Ursillo, Catherine/ 1040 Park Ave, New York, NY .... (212) 722-9297
Uzzle, Burk/ 831 Beechwood Dr., Havertown, PA .... (215) 896-6168
Vaeth, Peter/ 295 Madison Avenue, New York, NY .... (212) 685-4700
Valentin, Augusto/ 202 E. 29th Street 6th Floor,
    New York, NY.. (212) 532-7480
Valerio, Gary/ 278 Jay St., Rochester, NY .... (716) 352-0163
Vallini Productions/ 43 E. 20th Street 2nd Floor,
    New York, NY.. (212) 674-6581
Van Camp, Louis/ 535 Broadhollow, Melville, NY .... (516) 752-1511
Van Nes, Hans/ 431 E. 90th Street, New York, NY .... (212) 876-4900
Van Petten, Rob/ Boston, MA .... (617) 426-8641
Van Schalkwyk, John/ 50 Melcher Street, Boston, MA .... (617) 542-4825
Varnedoe, S/ 12 W 27th St, New York City, NY .... (212) 679-1230
Varon, Malcolm/ 125 Fifth Avenue, New York, NY .... (212) 473-5957
Vartoogian, Jack/ 262 W 107th St Apt 6A, New York, NY .... (212) 663-1341
Vassiliev, Nina/ 145 E. 17th Street, New York, NY .... (212) 473-0190
Vatz, Betty/ 411 West End Avenue, New York, NY .... (212) 724-5089
Vaughan, Ted/ 423 Doe Run Road, Manheim, PA .... (717) 665-6942
Vendetti, Charles/ 85 Airport Rd, Hartford, CT .... (203) 246-7491
Vendikos, Tasso/ 20 E. 20th Street, New York, NY .... (212) 286-9775
Verdi, Richard/ 36 E 23rd St, New York, NY .... (212) 228-1424
Vericker, Joseph P./ Box 390 Throggs Neck, Bronx, NY .... (212) 863-9801
Vest Michael Photography/ 40 West 27th Street, New York, NY.... (212) 532-8331
Vhandy Productions Inc/ 225 A E 59th, New York, NY .... (212) 759-6150
Vicari, Jim/ 8 E. 12th Street, New York, NY .... (212) 675-3745
Vickers, Camille/ 200 West 79 St PHA, New York, NY .... (212) 580-8649
ViCom PhotoGraphics/ 12 N Washington Street, Rockville, MD..... (301) 424-1230
Vidal, Bernard/ 853 Seventh Avenue, New York, NY .... (212) 582-3284

Vidol, John/ 37 W. 26th Street, New York, NY .... (212) 889-0065
Vidor, Peter L Photography/ 70 Chestnut Street,
    Morristown, NJ .... (201) 267-1104
Viertel, Janet/ 180 S. Broadway, White Plains, NY .... (914) 948-1300
Villota, Luis/ 300 E. 51st Street, New York, NY .... (212) 758-5791
Vine, David/ 873 Broadway, New York, NY .... (212) 505-8070
Vishniac, Roman/ 219 W. 81st Street, New York, NY .... (212) 787-0997
Vista Images/ 32 Bella Vista, Locust Valley, NY .... (516) 674-3480
Vlamis, Suzanne/ 405 East 82 Street, New York, NY .... (212) 879-4587
Vogel, Allen/ 126 Fifth Avenue, New York, NY .... (212) 675-7550
Vogel, Rich Studio/ 119 West 23rd Street, New York City, NY ...... (212) 741-5330
Vogue Wright Studios Inc/ 423 W 55th Street, New York, NY .... (212) 977-3400
Volkmann, Roy/ 6 W 32nd St, New York City, NY .... (212) 594-8204
Von Hassell, Agostino/ 277 W. 10th Street Penthouse D,
    New York, NY .... (212) 242-7290
Von Hoffmann, Bernard/ 2 Green Village Road, Madison, NJ .... (201) 377-0317
Voscar the Maine Photogrphr/ PO Box 661, Presque Isle, ME ...... (207) 769-5911
Vos, Gene/ 440 Park Avenue S., New York, NY .... (212) 685-8384
VULLO, PHILLIP/ 565 Dutch Valley Rd., Atlanta, GA .... (404) 874-0822
    See our ad on page 323
Wachter, Jerry/ 1410 Bare Hills Ave, Baltimore, MD .... (301) 337-2977
Wackerbarth, Horst/ New York, NY .... (213) 383-0498
Waggaman, John/ 2746 N. 46, Philadelphia, PA .... (215) 473-2827
Wagner, Daniel/ 2 W. 32 St., New York, NY .... (212) 563-1789
Wagner, David A/ 156 Fifth Avenue, New York, NY .... (212) 741-1171
Wagoner, Robert/ 150 Fifth Ave. #220, New York, NY .... (212) 807-6050
WAHLSTROM, RICHARD PHOT., INC./ 650 Alhabama St.,
    San Francisco, CA .... (415) 550-1400
    See our ad on pages 324, 325
Waine, Michael/ 873 Broadway, New York, NY .... (212) 533-4201
Walch, Robert/ 310 West Main St, Kutztown, PA .... (215) 683-5701
Walden, Bob/ 21-45 28th St, Astoria, NY .... (212) 204-1938
Waldinger, Conrad Photography/ 3158 Webster Ave, Bronx, NY .... (212) 547-0555
Waldo, Maje/ 873 Broadway, New York, NY .... (212) 475-7886
Walker, John/ 153 W. 27th St., New York, NY .... (212) 929-0269
Wallis, Jake/ New York, NY .... (212) 684-4255
Walsh, Bob Medical Adv Photo/ 231 East 29 St, New York, NY ..... (212) 684-3015
Walsh Photocommunications/ 6564 Ridings Rd, Syracuse, NY .... (315) 463-6807
Waltzer, Bill Photography/ 110 Greene Street, New York, NY .... (212) 925-1242
Waltzer, Carl/ 873 Broadway Room 412, New York, NY .... (212) 475-8748
Walz, Barbra/ 143 W 20th, New York, NY .... (212) 242-7175
Wanamaker/ Box 2800, Darien, CT .... (203) 655-8383
Wang Studio Inc., John/ 30 E. 20th Street, New York, NY .... (212) 982-2765
Ward, Anthony/ 361 Cadwalader Ave, Elkins Park, PA .... (215) 572-6164
Warren, M E Gallery/ 48 Maryland Avenue, Annapolis, MD .... (301) 974-0444
Warsaw Photographic Assoc. Inc/ 36 East 31 Street,
    New York, NY .... (212) 725-1888
Warwick, Ben/ 100 Fifth Ave, New York, NY .... (212) 243-1806
Wasinski, Alex/ 119 W. 23 St., New York, NY .... (212) 989-0455
Watanabe, Nana/ 31 Union Sq W, New York City, NY .... (212) 741-3248
WATSON, ALAN/ 635 State St., San Diego, CA .... (619) 239-5555
    See our ad on page 326
Watson, Albert M./ 237 E. 77th Street, New York, NY .... (212) 628-7886
Watson, Ross H./ 859 Lancaster Ave., Bryn Mawr, PA .... (215) 527-1519
Watson, Tom/ 2172 W. Lake Road, Skaneateles, NY .... (315) 685-6033
Watts, Cliff/ 103 5th Avenue, New York, NY .... (212) 989-8235
Weber, Alan K./ 156 Fifth Ave. #701, New York, NY .... (212) 255-4317
Weber, Bruce/ 135 Watts Street, New York, NY .... (212) 226-0814
Weckler, Chad/ 256 Fifth Ave. 4th Fl., New York, NY .... (212) 868-3370
Weidling, Mark/ 1501 Ammer Rd., Glenview, IL .... (312) 998-5839
Weidman, H. Mark/ 2112 Goodwin Ln., North Wales, PA .... (215) 646-1745
Weigand, Tom/ 717 N. 5th St., Reading, PA .... (215) 374-5751
Weihs, Tom/ 121 E. 24th St., New York, NY .... (212) 673-7767
Weinberg, Abe/ 1230 Summer Street, Philadelphia, PA .... (215) 567-5454
Weinberg, Michael S. Studio/ 5 East 16th Street,
    New York, NY .... (212) 691-0713
Weiner, Randy/ 217 E. 84 St. #2c, New York, NY .... (212) 288-3518
Weinik, Susan Aimee/ 405 E. 63rd Street, New York, NY .... (213) 838-0111
Weinstein, Todd/ 47 Irving Pl, New York, NY .... (212) 254-7526
Weir, Jay/ 29 Washington Ave., Danbury, CT .... (203) 743-6449
Weisenfeld, Stanley/ 135 Davis Street, Painted Post, NY .... (607) 962-7314
Weiss, Michael Studio Inc/ 10 W 18th, New York, NY .... (212) 929-4073
Weitz, Allan/ 373 Park Ave. S., New York, NY .... (212) 725-8041
Weidlein, Peter King/ 122 West 26th Street 12th Fl,
    New York, NY .... (212) 989-5498

Weldon, Mort/ 473 Winding Rd N, Ardsley, NY .... (914) 693-4005
Weller, Bruce/ 6508 Crestwood Rd., Baltimore, MD .... (301) 327-4587
Wellington/ 175 Fifth Ave, Suite 3337, New York, NY .... (212) 271-7462
Welsch, Ulrike/ 42 Elm, Marblehead, MA .... (617) 631-1641
Wendler, Hans/ RFD 1 PO Box 191, Epsom, NH .... (603) 736-9383
Werner, Perry Alan/ 21 Sheridan Avenue, Mt Vernon, NY .... (914) 699-3637
West, Bonnie/ 156 Fifth Ave., New York, NY .... (212) 929-3338
West, Charles H./ 304 Henry Street Apt. 4A, Brooklyn, NY .... (212) 624-5920
West, Jerry/ 140 W. 57th Street, New York, NY .... (212) 245-2416
Wexler, Ira/Photography/ 4893 Macarthur Blvd. N.W.,
    Washington, DC .... (202) 337-4886
Weydig, Kathy/ 276 Myrtle Ave., Bridgeport, CT .... (203) 367-8948
Wheeler, Gary/ 44 W. 36th Street, New York, NY .... (212) 239-8187
Wheeler, Nick/ Turner & Pierce, Townsend, MA .... (617) 597-2919
Whitaker, Ross/ 156 Fifth Ave, New York, NY .... (212) 691-0892
White, Anne B./ 170 E 88 St Apt 8H, New York, NY .... (212) 860-1776
White Bill Studio/ 31 W 31 St, New York, NY .... (212) 947-9575
White, Frank/ 18 Milton Pl, Rowayton, CT .... (203) 866-9500
Whitehead, Buz/ 328 East 9th Street, New York, NY .... (212) 674-1473
Whitehurst, Wm./ 32 W. 20 St., New York, NY .... (212) 206-8825
White, Joel/ 61 Jane St, New York City, NY .... (212) 691-6401
White, John/ New York, NY .... (212) 691-1133
White Light Inc/ 186 Greenwood Ave, Bethel, CT .... (203) 743-3834
Whitely, Howard/ 60 E. 42nd Street, New York, NY .... (212) 490-3111
White, Saul/ 270 Hammelton Road, Chappaqua, NY .... (914) 238-6188
White, Sharon/ 144 Moody Street, Waltham, MA .... (617) 891-6011
White-Spite/ 115 W 29th, New York, NY .... (212) 564-0875
Whitley, Dianna/ 235 E. 22nd Street, New York, NY .... (212) 532-4616
Whittington, Robert/ 347 W 39th St, New York City, NY .... (212) 947-5689
Wickham, Reginald/ 220 Voorhees St, Teaneck, NJ .... (201) 833-1748
Wick, Walter/ 119 W 23rd Str, New York, NY .... (212) 243-3448
WIEN, JEFFREY/ 160 Fifth Ave., New York, NY .... (212) 243-7028
    See our ad on page 327
Wier, John Arthur/ 38 E. 19th St. 8th Fl., New York, NY .... (212) 477-5107
Wier, Terry/ 38 East 19, New York, NY .... (212) 477-5107
Wilcox, Elizabeth/ 260 Rock House Road, Easton, CT .... (203) 268-8361
Wilcox, Shorty/Dpi/ 521 Madison Ave., New York, NY .... (212) 246-6367
Wilding, Jack/ 12 W 27th St, New York City, NY .... (212) 696-9609
WILKES, STEPHEN/ 48 E. 13th St., New York, NY .... (212) 475-4010
    See our ad on pages 328-331
Willasch, Robert/ 3b Torlina Ct., Baltimore, MD .... (301) 298-5074
Williams, Larry/ 43 W. 29th Street, New York, NY .... (212) 684-1317
Williams, Lawrence/ 9101 W. Chester Pike, Upper Darby, PA ...... (215) 789-3030
Williamson, Richie/ 514 W 24th, New York, NY .... (212) 362-9546
Williams, Ron/ 1703 Walnut Street, Philadelphia, PA .... (215) 563-0880
Williams, W G/ 1100 17th St. NW, Suite 1000, Washington, DC .... (202) 296-4414
Williams, Woodbridge/ PO Box 11, Dickerson, MD .... (301) 972-7025
Wilson, Michael Photography/ 441 Park Ave South,
    New York, NY .... (212) 683-3557
Wilson, Paul S/ 1225 Spring Street, Philadelphia, PA .... (215) 564-2772
Wilson, Robert L./ PO Box 1742, Clarksburg, WV .... (304) 623-5368
Wilt, Byron/ Rd 21 Box 117, Dover, PA .... (717) 843-2215
Wing, Peter/ 56-08 138th St, Flushing, NY .... (718) 762-3617
Wing Studio/ 30 W. 26th Street, New York, NY .... (212) 620-0944
Wironen, Inc./ 249 Timpany Blvd., Gardner, MA .... (617) 632-1714
Wirtz, Harry Words & Pictures/ Rd. 4 Box 301 Wood St.,
    Mahopac, NY .... (914) 526-2769
Witlin, Ray/ 245 W. 107th Street, New York, NY .... (212) 866-7625
Witte, Michael C/ Voorhis Point, S Nyack, NY .... (914) 358-9095
Wohlfahrt Studios Inc/ 15 W 36th, New York, NY .... (212) 947-7150
WOJCIK, JAMES/ 95 Vandam St., New York, NY .... (212) 807-0593
    See our ad on page 332
Wolf, Bernard/ 214 E 87th, New York, NY .... (212) 427-0220
Wolf, Bruce/ 123 W. 28th St., New York, NY .... (212) 695-8042
Wolfe, Simon/ 1040 Second Avenue, New York, NY .... (212) 758-7365
Wolf, Henry/ 167 E. 73rd Street, New York, NY .... (212) 472-2500
Wolfson, Robert Photographers/ 156 Fifth Avenue Suite 327,
    New York, NY .... (212) 924-1510
Wolosker, Steven/ 762 Madison Ave, New York City, NY .... (212) 288-8989
Wong, Leslie/ 303 W. 78th St., New York, NY .... (212) 595-0434
Wood, Richard/ 25 Thorndike St, Cambridge, MA .... (617) 661-6856
Wood, Susan/ 641 Fifth Avenue, New York, NY .... (212) 371-0679
Wormser, Richard L./ 800 Riverside Drive, New York, NY .... (212) 928-0056
Wrenn, Bill/ 403 Riversville Rd., Greenwich, CT .... (203) 869-5628
Wright, Jeri/ PO Box 7, Wilmington, NY .... (518) 946-2658

STOCK PHOTO HOUSES/East

Wright, Mac Studio/ RD4 Box 248 E Main St, Chester, NJ .... (201) 879-4545
Wu, Ron Studios Inc/ 179 St Paul St, Rochester, NY .... (716) 454-5600
Wurster, George/ 22 Hallo Street, Edison, NJ .... (201) 225-0409
Wyatt, Chad Evans/ 2325 42nd Street NW, Washington, DC .... (202) 337-2641
Wyman, Ira/ 14 Crane Avenue, West Peabody, MA .... (617) 535-2880
Yablon, Ron/ P.O. Box 128, Exton, PA .... (215) 363-2596
Yaeger, H/ 8 Gramercy Park S, New York City, NY .... (212) 777-6225
Yamashiro, Tad/ 224 E. 12th Street, New York, NY .... (212) 473-7177
Yee, Tom/ 30 W 26th St, New York City, NY .... (212) 242-0301
Young, Bob Photography, Inc./ 1445 Main St., Rahway, NJ .... (201) 381-6190
Young, Ellan/ 86 Prospect Drive, Chappaqua, NY .... (914) 238-4837
Young, James/ 110 W. 25th Street, New York, NY .... (212) 924-5444
Young, Rick Photography/ 27 West 20th Street, New York, NY ..... (212) 929-5701
Zack, Memo/ 39 W. 67th Street, New York, NY .... (212) 787-1658
Zack, Patrick/ 1099 First Avenue Apt. 5RN, New York, NY .... (212) 758-7030
Zager, Howard/ 450 W. 31st Street, New York, NY .... (212) 239-8082
Zajack, Greg/ 57 W. 19th St., New York, NY .... (212) 206-0394
Zakarian Inc., Aram/ 25 E. 20th Street, New York, NY .... (212) 674-3680
Zander Photography Inc/ 30 W. 26th Street, New York, NY .... (212) 620-0944
Zanetti, Gerald Assoc Inc/ 139 Fifth Avenue, New York, NY .... (212) 473-4999
Zappa Studios/ 28 E 29th, New York, NY .... (212) 532-3476
Zapp, Carl/ 873 Broadway, New York, NY .... (212) 505-0510
Zarember, Sam/ 26 Old S Salem Rd, Ridgefield, CT .... (203) 438-4472
Zenrich, Alan/ 78 Fifth Ave., New York, NY .... (212) 807-1551
Zeschin, Elizabeth/ 70 West 68 Street, New York, NY .... (212) 496-9219
Ziff Davis Publ. Co./ One Park Ave., New York, NY .... (212) 503-3500
Zimmerman, John/ 200 E. 62nd Street, New York, NY .... (212) 935-5027
Zingler Joseph/ 18 Desbrosses Street, New York, NY .... (212) 226-3867
Zlotnik, Charlyn/ 17 6th Avenue, New York, NY .... (212) 226-4149
Zmiejko, Tom/ PO Box 126, Freeland, PA .... (717) 636-2304
Zoiner, John/ 12 W. 44th Street, New York, NY .... (212) 972-0357
Zubkoff, Earl/ 2426 Linden Ln, Silver Spring, MD .... (301) 585-7393
Zuk, Tom/ 36 E 23rd, New York, NY .... (212) 475-0309
Zuretti Jr., Charles/ 156 Fifth Avenue Room 1301,
    New York, NY.. (212) 924-9412
Zweifel, Michael/ P.O. Box 213, Coopersbury, PA .... (212) 477-5629

STOCK PHOTO HOUSES

AFTER IMAGE, INC./ 3807 Wilshire Suite 250, Los Angeles, CA..... (213) 467-6033
American Library Color Slide C/ New York City, NY................... (212) 255-5356
Arnold, Peter/ 1466 Broadway, New York, NY .... (212) 840-6928
Art Resources Inc/ 65 Bleecker Street, New York, NY .... (212) 505-8700
Authenticated News Int/ 29 Katonah Ave, Katonah, NY .... (914) 232-7726
Barksdale, William E Agri Phot/ PO Box 17726, Memphis, TN....... (901) 767-9540
Berenholtz Stock Photos/ 600 W. 111th St., New York, NY .... (212) 749-0644
Bettman Archive/ 136 E 57th St, New York City, NY .... (212) 758-0362
Camerique Stock Photography/ P.O. Box 175, Blue Bell, PA .... (215) 272-7649
Camerique Stock Photography/ 45 Newbury St, Boston, MA .... (617) 267-6450
Chandoha, Walter/ RFD 1 PO Box 287, Annandale, NJ .... (201) 782-3666
Cohen, Ken/ 200 E. 17th Street, New York, NY .... (212) 674-1831
Coleman, Bruce Inc/ 381 Fifth Avenue, New York, NY .... (212) 683-5227
Colour Library Intl, Ltd/ 99 Park Ave, New York, NY .... (212) 557-2929
Culver Pictures Inc/ 660 First Ave, New York City, NY .... (212) 684-5054
Degginger, Edward R./ PO Box 186, Convent Station, NJ .... (201) 267-4165
Design Conceptions/ 112 Fourth Avenue, New York, NY .... (212) 254-1688
Design Photographers Intl/ 521 Madison Avenue, New York, NY .. (212) 752-3930
Devaney Stock Photos/ 122 E. 42nd St., New York, NY .... (212) 767-6900
De Wys, Leo/ 200 Madison Avenue, New York, NY .... (212) 689-5580
Eastern Photo Service/ 12 E 36th St, New York City, NY .... (212) 689-5580
Editorial Photocolor Archives/ 65 Bleecker Street, 9th Floor,
    New York, NY.. (212) 505-8700
Esto Photographics Inc/ 222 Valley Pl, Mamaroneck, NY .... (914) 698-4060
Finley Photographics Inc/ 405 Lexington Ave, New York, NY .... (212) 697-9161
Focus On Sports Inc./ 222 E. 46th Street, New York, NY .... (212) 661-6860
Food Stock/ 320 E. 39th St., New York, NY .... (212) 679-8157
Forbert David J Shostal Asso/ 164 Madison Ave, New York, NY ... (212) 686-8850
Four By Five/ 485 Madison Ave, New York, NY .... (212) 355-2323
Galloway, Ewing/ 1466 Broadway, New York, NY .... (212) 719-4720
Gamma-Liaison Photo Agency/ 150 East 58th Street,
    New York, NY.. (212) 888-7272
Gates, Ralph Worldwide Photos/ 364 Hartshorn Drive P O Box233,
    Short Hills, NJ... (201) 379-4456
Gatewood, Charles/ Box 745, Woodstock, NY .... (914) 246-5723
Globe Photos, Inc./ 275 Seventh Ave., New York, NY .... (212) 689-1340

Goltzer, Seth/ P.O. Box 5092, Westport, CT .... (203) 222-0462
Gordon, Joel/ 112 Fourth Ave., New York, NY .... (212) 254-1688
Granger Collection, The/ 1841 Broadway, New York City, NY........ (212) 586-0971
Grinberg,Sherman Film Librarie/ 630 Ninth Ave,
    New York City, NY.. (212) 765-5170
Hackett, Gabriel D/ 130 W. 57th Street, New York, NY .... (212) 265-6842
Hahn Graphic/ 1035 Dewey Ave, Rochester, NY .... (716) 254-5705
Heilman, Grant/ Box 317, Lititz, PA .... (717) 626-0296
Heimann-Hubbard Std./ Stock Photo Hse. 61 Lispenard,
    New York, NY.. (212) 925-4514
Heller, Gary/ 251 Park Ave S, New York, NY .... (212) 777-4210
Hirsch Photo/ 699 Third Ave, New York, NY .... (212) 557-1150
Images Press Services Inc/ 7 East 17th Street, New York, NY .... (212) 675-3707
Index/Stone/ 126 Fifth Ave. 8 Fl., New York, NY .... (212) 929-4644
Index/Stone Int'L., Inc./ 126 Fifth Ave., New York, NY .... (212) 929-4644
International Stock Photo/ 113 East 31st Street,
    New York, NY.. (212) 696-4666
Kaplan, Peter J. Photography/ 924 West End Avenue,
    New York, NY.. (212) 222-1193
Keystone Press Agency Inc/ 202 E 42 St, New York, NY .... (212) 924-8123
Kinne, Jane S./ 60 E. 56th Street, New York, NY .... (212) 758-3420
Kramer Joan and Associates Inc/ 720 Fifth Avenue,
    New York, NY.. (212) 224-1758
Kreis, Ursula G/ 63 Adrian Avenue, Bronx, NY .... (212) 562-8931
Laird, Richard Photography/ 414 W 22nd St,
    New York City, NY.. (212) 675-2138
Lambert Studios, Harold M Inc/ PO Box 27310,
    Philadelphia, PA.. (215) 224-1400
Landslides & Aerial Photograph/ 77 Conant Road, Lincoln, MA...... (617) 259-8310
Lewis, Frederic Inc/ 15 West 38th Street, New York, NY .... (212) 921-2850
Life Picture Service/ Time & Life Bldg, New York City, NY .... (212) 841-4800
MacLaren, Mark/ 430 E. 20th Street, New York, NY.................. (212) 674-8615
Maisel, Jay/ 190 Bowery, New York, NY .... (212) 431-5013
McConnell McNamara & Co/ 182 Broad St, Wethersfield, CT .... (203) 563-6154
Medichrome/ 271 Madison Avenue, New York, NY .... (212) 679-8480
Memory Shop Inc/ 109 E 12th St, New York City, NY .... (212) 473-2404
Mogeriey, Jean/ 220 E. 65 St. #8d, New York, NY .... (212) 758-4068
Monkmeyer Press Photo Agcy/ 118 E 28th, New York, NY .... (212) 689-2242
Movie Star News/ 134 West 18th Street, New York, NY .... (212) 620-8160
M Y Creative Svc Ltd/ 22 Irving Pl, New York City, NY .... (212) 674-4182
Niccolini, Dianoara/ 356 E 78th, New York, NY .... (212) 288-1698
Philiba, Allan A/ 3408 Bertha Dr, Baldwin, NY .... (212) 286-0948
Photo Associates News Service/ PO Box 306, Station A,
    Flushing, NY... (212) 961-0909
Photofile International/ 32 East 31 St, New York, NY .... (212) 989-0500
Photonet/ 250 West 57 Street, New York, NY .... (212) 254-4070
Photoquest Int'l Inc/ 521 Madison Ave, New York, NY .... (212) 986-1224
Photo Researchers/ 60 East 56th Street, New York, NY .... (212) 758-3420
PHOTO RESEARCHERS/ 60 E. 56th St., New York, NY.............. (212) 758-3420
    See our ad on page 335
Photounique/ 1328 Broadway, Penthouse, New York, NY .... (212) 244-5511
Picture Cube/ 89 State St, Boston, MA .... (617) 367-1532
Pixelnet/ 253 Martens Ave., Mountain View, CA.........................
Plessner International/ 95 Madison Ave., New York, NY .... (212) 686-2444
Rainbow/ Main Street, Box 573, Housatonic, MA.:.................... (413) 274-6211
Roberts, H Armstrong Inc/ 420 Lexington Ave - Rm 2914,
    New York, NY.. (212) 682-6626
Roberts, H Armstrong Inc/ 4203 Locust Street,
    Philadelphia, PA.. (215) 386-6300
Sanford, Eric/ 219 Turnpike Road, Manchester, NH .... (603) 624-0122
Scala Fine Arts/ 65 Bleecker St, 9th Floor, New York, NY .... (212) 505-8700
Science Photo Library Int'l In/ 118 E 28th St, New York, NY........ (212) 683-4028
Sieb, Fred Photography, Inc/ Box 900 Birch Hill Road,
    North Conway, NH .... (603) 356-5879
Skyline Features, Inc./ 352 W. 15 St. #401, New York, NY .... (212) 242-4433
Sotheby Park Bernet Photograph/ 65 Bleecker Street,
    New York, NY.. (212) 505-8700
Southern Light Stock Agency/ P.O. Box 969, Pittsboro, NC .... (919) 542-4500
Spectragraphics/ 4 Brayton Ct, Commack, NY .... (516) 499-3100
Sports Illustrated Pictures/ Time & Life Bldg.,
    New York, NY.. (212) 841-2803
Sports Photo File Inc./ 24 W. 46th Street, New York, NY .... (212) 719-3565
Stock Boston Inc/ 36 Gloucester St, Boston, MA .... (617) 266-2573
Stock Market Photo Agency NY/ 1181 Broadway, New York, NY.... (212) 684-7878
Stock Photogrpahy Co./ 230 Park Ave. Ste. 923, New York, NY..... (212) 490-6490

STOCK PHOTO HOUSES/East

Stockphotos Inc/ 275 7th Avenue, New York, NY .... (212) 421-8980
Stock Shop Inc, The/ 271 Madison Avenue, New York, NY .... (212) 679-8480
Stockshop/Medichrome/ 271 Madison Ave, New York, NY .... (212) 679-8480
Sygma/ 225 W 57th, New York, NY .... (212) 765-1820
Tamin Stock Photos Inc/ 144 W 27st 2nd Fl, New York, NY .... (212) 807-6691
Taurus Photos/ 118 E. 28th Street, New York, NY .... (212) 683-4025
Three Lions/ 145 E 32nd St, New York City, NY .... (212) 725-2242
TIB THE IMAGE BANK/ 633 Third Ave., New York, NY .... (212) 953-0303
Uniphoto Picture Agency/ 1071 Wisconsin Avenue,
     Washington, DC .... (202) 333-0500

United Press Int'l Newspicture/ 220 E 42nd St,
     New York City, NY.. (212) 850-8600
Wasinski, Alex/ 119 W 23rd, New York, NY............................ (212) 989-0455
WEST STOCK, INC./ 157 Yesler Ste. 600, Seattle, WA .... (206) 621-1611
    See our ad on pages 336-339
Wide World Photos Inc/ 50 Rockfeller Plz, New York City, NY ...... (212) 621-1930
Wilcox Collection, the/ 521 Madison, New York, NY .... (212) 752-3930
Willoughby Peerless/ 116 W 32nd St, New York, NY .... (212) 564-1600
Woodfin Camp & Associates/ 415 Madison Avenue, New York, NY . (212) 750-1020
Woodfin Camp, Inc./ 925 1/2 F St. N.W., Washington, DC........... (202) 638-5750

REPS: ILLUSTRATORS AND PHOTOGRAPHERS

Abbey, Ken/ 421 7th Ave, New York, NY .... (212) 947-7577
Adams, Kris / Olbrys, Ellen/ 62 W 45th St, New York, NY .... (212) 869-4170
Adamus, Ray/ 22 W 38 Rm 1004, New York, NY .... (212) 719-5514
American Soc of Picture Profes/ Box 5283 Grand Central Station,
   New York, NY .... (212) 682-6626
ANTON, JERRY/ 107 E. 38th St., New York, NY .... (212) 689-5886
   See our ad on pages 13-15
Arnold, Peter Inc/ , NY .... (212) 840-6928
ARTISTS ASSOCIATES/ 211 E. 51st St., New York, NY .... (212) 755-1365
   See our ad on pages 16-21
ARTISTS INTERNATIONAL/ 225 Lafayette St. #1102,
   Soho, NY .... (212) 334-9310
   See our ad on pages 22-25
Arton Assoc Inc/ 216 East 45th St, New York, NY .... (212) 661-0850
ART STAFF, INC./ 1200 City National Bank Bldg.,
   Detroit, MI .... (313) 963-8240
   See our ad on pages 26-31
ATOLS, MARY/ 229 W. Illinois St., Chicago, IL .... (312) 828-9272
   See our ad on pages 272, 273
Badin, Andy/ 333 E 49th Street, New York, NY .... (212) 980-3578
Bahm, Darwin/ 6 Jane St, New York, NY .... (212) 989-7074
Bancroft, Carol/ 185 Goodhill Rd, Weston, CT .... (203) 226-7674
Basile, Ronald C./ 1328 Broadway, Penthouse, New York, NY .... (212) 244-5511
Becker, Noel/ 150 West 55 Street, New York, NY .... (212) 757-8987
Beilin, Frank/ 405 E. 56th Street, New York, NY .... (212) 751-3074
Berns, Jim/ 140 Riverside Dr. #10l, New York, NY .... (212) 724-4655
Bernstein & Andriulli, Inc/ 60 E. 42nd Street, New York, NY .... (212) 682-1490
Berthezene, Cindy/ 315 West 54th Street, New York, NY .... (212) 245-6584
Black, Joel P./ 540 Fort Washington Ave., New York, NY .... (212) 781-1055
Bloncourt, Nelson/ 300 West 23 St, New York, NY .... (212) 243-4248
Boghosian, Marty/ 7 E. 35th Street, New York, NY .... (212) 685-8939
Booth, Tom/ 425 W 23rd St Suite 17A, New York, NY .... (212) 243-2750
Brackman, Henrietta/ 415 E. 52nd Street, New York, NY .... (212) 753-6483
Brindle, Carolyn and Partner/ 203 E. 89th Street #3D,
   New York, NY .... (212) 831-1572
Brody, Anne/ 55 Bethune St, New York, NY .... (212) 242-1407
Brown, Doug/ 400 Madison Ave Room 801, New York, NY .... (212) 980-4971
BRUCK, J. S./ 157 W. 57th St., New York, NY .... (212) 247-1130
   See our ad on pages 40-65
Bruck, Nancy/ 315 East 69th Street, New York, NY .... (212) 288-6023
Bruml, Kathy/ 262 West End Avenue, New York, NY .... (212) 874-5659
Bush, Nan/ 135 Watts St, New York, NY .... (212) 226-0814
Cafiero, Charles-John/ 294 Elizabeth St, New York, NY .... (212) 777-2616
Cahill, Joseph H./ 135 E. 50th Street, New York, NY .... (212) 751-0529
Camp, Woodfin, Inc./ 925 1/2 F St. N.W., Washington, DC .... (202) 638-5705
Caputo, Elise/ 60 E. 42nd St. Ste. 1805, New York, NY .... (212) 949-2440
Carp, Stanley/ 8 East 48th Street, New York, NY .... (212) 759-8880
Casey, Marge & Arroyo, Lou/ 245 E. 63rd St., New York, NY .... (212) 486-9575
Chalek, Rick/ 9 E. 32nd St., New York, NY .... (212) 688-1080
Chandoha, Sam/ Rd 1 PO Box 287, Annandale, NJ .... (201) 782-3666
Chapnick, Ben/ 450 Park Avenue S., New York, NY .... (212) 679-3288
Chie/ 15 East 11th Street, New York, NY .... (212) 243-2353
Chislovsky, Carol, Inc./ 420 Madison Ave., New York, NY .... (212) 980-3510
COBB, LISA & ASSOCIATES/ 3416 Main St., Dallas, TX .... (214) 939-0032
Cohen, Paul/ 260 W 36th St, New York, NY .... (212) 279-0900
COLEMAN, WOODY PRESENTS, INC./ 1295 Old River Rd.,
   Cleveland, OH .... (216) 621-1771
   See our ad on pages 71-77
Collignon, Daniele/ 200 W. 15th St., New York, NY .... (212) 243-4209
Correia, Joseph A./ 11 Cabot Road, Woburn, MA .... (617) 933-8090
Cosimos Studio/ 35 W. 36th Street, New York, NY .... (212) 563-2730
Crabb, Wendy/ 320 E 50th St, New York, NY .... (212) 355-0013
Crandall Color/ 2001 W Main St, Stamford, CT .... (203) 327-9100
Debacker, Clo/ 29 E. 19th Street, New York, NY .... (212) 420-1276
DEDELL, JACQUELINE/ 58 W. 15th St., New York, NY .... (212) 741-2539
   See our ad on pages 84, 85
Dellacroce, Julia/ 226 E. 53rd St. #3c, New York, NY .... (212) 580-1321
Delvecchio, Lorraine/ 3156 Baisley Avenue, Bronx, NY .... (212) 829-5194
Design Management Institute/ 621 Huntington Ave.,
   Boston, MA .... (617) 232-4496
Deverin, Daniele/ 226 E 53rd, New York, NY .... (212) 755-4945
Dewan, Michael/ 250 Cabrini Blvd, New York, NY .... (212) 927-9458
Dewey, Frank/ 420 Lexington Avenue, New York, NY .... (212) 688-4555
Dickinson, Alexis M A/ 21 East 22nd St 11F,
   New York City, NY .... (212) 473-8020

DiMartino, Joseph/ 200 E 58th, New York, NY .... (212) 935-9522
DiParisi, Peter Photo Rep/ 54 W. 39th Street, New York, NY .... (212) 840-8225
DPI-Alfred Forsyth/ 521 Madison Ave., New York, NY .... (212) 752-3930
Drexler, Sharon/ 451 Westminster Road, Brooklyn, NY .... (212) 284-4779
Dubner, Logan/ 342 Madison Ave, New York, NY .... (212) 883-0242
Dweck, Michael & Co/ 36 W 34th St, New York, NY .... (212) 695-2330
ELLA/ 229 Berkeley St., Boston, MA .... (617) 266-3858
   See our ad on pages 90, 91
Erlacher, Bill/ 211 E. 51st Street, New York, NY .... (213) 755-1365
Feder, Ted/ 65 Bleecker Street 9th Floor, New York, NY .... (212) 505-8700
Feldman, Robert/ 171 First Ave, New York, NY .... (212) 473-2500
Fischer, Bob/ 135 E. 54th Street, New York, NY .... (212) 755-2131
Fisher, Alison/ 186 South Street, Boston, MA .... (617) 426-5731
Forsyth, Alfred W/ 521 Madison Ave, New York, NY .... (212) 752-3930
Foster, Peter/ 870 United Nations Plaza, New York, NY .... (212) 593-0793
Freelancenter, Inc/ 353 Lexington Avenue, New York, NY .... (212) 683-6969
Gargagliano, Tony/Barb Rindner/ 216 E 45th St, New York, NY .... (212) 661-0850
Garten, Jan & Jack/ 275 Central Park West, New York, NY .... (212) 787-8910
Gelman, Barbara/ 181 East 78th Street, New York City, NY .... (212) 620-0917
Geng, Maud/ 13 Gloucester St, Boston, MA .... (617) 236-1920
Giandomenico, Terry (Rep)/ 13 Fern Ave, Collingswood, NJ .... (609) 854-2222
Ginsburg, Michael & Associates/ 339 E. 58th St.,
   New York, NY .... (212) 628-2379
Glover, Cynthia/ 2502 Eutaw Place #2-B, Baltimore, MD .... (301) 728-7309
GOLDMAN, DAVID AGENCY/ 18 E. 17th St., New York, NY ...... (212) 807-6627
   See our ad on page 114
Goldstein, Michael/ 107 W. 69th Street, New York, NY .... (212) 874-6933
Goodman, Lou/ 322 Summer, Boston, MA .... (617) 542-8254
Goodwin, Phyllis A./ 10 E. 81st Street, New York, NY .... (212) 570-6021
Gordon Associates, Barbara/ 165 E. 32nd Street,
   New York, NY .... (212) 686-3514
Gould, Stephen Jay/ 225 E. 31st Street, New York, NY .... (212) 686-1690
Green, Anita/ 160 E 26th, New York, NY .... (212) 532-5083
Greenblatt, Eunice/ 370 E 76th, New York, NY .... (212) 772-1776
Grey, Barbara/ 1519 50th St, Brooklyn, NY .... (212) 851-0332
Grien, Anita/ 155 E 38th Street, New York, NY .... (212) 697-6170
Griffith, Valerie/ 10 Sheridan Square, New York, NY .... (212) 675-2089
Hankins & Tegenborg Ltd./ 310 Madison Ave. #1225,
   New York, NY .... (212) 867-8092
Head, Olive/ 90 Riverside Drive 16F, New York, NY .... (212) 580-3323
Heyl, Fran/ 230 Park Ave. Ste. 2525, New York, NY .... (212) 687-8930
Hoeye, Michael W./ 120 W. 70th Street, New York, NY .... (212) 362-9546
Hollyman, Audrey/ 300 E. 40th Street, Ste. 19R,
   New York, NY .... (212) 867-2383
Holt, Rita Assoc/ 280 Madison Avenue, New York, NY .... (212) 683-2002
Hovde, Nob Associates/ 829 Park Ave, New York, NY .... (212) 753-0462
HULL, SCOTT/ 20 Lynn Rae Cir., Dayton, OH .... (513) 433-8383
   See our ad on page 106
Image Bank/ 633 Third Avenue, New York, NY .... (212) 953-0303
Jacobsen Vi Co Studio/ 333 Park Ave S 2nd Fl, New York, NY ..... (212) 677-3770
Jedell, Joan/ 370 E. 76th Street, New York, NY .... (212) 861-7861
Johnson, Evelyne/ 201 E. 28th Street, New York, NY .... (212) 532-0928
Jossel, Marguerite/ 4 Gramercy Park W, New York, NY .... (212) 673-3522
Kahn, Harvey Assoc/ 50 East 50th Street, New York, NY .... (212) 752-8490
Kammler, Fredric/ 225 E 67th, New York City, NY .... (212) 249-4446
Kane, Barney & Friends/ 120 E. 32nd Street, New York, NY .... (212) 689-3233
KAPLAN, HOLLY/ 35 N. 36th St., New York, NY .... (212) 563-2730
   See our ad on pages 216, 217
Keating, Peggy/ 30 Horatio Street, New York, NY .... (212) 691-4654
Kenney, Ella/ 229 Berkeley #52, Boston, MA .... (617) 266-3858
Kenney, John Associates/ 342 Madison Ave., New York, NY .... (212) 697-8370
Kent Creative Group/ 5 E. 16th Street, New York, NY .... (212) 929-5596
Kilpatrick, Holly J./ 440 W. 34th #13e, New York, NY .... (212) 563-0227
Kim/ 209 E. 25th Street, New York, NY .... (212) 679-5628
Kimche, Tania/ 470 W. 23rd Street, New York, NY .... (212) 242-6367
KIRCHOFF/ 866 United Nations Plz., New York, NY .... (212) 644-2020
   See our ad on page 115
Klein, Leslie D./ 104 W. 40th St. #111, New York, NY .... (212) 683-5454
Klimt, Bill & Maurine/ 15 W. 72nd St., New York, NY .... (212) 799-2231
Kopel, Shelly & Associates/ 342 Madison Ave, New York, NY ...... (212) 986-3282
Kreis, Ursula G/ 63 Adrian Ave, New York, NY .... (212) 562-8931
Krieger, Harold/ 225 E 31st, New York, NY .... (212) 686-1690
Lamont, Mary/ 200 W. 20th Street, New York, NY .... (212) 242-1087
LANDER, JANE ASSOC./ 333 E. 30th St., New York, NY .... (212) 679-1358
   See our ad on page 120

Lane, Judy/ 444 E. 82nd Street, New York, NY .... (212) 861-7225
Larkin, Mary/ 308 E 59th St, New York, NY............................. (212) 308-7744
Lavaty Artists Representatives/ 50 East 50th St,
  New York, NY.. (212) 355-0910
Leach, Martin/ 114 E. 25th Street, New York, NY..................... (212) 260-5700
Lee, Alan/ 33 E 22nd, New York, NY...................................... (212) 673-2484
Lee, Barbara/ 307 W. 82nd Street, New York, NY..................... (212) 724-6176
Leff, Jerry/ 342 Madison Ave. #949, New York, NY .... (212) 697-8525
Leff, Wilma/ 342 Madison Ave, New York, NY .... (212) 697-8525
Legrand, Jean-Yves/ 41 W. 84th Street, New York, NY .... (212) 724-5981
Leonian, Edith/ 220 E. 23rd Street, New York, NY .... (212) 989-7670
Levin, Bruce Associates/ 1691 Third Ave. 3a, New York, NY .... (212) 410-0123
Lewin, Chuck/ 242 E. 19th Street, New York, NY .... (212) 228-5530
Li, Liz/ 260 Fifth Avenue, New York, NY .... (212) 889-7067
Lindgren, Pat/ 194 Third Avenue, New York, NY...................... (212) 475-0440
Locke, John-Studios, Inc/ 15 East 76th St, New York, NY .... (212) 288-8010
Lott, George/ 60 E. 42nd Street, New York, NY........................ (212) 687-4185
Madris, Stephen/ 445 E. 77th Street, New York, NY .... (212) 744-6668
MANASSE, MICHELE/ 1960 Broadway #2 E., New York, NY ...... (212) 873-3797
  See our ad on page 160
Mandel, Bette/ 265 E 66th, New York, NY............................... (212) 737-5062
Marek/ 160 Fifth Ave, New York, NY .... (212) 924-6760
MARIE, RITA & FRIENDS/ 6376 W. 5th St.,
  Los Angeles, CA.. (213) 934-3395
  See our ad on pages 131-137
Mariucci, Marie/ 32 W 39th Street 8th Floor, New York, NY .... (212) 944-9590
Marshall, Edith Paul/ 40 W. 77th Street, New York, NY .... (212) 877-3921
Mason, Kathy/ 101 W. 18th Street, New York, NY .... (212) 855-9074
Mathias, Cindy/ 7 E 14th, New York, NY................................. (212) 741-3191
Mattelson, Judy/ 88 Lexington Avenue, New York, NY .... (212) 684-2974
Mautner, Jane/ 85 Fourth Avenue, New York, NY .... (212) 777-9024
McLoughlin, James/ 12 W. 32nd Street, New York, NY .... (212) 244-1595
MCNAMARA ASSOCIATES, INC./ 1250 Stephenson Hwy.,
  Troy, MI .... (313) 583-9200
  See our ad on pages 140-143
McNamara, Paula B/ 182 Broad Street, Wethersfield, CT .... (203) 563-6154
Melsky, Barney/ 157 E. 35th Street, New York, NY .... (212) 532-3311
Mendelsohn, Richard Assoc/ 353 W 53rd, New York, NY .... (212) 682-2462
Mendola, Joseph/ 420 Lexington Ave., New York, NY .... (212) 986-5680
Mercier, Louis/ 342 Madison Avenue, New York, NY .... (212) 972-1701
Metz, Bernard/ 43 E. 19th St., New York, NY .... (212) 254-4996
Metzger, Rick/ 200 Fellview Terr, Stoneham, MA .... (617) 665-0622
Miller, Marcia/ 60 E 42nd, New York, NY................................ (212) 929-1107
Milsop, Frances/ 514 E. 83rd Street, New York, NY .... (212) 794-0922
Mintz, Les/ 111 Wooster St. #PHC, New York, NY .... (212) 925-0491
Moretz, Eileen/ 141 Wooster Street, New York, NY .... (212) 254-3766
Morgan, Vicki/ 194 Third Avenue, New York, NY .... (212) 475-0440
Mosel, Sue/ 310 E 46th, New York, NY................................... (212) 599-1806
Moshe,/ 63 East 9 St, New York, NY...................................... (212) 477-3129
MOSKOWITZ, M. REPRESENTS, INC./ 342 Madison Ave.,
  New York, NY.. (212) 719-9879
Moss, Eileen/ 333 E 49th St, New York, NY............................. (212) 980-8061
Mulvey Associates, Inc/ 1457 Broadway, New York, NY.............. (212) 840-8223
NEWBORN, MILTON/ 135 E. 54th St., New York, NY................ (212) 247-1130
Niaki, Rosemary/ 65 Central Park West, New York, NY .... (212) 877-6386
Nichols, Eva/ 1241 University Avenue, Rochester, NY .... (716) 275-9666
Opticalusions/ 9 E. 32nd St., New York, NY............................ (212) 688-1080
O'Rourke Associates/ 200 E. 62nd Street, New York, NY .... (212) 935-5027
Oye, Eva/ 307 E 44th St, New York, NY.................................. (212) 286-9103
Palmer-Smith Assocs., Glenn/ 160 Fifth Avenue, New York, NY ..... (212) 807-1855
Palulian, Joanne/ 18 McKinley Street, Rowayton, CT .... (203) 866-3734
Parvis, Frank/ 15 Washington Pl, New York, NY....................... (212) 473-5868
Penny & Stermer Group/ 114 E. 32nd St., New York, NY .... (212) 685-2770
Penny, Barbara Associates Inc/ 114 E 32nd St Suite 902,
  New York, NY.. (212) 685-2770
Photo Agents Ltd, Gary Lerman/ 40 East 34th Street,
  New York, NY.. (212) 683-5777
Photo Rep/ 156 Fifth Avenue #900, New York, NY................... (212) 675-2727
Pohl, Jacqueline/ 2947 Jackson, San Francisco, CA................... (415) 563-8616
Popper, Serge/ 315 E 68 St, New York City, NY........................ (212) 879-6200
POTTS, CAROLYN & ASSOCIATES/ 3 E. Ontario #25,
  Chicago, IL.. (312) 935-1707
  See our ad on pages 154, 155
Prof Women Photographers Inc/ 43 W 22nd, New York, NY .... (212) 255-9678
Push Pin Lubalin Peckolick/ 67 Irving Pl, New York, NY.............. (212) 674-8080

Quercia, Matt/ 78 Irving Place, New York, NY .... (212) 477-4491
Rapp, Gerald & Cullen/ 108 East 35th Street, New York, NY .... (212) 889-3337
Ray, Marlys/ 350 Central Park West, New York, NY .... (212) 222-6194
Reese, Kay & Associates, Inc./ 156 Fifth Ave., New York, NY .... (212) 924-5151
Renard, Madeline/ 501 Fifth Ave, New York, NY .... (212) 490-2450
Rentmeester, Co/ 435 W 23rd St, New York, NY .... (212) 243-2750
Richards, Gary/ 1462 First Ave, New York, NY.......................... (212) 861-8374
Riley, Edward T., Inc/W. Stillman/ 215 E. 31 St., New York, NY ..... (212) 684-3448
Rosenberg, Arlene/ 373 W. 11th St., New York, NY .... (212) 675-7983
Rostaing, Anne/ 26 Bowery, New York, NY .... (212) 349-6351
Rubin, Elaine/ 301 E 38th St #17J, New York, NY .... (212) 725-8313
Rudoff, Stan Assocs/ 271 Madison Ave, New York, NY .... (212) 679-8780
Russo, Karen/ 175 W. 92nd Street, New York, NY .... (212) 749-6382
Sacramone/Valentine/ 302 W 12th, New York, NY .... (212) 929-0487
Samuels, Rosemary/ 39 E 12th, New York, NY.......................... (212) 477-3567
Sander, Vicki/ 48 Gramercy Park N. #3B, New York, NY .... (212) 674-8161
Sands, Laura/ 873 Broadway, New York, NY .... (212) 505-5600
Saunders, Michele/ 309 W 76th St, New York City, NY .... (212) 496-0268
Schickler, Paul/ 135 E. 50th Street, New York, NY.................... (212) 355-1044
Schub & Bear/ 136 E 57th St, New York, NY .... (212) 246-0679
Seeman, Ed - the Rep Force/ 310 E. 46th Ste. 6g,
  New York, NY.. (212) 682-3012
SEIGEL, FRAN/ 515 Madison Ave., New York, NY .... (212) 486-9644
  See our ad on page 80
Setter, Frank/ 400 E 78th, New York, NY .... (212) 249-3138
Shamilzadeh, Sol/ 1155 Broadway, New York, NY .... (212) 532-1977
Shapiro, Elaine/ 369 Lexington Avenue, New York, NY .... (212) 867-8220
Shepherd, Judith/ 186 E 64 St, New York, NY.......................... (212) 838-3214
Sigman, Joan/ 336 E. 54th Street, New York, NY .... (212) 832-7980
S I International/ 43 E 19th Street, New York, NY .... (212) 254-4996
Silva-Cone Studios/ 260 W. 36 St. 7 Flr., New York, NY .... (212) 279-0900
Simoneau, Christine/ 236 E. 33rd St., New York, NY .... (212) 696-2085
Skyline Features, Inc./ 352 W. 15 St. #401, New York, NY .... (212) 242-4433
Slome, Nancy/ 121 Madison Ave., New York, NY .... (212) 685-8185
Smith, Emily/ 30 E. 21st Street, New York, NY .... (212) 674-8383
Sokolsky, Stanley/ 322 E. 39th Street, New York, NY .... (212) 686-5000
Solomon, Richard/ 121 Madison Avenue, New York, NY .... (212) 683-1362
S P A R/ 1123 Broadway Room 914, New York, NY .... (212) 924-6023
Spiers, Herb/S.I. Int'L./ 43 E. 19th St., New York, NY .... (212) 254-4996
Stogo, Donald R Associates/ 310 E 46th St, New York, NY .... (212) 490-1034
Stoller, Erica/ 222 Valley Place, Mamaroneck, NY .... (914) 698-4060
Storyboards/ 62 W. 45th Street, New York, NY .... (212) 869-4170
STRINGER, RAYMOND/ 251 W. 30th St. 5E, New York, NY .... (212) 760-0919
  See our ad on page 10
Studio Suppliers Assoc/ 548 Goffle Rd, Hawthorne, NJ .... (201) 427-9384
Susse, Ed/ 36 E. 20th St, New York, NY .... (212) 477-0674
Tannenbaum, Dennis/ 286 Fifth Avenue, New York, NY .... (212) 279-2838
Trapido, Paul/ 185 Duane Street, New York, NY .... (212) 219-2199
Ursula/ 63 Adrian Avenue, Bronx, NY .... (212) 562-8931
Van Arnam, Lewis/ 154 W 57 St Studio 405, New York, NY .... (212) 541-4787
Ventura Associates Inc./ 200 Madison Avenue, New York, NY ...... (212) 889-0707
Walker, Eleanora/ 120 E 30th, New York, NY .... (212) 689-4431
Wasserman, Ted Associates/ 331 Madison Ave, New York, NY....... (212) 867-5360
Watterson, Libby/ 350 E 30th St, New York City, NY .... (212) 696-1461
Wayne, Philip/ 66 Madison Ave, New York, NY .... (212) 889-2836
Wein, Gita/ 320 E 58th, New York, NY .... (212) 759-2763
Weissberg, Elyse/ 299 Pearl Street, New York, NY .... (212) 406-2566
WELLS, SUSAN/ 5134 Timber Trail N.E., Atlanta, GA .... (404) 255-1430
  See our ad on page 179
Wheeler, Paul/Wheeler Pictures/ 50 W. 29th St.,
  New York, NY.. (212) 696-9832
Wolfe, Deborah Ltd/ 731 North 24th Street, Philadelphia, PA .... (215) 232-6666
Yellen, Bert/ 575 Madison Ave Suite 1006, New York, NY .... (212) 605-0555
Young, Diane/ 10 West 18 Street, New York City, NY .... (212) 255-2515
Zanetti, Lucy/ 139 Fifth Avenue, New York, NY .... (212) 473-4999

PRINTING, PRODUCTION

PRINTS, CHROMES, RETOUCHERS

Able Art Service/ 8 Winter St, Boston, MA .... (617) 482-4558
Adams & Abbott Inc/ 46 Summer, Boston, MA .... (617) 542-1257
Adams Photoprint/ 250 W 57 St, New York, NY .... (212) 247-4637
Ad-Link/ 37 W 47th, New York, NY...................................... (212) 382-0266
Albert Appel/ 119 West 23 St, New York, NY .... (212) 989-6585
Alfie Custom Color/ 155 N Dean St, Englewood, NJ .... (201) 569-2028
Alves Photo Service/ 14 Storrs Ave, Braintree, MA .... (617) 843-5555
American Blue Print Co Inc/ 7 E 47th St, New York, NY .... (212) 751-2240
American Photo Print Co/ 285 Madison Ave, New York, NY........ (212) 532-2424
American Photo Print Co/ 350 Fifth Ave, New York, NY .... (212) 736-2885
Anselmo Studio/ 211 East 51st St., New York, NY .... (212) 753-1606
Apco-Apeda Photo Co/ 250 W 54th St, New York, NY .... (212) 586-5755
Appel, Leon Associates/ 2 W 46th St, New York, NY................. (212) 840-6633
Arnow, Catherine Inc/ 230 E 44th St, New York, NY .... (212) 692-9373
ASAP Photolab Inc/ 40 E 49th St, New York, NY .... (212) 832-1223
Asman Custom Photo Service Inc/ 926 Pennsylvania Avenue SW,
      Washington, DC .... (202) 547-7713
Atlantic Blue Print Co/ 575 Madison Ave, New York, NY .... (212) 755-3388
AT&S Retouching Svcs/ 230 E 44th St, New York, NY .... (212) 986-0977
Aurora Retouching/ 19 W 21st St, New York, NY..................... (212) 255-0620
Authenticolor, Inc./ 227 E. 45th St., New York, NY.................
AZO Color Labs/ 149 Madison Ave, New York, NY .... (212) 982-6610
Belart Assocs/ 515 Madison Ave, New York, NY .... (212) 753-2625
Bellis, Dave/ 155 E 55th, New York, NY .... (212) 753-3740
Bell-Taitt, Carolyn/ Room 1221 10 W 33rd St, New York, NY ...... (212) 947-9449
Kaufmann, Peter H.-Berkey K&L/ 222 E 44th St, New York, NY .... (212) 661-5600
Bishop Retouching Inc/ 236 E 36th St, New York, NY .... (212) 889-3525
Blae, Ken Retouching Inc/ 1501 Broadway, New York, NY .... (212) 869-3488
Blow-Up/ 2441 Maryland Ave, Baltimore, MD......................... (301) 467-3636
Bluestone Photoprint Co Inc/ 19 W 34th St, New York, NY .... (212) 564-1516
Bonaventura Studio/ 307 E 44th St, New York, NY .... (212) 687-9208
Boris Color Labs Inc/ 35 Landsdowne St, Boston, MA .... (617) 437-1152
Carlson & Forino Studios/ 230 E 44th St, New York, NY .... (212) 697-7044
Carroll, Joan/ 7 Peter Cooper Rd, New York, NY .... (212) 473-5445
Cavalluzzo, Dan/ 49 W 45th St, New York, NY....................... (212) 921-5954
CCS Company/ 330 E 59th, New York, NY.............................. (212) 752-2330
Certified Color Service/ 330 E 59th St, New York, NY .... (212) 752-2330
Chroma Copy/ 348 Fairfield Ave, Stamford, CT .... (203) 356-0170
Chroma Copy/ 2314 Market St, Philadelphia, PA .... (215) 561-2661
Chroma Copy/ 364 Boylston St, Boston, MA .... (617) 262-3020
Chroma Copy/ 227 E. 56th St., New York, NY .... (212) 421-4440
Chromeprint/ 104 E 25th St, New York, NY .... (212) 228-0840
Colmer, Bryan/ 310 E. 46th Street, New York, NY .... (212) 682-3012
Colorama/ 370 W 35th St, New York, NY .... (212) 279-1950
Coloratura/ P.O. Box 1749 67 Brookside, Boston, MA............... (617) 522-5132
Color By Pergament/ 305 E 47th St, New York, NY .... (212) 751-5367
Color Design Inc/ 19 West 21 St, New York, NY...................... (212) 255-8103
Colorfax Laboratories Inc/ 11961 Tech Rd, Silver Spring, MD ...... (301) 622-1500
Colorite Film Processing Labs/ 115 E 31st St, New York, NY....... (212) 532-2116
Color Perfect Inc/ 200 Park Ave S, New York, NY .... (212) 777-1210
Color Unlimited Inc/ 443 Park Ave S, New York, NY .... (212) 889-2440
Columbia Blue & Photoprint Co/ 14 E 39th St, New York, NY...... (212) 532-9424
Complete Photo Service/ 703 Mt Auburn, Cambridge, MA .... (617) 864-5954
Compo Stat Svce/ 18 E 48th St, New York, NY .... (212) 758-1690
Consolidated Poster Svce/ 341 W 44th St, New York, NY .... (212) 581-3105
Copytone/ 8 W 45th St, New York, NY .... (212) 575-0235
Cortese, Phyllis/ 12 W 27th St, New York, NY .... (212) 696-0288
Cosmic Sound-Delight Inc/ 225 East 43rd Street,
      New York, NY.. (212) 688-8686
Crandall, Robert Associates/ 306 E 45th St, New York, NY .... (212) 661-4710
Creative Color/ 25 West 45 St, New York, NY .... (212) 764-3077
Crowell, Joyce Studio/ New York, NY .... (212) 683-3055
Crown Photo/ 370 W 35th St, New York, NY .... (212) 279-1950
Darkroom Inc, The/ 222 E 46th St, New York, NY .... (212) 687-8920
Davis-Ganes/ 15 E 40th St, New York, NY .... (212) 687-6537
Diamond, Richard/ 50 E 42nd St, New York, NY .... (212) 697-4720
Diana Studio/ 301 West 53rd St, New York, NY .... (212) 757-0445
Dimension Color Labs Inc/ 28 W 39th St, New York, NY .... (212) 354-5918
Dipierro-Turiel/ 210 E 47th St, New York, NY........................ (212) 752-2260
Dorsey's, Jeannie Airbrush Stu/ PO Box 314 Rt 140,
      Gilmanton, NH... (603) 267-8779

Dunlop Custom Photolab Svc/ 2321 4th St NE, Washington, DC.... (202) 526-5000
Durkin, Joseph/ 25 Huntington Ave, Boston, MA .... (617) 267-0437
Dzurella, Paul Retouching/ 15 W 38th, New York, NY............... (212) 840-8623
Ecay, Thom Retouching/ 49 West 45th Street, New York, NY....... (212) 840-6277
Equitable Blueprint/ 799 Seventh Ave, New York, NY .... (212) 962-5672
Evan Avedisian Distesan Color/ 29 West 38th Street,
      New York, NY.. (212) 697-4240
Filmstat/ 520 Fifth Ave, New York, NY .... (212) 840-1676
Fine-Art Color Lab Inc/ 221 Park Ave S, New York, NY .... (212) 674-7640
Finley Photographics Inc/ 488 Madison Ave, New York, NY .... (212) 688-3025
Finley Photographics/ 405 Lexington Ave, New York, NY .... (212) 986-7920
Fodale Studio/ 247 East 50th St., New York, NY .... (212) 755-0150
Forway Studios/ 441 Lexington Ave, New York, NY .... (212) 661-0260
Foto Fidelity Inc/ 35 Leon, Boston, MA................................ (617) 267-6487
Four Colors Photo Lab Inc/ 10 E 39th St, New York, NY .... (212) 889-3399
Franklin Photos/ 353 W 48th, New York, NY .... (212) 246-4255
Frenchy's Color Lab Inc/ 10 E 38th St, New York, NY .... (212) 889-7787
Frey, Louis Co Inc/ 18 E 50th St, New York, NY .... (212) 791-0500
Friedman, Estelle/ 160 E 38th St, New York, NY .... (212) 532-0084
Full Frame Productions, Inc./ 36 Bromfield St., Boston, MA .... (617) 423-9254
Gads Color/ 30 East 42nd Street, New York, NY .... (212) 687-5911
Gayde, Richard/ 515 Madison Ave, New York, NY .... (212) 421-4088
GFI Printing & Typesetting/ 2 Highland St, Port Chester, NY .... (914) 937-2823
Gilbert Studio/ 127 W. 24th St., New York, NY .... (212) 683-3472
Gould, David/ 76 Coronado St, Atlantic Beach, NY.................. (516) 371-2413
Graphic Systems/ 33 W. 17th St., New York, NY .... (212) 242-8787
Gray, George Studios/ 230 E 44th St, New York, NY................. (212) 661-0276
Greenleaf Associates/ 42 Greenleaf Street, Malden, MA .... (617) 321-6881
Greller, Fred/ 325 E 64th St, New York, NY .... (212) 535-6240
Grubb Retouching Inc Color BW/ 155 Riverside Dr,
      New York, NY.. (212) 873-2561
G S Lithographers/ 1 Kero Road, Carlstadt, NJ .... (201) 933-8585
G W Color Lab Inc/ 36 E 23rd St, New York, NY .... (212) 677-3800
Hill, Murray Photo Print Inc/ 32 W 39th St, New York, NY......... (212) 921-4175
H T J Adstat Reproductions/ 515 Madison Ave, New York, NY ..... (212) 755-0429
Hudson Reproductions Inc/ 76 Ninth Ave, New York, NY........... (212) 989-3400
H-Y Photo Service/ 16 E 52nd St, New York, NY..................... (212) 371-3018
Ideal Photographic Corp/ 160 W 46th, New York, NY .... (212) 819-0359
Image Inc/ 1919 Penn Ave NW, Washington, DC .... (202) 833-1550
Industrial Color Lab/ 9 Proctor St PO Box #563,
      Framingham, MA .... (617) 872-3280
Jaeger, Elliot Retouching/ 49 West 45 Street, New York, NY....... (212) 840-6278
Jellybean Photographic/ 99 Madison Ave, New York, NY .... (212) 679-4888
J M W Studio Inc/ 230 East 44th Street, New York, NY .... (212) 986-9155
Jones, Barry Retouching/ 2725 Mary St, Easton, PA................. (215) 253-3709
J&R Color Lab/ 29 W 38th Street, New York, NY .... (212) 869-9870
Just Dupes/ 105 Fifth Ave 9D, New York, NY .... (212) 255-4047
Katz, David Studio/ 6 East 39th St, New York, NY .... (212) 889-5038
Kennedy, Kathy Photo Works/ 119 W 23rd St, New York, NY ...... (212) 255-4382
K E W Color Labs/ 112 Main St, Norwalk, CT......................... (203) 853-7888
KG&R Studios/ 56 W 45th St, New York, NY .... (212) 840-7930
K G & R Studios Inc/ 56 W 45th St, New York, NY .... (212) 840-7930
Kling, Al/ 25 West 45th St, New York, NY .... (212) 575-5600
Kurahara, Joan/ 611 Broadway, New York, NY .... (212) 505-8589
Laferla, Sandro/ 135 W. 14th St., New York, NY .... (212) 620-0693
Langen & Wind/ 265 Madison Ave, New York, NY .... (212) 686-1818
Larson Color Lab/ 123 Fifth Ave, New York, NY .... (212) 674-0610
Laumont Color Lab Inc/ 333 W 52nd, New York, NY .... (212) 245-2113
Lieberman, Kenneth/ 69 Fairview, Searingtown, NY .... (516) 621-3084
Lindstrom, Ozzie/ 79 Midwood Rd, Glen Rock, NJ .... (212) 391-2085
Loonan, Matthew Adv Inc/ 121 Varick St, New York, NY .... (212) 255-7463
Loy-Taubman Inc/ 34 E 30th St, New York, NY .... (212) 685-6871
Lucas, Bob/ 10 E 38th St, New York, NY .... (212) 725-2090
Lukon Art Service Ltd/ 24 W 45th St, New York, NY .... (212) 575-0474
Makepeace, B L Inc/ 1266 Boylston St, Boston, MA .... (617) 267-2700
Mancaruso, Ann/ 5 West 46 Street, New York, NY .... (212) 840-0215
Mandl, Bela Retouching/ 325 E 57th St, New York, NY............. (212) 355-0478
Manna Color Labs Inc/ 42 W 15th St, New York, NY .... (212) 691-8360
Mann & Greene Color Inc/ 320 East 39 Street, New York, NY...... (212) 481-6868
Marshall, Henry/ 6 E 39th St, New York, NY .... (212) 686-1060
Martin/Arnold Color Systems In/ 150 Fifth Ave, New York, NY .... (212) 675-7270
Martin, Tulio G/ 234 West 56th Street, New York, NY .... (212) 245-6489
Mask-O-Neg/ 33 W 34th, New York, NY .... (212) 947-5121
Mayer, Kurt Color Laboratories/ 1170 Broadway, New York, NY.... (212) 532-3738
McCurdy & Cardinale Color Lab./ 65 W. 36 St., New York, NY...... (212) 695-5140

Mc Williams, Clyde Studios/ 151 West 46th St, New York, NY ...... (212) 221-3644
Medina Studios/ 141 E 44th St Room 808, New York, NY .... (212) 867-3113
Meehan-Tooker Co/ E Rutherford, NJ .... (201) 933-9600
Micolupo, Dominick - Retoucher/ 289 Garfield Pl.,
  Brooklyn, NY .... (718) 638-4025
Miller, Norm Assoc/ 17 E 48th St, New York, NY .... (212) 752-4830
Modernage Photo Services/ 1150 Ave of the Americas,
  New York, NY .... (212) 997-1800
Moser, Klaus T, Ltd/ 127 East 15th Street, New York, NY .... (212) 475-0038
Motal Custom Darkrooms/ 25 W 45th St, New York, NY .... (212) 719-5454
Muggeo, Sam/ 63 Hedge Brook Lane, Stamford, CT .... (212) 972-0398
Multimedia/Color Pre Press Svc/ 407 Park Ave. S.,
  New York, NY .... (212) 889-2189
Myers, Barry Studio Inc/ 1501 Broadway, New York, NY .... (212) 997-1930
My Lab Inc./ 117 E 30th St, New York, NY .... (212) 686-8684
Nohe, Albert and Associates/ 925 Penn Ave, Pittsburgh, PA........ (412) 471-9979
Northeast Color Research Inc/ 40 Cameron Ave Box 358,
  Somerville, MA .... (617) 666-1161
North Light Inc/ 39 West 32 St, New York, NY .... (212) 563-7325
On Target Graphic Svcs Inc/ 1185 E. Putnam Ave.,
  Riverside, CT .... (203) 637-8300
Ornaal Color Photos/ 24 W 25th St, New York, NY .... (212) 675-3850
Paccione, E S Inc/ 150 E 35th, New York, NY .... (212) 889-2790
Palevitz, Bob/ 333 E. 30th St, New York, NY .... (212) 684-6026
Paper Faces/ 412 E 59th St, New York, NY......................... (212) 838-1923
Photo Exchange, The/ 1 W 20th, New York, NY..................... (212) 675-6582
Photographic Color Specialists/ 10-36 47th Rd,
  Long Island, NY .... (212) 786-4770
Photographics Unlimited/ 43 W 22nd St, New York, NY .... (212) 255-9678
Photorama/ 239 W 39th St, New York, NY .... (212) 354-5280
PIC Color Corp/ 25 W 45th, New York, NY .... (212) 575-5600
Precision Chromes Inc/ 310 Madison Ave, New York, NY.......... (212) 687-5990
Preferred Photographic Co/ 165 W 46th St, New York, NY.......... (212) 382-0237
PROFESSIONAL COLOR SERVICE/ 14910 Burbank,
  Van Nuys, CA .... (818) 787-7333
Prussack, Phil Studio/ 155 E 55th St, New York, NY .... (212) 755-2470
Quality Color Laboratory Inc/ 305 E 46th St, New York, NY .... (212) 753-2200
Raffi Custom Photo Lab/ 21 W 46th, New York, NY .... (212) 719-2727
Ramer, Joe Associates/ 509 Madison Ave, New York, NY .... (212) 751-0894
Rasulo Graphic Service/ 36 East 31, New York, NY .... (212) 686-2861
Ratigan, William P./ 189 Second St., Troy, NY .... (518) 272-2626
Regal Velox/ 25 W 43rd St, New York, NY .... (212) 840-0330
Renaissance Retouching/ 136 W. 46th St., New York, NY .... (212) 575-9744
Replichrome/ 7 East 17th Street, New York, NY .... (212) 929-0409
Reproduction Color Specialists/ 9 E 38th St, New York, NY......... (212) 683-0833
Retouchables, The/ 104 E 40 St Ste 307, New York, NY .... (212) 867-4225
Retouchers Gallery/ 160 E 38th St, New York, NY .... (212) 697-6544
Retouching Graphics Inc/ 321 E. 54th St. Apt. 3c,
  New York, NY .... (212) 838-1867
Retouching Inc/ 9 E 38th St, New York, NY .... (212) 683-4188
Riter, Warren/ 2291 Pennfield Rd, Pennfield, NY .... (716) 381-4368
Rivera and Schiff Assoc Inc/ 21 W 38th St, New York, NY .... (212) 354-2977
Robotti, Tho./ 5 W. 46 St., New York, NY.......................... (212) 840-0215
Rogers Color Laboratory Corp/ 165 Madison Ave, New York, NY.... (212) 683-6400
Rothman, Henry/ 6927 N 19th St, Philadelphia, PA .... (215) 424-6927
R&R Graphics Inc/ PO Box 623, Orange, CT .... (203) 795-0565
Ruggiero, Marie/ 141 E 44th St, New York City, NY .... (212) 697-5430
Ruhl, Dick/ 835 3rd Ave., New York, NY .... (212) 838-4808
Russo Photographic Services/ 305 E 46th St, New York, NY .... (212) 421-5550
R & V Studio/ 32 W 39th, New York, NY .... (212) 944-9590
Sa-Kura Retouching/ 123 W 44 Street, New York, NY .... (212) 764-5944
Sanchez, Edward/ 220 E. 23rd Street, New York, NY .... (212) 683-7897
San Photo Art Service/ 165 West 29th Street, New York, NY ...... (212) 594-0850
Santopadre, Charles/ 420 Lexington Ave, New York, NY .... (212) 986-5154
Scala Fine Arts/ 65 Bleecker Street 9th Floor, New York, NY...... (212) 673-4988
Schiavone, Joe/ 301 W. 53rd St. Apt. 4e, New York, NY........... (212) 757-0660
Schiftan, Alfred Inc/ 460 Park Ave S, New York, NY .... (212) 532-1984
Scope Assoc/ 11 E 22nd St, New York, NY .... (212) 674-4190
Scott, Diane Associates Inc/ 339 E 58th St, New York, NY......... (212) 355-4616
Sharkey, Dick Studio, the/ 301 West 53rd St, New York, NY ...... (212) 265-1036
Shaw, Rik Associates/ 250 West 54 Street, New York, NY .... (212) 757-3988
Shields, Houston & Assoc/ 145 E 49th St, New York, NY .... (212) 753-7760
Simmons-Beal/ 3 E 40th St, New York, NY .... (212) 532-6261
Sklarsky, Louis/ 135 West 36, New York, NY...................... (212) 695-7454
Skoglund Studios/ 279 E 44th, New York, NY...................... (212) 986-1841

Skollar, Bill/ 270 W 17th Street, New York, NY .... (212) 255-3739
Spano/Roccanova Retouching Inc/ 16 W 46th St, New York, NY ... (212) 840-7450
Spector, Hy Studios/ 56 W 45th St, New York, NY .... (212) 221-3656
Spectrum Creative Retouchers I/ 230 E 44th St, New York, NY..... (212) 687-3359
Speed Graphics/ 150 East 58th Street, New York, NY.............. (212) 371-1362
Spiegel, Len/ 40 E 49 St, New York, NY............................ (212) 832-1223
Stanley, Joseph/ 211 W 58th St, New York, NY .... (212) 246-1258
Stat Store Inc/ 148 5 Ave, New York, NY .... (212) 929-0566
Stevens, Wm Photo Retouching/ 353 East 77th Street,
  New York, NY .... (212) 628-6484
Stewart Color/Ken Lieberman/ 563 Eleventh Ave, New York, NY ... (212) 868-1440
Studio 55/ 170 Reynolds Ave, Bronx, NY .... (212) 840-0920
Studio 6 Inc/ 346 Boston Post Rd, Sudbury, MA .... (617) 443-5101
Subtractive Technology/ 338 Newbury St, Boston, MA .... (617) 261-1887
Superior Photo Retouching Svc/ 1955 Mass Ave, Cambridge, MA ... (617) 661-9094
Superphoto/ 165 Madison Ave, New York, NY...................... (212) 686-9510
Tanksley, John/ 210 E 47th, New York, NY .... (212) 752-1150
Tartaro Color Lab/ 29 W 38th St, New York, NY .... (212) 840-1640
Technical Photography Inc/ 1275 Bloomfield Avenue,
  Fairfield, NJ .... (201) 227-4646
Terzo, Sal/ 49 W 45th St, New York, NY .... (212) 730-1660
Trio Studio/ 18 E 48th St, New York, NY .... (212) 752-4875
TRP Slavin Colour Services Ltd/ 920 Broadway, New York, NY..... (212) 674-5700
Ultima Color/ 550 West 43rd, New York, NY .... (212) 239-4646
Ultimate Image/ 443 Park Ave South, New York, NY .... (212) 683-4838
Van Vort, Donald D/ 71 Capital Hts Rd, Oyster Bay, NY.......... (516) 922-5234
Venezia, Don Retouching/ 40 E 54th St, New York, NY .... (212) 832-8829
Vidachrome Inc/ 25 W 39th St, New York, NY .... (212) 391-8124
VonEiff, Damon Retoucher/ 930 F Street NW #812,
  Washington, DC .... (202) 347-2788
Wagner Photoprint Co/ 121 W 50th St, New York, NY .... (212) 245-4796
Ward, Jack Color Services Inc/ 220 E 23rd, New York, NY .... (212) 725-5200
Way Color Inc/ 420 Lexington Ave, New York, NY................. (212) 687-5610
Weber, Martin J/ 171 Madison Ave, New York, NY................. (212) 532-2695
Weiman & Lester Inc/ 21 E 40th St, New York, NY .... (212) 679-1180
Weinstock, Bernie/ 162 Boylston, Boston, MA..................... (617) 423-4481
Wilen, Herb/ 225 E 57th, New York, NY .... (212) 688-1938
William, Stevens Photo Retouch/ 353 East 77th, New York, NY..... (212) 628-6484
Wilson, Paul/ 25 Huntington Ave, Boston, MA .... (617) 437-1236
Wind, Gerry & Associates/ 265 Madison Ave, New York, NY .... (212) 686-1818
Winter, Jerry Retouching/ 333 East 45 St Apt 31C,
  New York, NY .... (212) 490-0876
Wolf, Bill/ 212 East 47th Street, New York, NY .... (212) 697-6215
Wolsk, Bernard Inc/ 509 Madison Ave, New York, NY .... (212) 751-7727
Zazula, Hy Associates/ 2 W. 46th St., New York, NY .... (212) 819-0444
Zazula, Hy Assoc Inc/ 2 W 46th St, New York, NY .... (212) 819-0444

PRINTERS AND ENGRAVERS

Ace Offset Service Inc/ 200 Hudson St, New York, NY .... (212) 431-5222
Acme Printing Co Inc/ 4 Colby, Medford, MA .... (617) 395-7150
Adams Group Inc, The/ 225 Varick, New York, NY .... (212) 255-4900
A-Del Lithographics/ 111 Eighth Ave Suite 1515,
  New York, NY .... (212) 924-6969
Adler Printing Company/ 28 Kansas Street, Hackensack, NJ .... (201) 343-3358
Adlon Press/ 37 W 20th St, New York, NY......................... (212) 929-8675
Advance Printing Co Inc/ 345 Hudson St, New York, NY .... (212) 924-8940
Advertisers Assocs Inc/ 1627 Penn Ave, Pittsburgh, PA .... (412) 281-6144
A & H Litho/ 481 Washington St, New York, NY .... (212) 925-5593
Alexander & Pamaro Inc/ 40-20 22nd St, Long Island Cty, NY...... (212) 784-3201
Alexographic Press Inc/ 225 Varick St, New York, NY .... (212) 243-0146
A&L Litho Service Inc/ 175 Varick St, New York, NY .... (212) 255-2827
Alpine Press Inc, The/ 100 Alpine Cir, Stoughton, MA .... (617) 341-1800
Ambassador Arts, Inc/ 122 W 27th Street, New York, NY .... (212) 243-4290
American Bank Note Co/ 70 Broad St, New York, NY .... (212) 542-9200
American Colormatic Co Inc/ 70 Birch Street, Abington, MA .... (617) 337-9367
American Lithotone/ 1133 Broadway, New York, NY............... (212) 929-8393
American Press Inc/ 3701 Hwy 33, Neptune, NJ .... (201) 367-2914
Ampco Printing-Advertisers Off/ 125 West End Ave,
  New York, NY .... (212) 799-3900
Amsel Litho Corp/ 270 Lafayette St, New York, NY .... (212) 925-8575
Arcata Pub Group/ 1185 Sixth Ave, New York, NY .... (203) 846-6000
Argold Press Inc/ 32 West 22nd St, New York, NY................. (212) 675-3800
Art Graphics Litho Corp/ 1328 Broadway, New York, NY .... (212) 695-7430
Art Litho Co/ 1500 W Patapsco Ave, Baltimore, MD .... (301) 355-3200

ARW Productions/ 404 Park Ave South, New York, NY .... (212) 889-5085
Associated Offset Co Inc/ 599 11th Ave, New York, NY .... (212) 974-1963
Associative Adv./Sotoco/ 39 High Street, Passaic Park, NJ .... (201) 471-1170
Astoria Press Inc/ 435 Hudson St, New York, NY .... (212) 255-6768
Atwater Press Inc/ 207 W 25th St, New York, NY .... (212) 675-2710
Bailey Press/ 251 Causeway, Boston, MA .... (617) 523-1938
Banner House Printing/ 6 Murray St, New York, NY .... (212) 732-2280
B A T Litho Publishing Corp/ 37 E 18th St, New York, NY .... (212) 982-8120
Baum Printing Inc/ 9985 Gantry & Geiger Rds,
  Philadelphia, PA .... (215) 671-9500
Bayberry Printing & Lithograph/ 148 Lafayette St,
  New York, NY .... (212) 966-2217
Beach Publishing&Printing, Co./ Rt. 26 at Central Ave.,
  Ocean View, DE .... (302) 539-3728
Beacon Press Inc, The/ 225 Varick St, New York, NY .... (212) 691-5050
Beacon Printing Co/ 270 Lafayette St, New York, NY .... (212) 925-7618
Beck Engraving/ 2100 Cabot Blvd West, Langhorne, PA .... (215) 752-8010
Beck Engraving/ 2 Pennsylvania Plaza Suite1528,
  New York, NY .... (212) 564-1916
Beechwood Press Inc/ 4100 Palisade Ave, Union City, NJ .... (201) 866-5000
Bell Photo Engraving Co/ 2809 Jeannette St, Union City, NJ .... (201) 867-3281
Bergen Lithographers Inc/ 55 Veterans Blvd, Carlstadt, NJ .... (212) 736-8430
Berkshire Printing Ent Ltd Inc/ 100 Ave of the Americas,
  New York, NY .... (212) 925-4428
Blair Graphics/ 9 West 57th Street, New York, NY .... (212) 838-9191
Blum Assoc Inc/ 186 Lincoln Street, Boston, MA .... (617) 426-6733
Bradford & Bigelow Inc/ Us Rt 1, Danvers, MA .... (617) 599-9333
Bridge Lithographic/ 160 Varick St, New York, NY .... (212) 989-2650
Brockton Photo Engraving Co/ PO Box 1444 165 Court St,
  Brockton, MA .... (617) 586-6004
Brod Printing & Lithographing/ 509 Madison Avenue,
  New York, NY .... (212) 838-6636
Brooklyn Press Inc/ 59 Lawrence St, Brooklyn, NY .... (212) 625-4100
Brose Offset Lithographing Co/ 345 Hudson Street,
  New York, NY .... (212) 989-2650
Brunel, Jean/ 143 Franklin St, New York, NY .... (212) 226-3009
Bryant Press Inc/ 52 E 19th St, New York, NY .... (212) 254-5122
Burton Color Lithograph Co/ 480 Canal St, New York, NY .... (212) 226-7757
Burton-Quaker Corp/ 406 W 31st St, New York, NY .... (212) 279-7375
Caltone Lithographers Inc/ 406 W 31st St, New York, NY .... (212) 594-2424
Canterbury-Perfect Press Inc/ 406 W 31st St, New York, NY .... (212) 868-1000
Capitol Lithographers Inc/ 45 W 18th St, New York, NY .... (212) 924-6300
Cardinal Lithographers/ 38-09 43rd Ave, Long Island Cty, NY ...... (212) 392-9600
Cardinal Photo Engraving/ 270 Lafayette, New York, NY .... (212) 431-9770
Carillon Lithographing Corp/ 37 E 18th St, New York, NY .... (212) 254-5840
Carnival Press Inc/ 200 Entin Rd, Clifton, NJ .... (201) 470-8100
Case Hoyt Color Printers/ 810 Seventh Ave, New York, NY .... (212) 489-1991
Case-Hoyt Corp/ PO Box 259, Rochester, NY .... (716) 232-6840
Central Engraving Co/ 156 Carter Street, Chelsea, MA .... (617) 426-9546
Century Reproductions/ 93 Audubon St, New Haven, CT............. (203) 777-7288
Certified Ptg Co Inc/ 342 Madison Ave, New York, NY .... (212) 490-3993
Charden T-Shirt Printers/ 69 King St, Dover, NJ .... (201) 328-1444
Cherry Lane Lithog Corp/ 1478 Old Country Rd, Plainview, NY .... (212) 895-4082
Citation Photo Engraving Corp/ 54 W 22nd St, New York, NY....... (212) 242-1662
Coe Displays/ 51 W 21st, New York, NY .... (212) 924-4560
Cogens/ 135 Washington St, Providence, RI .... (401) 421-4436
Colish, A/ 40 Hartford Ave, Mt Vernon, NY .... (212) 409-3800
Collier Graphic Services/ 240 West 40th Street,
  New York, NY .... (212) 840-0440
Colonial Graphics/ 92 Maryland Ave, Paterson, NJ .... (201) 345-0600
Colorama Press Inc/ 420 Valley Brook Ave, Lyndhurst, NJ .... (201) 933-5660
Color Lithographers Inc/ 225 Varick St, New York, NY .... (212) 255-3200
Colorpress/ 21 Dwight Pl, Fairfield, NJ .... (201) 575-7555
Color-Vu Corporation/ 6 N Pearl St, Portchester, NY .... (914) 937-0990
Columbia Lithographic Co Inc/ 1 Bridge Plaza North Ste 240,
  Fort Lee, NJ .... (212) 725-5777
Columbia Printing Co/ 32 W 40 St #2S, New York, NY............... (212) 382-3740
Comet Press/ 122 E 42 Street, New York, NY .... (212) 924-6700
Confort & Co/ 47-47 Austell Pl, Long Island, NY .... (212) 729-8900
Consolidated/Drake Press/ 5050 Parkside Ave,
  Philadelphia, PA .... (215) 879-1400
Continental Color Inc/ 245 Seventh Ave, New York, NY .... (212) 243-7077
Copley-Litho Inc/ 180 Varick St, New York, NY .... (212) 620-0640
Copy Shop, The/ 275 Seventh Ave, New York, NY .... (212) 924-2700
Craftsman Color Lithographers/ 40 West 25th Street,
  New York, NY .... (212) 675-8200

Creative Lithography Inc/ 263 9th Ave, New York, NY .... (212) 691-9930
Custom Offset Inc/ 180 Varick St, New York, NY..................... (212) 243-4804
Daniels Printing Co/ 40 Commercial, Everett, MA .... (617) 389-7900
Darcy Printing/ 225 Varick St, New York, NY .... (212) 924-1554
Dartmouth Press/ 333 Hudson St, New York, NY .... (212) 929-4508
Dart Printing/ 195 Hudson St, New York, NY .... (212) 925-9533
Davis-Delaney-Arrow/ 141 E 25th St, New York, NY .... (212) 686-2500
Davis Printing Corp/ 640 Dell Rd, Carlstadt, NJ .... (201) 935-5100
Dell Graphics Inc/ 207 W 25th St, New York, NY .... (212) 989-3434
Delta Press/ 100 Sixth Ave, New York, NY.......................... (212) 966-6556
Design Press/ 119 W 23rd St, New York, NY .... (212) 675-2747
Direct Press/Modern Litho/ 386 Oakwood Road,
  Huntington Sta., NY .... (516) 271-7000
D&L Offset Lithography & Co/ 100 Sixth Ave, New York, NY .... (212) 226-3770
Donnelley, R R & Sons Co/ 100 Park Ave, New York, NY .... (212) 490-9500
DV Printing/ 228 E 45th, New York, NY............................ (212) 490-3620
Dynamic Litho Corp/ 16-11 Morenci Lane, Littleneck, NY .... (212) 736-1410
Eastern Reproduction Engravers/ 1250 Main Street,
  Waltham, MA .... (617) 893-0555
Eastern Systems Inc/ 545 W 45th St, New York, NY .... (212) 245-8800
Eastman-Aver Corp/ 19 W 24th St, New York, NY.................. (212) 929-7946
Edinboro Offset Co Inc/ 201 South St, Boston, MA .... (617) 542-0908
Edison Litho/ 418 W 25th, New York, NY........................... (212) 741-2212
Eilert/Appleton Printing Corp/ 318 W 39th St, New York, NY....... (212) 563-0300
Einson Freeman Inc/ 20-10 Mappel Av, Fairlawn, NJ .... (201) 423-1900
Elm Press Co/ 38 E 29th St, New York, NY .... (212) 242-1277
Empire Color Lithographers Inc/ 200 Varick St, New York, NY ..... (212) 924-7866
Esquire Photo Engraving Co Inc/ 4 W 22nd St, New York, NY....... (212) 929-4527
Excel Printing Co. Inc/ 160 Fifth Avenue, New York, NY........... (212) 986-3122
Fenn & Fenn Lithographers/ 75 Varick St, New York, NY .... (212) 925-4800
Fidelity Press/ 2401 Revere Beach Pky, Everett, MA................ (617) 389-6220
Fine Arts Reproductions Co Inc/ 132 Lafayette St,
  New York, NY .... (212) 226-1607
Four Seasons Litho/ 275 Northern Blvd, Great Neck, NY .... (212) 895-7500
Fox Color Separations/ 290 N. Benson Ave. #1, Upland, CA......... (714) 981-5050
Froelich/Greene Litho Corp./ 250 Hudson St, New York, NY........ (212) 691-2450
Gair Mark Press Inc/ 1839 Elizabeth Ave, Rahway, NJ .... (201) 574-3870
General Offset Co Inc/ 234 16th St, Jersey City, NJ .... (212) 925-1700
General Process Corp/ 232 Madison Ave, New York, NY .... (212) 689-9560
Georgian Press Inc, The/ 175 Varick St, New York, NY .... (212) 924-4820
Gerding Printing Co., Inc./ 1600 Eastern Ave, Baltimore, MD....... (301) 276-0800
Gerson Offset/ 333 Hudson St, New York, NY .... (212) 924-5910
Geyer Printing Co Inc/ 3700 Bigelow Blvd, Pittsburgh, PA .... (412) 682-3633
Gramercy Lane Photo Engr/ 114 W 26th St, New York, NY .... (212) 691-9898
Graphic Color Plate Inc./ 230 Park Ave, New York, NY .... (212) 986-3840
Great Lakes Press Corp/ 1441 Broadway, New York, NY .... (212) 944-2020
Griffith, Dexter Inc/ 38 W 21st St, New York, NY .... (212) 243-8400
Grinnell Litho Co Inc/ 185 Grant Ave, Islip, NY .... (516) 581-3300
Grinthal Press Inc/ 45 W 18th St, New York, NY .... (212) 741-0050
G. S. LITHO/ 1 Kero Rd., Carlstadt, NJ .... (201) 933-8585
  See our ad on page 16
Hanover Lithographing Inc/ 131 Varick St, New York, NY .... (212) 989-1710
Harlin Litho/ 48 W 21st, New York, NY .... (212) 675-2035
Harvest Printing Co/ 250 W 54th St, New York, NY .... (212) 246-8635
Head, John R. Printing Co Inc./ 250 W Broadway,
  New York, NY .... (212) 431-4960
Herbick & Held Printing/ 1117 Wolfendale St, Pittsburgh, PA .... (412) 321-7400
Herrmann Printing & Litho Inc/ 7810 Tioga St,
  Pittsburgh, PA .... (412) 243-4100
Herst Litho Inc/ 620 12th Ave, New York, NY .... (212) 245-4666
Hill, Murray Press/ 225 W 34th St, New York, NY .... (212) 563-0364
Hopp Press Inc, The/ 460 W 34th St, New York, NY .... (212) 279-1800
Horan Engraving Co/ 44 W 28th St, New York, NY .... (212) 689-8585
Hudson Printing Co Inc/ 200 Hudson St, New York, NY .... (212) 966-5400
Hughes Printing/ 675 Third Ave, New York, NY .... (212) 972-0540
Hughes Printing of Conn Inc/ 60 Merritt Blvd, Trumbull, CT........ (203) 377-0707
Impact Designs/ 200 Eagle Road Suite 2, Wayne, PA .... (215) 688-0540
Infinity Pixel Inc/ 28 Ormond Park Rd, Brookville, NY .... (516) 626-9500
Instant Type Inc/ 99-19 70th Ave, Forest Hills, NY .... (212) 459-5000
Intaglio Service Co. of N Y/ 40 West 25th Street, New York, NY ...... (212) 924-8277
Intermedia Consultants, Inc./ 335 West 87th Street,
  New York, NY .... (212) 580-9177
Jaylen Lithographers/ 175 Varick St, New York, NY .... (212) 924-6100
Jeremy Printing Corp/ 200 Hudson St, New York, NY .... (212) 966-2223
Jurist Co Inc/ 175 Varick St, New York, NY .... (212) 243-8008

Jurist, Harvey Co Inc/ 350 Hudson Street, New York, NY .... (212) 242-1120
Karr Graphics Corp/ 100 Ave of the Americas, New York, NY........ (212) 966-6000
Kaufmann Press Inc, The/ 4100 Palisade Ave, Union City, NJ .... (201) 866-6977
Kenner Printing Co Inc/ 418 West 25th St, New York, NY .... (212) 807-8800
Kerner Printing Co Inc/ 207 W 25th St, New York, NY.............. (212) 989-5464
Kim Lithographing Corp/ 158 W 27th St, New York, NY .... (212) 989-1250
KLN Publishing Services Inc/ 36 E 30th St, New York, NY .... (212) 686-8200
Koppel, Thomas A & Son Co Inc/ 228 E 45th St, New York, NY..... (212) 687-8556
Kordet Graphics Inc/ 15 Neil Court, Oceanside, NY .... (212) 322-6951
Kroll Stationers Inc/ 145 E 54th St, New York, NY .... (212) 541-5000
Krueger, W A Co/ 6 Beacon Street, Boston, MA .... (617) 227-6785
Krueger, W A Co/ 777 Third Ave, New York, NY .... (212) 826-1030
Kubes, Victor O/ 207 W 25 St, New York, NY .... (212) 989-5464
Lakeland Press/ 215 Park Ave S, New York, NY .... (212) 673-5800
Lanman Co, the/ 10 E 21st Street, New York, NY .... (212) 697-6910
Lasalle Litho Corp/ 52 E 19th St, New York, NY.................. (212) 674-4700
Lasky Co/ 67 E Willow St, Millburn, NJ .... (212) 757-8106
Latham Process Corp/ 200 Hudson St, New York, NY .... (212) 966-4500
Laurel Printing Inc./ 375 Executive Blvd., Elmsford, NY .... (914) 592-5600
Lawrence Lithographers Ltd/ 545 W 45th St, New York, NY .... (212) 489-1210
Lebanon Valley Offset Co Inc/ 40 W 40th St, New York, NY ...... (212) 840-5113
Leebo Printing Co/ 207 W 25th St, New York, NY .... (212) 989-8444
Lehigh Press Inc/ Pennsauken, NJ .... (609) 665-5200
Lenz & Riecker Inc/ 135 W 50th St, New York, NY .... (212) 581-9725
Lerman Graphics/ 230 W 17th St, New York, NY .... (212) 255-9660
Leslie Litho Corp/ 200 E 30th St, New York, NY .... (212) 679-1909
Levine Bros Inc/ 111 Eighth Ave, New York, NY .... (212) 929-8956
Liberty-York Graphic/ 171 Greenwich Street, Hempsted, NY......... (516) 481-8500
Lichtman, Cathy Photograp Prin/ 5 East 17 Street,
    New York, NY.. (212) 924-2500
Lincoln Graphic Arts Inc/ 475 Park Ave S, New York, NY.......... (212) 532-4004
Lind Brothers/ 111 Eighth Ave, New York, NY .... (212) 924-9280
Lithochrome/ 291 Weidner Rd, Rochester, NY..................... (716) 328-2750
Litho 45 Corp/ 406 W 31 St, New York, NY .... (212) 244-4970
Lithocraft Inc/ 50 Broad St, Carlstadt, NJ .... (201) 939-6440
Litho Masters Inc/ 55 Veterans Blvd, Carlstadt, NJ .... (201) 933-5162
Litho Plus Inc/ 33 E 21st St, New York, NY .... (212) 989-6800
Litho Prepsters Inc./ 115 West 29th Street, New York, NY .... (212) 868-5885
Longacre Press, The/ 85 Weyman Ave, New Rochelle, NY........... (212) 824-8558
Lou-Art Offset Co Inc/ 27 W 24 St, New York, NY .... (212) 675-5920
Lynn Art Offset Corp/ 333 Hudson, New York, NY .... (212) 675-7065
Mahl, Herman M/ 520 Albermarle Rd, Cedarhurst, NY .... (516) 295-5456
Mail & Express Printing Co/ 225 Varick St, New York, NY .... (212) 255-4900
Major Press/ 448 West 16th Street, New York, NY .... (212) 255-7008
Mallon, Peter F Inc/ 45-29 Court Sq, Long Island, NY .... (212) 786-2000
Manchester Press/ 111 Eighth Ave, New York, NY .... (212) 924-3690
Manhardt-Alexander Inc/ 25 West 43rd St, New York, NY .... (212) 221-6130
Manhattan Litho Corp/ 350 Hudson St, New York, NY .... (212) 243-8495
Mann/ 100 Sixth Street, New York, NY .... (212) 966-0402
Mansfield Press Inc/ 620 Twelfth Ave, New York, NY .... (212) 265-5411
Marand Lithographers Inc/ 152 W 25th St, New York, NY .... (212) 989-7999
Martin Lithographers Inc/ 10 Skyline Dr, Plainview, NY .... (212) 895-1414
Mascon Printing/ 145 Hudson St, New York, NY .... (212) 966-1777
Mastercraft Lithographers Inc/ 39-01 Queens Blvd,
    Long Island, NY .... (212) 361-7979
Master Eagle Photoengraving Co/ 40 West 25th Street,
    New York, NY.. (212) 924-8277
Medallion Assocs Ltd/ 37 W 20th St, New York, NY .... (212) 929-9130
Medallion Graphics Inc/ 150 Varick St, New York, NY .... (212) 924-1056
Mercury Photo Engravers Corp/ 244 W 49th St, New York, NY .... (212) 489-1855
Midstate Printing/ 230 Ainsley Dr, Syracuse, NY .... (315) 475-4101
Miller, George C & Son Inc/ 20 W 22nd St, New York, NY .... (212) 255-7284
Mill River Press Inc/ 116 Nassau St, Brooklyn, NY .... (212) 875-5832
MJ Offset Corp/ 115 W 27th St, New York, NY .... (212) 242-8655
Mobray Engraving/ 222 W Exchange St, Providence, RI .... (401) 861-1000
Moffa Press Inc/ 351 W 52nd St, New York, NY .... (212) 582-9290
Mohican Press Inc/ 54 W 21st St, New York, NY .... (212) 929-4040
Monarch Services Inc/ 4517 Harford Rd, Baltimore, MD........... (301) 254-9200
Morris Engraving Co/ 30 E 20th St, New York, NY............... (212) 475-7550
M R Printing/ 9 E 38th St, New York, NY .... (212) 889-3430
National Bickford Foremost/ 10 Park Lane, Providence, RI.......... (401) 944-8400
National Reproductions/ 130 Cedar St, New York, NY............. (212) 349-1400
National Reprographics Inc/ 110 W 32nd St, New York, NY .... (212) 736-5674
Neff Lithographing Co/ 233 Spring St, New York, NY .... (212) 255-4690
Newark Printing Co Inc/ 31 Division St, Newark, NJ .... (201) 621-9090

New England Lithograph Co Inc/ 9 Melcher, Boston, MA .... (617) 482-7711
Newport Graphics Inc/ 80 Varick St, New York, NY .... (212) 925-5500
New Victoria Printers Inc/ 7 Bank St, Lebanon, NH .... (603) 448-2264
New York City Press Inc/ 207 W 25th St, New York, NY .... (212) 334-9863
Noral Color Corp/ 211 W 56th St, New York, NY .... (212) 582-6150
Olympic Litho Corp./ 116 Nassau Street, Brooklyn, NY .... (718) 522-2400
Omega Graphics Inc/ 230 W 55 Street, New York, NY.............. (212) 686-5320
Open Studio Ltd/ 187 E Market St, Rhinebeck, NY .... (914) 758-8163
Oxford Litho Co Inc/ 111 8th Ave, New York, NY .... (212) 557-9020
Pan American Lithographing Cor/ 175 Varick St, New York, NY..... (212) 989-7250
Pandick Press Inc/ 345 Hudson St, New York, NY .... (212) 741-5555
Panorama Press/ 460 W 34th, New York, NY .... (212) 594-6220
Pearl, Paul Ltd/ 180 Varick St, New York, NY................... (212) 989-0738
Pearl-Pressman-Liberty/ Fifth & Poplar Sts,
    Philadelphia, PA .... (215) 925-4900
Pearl Process Inc/ 170 Varick St, New York, NY................. (212) 242-4934
Pedeco Printing/ 480 Canal St, New York, NY .... (212) 966-5200
Penco Graphics Inc/ 150 Varick St, New York, NY .... (212) 675-3360
Perni Color Process Corp/ 170 Varick St, New York, NY .... (212) 242-4660
Peter Print Graphics/ 740 Broadway, New York, NY .... (212) 533-2570
Photo Comp Press/ 410 West Street, New York, NY .... (212) 675-0606
Photogravure & Color Co/ Grand & Barrett, Moonachie, NJ .... (212) 924-4840
Phototype Engraving Co/ 7890 Airport Highway,
    Pennsauken, NJ .... (609) 663-4100
Pictorial Powers Inc/ 151 W 40th St, New York, NY .... (212) 840-6460
Pilot Photo Engraving/ 150 W 22nd, New York, NY.............. (212) 691-1616
Pioneer-Moss Inc/ 460 W 34th St, New York, NY .... (212) 947-1550
Plaza Publicity Design & Print/ 56 Vandan, New York, NY .... (212) 807-7086
Polychrome Lithography Co Inc/ 15 W 44th St, New York, NY ..... (212) 840-2930
Port City Press/ 500 Fifth Ave, New York, NY .... (212) 921-9166
Poster Printing Litho&Silk Scr/ 104 E 40th Street,
    New York, NY... (212) 889-4392
Precision Printers Inc/ 16 W 32nd, New York, NY .... (212) 760-0123
Prestone Printing Co Inc/ 450 Seventh Ave, New York, NY......... (212) 695-6441
Pride Offset/ 685 W Shore Rd, Warwick, RI .... (401) 737-2300
Prieston Photo Engraving/ 124 W 24th, New York, NY............ (212) 243-5335
Princeton Polychrome Press/ 861 Alexander Road,
    Princeton, NJ .... (609) 452-9300
Printers Ink, The/ P.O. Box 444, East Northport, NY .... (516) 368-2919
Print Shop Inc, The/ 406 W 31 St, New York, NY .... (212) 736-9603
Pro Color Inc/ 940 Federal Rd, Brookfield, CT .... (203) 775-3155
Promotion Graphics Assoc of Ny/ 160 Varick St, New York, NY..... (212) 989-1376
Publishers Production Int'l/ 940 E 149th St, Bronx, NY .... (212) 292-5536
Quadri Inc/ 10-25 45th Rd, Long Island, NY .... (212) 361-8484
Quality House of Graphics/ 47-47 Van Dam St,
    Long Island Cty, NY .... (212) 784-7400
Raleigh Lithograph Corp/ 100 Ave of the Americas,
    New York, NY.. (212) 966-1880
Ramapo Litho Corp/ 225 Varick St, New York, NY............... (212) 924-2230
Rapoport Printing Corp/ 195 Hudson St, New York, NY .... (212) 226-5501
Redi Decal Co/ 5 Belmont Place, Hicksville, NY .... (516) 938-7197
Redler Inc/ 32-02 Queens Blvd, Long Island Cty, NY .... (212) 729-8080
Regensteiner Printing Group/ 30 Rockefeller Plz,
    New York, NY.. (212) 489-6991
Regina Services Corp/ 180 Varick St, New York, NY .... (212) 777-6700
Reilly New York Graphics/ 540 West 48th Street,
    New York, NY.. (212) 489-7800
Remco/ 54 W 21st St, New York, NY .... (212) 242-4647
Revere Press Inc/ 1001 E Venango St, Philadelphia, PA.............. (215) 425-7600
R I Lithograph/ 35 Monticello Pl, Pawtucket, RI .... (401) 725-0500
Riviera Lithographs/ 45 E 20th St, New York, NY............... (212) 475-8474
Rochester Empire Graphics/ 1260 Lyell Ave, Rochester, NY .... (716) 458-9700
Rolls Offset Printing/ 304 E 45th, New York, NY .... (212) 599-1234
Rothchild Printing Co Inc/ 7900 Barnwell Ave, Elmhurst, NY........ (212) 899-6000
Roycliff Assoc Inc/ 50 John St, Stamford, CT................... (203) 325-1531
Rumford Press/ 475 Park Ave S, New York, NY .... (212) 725-1900
Salzer & Co Inc/ 15 W 38th St, New York, NY .... (212) 840-8498
Sanders Printing Corp/ 350 Hudson St, New York, NY .... (212) 691-1070
Sandy-Alexander/ 645 W 44th, New York, NY .... (212) 765-3035
Schubert, Howard Co Inc/ 51 Rushmore, Westbury, NY .... (212) 895-5280
Scientific Color-Graphics/ 220 W 19th, New York, NY .... (212) 924-5232
Scott Printing SD/ 145 Hudson St, New York, NY .... (212) 226-7100
Seaboard Lithograph Corp/ 37 E 18th St, New York, NY.......... (212) 475-3481
Semline Inc/ 180 Wood Rd, Braintree, MA .... (617) 843-8100
Service Litho Inc/ 505 Kennedy Blvd, Somerdale, NJ .... (609) 346-1515

Seville Graphics Corp/ 150 Varick St, New York, NY.................. (212) 924-1057
Shaw Press, Inc./ 55 Vandam St., New York, NY .... (212) 675-2430
Shear & Son/ 200 Hudson St, New York, NY .... (212) 925-2842
Spartan Offset Printing Co/ 55 Webster Ave,
   New Rochelle, NY.. (914) 576-7330
Specialty Printers of America/ 700 E Parker St,
   Scranton, PA... (717) 342-2203
Spectrum Printing/ 150 Varick St, New York, NY .... (212) 255-3131
Speed-O-Lite Offset/ 531 W 25th, New York, NY .... (212) 242-6666
Spiral Binding Co Inc/ 2 Bridewell Pl, Clifton, NJ .... (201) 471-2800
Sterling Regal Inc./ 304 E. 45th St., New York, NY .... (212) 661-0100
Sterling-Roman Press Inc/ 75 Varick Street, New York, NY.......... (212) 226-1800
Stern Graphics/ 355 Great Neck Rd, Great Neck, NY .... (516) 829-5274
Stevens-Bandes/ 180 Varick St, New York, NY .... (212) 675-1128
Stones/ 44 Brattel St, Cambridge, MA .... (617) 495-0200
Stuart Color Graphics/ 406 W 31st St, New York, NY .... (212) 354-2214
Suburban Publishers/ 50 W 23rd, New York, NY .... (212) 255-8303
Sun Press Inc/ 22-14 40th Ave, Long Island Cty, NY .... (212) 706-0522
Swift, John S Co/ Teterboro, NJ .... (201) 288-2050
Tabard Press Corp, the/ 345 Hudson St, New York, NY .... (212) 924-6260
Tenny Graphics Inc/ 216 E 45th St, New York, NY .... (212) 245-6050
Thebault, L P Company/ Pomeroy Road, Pasippany, NJ .... (201) 884-1300
Thorner-Sidney Press Inc/ 808 Seneca, Buffalo, NY .... (716) 856-4500
TMQ Lithographers/ 153 W 27th St, New York, NY .... (212) 255-0555
Todd Photoprint Inc/ 1600 Broadway, New York, NY .... (212) 245-2440
Triangle Engraving Co/ 229 W 28th St, New York, NY .... (212) 736-8880
Tri-Lon Color Lithographers Lt/ 54 W 21st St, New York, NY....... (212) 255-6140
Trucraft Printing/ 31 W 46th St, New York, NY .... (212) 719-4125
Truglio,Frank & Assoc.Retouch./ 835 3rd Ave, New York, NY ..... (212) 371-7635
2001 Color Seps, Inc/ 135 W 27th, New York, NY .... (212) 691-3000
United Lithographing Corp/ 599 11th Ave, New York, NY .... (212) 246-9750
United Printing/ 55 Colorado Ave, Warwick, RI .... (401) 739-5600
Universal Engraving Co/ 229 W 28th St, New York, NY .... (212) 239-4870
Walker, Johnnie Press/ 128 Lafayette St, New York, NY .... (212) 226-2700
Walker-Prismatic Engraving Cor/ 141 E 25th St, New York, NY..... (212) 689-5353
Wallace Press/ 200 South S, New Providence, NY .... (201) 464-2216
Weber Lithography Inc/ 20 Vandam St, New York, NY .... (212) 243-6755
Wellesley Engravers Inc/ #3 Crest Rd, Wellesley, MA............... (617) 235-3468
West Side Printing & Litho Co/ 99 Madison Ave, New York, NY.... (212) 532-3300
Whitehall Press Inc/ 110 Greenwich St, New York, NY .... (212) 349-6275
Wilbar Photoengraving Co Inc/ 420 Lexington Ave,
   New York, NY.. (212) 247-7500
Winson Litho Inc/ 44-02 11th Street, Long Isle City, NY............ (212) 729-8787
Winthrop Printing Co Inc/ 235 Old Colony Avenue, Boston, MA..... (617) 268-9660
Wintry Press Ltd/ 100 Ave of the Americas, New York, NY......... (212) 219-0700
Wittenstein, Doris Graphic Des/ 430 Lafayette Street #3R,
   New York, NY.. (212) 475-7552
Woodbury & Co Inc/ 485 Fifth Ave, New York, NY .... (212) 683-0851
Wood Press, The/ 515 E 41st St, Paterson, NJ....................... (201) 684-4472
World Color Press/ 485 Lexington Ave, New York, NY.............. (212) 986-2440
Wright Company Inc., The/ 4 Munroe St, Cambridge, MA .... (617) 547-7200
Zap, John Printing/ 23 W 36th St 6th Fl, New York City, NY....... (212) 736-4379
Zarrett Graphics Corp/ 150 Fifth Ave, New York, NY .... (212) 989-6226

TYPOGRAPHERS

AA Typeart Service/ 420 Lexington, New York, NY .... (212) 986-9468
Adcraft Typographers/ 300 Park Ave S, New York, NY .... (212) 245-3434
Adroit Graphic Composition Inc/ 537 Greenwich St,
   New York, NY.. (212) 243-1929
Advani Typographic Associates/ 380 Lafayette St,
   New York, NY.. (212) 475-0840
Advertising Agencies Svce Co/ 216 E 45th St, New York, NY .... (212) 687-0590
Alchus Publications/ 141 S Harrison St, E Orange, NJ .... (201) 673-8560
Almore Graphics/ 48 W 48th Street, New York, NY .... (212) 221-8585
American Typecrafters Inc/ 132 W 21, New York, NY............... (212) 807-1750
AM Varityper/ 11 Mount Pleasant, East Hanover, NJ .... (201) 631-8134
Antiquated Typographers/ 406 W 31st St, New York, NY .... (212) 695-2404
Armstrong, Walter T Inc/ 1309 Noble St, Philadelphia, PA .... (215) 592-7474
Arrow Typographers/ 2-14 Liberty St, Newark, NJ................... (201) 622-0111
Artists Classified/ 260 5th Avenue, New York, NY .... (212) 889-7424
Artography Inc/ 311 W 43rd St, New York, NY .... (212) 582-0466
Asterisk Typographers/ 363 Seventh Ave, New York, NY .... (212) 736-9022
Bair, Estelle/ 1777 Walton Rd, Blue Bell, PA .... (215) 542-7790
Batsch Spectracomp/ 17 South 19 Street, Camp Hill, PA .... (717) 761-3260

Baumwell, M J Typography/ 331 E 38th St, New York, NY........... (212) 661-8787
Biel, Robert Assoc/ 87 Greenwich Ave, Greenwich, CT .... (203) 622-6630
Black Inc/ 165 W 46th, New York, NY................................ (212) 819-0045
Bluestein, Deborah/ 422 S. Main Street, Bradford, MA.............. (617) 374-1309
Bolhack, Samuel Inc/ 381 Park Ave S, New York, NY .... (212) 696-4430
Boro Typographers/ 37 E 21st St, New York, NY .... (212) 475-7850
Cahill Graphics/ 85 Crooks Ave, Clifton, NJ.......................... (201) 772-3300
Capitol-Crosby Typographers In/ 130 Crosby St, New York, NY ..... (212) 966-5750
Cardinal Type Svce Inc/ 545 W 45th St, New York, NY .... (212) 489-1717
Carnase Typography/ 145 E 32nd St, New York, NY .... (212) 679-9880
Catherine Graphics/ 350 W 31st, New York, NY .... (212) 736-1130
City Typographic Service Inc/ 387 Park Ave S, New York, NY ...... (212) 686-2760
Cold Comp/ 810 Penn Ave, Pittsburgh, PA............................ (412) 281-5556
Cold Font/ 363 Seventh Ave, New York, NY .... (212) 736-5310
Comet Typographers Inc/ 21 Newtown Rd, Plainview, NY........... (516) 293-2229
Commercial Typographers/ 122 W 26th, New York, NY .... (212) 243-7503
Compmasters/ 34 W 15th St, New York, NY.......................... (212) 924-1729
Compo-Set Typographers Inc/ 200 Hudson St, New York, NY....... (212) 431-4515
Composing Room of Long Island/ 355 Great Neck Road,
   Great Neck, NY.. (516) 829-5274
Composing Room of N E/ 131 Beverly St, Boston, MA............... (617) 742-4866
Compugraphic/ 80 Industrial Way, Wilmington, MA .... (617) 944-6555
Concord Typographic Service In/ 212 Fifth Ave, New York, NY ..... (212) 889-2293
Cresset/Baxter & Spencer Inc/ 110 Greenwich St,
   New York, NY.. (212) 766-9400
C T C/ 7 W 36th St, New York, NY .... (212) 594-3434
Davis & Warde Inc/ 704 Second Ave, Pittsburgh, PA................ (412) 261-1904
Designed Word, the/ 56 W 22nd St, New York, NY .... (212) 675-1171
Design Typographers Inc/ 1220 Broadway, New York, NY .... (212) 947-2299
Dotto Reproductions/ 178 Ocean Avenue, Jersey City, NJ .... (201) 333-0444
Dusch Graphics Inc/ 201 E Grove St, Westfield, NJ .... (201) 233-6292
East Coast Advertising/ 318 E. Main St., Salisbury, MD .... (303) 546-3728
Elizabeth Typesetting Co/ 26 N 26th St, Kenilworth, NJ .... (201) 241-6161
Elroy Typesetting/ 52 E 19th, New York, NY .... (212) 674-1220
Empire Typographers/ 28 W 23rd St, New York, NY .... (212) 741-1150
Etc Graphics, Inc./ 386 Park Ave S, New York, NY .... (212) 889-8777
Expert Type/ 44 W 28th Street, New York, NY .... (212) 532-6222
FACT Typographers Inc/ 29 W 38th St, New York, NY.............. (212) 221-1565
Fine Art Typographers/ 25 W 39th St, New York, NY .... (212) 398-9640
Foto-Ready Production/ 350 E 13th, New York, NY.................. (212) 473-2913
Franklin Typographers Inc/ 225 W 39th St, New York, NY .... (212) 736-4707
Gemini Composition/ 208 W 30th, New York, NY .... (212) 736-8877
Gerard Assoc Photo Type/ 163 W 23rd St, New York, NY .... (212) 691-4960
Graphactory/ 627 Greenwich Street, New York, NY .... (212) 929-3985
Graphic Type Setting/ 36 W Broadway, S Boston, MA............... (617) 269-4266
Graphic Word, The/ 80 Eighth Ave, New York, NY................... (212) 924-1111
Gross, J.J. & Co./ 11 West 25th Street, New York, NY .... (212) 989-9600
Haber Typographers Inc/ 115 W 29th St, New York, NY .... (212) 594-9000
Hamilton Phototypesetting/ 171 Ingram Ave, Pittsburgh, PA........ (412) 922-5176
Harlowe Typography Inc/ 3512 Bladensburg Rd, Brentwood, MD ... (301) 277-8311
Hartog Phototype Inc/ 475 Fifth Ave, New York, NY .... (212) 689-7141
Henricks, Charles/ 75 Varick St, New York, NY .... (212) 925-1572
Hesco/ 50 W 23rd, New York, NY .... (212) 242-4559
H&H Typographic Svce/ 1117 Wolfendale St, Pittsburgh, PA....... (412) 359-2548
Hodges Typographers/ 8814 Brookville Rd, Silver Spring, MD ...... (301) 585-3601
I G I/ 160 Fifth Ave, New York, NY .... (212) 243-0404
Infocomp Inc/ 2611 Stayton St, Pittsburgh, PA...................... (412) 321-9100
Innovative Graphics Int'l Ltd/ 160 Fifth Ave, New York, NY .... (212) 243-0404
Island Compositions Inc/ 287 Skidmore Rd, Deer Park, NY .... (516) 242-4880
Island Typographers/ 6 Burns Avenue Box 1, Hicksville, NY......... (516) 931-2282
Johnson/Ken-Ro Inc/ 393 S Main St, Freeport, NY .... (212) 441-4407
J R I Graphic Communications/ 73 Rudolph Ave,
   Elmwood Park, NJ .... (201) 797-0170
Justified Type Inc/ 528 Clinton Ave, Bridgeport, CT.................. (203) 579-1717
Kalafatis, George/ 3 Anthony Rd, Lexington, MA..................... (617) 862-2338
Klass Advertising/ 112 Broadway, Malverne, NY .... (516) 887-7878
Kommel, Marvin Prods Inc/ 219 E 44th St, New York, NY .... (212) 682-3498
Latent Lettering Co., Inc./ 29 W. 38 St., New York, NY.............. (212) 221-0055
L&B Typo Inc/ 2283 South Ave, Scotch Plains, NJ .... (201) 889-4404
L-C Graphics/ 1096 Rt 22 W, Mountainside, NJ .... (201) 654-8080
LCR Graphics Inc/ 254 W 31st St, New York, NY .... (212) 564-1385
Lettick Typografic Inc/ 227 Wheeler Ave, Bridgeport, CT .... (203) 367-6491
Lettra Graphics Inc/ 364 Manville Rd, Pleasantville, NY .... (914) 769-1955
Lincoln Typographers Inc/ 1140 Broadway, New York, NY.......... (212) 679-7933
Litho Composition Co/ 281 Summer St, Boston, MA................. (617) 482-3236

Lloyd & Germain Typographics/ 17 West 45 Street, New York, NY .... (212) 840-2299
Madison Type/ 232 Madison Avenue, New York, NY .... (212) 889-9840
Malin Typographers Inc/ 270 Lafayette St, New York, NY .... (212) 966-4214
Mangis Typographic Service/ 412 First Ave, Pittsburgh, PA .... (412) 261-0596
Mar•X Myles Composition Inc./ 271 Madison Ave, New York, NY... (212) 683-2100
Master Eagle/ 40 W 25th, New York, NY .... (212) 691-1660
M C S Inc/ 110 West 40th Street, New York, NY .... (212) 840-1327
Meyer, John C & Son Inc/ 432 N Sixth St, Philadelphia, PA .... (215) 627-4320
Michi Japanese/ 141 E 44th, New York, NY .... (212) 883-1215
MKP/ 219 E 44th, New York, NY .... (212) 682-3498
M&M Typographers Inc/ 45 W 18th St, New York, NY .... (212) 243-4645
Monotype Composition Co/ 645 Summer, South Boston, MA .... (617) 269-4188
Monroe Typesetting Service Inc/ 284 N Eighth St, Prospect Park, NJ .... (201) 595-6544
Multilanguage Typographers Inc/ 22-14 40th Ave, Long Island, NY .... (212) 392-6180
Nassau Typographers Inc/ 111 Express, Plainview, NY .... (212) 762-8107
One Seven Typographers/ 491 Broadway, New York, NY .... (212) 226-3481
Ortiz, Armand Typographic Co/ 260 W 29th St, New York, NY ..... (212) 947-3848
O'Sullivan Typographers Inc/ 491 Broadway, New York, NY .... (212) 226-3481
Panagraphics Corp./ 774 Fillmore Ave., Buffalo, NY .... (716) 852-8211
Pastore De Pamphilis Rampone/ 145 E 32nd St, New York, NY..... (212) 889-2221
PHP Typography Inc/ 125 S Ninth St, Philadelphia, PA............. (215) 922-8700
Positive Type/ PO Box 541, Millerton, NY .... (518) 789-3865
Post Graphics Inc/ 463 Barell Ave, Carlstadt, NJ .... (201) 933-6363
Primar Typographers Inc/ 85 Washington St, New York, NY .... (212) 269-7916
Prototype/ 119 W 23rd St, New York, NY.......................... (212) 807-8797
Pulsar Graphics Inc/ 200 Craig Rd, Freehold, NJ .... (201) 780-2880
Purveyors of the Printed Word/ 155 Bank St, New York, NY .... (212) 929-1575
Quinn Lee Daniel/ 20 Lincroft Ave, Old Bridge, NJ .... (201) 679-6279
Reproduction Typographers/ 244 W First Ave, Roselle, NJ........... (201) 241-3200
Rockland Typographical Svcs/ 577 North Rt 303, Blauvelt, NY...... (914) 358-3960
Royal Composing Room Inc/ 387 Park Ave S, New York, NY........ (212) 889-6060
Scarlett Letters Inc./ 75 Spring Street, New York, NY .... (212) 966-3560
Schiller, J Inc/ 37 Meridian Rd, Edison, NJ .... (201) 549-6500
Set-Rite Typographers Inc/ 49 E 21st St, New York, NY .... (212) 777-7750
Sevell, Sid/ 25 West 43, New York, NY .... (212) 840-3300
Snyder Graphics/ 25-29 N Broadway, Yonkers, NY .... (914) 476-8500
SR Linotypers Inc/ 270 Lafayette St, New York, NY .... (212) 925-5190
Stewart Color Lab/ 563 Eleventh Ave, New York City, NY .... (212) 868-1440
Stuart, Edwin H Inc/ 422 First Ave, Pittsburgh, PA .... (412) 261-3896
Swift Typography/ 200 Hudson St, New York, NY .... (212) 925-3680
Techni-Process Lettering/ 216 E 45th St, New York, NY .... (212) 867-0840
TGC/ 305 E 46th St, New York, NY .... (212) 754-9500
T G I/ 221 Park Ave S, New York, NY .... (212) 777-3900
Thomas, John J & Sons Inc/ 121 Fulton St, New York, NY .... (212) 233-5548
Thumb Print Inc/ 44-09 43rd Ave, Sunnyside, NY .... (212) 786-6431
Tone Graphics Inc/ 27 W 24th St, New York, NY .... (212) 675-8900
Topel Typographic Corp/ 27 W 24th St, New York, NY .... (212) 924-4180
Trade Typographers Inc/ 1433 P St Nw, Washington, DC .... (202) 667-3420
Tri-Arts Press/ 331 E 38th St, New York, NY .... (212) 686-4242
Type For U/ 4 Brattle St, Cambridge, MA .... (617) 661-1215
Type Group Inc, The/ 40 West 25th Street, New York, NY .... (212) 691-1670
Type House Inc/ 60 Connolly Pky, New Haven, CT .... (203) 288-8481
Typographic Designers Inc/ 216 E 45th St, New York, NY .... (212) 687-4372
Typographic House/ 63 Melcher, Boston, MA .... (617) 482-1719
Typographic Images Inc/ 9 E 37th St, New York, NY .... (212) 889-8510
Typographics Comm/ 305 E 46th, New York, NY .... (212) 754-9500
Typographics Plus Inc/ 16 W 46th St, New York, NY .... (212) 869-8440
Unitron Graphics/ 180 Varick St, New York, NY .... (212) 255-5500
U S Lithograph, Typographers/ 853 Broadway, New York, NY ...... (212) 673-3210
Varityper/ 11 Mt Pleasant Ave, E Hanover, NJ .... (201) 887-8000
Verilen Graphics/ 3 E 40th Street, New York, NY .... (212) 686-7774
Vulcan Typography Co/ 216 E 45th St, New York, NY .... (212) 557-4990
Wertheim Co/ 75 Varick St, New York, NY .... (212) 966-5913
Western Inc/ 33A Harvard Street, Brookline, MA .... (617) 277-6700
Willmann Paper/ 315 Hudson St, New York, NY .... (212) 989-2700
World Typeface Center Inc/ 145 E 32nd St, New York, NY .... (212) 685-4374
Zimmering & Zinn/ 50 W 23rd St, New York, NY .... (212) 989-3151
Zip Print Inc/ 666 Anderson Ave, Cliffside Park, NJ............... (201) 461-3555

PAPER SUPPLIERS

Accurate Envelope Co Inc/ 320 Lafayette St, New York, NY .... (212) 431-5200
Allan & Gray Corp/ 111 Eighth Ave, New York, NY................. (212) 741-5522
Allied Paper/ 60 East 42 St, New York, NY........................ (212) 661-7755
Alling and Cory/ N Division & Elm Sts, Buffalo, NY .... (716) 852-7200
Alling and Cory/ PO Box 60, Utica, NY .... (315) 736-0111
Alling and Cory/ PO Box 4887, Syracuse, NY .... (315) 432-1200
Alling and Cory/ 55 Snowdrift Rd, Fogelsville, PA................ (215) 395-4200
Alling and Cory/ 485 Terminal St, Camp Hill, PA .... (717) 761-6064
Alling and Cory/ 1300 W Lehigh Ave, Philadelphia, PA .... (215) 223-7700
Alling and Cory/ 2820 W 21st St, Erie, PA........................ (814) 838-3535
Alling and Cory/ Rocky Glen Rd, Moosic, PA .... (717) 342-0213
Alling and Cory/ 2920 New Beaver Ave, Pittsburgh, PA .... (412) 734-2000
Alling and Cory/ 802 Ruffner Ave, Charleston, WV .... (304) 346-0788
Alling and Cory/ 6th St & Boltline Rr, Fairmont, WV .... (304) 363-6500
Alling & Cory/ 30-35 Thomson Ave, Long Island Cty, NY.......... (212) 784-6200
American Printing&Envelope Co/ 900 Broadway, New York, NY .... (212) 475-1204
Ampad Inc/ Holyoke, MA... (413) 536-3511
Andrews/Nelson/Whitehead/ 31-10 48th Ave, Long Island Cty, NY .... (212) 937-7100
Andrews Paper House of York In/ 400 Mulberry St, York, PA...... (717) 846-8816
Antietam Paper Co Inc/ 106 Oakmont Drive, Hagerstown, MD ..... (301) 739-0600
Arrow Paper Co/ 36-24 23rd, Long Island Cty, NY .... (212) 361-1000
Baldwin Paper Co/ 161 Ave of the Americas, New York, NY .... (212) 255-1600
Baltimore-Warner Paper Co/ 1201 67th St, Baltimore, MD .... (301) 866-1500
Barton Duer & Koch Paper Co/ 2420 Schuster Dr, Cheverly, MD ... (301) 322-3300
Beekman Paper Co Inc/ 137 Varick St, New York, NY .... (212) 242-4100
Bulkley Dunton/ 295 Fifth Ave, New York, NY .... (212) 679-5050
Capital Paper Co Inc/ 123 W 19th St, New York, NY .... (212) 255-5010
Carter Rice/ 330 Nutmeg Rd S, S Windsor, CT .... (203) 528-9351
Carter Rice/ 66-D Industry Ave, Springfield, MA .... (413) 788-0901
Carter Rice Storrs & Bement/ 51 Railroad Ave, West Haven, CT.. (203) 932-2202
Carter Rice Storrs & Bement/ 273 Summer St, Boston, MA .... (617) 542-6400
Carter Rice Storrs & Bement/ 402 Walcott St, Pawtucket, RI....... (401) 723-6400
Case Paper Co Inc/ 23-30 Bordon Ave, New York, NY .... (212) 361-9000
Central Paper Co/ 1004 Whitehead Rd Ext, Trenton, NJ .... (609) 883-7500
Champion Int'l Corp/ One Champion Plz, Stamford, CT .... (203) 358-7000
Champion Papers/ 805 3rd Ave, New York, NY .... (212) 758-5950
Charrette/ 31 Olympia Ave, Woburn, MA .... (617) 935-6010
Connecticut Valley Paper & Env/ 134 Chelmsford St, N Billerica, MA.. (617) 935-4488
Consolidated Papers Inc/ 1 Penn Plz, New York, NY .... (212) 736-1550
Copco Papers Inc/ 5 Royal Dr, Mckees Rocks, PA .... (412) 771-3660
Copco Papers Inc/ 1537 Hansford, Charleston, WV .... (304) 346-0727
Craig Envelope/ 12-01 44th Ave, Long Island Cty, NY............. (212) 786-4277
Crane & Co Inc/ Dalton, MA .... (413) 684-2600
Crestwood Paper Co Inc/ 315 Hudson Street, New York, NY .... (212) 989-2700
Cross-Siclare/ 125 Lake Ave, Staten Island, NY .... (212) 442-8900
Darragh Paper Co/ 1000 McKee Ave, Mckees Rocks, PA .... (412) 771-1855
Dennison Mfg Co/ 300 Howard St, Framingham, MA .... (617) 879-0511
Dimayo Packaging Inc/ 4801 Dell Ave, N Bergen, NJ .... (201) 867-1500
Dri Mark Products Inc/ 15 Harbor Park Drive, Port Washington, NY .... (516) 484-6200
Empire Paper Corp/ 1033 Massachusettes Ave, Boston, MA......... (617) 427-0076
Envelope Convertors Inc/ 100 Morgan Ave, Brooklyn, NY .... (212) 386-6000
Envelope Factory, The/ 2031 42nd Street, North Bergen, NJ........ (212) 564-6310
Esleeck Mfg Co/ Canal St, Turners Falls, MA .... (413) 863-4326
Franklin-Cowan Paper Co/ 210 Ellicott St, Buffalo, NY .... (716) 854-5954
Fraser Paper Ltd/ 2 Greenwich Plz, Greenwich, CT .... (203) 661-3040
Garrett-Buchanan Co/ 9525 Berger Rd, Columbia, MD .... (301) 730-8085
General Envelope Co Inc/ 1010 44th Ave, New York, NY .... (212) 242-1151
General Paper Corp/ Sexton Rd, Mckees Rocks, PA .... (412) 771-3515
Gilbert Paper/ 200 Park Avenue, New York, NY................... (212) 949-1046
Glatfelter, P H Co/ 228 S Main St, Spring Grove, PA.............. (717) 225-4711
Goodkin, M P Co/ 140-146 Coit St, Irvington, NJ .... (201) 371-1199
Gotham Paper Co Inc/ 560 Ferry St, Newark, NJ .... (201) 589-1660
Gould Paper Corp/ 315 Park Ave South, New York, NY .... (212) 505-1000
Hammermill/ 101 Park Ave Room 2507, New York, NY .... (212) 949-5757
Hammermill Paper Co/ Erie, PA .... (814) 456-8811
Hobart/McIntosh Paper Co/ 51 E 42nd St, New York, NY .... (212) 697-5320
Hollingsworth & Vose Co/ 112 Washington St, E Walpole, MA...... (617) 668-0295
Holyoke Card & Paper Co/ PO Box 3450, Springfield, MA .... (413) 732-2107

Hudson Valley Paper Co/ 981 Broadway, Albany, NY .... (518) 436-8481
Hudson Valley Paper Co/ 107 Brink St, Endwell, NY................... (607) 748-7315
International Paper/ 77 W 45th, New York, NY .... (212) 536-6000
James River Corp./ Adams, MA .... (413) 743-0290
James River Corp./ Groveton, NH .... (603) 636-1154
James River Corp/ Southampton, PA .... (215) 364-3900
Lehigh Valley Paper/ P O Box 1029, Allentown, PA .... (215) 434-9571
Lewmar Paper Co/ 370 Adams St, Newark, NJ .... (201) 589-2800
Lexington Paper Co/ 157 Hobart, Hackensack, NJ .... (201) 487-2306
Lindenmeyr Paper Co./ 42 Rumsey Rd, E Hartford, CT .... (203) 289-6444
Lindenmeyr Paper Co./ 53rd Ave at 11th St,
    Long Island Cty, NY .... (203) 637-4381
Lindenmeyr Paper Co./ 35 Mt Washington Ave, Boston, MA .... (617) 268-9280
Lindenmeyr Paper Co./ 245 Butler Ave, Lancaster, PA............... (717) 397-2111
Lindenmeyr Paper Co/ 919 Wallace St, Philadelphia, PA .... (215) 235-9000
Linweave Fine Paper Inc/ 10 Linweave Drive, Holyoke, MA .... (413) 536-6410
Lorles Paper Co/ 465 Alfred Ave, Teaneck, NJ .... (201) 833-2311
Lowe Paper Co/ River Street, Ridgefield, NJ .... (201) 945-4900
Ludlow Corp/ 145 Rosemary St, Needham Hts, MA .... (617) 444-4900
Makepeace, B. L./ 125 Guest Street, Boston, MA..................... (617) 782-3800
Mead Corp/ 10 High St, Boston, MA .... (617) 426-4400
Mead Merchants/ S 17th St & Merriman St, Pittsburgh, PA .... (412) 481-2800
Millar, Geo W & Co Div G W M/ 161 Ave of the Americas,
    New York, NY... (212) 741-6100
Millcraft Paper Co/ 6125 Wattsburg Rd, Erie, PA .... (814) 825-3070
Millers Falls Paper Co/ Millers Falls, MA........................... (413) 659-3911
Milton Paper Co Inc/ 100 W 22nd, New York, NY.................... (212) 929-6721
Milton Paper Co of NJ/ 40 Jackson St, Passaic, NJ .... (212) 929-6721
Mohawk Paper Mills Inc/ 465 S Saratoga St, Cohoes, NY .... (518) 237-1740
Monadnock Paper Mills Inc/ Bennington, NH .... (603) 588-3311
Morris Paper Co/ 21st St, Pittsburgh, PA .... (412) 471-2500
Munroe, D F/ 440 Chauncy St Rt 106 PO 228, Mansfield, MA ...... (800) 343-7782
Munroe, D. F./ 351 Middlesex Ave, Wilmington, MA.................. (617) 944-4750
Newbrook Paper/ 32 Bleecker St, New York, NY...................... (212) 966-0100
Old Colony Envelope Co/ Westfield, MA .... (413) 568-2431
Olympic Paper Co/ 75 Varick St, New York, NY .... (212) 925-4050
Paper Mart Inc, The/ 120 Dorsa Ave, Livingston, NJ................. (201) 994-1500
Paper Merchants/ 500 State Rd, Bensalem, PA .... (215) 637-1900

Parsons, Frank Paper Co Inc/ 2270 Beaver Rd, Landover, DC .... (301) 386-4700
Parsons Paper Div/ Holyoke, MA..................................... (413) 532-3222
Paterson Card & Paper Co/ 730 Madison Ave, Patterson, NJ .... (201) 278-2410
Postal Envelope/ 54 Bleecker St, New York, NY .... (212) 966-1953
Pratt Paper Co/ 10 High St, Boston, MA .... (617) 482-4455
Rice, C M Paper Co/ Riverside Ind Park, Portland, ME............... (207) 797-3300
Rice, C M Paper Co/ 276 N State St, Concord, NH .... (603) 225-6678
Rising Paper Co/ Park St, Housatonic, MA............................ (413) 274-3345
RIS Paper Co/ 499 Wildwood, Woburn, MA........................... (617) 938-1800
Ris Paper Co Inc/ 45-11 33rd St, Long Island Cty, NY .... (212) 392-8100
Royal Paper Corp/ 210-216 Eleventh Ave, New York, NY .... (212) 924-3400
Royal Paper of NJ/ 400 Brighton Rd, Clifton, NJ.................... (212) 695-5464
Saxon Industries/ 1230 Ave of the Americas, New York, NY .... (212) 246-9500
Saxon Paper-New York/ 30-10 Starr Avenue,
    Long Island Cty, NY .... (212) 937-6100
Seneca Paper/ 48 King St, Rochester, NY .... (716) 328-9300
Sheaffer Eaton Div of Textron/ 75 South Church Street,
    Pittsfield, MA .... (413) 499-2210
Sloves Organization/ 601 W 26th St, New York, NY .... (212) 620-2830
Strathmore Paper Co/ S Broad St, Westfield, MA..................... (413) 568-9111
Strathmore Paper Co/ 101 Park Avenue Rm 2507, New York, NY .. (212) 949-5888
St Regis Paper Co/ 237 Park Ave, New York, NY .... (212) 808-6000
Union Camp/ 1600 Valley Rd, Wayne, NJ .... (201) 628-9000
Union Card & Paper Co Inc/ 537 Greenwich St, New York, NY...... (212) 691-8700
Virginia Paper Co/ 3310 75th Ave, Landover, MD .... (301) 341-5700
Walker Goulard Plehn Co Inc/ 1225 Franklin Ave,
    Garden City, NY... (516) 683-3390
Warren, S D/ 225 Franklin St, Boston, MA........................... (617) 423-7300
Westvaco Corporation/ 299 Park Ave, New York, NY .... (212) 688-5000
Weyerhaeuser Co/ 1 Plymouth Meeting, Plymouth Mtng, PA........ (215) 825-1110
Weyerhaeuser Co./ 2 Greenwich Plz, Greenwich, CT.................. (212) 822-3500
Whitaker Paper Co/ 1005 Beaver Ave, Pittsburgh, PA .... (412) 322-6500
Wilson, R D & Sons & Co/ PO Box 1486, Clarksburg, WV .... (304) 624-7549
Wilson, R D & Sons & Co/ First & Juliana St,
    Parkersburg, WV.. (304) 422-6479
W W F Paper Corp/New England/ 440 Rutherford Ave,
    Charlestown, MA .... (617) 242-5540
WWF Paper Co, The/ 185 Madison Ave, New York, NY............... (212) 684-1200
Wyman, Donald Inc/ 176 Federal, Boston, MA .... (617) 426-6282

TALENT, MISC. SERVICES

ACTORS, MODELS, TALENT

ABC-TV Casting/ 1330 Sixth Ave, New York, NY .... (212) 887-7777
Abetter Cork/ 262 Mott St, New York, NY .... (212) 925-7755
Abrams Artists & Associates Lt/ 420 Madison Ave--14th Floor,
   New York, NY .... (212) 935-8980
Action Models Inc/ 136 W 32nd St Rm 604, New York, NY .... (212) 279-3720
Act 48 Mgmt/ 1501 Broadway, New York, NY .... (212) 354-4250
Actors Group Agency/ 157 W 57th, New York, NY .... (212) 245-2930
Adams, Bret/ 448 West 44th St, New York, NY .... (212) 765-5630
Agency for Models, the/ 108 A Appleton St, Boston, MA.............. (617) 267-4211
Agency for Performing Arts/ 888 7th Ave, New York, NY .... (212) 582-1500
Agents for the Arts/ 1650 Broadway, New York, NY .... (212) 247-3220
Albert, Mildred L/ 137 Newbury St, Boston, MA........................ (617) 266-1282
All Media Productions/ 1 Bay St, Boston, MA............................ (617) 482-8983
All Tame Animals Inc/ 37 West 57th St, New York City, NY .... (212) 752-5885
All The Way Live/ 306 N Market St, Wilmington, DE .... (215) 324-1765
Amato, Michael/ 1650 Broadway, New York, NY .... (212) 247-4456
Amberley Stables Inc/ Mckinstry Rd, Gardiner, NY .... (914) 255-0982
Ambrose Co, The/ 1466 Broadway, New York, NY .... (212) 921-0230
American Drapery/Carpet/ 257 Park Ave S, New York, NY .... (212) 477-9400
American Int'l Talent/ 166 W 125th St, New York City, NY .... (212) 663-4626
American Musicians Union, Inc./ 8 Tobin Court, Dumont, NJ .... (201) 384-5378
American Program Bureau/ 850 Boylston Street,
   Chestnut Hill, MA .... (617) 731-0500
American Talent Int'l/ 888 Seventh Ave, New York, NY .... (212) 977-2300
Anderson, Beverly/ 1472 Broadway, New York, NY .... (212) 944-7773
Animal Actors Int., Inc./ Rd. 3 Box 221, Washington, NJ .... (201) 689-7539
Art Flag Co/ 6 West 18th St, New York, NY .... (212) 473-8282
Artists Supply House/ 448 Market St, Saddlebrook, NJ .... (201) 843-7828
Associated Artists Talent Agcy/ 311 West 43rd St 606,
   New York, NY .... (212) 974-0044
Associated Booking Corp/ 1995 Broadway, New York City, NY ..... (212) 874-2400
Astor, Richard/ 1697 Broadway, New York City, NY .... (212) 581-1970
Baldwin-Scully/ 501 Fifth Ave, New York, NY .... (212) 922-1330
Barbizon Agency/ 3 E 54th St, New York City, NY .... (212) 371-3617
Barbizon Agency/ 480 Boylston St, Boston, MA......................... (617) 266-6980
Barbizon Agency/ 4550 Montgomery Ave, Washington, DC .... (301) 656-5996
Barbizon Agency/ 80 Broad St, Red Bank, NJ .... (201) 842-6161
Barbizon Agency/ 2816 Morris Ave, Union, NJ .... (201) 964-8925
Barbizon Agency/ 1675 White Horse-Mercerville, Trenton, NJ........ (609) 586-3310
Barry Agency/ 165 W 46th, New York, NY .... (212) 869-9310
Bauman & Hiller/ 250 W 57th, New York, NY .... (212) 757-0098
Beauty Bookings/ 130 W 57th St, New York City, NY .... (212) 977-7157
Bee Beck Talent/ 45 W 45th, New York, NY .... (212) 944-5724
Beilin, Peter Agency Inc/ 230 Park Ave, New York, NY .... (212) 949-9119
Berlin, Lisa Management Inc/ 253 West 72 Street,
   New York City, NY .... (212) 877-6187
Berloni, Wm Theatrical Animals/ 314 W 52nd Street,
   New York City, NY .... (212) 974-0922
Big Beauty Models/ 159 Madison Ave, New York City, NY .... (212) 685-1270
Birnbaum, Charlotte (Voice Ov)/ 32 Lynah Road, Stamford, CT ..... (203) 968-0583
Bishop, Kearney/ 1697 Broadway, New York, NY .... (212) 581-6200
Bloom, Michael J/ 400 Madison Ave, New York City, NY .... (212) 832-6900
Boston Agency, The/ 350 Beacon Street, Boston, MA.................. (617) 247-0200
Brats/ 527 Madison Avenue, New York, NY .... (212) 752-6090
Brennan, Gloria International/ 1720 Belmont Ave,
   Baltimore, MD .... (301) 484-2766
Brinker, Jane Ltd/ 51 W 16th, New York, NY .... (212) 924-3322
Broadcast Business Consultants/ 10 E. 40th St.,
   New York, NY .... (212) 679-4970
Brown, Deborah Casting/ 250 W. 57th St. #2608, New York, NY .. (212) 581-0404
Buchwald, Don & Assoc/ 10 E 44th, New York, NY .... (212) 867-1070
Cameo Kids Casting/ 392 Boylston St, Boston, MA .... (617) 536-6004
Canales, Louis, Inc/ 300 East 46 St, New York City, NY .... (212) 986-8422
Carroll, James/ 9204 Summit Rd., Silver Spring, MD .... (301) 588-8324
Carter, Kit Casting Director/ 160 W. 95 St., New York, NY .... (212) 864-3147
Casting Company, The/ 636 Beacon St, Boston, MA .... (617) 536-0881
Cataldi, Richard/ 180 7th Avenue, New York, NY....................... (212) 741-7450
CBS-TV Casting/ 51 W 52nd, New York, NY .... (212) 975-2263
Central Casting/ 330 N. Charles St. #612, Baltimore, MD........... (301) 962-8272
Charney, Sue Models Ltd/ 641 Lexington Ave,
   New York City, NY .... (212) 751-3005
Claire Casting/ 118 E 28th St, New York, NY .... (212) 889-8844

Click Model Management Inc/ 881 7th Ave Carnegie HI #1110,
   New York, NY .... (212) 245-4306
Colello, Jac/ 201 E. 17th St., New York, NY .... (212) 505-7848
Coleman-Rosenberg/ 667 Madison Ave, New York City, NY.......... (212) 838-0734
Collier Bob Sucess Seminars/ 1560 Broadway Suite 509,
   New York, NY .... (212) 719-9636
Colquhoun, Mary Casting/ 47 W 68th St, New York, NY .... (212) 877-3176
Complete Casting/ 240 West 44th Street, New York, NY .... (212) 382-3835
Conover, Joyce Agency/ 33 Gallowae, Westfield, NJ .... (201) 232-0908
Contact Studios/ 165 W 47th, New York, NY .... (212) 354-6400
Contemporary Casting Ltd/ 16 W 46th, New York, NY .... (212) 575-9450
Cooper, Bill Assoc/ 224 W 49th, New York, NY .... (212) 307-1100
Copley 7 Models & Talent/ 29 Newbury Street, Boston, MA .... (617) 267-4444
CTP Casting/ 22 W 27th, New York, NY .... (212) 696-1100
Cunningham, Wm D/ 919 Third Ave, New York, NY .... (212) 832-2700
David's Outfitters/ 36 W 20th St, New York, NY .... (212) 691-7388
Dawn Animal Agency Inc/ 160 W 46th St, New York City, NY ...... (212) 575-9396
Deacy, Jane/ 300 E 75th, New York, NY .... (212) 752-4865
Deanda, Ramon/ PO Box 362 Planetarium Station, New York, NY .. (212) 580-2236
Deron, Johnny/ 30-63 32nd St, Astoria, NY .... (212) 728-5326
De Seta, Donna Casting/ 424 West 80th Street, New York, NY ..... (212) 239-0988
DHKPR/ 165 West 46th Street Suite 710, New York, NY .... (212) 869-2880
Diaz, Oliverio/ 866 Broadway, New York, NY .... (212) 475-7080
Dillworth, Francis/ 496 Kinderkamack Rd, Oradell, NJ .... (201) 265-4020
Dipene, Cunningham Escott/ 919 Third Ave, New York City, NY .... (212) 832-2700
DMI Talent Assoc Faces&Fashion/ 250 W 57th St Ste 713,
   New York, NY .... (212) 264-4650
Double Take/ 1501 Broadway, New York City, NY .... (212) 354-4250
Draper, Stephen/ 37 W 57th, New York, NY .... (212) 421-5780
Dreamweavers - Female Athletes/ 110 W. 40th St. #501,
   New York, NY .... (212) 869-2172
Duffy & Quinn/ 366 Fifth Ave, New York, NY .... (212) 688-2885
Dulcina Eisen Assoc/ 154 E 61st, New York, NY .... (212) 355-6617
East, Phillip/ 6108 S. Kimbark, Chgo. New York, NY .... (212) 246-8484
Wagner, Leslie/ 527 W 110th, New York, NY .... (212) 662-7584
Elite Model Management/ 150 E 58th St, New York, NY .... (212) 888-6299
Elliott, Tom Productions/ 276 Cambridge St. Ste. 4,
   Boston, MA .... (617) 227-7277
Entertainment Unlimited Artist/ 64 Division Ave,
   Levittown, NY .... (516) 735-5550
Evans, Pat Models/ 3850 H.M.T. W. Ste. 6c, Riverdale, NY .... (212) 884-4785
Faces International/ 8833 Sunset Blvd, Penthouse,
   Los Angeles, CA... (213) 463-2237
Fay, Sylvia/ 71 Park Ave, New York, NY .... (212) 889-2626
Feiden, Margo Galleries/ 51 E 10th, New York, NY .... (212) 677-5330
Ferrari, Richard Management/ 74 Riverside Drive Loft 2R,
   New York, NY .... (212) 877-1214
Feuer & Ritzer/ 1650 Broadway, New York, NY .... (212) 765-5580
Fields, Marje/ 165 W 46 Room 1205, New York City, NY .... (212) 581-7240
Fifi Oscard/ 19 W 44th, New York, NY .... (212) 764-1100
Finger, Leonard/ 1501 Broadway, New York, NY .... (212) 944-8611
Flight 485/ 295 Madison Ave, New York City, NY .... (212) 751-6522
Ford Model Shoppe/ 176 Newbury St., Boston, MA.................... (617) 266-6939
Ford Models Inc/ 344 E 59th St, New York City, NY .... (212) 753-6500
Foster-Fell/ 26 W 38th, New York, NY .... (212) 944-8520
4-B Talents/ 1697 Broadway, New York, NY .... (212) 246-1606
Funny Face/ 527 Madison Ave, New York, NY........................... (212) 752-4450
Gage Group/ 1650 Broadway, New York, NY .... (212) 541-5250
Galvin Associates/ 163-21 Depot Rd, Flushing, NY .... (212) 445-4110
Garcia-Make-Up & Hair/ 240 E 27th St, New York City, NY .... (212) 889-3028
George, Margo/ 159 West Main St PO Box 645, Goshen, NY........ (914) 294-8144
Gilbert the Magician/ 60 E 42nd, New York, NY .... (212) 687-4185
Gilla Roos Ltd/ 527 Madison Ave, New York, NY .... (212) 758-5480
Ginori Fifth Ave/ 711 Fifth Ave, New York, NY .... (212) 752-8790
Grant, Peggy Assoc/ 1650 Broadway, New York, NY................... (212) 586-1452
Greco, Maria Casting/ 888 8th Ave, New York, NY .... (212) 757-0681
Greenman, Leon R Inc/ 21 Park Pl, New York, NY .... (212) 227-1761
Hadley, Peggy Ltd/ 250 W 57th, New York, NY .... (212) 246-2166
Hanns Wolters/ 10 W. 37th St., New York, NY.......................... (212) 714-0100
Hart Agency, The/ 137 Newbury St, Boston, MA........................ (617) 262-1740
Harth, Ellen Inc/ 149 Madison Ave, New York, NY .... (212) 686-5600
Hartig, Michael Agency Ltd/ 527 Madison Ave,
   New York City, NY .... (212) 759-9163
Healy, Bob/ 912 Curtis Avenue, Point Pleasant, NJ .... (201) 899-4740
Hempstead China/ 27 William St, New York, NY .... (212) 344-6970

Henderson/Hogan/ 200 W 57th, New York, NY.......................... (212) 765-5190
Henry, June/ 119 W 57th, New York, NY................................... (212) 582-8140
Herman & Lipson Casting Inc/ 24 W 25th, New York, NY .... (212) 807-7706
Hertz Rent-A-Car/ 501 W. Lombard St., Baltimore, MD .... (301) 332-0016
Hesseltine/Baker/ 165 West 46th Room 409, New York, NY........ (212) 921-4460
Hudson's/ 93 Third Ave, New York, NY................................... (212) 598-0020
Hughes/Moss Casting Ltd/ 311 W 43rd St, New York, NY .... (212) 307-6690
Hunt, Diana/ 44 W 44th, New York, NY................................... (212) 391-4971
Hyde-Hamlet Casting Inc/ 165 West 46th St Suite 1115,
    New York, NY.. (212) 730-1842
IMC/ME Model Management/ 120 W 41st St 5th Fl, NY, NY....... (212) 869-8590
In-Casting/ 220 E 63rd, New York, NY.................................... (212) 752-5833
International Legends Inc/ 40 E 34th St Ste 1600,
    New York, NY.. (212) 684-4600
International Model Agency/ 232 Madison Ave Ste 609,
    New York, NY.. (212) 686-9053
Int'l Creative Mgt Inc/ 40 W 57th, New York, NY..................... (212) 556-5600
Ivry, Marian Agency/ 1650 Broadway, New York, NY................ (212) 586-2760
Jan J Agency Inc/ 222 E 46th St, New York City, NY.................. (212) 490-1875
Johnson-Liff/ 1501 Broadway, New York, NY........................... (212) 391-2680
Johnston Agency/ 4 Bramble Ln., Riverside, CT .... (203) 637-5949
Jordan, Joe Talent/ 200 W 57 St, New York, NY...................... (212) 582-9003
Kabram & Sons/ 257 Bowery, New York, NY............................ (212) 477-1480
Kahn, Jerry Inc./ 853 Seventh Ave. Suite 7C, New York, NY ...... (212) 245-7317
Kahn, Tony/ 18 Addison St., Arlington, MA............................. (617) 646-5649
Kara, Michael/ 641 West 59th St, New York, NY...................... (212) 582-0132
Kay Models, Ltd/ 328 E 61st St, New York, NY .... (212) 308-9560
Kebbe, Charles Associates/ 33 W 60th St, New York, NY .... (212) 490-1773
Kennedy Artists Reps/ 881 Seventh Ave, New York City, NY ...... (212) 675-3944
Kid, Bonnie Agency/ 250 W 57th St, New York City, NY............. (212) 246-0223
King, Archer Ltd/ 1440 Broadway, New York City, NY................ (212) 764-3905
Kirk, Roseanne/ 527 Madison Ave, New York, NY .... (212) 888-6711
Klein, Maryellen/ 330 E. 33rd St., New York, NY...................... (212) 683-6351
KMA Assoc/ 303 W 42nd, New York, NY................................. (212) 581-4610
Kolmar-Luth/ 1501 Broadway Suite 201, New York, NY............. (212) 730-9500
Kornblau Voice-Model-Acting/ B-6 Sea Aire, Somers Point, NJ ...... (609) 927-8983
Kramer/Nigro Co/ 234 West 81st, New York, NY .... (212) 580-6898
Kressel, Lynn/ 157 W 57th, New York, NY............................... (212) 581-6990
Kumin, Sihon E Casting/ 250 West 57th Street, New York, NY...... (212) 245-7670
Lakin, Gaye/ 345 E. 81st St., New York, NY............................ (212) 861-1892
Lantz Office/ 888 7th Ave, New York, NY .... (212) 586-0200
Larner, Lionel/ 850 Seventh Ave, New York, NY .... (212) 246-3105
Lawrence, Joanna Agency Inc/ 82 Patrick Rd, Westport, CT .... (203) 226-7239
L B H Assoc Ltd/ 1 Lincoln Plz, New York, NY......................... (212) 787-2609
Leaverton Assoc/ 1650 Broadway, New York, NY..................... (212) 541-9640
Leighton, Mr Jan Voices-Actor/ 205 W 57 St., New York, NY...... (212) 757-5242
Lenny, Jack Assoc/ 140 W 58th St, New York City, NY .... (212) 582-0270
Lewis, Lester/ 110 W 40th, New York, NY............................... (212) 921-8370
L'Image Model Management Inc/ 114 E. 32 St., New York, NY..... (212) 725-2424
Little Women/ New York, NY... (212) 685-1270
Long Island Game Farm & Zoo/ Chapman Blvd, Manorville, NY ..... (516) 878-6644
Love, Harriet/ 412 W Broadway, New York, NY .... (212) 966-2280
Malige, Didier (Hair By)/ 105 West 55 Street, New York, NY....... (212) 245-0200
Manhattan Doll Hospital/ 176 Ninth Ave, New York, NY .... (212) 989-5220
Mannequin Models Inc/ 730 Fifth Ave, New York City, NY .... (212) 586-7716
MariellaSmithMasters, Makeup/ 105 West 55 Street,
    New York, NY.. (212) 245-0200
Martinelli Attractions/ 888 Eighth Ave, New York, NY.............. (212) 586-0963
Matama/ New York, NY.. (212) 580-2236
McCorkle-Sturtevant Casting Lt/ 240 W 44th, New York, NY ...... (212) 888-9160
Mccullough Models & Talent/ 8 S Hanover Ave,
    Atlantic City, NJ... (609) 822-2222
McDermott, Marge/ 216 E 39th St, New York, NY.................... (212) 889-1583
MCL Casting/ 160 W 46th St, New York, NY............................ (212) 921-9488
Media Power Associates/ 2127 Maryland Ave., Baltimore, MD....... (301) 243-6716
Meredith Agency, The/ 91 Overlook Ave, Wayne, NJ .... (201) 694-7802
M E W Agency/ 370 Lexington Ave, New York, NY.................... (212) 889-7272
MHR Group, The/ 436 Ferry St., Newark, NJ........................... (201) 589-3966
Midiri Models Inc/ 1920 Chestnut St, Philadelphia, PA .... (215) 561-5028
Miller, Eleanor C./ 29 W. Indiana Ave., Beach Haven, NJ .... (609) 492-4112
MMG / Marcia's Kids/ 250 W 57th St, New York, NY .... (212) 246-4360
MMI/John Casablancas/ 123 East 54 Street, New York, NY .... (212) 980-8339
Model Shoppe, The/ 176 Newbury St, Boston, MA .... (617) 266-6939
Models/Models/ 37 E 28th St, New York City, NY .... (212) 685-0053
Models Service Agency/ 1457 Broadway, New York, NY............. (212) 944-8896

Morris, William/ 1350 Ave of the Americas,
    New York City, NY.. (212) 586-5100
Mystique Model Management/ 36 E 23rd St, New York, NY .... (212) 228-1424
National Talent Associates/ 186 Fairfield Rd, Fairfield, NJ .... (201) 575-7300
National Talent Associates/ 40 Railroad Avenue,
    Valley Stream, NY.. (212) 343-6730
Navarro/Bertoni/ 25 Central Pk W, New York, NY.................... (212) 765-4251
News & Entertainment Corp, The/ 230 West 55 Street,
    New York, NY.. (212) 765-5555
NY Pyrotechnic Prod Co Inc/ Assoc Rd, Bellport Li, NY.............. (516) 286-0088
One Woman Antique Clothing/ 336 Columbus Ave, New York, NY .. (212) 724-2223
Oppenheim-Christie/ 565 Fifth Ave, New York, NY................... (212) 661-4330
Oscard, Fifi Assoc Inc/ 19 W 44th St, New York City, NY .... (212) 764-1100
Ostertag, Barna/ 501 Fifth Ave, New York, NY........................ (212) 697-6339
Our Agency/ 19 W. 34. St. #700, New York, NY .... (212) 736-9582
Packwood, Harry/ 342 Madison Ave Ste 1912, New York, NY ...... (212) 682-5858
Palmer, Dorothy/ 250 W 57th, New York, NY.......................... (212) 765-4280
Pasciuto, Joanne Inc/ 1457 Broadway, New York, NY............... (212) 944-6420
Pipino, Marc (Hair By)/ 105 West 55 Street, New York, NY .... (212) 245-0200
Plus Model Management/ 49 W 37th St, New York City, NY........ (212) 997-1785
Poko Puppets Inc/ 12 Everit St, Brooklyn, NY .... (718) 522-0225
Precola Devore Model Agency/ 1341 G St NW Colorado Bldg,
    Washington, DC... (202) 347-2997
Premier Talent/ 3 E 54th, New York, NY .... (212) 758-4900
Pretty People & Co., Ltd./ 296 Fifth Ave. 5th Flr. Ph.,
    New York, NY.. (212) 714-2060
Print Place, The/ 510 Madison Ave, New York, NY................... (212) 753-3810
Profiles Div Kronic&Kelly Agy/ 171 Madison Ave Suite 1314,
    New York, NY.. (212) 684-5223
Pulvino & Howard/ 215 Park Ave S, New York, NY .... (212) 477-2323
Rapp, Charles Ents/ 1650 Broadway, New York, NY .... (212) 247-6646
Reed,Sweeney, Reed Casting Inc/ 1780 Broadway, New York, NY... (212) 265-8541
Reminiscence/ 175 MacDougal St, New York, NY..................... (212) 477-4051
Rogers, Wallace Inc/ 160 E 56th, New York, NY...................... (212) 755-1464
Roos, Gilla Ltd/ 555 Madison, New York City, NY .... (212) 758-5480
Rubinstein, Bernard/ 215 Park Ave S, New York, NY .... (212) 460-9800
Ryan, C V Enterprises/ 200 W 57th St, New York City, NY .... (212) 245-2225
Sagarino, Don Studios/ 606 Farmington Avenue, Hartford, CT ...... (203) 236-5897
Sanders, Honey/ 229 W 42nd, New York, NY........................... (212) 947-5555
Sanford Leigh/ 527 Madison Ave, New York, NY .... (212) 752-4450
Savina And The Jazztet/ 825 Madison Avenue, New York, NY........ (212) 734-4000
Schuller Talent Inc/ 667 Madison Ave, New York City, NY .... (212) 758-1919
Schur, Edie F., Inc./ 176 E. 71 St., New York, NY..................... (212) 734-5100
Schwab, Anne Model Store/ 1529 Wisconsin Avenue NW,
    Washington, DC... (202) 333-3560
Scott, Dick Ents/ 159 W 53rd, New York, NY .... (212) 246-6096
Senatore, Peggy/ 515 E. 79 St., New York, NY .... (212) 675-8800
SERENDIPITY MODELS&TALENT LTD/ 3130 Maple Drive NE Ste. 19,
    Atlanta, GA.. (404) 237-4040
Shapiro, Barbara Casting/ 111 W 57th, New York, NY .... (212) 582-8228
Silver, Monty/ 200 W 57th, New York, NY.............................. (212) 765-4040
Smith, R L Models/ 171 Madison Ave, New York, NY .... (212) 889-2283
Smith, Susan Agency, The/ 850 Seventh Ave,
    New York City, NY.. (212) 581-4490
Soglio, Anthony/ 423 Madison Ave, New York, NY .... (212) 751-1850
Soho Rep Thr/ 19 Mercer St, New York, NY .... (212) 925-2588
Starchild, Adam/ Box 5474, New York, NY............................. (212) 972-1020
Starkman Agency Inc/ 1501 Broadway, New York City, NY......... (212) 921-9191
Stein, Lillian/ 1501 Broadway, New York, NY .... (212) 840-8299
STE Representation Limited/ 888 Seventh Ave, New York, NY........ (212) 246-1030
S T E Representation Ltd/ 888 Seventh Ave,
    New York City, NY.. (212) 246-1030
Sullivan, Abby Casting/ 7816 Blackberry Ave., St. Louis, MO .... (314) 726-4596
Sutor, Paula/ 5 North Square, Boston, MA.............................. (617) 367-2234
Talent Reps Inc/ 20 E 53rd, New York, NY............................. (212) 752-1835
Taylor Royal Casting/ 2308 S Road, Baltimore, MD................... (301) 466-5959
Tent & Trails/ 21 Park Pl, New York, NY................................ (212) 227-1760
Thomas, Jean Inc/ 260 Fifth Ave, New York, NY...................... (212) 683-2111
Thomas, Michael/ 22 E 60th, New York, NY............................ (212) 755-2616
Todd, Joy/ 250 W 57th, New York, NY .... (212) 765-1212
Troy, Gloria/ 1790 Broadway, New York, NY .... (212) 582-0260
Universal Attractions/ 218 W 57th St, New York, NY .... (212) 582-7575
Universal Images/ 505 Fifth Ave., 10th Floor, New York, NY .... (212) 661-3896
Wandon Music Company/ P O Box 1436 FDR Station,
    New York, NY.. (212) 772-1068

Waters, Bob/ 510 Madison Ave, New York, NY........................... (212) 593-0543
Weber, Joy Casting/ 250 W 57th St, New York, NY.................... (212) 245-5220
Weinstein, Jordan/ P.O. Box 215, Boston, MA........................... (617) 267-5096
Weist-Barron School for Acting/ 35 W 45 St, New York, NY........ (212) 840-7025
Wilhelmina Models Inc/ 9 E 37th St, New York City, NY............. (212) 532-7141
Willoughby, Anita/ 267 E. 7th Street, New York, NY.................. (212) 673-1448
Witt, Peter Assoc Inc/ 215 E 79th St, New York City, NY............ (212) 861-3120
Wolters, Hans/ 342 Madison Ave, New York, NY....................... (212) 867-9177
World Wide Modeling Inc/ 40 West 39th Street, New York, NY .... (212) 354-7575
Wright, Ann Representatives/ 136 E 57th St, New York, NY......... (212) 832-0110
Writers & Artists Agency/ 162 W 56th, New York, NY................. (212) 246-9029
Zakin, Dube Ballet & Dance Mgt/ 1841 Broadway, New York, NY .. (212) 582-0140
Zimmerman, Paul Richard/ One Fox Hollow Court,
    Woodclif Lake, NJ... (201) 573-1991
Zirpoli, Dan/ 8204 Yarborough Rd., Towson, MD..................... (301) 685-2370
Zoli/ 146 E 56th St, New York City, NY................................... (212) 758-5959

PROPS, SERVICES, LOCATIONS, SUPPLIES

AAA Appliance Rental/Sales/ 40 W 29th, New York, NY .... (212) 686-8884
AAA Chair & Table Renting/ 561 W 179th, New York, NY .... (212) 927-0200
AAA U-Rent/ 53 Thayer St, New York, NY................................ (212) 568-0859
AA Feather Co/ 16 W 36 St, New York, NY.............................. (212) 695-9470
Abacus Plastic/ 135 West 26th Street, New York, NY................. (212) 807-7966
Abbey Locksmiths/ 1558 Second Avenue, New York, NY............ (212) 535-2289
Abbey Shade/ 1336 Second Ave, New York, NY .... (212) 879-8500
Abet Rent A Fur/ 307 Seventh Ave., New York, NY .... (212) 989-5757
A&B Smith Co/ 819 Liberty Ave, Pittsburgh, PA .... (412) 242-5400
Abstracta Exhibit & Display S/ 38 W 39th St, New York, NY .... (212) 944-2244
Accurate Signs/ 154 Reade Street, New York, NY .... (212) 966-0433
Ace Baby Furniture/ 4855 Broadway, New York, NY .... (212) 567-0320
Ace Rosa Pen Co., Inc./ 155 Park Ave, Lyndhurst, NJ .... (201) 939-1112
Acme Safe Co Inc/ 150 Lafayette, New York, NY...................... (212) 226-2500
Actors Tv Studio/ 1026 Third Ave, New York, NY...................... (212) 371-4244
Adcom Inc/ 2225 N Charles St, Baltimore, MD .... (301) 243-4220
Adcom Inc/ 15815 S Fredrick Rd, Rockville, MD....................... (301) 948-3605
Adirondack Chair/ 219 E 42nd, New York, NY .... (212) 972-1700
Advance Imports/ 431 Ferry St, Newark, NJ............................. (201) 344-1171
Advance Productions Inc/ 29 E 32nd St, New York, NY.............. (212) 686-5244
Adwell Audiovisual Co Inc/ 158 Main St PO Box 67,
    Hempstead, NY .... (212) 343-4462
Agfa-Gevaert/ 275 North St, Teterboro, NJ.............................. (201) 288-4100
AIC Photo, Inc./ 168 Glen Cove Rd, Carle Place, NY................. (516) 742-7300
Albany (NY) Market Research Co/ 167 Chestnut St.,
    Albany, NY .... (518) 463-0092
Alba's Parrot Fantasies/ 1935 New York Ave,
    Huntington Sta, NY.. (516) 271-6953
Alcamo/ 541 W 22nd, New York, NY..................................... (212) 255-5224
Alessandro, Danny/Jacks, Edwin/ 1156 Second Ave,
    New York, NY... (212) 421-1928
Algonquin Hotel/ 59 W 44th St, New York, NY......................... (212) 840-6800
Alizah Cruises/ Nantucket Boat Basin, Nantucket, MA.............. (617) 228-4409
All Languages Svc/ 545 Fifth Ave, New York, NY...................... (212) 986-1688
All-Mobile Video/ 630 Ninth Ave, New York, NY....................... (212) 757-8919
All Tame Animals/ 37 W 57th St, New York, NY........................ (212) 752-5885
Alonzo, Louis (Hair By)/ 105 West 55 Street, New York, NY........ (212) 245-0200
Amalgamated Cordage Corp/ 34 Harbor Park Dr,
    Port Washington, NY.. (516) 484-0780
Amber Artist & Drafting Materi/ 1133 Broadway, New York, NY.... (212) 243-3600
America Hurrah Antiques/ 766 Madison Avenue, New York, NY..... (212) 535-1930
American Hobby Ctr/ 146 W 22nd, New York, NY...................... (212) 675-8922
American Navel Instruments Cor/ 112 Hudson St, New York, NY... (212) 966-7300
American Olean Tile Co/ 150 E 58th, New York, NY .... (212) 688-1177
American Pre-Production Co/ 441 Park Ave S,
    New York City, NY... (212) 679-7924
Amer Soc of Mag Photographers/ 205 Lexington Ave,
    New York, NY... (212) 889-9144
Angelo's/ 146 W 83 Rd St, New York, NY................................ (212) 262-1127
Anichini Gallery/ 7 E 20th, New York, NY................................ (212) 982-7274
Animal Actors Int., Inc./ Rd. 3 Box 221, Washington, NJ........... (201) 689-7539
Animal Outfits for People/ 252 W. 46th St., New York, NY .... (212) 840-6219
Anthony, Michael (Hair By)/ 105 West 55 Street,
    New York, NY... (212) 245-0200

Antique Auto Props/ E. Rutherford, NJ .... (201) 438-9628
Arbee Men's Wear/ 1598 Second Ave, New York, NY............... (212) 737-4661
Ardon, E J/ 176 Brookline, Boston, MA.................................. (617) 536-5120
Aristo Import/ 15 Hunt Road, Orangeburg, NY......................... (914) 359-0720
Arkin-Medo/ 30 E 33rd St, New York, NY................................ (212) 685-1969
Armacost, Julie/ 6 Rockwood P, Edgewater, NJ .... (201) 224-8639
Arthritis Foundation Shop, The/ 1407 Second Ave - 234 E 75 St,
    New York, NY... (212) 535-6666
Artistic Brush Mfg Co/ 103 Central Ave, Clifton, NJ .... (201) 546-1200
Artistic Model Design/ 37 E 29th St, New York, NY................... (212) 684-6093
Artistic Neon By Gasper/ 76-19 60th Lane, Glendale, NY .... (212) 821-1550
Arts & Flowers/ 126-15 89th Ave, Richmond Hill, NY .... (212) 847-4414
A & S Book Co/ 274 W 43rd, New York, NY............................. (212) 695-4897
Ash, Sam/ 160 W 48th, New York, NY.................................... (212) 245-4778
Astor Wines & Spirits/ 12 Astor Pl, New York, NY .... (212) 674-7500
Athenian Gift Shop/ 323 W 42nd, New York, NY .... (212) 247-6244
A Tisket A Tasket/ 993 Second Avenue, New York City, NY .... (212) 308-4066
Atlantic Audio-Visual Corp/ 630 Ninth Ave, New York, NY.......... (212) 581-4004
Atlantic Camera Repair Corp/ 276 Higbie Lane,
    West Islip, NY .... (516) 587-7959
Audio Visual Dynamics/ 8 Budd St., Morristown, NJ .... (201) 993-8500
Aukshunas, Jane/ 366 Harvard St., Cambridge, MA .... (617) 492-2474
Austin Ltd/ 140 E 55th St, New York, NY................................ (212) 752-7903
Avcom Motion Pic Supp & Equip/ 1697 Broadway, New York, NY.. (212) 581-7455
Azteca/ 409 Amsterdam Ave, New York, NY............................ (212) 869-3666
Azuma/ 666 Lexington Ave, New York, NY.............................. (212) 752-0599
Bailey Designs/ 110 Williams St, Malden, MA.......................... (617) 321-4448
Baldassano, Irene/ 16 West 16 Street, New York, NY................ (212) 929-0186
Barbizon Light/ 3 Draper St, Woburn, MA............................... (617) 935-3920
Barclay Church Supply/ 16 Warren St, New York, NY .... (212) 267-9432
Bar Mart Corp/ 123 Bowery, New York, NY .... (212) 226-7148
Barnes, E J/ 630 Ninth Ave, New York, NY .... (212) 757-6600
Barth, Mary/ 70-11 Juno St, Forest Hills, NY .... (212) 261-6290
Bass, Anne/ 23 Barrow St, New York City, NY......................... (212) 741-0924
Baxter Costume/ 24 Lincoln St, Boston, MA............................ (617) 426-5494
Bazaar De La Cuisine/ 1003 Second Ave, New York, NY............ (212) 421-8028
B'Cast Traffic & Residuals/ 666 Third Ave, New York, NY .... (212) 682-5200
Bedworks/ 121 W 19th, New York, NY.................................... (212) 777-5640
Bee, Jay/ 134 W Twenty Six Street, New York, NY .... (212) 564-5860
Beemak Plastics/ P.O. Box 46098, Los Angeles, CA .... (213) 876-1770
Beethoven Pianos/ 1645 First Ave, New York, NY .... (212) 288-2099
Beinner, Michael D Public Rel./ 342 Madison Ave,
    New York, NY... (212) 986-5758
Belden (Lee Filters)/ 534 W 25th, New York, NY .... (212) 691-1910
Bergman, L V & Assoc Inc/ E Mountain Rd S, Cold Spring, NY...... (914) 265-3656
Berlin, Irving/ 14 E 37th, New York, NY .... (212) 532-3600
Berlitz Svcs/ 40 W 51st, New York, NY.................................. (212) 765-1000
Bernco Specialty Advertising/ 300 Hempstead Turnpike,
    West Hempstead, NY .... (516) 681-7676
Bernstein, Leo D & Sons/ 30 W 29th St, New York, NY.............. (212) 683-2260
Zimmerman, P./ P.O. Box 11, S. Britain, CT............................ (203) 744-0000
Beseler, Charles Co/ 8 Fernwood Rd, Florham Park, NJ............. (201) 822-1000
Bill's Flower Market Inc/ 816 Ave of the Americas,
    New York City, NY... (212) 889-8154
Bink & Bink/ 80 Second Ave., New York, NY .... (212) 460-5826
Binney & Smith Art Materials/ 1100 Church Ln, Easton, PA .... (215) 253-6271
Blake Films Inc/ 160 Southampton St, Boston, MA .... (617) 445-4700
Blatt/ 809 Broadway, New York, NY....................................... (212) 674-8855
Blaustein Print & Hardware/ 304 Bleecker St, New York, NY ...... (212) 255-1073
Blue Baron Cadillac Limousine/ 90 Jerico Turnpike,
    Floral Park, NY .... (212) 347-3666
Bogart Eleanor/Make-Up/ 243 W 72nd, New York, NY .... (212) 496-6421
Boland, Bryan J/ Pine Dr RFD 2, Burlington, CT .... (203) 673-1307
Bollei, Gerard / Hair/ 160 Fifth Ave, New York, NY .... (212) 924-6760
Boston Camera Rental Company/ 607 Boylston Street,
    Boston, MA.. (617) 262-6161
Boston Gaffers/Blake Films/ 160 Southampton St., Boston, MA .... (617) 445-4700
Bourges Color Corp/ 20 Waterside Plz, New York, NY............... (212) 725-0800
Brandon Memorabilia/ 222 E 51st St, New York City, NY .... (212) 593-2794
Brass By Ben Karpen/ 212 E 51st St, New York City, NY .... (212) 755-3450
Brenner Sawdust Co Inc/ 26 Kent St, Brooklyn, NY.................. (212) 383-2455
Bridge Kitchenware/ 214 E 52nd, New York, NY .... (212) 688-4220
Brill, Ralph Associates/ Box 200, Garrison, NY........................ (914) 265-3060
Bring Sailing Back C/O Petrel/ Battery Park, New York, NY......... (212) 825-1976
Broadcast Business Consultants/ 10 East 40th Street,
    New York, NY... (212) 679-4970

TALENT, MISCELLANEOUS SERVICES/East

Broadway Arts/ 1755 Broadway 4th Floor, New York, NY .... (212) 586-7947
Broadway Lumber/ 557 Broadway, New York, NY .... (212) 226-0768
Broadway Panhandler/ 520 Broadway, New York, NY .... (212) 966-3434
Broderson, Charles/ 873 Broadway, New York, NY .... (212) 925-9392
Brody, David A/ 84-50 Austin St, New York City, NY .... (212) 873-1300
Brooklyn Model Works, Inc./ 60 Washington Ave.,
    Brooklyn, NY.. (718) 834-1944
Brooks, Robert/ 235 E 53rd, New York, NY........................... (212) 486-9829
Brown, Arthur & Bro/ 2 W 46th, New York, NY .... (212) 575-5555
Brown,Iris Victorian Doll & Mi/ 253 E 57th St, New York, NY ...... (212) 593-2882
Brusock, Jim / Make-Up/ 160 Fifth Ave., New York, NY .... (212) 924-6760
Budget Uniform Ctr/ 110 E 59th, New York, NY .... (212) 593-0965
Buffet Caterers/ 308 Knickerbocker Ave, Brooklyn, NY .... (212) 821-6369
Burton, Kate Casting/ 226 W 11th St, New York City, NY........... (212) 243-6114
Cambridge-Essex Stamp/ 500 Eighth Ave 10th Floor,
    New York, NY.. (212) 279-3722
Camera Barn/ 1272 Broadway, New York, NY .... (212) 947-3510
Camera Mart Inc, The/ 456 W 55th St, New York, NY .... (212) 757-6977
Camera Service Center Inc/ 625 W 54th St, New York, NY.......... (212) 757-0906
Camrod (Hondas)/ 610 W 57th, New York, NY .... (212) 582-7444
Candle Shop, The/ 118 Christopher St, New York, NY .... (212) 989-0148
Canon USA Inc/ One Canon Plz, Lake Success, NY .... (516) 488-6700
Capo, Michael Antiques/ 831 Broadway, New York City, NY ...... (212) 982-3356
Cappy & Co Inc/ 323 Blvd of the Allies, Pittsburgh, PA............. (412) 281-2133
Capsouto Freres/ 451 Washington St, New York, NY .... (212) 966-4900
Captain Haggerty's Dogs/ 1748 First Ave., New York, NY .... (212) 410-7400
Cardel Ltd/ 615 Madison Ave, New York, NY.......................... (212) 753-8880
Carey Cadillac Renting/ 41 E 42nd, New York, NY .... (212) 599-1122
Carmichael-Moore, Bob Inc/ PO Box 5, New York, NY .... (212) 255-0465
Carroll Musical Instrument Svc/ 351 W 41st St,
    New York City, NY.. (212) 868-4120
Casa Latina Music/ 345 W 58th, New York, NY .... (212) 582-5705
Casa Moneo/ 210 W 14th, New York, NY .... (212) 929-1644
Cavedon Associates/ 164 Newbury St, Boston, MA.................. (617) 266-1447
Central Skin Diving/ 160-09 Jamaica Ave, Jamaica Queens, NY..... (212) 739-5772
Century Lumber/ 1875 Second Ave, New York, NY .... (212) 876-1100
Chance's Restaurant/ 14 E 58th, New York, NY .... (212) 832-2882
Chapin, Spence Thrift Shop/ 1424 Third Ave, New York, NY ...... (212) 737-8448
Charrette/ 215 Lexington Ave, New York, NY .... (212) 683-8822
Charrette Corp/ 1 Winthrop Sq, Boston, MA.......................... (617) 935-6000
Chartpak/ One River Rd, Leeds, MA.................................... (413) 584-5446
Chateau Theatrical Animals/ 608 W 48th St,
    New York City, NY.. (212) 246-0520
Chauffeurs Unlimited/ 310 West End Ave, New York, NY .... (212) 874-3858
Chelsea Thr Ctr/ 407 W 43rd, New York, NY .... (212) 541-8394
Chenko Studio/ 167 W 46th St, New York City, NY .... (212) 944-0215
Cheverton, Linda/ 150 9th Ave, New York, NY .... (212) 691-0881
Chic Display/ 142 W 14th, New York, NY .... (212) 924-3720
Childcraft/ 155 E 23rd St, New York, NY .... (212) 674-4754
Children's Entertainment/ 17 W 32nd, New York, NY .... (212) 244-0265
Christofle at Baccarat/ 55 E 57th, New York, NY .... (212) 826-4100
Christo-Vac-Costume Armour/ Shore Rd PO Box 325,
    Cornwall-Hudson, NY.. (914) 534-9120
Cine 60/ 630 Ninth Ave, New York, NY .... (212) 586-8782
Cinergy Communications Corp/ 321 W. 44th Street,
    New York, NY.. (212) 582-2900
Cine Studio/ 241 W 54th St, New York, NY .... (212) 581-1916
Cinnabar/ 1027 N. Orange Dr., Hollywood, CA...................... (213) 461-3834
Circle Ice & Cube Co/ 491 Tenth Ave, New York, NY .... (212) 873-7469
Circle Line/ Pier 83 Foot of W 43rd, New York, NY .... (212) 563-3200
City Knickerbocker Lighting/ 781 Eighth Ave, New York, NY ...... (212) 586-3939
Claremont Riding Academy/ 175 W 89th St, New York, NY .... (212) 724-5100
Clarence House/ 40 E 57th, New York, NY .... (212) 752-2890
Clarke, Jeff & Sons/ 530 Westport Av, Norwalk, CT................. (203) 846-1617
Classic Limousine Service/ 34 Union Park, Boston, MA .... (617) 266-3980
Clock Hutt/ 1050 Second Ave, New York, NY .... (212) 759-2395
Cloder Corporation/ 49 Ann St, New York, NY .... (212) 962-1600
Clove Lake Stables/ 1025 Clove Rd, Staten Island, NY .... ( ) 448-1414
Colello, Jac/ 201 East 17th St, New York City, NY.................. (212) 505-7848
Colette French Pastry/ 1136 Third Ave Betw 66&67th,
    New York, NY.. (212) 988-2605
Collector's Cabinet, The/ 153 E 57th, New York, NY .... (212) 355-2033
Collegium Sound/ 35-41 72nd St, Jackson Heights, NY............. (718) 426-8555
Comprehensive Svc/ PO Box 881 Times Square St, New York, NY .. (212) 586-6161
Consultants for Talent Payment/ 22 West 27th Street Suite 1000,
    New York, NY.. (212) 696-1100

Continental Felt Co Inc/ 22 W 15th St, New York, NY .... (929) 526-5262
Continental Productions/ 40 E 34th, New York, NY.................. (212) 986-8584
Cooper Classics, Ltd./ 132 Perry St., New York, NY .... (212) 929-0094
Corporate Comm. Consultants/ 5848 Douglas Street,
    Pittsburgh, PA... (412) 422-5339
Cosby, Gerry & Co/ 3 Penn Plz, New York, NY...................... (212) 563-6464
Costume Armour Inc/ Shore Rd PO Box 325,
    Cornwall-Hudson, NY.. (914) 534-9120
Country Floors/ 300 E 61st, New York, NY .... (212) 758-7414
Creative Consumer Resources/ 284 Lincoln Blvd.,
    Middlesex, NJ.. (201) 469-9044
Creative Ideas/ 143 State St., Bangor, ME .... (207) 945-3105
Cross, Mark/ 645 Fifth Ave., New York, NY .... (212) 308-6600
Crystal Aquarium/ 1659 Third Ave, New York, NY.................. (212) 534-9003
Crystal Clear Importing Co/ 220 Fifth Ave, New York, NY .... (212) 683-6272
Curtain Up/ 402 W 43rd St, New York, NY........................... (212) 564-7272
Cycle Service Center Inc/ 74 Ave of the Americas,
    New York City, NY.. (212) 925-5900
Daines, David/ 833 Madison Ave, New York City, NY.............. (212) 535-1563
Dallek Inc/ 269 Madison Avenue, New York, NY .... (212) 684-4848
Darby Tent Co/ 77-22 164 St, Flushing, NY .... (212) 591-5300
D'Arcy, Timothy/ 43 W 85th St, New York City, NY .... (212) 580-8804
Davis Keniston/ 18 University Rd. #2, Brookline, MA .... (617) 566-1252
Dayton Record Store/ 824 Broadway, New York, NY............... (212) 254-5084
Delaware State Travel Service/ 99 Kings Highway PO Box 1401,
    Dover, DE... (800) 441-8846
Delsemme's Artists' Materials/ 27 W 14th St, New York, NY ...... (212) 675-2742
Demarest, Charles/ PO Box 238, Bloomingdale, NJ .... (201) 492-1414
De May, Anthony / Hair/ 160 Fifth Ave., New York, NY .... (212) 924-6760
Designs by Nita-Floral & Trees/ 856-D Jericho Turnpike,
    Huntington, NY.. (516) 423-1593
Deutsch/ 196 Lexington Ave, New York, NY .... (212) 683-8746
Deux, Pierre Antiques/ 369 Bleecker St, New York, NY............ (212) 243-7740
Dickinson Direct Response/ 67 Federal Avenue, Quincy, MA ...... (617) 471-9222
Diebold Inc/ 405 Lexington Ave, New York, NY .... (212) 687-7475
Directors' Studio/ 527 W 45th St, New York, NY .... (212) 581-2050
Dixie Foam/ 20 E 20th, New York, NY .... (212) 777-3626
DOI Camera Place/ 342 Madison Ave, New York, NY .... (212) 661-0876
Dongia Textiles/ 973 Third Ave, New York, NY .... (212) 477-9877
Door Store/ 210 E 51st, New York, NY .... (212) 753-2280
Duns Marketing Services Ex Lts/ One Penn Plaza Suite 4520,
    New York, NY.. (212) 971-9277
Dykes Lumber/ 348 W 44th, New York, NY .... (212) 246-6480
Dynamic Interiors/ 760 McDonald Ave, Brooklyn, NY.............. (212) 435-6326
Eagle Master Locksmiths/ 306 Third Ave, New York, NY .... (212) 532-1075
Eagle Regalia/ 7 Daey Street, New York, NY......................... (212) 962-2260
Eagle Supply Co/ 327 W 42nd St, New York, NY .... (212) 246-6180
Ealing Corp, The/ 22 Pleasant St, S Natick, MA .... (617) 655-7000
Eastern Artists/ 352 Park Ave. S., New York, NY .... (212) 725-5555
Eastman Kodak/ 1133 Sixth Ave, New York, NY .... (212) 930-7800
Eastman Kodak Co/ 343 State St, Rochester, NY .... (716) 724-4000
Eaves/ 21-07 41st Ave, Long Island Cty, NY.......................... (212) 729-1010
Echo Antiques/ 415 Third Ave, New York, NY .... (212) 689-4241
Eckstein, Warren's Master Dog/ 3586 Maple Ct, Oceanside, NY..... (316) 764-2683
Eclectic Properties, Inc./ 204 West 84th Street,
    New York, NY.. (212) 799-8963
Economy Badge/ 38 W 32nd, New York, NY .... (212) 736-1215
Editing Machine, The/ 630 Ninth Ave, New York City, NY.......... (212) 757-5420
18th St Playhouse/ 145 W 18th St, New York, NY .... (212) 243-8643
Elon Inc/ 150 E 58th, New York, NY .... (212) 759-6996
Empire Artists Materials/ 851 Lexington Ave, New York, NY .... (212) 737-5002
Encore Props/ 410 W 47th St, New York City, NY .... (212) 246-5237
Epstein, M & Son Inc/ 809 Ninth Ave, New York, NY .... (212) 265-3960
Faber-Castell Corp/ 41-47 Dickerson PO Box 7099, Newark, NJ..... (201) 484-4141
Fabulous Fakes-Modelmaking/ 18 E 18th St, Studio 4E,
    New York, NY.. (212) 807-8562
F A O Schwarz/ 745 Fifth Ave, New York, NY .... (212) 644-9400
Farkas Films Inc/ 385 Third Ave, New York City, NY .... (212) 679-8212
F & B/Ceco/ 315 W 43rd, New York, NY .... (212) 974-4600
Feature Systems/ 512 W 36th, New York, NY .... (212) 736-0447
Federal Restaurant Supply/ 202 Bowery, New York, NY .... (212) 226-0441
Feder, Louis/ 14 E 38th, New York, NY .... (212) 686-7701
Felner, Robert/ 55 West 75 Street, New York, NY .... (212) 580-8132
Ferco Inc/ 707 11th Ave, New York, NY.............................. (212) 245-4800
Ferraro, Joan/ 105 West 77 St, New York, NY .... (212) 877-4949

TALENT, MISCELLANEOUS SERVICES/East

Fiberbilt Cases/ 601 W 26th St, New York, NY .... (212) 675-5820
Filmlab/ 21 W 46th, New York, NY .... (212) 221-8435
Films Inc/ 440 Park Ave S, New York, NY .... (212) 889-7910
Filmtrucks Inc/ 601 West 29th Street, New York, NY .... (212) 868-7065
Fina, Michael C Co/ 580 Fifth Ave, New York, NY .... (212) 757-2530
Finneran, Kathy & Bill/ 40 Great Jones St., New York, NY .... (212) 473-6312
First Federal Coin Exchange/ 915 Broadway, New York, NY .... (212) 420-9696
First Impressions/ PO Box 398, Oldwick, NJ .... (201) 832-2626
511 Producers Service Corp/ 511 West 54 St, New York, NY .... (212) 581-4491
Flax, Sam/ 743 Third Ave, New York, NY .... (212) 620-3050
Florentine Craftsmen/ 654 First Ave, New York, NY .... (212) 532-3926
Focarino Studio, The/ 31 Deep Six Drive, East Hampton, NY .... (516) 324-7637
Ford, Rita Inc/ 19 E 65 St, New York, NY .... (212) 535-6717
Forrest Sign Co/ 949 Second Ave, New York, NY .... (212) 986-6260
Forsyth Monument Works, Inc./ 172 Suffolk St., New York, NY .... (212) 473-2388
Fortunoff/ 681 Fifth Ave, New York, NY .... (212) 758-6660
Freeman, Susan/ 1158 5th Ave, New York, NY .... (212) 534-5244
French & Spanish Book Corp/ 610 Fifth Ave, New York, NY .... (212) 581-8810
FR Film/ 15 W 45th, New York, NY .... (212) 221-4399
Friedman, A. I., Inc./ 25 W. 45th St., New York, NY .... (212) 575-0200
Friedman, Jane/ 30 Westminster Dr, Croton-Hdsn, NY .... (914) 739-9118
Fur Pillow & Rug Co/ PO Box 66, New York, NY .... (212) 688-1528
Gadbois, Maggie/ 303 Park Ave So #408, New York, NY .... (212) 254-4653
GAF/Sears&Roebuck Co/ Binghampton, NY .... (607) 729-6555
Gallery 10/ 21 Greenwich Ave, New York, NY .... (212) 929-9411
Garkowski, Annette/ New York, NY .... (718) 835-1938
Gavel, Deborah/ 26 Worcester Sq., Boston, MA .... (617) 262-2195
Gazebo, The/ 660 Madison Ave, New York, NY .... (212) 832-7077
Geiger, Pamela (Hair & Makeup)/ 105 West 55 Street,
New York, NY .... (212) 245-0200
General Camera Corp/ 540 W 36th, New York, NY .... (212) 594-8700
General Pencil Co/ 67 Fleet St, Jersey City, NJ .... (201) 653-5351
Gene's/ 242 E 79th, New York, NY .... (212) 249-9218
Gerard, Barbara/ 823 Park Ave, New York City, NY .... (212) 628-4524
Gerdau, Otto/ 82 Wall St, New York, NY .... (212) 709-9600
Giant Umbrella/ 112 W 34th St Rm 453, New York, NY .... (212) 279-8405
Giardinelli Band Instrument Co/ 151 W 46th, New York, NY .... (212) 575-5959
Giger, Ed/ 12 Church Street, Middletown, NJ .... (201) 671-1707
Girl/Scout Locations/ 1 Hillside Ave, Port Washington, NY .... (516) 883-8409
Gittler, Barbara Company/ 157 West 57th Street Suite 700,
New York, NY .... (212) 246-8282
Giurdanella Bros/ 178 First Ave, New York, NY .... (212) 228-2000
Gladstone/ 16 W 56th, New York, NY .... (212) 245-5950
Glassmasters Guild/ 621 Ave of Amers at 19 St, New York, NY .... (212) 924-2868
Goday, Dale & Assoc/ 55 E 11th St, New York City, NY .... (212) 586-6300
Golden Office Interiors Inc/ 574 5th Ave, New York, NY .... (212) 719-5150
Gold, Judy/ 40 Sulgrave Rd, Scarsdale, NY .... (914) 723-5036
Gong, Julie/ 395 Degraw St., Brooklyn, NY .... (718) 855-3537
Gordon Novelty/ 933 Broadway, New York, NY .... (212) 254-8616
Gothic Cabinet Craft/ 201 First Ave, New York, NY .... (212) 674-1090
Gothic Lumber/ 698 Second Ave, New York, NY .... (212) 683-0410
Governor's Office of Economic/ Bldg 6 Rm 517B Capitol Complex,
Charleston, WV .... (304) 348-2234
Graf, Philip/ 979 Third Ave, New York, NY .... (212) 755-1448
Grand Central Artists Material/ 18 E 40th St, New York, NY .... (212) 679-0023
Great Locations/ 97 Windsor Rd, Tenafly, NJ .... (201) 567-1455
Great Oak Landing/ Box 527, Chestertown, MD .... (301) 778-2100
Greenwich Nursery & Plants/ 506 Ninth Ave, New York, NY .... (212) 947-1170
Grumbacher, M Inc/ 460 W 34th St, New York, NY .... (212) 279-6400
G & R Video/ 300 Park Ave South, New York, NY .... (212) 533-1887
G & T Harris/ 523 West One Twenty One Street, New York, NY .... (212) 866-2307
Guccione/ 333 W 39 St, New York City, NY .... (212) 279-3602
Guitarras, Juan Orozco/ 155 Sixth Ave, New York, NY .... (212) 691-8620
Haberman M&I Jewelers/ 122 East 42nd St, New York, NY .... (212) 697-5270
Hackman, Aaron/ 165 W 23rd, New York, NY .... (212) 242-7877
Hammacher Schlemmer/ 145 E 57th, New York, NY .... (212) 421-9000
Hampton TV & Appliances/ 401 Park Ave S, New York, NY .... (212) 532-9700
Handloser Sandy - Stylist/ 752 West End Av, New York, NY .... (212) 222-4665
Hannett-Morrow Wallcoverings/ 979 3rd Ave, New York, NY .... (212) 935-3380
Hansen, Ed/ 111 W. 24th Street, New York, NY .... (212) 242-1504
Hansen, Joseph C/ 423 West 43rd Street, New York, NY .... (212) 246-8055
Harlequin/ 203 W 46th, New York, NY .... (212) 819-0120
Harley-Davidson of NYC/ 40-01 Northern Blvd,
Long Is City, NY .... (212) 786-8700
Harrington, Susie/ 6151 Liebig Ave, Bronx, NY .... (212) 581-6470
Harris, A T Corp/ 47 East 44th Street, New York, NY .... (212) 682-6325
Hart, Edna/ 162 Ninth Ave, New York City, NY .... (212) 242-2850
Hartigan, Gail M./ 7513 Carroll Ave., Takoma Park, MD .... (301) 270-9538
Hatfield's Color Shop/ 859 Boylston, Boston, MA .... (617) 267-7511
Heller, Ann/ 7816 Third Ave, Brooklyn, NY .... (212) 238-5454
Hess Repairs/ 200 Park Ave S, New York, NY .... (212) 260-2255
Hewig & Marvic/ 136 E 57th, New York, NY .... (212) 752-3224
Heydenryk/ 417 E 76th, New York, NY .... (212) 249-4903
Hilliard, Alex (Hair By)/ 105 West 55 Street, New York, NY .... (212) 245-0200
Honeywell/ 24-30 Skillman Ave, Long Isl City, NY .... (212) 392-4300
Hornmann/ 304 W 34th, New York, NY .... (212) 279-6079
Horseman V Antiques/ 348 Third Ave, New York, NY .... (212) 683-2041
Hough, Therese/ 11 Fifth Ave, New York City, NY .... (212) 673-4100
House of Oldies/ 35 Carmine St, New York, NY .... (212) 243-0500
House of Screens/ 219 E 89th, New York, NY .... (212) 534-8773
Howe Floral Co., Inc./ 171 W. 23rd St., New York, NY .... (212) 691-4381
Howe Furniture Corp/ 155 E 56th St, New York, NY .... (212) 826-0280
Hudson Photographic Ind Inc/ 2 S Buckhout St, Irvington, NY .... (914) 591-8700
Hudson River Day Line/ Pier 81 Foot of W 41st, New York, NY .... (212) 279-5151
Hunt Manufacturing Co/ 1405 Locust St, Philadelphia, PA .... (215) 732-7700
IFR Furniture Rentals/ 540 Atlantic Ave, Boston, MA .... (617) 542-7255
Ilford Inc/ W 70 Century Rd, Paramus, NJ .... (201) 265-6000
Ilnseher,Francois(Hair&Makeup)/ 105 West 55 Street,
New York, NY .... (212) 245-0200
In/Sight Direct Marketing/ 3000-50 Stevens Street,
Oceanside, NY .... (516) 678-2367
International Photo Optical As/ 1560 Broadway, New York, NY .... (212) 869-3560
Inter Video/ 3220 Burbank Blvd., Burbank, CA .... (818) 843-3633
Iredale Assoc/ 271 Madison Ave, New York, NY .... (212) 889-7722
Irving's Food Center/ 4801 Metropolitan Ave, Ridgewood, NY .... (212) 757-2753
Irvington House Thrift Shop/ 1534 Second Ave, New York, NY .... (212) 879-4555
Island Camera/ 228 Rt 109, E Farmingdale, NY .... (516) 293-8910
Jackie's Limousine & Location/ 1229 E 82nd St, Brooklyn, NY .... (212) 763-9668
Jankovic, Paul Mktng Research/ P.O. Box 505,
Bethany Beach, DE .... (301) 546-3728
Janovic Plaza/ 1150 3rd Ave, New York, NY .... (212) 772-1400
Jaybee Photo Suppliers Inc/ 636 Avenue of Americas,
New York, NY .... (212) 929-2222
Jenrette, Pamela/ 300 Mercer St, New York, NY .... (212) 673-4748
Jewelite Signs & Letters Inc/ 154 Reade Street,
New York, NY .... (212) 683-4474
Johnson Artist Materials Inc/ 355 Newbury St, Boston, MA .... (617) 536-4065
Joy Products/ 25 West 45 Street, New York, NY .... (212) 869-3743
J S L Video Services, Inc/ 25 W 45th, New York, NY .... (212) 575-5082
Juchnewicz, Joan/ 272 Ave. F, Bayonne, NJ .... (201) 436-6721
Jungle Red Studios/ 20 Desbrosses St, New York, NY .... (212) 226-1811
Kaltenback, Kurt Lightbanks/ 100 Hudson Harbor,
Edgewater, NJ .... (201) 224-9253
Kaplan, Howard/ 35 E Tenth St, New York City, NY .... (212) 674-1000
Kapp & Strobel/ 32 Union Sq, New York, NY .... (212) 473-2639
Katz, Ruth J/ 2109 Broadway, New York City, NY .... (212) 870-1471
Kauffman, H & Sons/ 139 E 24th St, New York, NY .... (212) 684-6060
Kaufman/Astoria Studio/ 34-31 35th St, Astoria, NY .... (212) 392-5600
Kaufman Surplus Inc. Army&Navy/ 319 W 42nd St, New York, NY. (212) 757-5670
Kaye, Sandye/ 1010 Saint Paul Street, Baltimore, MD .... (301) 661-6610
Kea Cosmetics Inc/ 90 13th Ave, Ronkonkoma, NY .... (516) 467-0722
Keeble-Cavaco/ 853 Seventh Avenue, New York, NY .... (212) 582-3473
Kelly, Bob/ 151 W 46th, New York, NY .... (212) 819-0030
Kempler, George J/ 160 Fifth Ave, New York City, NY .... (212) 989-1180
Kenmore Furniture Co Inc/ 156 E 33rd St, New York City, NY .... (212) 683-1888
Kerygma Media Int'L. Ltd./ 601 River Rd., Sykesville, MD .... (301) 442-1752
Kimmel, Lily Associates/ 12 E 86th St, New York, NY .... (212) 532-2925
Kirk-Brummel/ 979 Third Ave, New York, NY .... (212) 477-8590
Klein, Lee Associates/ 6 Peter Cooper Road, New York, NY .... (212) 254-2070
Klein, Maryellen/ 330 East 33rd Street, New York, NY .... (212) 683-6351
Kleinsleep/ 149 W 24th St Advertising & Pr, New York, NY .... (212) 807-1990
Klem, Tom 3D Models/ 85 Leonard Street 4th Floor,
New York, NY .... (212) 431-4059
Kliegl Bros/ 32-32 48th Ave, Long Island Cy, NY .... (212) 786-7474
Koh-I-Nor Rapidograph Inc/ 100 North St, Bloomsbury, NJ .... (201) 479-4124
Konica/ 25-20 Brooklyn-Queens Expy, Woodside, NY .... (212) 932-4040
Kracker Factree Speci Effects/ 5604 Ashbourne Rd.,
Baltimore, MD .... (301) 242-2895
Krasilovsky/ 150 Lafayette, New York, NY .... (212) 226-2500
Kristina-Fashion Stylist/ 41 Dupont Avenue, Piscataway, NJ .... (201) 752-2338

Kugel, F.N. Associates/ PO Box 374, Rockland, MA .... (617) 871-1900
Kulicke Frames/ 601 W 26th St, New York, NY .... (212) 924-6660
Kuttner Antiques/ 36 E 20th St, New York, NY .... (212) 228-6375
La Belle Epoque Ballroom/ 827 Broadway, New York, NY .... (212) 254-6436
La Belle/NY/ 330 West 58 Street Suite 5C, New York, NY .... (212) 582-8296
La Ferla, Sandro Backdrops/ 135 West 14, New York, NY .... (212) 620-0693
Lake, Cathlin/ 348 E. 66 St., New York, NY .... (212) 794-2976
Lakin, Gaye - Stylist TV-Print/ 345 E. 81st Street,
   New York, NY .... (212) 861-1892
Lambert Co Inc/ 920 Commonwealth Ave, Boston, MA .... (617) 232-8551
Langnickel Artist Brushes/ 229 West 28th St, New York, NY .... (212) 563-9440
Lav, Brian/ 821 Jersey Avenue, Apt 3G, Elizabeth, NJ .... (201) 289-5973
Lazar,Cathy Costumes•Softprops/ 155 E 23rd St,
   New York City, NY .... (212) 473-0363
Leach, Ed Inc/ 160 Fifth Avenue, New York City, NY .... (212) 691-3450
Leach, G & W Company/ 1242 Brighton Road, Pittsburgh, PA ...... (412) 322-3288
Lee Lighting America/ 534 W 25th St, New York, NY .... (212) 691-1910
Lee, Nora, Stylist/ 162 W 56th St, New York City, NY .... (212) 245-5218
Lee's Art Shop/ 220 W. 57 St., New York, NY .... (212) 247-0110
Lees Keystone Inc/ 23 E 26th, New York, NY .... (212) 689-7727
Lee's Studio Gallery/ 211 West 57th St, New York City, NY .... (212) 265-5670
Leitner Uniforms/ 26 Bowery, New York, NY .... (212) 267-8740
Le Noble/ 500 W 52nd, New York, NY .... (212) 246-0150
Lens & Repro Equip Corp, the/ 33 W 17th St, New York, NY .... (212) 675-1900
Letraset/ 40 Eisenhower Dr, Paramus, NJ .... (201) 845-6100
Let There Be Neon/ 451 W. Broadway, New York, NY .... (212) 473-7370
Levy, Jacquelyn/ 89 Fairview Dr, Searingtown, NY .... (516) 484-1622
Limobile/ 63 Gansevoort Street, New York, NY .... (212) 989-2330
Linden Exhibits Inc/ 1135 W Elizabeth Ave, Linden, NJ .... (201) 862-1492
Lloyd's Limousine Ltd/ PO Box 23, Bayside, NY .... (718) 631-4403
Locate Market, The/ 1729 Second Avenue, New York, NY .... (212) 534-8997
Location Connection Inc, The/ 31 E 31st St, New York, NY .... (212) 684-1888
Location Hunter, The/ 16 Iselin Ter, Larchmont, NY .... (914) 834-2181
Location Locators/ 225 E 63rd St, New York City, NY .... (212) 832-1866
Locations Paula Wolfson-Krauss/ 277 W. 10th St.,
   New York, NY .... (212) 741-3048
Locations Unlimited/ 90 Brayton St, Englewood, NJ .... (201) 567-2809
Loeb, Paul/ 755 W End Ave, New York City, NY .... (212) 864-7020
Lovelia Enterprises, Inc./ 356 E. 41st St., New York, NY .... (212) 490-0930
Lowe, James Autographs/ 667 Madison Ave, New York, NY .... (212) 889-8204
Lowel-Light Mfg/ 475 10th Ave, New York, NY .... (212) 947-0950
Lucidity/ 775 Madison Ave, New York, NY .... (212) 861-7000
Lutz, Robin Home Ec./ 8999 Sidelong Pl., Columbia, MD .... (301) 730-2567
Luxo Lamp Co/ Monument Park, Port Chester, NY .... (914) 937-4433
Lynch, Sharon/ 320 W 55th St, New York City, NY .... (212) 582-4449
Madison Hardware/ 105 E 23rd, New York, NY .... (212) 777-1110
Magickal Childe/ 35 W 19th, New York, NY .... (212) 242-7182
Magic Marker Industries Inc/ 467 Calhoun St, Trenton, NJ .... (609) 392-3071
Maglione, Marcia/ 381 Hanover St, Boston, MA .... (617) 367-0695
Magna Tech Electronic/ 630 Ninth Ave, New York, NY .... (212) 586-7240
Maine State Development Off/ 193 State St, Augusta, ME .... (207) 289-2656
Maller, Bonnie (Makeup By)/ 105 West 55 Street,
   New York, NY .... (212) 245-0200
Mallie, Dale & Co Inc/ 40 Stevens Pl, Lawrence, NY .... (516) 239-8782
Mallie, Dale & Co Inc/ 35-30 38th Street Astoria Stud,
   Astoria, NY .... (212) 706-1233
Manhattan Model Shop/ 40 Great Jones St, New York, NY .... (212) 473-6312
Manhattan Shade/ 1297 Third Ave, New York, NY .... (212) 288-5616
Maniatis, Michael/ 48 W. 22nd St., New York, NY .... (212) 620-0398
Mannino, Robert/ 340 E 57th St, New York City, NY .... (212) 486-1299
Manny's/ 156 W 48th, New York, NY .... (212) 819-0576
Marek Co/ 160 Fifth Ave, New York, NY .... (212) 924-6760
Marion and Company Inc/ 315 West 39th Street 16 Floor,
   New York, NY .... (212) 594-1848
Mark L V Frames/ 330 Hudson Street, New York, NY .... (212) 620-0522
Marks, Arthur Unltd/ 140 E 40th St, New York City, NY .... (212) 685-2761
Martin, Alice Manougian/ 239 E 58th St, New York City, NY ...... (212) 688-0117
Martin Audio Video Corp/ 423 W 55th, New York, NY .... (212) 541-5900
Martin Paint Centers/ 1489 Third Ave, New York, NY .... (212) 650-9563
Martin Paint Centers/ 308 W 125th, New York, NY .... (212) 864-9712
Maryland Film Commission/ 45 Calvert Street, Annapolis, MD ...... (301) 269-3577
Marymount Manhattan Theatre/ 221 E 71st St,
   New York, NY .... (212) 472-3800
Maslansky, Stephanie/ 49 Grove Street #6C,
   New York City, NY .... (212) 206-1243

Mason's Tennis Mart/ 911 7th Ave, New York City, NY .... (212) 757-5374
Massachusetts Film Bureau/ 100 Cambridge St (13th Floor),
   Boston, MA .... (617) 727-3330
Master & Talent Inc/ 1139 Foam Pl, Far Rockaway, NY .... (516) 239-7719
Matenciot, Andre Co Inc/ 979 3rd Ave, New York, NY .... (212) 486-9064
Mayer, Joseph/ 22 W 8th Street, New York, NY .... (212) 674-8100
Mayor's Office of Film/ 110 W. 57th Street, New York, NY .... (212) 489-6710
Mazzei, Michael / Hair/ 160 Fifth Ave., New York, NY .... (212) 924-6760
McConnell and Borow/ 10 E 23rd St, New York, NY .... (212) 254-1486
McKenna, Ann/ 41 Dekalb Pl., Morristown, NJ .... (201) 267-8693
McKnight, Sam (Hair By)/ 105 West 55 Street, New York, NY ...... (212) 245-0200
M C S, Inc./ P O Box 728, Up Montclair, NJ .... (201) 746-7385
Mellor Gym/ 21 West Thirty Eight Street, New York, NY .... (212) 685-0790
Mendez, Raymond A./ 220 W. 98th St. Apt. 12b, New York, NY .... (212) 864-4689
Mergenthaler Linotype Co/ 201 Old Country Rd, Melville, NY ...... (516) 673-4197
Merit Photo Shop/ 550 Eighth Ave, New York, NY .... (212) 730-7430
Meta Photo Supply Co/ 244 Madison Ave, New York, NY .... (212) 725-0962
Meyer, Jimmy & Co/ 428 W 44th St, New York City, NY .... (212) 947-8115
Meyer, N S/ 42 E 20th, New York, NY .... (212) 533-1000
Meyers, Pat/ 436 W 20th St, New York City, NY .... (212) 620-0069
MHR Group, The/ 436 Ferry St, Newark, NJ .... (201) 589-3966
Mickiewicz, Robert A, Esq/ 7 Whittemore Terrace, Boston, MA ...... (617) 436-6438
Milan Lab/ 57 Spring St, New York, NY .... (212) 226-4780
Miller, L Matthew Assoc/ 48 W 21st, New York, NY .... (212) 741-8011
Miller, Lorna B/ 2 Horatio St, New York City, NY .... (212) 243-3599
Mills, Joey/Make-Up/ 160 Fifth Ave, New York, NY .... (212) 924-6760
Milne, Judith and James Inc/ 524 E 73rd St 5th Fl,
   New York, NY .... (212) 472-0107
Minolta Corp/ 101 Williams Dr, Ramsey, NJ .... (201) 825-4000
Minskoff Rehearsal/ 1515 Broadway, New York, NY .... (212) 575-0725
Miranda Designs/ 745 President, Brooklyn, NY .... (212) 857-9839
Miya Shoji Screens/ 107 W 17th, New York, NY .... (212) 243-6774
Moda 700/ 700 Madison Ave, New York City, NY .... (212) 935-9188
Model's Mart Ltd/ 17 E 48th St, New York, NY .... (212) 688-6215
Modern Artifical Flowers/ 517 W 46th St, New York, NY .... (212) 265-0414
Moderne Copy Advertising/ 185 Millbury Ave, Millbury, MA .... (617) 865-2361
Modern Miltex Corp/ 280 E 134th St, Bronx, NY .... (212) 585-6000
Mokus - Stylist/ 247 W 35th St, New York City, NY .... (212) 279-4926
Moontaro, Tanna/ 56 Seventh Ave, New York, NY .... (212) 242-1138
Moore, Elyse/ 77 W 55th St, New York City, NY .... (212) 757-3837
Moore Push-Pin Co/ 1300 E Mermaid Ln, Wyndmoor, PA .... (215) 233-5700
Moormends/ 1228 Madison Ave, New York, NY .... (212) 289-3978
Morelli Ballet/ 69 W 14th, New York, NY .... (212) 242-1903
Morilla Inc/ 211 Bowers St, Holyoke, MA .... (413) 538-9250
Morrell & Co/ 307 E 53rd, New York, NY .... (212) 688-9370
Morrison, J Better Cars, Inc/ 117 Third Street,
   Garden City L I, NY .... (516) 741-1322
Moshy Bros/ 89 Chambers St, New York, NY .... (212) 227-6267
Mothers Sound Stage/ 210 E 5th St, New York, NY .... (212) 260-2050
Motion Picture Ent., Inc./ Box 276, Tarrytown, NY .... (212) 245-0969
Hartwell Motors/ 134 East 70 St, New York, NY .... (212) 734-4000
Movie Cars/Promotional Cars/ 825 Madison Ave. Ste. 3r,
   New York, NY .... (212) 734-4000
M P E/ Box 276, Tarrytown, NY .... (212) 245-0969
MPO Videotronic Projector Co/ 619 W 54th St, New York, NY ...... (212) 708-0550
Mulder/Goodwin Studio/ 1200 Broadway 2c, New York City, NY ... (212) 689-9037
Muppets Meeting Films/ 117 E 69th, New York, NY .... (212) 794-2400
Murphy Door Bed Co/ 40 E 34th, New York, NY .... (212) 682-8936
Murray, William/ 40 West 70th Street Studio 6B,
   New York, NY .... (212) 724-1510
Museum Books Inc/ 6 W 37 St 4th Floor, New York, NY .... (212) 563-2770
Music Inn/ 169 W 4th, New York, NY .... (212) 243-5715
MVP Productions/ 453 W 47th, New York, NY .... (212) 245-8027
Nagra Magnetic Recorders Inc/ 19 W 44th St, New York, NY .... (212) 840-0999
Natasi Make-Up/ 1514 91st St, N Bergen, NJ .... (201) 869-7668
Nat'l Tile & Marble/ 165 E 109th, New York, NY .... (212) 427-7525
Needles, Frances/ 75 Henry St, Brooklyn, NY .... (212) 852-4877
Neptune Corp/ 619 West 54th Street, New York, NY .... (212) 765-4785
Neptune Photo Inc/ 739 Franklin Ave, Garden City, NY .... (516) 741-4484
Newbery, Tom/ Ridge Rd, Glen Cove, NY .... (516) 759-0880
Newel Art Galleries Inc/ 425 E 53rd St, New York City, NY .... (212) 758-1970
New England Make-Up Effects/ 100 Boylston St., Boston, MA ...... (617) 542-8138
New Hampshire Film Bureau/ 105 Loudon Rd, Concord, NH .... (603) 271-2598
New Jersey Mot Pic & Tv Comm/ Gateway One, Newark, NJ .... (201) 648-6279
New York Central Supply Co/ 62 Third Ave, New York, NY .... (212) 473-7705

New York Flash Rental/ 156 Fifth Ave, New York, NY .... (212) 741-1165
Niccolini Antique Rentals/ 114 E 25 St, New York, NY .... (212) 254-2900
Nikon Inc/ 623 Stewart Ave, Garden City, NY .... (516) 222-0200
Nile/ 200 W 79th St, New York City, NY .... (212) 580-7571
95th St Studio, The/ 206 E 95th St, New York City, NY .... (212) 683-6311
North American Video/ 423 E 90th St, New York City, NY .... (212) 369-2552
North Light Studios/ 122 W. 26 12th Fl., New York, NY .... (212) 989-5498
Nostalgia Alley/ 547 West 27th Street, New York City, NY .... (212) 695-6578
Novellino, Nino/ PO Box 325 Shore Rd, Cornwall Hudson, NY ..... (212) 585-1199
Novel Pinball & Juke Box Co/ 593 Tenth Ave, New York, NY ...... (212) 736-3868
NY Awning/ 210 W 90th, New York, NY .... (212) 265-2900
NY Blackboard/ 45 Corsby St, New York, NY .... (212) 966-0555
N Y C Film Commission/ 110 W 57th St, New York City, NY .... (212) 489-6714
NYC Transit Auth/ 370 Jay St, Brooklyn, NY .... (212) 330-3140
NY Flameproofing/ 635 N 23 St, New York, NY .... (212) 924-7200
N Y Frame & Picture Co/ 29 John St, New York, NY .... (212) 233-3205
NY State Ofc of Motion Picture/ 230 Park Ave, New York, NY .... (212) 949-8514
Obsolete Fleet Daniel List,The/ 45 Christopher St,
    New York, NY .... (212) 255-6068
Olden Camera & Lens Co Inc/ 1265 Broadway, New York, NY ...... (212) 725-1234
Old Print Shop/ 150 Lexington Ave, New York, NY .... (212) 683-3950
Oliphant, Sarah/ 38 Cooper Sq., New York, NY .... (212) 741-1233
Olympic Designs/ 141 Fifth Ave, New York, NY .... (212) 533-0843
On Site Testing/ 141 Fifth Avenue, New York, NY .... (212) 753-9215
Orange Front Art Supply/ 224 Front St, Hempstead, NY .... (516) 481-6464
Orefice, Jeanette/ 51 Joralemon St., Brooklyn, NY .... (718) 852-2418
Ouellette, Dawn/ 336 E 30th St, New York City, NY .... (212) 868-1121
Overland Stage Company/ 511 West 54th Street, New York, NY ... (212) 581-4469
Ozalid Corp/ 1000 MacArthur Blvd, Mahwah, NJ .... (201) 529-3100
Packard Electronics Co/ 33 Union Sq W, New York, NY .... (212) 691-6111
Packer, J & Son/ 824 Lexington Ave, New York, NY .... (212) 838-5488
Palette Art Co Inc, The/ 436 Madison Ave, New York, NY .... (212) 753-7338
Palmer, Barbara/Wardrobe Spec/ New York City, NY .... (212) 580-4380
Pampered Kitchens/ 21 E 10th, New York, NY .... (212) 982-0340
Panasonic Company/ 1 Panasonic Way, Secaucus, NJ .... (201) 348-7000
80 Papers/ 80 Thompson St., New York, NY .... (212) 966-1491
Paper White Florists/ 80 2nd Ave, New York, NY .... (212) 477-3361
Paradise Design/ 800 Sixth Ave, New York, NY .... (212) 684-3397
Paragon/ 867 Broadway, New York, NY .... (212) 255-8036
Paramount Gallery/ 58 E 11th, New York, NY .... (212) 777-9131
Party Bazaar/ 390 Fifth Ave, New York, NY .... (212) 695-6820
Paul Assoc/ 155 E 55th, New York, NY .... (212) 755-1313
Peacock, Linda/ 28 W 86th St, New York City, NY .... (212) 580-1422
Pegasus Productions Puppets/ P O Box 470 Times Square Sta,
    New York, NY .... (212) 239-4920
Pennington Enterprises Ltd./ 72 Edmund St., Edison, NJ .... (201) 985-9090
Pennsylvania Film Office/ 461 Forum Bldg, Harrisburg, PA .... (717) 787-5333
Penny Whistle Toys/ Columbus & 81st, New York, NY .... (212) 873-9090
Pentalic Corp/ 132 W 22nd St, New York, NY .... (212) 989-4664
People For Dogs/ 310 W 87 St, New York, NY .... (212) 580-7539
Performance Lighting/ 2741 Noblestown Rd., Pittsburgh, PA ...... (412) 922-0900
Philips Television Systems/ 900 Corporate Dr, Mahwah, NJ .... (201) 529-1550
Photo Exchange/ 1 W 20th St, New York, NY .... (212) 675-6582
Photo-Graphic Apparatus Syst/ 380 Fourth Ave, Brooklyn, NY .... (212) 522-4200
Photomart 49th Ltd/ 30 Rockefeller Plz, New York, NY .... (212) 582-4996
Photo Resources/ 156 5th Ave, New York, NY .... (212) 243-2554
Photo-Tech Repair Svce/ 132 Fourth Ave, New York, NY .... (212) 673-8400
Photo-Tekniques Ltd/ 119 Fifth Ave, New York City, NY .... (212) 254-2545
Phyllis Exotic Plants/ 78 St Marks Ave, Brooklyn, NY .... (212) 783-9799
Pietsch, Barbara/ 126 Powell Ln., Upper Darby, PA .... (215) 352-8924
Pioneer Piano/ 934 Eighth Ave, New York, NY .... (212) 586-3718
Place for Antiques, The/ 993 Second Ave, New York, NY .... (212) 475-6596
Plant Specialists, Inc/ 42-25 Vernon Blvd, Long Island, NY ...... (212) 392-9404
Plastic Reel Corp of America/ 475 Boulevard,
    Elmwood Park, NJ .... (201) 796-6600
Plaza Artist Materials Inc/ 173 Madison Ave, New York, NY ...... (212) 689-2870
Plexability Ltd/ 200 Lexington Ave, New York City, NY .... (212) 679-7826
Plexi-Craft/ 514 W 24th, New York, NY .... (212) 924-3244
Polaroid Corp/ 549 Technology Sq, Cambridge, MA .... (617) 577-2000
Polk's Model Craft/ 314 Fifth Ave, New York, NY .... (212) 279-9034
Port Authority of NY & NJ/ 1 World Trade Ctr Rm 68 West,
    New York, NY .... (212) 466-7854
Poster America/ 174 Ninth Ave, New York, NY .... (212) 691-1615
Poster Originals/ 924 Madison Ave, New York, NY .... (212) 861-0422
Pottery Barn/ 117 E 59th, New York, NY .... (212) 741-9132

Pottery Barn/ 231 Tenth Ave, New York, NY .... (212) 741-9140
Powers, James Inc/ 12 E 41st St, New York City, NY .... (212) 686-9066
Pragan Camera Store/ 215 W 14th St, New York, NY .... (212) 929-3910
Prince, Julie-Masks & Lifemask/ 141 E 56th Street,
    New York City, NY .... (212) 486-9249
Pro-Com Systems/ 5001 Baum Blvd, Pittsburgh, PA .... (412) 621-1950
Professional Camera Repair/ 37 W 47th, New York, NY .... (212) 382-0550
Professional Photo Supply/ 141 West 20th Street,
    New York, NY .... (212) 924-1200
Projection Systems Int'l/ 219 East 44th Street,
    New York, NY .... (212) 682-0995
Promo. Finders-Free Srce. Ser./ 200 Park Ave. Ste. 230,
    New York, NY .... (212) 972-1212
Prop House Inc, The/ 76 Ninth Ave, New York, NY .... (212) 691-9099
Pro Piano/ New York, NY .... (212) 582-6798
Proposition Rentals/ 15 W 38th St, New York City, NY .... (212) 944-1969
Prop Shop Inc/ 26 College Pl, Brooklyn Hts, NY .... (718) 522-4606
Purcell, E., Dressmaker/Tailor/ 105 Sullivan Street,
    New York, NY .... (212) 925-1962
Q-TV/ 33 W 60th, New York, NY .... (212) 765-4200
Quality House Interior Service/ 1455 Cromwell Ave,
    Bronx, NY .... (212) 992-5600
Quarry/ 183 Lexington Ave, New York, NY .... (212) 679-2559
Rackoff, Murray/ 22 W 48th, New York, NY .... (212) 869-5093
Rafferty Communicators/ 12 E. 46th Street, New York, NY .... (212) 661-7120
Rafik Film Supplies/ 814 Broadway, New York, NY .... (212) 475-9110
R. B. Studios/ 235 Park Avenue South, New York, NY .... (212) 505-7474
RCA Svc Co/ 300 G Corporate Court, South Plainfiel, NJ .... (800) 631-8823
Record Hunter/ 507 Fifth Ave, New York, NY .... (212) 697-8970
Renny/ 27 E 62nd, New York, NY .... (212) 371-5354
Renrose Locations, Ltd./ 4 Sandalwood Dr., Livingston, NJ ...... (201) 992-4264
Resale Dress Shop/ 1041 Madison Ave, New York, NY .... (212) 737-7273
Rhode Island Tourist Promo/ 7 Jackson Walkway,
    Providence, RI .... (800) 556-2484
Rich Art Color Co Inc/ 109 Graham Ln, Lodi, NJ .... (201) 777-8844
Ridge, John Russell/ 463 West Street, New York City, NY .... (212) 929-3410
Ridge Radio & TV/ 51 University Pl, New York, NY .... (212) 673-6400
Rindner, Jack N Assoc/ Tinton Falls, NJ .... (201) 542-3548
Ritz Logistical Services Ltd./ 115 West 73rd Street,
    New York, NY .... (212) 864-2200
Ritz Thrift Shop/ 107 W 57th, New York, NY .... (212) 265-4559
Robinson, James (Antique)/ 15 E 57th, New York, NY .... (212) 752-6166
Rockin' Relix,Inc/Button Prods/ 1734 Coney Island,
    Brooklyn, NY .... (212) 645-0818
Rogers, William Backdrops/ 156 Fifth Avenue, New York, NY ..... (212) 206-0016
Ronan, T J Paint Corp/ 749 E 135th St, Bronx, NY .... (212) 292-1100
Root Al, Company/ PO Box 357, Fogelsville, PA .... (215) 285-2778
Rosemary's Cakes/ 299 Rutland Ave, Teaneck, NJ .... (201) 833-2417
Rosetta/ 21 W 46th, New York, NY .... (212) 247-6430
Ross-Gaffney Inc/ 21 West 46 St, New York, NY .... (212) 719-2744
Rossi, E/ 191 Grand St, New York, NY .... (212) 966-6640
Ross, Penny/ 1521 Forest Glen Rd., Silver Spring, MD .... (301) 681-6665
Roth Import Co/ 13 W 38th, New York, NY .... (212) 221-8896
Rubies Costumes/ 120-08 Jamaica Ave, Richmond Hill, NY ...... (212) 846-1008
Rug Warehouse, The/ 2222 Broadway, New York, NY .... (212) 787-6665
Russal, Varcra/ 326 E. 65th Street Studio #3, New York, NY ..... (212) 737-9520
Sage Studios Inc./ 245 E. 84th Street, New York, NY .... (212) 988-0500
Sam Goody's/ 666 Third Ave, New York, NY .... (212) 986-8480
Sanford, H C Associates Inc/ 305 E 46th St, New York, NY ...... (212) 832-0066
Sanlu Art Industries/ 25 East 28th Street, New York, NY .... (212) 620-3000
Sanra/ 220 E 26th St, New York City, NY .... (212) 685-7153
Sapan, Jason Holographic/ 240 E 26th, New York, NY .... (212) 686-9397
Say It in Neon Inc/ 434 Hudson St, New York, NY .... (212) 691-7977
Schachter's Babyland/ 81 Ave A, New York, NY .... (212) 777-1660
Schartz, William A & Son/ 173 Christopher St, New York, NY ... (212) 675-1919
Schenkel, Edna Location Hunter/ 16 Iselin Ter.,
    Larchmont, NY .... (914) 834-2181
Schirmer Music/ 40 W 62 Street, New York, NY .... (212) 541-6236
Schnoodle Studios/ 54 Bleecker St, New York City, NY .... (212) 431-7788
School Products Co, The/ 1201 Broadway, New York, NY .... (212) 679-3516
Schur Sylvia Creative Food Ser/ 14 Lawton St Library Plaza,
    New Rochelle, NY .... (212) 772-0514
Schwartz, M & Sons/ 45 Hofman Ave, Hauppauge, NY .... (212) 895-6125
Science Faction Corp/ 333 West 52nd Street, New York, NY ..... (212) 586-1911
Scott, Arthur (Hair&Makeup By)/ 105 West 55 Street,
    New York, NY .... (212) 245-0200

I N S P I R

Inspiration. It's that elusive, precious creative thought—that flash of imagination that solves a stubborn problem, ignites great ideas. It's fresh insight, a new way of seeing. And there's no better resource to turn to when you're looking for fresh vision than ROTOVISION. ROTOVISION'S ART DIRECTORS' INDEXES constitute the world's most complete international anthology of fine commercial work by illustrators, designers, graphic artists

American Illustration, Design and Photography

No art director should be without these rich collections of the finest American illustration and photography. Page after page, you'll find the work of America's best illustrators, designers and photographers, presented in an impressively beautiful format. No matter what your needs, you're bound to find the right artist for your next job in these superbly reproduced portfolios. PLUS! Each volume also contains the CREATIVE SERVICES DIRECTORY, a comprehensive reference to creative services throughout the U.S. The Directory is divided by region for easy use. For your next project, why not choose from the best?

ADWEEK/ADI 9: 340 pp., all color;

ADWEEK/ADI 10: 450 pp., all color;

ADWEEK/ART DIRECTORS' INDEX 9 & INDEX 10

$27.50 #01-09 $35.00 #01-10

Worldwide Illustration, Graphics and Design

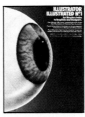

A collector's item that belongs in every studio's library of international art and design, this book represents the early work of 300 fine artists. You'll find a wealth of innovative techniques and imaginative visuals that will spur your own creative imagination into working overtime!

ILLUSTRATOR ILLUSTRATED NO. 1

320 pp.; 200 color

$50.00 #02-01

Three hundred of the world's finest artists from 19 countries display the best work in this superb volume. From editorial art to packaging, this rich source of inspiration is a collection of beautifully reproduced commercial art from around the world.

ILLUSTRATOR ILLUSTRATED NO. 2

384 pp.; more than 1,000 ill.

$55.00 #02-02

Worldwide Photography

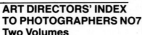

The language of creativity is universal, and nowhere is that more evident than in these stunning collections. Photographers from 34 nations show how the world sees itself through advertising—with unbelievable impact. A fantastic creative and production resource. Volume 1 of each edition covers Europe; Volume 2 covers Asia, Australasia and the Americas.

NO. 7, Vol. 1: 416 pp., 320 in color.

NO. 7, Vol. 2: 416 pp., 320 in color.

NO. 8: Vol. 1: 424 pp., 330 in color.

NO. 8: Vol 2: 440 pp., 360 in color.

NO. 9: Vol. 1: 392 pp., 320 in color.

No. 9: Vol 2: 352 pp., 300 color.

ART DIRECTORS' INDEX TO PHOTOGRAPHERS NO7 Two Volumes

$40.00 #01-071 $40.00 #01-072

ART DIRECTORS' INDEX TO PHOTOGRAPHERS NO8 Two Volumes

$45.00 #01-081 $45.00 #01-082

ART DIRECTORS' INDEX TO PHOTOGRAPHERS NO9 Two Volumes

$47.50 #01-091 $47.50 #01-092

The Master Collection

This beautiful collection of photographs by the Swiss photographer, Christian Vogt, is an expression of pure joy—joy in work, joy in life. It includes many of the photographs exhibited in Europe and the United States within the last 10 years. This book is a must for every complete photographic library.

CHRISTIAN VOGT, PHOTOGRAPHS

$35.00 #04-01 96 pp.; 32 color

When Christian Vogt asked 52 women to "make a sensual image of themselves," the only condition was that a simple box, a studio prop, remain. The 82 duo-tone images which make up this book constitute an erotic, revealing and touching testimony to both the women and the photographer.

88 pp. duo-tone 16 pp. text

CHRISTIAN VOGT, IN CAMERA

$25.00 #05-02

Brazilian photographer Alecio de Andrade catches the poetry of Paris, his adopted city, in these sensitive, loving photographs. The complexity of contrasts in these elegant duo-tones captures the spirit of this fabled city in an original, fresh view.

120 pp. duo-tone; 24 pp. text.

PARIS, THE ESSENCE OF AN IMAGE

$20.00 #04-02

Disturbing ... sensual ... photographs in which the camera is the inner eye of this perceptive Czech photographer. Saudek captures the soul of a people living their lives in glory and in defeat. Many of these telling photographs are published for the first time in this absorbing volume.

THE WORLD OF JAN SAUDEK

$35.00 #04-03 66 pp. duo-tone; 46 color; 32 pp. of text

ATION

and photographers. Each beautifully bound volume is printed in Europe on the best coated stock; each artist's work, whether in subtle black-and-white or vivid color, is faithfully reproduced. Keep inspiration on *your* shelf; turn to these superb worldwide idea sources and meet the finest artists from 34 countries. Inspiration. From ROTOVISION. Be inspired—use the coupon below to discover the ROTOVISION collection.

British Illustrators and Designers

ILLUSTRATOR ILLUSTRATED NO. 3

9.50   **#02-03**

Own this volume, and you'll have samples from more than 1,000 illustrators and designers from 24 countries—a huge portfolio of work rich in creativity, originality and fresh approaches. Puzzling over how to handle your latest assignment? For fresh creative views, see what's happening around the world!

384 pp.; over 1,000 color ill.

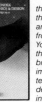

ILLUSTRATOR ILLUSTRATED NO. 4

$55.00   **#02-04**

Tour the world through the eyes of the best commercial artists and designers from 18 countries. You'll be amazed at the rich variety of brilliant work: vivid impact, innovative technique, and delightfully original interpretations of the marketplace. A must for any up-to-date library of design and illustration.

320 pp.; 210 color.

IMAGES 7

$35.00   **#0307**

IMAGES 8

$37.50   **#03-08**

Here's unusual inspiration in two volumes direct from Great Britain. More than 500 pieces from two juried expositions, chosen by London's Association of Illustrators, these works by professionals and students include advertising, editorial, book illustration, graphic design and experimental work. If you need fresh vision, expanded creative horizons, browse through this superbly reproduced collection. The cream of more than 4,000 entries, it's the best in British commercial art!

IMAGES 7: 240 pp.; 250 pieces; 200 color.

IMAGES 8: 240 pp.; 250 pieces;

Send inspiration quick! Please rush me the work of the world's finest artists and photographers in the ROTOVISION books I've marked below, indicating quantity:

American Illustration, Design and Photography:

____ Index 9 (#01-09) @ $27.50 ea.
____ Index 10 (#01-10) @ $35.00 ea.

Worldwide Illustration, Graphics and Design:

____ Illustrator Illustrated 1 (#02-01) @ $50.00 ea.
____ Illustrator Illustrated 2 (#02-02) @ $55.00 ea.
____ Illustrator Illustrated 3 (#02-03) @ $49.50 ea.
____ Illustrator Illustrated 4 (#02-04) @ $55.00 ea.

Worldwide Photographers:

____ ADI to Photographers, Index 7 Vol. 1 (#01-07,1) @ $40.00 ea.
____ ADI to Photographers, Index 7 Vol. 2 (#01-07,2) @ $40.00 ea.
____ ADI to Photographers, Index 8 Vol. 1 (#01-08,1) @ $45.00 ea.
____ ADI to Photographers, Index 8 Vol. 2 (#01-08,2) @ $45.00 ea.
____ ADI to Photographers, Index 9 Vol. 1 (#01-09,1) @ $47.50 ea.
____ ADI to Photographers, Index 9 Vol. 2 (#01-09,2) @ $47.50 ea.

British Illustrators and Designers:

____ Images 7 (#03-07) @ $35.00 ea.
____ Images 8 (#03-08) @ $37.50 ea.

The Master Collection:

____ Christian Vogt, Photographs (#04-01) @ $35.00 ea.
____ Christian Vogt, In Camera (#05-02) @ $25.00 ea.
____ Paris, Alecio de Andrade (#04-02) @ $20.00 ea.
____ The World of Jan Saudek (#04-03) @ $35.00 ea.

Name _____

Company _____

Address _____

City _____

State _____   Zip _____

Total Sales Price of Book(s) _____
Shipping Charges (allow $4/book) _____
Total Amount of Order _____

Please charge my ___ VISA ___ Master Card ___ Check enclosed
Account No. _____
Expiration Date _____ Telephone _____
Signature _____

RotoVision

Send to:
ADWEEK/
Rotovision Books
820 Second Avenue
New York, NY 10017

Payment must be sent with order. Make checks payable to ADWEEK. Please allow 8-10 weeks for delivery. Include $4.00 per book for shipping charges.

Scull Limousine/ 104 West 17 Street, New York, NY .... (212) 807-0472
Sculpture Assoc. Ltd., Inc./ 40 E. 19th St., New York, NY............ (212) 777-2400
Scupp, Kathleen/ 36 Gramercy Pk, New York City, NY .... (212) 673-7960
Seal-O-Matic Corp/ 900 Passaic Ave, E Newark, NJ .... (201) 481-6500
Seal Prod Inc/ 550 Spring St, Naugatuck, CT........................ (203) 729-5201
Seashells Unltd. Inc./ 590 Third Ave, New York, NY................ (212) 532-8690
Segall, Rachel Lulov/ 540 Main St, New York City, NY .... (212) 308-3568
Seguin Mirror & Brass Inc/ 202 E 70th St, New York, NY............ (212) 628-1460
Senatore, Peggy/ 515 East 79th St, New York, NY .... (212) 675-8800
Serendipity Three/ 225 E 60th St, New York City, NY................ (212) 838-3531
Service Party Rental/ 521 E 72nd, New York, NY .... (212) 288-7384
Set Shop, the/ 3 W. 20th St., New York, NY .... (212) 929-4845
Seymour, Celeste/ 130 E 75th St, New York City, NY .... (212) 744-3545
Shadovitz Bros Distrs Inc/ 1565 Bergen Street, Brooklyn, NY .... (212) 774-9100
Sheeran, Kay/ 530 Valley Rd, Upper Montclair, NJ.................... (201) 744-0333
Sherman, Nat/ 711 Fifth Ave, New York, NY .... (212) 751-9100
Sherwood, Karen/ 106 E. 30 St. #1f, New York, NY .... (212) 532-0833
Showroom Outlet/ 635 W 55th, New York, NY .... (212) 581-0470
Sigal, Barry/ 105 E. 38 St., New York, NY .... (212) 684-3416
Simco/ 245 Seventh Ave, New York, NY .... (212) 242-0450
Sinar Bron Inc/ 23 Progress St, Edison, NJ .... (201) 754-5800
Sisko, Bob Enterprises/ 36 Warwick St, Newark, NJ .... (201) 589-7590
Sklarsh, Shelle/ 57 W 73rd St, New York City, NY .... (212) 873-3335
Slote, Ina/ 7 Park Ave, New York, NY .... (212) 679-4584
Smiley Associates Inc/ 215 Park Ave South, New York, NY.......... (212) 673-9276
Smith, Randy/ 123-35 82nd Rd., Kew Gardens, NY .... (212) 263-6655
Smith & Watson/ 305 E 63rd St, New York City, NY .... (212) 355-5615
Soho Music Gallery/ 26 Wooster St, New York, NY .... (212) 966-1637
Sokolec/ 154 E 61st St, New York City, NY .... (212) 888-6030
Soldier Shop/ 1222 Madison Ave, New York, NY .... (212) 535-6788
Sonocraft Corp/ 360 W 31st St, New York, NY .... (212) 760-9300
Sony/ Sony Drive, Park Ridge, NJ.................................. (201) 930-1000
Sound Assoc/ 424 W 45th, New York, NY .... (212) 757-5679
Spanish Music Center/ 319 W 48th, New York, NY .... (212) 582-4280
Speakeasy Antiques/ 799 Broadway, New York, NY .... (212) 533-2440
Specht, Meredith/ 166 E 61st St, New York City, NY .... (212) 832-0750
Spectrum Helicopters Inc/ 45 Bergen Turnpike,
    Ridgefield Park, NJ .... (201) 641-3113
Spiratone/ 130 W. 31st Street, New York, NY...................... (212) 594-5267
Sports Locker/ 625-A Eighth Ave, New York, NY .... (212) 695-3479
Spots Alive Consultants Inc/ 342 Madison Avenue,
    New York, NY .... (212) 953-1677
Staging Techniques/ 342 W 40th St, New York, NY .... (212) 736-5727
Starbuck Studio/ 60 W. 22nd St., New York, NY .... (212) 255-2857
Staten Island Ferry/ Battery Maritime Bldg, New York, NY.......... (212) 806-6901
Steiman, H & Sons/ 164 Perry St, New York, NY .... (212) 243-7128
Steinberg & Dubin/ 245 E Houston St, New York, NY .... (212) 475-7697
Stein, Jack Make-Up Center/ 80 Boylston St, Boston, MA .... (617) 542-7865
Strawberries Finders Service/ Bucks County,
    Riegelsville, PA .... (215) 346-8000
Strettels, Jo / Make-Up/ 160 Fifth Ave., New York, NY .... (212) 924-6760
Studio 39/ 144 E 39th, New York, NY .... (212) 685-1771
Studio 84/ 245 E 84th, New York, NY .... (212) 988-3700
Studio Film & Tape/ 630 Ninth Ave, New York, NY .... (212) 977-9330
Stupell, Carole Ltd/ 61 E 57th, New York, NY .... (212) 260-3100
Stuyvesant Bicycle/ 349 W 14th, New York, NY .... (212) 675-2160
Suffolk County Dept of Econ/ 4175 Veterans Hwy,
    Ronkonkoma, NY .... (516) 588-1000
Sukon Group/ 355 Lexington Avenue, New York, NY................ (212) 986-2290
Sundial Mirror/ 1491 First Ave, New York, NY .... (212) 734-0838
Suns Sporting Goods/ 24 W 23rd, New York, NY .... (212) 675-3766
Supersnipe/ PO Box 1102 Gracie Station, New York, NY .... (212) 879-9628
Supplyline/ Post Office Box 915, Barnstable, MA .... (716) 586-8137
Syd-Art Novelty/ 2643 Grand Ave, Bellmore, NY .... (212) 243-4633
Taj Persian & Oriental Rugs/ 255 Fifth Ave, New York, NY .... (212) 889-7697
Tannen's Magic Manuscript Ltd/ 6 W 32nd St, New York, NY ...... (212) 541-9550
Tape City International/ 404 Park Ave S, New York, NY .... (212) 679-1606
Tasty Props/ 320 E. 39th St., New York, NY .... (212) 679-8157
Technisphere Corporation/ 215 E 27th St, New York, NY .... (212) 889-9170
Tekno Inc/ 15 E 30 St, New York, NY .... (212) 889-5080
Tender Buttons/ 143 E 62nd, New York, NY........................ (212) 758-7004
Tepee Town/ 625 8th Ave Port Auth Bus Ter, New York, NY ...... (212) 563-6430
Terminal/ 166 W 48th, New York, NY .... (212) 869-5270
Terrestris Greenhouses/ 409 E 60th St, New York, NY .... (212) 758-8181
Terzis, Jon J/ 655 Ave of the Americas, New York City, NY .... (212) 929-5174

Theatre Opera Music Inst/ 23 W 73rd, New York, NY .... (212) 787-3980
Things Antique/ 483 Amsterdam Ave, New York, NY................ (212) 873-4655
31st Realty Associates/ 450 W 31st St, New York City, NY .... (212) 947-0811
3M Company/ 15 Henderson Dr, West Caldwell, NJ .... (212) 285-9600
Tiffen Manufacturing/ 90 Oser St, Happauge, NY .... (212) 895-6240
Todd, Jeanine/ 360 W 22nd St, New York, NY .... (212) 929-4850
Tomoko / Make-Up & Hair/ 160 Fifth Ave., New York, NY .... (212) 924-6760
Top Notch Art Materials/ 819 Penn Ave, Pittsburgh, PA .... (412) 355-0444
Townsend's Fabulous Fakes Inc./ 18 E. 18 St., New York, NY ...... (212) 807-8562
Toy Balloon Corp/ 204 E 38th, New York, NY...................... (212) 682-3803
Traflix/ 59 E 54th, New York, NY.................................. (212) 755-5515
Tranum Robertson Hughes/ 2 Dag Ham Plz, New York, NY .... (212) 371-7500
Triton Gallery/ 323 W 45th, New York, NY .... (212) 765-2472
Trupp, Terri/ 2914 Miles Ave, Baltimore, MD...................... (301) 462-4085
Tudor Electrical Supply/ 222 E 46th, New York, NY .... (212) 867-7550
Uchida of America Corp/ 69 34 51 Ave, Woodside, NY.............. (212) 779-0400
Uhlfelder, Leo & Company/ 420 S Fulton Ave, Mt Vernon, NY...... (212) 293-4554
Ulano/ 255 Butler St, Brooklyn, NY .... (212) 643-1770
Uncle Sam Umbrella Shop/ 161 W 57th, New York, NY............ (212) 582-1976
Unger, Captain Howard (Boats)/ 80 Beach Road,
    Great Neck, NY .... (516) 829-9800
Unicorn/ 26 Greenwich Ave, New York, NY........................ (212) 989-6160
Union Instrument Co/ 300 Corpate Court, S Plainfield, NJ .... (201) 756-6868
Union Rubber Inc/ 232 Allen St, Trenton, NJ...................... (609) 396-9328
Unique Clothing Warehouse/ 718 Broadway, New York, NY .... (212) 674-1767
Variety Scenic Studios/ 25-19 Borden Ave,
    Long Island Cty, NY .... (212) 392-4747
Vermont Film Bureau/ 134 State St., Montpelier, VT .... (802) 828-3236
Veterans Caning/ 550 W 35th, New York, NY .... (212) 868-3244
Victoria, Elaine/ 60 East 12th Street, New York, NY .... (212) 807-1069
Video Corp of America/ 1913 Rte 27, Edison, NJ .... (201) 572-3300
Videofilm Systems, Inc./ 116 County St., Norwalk, CT .... (203) 866-7319
Video Strategies USA/ 1995 Broadway, New York, NY .... (212) 496-8600
Village Stripper, The/ 519 Hudson, New York, NY .... (212) 929-4180
Voyager Emblems, Inc./ 3707 Lockport Road, Sanborn, NY .... (716) 731-4121
Wagner, Sherle/ 60 E 57th, New York, NY .... (212) 758-3300
Walbead/ 29-76 N Boulevard, Long Island Cty, NY................ (212) 392-7616
Walker, Barbara/ 400 W End Ave, New York City, NY .... (212) 580-0739
Walker Mineral/ 995 First Ave, New York, NY...................... (212) 838-1444
Wallpaper Mart/ 187 Lexington Ave, New York, NY .... (212) 889-4900
Wallpapers East/ 1190 3rd Ave, New York, NY .... (212) 861-9420
Walsh, Honore/ 310 E 75th St, New York City, NY .... (212) 737-7107
Warner, Kim Freelance Stylist/ 222 W. 23 St. Suite 703,
    New York, NY .... (212) 924-2566
Watson, Elizabeth/ 237 East 77th Street, New York, NY .... (212) 628-7886
Watson, Lorye/ 420 W 46th St, New York City, NY .... (212) 247-6639
Wax, Morton Dennis & Associates/ 200 West 51st Street,
    New York, NY .... (212) 247-2159
Weber, F Div/ Wayne & Windrim Ave, Philadelphia, PA.............. (215) 329-6900
Weiss, David Importers/ 969 Third Ave, New York, NY .... (212) 755-1492
Weist-Barron School of Tv Comm/ 35 W 45th St, New York, NY .... (212) 840-7025
Werth, Al Inc/ 203-05 W 38th, New York, NY .... (212) 921-0177
West Side Screenings/ 311 W 43rd, New York, NY .... (212) 246-3838
Whole Art/ 259 W 30th Street, New York City, NY .... (212) 868-0478
Wicker Garden-Baby/ 1320 Madison Ave, New York, NY .... (212) 348-1166
Wicker Garden, The/ 1318 Madison Ave, New York City, NY........ (212) 410-7000
Wickery, The/ 342 Third Ave, New York, NY...................... (212) 889-3669
Wild, H L/ 510 E 11th, New York, NY .... (212) 228-2345
Wilson, Patti/ 110 Chambers St, New York City, NY .... (212) 285-1154
Winnie, Joanne/ 1780 Strawberry Road, Mohegan Lake, NY........ (914) 528-0545
Winsor & Newton/ 555 Winsor Dr, Secaucus, NJ .... (201) 864-9100
Winston, Harry/ 718 Fifth Ave, New York City, NY .... (212) 245-2000
Winston, Mary Ellen/ 11 East 68 Street, New York, NY .... (212) 879-0766
Winters, Patricia J./ 215 E. 68th Street, New York, NY .... (212) 249-6337
Wizardworks/ 67 Atlantic Ave, Brooklyn, NY...................... (212) 349-5252
Wizardworks/ 47 Murray St., New York, NY .... (212) 349-5252
Yellowbox, Inc/ 47 E 34th St, New York City, NY .... (212) 532-4010
YK Video/ 432 Park Ave S, New York, NY .... (212) 686-8515
Ynocencio, Jo/ 302 E 88th St, New York City, NY .... (212) 348-5332
York Floral Co., Inc./ 804 Sixth Ave., New York, NY .... (212) 686-2070
Zabel/ 125 Washington Pl, New York City, NY .... (212) 242-2459
Zeller, Gary Special Effects/ 40 W 39th St, New York, NY.......... (212) 869-8636

COPYWRITERS

Adler, Lawrence J./ 324 East 74th St., New York, NY .... (212) 744-4327
Ad Works/ P O Box 575, Bedford, NY..................................... (914) 234-9494
Ahrend Associates/ 79 Madison Ave, New York, NY.................... (212) 685-0033
Ahrens, Roger Advertising PR/ 5 Riverside Drive,
   New York, NY.. (212) 580-8814
Anderson, Carolyn T./ 2409 Emmitsburg Road, Gettysburg, PA...... (717) 334-2873
Arlen Communications Inc./ 7315 Wisconsin Ave #600E,
   Bethesda, MD... (301) 656-7940
Barkus, Ted Company Inc/ 225 S. 15th St., Philadelphia, PA .... (215) 545-0616
Biondo Custom Copywriters/ Post Office Box 350,
   Woodmere, NY.. (516) 374-6048
Blate, Samuel R. Associates/ 10331 Watkins Mill Dr.,
   Gaithersburg, MD .... (301) 840-2248
Brick, Monte-Wordsmith/ 6 Inwood Place, Melville, NY .... (516) 549-9640
Browne Charlie Communications/ Hawthorne Hill Road,
   Newtown, CT... (203) 426-0287
Brunkus, Denise/ 67 Pines Lake, Wayne, NJ .... (201) 835-4154
Caruba Organization, The/ 9 Brookside Rd.-Box 40,
   Maplewood, NJ .... (201) 763-6392
Certner, Andrew/ 41 Terkuile Road, Montvale, NJ .... (201) 391-9279
Cheapskate Copywriters/ Post Office Box 350, Woodmere, NY ...... (516) 374-6048
Clarke and Corcillo/ 530 Westport Ave., Norwalk, CT................. (203) 846-1617
Collateral-To-Go/ 60 Overlook Road, Montclair, NJ .... (201) 746-1351
Communications Counselors/ 380 Essex Ave, Bloomfield, NJ......... (201) 743-9661
Consolidated Marketing Servcs./ 51 East 42nd St #517,
   New York, NY... (212) 688-8797
Cope, Lawrence L./ 5407 Newington Rd., Bethesda, MD............. (301) 656-8745
Copy Creations-Sandi Lifschitz/ 209 E 56th St Suite 8H,
   New York, NY... (212) 826-6766
Copy Shoppe, The/ 280 Madison Avenue, New York, NY .... (212) 679-COPY
Copy-That-Clix/ P O Box 102, Lefferts Station, Brooklyn, NY .... (718) 756-1712
Cowan, William M./ 1743 Beacon St, Waban, MA .... (617) 244-7182
Creatique/ 290 Jefferson Ave, Cresskill, NJ .... (201) 567-0436
Creative Copy Center, A/ 1529 Wisconsin Avenue NW,
   Washington, DC .... (202) 333-3560
Creative/Industrial Writing/ 297 State Street, Brooklyn, NY .... (212) 852-0055
Dernbach Associates Inc/ Pipe Stave Hollow Road, Box405,
   Miller Place, NY.. (516) 473-5546
Direct Response Copy Mistress/ 36 North Moore Street, 2W,
   New York, NY... (212) 431-4461
Direct Response,The,TV Writer/ 23 Vanderburgh Avenue,
   Larchmont, NY.. (914) 834-1607
DR & Associates/ 212 Beech View Ct., Towson, MD .... (301) 296-8598
Drooz, Geri/ 160 Willowcrest Dr, Rochester, NY .... (716) 461-1047
Essential Radio Service, The/ 210B Morristown Road,
   Matawan, NJ .... (201) 583-8858
Fitzgerald-McArdle, Debbie/ 3840 Calvert St NW,
   Washington, DC .... (202) 965-0817
Forsman, Donna/ R D 1 Box 154, Orrtanna, PA .... (717) 642-8195
Gewirtz, Sheldon/ 280 West 86th Street, New York, NY .... (212) 877-3927
Hays, Elizabeth Advertising/ 370 Church Street, Lodi, NJ........... (201) 365-1875
Healy, Bob/ 912 Curtis Ave., Point Pleasant, NJ....................... (201) 241-3030
Hirsh, Jeff/ P.O. Box 124, Haworth, NJ .... (201) 384-7086
Holmes, Bruce/ 2802 Village Drive, Brewster, NY .... (914) 278-9662
Huber, John Communications/ 258 Silver Spring Road,
   Wilton, CT .... (203) 762-7087

Inter-Presse De France/ 100 Beekman Street, New York, NY......... (212) 285-1872
Johnson, Ray/ 21 Whit's End, Concord, MA............................. (617) 369-3515
Jordan, Jim Topcopy/ 514 South Aurora St, Ithaca, NY.............. (607) 272-1323
Kaplan, Jim Direct Marketing/ 67-50B 188 St,
   Fresh Meadows, NY .... (212) 591-3089
K A S T Communications Inc/ 22 East 36 St Suite 3C,
   New York, NY... (212) 889-7993
Kean Communications/ 36-08 21st Ave, Long Island Cy, NY .... (212) 728-8192
Kean, Jack/ 36-08 21st Avenue, New York, NY......................... (212) 728-8192
Kimmel,Lynn/Med/Consumer/Promo/ 353 West 19 Street,
   New York, NY... (212) 741-1950
Ad Works, the/ 4 Gorham Avenue, Westport, CT .... (203) 227-2990
Lareau & Associates/ 140 West End Ave, New York, NY.............. (212) 877-6533
Lasky, Carol/ 10 Thacher St. Ste. 112, Boston, MA .... (617) 720-4440
Leon, George DeLucenay/ 297 State St, New York, NY .... (212) 852-0055
Lerman, Maury/ 425 East 58 Street, New York, NY .... (212) 421-2149
Levin, Joel/ Box 142, New York, NY .... (212) 861-3300
Linder,.Lou/ 500 East 77th Street, New York, NY .... (212) 705-1345
Madison Avenue & Elm Inc./ 29 Haviland St.,
   South Norwalk, CT... (203) 853-3363
Media Power Associates/ 2127 Maryland Ave., Baltimore, MD....... (301) 243-6716
Mendelsohn, Dick Inc/ 119 West 77 Street, New York, NY .... (212) 787-1386
Miller, Eric/ 135 Willow St, Brooklyn Hts, NY .... (212) 852-3344
Morris Associates/ 14 Westview Ave #714, Tuckahoe, NY .... (914) 779-9425
Mylasco Marketing/ 215 West 75 Street, New York, NY .... (212) 724-4519
News & Farmer/ P.O. Box 459, Preston, MD .... (301) 673-7131
Olmsted, Pete/ 13 Spring St, Cambridge, NY .... (518) 677-5560
Oops, Inc./ Box 111, Conway, MA .... (413) 369-4925
Pelletier, Tom/ 45L Derryfield Road, Derry, NH........................ (603) 434-7372
Please Release Me-PR & Adv/ 252 Jewett Avenue #1,
   Jersey City, NJ .... (201) 435-7972
Pro/Creatives Co/ 25 W Burda, Spring Valley, NY..................... (914) 356-4623
Queens Ad Service/ 15-27 Parsons Blvd, Whitestone, NY .... (718) 746-8331
Really Good Copy Company/ 76 Whiting Lane,
   West Hartford, CT... (203) 233-6128
Reid, Derk Healthcare Copy/ Box 410 North Hollow.Rd,
   Stowe, VT .... (802) 253-9519
Rensch, Randall/ 440 East 62nd St., New York, NY................... (212) 223-0839
Ruben, JJ Copyartiste/ 947 First Ave, New York, NY .... (212) 758-0098
Schneider & Associates/ 127 E. 59th St., New York, NY .... (212) 421-1950
Scott, John M., Jr./ 24 Fifth Ave., New York, NY .... (212) 674-6531
Silver, Martin J./ 559 Arlington Pl, Cedarhurst, NY .... (516) 295-2568
Smith, Carol E./ 5 Dana Dr. #15, Hudson, NH .... (603) 883-7016
Smith, Della/ 72 West 82 Street No 3R, New York, NY .... (212) 595-0378
Soslow, Robin/ 7508 N Arbory Way, Laurel, MD....................... (301) 498-8740
Springer, Eunice Advertising/ 115 West 57 Street,
   New York, NY... (212) 582-9377
Stroud Mgmt/ 18 E 48th, New York, NY .... (212) 688-0226
Thompson, D R Enterprises/ 3420 112th Street, Queens, NY .... (212) 949-4940
West, Ben the Writer/ 19 Francis Road, E. Brunswick, NJ .... (201) 254-9260
Wetjen, Amy J.-Freelance Copy/ 33 Pine Street, Trumbull, CT....... (203) 268-0422
Williams, W. G., Assoc., Inc./ 1100 Seventeenth St. N.W.,
   Washington, DC .... (202) 463-8017
Yale, David R./ 234 Fifth Ave. Ste. 304, New York, NY .... (212) 686-4720
Zackowitz, Allan/ 5474 Treefrog Place, Columbia, MD .... (301) 596-6759
Ziff, Gilbert E/ 444 Central Park W, New York, NY .... (212) 222-5684
Zukowski, Daniel B/ PO Box 16, New Hyde Park, NY .... (516) 488-6691

Kinetics/1985

444 North Wabash Avenue
Chicago, Illinois 60611
Tel. 312-644 2767

We produce special effects and animation for film. In our Chicago studio, we operate a CINETRON/OXBERRY 1100B motion-control animation stand, as well as two OXBERRY optical printers and a MITCHELL STANDARD camera for table top and stage model photography.

We submit the frames below for your perusal. To see them in motion, please call for our reel. We bring to our clients a unique vision and ability to solve technical and design problems elegantly, on schedule and on budget.

Our staff includes:
George Eastman/Creative Director
Joe Calomino/Director-Animator
Don Hoeg/Director-Designer
Ron Fleischer/Director-Cameraman
Daniella Violet-Green/Executive Producer